Peter Norton's
Complete Guide to Norton SystemWorks 2.0

Peter Norton
Scott H. A. Clark

SAMS

A Division of Macmillan Computer Publishing
201 West 103rd Street, Indianapolis, Indiana 46290 USA

W9-AUD-308

Peter Norton's Complete Guide to Norton SystemWorks 2.0

Copyright © 1999 by Peter Norton

International Standard Book Number: 0-672-31528-9

Library of Congress Catalog Card Number: 99-88327

Printed in the United States of America

First Printing: April 1999

02   01   00   99   4   3   2   1

Trademarks

All terms mentioned in this book that are known to be trademarks or service marks have been appropriately capitalized. Sams Publishing cannot attest to the accuracy of this information. Use of a term in this book should not be regarded as affecting the validity of any trademark or service mark.

Warning and Disclaimer

Executive Editor
Angela Wethington

Acquisitions Editor
Jamie Milazzo

Development Editor
Joyce Nielsen

Managing Editor
Tom Hayes

Project Editor
Damon Jordan

Copy Editor
Victoria Elzey

Proofreader
John Rahm
Tricia Sterling

Indexer
Larry Sweazy

Technical Editors
Nancy Ives
Curtis Knight
Craig Sparks
Nancy Sparks
Brendon Woirhaye

Production
Lisa England
Brad Lenser

Contents at a Glance

Appendixes

Contents

Dedication

For Lori Harris

and a friendship that shines
so brightly
I could never choose
No choices whatsoever.

With Love, from Scott

Acknowledgments

First, I would like to extend sincerest of thanks to Winston Steward. Winston stepped in and authored the Norton AntiVirus, Norton UnFormat, and System Information chapters. He did a great job. This project couldn't have been completed without him.

It would not have been possible for me to have asked for a better acquisitions editor at Macmillan Computer Publishing than Jamie Milazzo. Her enthusiasm, encouragement, and hard work were invaluable to me long before this project was off the ground and long after it was complete. Thanks, Jamie!

Joyce Nielsen, my developmental editor, was an incredible working partner. Her eye for detail, her sense of what the book was trying to achieve and where it was going, and her dedication all changed and improved this book tremendously. I hope to have the privilege of working with her again.

Absolutely instrumental were the software designers at Symantec. In alphabetical order, Sarah Hicks, Kevin Li, David Loomstein, Marian Merritt, Dana Prussoff and Peder Ulander repeatedly went above and beyond the call of duty to get me what I needed to do this book properly. They provided me with an early beta of the suite, but, most importantly, they provided me with their own time and resources. Software design is one field that your free time is sometimes measured in hours, not days, but these people gave me their gracious assistance every time I turned to them for help. Connections between me and these project managers were priceless. All the time that Peder, Dana, Marian, David, Kevin, and Sarah gave me was time I knew they didn't really have. I can't thank them enough.

Also instrumental was Damon Jordan, the project editor on this title. Damon put in hours and effort far above and beyond the call of duty. His enthusiasm for this project and his dedication to it simply made it happen. He's amazing.

On the technical side, Nancy Ives, Nancy Sparks, and Craig Sparks, all Symantec specialists, toiled and researched to make sure that every word you read here is correct and in sync with what you'll find in your own SystemWorks suite. Thank you all!

As she has been on many Norton projects, Angie Wethington, Executive Editor at Macmillan Computer Publishing, was a superb facilitator for the entire book.

Matt Wagner, my agent at Waterside Productions, Inc., deserves immeasurable credit for putting it all together and getting all of us in touch.

Thanks also to Margot Maley, of Waterside Productions, Inc., for bringing Winston into the fold.

To Casey and Lisa Kammel, eternal thanks for changing my life.

Warm regards to all,

Scott

About the Authors

Computer software entrepreneur and writer **Peter Norton** established his technical expertise and accessible style from the earliest days of the PC. His Norton Utilities was the first product of its kind, giving early computer owners control over their hardware and protection against myriad problems. His flagship titles, Peter Norton's DOS Guide and Peter Norton's Inside the PC (Sams Publishing) have provided the same insight and education to computer users worldwide for nearly two decades. Peter's books, like his many software products, are among the best-selling and most-respected in the history of personal computing.

Peter Norton's former column in PC Week was among the highest-regarded in that magazine's history. His expanding series of computer books continues to bring superior education to users, always in Peter's trademark style, which is never condescending nor pedantic. From their earliest days, changing the "black box" into a "glass box," Peter's books, like his software, remain among the most powerful tools available to beginners and experienced users, alike.

In 1990, Peter sold his software development business to Symantec Corporation, allowing him to devote more time to his family, civic affairs, philanthropy, and art collecting. He lives with his wife, Eileen, and two children in Santa Monica, California.

Scott Clark's sometimes formal, sometimes informal exploration of personal computers began while he was in high school (where he served as the school's network administrator) and continued through his college years. He is a graduate of Boston University, where he was a Trustee Scholar and a University Scholar in the University Professors Program for Interdisciplinary Studies.

Scott was brought on as Executive Editor of Peter Norton's computer books upon his graduation in 1989, and became the Director of the series in 1992. Since that time he has overseen the creation of every new edition and new title in the series, editing and writing for many of them, and working with several publishers.

In 1996 he served as primary author for the Sams publication of the best-selling sixth edition of Peter Norton's flagship title, *Inside the PC* and was a major contributor to PC Press' premier title, *The Complete Family PC Encyclopedia.* He resides in Southern California in a house full of Disney collectibles.

Tell Us What You Think!

As the reader of this book, *you* are our most important critic and commentator. We value your opinion and want to know what we're doing right, what we could do better, what areas you'd like to see us publish in, and any other words of wisdom you're willing to pass our way.

As the Executive Editor for the General Desktop Applications team at Macmillan Computer Publishing, I welcome your comments. You can fax, email, or write me directly to let me know what you did or didn't like about this book—as well as what we can do to make our books stronger.

Please note that I cannot help you with technical problems related to the topic of this book, and that due to the high volume of mail I receive, I might not be able to reply to every message.

When you write, please be sure to include this book's title and author, as well as your name and phone or fax number. I will carefully review your comments and share them with the author and editors who worked on the book.

Fax: 317-581-4770

Email: awethington@mcp.com

Mail: Angela Wethington
              Executive Editor
              General Desktop Applications
              Macmillan Computer Publishing
              201 West 103rd Street
              Indianapolis, IN 46290 USA

Foreword

Dear Reader,

Thank you for purchasing *Peter Norton's Complete Guide to Norton SystemWorks*. I hope you find this book to be a valuable reference to helping you get the most from Norton SystemWorks.

Norton SystemWorks 2.0 was developed to provide you with an easy, integrated solution to keep your computers well maintained and problem free. By integrating the complete and most recent versions of our most popular utility products—Norton Utilities, Norton AntiVirus, Norton CleanSweep, Norton CrashGuard and Norton Web Services—we have provided peace of mind that you have the tools to keep doing what you really want to do on your computer. That means surfing the Internet, home banking, playing games, working with your kids on educational programs, and all the thousands of things you use your computer for.

Peter Norton's Complete Guide to Norton SystemWorks will provide you with a more thorough understanding of the benefits of Norton SystemWorks. It will also give you better understanding of the tools and utilities included—why they should be used, when they should be used, and how they should be used.

Beginning with the easy installation of Norton SystemWorks, you will immediately discover the advantages of purchasing an integrated suite of utilities over purchasing a bundle of products. These benefits include a single installation, a single registration, and a single reboot. These products were developed to work together, act compatibly, providing you with the best—and smartest!—way to keep your computer working.

Norton Utilities, the number one problem-solving software for over fifteen years, is the industry leader in detecting, repairing, and preventing major and minor computer problems. Additionally, Norton Utilities includes easy-to-use programs that will optimize your system to run faster—at peak efficiency.

Norton AntiVirus, the world's best-selling antivirus software, protects your PC with the most popular and most powerful antivirus capabilities available. Whether you're on the Internet, sharing disks, or multiple users are sharing your computer, you want to be protected from all the viruses that could infect your system. And if a virus is detected, Norton AntiVirus will fix your files and purge the virus from your system. Norton AntiVirus gives you peace of mind that whatever you're doing on your PC, you will be protected.

Norton CleanSweep is the safest, most thorough means of removing programs and files from your computer. This award-winning uninstaller also makes it easy for you clean out Internet "junk," store seldom-used programs you may not want to remove, and move programs to new disks or partitions.

Norton CrashGuard gives you more power to save your work from crashes. When your system or application experiences a crash, you want to make sure that you're protected from data loss. Norton CrashGuard provides you with easy-to-use steps to guide you through the crash to make sure you stay protected.

Norton Web Services keeps your system updated with the latest virus definitions, software updates and hardware drivers. By connecting to our Norton Web Services web site, LiveUpdate Pro will search the Internet and easily download and install the updates for your specific system.

I hope that with all of the examples, screen shots, and helpful tips included in *Peter Norton's Complete Guide to Norton SystemWorks 2.0*, you'll be quickly on your way to maintaining and protecting your PC.

Again, thank you for purchasing this book and using Norton SystemWorks 2.0. Together they'll provide you with the smartest way to keep your computer working.

Sarah Hicks, Group Product Manager
Symantec Corporation

PART I

Introduction to Norton SystemWorks

Introduction

More than 15 years ago, when personal computers were still very much in their primordial stages, Peter Norton recognized that there was no technical reason why files that were deleted by accident had to be considered lost forever. Many people—himself included—had lost important data to accidental erasure, but Peter was the first ever to do anything about it. Thus, Norton UnErase was created and the Norton Utilities were born. The Norton Utilities quickly expended to provide tools to watch for and recover from serious problems, like Norton Disk Doctor; to maximize the potential performance of any PC, like Norton Speed Disk; to make working in the text-based DOS environment more tolerable and efficient, like The Norton Commander; to provide users with vital information about their PC and its components, like Norton Diagnostics; and so on. When Microsoft Windows first came on the scene, the Norton Utilities were there. New components were added as new issues developed—Norton AntiVirus, to protect against outside attacks, and Norton CrashGuard to, in a sense, protect against attacks from within.

In September of 1998, all of these components were brought together for the first time in one suite of tools: Norton SystemWorks 2.0. A highly-integrated utility environment, Norton SystemWorks 2.0 provides all the functionality of each major Norton utility product, plus the qualitative benefit of all these products working together.

Norton SystemWorks 2.0

The Norton SystemWorks 2.0 components can be broken up into six major categories: Norton Utilities components, Norton AntiVirus, Norton CrashGuard, Norton CleanSweep, Norton Web Services, and the Professional or Basic Bonus Pack. Since its initial release, there have already been some changes and improvements to the Norton SystemWorks suite of products. This book provides the latest-breaking news and information regarding all of these cutting-edge tools. In the following sections, we'll examine each major SystemWorks 2.0 component and its various pieces.

The Norton Utilities

The primary member of Norton SystemWorks 2.0 is the award-winning collection of tools making up the Norton Utilities. Here is a quick look at each utility and what it can do for you:

- **Image** places a snapshot of your system's vital disk information onto a dedicated area of each drive. This information can be vital to repairing the drive with other Norton Utilities tools.

- **Norton Connection Wizard** checks the health and stability of your modem and dial-up connections, helping maximize the quality of your online experiences.

- **Norton Disk Doctor** analyzes your drives, checking for myriad problems and damage, both major and minor. Norton Disk Doctor can repair these problems automatically before your data ever becomes endangered.

- **Norton File Compare** will show you the differences between two files or two Windows Registry keys, enabling you to undo selected changes interactively.

- **Norton Protection** safeguards every file deleted on your Windows 95 or Windows 98 PC. Recovery of any deleted file is 100% guaranteed so long as the file is under Norton Protection. Even temporary and overwritten files can be recovered if they have been protected with the Norton Protected Recycle Bin.

- **Norton Optimization Wizard** will fine-tune your Windows Registry and your Windows Swap File for maximum system performance. It can even relocate your swap file on your fastest drive!

- **Norton Registry Editor** provides a sophisticated tool for expert users to read and manually modify the Windows Registry and a variety of application- and hardware-related initialization files. Unlike Microsoft REGEDIT, Norton Registry Editor provides advanced undo capability and modification tracking.

- **Norton Speed Start** works under Windows 95 to provide launching acceleration of up to 50 percent. Speed Start works entirely in the background and uses few system resources. On a Windows 98 PC, this same functionality is provided by Speed Disk and the operating system itself.

- **Norton System Check** combines other key Norton Utilities components together in one place, allowing you to check every major aspect of your system's integrity— from disks to the Registry—and repair problems before they endanger your work.

- **Norton System Doctor** is often referred to as the early warning system driving Norton SystemWorks. System Doctor constantly monitors a variety of system and drive characteristics—which you select—and can alert you to growing problems before your productivity or data is ever at risk. In many cases, the System Doctor sensors can even repair detected problems without ever interrupting your work.

- **Norton WinDoctor** safeguards against problems with the Windows Registry. It can detect Registry key errors and can prompt you to remove entries which refer to antiquated hardware or uninstalled software. WinDoctor can check to verify that all of your application components are installed where they are supposed to be. In this way, WinDoctor guarantees that your applications, as well as their operating environment, are stable and reliable.

- **Norton Registry Tracker** monitors modifications made to the Windows Registry, enabling you to undo changes which generate system trouble or are simply undesirable.

- **Rescue** and **Norton Zip Rescue** provide a means by which your system may be restarted—either in DOS or Windows—even after catastrophic damage has occurred. Rescue will then automatically run the Rescue Recovery Wizard, enabling almost any kind of drive and system-file problem to be repaired.

- **Space Wizard** enables you to search for unused and unnecessary files and delete, relocate, or compress them, increasing available free space on your drives.

- **Speed Disk** optimizes the location of files on your hard drive based on how you use them. Commonly used files and directories are given priority placement at the front of the drive, speeding their access times. In conjunction with the Norton Optimization Wizard, Speed Disk will defragment and relocate your Windows Swap File, potentially accelerating every Windows task you perform.

- **System Information** provides you with a single location from which you can check your system's hardware and software configuration and perform a variety of benchmark tests to analyze system performance.

- **UnErase Wizard** works in conjunction with Norton Protection to interactively and painlessly bring back deleted files from the dead.

- **WipeInfo** allows you to dramatically increase your privacy by deleting files and folders in a way that no one can ever retrieve them. You can also wipe your drives' free space, making long-deleted files unavailable forever.

Norton AntiVirus

The second major component of Norton SystemWorks 2.0 is Norton's industry-dominating and award-winning virus protection and eradication software, Norton AntiVirus. The following features are included with Norton AntiVirus:

- **ActiveX** and **Java Detect** watch for suspect code downloaded in ActiveX applets and Java objects.

- **Auto-Protect**, runs continuously in the background, using almost no system resources but constantly watching for virus code and attack. Auto-Protect will also guard against Macro viruses hidden within document files.

- **Bloodhound**, Norton's proprietary heuristic technology, enables Norton AntiVirus to detect viruses which are totally new—those not yet included in the NAV virus definitions. It does this by creating a virtual PC on which suspected viral code is run, and the results analyzed. This non-existent system takes the "hits," leaving your actual system safe. Bloodhound heuristic technology will catch over ninety percent of all unknown macro viruses and over eighty percent of all unknown file viruses.

- **Quarantine** safely isolates files which may contain viruses or Trojan horses, giving you time to download new virus definitions and re-analyze the files for safety before accidentally using them.

- **Repair Wizard**, an interactive, step-by-step tool, uses the familiar Windows wizard panels to guide you through the process of removing any detected virus from your PC.

- **Striker** uses patent-pending technology to detect and eradicate polymorphic viruses—viruses which change every time a new file is infected. Traditionally nearly impossible to stop, Striker uses a "Virtual PC," like Bloodhound, to safely activate, analyze, and destroy these pernicious viruses.

- **Virus Sensor** works in conjunction with Auto-Protect to not detect viruses *per se*, but to detect virus-like behavior. The sudden command to delete huge numbers of files, or to reformat a hard disk, will be caught by Virus Sensor, which alerts Norton AntiVirus to investigate the code generating the command. This is another line of defense against new, undefined viruses and Trojan horses.

Norton CleanSweep

Norton CleanSweep provides you with an easy-to-use way to monitor the installation of new software and to remove software, guaranteeing that *all* of that software's components—including stray Registry entries—are deleted, too. CleanSweep also provides a suite of tools which can help you eliminate unnecessary files of all kinds from your disks and maximize your valuable free drive space.

Norton CrashGuard

Norton Anti-Freeze and **CrashGuard** provide dramatically new ways of intercepting and preventing crashes from ever happening. Nevertheless, in instances when a crash does occur, the Crash Recovery Assistant guides you through the process of saving data from within the crashed application and closing frozen applications before other applications are stopped in their tracks.

Norton Web Services

With **Norton Web Services**, you can receive timely updates to your Norton software as well as all other major software and hardware on your PC. You'll also find some high-tech support options to answer your questions quickly. Norton Web Services includes the following components:

- **LiveUpdate Pro** provides you with a Web-based means for keeping not just your Norton SystemWorks software, but all major software on your PC up-to-date. You can quickly select and download hardware drivers and a wide variety of enhancement software to improve your own productivity.

- **Technical Chat** allows you to chat in real time with Symantec technicians, troubleshooting your Norton software and your system itself on a per-use basis.

6A

The Bonus Pack

The SystemWorks bonus pack includes tools to address the broad needs of mobile users, Web site designers, and many others. Its components include:

- **Norton 2000 Bios Check and Fix** guarantees that your PC's BIOS and Real Time Clock, which provide for the plurality of your PC's date-related needs, are fully Y2K compatible.

- **Norton Secret Stuff** provides a complete solution by which you can secure and encrypt files on your PC and files you send in email. Once encrypted, using a password you select, no one who is not in possession of the password can open the protected files.

- **Norton Mobile Essentials** gives you a way to establish a host of customized configurations for each of your various remote working locations. If you work at a variety of offices around the country or around the world, or if you simply travel regularly for any reason, NME will set up your notebook computer to work precisely as you wish it to while you're at each location away from home. Everything from dial-up numbers to calling-card settings can be securely stored, and made available in an instant.

- **Visual Page** provides a graphical environment in which World Wide Web pages may be designed as easily as a letter can be typed or a picture drawn. No technical knowledge of the workings of HTML are required, but HTML is fully supported in this powerful design tool.

- **WinFax** provides fax capabilities to users of Windows 98.

OR 6B

The Professional Pack

The SystemWorks Professional Pack provides two additional tools which address the needs of the more advanced user.

- **Norton 2000** is a complete Y2K solution for the power user. It can analyze every application on your PC and can compensate for and correct a wide range of Y2K incompatibilities. In addition, Norton 2000 will scan all of your data files, looking for and, optionally, correcting year-2000 incompatible dates. You can generate fully customizable reports detailing the Y2K-related problems of any PC. Norton 2000, of course, also provides the same BIOS and System Date checking as the Norton 2000 BIOS Check and Fix, included in the SystemWorks Bonus Pack.

- **Norton Ghost** makes moving from one PC to another—a new one, for example—almost painless. With Norton Ghost, you can make an exact duplicate of your existing hard drive, including the Windows Registry and other configuration files, and then copy the old drive to a new drive *in toto*. Norton Ghost completely solves the problem of having to reinstall all of your software.

How This Book Is Organized

This Introduction has, hopefully, given you a preliminary understanding of what Norton SystemWorks is, what it does, and how all of its pieces work together to maximize productivity and protect data. In the following chapters, you'll learn how to get the most out of every Norton SystemWorks component. The book is organized in accordance with some broad aspects of what the integrated parts of SystemWorks do. Part I focuses on ways SystemWorks protects your PC from problems and prevents them from happening in the first place. Part II addresses a wide range of recovery issues—things to do to repair existing difficulties. Part III teaches you how to use Norton SystemWorks to dramatically improve your PC's performance and to customize its working to your tastes.

Conventions Used in This Book

This book uses the following conventions:

File | Open	Menus and selections on them are separated by a vertical bar.
Program Files\Norton SystemWorks\ Norton Utilities	The names of folders are separated by back slashes.
monospace	It's important to differentiate the text that you see on the screen, or that appears within a file and so on, from the text that explains it. I've used monospace type to make this differentiation.
Bold	Bold text is used to designate items that you type (for example, at the command line).
ALL CAPS	Commands use all capital letters. Some Registry entries also use all caps even though they aren't all commands. Normally you'll type a command at the DOS prompt or within the Run dialog box. If you see all caps somewhere else, it's safe to assume that the item is a case-sensitive Registry entry or some other value. Filenames also appear in all caps.

Special Elements

Each chapter is peppered with tips for ways to use SystemWorks you might not have considered and occasional cautions alerting you to issues that could reduce the protection provided to you by Norton SystemWorks. As you read, you'll encounter the following special elements:

Note: Notes draw your attention to side issues, considerations, and opportunities for using SystemWorks which just don't fit into the flow of the main text.

Tip: Tips recommend some specific ideas for using SystemWorks that might significantly add to your productivity.

Caution: Cautions indicate a sidebar containing serious considerations that could jeopardize the safety of your data or could dramatically hinder your own productivity.

TECHNICAL NOTE

Technical Notes indicate that the information in the accompanying sidebar is of a more technical nature. This doesn't necessarily mean it's information for power-users only. You'll find technical notes used throughout the text to give you some technical background you may want to know to better understand the discussion in the main text.

PETER'S PRINCIPLE

Peter's Principle sections provide you with some practical, hands-on suggestions for using the SystemWorks components in the spirit of Peter Norton.

FAT32

FAT32 sections, which you will encounter only occasionally, draw your attention to the one or two places in which a Norton SystemWorks component behaves differently on a FAT32 drive than it does on a FAT16 drive.

WINDOWS 98

You'll only see Windows 98 sections once or twice, but they indicate when some aspect of Norton SystemWorks behaves differently under Windows 98 than it does under Windows 95.

When Bad Things Happen to Good Computers

When the general public first started hearing about computers back in the 1940s, among the many fantastical images that danced in their heads was that of the perfect machine. The computer was—or would someday be—a device that could perfectly calculate anything you asked of it. It could accept a query from you and return information that answered your questions perfectly. It could take over the tasks of thousands of people and run our homes, schools, and cities perfectly. A computer was exactly what you needed if you wanted your rocket to launch—or your missile to land—perfectly.

The fact that all this was perfectly ludicrous didn't sink into the mainstream public until nearly four decades later, when the first of us invited a computer into our homes. We all learned—and new users continue to learn today—that perfection was indeed an elusive goal. A computer was, and is, only as "perfect" as the women and men who design and program it. In other words, it's not perfect at all. Certainly, computers can perform flawlessly when they have been programmed flawlessly, and no one would question that we have achieved a level of reliability today that makes us—well, some of us—comfortable with the fact that our lives today are truly run on computers, if not by computers.

Like good people, today's good computers perform deeds that the rest of us would be hard-pressed to live without. But, also like good people, with our carefully evolved 2,000-plus body parts and our billions of cells, good computers still have bad days. Sometimes these days result from one otherwise good computer's influence over another good computer, with unpredicted results. Sometimes aging parts fail. Sometimes all the good people in the world can't compensate for the deeds of one really bad person. And sometimes, of course, a good computer's programming just isn't as flawless as it might otherwise be.

One of Those Days...

It's part of the nature of human beings to make mistakes. We would all like to think that, in contrast, it's part of the nature of computers to avoid mistakes. And many of them do much of the time. But the fact remains that it is the nature of computers, like people, to fail. What you can do about those failures—not just how you handle them when they occur, but what you can do to prevent them from happening in the first place—is what this book, and the Norton SystemWorks suite of utility products, is all about.

Complexity Approaches Chaos

Some of the failures that we experience with our computers are the direct result of the demands we place on them. As mainstream personal computers have evolved from the Apple II+, to the IBM PC, to the Apple Macintosh, to today's workstations running Windows 98 and Windows NT, we've come a long way from expecting our computers to add up our shopping bills or "take a letter." Today, it's just as likely to find a personal computer managing the bills of a multimillion-dollar company and editing our letters! When Bill Gates said in the early 1980s that no one would ever need more than 640K of memory in his or her computer, it wasn't because he was shortsighted. The fact is that you and I are using our personal computers daily for tasks that were inconceivable then.

Of course, to meet today's demands, today's PC is a far cry from the simplicity of yesterday's. Indeed, even individual chips inside your PC are more complex than the most sophisticated computer of any kind just 20 years ago. In addition to new hardware, huge quantities of code had to be written at each step in the PC's evolution to support our demands for better user interfaces, faster performance, and even better games. As it turns out—and as you might suspect—it is their empowering complexity that also plays a major role in giving our computers some very bad days.

It's useful to think of the Windows 98 operating system—actually, any modern operating system—as a massive machine. To perform its function properly, every part of Windows relies on the fact that every other part is in its proper place, is properly lubricated, and is working as perfectly as possible. In turn, every application we run requires the same of itself as well as of Windows. The 24×18-inch box that sits under your desk is a productivity factory containing literally millions of parts, all of which have to work if you're going to. When a piece is out of place or is improperly configured, all the other pieces that rely on it may also fail, cascading into one of a variety of error messages that we have all come to dread.

Incompatible "Parts"

Of course, as the complexity of our PCs has increased, it has been necessary to abandon old ways of doing things for new, faster, or more efficient techniques or technologies. Each such abandonment can expose the machine to failure. This is because an old piece of software or hardware might have been created to make use of the old methodology that no longer exists. Although Microsoft has gone to great lengths to track "retired" techniques and to be certain that new operating system elements handle antiquated software as well as possible, perfection remains as elusive as ever.

Human Weakness

Perfection also remains elusive because the people who write operating systems are no more perfect than the rest of us. As a result, issues sometimes get overlooked.

It's also true that many software developers often create their own, unique ways of achieving key tasks for reasons of patent, copyright, or copy-protection—and some of that becomes incompatible as the operating system is updated. It's unreasonable to think that even a company with the resources of Microsoft could own a copy of every piece of software ever written and be aware of any incompatibilities that might develop as Windows changes.

Bugs

Similarly, software developers—and, of course, this includes Microsoft—sometimes err. Errors that occur in either computer software or in hardware itself are commonly known as "bugs," and a large number of the errors that we users encounter on our PCs occur because of these bugs. Software developers may mis-implement a request to the operating system, causing the OS to shut down the offending application when the flawed request is made. Similarly, a typographical error in text that we barely notice—especially in those cases where a missing letter nevertheless creates another valid word—as with "wasp" and "was"—might cause a computer program to attempt to access the wrong device, the wrong bit of memory, and so on, all of which could be fatal errors. In other instances, the errors are those of omission: A software developer may have insufficiently tested a product, and an unforeseen circumstance—such as a calculation that attempts to divide by zero, which is a mathematical impossibility—may cause a "crash."

In the best of all possible worlds, all software developers would be successful and would aggressively track down and repair bugs as they are discovered. Indeed, this process of updating or "patching" software is very common; we return to that theme in Chapter 19, "Norton Web Services: Your Current Computer," when we discuss Norton Web Services and LiveUpdate Pro. Sadly, however, all software companies are not successful, and buggy software may be orphaned with no one to repair it.

You and Me

Tragically, the litany of human errors concludes with those that you and I make. We delete the wrong files. We click OK when we intend to click Cancel. We try to accomplish too many tasks simultaneously. We don't shut down our PCs properly. We dump coffee where coffee was never intended to go. Each of us has made hundreds of these kinds of mistakes while going about the daily tasks of our lives, and most of us have experienced that dreadful sinking feeling as we realize what we've done to our computers and to ourselves. It's no exaggeration to say that a lifetime of work can be destroyed in a few seconds.

Compounding the actual mistakes we make are all the human factors for which we really can't compensate in advance. Many employees may be expected to make use of the same

PC, and someone may unknowingly destroy someone else's work. Simply changing certain operating parameters may make it appear that hours of labor have been lost—and they might actually become lost if you don't determine what has been changed before you go about trying to reconstruct something that is merely hiding. A well-meaning janitor may water your office plants and set them to drip, unknowingly, into your PC (don't laugh, it's a true story). Less innocently, a dismissed employee may attempt to do far more damage than merely taking the office's last pad of sticky notes.

At home, the PC can also be exposed to the ministrations of children, who may inadvertently place all your tax records in the recycle bin. Children also have tempers, but they may not understand the possible scope of their malicious mischief as an adult would. Your son or daughter will not understand how angrily deleting "only one folder" got them grounded into the afterlife. Allowing the family cat to sleep on the PC monitor may only be precious until her random footsteps on your keyboard fall on the Delete key—or worse.

Finally, human-created computer viruses can endanger any data or software that resides on the computer they infect, or on any computer connected to that computer. Much has been written in the popular press about computer viruses passing via online connections to the Internet or online service providers. A virus was even passed once on floppy disks from a very large software developer because the disk duplicator had infected systems. While such instances are unlikely—and are as newsworthy as they are largely because of how unlikely they are—they nevertheless occur. Keep in mind, too, that a computer virus won't care if you're its intended target or not.

Hardware and Media Life Expectancy

Having looked at all the ways that people can fail computers—programming them wrong, using them wrong, pouring the wrong liquids into them, and so on—it is rather refreshing to realize that computers themselves also fail. Just as most of us expect our car-repair bills to start skyrocketing around 100,000 miles, computer parts are also subject to the Second Law of Thermodynamics. Basically put, stuff wears out. It's true that much of what is inside your PC's case is delightfully solid-state and, therefore, subject to very little daily wear and tear. At the same time, it's sobering to remember that the one place inside your PC that has parts that move more or less constantly—your hard disks—is the one place where everything that is important to you is stored. Hard disk motors are more sophisticated than ever, and the precision and reliability with which the read/write heads move across the disk platters is very high. Still, problems can occur.

Mechanical failure aside, the magnetic markings used to divide the space on your hard drives into organizational units (known as tracks and sectors) can slowly fade over time. If this process continues for too long, it can become impossible to retrieve your valuable data, even if the data themselves are still perfectly intact.

Despite their inherent stability, hardware chips do break. Power surges from electrical storms or even static electricity can expose the insides of your PC to voltages thousands of times higher than those for which they were designed. If this kind of disaster occurs while your PC is performing a read or a write to your hard disk, this hardware problem can turn immediately into a software problem.

Contacts between components inside your PC can also become unreliable because of dust and grime sucked into your PC by its fan. (In some systems, PC's are considered so vital that all the air that passes into them goes through a HEPA-grade filtration system just to eliminate this kind of problem.) In such circumstances, important data or commands may not move properly through your PC, and the tasks you think you are performing might not, in fact, be taking place, even though no error may be reported. Additionally, unreliable, dirty contacts may contribute to the likelihood that stray static electricity may jump from one component to others inside your PC, causing damage as it moves. Perhaps worst of all, unreliable contacts can make it appear that a functioning device has failed. The dire consequences of reformatting a perfectly healthy hard disk seem obvious.

Incremental Performance Degradation

A final kind of "bad thing" that can happen to an otherwise "good" PC simply results from poor system maintenance. In some ways, this could be considered an error of human omission, but this problem manifests itself in unique ways that bear mentioning on their own. If you've spent much time working with computers—or with people who do—you very likely have heard stories of computers that suddenly seem to work slower and slower, as though they are getting weary with endless word processing.

What is most likely happening in all these cases is that, through the normal process of storing, deleting, storing, and deleting data, the organization of a PC's hard disk—in this instance, the organization that the PC uses to find your data and programs, not the directories and folders that we see every day—looks more like the pantry after a large, Southern California earthquake. Yes, you could separate the peas from the soup and the spilled salt from the spilled pepper, but it would take you forever. In the same manner, it takes your computer longer and longer to find your data, to run your programs, and to maintain itself when all the bits and pieces it requires are scattered across your hard disks.

> **Note:** In technical jargon, the scattering of data across a hard disk is known as *fragmentation*. Fragmentation occurs as your computer becomes incapable of storing a file's data in contiguous locations on your disks. Why and when this occurs—and what you can do about it—is the subject of Chapter 17, "Norton Utilities: Getting It Together with Norton Optimization Wizard, Speed Disk, and SpeedStart."

As a result of this scattering, the read/write heads of your hard disks must move more to gather or store the data you and your applications require. As this fragmenting worsens, the time involved in these head movements becomes ever larger, commonly giving the impression that the PC is working slower.

An unfortunate side effect of all of this—as if a slow PC weren't enough—is that all those head movements put additional wear and tear on your drive's mechanical systems. Additionally, the integrity of your data itself can be endangered by a severely fragmented disk. You can read more about such issues in Chapter 17.

A different cause of a degraded performance can be an improperly maintained Windows Registry. Replacing the many .INI (initialization) files in the C:\WINDOWS folder, the Windows Registry was designed to provide a single place in which every application you ever install can maintain the configuration data it needs to operate properly. The cliché of storing all your eggs in one basket applies here, however: A sufficiently damaged Registry prevents your computer from booting at all. A large quantity of useless, anti-quated Registry entries may add significant amounts of time to that required to process reads from and writes to the Registry. When this extra time occurs repeatedly, it can slow down your computer's performance and your productivity.

The Importance of Backups

While you're thinking about all the things that can go wrong with and around your PC, take a few moments to think about one of the smartest, easiest things you can do to com-pensate for all the dangers that threaten your data: maintain backups. That is, make a copy of all the important data on your hard disk(s) so that, if disaster strikes, it isn't your life or livelihood on the line. Which of the data on your hard disk is important? Every byte. The valuable content you create with your word processing, database, or graphic programs has *no* value if your application has been damaged and won't run. Granted, in many instances, it is easiest to simply reinstall any piece of "broken" software rather than restoring it from a backup. For this reason, many people choose to back up only their data files. There is nothing inherently wrong with this strategy—and it is, in fact, what most people do.

A counter-example to this, however, might be the plight of someone who purchased Microsoft Word 6, then purchased the upgrade to Word 7, then installed SR-1 and now SR-2. Even if you've retained at least Disk One—which the Word 7 upgrade will require to reinstall—from your ancient Microsoft Word 6 package, you've now got at least three updates to run through to verify that all your files are the proper, most-recent application files. With a backup of the application, restoring files might be quicker. The issue of what to back up is one that each user must evaluate personally. Don't be discouraged from backing up *anything* because backing up *everything* just takes too long. At a mini-mum, always protect your precious data files.

Backing Up Is Your Best Protection Value

So, what exactly is involved in backing up those millions of bytes on your hard disk? How can it be done reliably? And how should it be done to maximize your safety and minimize your inconvenience?

First, you must obtain appropriate backup hardware. In most cases, this will be a tape drive of some capacity that connects to your PC either internally or externally. Pricing for tape drives is as varied as the speed and capacities of the drives themselves. A good tape drive may seem expensive, but consider the value of everything you are protecting through its purchase and use. If your finances are such that purchases of a couple hundred dollars must be planned, I urge you to budget for backup hardware for your PC. The return can be incalculable.

After you decide to acquire backup hardware, you must decide what best suits your needs. The chief issue here is capacity. Smaller media are less expensive, but they may require you to use several disks or tapes to back up your entire computer system. Worse, using smaller media requires you to change media several times during a backup; this inconvenience may lead you to abandon backing up altogether, at which point your entire investment, however small or large, is wasted. I generally recommend that you select a capacity that is sufficient to hold at least the one primary hard drive you intend to back up. Usually, this will be your C: drive.

After you determine what capacity you reasonably require, your next decision is what media to use. Many choices exist, from tape drive, to Iomega ZIP and JAZ drives, to SyQuest cartridges, and even to rewritable CDs. The reason you must consider your capacity requirements first, however, is because that factor determines your media options. If you need to back up a hard drive containing 2GB of data files, then ZIP drives (with their 100MB capacity per disk) would be sorely inappropriate for the task. On the other hand, there's little reason to spend $1,000 on a high-capacity Digital Audio Tape (DAT) drive if you're backing up your notebook computer at college.

Many users have found that tape drives offer an acceptable balance of price and capacity, although they are usually your slowest backup option. On the other hand, if your backup process must stop after 100MB so you can insert a new disk, tape may be a good deal more efficient overall. CD-Recordable media offer permanence to those who require it, while rewritable CDs provide better permanence and speed than tape, but at a lower capacity and much higher cost. As with any purchase of hardware, you should do your best to evaluate your current and future requirements relative to the cost of the hardware and the media.

After you've selected and purchased your backup hardware, the most difficult part of backing up your computer reliably is complete. As you'll see, the rest of the process is delightfully automated. Backing up will almost never interrupt your work or require anything of you at all—except, of course, changing the tape. So how do you set up this behind-the-scenes wonder?

Every piece of backup software—and most backup devices now come with their own software—works more or less the same way. You have the opportunity to specify exactly what you want to back up, either your whole drive, your whole computer (all its drives at once), or selected files. You can also specify that only files that have been changed since your last backup get backed up, but we'll see that in a moment. To maximize the safety of your data, I recommend that you back up every file on your computer as your first backup job. Most backup software is also capable of checking over the tape once the backup is complete to verify that what was on your disks is, in fact, what was stored on tape. This can be a time-consuming process, but it's well worth doing—your computer can do this overnight; no interaction from you is required. When the process is complete, the software provides you with a report. Included in that report are any errors encountered. For this first backup, if any errors did occur, you should re-check your installation to make certain that everything is set up in accordance with the manufacturer's instructions. If this is the case, perform the complete backup again, and consult the hardware manufacturer's technical support if you still find errors.

Assuming no errors exist—and, in all likelihood, they won't—you can design the backup scheme you want to use. As mentioned previously, you have the option of either backing up everything on your computer every time you back up or having the backup software automatically back up only files that have changed since the previous backup. You can almost always configure a combination of these two as well, perhaps performing a complete backup every Friday evening and performing modified or incremental backups Monday through Thursday night. My strong recommendation is that you use at least this very scheme—backing up everything every night puts a little more wear and tear on your hardware, but it also affords a little extra security. Look at Figure 1.1 for an example of what this might look like in your backup software.

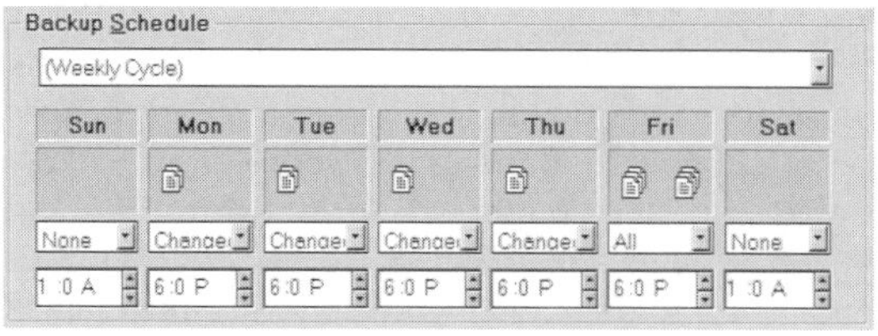

FIGURE 1.1

This chart gives an example of a good weekly backup plan.

You also should purchase five backup tapes, one for each work day of the week. Each morning, make it part of your daily habit to change to the next tape. The reason for this is simple: As they age, backup tapes can slowly stretch or distort, rendering them unreliable. By spreading your daily backups out across several tapes, you minimize the likelihood of discovering that the backup you really need rests on a damaged tape. Also, be sure to periodically verify the tape contents to be certain that your data is being stored reliably. All backup software provides this option, which is usually one of the preferences you select when you define a backup set. Doing this for one week out of every month—after all, you don't have to watch it happening or wait for it to finish if you set your backups to run while you're away or asleep—gives you the added assurance that the tape is actually storing your data reliably.

TECHNICAL NOTE

> Every file on your computer has a set of characteristics, or *attributes*, which give your PC more information about what the file contains and how it should be treated. Among these attributes—others of which include specifications identifying a file as a System file, an invisible or Hidden file, and whether the file should be treated as read-only (or not modifiable)—is the Archive attribute. When your backup software successfully stores a copy of a file onto tape, it sets the Archive attribute to indicate that the file was successfully archived to tape. Anytime thereafter, when the file is modified, the Archive attribute also changes. (The Archive attribute is sometimes called the *Archive bit*, for reasons that you can read about in Chapter 12, "Norton Utilities: The Laying-On of Hands and Norton Disk Editor.") When your backup software is configured to store only modified files, it looks at this attribute for every file on your computer, saving only those for which the Archive bit has been reset.

The Norton SystemWorks 2.0 suite of products does more than anything else available to keep your PC working reliably. As you continue reading and exploring each of the different products, give some serious consideration to the addition of backup hardware to your PC. It's absolutely one of your best protection values. With Norton SystemWorks behind you and a responsible backup plan at your side, the future ahead is as bright as you can make it. There's no better way to prevent bad things from happening to your good computer.

Norton SystemWorks Integrator: Putting It Together

After Norton SystemWorks 2.0 is properly installed, several key parts run automatically the first time you reboot Windows. Norton System Doctor, Norton AntiVirus, Norton CrashGuard, and Norton CleanSweep will all be working to check, monitor, and guarantee the integrity of your PC and your data. You'll read about all of these integrated components in detail in later chapters.

> **Note:** If you did not perform a Complete installation, your system's behavior after rebooting may differ slightly from what you've just read. This is normal. For more information about installing Norton SystemWorks, refer to Appendix B, "Installation Issues."

How do you access the parts of Norton SystemWorks that don't run automatically? And, incidentally, what is that weird icon with the bright blue letter "N" that has inserted itself into your system tray?

SystemWorks Integration

When Symantec was talking to users like you and me to find out what we want in a suite of integrated utilities, the most common answer they received was, perhaps not surprisingly, also the most obvious: a suite of integrated utilities needs to be integrated. Connected. Linked. Joined. Nobody wants to run the installation program 12 times—or run 12 different installation programs—to get software loaded on their PC. And after software is loaded, nobody wants to have to search at length to access it. As you no doubt already know, when you install software, pieces of it go here, pieces of it go there, but almost never do all the pieces go where you can find them. Even if you can find them, keeping all your software updated can be a tremendous chore. Visiting multiple Web sites and downloading updates and patches can take a large chunk of your time.

Finally, every piece of software works a little bit differently, and utility software, as a class, is notorious for cluttering up your System Tray with icons indicating various aspects of your system status and the software's status, and the price of cheese.

Norton SystemWorks integration lays all of that to rest. If you've already installed the software, you know that you only had to run one installation program—and it probably ran itself, if your CD-ROM plays discs automatically when you insert them. Unless you changed the defaults, all your Norton SystemWorks components were installed in a single folder, helpfully called "Norton SystemWorks." You were even able to register all the SystemWorks components online—and you only had to respond to one marketing survey! (Actually, you can even skip the survey.)

What makes Norton SystemWorks 2.0 truly special on a day-to-day basis, however, is the single entry it has placed near the top of your Start menu, as in Figure 2.1.

FIGURE 2.1

Norton SystemWorks places a single entry in your PC's Start menu.

This single entry gives you access to every aspect of Norton SystemWorks 2.0. This is your doorway to the Norton SystemWorks Integrator, which is your doorway to the entire suite. Figure 2.2 shows the main Integrator window.

FIGURE 2.2

The Norton SystemWorks Integrator is your doorway to the entire SystemWorks suite.

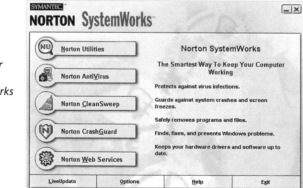

Norton SystemWorks Integrator

The SystemWorks Integrator consists of a mere nine buttons that put all of Norton SystemWorks at your fingertips. The remainder of this chapter will make you familiar with Integrator features, including the new Norton Tray Manager and unified LiveUpdate.

As you can see in Figure 2.2, the SystemWorks Integrator is comprised of three main areas, at the left, right, and bottom of the window. The right-hand area, or panel, is for informational purposes only. As you move your mouse cursor across the five icons in the left panel, the right panel updates, showing you key features of the Norton SystemWorks 2.0 component at which you're pointing. For example, in Figure 2.3, the mouse is pointing at Norton CleanSweep, one of the newest members of the Norton Utility family. (You'll read in depth about CleanSweep in Chapter 18, "Norton Utilities: More Room for your Stuff—Norton CleanSweep, Space Wizard, and WipeInfo.")

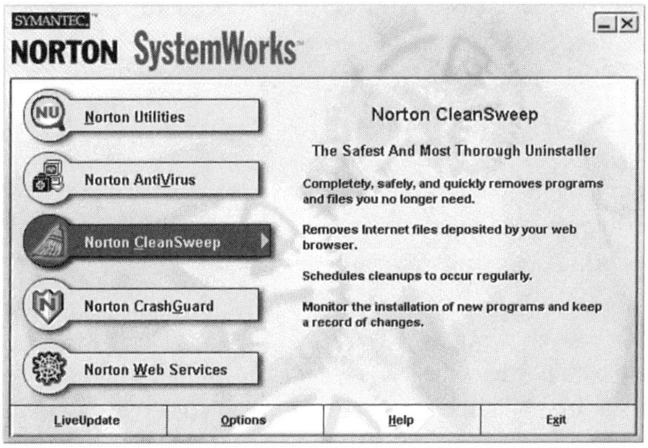

FIGURE 2.3

Point your mouse at any of the Norton SystemWorks components in the left panel and the right panel displays key features of that component.

Accessing any SystemWorks component is as simple as clicking its button in the left panel. In the case of Norton Web Services, at the bottom of the window, the Integrator will attempt to launch your Web browser—Norton Web Services features are all based on the World Wide Web. (You can learn about Norton Web Services in Chapter 19, "Norton Web Services: Your Current Computer.") If you click Norton AntiVirus, Norton CleanSweep, or Norton CrashGuard, you'll be taken directly to those major utilities.

Clicking the Norton Utilities button causes a slightly different result. Because so many smaller components make up the Norton Utilities, the Utilities has its own Integrator (see Figure 2.4). From here, you can quickly access any of the many Norton Utilities programs, as you'll see in a moment.

FIGURE 2.4

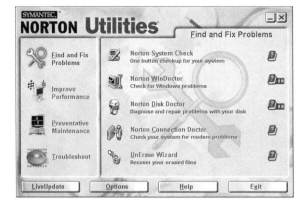

FIGURE 2.4

The Norton Utilities Integrator opens when you click Norton Utilities in the SystemWorks Integrator.

Service Buttons

Below the two main panels of the SystemWorks Integrator are four smaller buttons. These buttons give you access to several service-related features of the SystemWorks Integrator. Let's look at them from right to left.

Exit

The Exit button is fairly self-explanatory; click it and the SystemWorks Integrator quits. (Note that the Integrator's Exit button only closes the Integrator. It does not exit other SystemWorks components you have opened.)

Help

The Help button, when clicked, pops up a small menu of options. From here you can open a help file about the SystemWorks Integrator itself. From the Help button's menu you can retrieve a different help file which explains the wide variety of customer support options that are provided by Symantec to Norton SystemWorks 2.0 registered owners. You can also directly access the Symantec Web site by clicking the Integrator Help button and selecting Visit Symantec Web Site from the context menu.

At the bottom of the Help button's context menu is an item named About. As with most Windows applications, "About" provides you with general information about the software. Norton SystemWorks' "About" windows, however, do a good deal more.

As you can see in Figure 2.5, selecting About from the Help button menu opens a display that provides the version number and copyright information for the SystemWorks suite. Nothing unusual here. However, below that information are two areas you don't find in most applications. First, you can see that the copy of Norton SystemWorks used to create Figure 2.5 hasn't yet been registered. Registration is required to activate your rights to customer support as a legal owner of SystemWorks. Registration is also required before you can access LiveUpdate, about which you'll read in a moment. Registration also entitles you to receive information about updates and specially priced offers from Symantec.

Most users register the SystemWorks software at the end of the installation process. However, this is not required. If your modem is not installed or is not available when you install Norton SystemWorks—or if you want to put off registering for whatever reason— you can do so. This screen is an easy place to come when you are ready to register SystemWorks. Just click the Register Now button, and you are quickly stepped through a wizard that does most of the real work for you. (You can register one other way, which you'll read about in a few moments.)

FIGURE 2.5

Norton SystemWorks' About window shows information about the software and its registered owner.

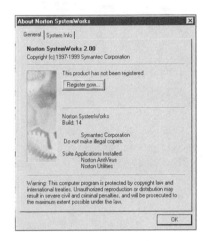

Below the Registration area is an animated scrolling display. Sorry, but technology just doesn't let me show you the animation here in the book. You'll have to take my word for it, or launch the Integrator and see for yourself! This display shows you more detailed information about the precise version of Norton SystemWorks 2.0 that you have installed. It also shows you the major SystemWorks components you have installed. If you're trying to locate a suite component and you can't seem to find it, take a look here: You might not have installed it in the first place!

Look back at Figure 2.5. This About window is also unusual because it consists of two different "tabbed" displays. You've probably already encountered tabs when you've used other standard Windows 95 and Windows 98 applications. Software designers use them to help gather related information together. For example, a program might gather all its customizable options together on several tabs so that they're intelligently organized—all the printing options together on a Print tab, for example—and easy to find.

By clicking the System Info tab, you display the window shown in Figure 2.6. You'll find a wealth of technical information about your PC. In fact, this is a miniature version of the Norton System Information tool you'll read about in Chapter 20, "Norton Utilities: Checking Your Own Nametag—System Info and Norton Diagnostics." Just click one of the five icons—System Properties, Memory Status, Display Settings, Library Versions, or Technical Support—to review the technical specs that are available under that category.

FIGURE 2.6

The System Info tab provides technical information about your PC, your copy of Windows, and Norton SystemWorks itself.

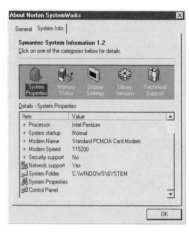

The information collected here can be useful to technical support personnel in the unlikely event that you ever need to call Symantec for help with Norton SystemWorks or one of its integrated components. The Library Versions section provides you with all the detailed version numbers for your installed Symantec software. Technical Support provides you with the telephone number for Symantec assistance as well as a shortcut icon you can double-click to go directly to Symantec's Web site. In the Memory Status section, a link to the Windows 98 Memory Troubleshooter is provided—assuming you're using Windows 98, just double-click the shortcut for help with memory-related problems. The System Properties section, shown in the previous figure, displays information about your PC and also provides shortcuts to your Control Panels, Network settings, and Windows System folder.

Options

The Options button in the SystemWorks Integrator drops down a small menu from which you can specify whether the Norton Tray Manager (which you'll read about soon) should load automatically at Windows startup or not. By default, the Tray Manager does load at startup; my recommendation is that you leave this option enabled unless someone in technical support asks you to turn it off as part of some troubleshooting process.

LiveUpdate

Last of the four service buttons at the bottom of your SystemWorks Integrator window is LiveUpdate. You'll read about LiveUpdate at length in Chapter 19. Briefly, LiveUpdate is a SystemWorks integrated component that allows you to connect to Symantec's host computer and check for new virus definitions for Norton AntiVirus and new versions and updates for all the Norton SystemWorks 2.0 suite. You can connect to the LiveUpdate host either via your existing Internet connection or by calling directly with your modem (if you don't have an Internet connection available).

A key new feature of Norton SystemWorks 2.0 is the capability of LiveUpdate to check for, download, and install updates for your entire SystemWorks suite all at once. You don't need to run LiveUpdate once to check for new virus definitions to keep your AntiVirus protection at its peak and then run it again to look for updates to the Norton Utilities or other SystemWorks components. LiveUpdate is now fully embedded in the SystemWorks Integrator. It can detect which SystemWorks components you have installed and can keep those components up-to-date automatically. After LiveUpdate is configured, it can work entirely behind the scenes on your behalf.

LiveUpdate is extremely easy to use, but if you're new to the idea of retrieving automatic online updates for your software, you may want to read the "LiveUpdate" section near the beginning of Chapter 19.

> **Note:** Don't confuse LiveUpdate with LiveUpdate Pro. The latter is a service provided as part of your subscription to Norton Web Services. Although LiveUpdate keeps all your Norton SystemWorks software current, LiveUpdate Pro can perform the same feat for all the major software installed on your PC! Unlike LiveUpdate, however, LiveUpdate Pro works only interactively. You log on to Norton Web Services and work with the LiveUpdate Pro online wizard to locate and retrieve updates. I'll talk about all of this in detail in Chapter 19.

The Norton Tray Manager

The newest SystemWorks Integrator component is another feature requested by scores of users: the Norton Tray Manager. You probably already know that the rectangular area at the right-hand side of your Windows taskbar is known as the *system tray* (see Figure 2.7). The purpose of the system tray is twofold. First, it provides a place for the display of your PC's clock. Second, and far more important, it provides a single, standard location where many applications can place an icon through which you can access some of its features. For example, the small speaker icon at the extreme-right of the system tray in Figure 2.7 gives me quick access to the volume settings for my PC.

The fact that applications can place icons into the system tray is sometimes a problem. Utility software can be particularly guilty of installing so many icons in the system tray that you can't reasonably remember what each one does, how to interact with it, or, ultimately, why you should care. Norton SystemWorks Integrator solves this problem. The Norton Tray Manager takes the various important Norton-related system tray icons and gathers them all together, "hiding them" behind a single icon until you need to use them. When you do want to use one of the features that is associated with a system tray icon, just point your mouse at the single Norton Tray Manager icon—that big, blue letter "N" that I mentioned early in this chapter—and the Norton system tray icons pop up, as shown in Figure 2.8. Move your mouse away and the icons disappear again. The Norton Tray Manager and SystemWorks Integrator keep your system tray neat and usable.

FIGURE 2.7

The Windows 98 taskbar consists of the Start menu button, shortcuts, open applications, and the system tray.

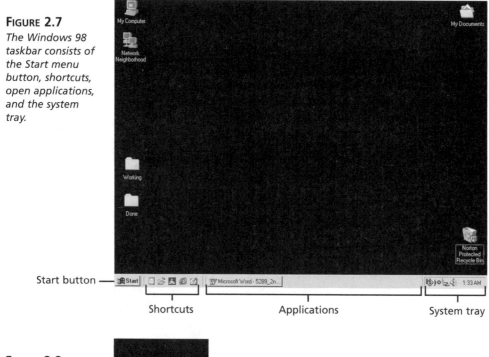

Start button

Shortcuts   Applications   System tray

FIGURE 2.8

Point your mouse at the Norton Tray Manager icon and all the Norton SystemWorks icons pop up, gathered neatly together. Move the mouse away and the Norton Tray Manager hides them from view again.

 — Norton Tray Manager Pop-up

Of course, if you don't want the Norton Tray Manager to load at Windows startup, you can easily achieve that: As you've read previously, the Options button on the SystemWorks Integrator lets you turn startup-loading on and off.

Additionally, once the Norton Tray Manager is running, you can associate or dissociate the SystemWorks icons. With the SystemWorks icons gathered, double-click the Norton Tray Manager icon (or right-click and select Ungroup Icons) to ungroup the icons. Double-click the Tray Manager icon again (or right-click and select Group icons) and the SystemWorks icons regroup.

Finally, notice that the Norton Tray Manager's blue letter N icon has a diamond-shaped background. Normally, this background is green. However, if one of the grouped SystemWorks icons requires your attention, the Tray Manager's background color turns red. So, for example, if System Doctor is running minimized and encounters a problem to which you should attend, the Tray Manager recognizes this fact and turns red. Thus, none of the various SystemWorks tray icons loses any functionality.

Using the Norton Utilities Integrator

You read previously that clicking Norton Utilities in the SystemWorks Integrator launches the Norton Utilities Integrator. The Norton Utilities Integrator, or NUI, works much the same as the SystemWorks Integrator, but with a few differences. Because the Norton Utilities Integrator must support many more options than the SystemWorks Integrator, the NUI's right-hand panel isn't merely informational; it's functional.

The highlighting halo around the icon next to the words "Find and Fix Problems" in the left-hand panel indicates that the five utilities shown in the right panel are associated with "Find and Fix" functionality. To launch any of the specific utilities, just click its name in the right panel. To open help with respect to an individual utility, click the small icon that has a book with a question mark on its cover to the right of the utility's name. In the case of a few utilities, a multimedia "tour" of the utility is available. Click the icon that looks like a strip of film to open help on the utility, and click Demo at the top of the help file.

FIGURE 2.9
Click one of the utility categories at the left to display links to the associated utilities in the right-hand panel.

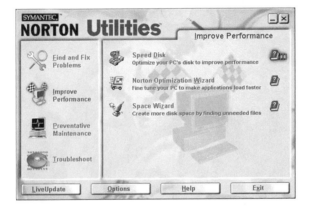

If you want to launch one of the utilities that is associated with a different type of functionality, just click the function type in the left-hand panel. As shown in Figure 2.9, the right-hand panel updates to show the utilities that perform that type of function.

On with the Show

Now that you have an understanding of the SystemWorks Integrator and Norton Utilities Integrator, you probably want to learn how to actually use the tools to which they give you access. The remainder of this book will help you do precisely that.

PART II

Protection and Prevention

Peter Norton

Norton Utilities: The System Doctor Is In

If you're concerned about the safety and health of your PC and the data it contains, you'll probably be using many of the different SystemWorks components on a regular basis. But, if you're wise, you'll use System Doctor continuously. Norton System Doctor is SystemWorks' and the Norton Utilities' front line of both defense and offense against almost anything that could endanger your data. (Pouring coffee into the system unit is another story, entirely.) System Doctor also provides a one-stop shop for a collection of performance monitoring and improvement tools, as well as diagnostic tools. In fact, although SystemWorks installed an icon on your desktop for the SystemWorks Integrator, you'll likely find that you access most of those tools through System Doctor.

Familiarizing you with System Doctor will give you an introductory understanding of virtually every aspect of Norton SystemWorks, so we'll start our exploration of this powerful software package here. Because one of the points of the System Doctor panel is that you're getting an integrated and, more importantly, unified interface to most of the Norton tools, there's a lot of commonality in how the different System Doctor tools can be configured. For that reason, I'll group the configuration how-to together near the end of this chapter, pointing out any significant differences you'll want to know about. You should also know that there are one or two differences between the sensors included with System Doctor in Norton SystemWorks and those that come with the stand-alone version of the Norton Utilities. I'll point out those differences as well, as we come to them.

Norton System Doctor, which was loaded as a component of the Norton Utilities when you installed Norton SystemWorks, isn't really one tool; it's a set of monitors or *sensors* which continually examine a variety of characteristics of your PC. All of these sensors can be easily configured to your tastes and needs, and will alert you when anything seems amiss. You will control exactly which sensors are active. Each active sensor can be displayed or hidden, as can the entire System Doctor *panel*, the customizable window in which sensors are displayed. You control how often each sensor checks up on your PC, and how it behaves when a concern arises. For problems that threaten the safety of your drives and data, you can even tell System Doctor to just fix whatever problems arise, without interrupting your work. System Doctor really is like having a private physician around; this one has nothing to do but watch out for your PC.

With that rather succinct introduction to System Doctor in hand, let's take some time to understand each of its different sensors, how they do what they do, and how you can make them work for you. Your data's safety, your PC's reliability, and its performance will all benefit from having a System Doctor in the house.

Sensors and Alarms

System Doctor's main panel, which you can see in Figure 3.1, consists of a collection of sensor displays which fit into a grid. (Your panel may look different than what you see here, and may consist of different default sensors depending on your system configuration, the number of drives on your system, and other factors.) It's this collective panel display which keeps you apprised of the health and welfare of your system. Each sensor you enable functions independently, watching out exclusively for the system characteristics for which it was designed. In a way, it's like having a panel of specialists at your beck and call, 24 hours a day, seven days a week. The different primary sensors—there are 38 of them—can be configured to display their examination results in a variety of different ways, which you'll read about later in this chapter.

> **Tip:** If you have closed your System Doctor panel, you can re-open it at any time by selecting Programs | Norton SystemWorks | Norton Utilities | Norton System Doctor from the Start menu. Similarly, if you've minimized System Doctor, clicking on its traffic light icon in the System Tray will maximize it.

First, let's look at what each sensor does. The sensors can be grouped into six fundamental categories, relevant to their type. These are disk-related sensors, system sensors, memory sensors, performance sensors, Internet and network sensors, and informative sensors. (Actually, all of System Doctor's sensors are informative, but the Information Sensors provide you with general information about your system as a whole, rather than keeping watch over a particular vital element.)

FIGURE 3.1
The Norton System Doctor panel consists of a number of sensor displays.

Disk-Related Sensors

There are eight different System Doctor sensors which watch over the condition and, moreover, the security of the precious data on your hard drive. You can see a collection of them in Figure 3.2. We'll look at the function of each one in turn, so that you'll understand when and whether you'll want to use each sensor.

FIGURE 3.2

This System Doctor panel shows all of the disk sensors active. Notice that three free space sensors are active, each showing the amount of free space on one of the hard drives.

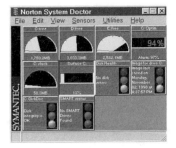

The Disk Doctor Sensor

By way of introduction to the Disk Doctor Sensor, I should explain that there are two different types of structures which exist on your hard disk. There are *physical* structures, like how many platters exist inside the box, and how many read/write heads, and so on. There are also *logical* structures which are created by software when the drive is partitioned and formatted. These logical structures are what bring organization to your data. They enable you to store and retrieve your files reliably and efficiently. Norton Disk Doctor, as you'll read about in Chapter 11, "Norton Utilities: The Disk Doctor Is In," is a powerful utility which checks the logical structures of your drives and verifies that those structures remain stable, clearly-defined, and ready to care for your data. These different structures, particularly the file allocation table which keeps track of where your files are located on the disk, are vital to ensuring your ability to save and load Windows, your applications, and your data.

The Disk Doctor sensor, here in System Doctor, regularly monitors your drives, looking for errors. These errors might manifest themselves as defects in the file allocation table, or two files which appear to be stored on the same place on disk—this is known as cross-linking—or places on disk where part of your system thinks a file is saved and part of your system doesn't. The sensor can be configured to perform these tests with the frequency you select. The sensor will also automatically run the full version of Norton Disk Doctor (if you wish it to do so) whenever problems are detected and will fix those problems while minimizing its interruption of your work. The Disk Doctor sensor works in the background, so you can work—or play—and keep your data secure at the same time.

As you can see in Figure 3.3, you can select to have several Disk Doctor sensors operative, each one watching over a different drive in your system, or you can set one Disk Doctor sensor to watch over all of your drives. You should choose one or the other of these options; activating more than one Disk Doctor sensor to check over all of your drives will significantly detract from the performance of your PC while those sensors perform their tests. With just one sensor watching each drive, or one watching all drives in succession, their testing will go unnoticed.

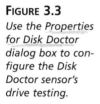

Figure 3.3

Use the Properties for Disk Doctor dialog box to configure the Disk Doctor sensor's drive testing.

You can also specify how often the sensor will check your drives using the Time between Drive Scans slide bar at the center of the dialog box. Two hours between scans is a reliable setting to select for a system used regularly. You may choose to test your drives less often if your PC is not used much, or more often if you often move large numbers of files around on your PC and want to be certain nothing ever goes wrong.

You can also set the Disk Doctor sensor to pause its drive testing for a period of time if the sensor detects that you are using your PC when it wants to check your drive. To do so, right-click on the face of the Disk Doctor sensor and select Properties from the pop-up menu. (This method, incidentally, is how you access the properties for all System Doctor sensors.) Once the Disk Doctor Sensor's properties are open, select the Drive tab. The system shown in Figure 3.3 will wait one minute before it continues its testing if it detects that you are performing other drive-related tasks, like saving or loading files. The reason for this is simple; every time you make a change to your drives, the Disk Doctor sensor needs to restart, making sure that whatever you changed hasn't created a problem. If not enough time passes between these restarts, you would eventually notice a performance drop because of them. Telling Disk Doctor to wait for a few minutes when it detects disk activity is based on a rather strange but proven principle: If a drive is accessed at any given moment, it will likely be accessed again soon. "Soon" is open to interpretation, but you can set the interpretation you like by using the Rescan Delay slide bar at the bottom of this sensor's Drive configuration tab.

The Disk Doctor sensor has the appearance of a traffic light, turning from green to red if difficulty arises. Many of the sensors can take on different appearances, displaying their test results to you as a traffic light, or a graph, or a percentage of some ideal system characteristic. The Disk Doctor sensor is an "all is well," or "all isn't well" kind of thing, so the traffic light is its only appearance.

The Disk Doctor Surface Test Sensor

The Disk Doctor Sensor only performs a subset of the tests which Norton Disk Doctor—an integrated part of Norton SystemWorks—can perform. One of the tests it does not perform is a check for physical damage to your drives' surfaces. Over time, a variety of problems on these surfaces can arise, any of which can cause irreparable data loss. The System Doctor Surface Test sensor can perform this surface test for you. It uses slack system time—that is, time when your PC's main processor, or CPU, is not heavily taxed—to periodically check your drives, looking for these surface problems as they just begin. As your CPU is needed to perform other tasks, the Surface Test sensor stops its work, and waits for the next chunk of idle time before continuing. In this way, as with the Disk Doctor sensor, you'll likely never notice that the Surface Test sensor is doing its job, watching over your data. Also like the Disk Doctor sensor, the Surface Test sensor can be configured to run Norton Disk Doctor automatically whenever any problems are detected. Alternatively, you can instruct the sensor to simply display an alarm—with or without an accompanying sound—to alert you to problems, letting you manually choose whether and when to repair them.

Unlike the Disk Doctor sensor, the Surface Test sensor can be configured to a number of different visual styles, as shown in Figure 3.4. In this case, each of the sensors will display the percentage of testing which has been completed, except for the stoplight, which will of course, display green until problems are detected. Certain sensor displays won't make any sense for a particular sensor, such as the histogram display for this sensor, but you can usually choose the display type you like best. (You've already seen one exception to this, of course: The Disk Doctor sensor can be displayed only as a traffic light.) All of these sensor display types are accessed though each sensor's Style tab, as you'll learn later in this chapter. For now, just be aware that they are available to you, so that when you start to customize your own System Doctor display, you'll be aware of everything in your toolbox.

FIGURE 3.4

The many faces of the Surface Test sensor. This figure also illustrates all of the different styles in which sensors can be displayed. Some styles are not available for some sensors.

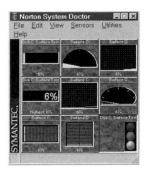

The Disk Health Sensor

The Disk Health sensor performs rather like a catch-all analyst, looking for problems in a variety of disk-related ways. Like the Disk Doctor sensor, it can safeguard the integrity of your file system. Like the Image and SMART sensors, which you'll read about in a few moments, it can verify that information maintained in your Norton Image files is up to date, and that your SMART-enabled hard drives are reporting no difficulties. The Disk Health sensor is also capable of automatically launching whatever Norton SystemWorks component is needed to repair any of these kinds of damage as they are detected. If you enable only one disk-related sensor, make it the Disk Health sensor. However, you'll get compounded protection when the other disk sensors are working for you as well—and certain functions, like checking for surface problems and fragmentation—are not performed by the Disk Health Sensor. Because it uses so little of your PC's processing power, I usually leave the Disk Health sensor enabled, along with the other disk-related sensors I use. I have the Disk Health sensor update itself only once a day, so it acts like a double-check against many of the other sensor functions. My data is worth it, and so is yours.

On Disk Health sensor's Measurement Properties tab, you'll notice that you can select the frequency of each of the Disk Health sensor's three primary tests, so that you can run certain checks—for example, the check of your Norton Image data—more often than the others. You'll notice on this sensor's Drive Properties tab that it, like the Disk Doctor sensor, can be configured to monitor all, or just one, of your drives. Like the Disk Doctor sensor, you should not enable multiple Disk Health sensors to check all drives. This can significantly slow your computer. Either enable multiple sensors, one for each drive, or enable one sensor only, checking all drives. Also like the Disk Doctor sensor, the Disk Health sensor can be displayed only as a traffic light.

The Disk Optimization Sensor

Norton Speed Disk is an integrated utility program which is part of the Norton Utilities and Norton SystemWorks. It makes a detailed analysis of your hard drives, checking for files which have become fragmented. That is, files whose content is not found in contiguous locations on disk, but has come to be spread around. How this happens and what its implications are is something you can read about in detail in Chapter 17, "Norton Utilities: Getting it Together with Norton Optimization Wizard, Speed Disk, and SpeedStart." For the time being, understand that a severely fragmented hard drive can seriously impact your PC's performance, and highly-fragmented files are quite a bit easier to damage than are those which are unfragmented. Additionally, as you'll read later when you learn about using Norton UnErase, it can be *much* easier to get back a deleted file if that file was not highly fragmented.

In order to keep tabs on this very important disk characteristic, keep the Disk Optimization sensor enabled in System Doctor. The sensor can be configured to display in a number of styles, but its basic functionality is to analyze the file allocation tables (FAT) of your drives and check to see what percentage of files are fragmented. As this number increases to some critical level which you can configure, the Disk Optimization sensor will either alert you to the problem, or it will automatically run the full version of Norton Speed Disk, repairing the problem in the background while you continue working. If you examine this sensor's Drive Properties tab (remember: right click on the sensor's face, and choose Properties from the menu) you'll notice that this sensor cannot be configured to check all drives. You should enable one Optimization sensor for each drive you want to check. This sensor is also like the Disk Doctor sensor, in that it will delay testing at times when you are using your drives. You can configure the length of that delay on the Drive Properties tab as well.

As with many sensors, this sensor can automatically run the relevant Norton SystemWorks utility to repair problems as it detects them. You can enable that property from the Alarm Properties tab, shown in Figure 3.5. Notice in the figure that Auto Trigger Level is checked and that the slide-bar in the middle of the panel is disabled. Many System Doctor sensors have a default trigger level—that is, the level above or below which an alarm is triggered or repair begins automatically—which is dynamically set by System Doctor itself. The Disk Optimization Sensor's automatic level is based on how much free space is available on your drive and how fragmented your files are when the alarm is enabled. To use that setting, just keep Auto Trigger Level checked. If you wish to set the trigger level yourself, uncheck the automatic trigger, and use the slide bar to set the alarm to the statistic you desire. The sensor shows the percentage of disk space that is *not* fragmented. For the drive represented in Figure 3.5, the Auto Trigger set the alarm at 97 percent. That means whenever more than three percent of this drive is fragmented, the drive will automatically be defragmented with Norton Speed Disk.

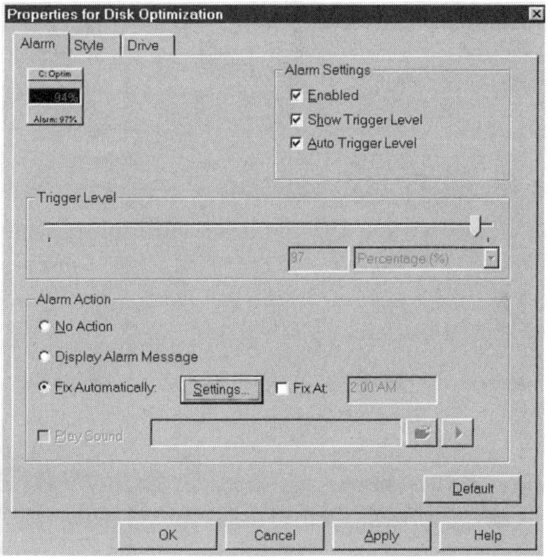

FIGURE 3.5

The Disk Optimization sensor's Alarm tab is similar in style to that of each of the other System Doctor sensors.

Figure 3.5 also shows the Alarm Action settings for this sensor. Again, these settings are common to most of the System Doctor sensors, so once you learn how to configure them for one sensor, you can configure them universally. When a sensor triggers an alarm, unless you configure the sensor differently, the alarm is displayed on screen, interrupting you briefly to draw your attention to the problem. If you wish to temporarily disable a sensor's alarms, but you don't want to disable that entire sensor, you can select No Action here. The sensor will continue to monitor and report its findings in the System Doctor panel, but nothing will be done about its alarms. Alternatively, you can select to have the problem fixed without your attention by selecting Fix Automatically. This option instructs the sensor to run the relevant utility—Speed Disk in this case—and appropriately repair the problem the sensor has detected.

Each utility operates somewhat differently, and you can click the Settings button here to bring up the configuration options for the relevant utility. When the sensor triggers an alarm and runs the integrated utility to automatically fix the trouble, it will use the settings you select through this Settings button. (You'll read about configuring each integrated SystemWorks component in that component's specific chapter.) Finally, you can choose to have repairs performed automatically, but only at a time you specify. So, for example, if you keep your PC powered-up all the time, you might want to have repairs made at 2 a.m., while you sleep.

> **Caution:** Be aware that several of the System Doctor sensors—the WinDoctor sensor, for example, which you'll read about later—will report serious problems with your PC which you should attend to as soon as possible. If you set repairs to only occur at a given time, you should train yourself to manually check the System Doctor panel on a regular basis. You'll want to make certain that you are not ignoring—or worse, compounding—problems whose repair should really not be delayed.

The Disk Slack Space Sensor

The System Doctor Slack Space sensor, reasonably enough, monitors the amount of slack space on your disks. Slack space is defined as space that has been assigned to a file, but which that file is not actually using. To understand what this means, you need to know a little bit about how files are stored on disk.

You may remember from reading previously about the Disk Doctor sensor that partitioning and formatting disks creates logical structures on them. These logical structures provide a method of organization by which your data can be stored and retrieved reliably. The most fundamental of these logical structures are known as "sectors," and these sectors have been grouped together into units known as "clusters." To keep the file system manageable, the file system designers in their wisdom have made one cluster the smallest amount of disk space that your PC can address. (If you like, you can think of clusters as mailboxes into which your data can be placed. Each such "mailbox" has its own unique address and "letters" cannot be placed in a partial mailbox. This analogy is far from perfect, but it may help you visualize the issues generally.)

The size of clusters on a hard disk has a direct correspondence to the total capacity of the disk—or, more accurately, the logical disk. A hard drive may have a total theoretical capacity of 9GB (gigabytes), but that drive can be partitioned into multiple logical disks, which the operating system will treat as though they were actually separate drives. It is the size of each of these logical disks that determines the size of cluster used for that particular logical disk. A DOS 16-bit file allocation table (FAT) limits the allowable partition size of a hard disk to 2GB, so a 4GB drive, for example, must be partitioned into two logical drives in order for it to be used. Each logical drive will have a capacity slightly less than the 2GB maximum allowed by the FAT. For drives with capacities over 1024MB, like almost all drives today, DOS uses a cluster size of 32KB, meaning that the smallest addressable space on the disk is 32KB. A direct consequence of this is that any file which is smaller than 32KB, still uses up 32KB of space when it is saved. (The reasons for this are now part of history. A "16-bit FAT" is called that because it uses numbers which are sixteen bits long to keep track of drive clusters. This limits the total number of clusters that can exist on a hard drive to 65,536, the largest number which fits into 16 bits. As a drive's capacity increases, the maximum number of clusters remains the same, so the size of each cluster must be increased to compensate.)

With Windows 95 OSR2—and in Windows 98—Microsoft introduced FAT32, a new 32-bit addressing scheme for keeping track of drive clusters on larger drives. With 32 bits available, the maximum number of clusters increases to a whopping 4,294,967,296! As a consequence, it's no longer necessary to sacrifice so much of your disk space to a mathematical limitation. Under FAT32, drives of greater than 512MB and less than 8GB capacity have a cluster size of a delightfully economical 4KB. Between 8GB and 16GB, cluster size is doubled to 8KB. A 16GB to 32GB drive will use a cluster size of 16KB, and only a massive drive of greater than 32GB capacity will require the use of 32KB clusters. (FAT32 supports drives of capacities less than 512MB, but you will not be given the opportunity to enable FAT32 on drives which are that small.)

Slack space, then, is the space that occurs in a cluster between the end of a file and the end of that cluster. Under the old FAT16, a 1KB file would create as much as 31KB of slack space! What a waste! Although, as you just read, FAT32 has solved much of this problem, not all drives that you may encounter will be FAT32 drives, and the Disk Slack Space sensor will let you know just how much of your drive—whether it's FAT16 or FAT32—is going to waste.

Note: Microsoft has provided a reliable utility, the FAT32 Drive Converter, for changing FAT16 drives into FAT32 drives. It's accessible through your Start menu by selecting Programs | Accessories | System Tools | Drive Converter (FAT32). If you have a lot of small files on your FAT16 drives, you may regain 40 percent or more of your drive space just by converting to FAT32! However, pay attention to the converter's warnings: Conversion to FAT32 is not reversible, and your drive will not be recognized by previous versions of Windows or DOS once you convert it. (Additionally, some older games or disk utilites may not run properly under FAT32.)

If you are not using a version of Windows 95 later than OSR2 or Windows 98, you must first upgrade to Windows 98 before you can use FAT32 and the FAT32 Drive Converter. If you are running Windows 95 OSR2 or Windows 98 but the converter does not appear in your Start menu, you can install it by inserting your Windows CD-ROM, opening the Add/Remove Programs control panel, selecting the Windows Setup tab, and adding it to your list of installed System Tools. To do this, select System Tools in the panel, then click the Details button. Place a checkmark next to the Drive Converter option, and click OK twice. The converter will load from your CD-ROM.

The Disk SMART Status Sensor

Self-Monitoring Analysis and Reporting Technology (SMART) is a new hardware technology which allows SMART-enabled hard drives to watch out for their own mechanical integrity and alert you if things begin to go wrong. Once warned, you can quickly copy all of your data from one drive to another, or to a backup tape, and remove the drive from your system for repair or disposal. The System Doctor SMART Status sensor converts the SMART data that these drives output into information you can use. Of course, if none of your drives has the SMART hardware built into it, there won't be any SMART data to report, and this sensor will tell you No SMART drives found. If you enable this sensor and get that message, you should disable the sensor and make room for another System Doctor tool which you can actually use.

The Disk Space Sensor

While the Disk Slack Space sensor alerts you to the presence of disk space you cannot directly use, the Disk Space sensor makes sure you know precisely how much space is left available which you can use. This sensor is highly configurable and can be made to show you either the amount of free space or the amount of disk space used. It can also measure that space in absolute terms (in other words, "let me know when I have only 10MB of free space left"), or as a percentage of total disk space (for example, "let me know when I have only five percent of my total disk space left"). It can display that information as a graphic, as a percentage, or it can tell you in kilobytes, megabytes, or gigabytes exactly how much space remains free (or is being used, depending on your preference).

Additionally, because free space is a characteristic which can change often and rapidly, this sensor gives you the option of seeing either the actual value or a decaying average. While the actual value will tell you exactly how much space is free at a given moment in time, the decaying average will tell you how much space is free, based on several measurements over a period of time you select. If, for example, you have a digital video editing application that creates a huge temporary file on disk while it runs, it might be much more important for you to know that, on average, you have 100MB of free space, rather than knowing that, at this very moment, you have 500MB of free space. This way, you can plan ahead for file-related activities which are liable to eat up space on a drive, possibly aborting themselves when free space becomes inadequate. When the alarm is triggered, as you can see in Figure 3.6, the sensor will give you the option of quickly freeing disk space by using the Norton Utilities Space Wizard.

FIGURE 3.6

System Doctor's space sensor alarm notifies you when it detects a low amount of free disk space.

The Image Sensor

Norton Image, a key part of Norton SystemWorks, which you'll read about in depth in Chapter 10, "Norton Utilities: More Than a Mirror, an Image," is a powerful tool which makes duplicate copies of vital parts of your drives—the boot areas, file allocation tables, and so on—and stores them so your drive can be reconstructed with relative ease in the case of a catastrophic failure. However, these files are only as useful as they are up-to-date. The System Doctor Image sensor will keep track of how recently your drives were Imaged and will alert you when too much time—defined by you—has passed since the last Imaging. The sensor can also launch Image automatically and perform an Image update without ever interrupting your work. If you look at this sensor's Drive Properties tab, you'll see that one Image sensor can monitor all, or just one, of your drives. Like the Disk Doctor sensor, which you read about earlier in this chapter, you should not set more than one Image sensor to watch over all drives. Also, like the Disk Doctor sensor, the Image sensor plays an all-or-nothing game, and can be displayed only as a stoplight.

As with all of the System Doctor sensors, how you use your PC should determine how you set the sensor. For many of the sensors and for many users, all of the default settings will be adequate. If you do an inordinate amount of file creation, deletion, moving, and so on, you'll want to set the Image sensor, and most of your other disk-related sensors, to update themselves more regularly. When it comes to the health of your drives, the more things change, the more you want to be certain they stay the same.

Memory Sensors

There are nine different System Doctor sensors which watch over your system's memory and resources. You can see a collection of them in Figure 3.7. By looking at each one in turn you will know what each one can do for you.

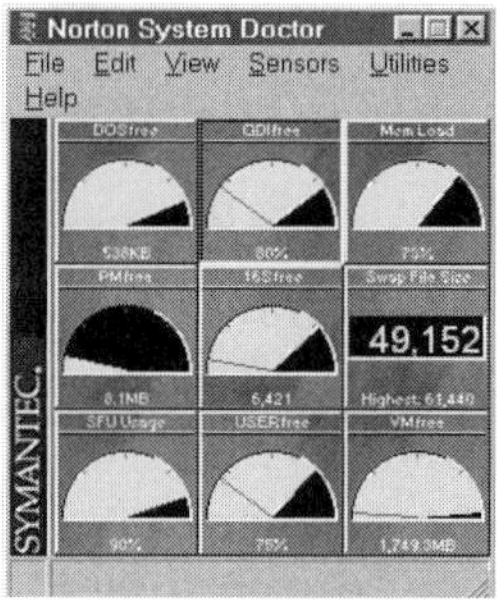

FIGURE 3.7
The collection of System DoctorMemory sensors.

The DOS Memory Sensor

The DOS Memory Sensor keeps track of how much conventional memory is available for use on your PC. Conventional memory is defined as the first 640K of physical RAM in your PC. Because of limitations in the architecture of both Windows and Intel processors—all of which are well beyond our scope here—DOS could originally only make direct use of this 640K range of memory. As applications became more and more complex, requiring more and more memory, any data that was needed had to be swapped or *paged* in and out of this 640K range. Today, any DOS real-mode device drivers which you load must be loaded into this conventional memory space. Fortunately, Windows 98 has replaced almost every conceivable real-mode driver with a protected mode driver which can be located and run anywhere in memory. You may, however, have a piece of hardware which cannot be supported by Windows 98 and still requires special real-mode drivers loaded either through your AUTOEXEC.BAT or CONFIG.SYS file, or both. There are also the (fortunately rare) pieces of antiquated DOS software—many of these are games—which can only run in part or in total within conventional memory. The DOS Memory sensor will let you know how much of this precious small range of memory is free for you to use for these purposes. The sensor can be configured to display in any of the various System Doctor styles, and can report its findings in terms of bytes available or a percentage of conventional memory free (or used, as you prefer). Like the Disk

Space sensor, which you read about earlier, you can also configure the DOS Memory sensor, and most of the other memory sensors, to display a decaying average, rather than an actual value.

The GDI Resources Sensor

Every application that runs under Windows, including Windows itself, requires GDI (graphic device interface) resources in order to run. These resources manage all of Windows' underlying graphical abilities, including the display of fonts. While virtual memory, which you'll read about shortly, can provide for a vast number of these resources, they are nevertheless finite in availability. As you run more and more programs simultaneously, these resources get used by those applications, and can run low. When that happens, Windows will display an out of memory error or, if you're running Norton SystemWorks, Norton CrashGuard will display the error. Although CrashGuard, which you'll read about at length in Chapter 8, "Norton CrashGuard: When Windows Breaks," will allow you to save your data out of a crashed program in most cases, such errors are still to be avoided when possible.

If you use a large number of programs at once, you can keep a watchful eye out for imminent problems by keeping the System Doctor GDI Resources sensor enabled. You can run out of GDI resources particularly quickly if you run a large number of older, 16-bit programs, such as those which were written to run under Windows 3.x. When the GDI sensor triggers, you should immediately quit as many applications as you can, beginning, of course, with any you are not currently using. Favor 16-bit applications over 32-bit applications in this quick shut-down process because the older 16-bit programs are far less stable and less tolerant of low resources than are their 32-bit cousins. Seriously consider upgrading any 16-bit software which you use commonly to a new 32-bit version if one is available. Your entire PC will be a more stable, reliable environment the less 16-bit software you make it endure.

Note: You can open Norton System Information (which you'll read about in depth in Chapter 20, "Norton Utilities: Checking Your Own Nametag—System Info and Norton Diagnostics") to see precisely what applications are running, and which are 32-bit and 16-bit. Right-click on the face of the sensor, and select Open System Information from the pop-up menu. Figure 3.8 shows a sample Memory tab in the System Information dialog box.

The GDI Resources sensor can be displayed in a number of styles, but measures only as a percentage of GDI resources available. The default setting of 20 percent is reasonable, but if you rapidly launch and quit many applications in a short period of time, you should probably enable the sensor's Decaying Average measurement property so you aren't surprised when your available resources suddenly drop well into the danger zone.

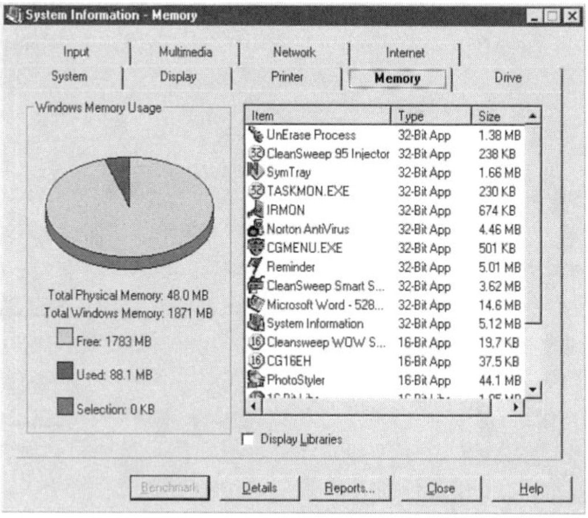

FIGURE 3.8

The System Information dialog box shows the memory and resources used by currently-running 16- and 32-bit applications.

The USER Resources Sensor

Related to GDI Resources, USER resources refer to memory space which has been set aside for Windows' own "User" module. This component of Windows manages a variety of issues relating to the user interface through which we mere mortals communicate with Windows and our applications. As more and more applications run, USER resources can run low. When this happens, on-screen menus, dialog boxes, buttons, and windows can display improperly or may refuse to display at all. The considerations for this sensor are similar to those for the GDI sensor. You should limit the number of 16-bit applications that you use and exit as many applications as you can any time the USER Resources sensor's alarm is triggered. You can open Norton System Information from this sensor's context menu as well or by double-clicking on the sensor and then double-clicking the System Information icon in the dialog box that opens.

The Selectors 16-Bit Sensor

In addition to requiring GDI and USER resources to run, older 16-bit applications, like those written for Windows 3.x, also require the use of "selectors." Selectors help Windows identify and manage areas of memory being used by 16-bit legacy applications, and there is a finite number of them available for the system to use. If you run several 16-bit applications at once, it is not at all inconceivable that you could run out of selectors, causing one or more—or all—of your 16-bit applications to crash. Although such crashes would commonly be caught by Norton CrashGuard, they should obviously be avoided if they can be. To do so, you should launch Norton System Information, as described in the previous section, and check to see which of your commonly-used applications are 16-bit. It's a good idea to upgrade those to 32-bit applications, either by buying a new version of the software, or by buying a piece of 32-bit software which performs the same functions. By their very nature, 16-bit applications are unstable beasts, and make Windows work much harder—and in significantly more complex ways—than do today's 32-bit applications. The more straightforward the running of Windows itself, the less likely you are to encounter difficulties. Until you are able to upgrade older software, however, keep the System Doctor Selectors sensor enabled, and watch out for your PC's precious resources to run low.

The Physical Memory Sensor

The System Doctor Physical Memory sensor keeps track of the amount of physical RAM available for your applications to use. If you refer back to Figure 3.7, you'll see the Physical Memory, or PM Sensor in the second row, at the extreme left. Notice in the figure that in this PC, which has 128MB of physical RAM, only 8.1MB of physical RAM was available for additional tasks. That means Windows, its disk cache, and the other applications running at the time were using almost 120MB of physical RAM. While Windows will provide significant virtual memory for your applications when physical RAM runs low, there is no question whatsoever that applications run much faster in physical RAM than they do in virtual memory.

The Virtual Memory Sensor

The Virtual Memory (VM) sensor keeps track of the amount of disk space available for use as virtual memory. As your computer's physical RAM fills (as, for instance, you run more and larger applications) Windows simulates the availability of additional RAM by creating a virtual memory, or *swap* file, into which and from which data is shuttled as more physical RAM is needed or as data already in virtual memory is needed for manipulation, respectively. Windows 95 and 98 are able to dynamically change the size of this swap file, so that it grows as you need more VM and shrinks to allow you to recapture drive space as your VM needs decrease. If your swap file drive is nearly full, however, you can actually run out of virtual memory. That can cause applications to crash. To avoid the problem, this sensor will apprise you of potential VM difficulties, so you can make more disk space necessary when problems arise.

Although System Doctor does not run them automatically to "fix" low Virtual Memory conditions, there are two Norton Utilities that dramatically increase the efficiency and availability of your Virtual Memory. First, the Norton Space Wizard—part of the Norton Utilities and integrated into Norton SystemWorks—can analyze your drives and help you select files to delete, making their drive space available. More important to virtual memory, however, is the Norton Optimization Wizard, or NOW. You'll read more about NOW in Chapter 17. In brief, NOW can analyze all of your drives, first making sure your fastest drive is being used for your virtual memory swap file. NOW will also set the Norton recommended parameters for your swap file, defragment it, and place it at the end of your fastest disk so that your virtual memory performance is not degraded by having the swap file fragmented. With this sensor enabled, you can see clearly how your system is using its virtual memory resources, and you can choose to use these other Norton tools to pump up your system's performance and your productivity, in one swoop.

The Swap File Sensor

System Doctor's Swap File sensor is, in some regards, the opposite of the Virtual Memory sensor. While the latter informs you as to how much disk space is available for Virtual Memory to use, the former enables you to see how much disk space is currently reserved for the swap file. The size of this file changes dramatically as you use Windows, depending on the demands of your applications. It can be useful to have a visual understanding of the largest and smallest size your swap file takes during your normal working day so that you can plan ahead when you start considering issues of free disk space, where to install applications, where to store all those pictures you've downloaded from the Internet, and so on. If your swap file commonly grows to use 90 percent of your total disk space, it would be foolish to reduce your available disk space by installing an application you know will take up 20 percent of what's available. So, by knowing the parameters of your swap file, you can maximize your performance by keeping enough space available for the file to grow into while you work. As you read in the previous section, the Norton Optimization Wizard can dramatically increase swap file performance—and thereby, system performance—by moving the swap file to your fastest drive or to the drive that has the most free space.

The Swap File Utilization Sensor

If you're really trying to tweak the last bit of performance out of your PC, there are many different things you can change—virtual memory settings, swap file locations, drive free space, fragmentation, and so on—which don't cost you a penny. On the other hand, sometimes you've just *got* to buy more physical RAM if you want your PC to work any faster. But how do you know when you're at that point? How do you know when you have done everything you can with the software and it's time to start adding hardware?

You know by using the System Doctor Swap File Utilization sensor. This sensor will tell you what percentage of the space currently reserved for your swap file is actually being used by your applications. Consider this scenario. You've got your swap file located on your fastest hard disk, thanks to the Norton Optimization Wizard, and there's nothing else on that disk—so there are no files you can delete to make more room for the swap file. By using the Swap File Utilization sensor to see how much of your swap file is actually being used, you can make the determination of whether or not you need to add physical RAM to your PC if you want to achieve greater performance. If most of your swap file is being used most of the time, then there's little question that your system would benefit from more physical RAM.

The Memory Load Sensor

The Memory Load sensor is closely related to the Swap File Utilization sensor. While the Swap File Utilization sensor keeps track of how much available swap file space is actually being used by applications, the Memory Load sensor performs the same function for physical RAM. When all of your physical RAM is being used, Windows must provide additional memory through Virtual Memory. Data that is not being used at a given moment is swapped out of RAM onto disk, in the VM swap file. When that data is needed again, it gets swapped back into RAM. Relative to the speed of physical RAM, all of this disk swapping takes forever. There's no question that you'll see your performance suffer from it.

The Memory Load sensor can be a bit confusing, inasmuch as a reading of 50% doesn't mean that half of your physical memory is in use, it means that all of your physical memory is in use… and that 50% of your total memory is being provided by RAM and half by Virtual Memory. To really simplify this, pretend for a moment you have a total of 1MB of physical RAM in your PC. If you see this sensor reporting 50%, then you know that you have a total of 2MB of usable RAM at that moment, 50% (1MB) of which is being provided by Virtual Memory, and 50% (1MB) of which is being provided by physical RAM (all of which—100%—is being used to achieve this). From the 50% point on up, your system will get slower and slower. There are a number of things you can consider doing when this sensor gives you this kind of a reading. First, run the Norton Optimization Wizard. It's one of the integrated tools of the Norton Utilities inside SystemWorks. The Optimization Wizard will analyze hard disk speed and free space issues and can relocate your swap file to another drive if better conditions can be found there. Second—and the Norton Optimization Wizard will do this automatically, as you can read about in Chapter 17—run Speed Disk to eliminate fragmenting in your files and in the swap file. This will bring out the best performance in whatever amount of virtual memory you have available. Finally, consider making the expense of adding RAM to your PC. Obviously, more physical RAM means more room to run your applications entirely in physical RAM, and there's no better way to maximize your performance than that.

System Sensors

There are nine System Doctor System sensors, but two of these—the two Norton AntiVirus sensors—are not recommended for use within SystemWorks. This is because the full Norton AntiVirus 5.0 product, complete with Auto-Protection in all operating modes at all times, is provided as part of SystemWorks. Contrastingly, the Norton Utilities stand-alone product contains only a limited version of the famous and award-winning Norton AntiVirus protection. The two virus-related sensors work together in the free-standing Norton Utilities product to monitor your PC for viruses—and to monitor System Doctor itself—to maintain up-to-date virus libraries and prevention/elimination technologies. (These are downloaded to your system through LiveUpdate.)

You can read much more about Norton AntiVirus in Chapter 9, "Norton AntiVirus: Infection Protection." The System Doctor AntiVirus sensor provides a subset of the technology found in the SystemWorks product. The threat of viruses is quite real, and obtaining the full AntiVirus package—along with all of the other Norton utilities—is a great reason to upgrade your stand-alone product to Norton SystemWorks. We'll take a look at the other seven sensors here. As you would expect already from your earlier reading, the two AntiVirus sensors—if they are present on your system—work and are configured using the same methods as other System Doctor sensors. (You'll read about general configuration issues at the end of this chapter.)

The Battery Power Sensor

The System Doctor Battery Power sensor is a useful little tool for monitoring the capacity of your notebook or laptop computer's battery. Much of this same functionality can be provided through your Windows Power Control Panel, which can display battery capacity in your System Tray. However, the sensor remains part of the System Doctor suite because many users, myself included, like to be able to have all of their diagnostic and informational tools in one place. The System Doctor panel provides me with one-stop-shopping, as it were. A glance at the panel tells me all I need to know about my entire computer.

The CPU (Central Processing Unit) Usage Sensor

The CPU Usage sensor enables you to monitor how much time your PC's main processor spends performing tasks, running commands, making calculations, and so on, contrasted with the amount of time it spends idle. If the CPU Usage sensor constantly indicates high usage, you should investigate the applications you are using at the time to verify first that they are 32-bit applications (16-bit applications will frequently use far more processor power than their 32-bit equivalents). Then check to see whether they are configured to properly make use of Windows resources (if they can be custom-configured).

A very high CPU usage can also indicate that you are running too many processes at once, either applications or device drivers—real-mode drivers in particular (those loaded through your CONFIG.SYS or AUTOEXEC.BAT files). It can also be an indication that your virtual memory settings may not be properly configured. (This is because the CPU is very involved in the swapping in and out of all of that data to and from disk.) If your CPU Usage sensor shows that your CPU is maxed-out most of the time, you should take a serious look at the readings displayed by the other System Doctor sensors. There may be steps you can take to reconfigure your system, optimize your drives, your hardware configurations, and your memory settings to lower the toll on your PC's processor and, ultimately, get better performance out of it. By default, this sensor has been configured to display as a Histogram, so that you can look back in time, as it were, and see which processes or applications caused your CPU to have its limits pushed. With that knowledge, you can change what you may need or want to change. (Be advised that certain individual processes, like loading files or launching an application, may cause your CPU to temporarily use 100%. This is entirely normal.) Note that some applications and utilities are designed to operate in the background using idle CPU time, and will cause Norton System Doctor to always report the CPU usage at 100%. This may be normal operation.

3c   ## The Norton CrashGuard Sensor

The CrashGuard sensor keeps a careful watch on the various resources (many of which you read about in the previous section on Memory sensors) which Windows and your applications require to run properly. The sensor is integrated fully with Norton CrashGuard, a component of Norton SystemWorks, and keeps track of crashes if they occur. If you examine this sensor's properties, as you can see in Figure 3.9, notice that this sensor, unlike the others, has three entirely unique properties tabs. One each for GDI Resources, USER Resources, and Virtual Memory. Each of these tabs controls functionality which essentially duplicates those three System Doctor sensors (all of which you read about in the previous section on Memory sensors). By using the CrashGuard sensor, you are essentially using all three of those sensors, unified into one display. You can adjust different settings for the CrashGuard sensor than those that you do for the individual sensors, if you have a reason to keep them both, or all, active. Notice, too, that the CrashGuard sensor, like the Disk Health sensor, reports its findings in an "everything is fine," or "something is wrong" manner—it can be displayed only as a traffic light. If you want the statistical information provided about the three Windows resources the CrashGuard sensor monitors, you will need to enable the other sensors as well.

Caution: Do not enable multiple CrashGuard sensors in the System Doctor panel. Doing so will unduly use possibly precious system resources.

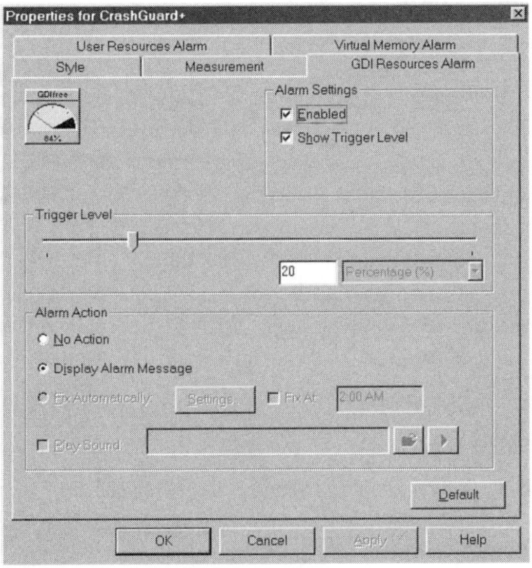

FIGURE 3.9

The properties for the CrashGuard sensor include three unique tabs which enable you to configure this sensor's specific functions.

The Open Files Sensor

This sensor keeps track of the number of files which are open on your computer. You're not limited in how many files you can have open under Windows, but you will notice significant performance degradation if you have too many files open at once.

If you notice that using a particular application seems to make your entire PC slow down, try enabling the Open Files sensor. Programs like drawing or photographic manipulation software often maintain huge numbers of files open at once, providing a variety of functionality, not the least of which is selective and multiple levels of "undo." The Open Files sensor will show you if that application causes the number of open files to jump dramatically. If it does, you may be able to re-configure the application to provide fewer levels of undo, or to make use of Windows resources more economically.

The Rescue Disk Sensor

Norton Rescue, which you will read about at length in Chapter 7, "Norton Utilities: Life Preserver on a (Rescue) Disk," is an integrated part of the Norton Utilities. Rescue will take a snapshot of all your drives' vital configuration characteristics, as well as the information necessary to boot your PC, start up Windows, and restore your entire Windows Registry. Additionally, your Rescue disk set will contain all the primary Norton repair tools—functioning either in DOS or in Windows itself, as you'll read in Chapter 7—necessary to provide a wide range of repair for most types of catastrophic drive failures and accidental deletion of data. However, like the Image files you read about earlier in this chapter, your Rescue disk set is only useful if it's up-to-date. To restore a current, damaged Registry with one that is weeks old, for example, could be as harmful as is the original Registry damage.

The Rescue Disk sensor will keep track of the age of your Rescue Disk set. Using a period of time you set, the sensor will alert you whenever that amount of time has passed since your Rescue set was last updated. Furthermore, the Rescue Disk sensor can be configured to automatically run the Rescue utility, both reminding you and allowing you to update your Rescue set whenever it does age inappropriately. Further, if you are making use of Rescue Folders or Norton ZIP Rescue rather than Rescue Disks, the Rescue sensor can actually update your Rescue files for you automatically, without interrupting your work. (There are serious trade-offs to consider with respect to Rescue Folders, however, which you can read about in the technical note in the Chapter 7 section titled "Floppy Creation.")

The Threads Sensor

The Threads Sensor can help you analyze the performance of your system with respect to its 32-bit applications and its 32-bit operating system. The jargon expression *threads* refers to a 32-bit application's ability to break its various complex processes apart into individual, distinct processes. Each of these individual processes is known as a thread, and your PC's CPU is capable of operating on many threads at a given time. In this way, this so-called "multi-threaded" characteristic can make a very significant contribution to your system's ability to efficiently multitask. You've already seen multi-threading at work if you have ever begun moving a file from one folder to another while another file is already being copied. You've also seen multi-threading if you have ever used a recent version of Adobe Photoshop, and noticed that you can perform a variety of tasks in the foreground while a time-consuming process is being performed in the background. Web browsers, too, can download and work with multiple elements simultaneously. Although the degree to which it works is debatable, multi-threading has also been used to allow you to cancel certain lengthy processes, like downloading figures or text from an online service, by pressing the Escape key while the data is pouring through your modem. With many threads running, however, system resources will be very highly taxed, and you will notice significant performance degradation. Anyone who has watched the mouse pointer jitter and jar across the screen while waiting for Adobe PageMaker or Photoshop to complete a complex task has experienced this. This sensor can contribute to your ongoing analysis of how many applications you can feasibly use at any one time, and whether or not your physical RAM is sufficient for your tasks.

The WinDoctor Sensor

Norton WinDoctor, which you will read about in Chapter 4, "Norton Utilities: The WinDoctor Is In," is one of the single most-useful components integrated into Norton SystemWorks and the Norton Utilities. WinDoctor can regularly and automatically scan your PC for all of the most common Windows-related problems. WinDoctor will detect Registry damage long before it manifests itself as a crashed operating system and lost data. WinDoctor can check for orphaned shortcuts, eliminating that tedious, "Windows is looking for…" message whenever you double-click a shortcut to a file that's been moved. Moreover, WinDoctor can repair all of these and many, many other problems.

The WinDoctor sensor in the System Doctor panel makes using WinDoctor completely automatic and unobtrusive. The sensor will run WinDoctor's collection of tests as often as you select. It is yet another of the "all or nothing" sensors, and so only displays as a traffic light. The WinDoctor sensor's great power really lies in its ability to automatically run the full WinDoctor repair utility and repair most Windows-related problems it encounters without ever disturbing your work. In fact, as this paragraph was typed, WinDoctor analyzed my Registry, my file system, my shortcuts, the deleted files in my Norton Protection Recycle Bin, and found three problems—which, I'll admit, I had artificially created to prove my point—and I would have never noticed the utility was running if I hadn't been watching for it.

Because it is both powerful and unobtrusive, I usually leave the WinDoctor sensor configured for checking the health of Windows 98 every day, with Fix Automatically always enabled on its Alarm Properties tab. Of course, if you don't want WinDoctor to perform its repairs automatically, you need not configure the sensor to do so. The WinDoctor utility provides a full system report that is quite informative. One of the nicest aspects of WinDoctor is that it creates an extensive Undo History, so any repair it makes that isn't to your liking can be reversed. If you do not enable any other System Doctor sensors, enable the WinDoctor sensor. You really can't go wrong.

Internet and Network Sensors

There are four sensors in System Doctor that provide performance-related analyses of your Internet and network connections. Of course, if you never go online, and if you're not on a LAN (local area network), you have no need to enable any of these four tools.

The Internet Packet Turnaround and Internet Speedometer Sensors

A detailed discussion of how data moves across and through the Internet is beyond what we want to examine here. However, you may already be aware that data of all types moves through the maze of the Internet in data bundles known as "packets." Analyzing how fast packets of data move between your computer and a remote Internet server can give you a good sense of how reliable and rapid your Internet connection is. If you're a user of IRC—Internet Relay Chat—you've doubtless experienced seeing "PING" appear hither and thither. When you "ping" another user, you're sending a packet of data out to his or her computer, and then the packet bounces back at you, and you're told how long it took for the round-trip. These two System Doctor sensors essentially perform the same function in the opposite manner. The Internet Packet Turnaround sensor will send out a packet of data to an Internet site which you specify (PING.SYMANTEC.COM is the default) and will measure the return-time of that packet against a *minimal* standard you set. The sensor will notify you if and when communication with the site you've selected is faster than the minimum level you select. This can be particularly useful if you are trying to establish a high-speed, reliable link to a specific site for the purposes of uploading or downloading data or participating in an online conference or whiteboard discussion.

The complementary sensor, Internet Speedometer, performs the same task, but alerts you when the speed of the connection you are testing drops *below* the level you select as being minimally acceptable.

Notice that both sensors have a properties tab that is unique to them alone, named "Site" under the sensors' preferences. This tab allows you to select an Internet site other than the default for speed testing. (Be aware that if you are working with a proxy server or if you are behind a firewall, these sensors may not function.)

The Network Reads and Network Writes (IPX) Sensors

Both the Network Reads and Network Writes sensors analyze the performance of your IPX (Novell NetWare compatible) network, returning information about how quickly you are able to read from or write to a network hard drive.

Performance Sensors

There are four main performance-related sensors—although you've already read how many of System Doctor's sensors reveal data relevant to the performance of your system—but there are actually a total of 78 different system properties which can be monitored through the combined cache, disk throughput, and Windows Performance sensors. We'll look at the first three main sensors before tackling the highly-configurable Windows Performance sensors.

The Cache Hits Sensor

5A

As Windows runs, it uses a significant portion of your physical RAM to provide you with a Disk Cache—that is, an area of memory set aside for the temporary storing of disk-based data you have used recently or are likely to use in the near future (an analysis based on processes which you have just performed). Because physical RAM is hundreds of times faster than your fastest hard drive, data stored in the disk cache is available almost instantly, relative to the time frame in which it would be available if it had to be loaded from disk. Thus, the disk cache plays a tremendously important role in accelerating the performance of your computer. The more data your operating system is able to provide to your applications from the cache, the faster everything will run. Conversely, the more often that needed data isn't in the cache—the more often it has to be loaded from one of your drives—the slower everything will run.

The Cache Hits sensor will give you an analysis of how regularly the data required by the operating system and your applications is found in the cache, and how regularly it must be loaded from disk. A cache hits average below about 70 percent could mean you are running too many applications or system threads at one time, limiting the availability of memory for the cache to use. To investigate this possibility, launch Norton System Information from the Start menu by selecting Programs | Norton SystemWorks | Norton Utilities | System Information and look at the Memory tab, which shows all of the various programs which are running. (You can also right-click on the sensor face and select Open System Information. This will take you directly to the Memory tab.) Additionally, you can add the Threads sensor from the Sensor menu, under System | Threads. Consider limiting the number of applications you run simultaneously. Windows will favor putting your applications into memory over creating more cache space—which is exactly what you want—but if your applications are disk-intensive, and your available cache is too small, things will become seriously bogged-down.

Another consideration, of course, to increase your cache hits is to increase the total amount of physical RAM present in your system. Windows will dynamically enlarge and shrink the cache to meet your working requirements, but the cache can't grow into memory that doesn't exist. For today's purposes, 64MB of RAM is really the functional minimum you want in your PC, if you're someone who values responsiveness.

The Cache Memory Utilization Sensor

5B

The Cache Hits sensor and the Cache Memory Utilization sensor are similar to the Swap File Size and Swap File Utilization sensors you read about earlier in this chapter. The Cache Utilization sensor keeps track of what portion—expressible as a percentage of total memory or as a specific figure of memory, in kilobytes or megabytes—of memory is being used for the disk cache. As with the Cache Hits sensor, this sensor is another way to analyze whether you're trying to make your PC do too much at once, and whether you should seriously consider adding physical RAM. You can use this sensor in combination with the Memory tab display in Norton System Information and the results of running the System Doctor Threads sensor to make those kinds of evaluations.

The Disk Throughput Sensor

As with the twin cache sensors, the Disk Throughput sensor is very useful in making fundamental analyses about how you use your computer and whether it has sufficient resources available to meet those needs. Measurements analyzing how quickly data moves from storage on your hard disks into memory and vice versa provide a meaningful contribution to all considerations of whether your PC's resources are insufficient to meet your requirements. This reading additionally reflects the presence of the Windows disk cache, and so provides an added sense of whether or not memory is available in quantity adequate to provide a suitably large cache. Finally, the reading obviously reflects the physical and data-transfer characteristics of your drives themselves. Having the best and the fastest hardware available may be relevant to neither your economic nor working realities. However, hardware that is too slow to do what you expect of it is no bargain. Yes, memory can be expensive, but your time has precious value too—regardless of what society has tried to teach you otherwise. I'm certain you'd rather spend that time with your friends and family of choice rather than with a box of metal, plastic, and pumped-up sand. These productivity sensors will help you make the evaluations you need to balance performance, productivity, and payment.

The Windows Performance Sensors

The Windows Performance sensors, which can be found in the Sensor menu under Performance | Windows Performance Stats, duplicate functionality found within Windows itself, for the purpose of giving you one convenient location from which to view and analyze all of your performance and system-health concerns: the System Doctor panel. The key to beneficial use of the Windows Performance sensors is, of course, selecting the sensor that monitors what you've changed in your PC to try to enhance its performance. And, in order to obtain meaningful data from the sensor, you need to use it before and after you make those changes, so you have something to compare. What follows in the next section is a brief description of each class of the sensors, followed by instructions on how to configure them. All the following sensors are accessed through the Windows Performance Stats dialog box, which you access from the Sensor menu under Performance | Windows Performance Stats.

Dial-Up Adapter Performance Sensor Specifics

If you have the Windows Dial-Up Adapter (commonly used for connecting to the Internet via a modem) installed on your system, this category of performance sensors will help you analyze the performance of your modem communications. Sensors provided are:

- Alignment Errors
- Buffer Overruns
- Bytes Received / Second
- Bytes Transmitted / Second
- Connection Speed
- CRC Errors
- Frames Received / Second
- Frames Transmitted / Second
- Framing Errors
- Incomplete Frames
- Overrun Errors
- Timeout Errors
- Total Bytes Received
- Total Bytes Transmitted

If you have made configuration changes with respect to your dial-up networking hardware, or if you have recently replaced a modem, upgraded it to a new technology standard, and so forth, these different sensors can help you determine whether the software
or hardware modification has improved your remote connections. Of course, it is important to remember that, with all things seemingly the same, you will still likely connect to
a remote site at a variety of rates. As you'll read about later in this chapter, to get meaningful analyses with these sensors, you should be certain to configure them to make their
analyses over an extended period of time.

Disk Cache Performance Sensor Specifics

The variety of disk cache-related sensors here provide some of the same functionality as
those you read about in the previous section. Additional tests are available here which
indicate problems encountered with respect to cache recycles. A cache recycle occurs
either when Windows needs to reduce the size of the cache to make physical RAM available for some other process, or when the cache is full and room must be made for new
data to be added. If cache recycles fail—which can be monitored by one of these sensors—it can indicate that the cache is full (in which case, you are probably attempting to
run too many applications at one time) or that physical RAM is insufficient for the
demand you are placing on your PC. The cache sensors are:

- Cache Buffers
- Cache Hits
- Cache Misses
- Cache Pages
- Failed Cache Recycles

- LRU Cache Recycles
- Maximum Cache Pages
- Minimum Cache Pages
- Random Cache Recycles

File System Performance Sensor Specifics

Many of these sensors duplicate functionality provided by the Norton sensors which you've already encountered earlier in this chapter. They are included here primarily for completeness, as I mentioned at the beginning of this discussion. One sensor, however, *Dirty Data*, is unique here, and tracks the amount of data which you have told Windows to write to disk but which Windows is holding in memory. In the event of a crash, this data is the most susceptible to loss. If you find that an unacceptably large amount of data is being held and that your system is already unstable, there are three steps you can take. First, of course, run the other Norton SystemWorks tools, Disk Doctor and WinDoctor in particular, to try to better stabilize your system. Second, use Norton System Information to track down and, if possible, eliminate 16-bit applications from your PC. Finally, and as a last resort, you can open the System Control Panel and select the File System button on the Performance tab. From there, select the Troubleshooting tab and place a check-mark in the box next to Disable Write-Behind Caching For All Drives. The amount of Dirty Data displayed by the sensor should drop to zero.

> **Caution:** Disabling write-behind caching will definitely negatively impact the performance of your PC. You should truly use it as a last resort, doing all you can to better stabilize your system as a whole, first.

The disk-cache sensors which are part of the Windows Performance sensors are:

- Bytes Read / Second
- Bytes Written / Second
- Dirty Data
- Reads / Second
- Writes / Second

Kernel Performance Sensor Specifics

The three Windows Kernel Performance sensors—Processor Usage, Threads and Virtual Machines—allow you to keep track of the demand your applications are placing on your PC's computing power. As you've read earlier in this chapter, a very large number of threads running will definitely see the slowing-down of each thread. The Virtual Machines sensor keeps track of how many virtual machines are running on your system. Windows itself uses one virtual machine, known as the System Virtual Machine, so this sensor will never show fewer than one virtual machine running. All of your 32-bit applications, the Windows interface, and your 16-bit Windows applications run within the System Virtual Machine. Each MS-DOS application you run, or each DOS-box you open from the Start menu's MS-DOS Prompt entry, runs in its own virtual machine. Each virtual machine acts like an entirely separate PC, providing each DOS application with the appearance of running all by itself and having complete control over all your system's ports and hardware.

The reasons for this are historical—if not hysterical. When MS-DOS applications were written, multi-tasking was yet to happen, and so each application essentially required that it be the only thing running. To facilitate compatibility with Windows and multitasking with Windows applications, the Windows System Virtual Machine creates these virtual machines, each of which runs in a special virtual 8086 operation mode of your PC's CPU, allowing your DOS applications to continue to believe they are each king of the hill. There are some modern exceptions to this: By using a special set of tools, some MS-DOS programs can now be run in protected mode, along with the rest of Windows. This enhances system performance tremendously. Every time your CPU has to work with one of the MS-DOS virtual machines, it has to switch itself into virtual 8086 mode and then back into protected mode to communicate with Windows. This enables Windows to be somewhat more in-charge than it would otherwise be, but all of those mode changes take significant time. If you've got a large number of virtual machines running on your PC, you can expect to see things operating at less than their potential performance.

Memory Manager Performance Sensor Specifics

The variety of Memory Manager Performance sensors are, for the most part, rather abstruse and arcane, relative to most users' interests. These sensors, like the other Windows Performance sensors, are accessed through the Windows Performance Sensors dialog box, by selecting Performance | Windows Performance Sensors from the System Doctor Sensor menu. Many of these sensors duplicate testing provided by the Norton sensors discussed previously. Others are particularly useful to computer programmers, allowing them to see how their applications and Windows interact. For reference, these sensors are:

- Allocated Memory
- Discards
- Disk Cache Size
- Instance Faults
- Locked Memory
- Locked Non-Cache Pages
- Maximum Disk Cache Size
- Mid Disk Cache Size
- Minimum Disk Cache Size

- Other Memory
- Page Faults
- Page-Ins
- Page-Outs
- Pages Mapped from Cache
- Swapfile Defective
- Swapfile in Use
- Swapfile Size
- Swappable Memory
- Unused Physical Memory

Microsoft Network Client and Server Performance Sensors

These two collections of sensors—the Microsoft Network Client and Server Performance Sensors—can be particularly useful to network administrators who are trying to troubleshoot problems across the network and improve its performance. The Client sensors—Bytes Read per Second, Bytes Written per Second, Number of Nets, Open Files, Resources, Sessions, and Transactions per Second—display very useful information which can help the Network Administrator track the impact of hardware and software changes to the network. They can also be used in determining whether network saturation times exist (that is, times at which the performance potential of the network is maxed-out). The Network Administrator can use this information to suggest changes in system policies that will be beneficial to everyone (for example, everyone backing up their local files to the server beginning at precisely 4:55 p.m. every afternoon might be less than a wonderful idea).

The Network Server sensors—Buffers, Bytes Read per Second, Bytes Written per Second, Bytes per Second, Memory, NBs, and Server Threads—provide similar functions, but for the server itself. These sensors can provide the Network Administrator with an indication that existing server hardware is growing inadequate to meet network demands. Additional physical RAM or additional processors might be needed to improve network-related user productivity. These sensors can also help detect system slack times, during which business-hours server maintenance can be performed while impacting a minimum number of individual users.

If you do not have a Microsoft Networking Client or Server installed on your system, these sensors will not be available to you.

Considerations for Configuring the Various Windows Performance Sensors

The Windows Performance Sensors may be exactly what you need to tell you what you want to know about your PC. Be aware, of course, that running a large number of these sensors can, in and of itself, impact your system's performance and thereby change the sensor readings. If you want an immediate response to a software configuration change you've made, you'll want to have the relevant sensor set to re-check its findings frequently. On the other hand, setting the sensor to update over a longer period of time is the technique to use when you're trying to determine use patterns and see the long-term or global effect of your performance modifications. Bear in mind that Windows must keep track of the sensor's readings and provide you with an average of those readings if you set the sensor to update its display infrequently. This can impact certain sensitive performance statistics, so keep a watchful eye out for variances seeming to appear from nowhere. It may be that you have just changed the sensor's time frame.

Informational Sensors

The final four System Doctor sensors provide information about your system and about Norton SystemWorks itself.

The Current Time and Date Sensor

The Current Time and Date sensor will provide you with a quick desktop reminder of what's going on in the world around you. You can change the font and size in which the time and date are displayed by this sensor to maximize its readability.

The LiveUpdate Sensor

The Norton Utilities LiveUpdate Sensor will remind you to keep all the Norton Utilities components as up-to-date as possible. LiveUpdate will guarantee that you always have the latest virus definitions and that you receive the benefit from any software enhancements or modifications Symantec releases. This sensor can be configured to automatically update your Norton Utilities software when the period of time you specify has passed. (Notice that this sensor is in the "all or nothing" family, and can only be displayed as a traffic light. The Norton Update sensor is one I always leave set to Hidden so that I can actively watch more vital aspects of my entire PC, but still maintain my Norton Utilities software. I recommend setting this sensor to check for updates every 30 days.)

The Protected Files Sensor

The Norton Protected Files sensor keeps track of the number of files present under Norton Protection. This matters because when you delete files, Norton Protection actually keeps a copy of them on disk for a period of time you specify. This can eat up otherwise valuable disk space. By configuring this sensor and Norton Protection individually, you can tell Norton Protection to save files for a period of time you designate, and you can tell this sensor to let you know if and when a very large number of files is being stored. In that circumstance, you may wish to run the Norton Protection Wizard (which you'll read about in Chapter 6, "Norton Utilities: Digging Through the Trash with Norton Protection,") and verify that you don't need the files Norton Protection is safeguarding. These files can then be safely purged by right-clicking the Recycle Bin and selecting Empty Norton Protected Files, recovering the disk space they were using.

6 D

The Windows Up Time Sensor

Finally, the Windows Up Time sensor shows you how much time has passed since
Windows was last started. This sensor can help you keep track of other people who may
be using your computer, and of the frequency with which system crashes cause your computer to be shut-down and rebooted. Now that the practice of leaving your PC on constantly is fairly widespread, the wisdom of occasionally restarting Windows just to allow
it to "clear its head" is something you should learn. By using this sensor to keep track of
how long Windows has been running, you can remind yourself to restart and thereby reset
Windows every five days, or however regularly you feel is appropriate. Finally, if you are
a system administrator, you may want to enable this panel to verify that hardware or software modifications have not increased a given workstation's tendency to crash.

System Doctor Sensor Histories

Most of the System Doctor sensors keep track of their readings and can display this history in an enlarged window view. For example, in Figure 3.10, you can see the Free
Space History for the C:\ drive. This window is accessed by right-clicking a sensor's
face and selecting Sensor History Window from the context menu, or by selecting a sensor and pressing Ctrl+H. (If Sensor History is disabled in the context menu, then that
sensor does not maintain a history. In such a case, pressing Ctrl+H won't do anything.)
The History window's time component, displayed as the horizontal axis, is determined
by the frequency with which the selected sensor is updated. In the case of Figure 3.10,
free space sensor is set to update every ten seconds. If the sensor were set to update once
an hour, the horizontal axis would reflect that setting. You'll also notice that the sensor
History window will provide you with information regarding the sensor's current reading, its highest and lowest reading since it was first enabled, its minimum and maximum
potential (in the case of the figure, no free space versus the size of my drive), and the
current alarm setting (in the figure, the alarm is set to alert me when less than one percent of my drive is free).

FIGURE 3.10

*You can display a
Sensor History for
the Free Space
sensor.*

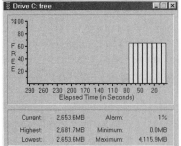

A sensor's history does not automatically reset when the sensor is disabled. In this way you can enable and disable a sensor over a period of time, checking for changes in current statistics versus historical ones. Each sensor's history is maintained within the Windows Registry and will be available even after your PC is shut down, until you reset the sensor. To do that, right-click the sensor's face, and select Reset from the context menu. If sensor history is valuable to you, use caution, there is no confirmation before the sensor history is reset.

Configuring the System Doctor Panel

You have already read how individual System Doctor sensors can be configured. Almost all sensors share the same Properties tabs, which are readily accessible by right-clicking a sensor's face and selecting Properties from the context menu. Alternately, you can double-click a sensor's face and choose Properties from the explanatory dialog box that will open. You can right-click most of the controls on the Properties tabs for specific help on what the control does. We can finish the discussion of Norton System Doctor by looking at how the panel, as a whole, can be configured.

Selecting When and How System Doctor Runs

You can select whether System Doctor runs automatically every time Windows starts. You can also decide whether you want the panel to display or whether you want it minimized, so that only the summary traffic light—green for "all okay"; red for "something's wrong"—displays in the System Tray. From the panel's View menu, select Options and click the Windows Settings tab. A checkbox in the Start Automatically with Windows will enable that functionality, while a checkbox in Start Minimized will place System Doctor's initial display in your System Tray, rather than on your desktop. (Click the Tray icon to view the entire panel.)

Adding, Removing, and Relocating Sensors

To add any of the Norton System Doctor sensors to the active System Doctor panel, click on the Sensors menu at the top of the panel and select first the sensor category, and then the individual sensor. It will appear at the end of the line of all current sensors.

Removing a sensor is just as easy; right-click on the sensor's face and select Remove from the context menu. (Notice that the context menus also show a Close option. This closes System Doctor as a whole, not just the individual sensor you've selected.)

To change the order in which sensors appear in the System Doctor panel, simply click your mouse on the sensor's face, hold the button down and drag the sensor to the location you desire. Other sensors will move out of the way to make space for the relocated sensor.

All of these settings are also available from the panel's View menu by selecting Options and then clicking on the Windows Settings tab. Sensors can be relocated within the panel by selecting their name in the Windows Settings tab and clicking the Up or Down button, as appropriate.

Resizing Sensors

All of the System Doctor sensors can be displayed in a variety of sizes, which can be set individually or globally. To resize just one sensor, open the Properties for that sensor and select the Style tab. Selecting the proper radio button for a Large or Small sensor size will change the sensor to that size when you click OK, as shown in Figure 3.11.

Notice, too, that you can select a sensor to be Hidden, such that its face does not display in the panel, but it continues to perform its monitoring tasks. You will still be alerted by alarms from this sensor, if you have the sensor configured in that manner, but you won't see it in the System Doctor display. To view all hidden sensors, you can right-click the face of any sensor and select Hidden Sensors from the View entry in the context menu. (You can also select Hidden Sensors from the panel's main View menu.)

FIGURE 3.11

Two System Doctor sensors, each shown in both Large and Small size.

You've probably already noticed that as you add and remove sensors, the System Doctor panel resizes itself to accommodate them. If you wish to manually reshape the panel, click the resize-icon at the bottom-right corner of the panel's window and drag the panel to the shape you desire. Reshaping is restricted by the sizes of the active sensors; System Doctor will not enable you to occlude a sensor's face. If you wish the panel to be smaller, set some of your sensors to their Hidden style, or remove them from the panel.

Resetting the Panel

If you have made a significant number of changes to the System Doctor panel, exploring the different sensors, moving them around, and so on, it may be easier for you to get the panel back to a reasonable configuration by resetting it, rather than by manually activating and deactivating multiple sensors. The default configuration set by System Doctor's designers provides excellent overall coverage for the most vital issues that the System Doctor sensors track. It is from this default configuration that you will likely build the configuration you actually desire. This can be done one of two ways. The easiest method is to select Options from the System Doctor View menu and click the Active Sensors tab. The Default button at the bottom-right corner of the tab will activate only the default sensors and will clear their histories, effectively resetting the entire panel. Alternatively, you can use the Run command from the Windows Start menu, and enter Sysdoc32.exe /reset into the Run window's file name panel and click OK.

Custom Sensor Configurations

If you like, you can establish a collection of different System Doctor panels, each of which monitors a different set of system characteristics. In this way, you can customize System Doctor to your current needs without manually disabling and enabling multiple sensors. You may, for example, normally want to monitor your own workstation's characteristics, but occasionally review how the network is performing. To create a customized configuration, enable and order the sensors you wish to display and select Save Configuration As from the panel's File menu. Give the configuration a name, such as "My PC" or "Network," and click OK. When you want to use the custom configuration, just load it from the Panel's File menu by selecting Open Configuration.

TECHNICAL NOTE

> At the time of this writing, the System Doctor EXE file takes no command-line arguments other than the /reset switch. You cannot, therefore, create customized shortcuts for your Taskbar or Start menu which launch System Doctor and load a specific custom configuration. (For example: SYSDOC32.EXE C:\PROGRAM FILES\NORTON SYSTEMWORKS\NORTON UTILITIES\NETW.NSD simply launches the most-recently used System Doctor configuration.) You must run System Doctor and select Load Configuration from the panel's File menu.

Panel Display Options

There are a number of ways to customize the manner in which the System Doctor panel is displayed. All of these are accessible through the panel's View menu. First among these is the option to turn the panel's title bar and menu off. If you can't find the View menu, chances are good that someone has found it before you. You can display the menu at any time by right-clicking the face of any sensor—the five entries at the bottom of every context menu are the equivalent of the panel's main menu. To turn the title bar and menu on or off, check or uncheck Show Title Bar in the panel's View menu. Pressing Ctrl+T will also toggle between showing and hiding the title bar and menu. You have the additional option of displaying or hiding the Symantec logo. Unchecking Show Symantec Logo in the View menu will allow you to recover a small amount of desktop space if you desire.

If you wish the System Doctor panel to float on top of all applications that you run under Windows, select Always on Top from the View menu. This can be particularly useful if you are in the middle of making software configuration changes and you want to immediately see whether your change has impacted your PC in the desired manner. Of course, the panel on top does occlude whatever is beneath.

You can also cause the panel to be "docked" to the screen, as shown in Figure 3.12. This locks the panel to the edge of the screen you select and effectively reduces the usable amount of screen space by the width of the panel. Be aware that you cannot move or re-order sensors while the panel is docked. An alternative to the loss of all that screen space is to activate the docked panel's Auto-Hide feature, also found on the View menu. In this manner, when an area of the screen other than the panel is selected, the panel "rolls away" into the screen edge, leaving only a thin line to indicate its presence. Pointing the mouse to that line at the screen edge "unrolls" the System Doctor panel. (You are probably already familiar with this type of functionality...the Windows Taskbar can also be docked to any of the screen edges you select, and will also Auto-Hide itself if you choose.)

Panel Appearance

In addition to the various panel settings discussed previously, you can create a variety of custom display options which impact the overall appearance of the panel. Each custom configuration you create can have its own custom appearance which will load with the configuration. Display schemes are largely a matter of aesthetics, but you may find that changing color combinations makes the sensors easier to read. You can also globally change the size and shape of sensors.

To begin creating a customized display, select Options from the panel View menu and click on the Sensor Appearance tab. At the top of the tab, the Scheme setting allows you to select a variety of bitmapped images that were loaded to your hard disk when Norton SystemWorks was installed. You can set the System Doctor panel to look like moon rocks, blue aluminum, or spray from a waterfall, among others. As you change to one of the saved display schemes, the color of display text will also change, to keep the sensors legible. You can also select any standard Windows bitmap (BMP) file to use as the background for your sensors. Simply click on the Folder icon near the bottom of the tab and navigate to the bitmap you want to use. The System Doctor panel will use a portion of that bitmap, beginning with the upper-left corner. If you want a pattern repeated throughout the System Doctor display, select a small bitmap, such as one of those provided by Microsoft as a background pattern for your Desktop.

Once you've selected a bitmap, you may need to change the colors System Doctor uses for text and its numeric displays. It's terribly hard to read black text against a black background. You can make these changes by selecting the various display components—text, graph color, and so on, from the Item drop-down menu, as shown in Figure 3.13. Once you've selected the screen element you wish to modify, you can change its color by clicking the Color button, or you can change its font and font size, assuming it's a text item, by clicking the Font button. (Bear in mind that if you dramatically increase the font size, you will want to increase the size of each sensor, so you can see all of the text. Sensors won't automatically stretch to fit the text.) The Color button takes you to the standard Windows color picker dialog, and the Font button lets you select from all installed fonts and font sizes and styles.

FIGURE 3.13
The Display Settings Tab with the Item drop-down visible.

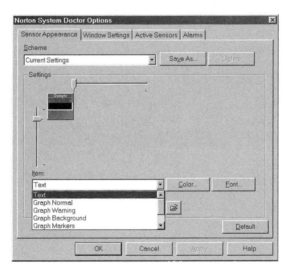

Finally, you can globally resize the System Doctor sensors by using the two slider bars which you can see in the middle of the tab in Figure 3.13. Sensors which you have set to Large in their own Style Properties will be twice as large as the sensor size you set here. By increasing the size of each sensor face, you can select a larger font, making all of the sensors more legible. Alternatively, you can reduce the sensor size, allowing more sensors to fit within the same-sized System Doctor panel.

Maintaining Your PC's Health with System Doctor

The System Doctor truly is at the heart of Norton SystemWorks. Virtually all system characteristics safeguarded by the various SystemWorks components can be monitored, configured, and run from within the System Doctor panel itself. Furthermore, you'll read in a number of places in this book that one of the most important tasks you can perform for the protection of your data is keeping the variety of Norton tools up-to-date. The System Doctor is the best, easiest way to remind yourself when your Image and Rescue data needs refreshing.

System Doctor need not be an intrusive part of your PC. You can keep it minimized all the time, only responding to alarms that sound at intervals you've selected. Or, you can have most System Doctor-monitored problems automatically repaired without your ever knowing they existed in the first place. If it sounds like I'm trying to convince you to use System Doctor, I am. It's a powerful tool in your collection of safety and performance utilities, and it's the core, unifying entity that draws all of your Norton SystemWorks protection together.

Peter Norton

Norton Utilities: The WinDoctor Is In

One of the newest Norton Utilities also happens to be one of the most important and most useful to Norton SystemWorks' overall plan for managing and maintaining the health of your PC and the safety of your data. As its name implies, Norton WinDoctor—introduced with version 3.0 in late 1997—watches over the health of Windows itself. In this chapter, you'll first learn what WinDoctor can do for you. Then, beginning in the section entitled, "Using WinDoctor and Configuring its Examinations," you'll learn how to work with WinDoctor's interface and customize it into your personal Windows physician.

Meet the Doctor

All your applications and all your data depend on Windows for literally everything, so if Windows gets sick, the problems can cascade through everything you do on your PC. If you're like most users, you've probably already discovered for yourself that this can happen with some regularity.

The reason for this is that Windows isn't a static environment. Like our own illness-susceptible bodies, Windows changes continuously as it's being used. Change can be good; change can be bad. Like ourselves, Windows doesn't exist in a plastic bubble—a plastic box, perhaps, but not a bubble. As a result, Windows gets exposed to myriad influences—including software you install, data you create, files you move across a local area network, and data that comes across the Internet—all of which can modify or otherwise impact Windows' functionality. And it's not just viruses that can harm your PC, although their threat is real. Any time you make changes to your operating environment—and even any time it makes changes to itself—you open the door to problems with incompatibilities, software bugs, and misconfigurations. You could spend hours of time running software you hate because you're afraid to install new applications, or you could use your PC to be what it was designed to be—a personal computer—and let WinDoctor take the responsibility for keeping Windows working.

Understanding the Examination

Whenever you go to the doctor for an examination, you've probably noticed that the poking and prodding is interspersed with a lot of questions and answers. Your doctor may also encourage you to ask her about the procedures she is performing. The benefit to this kind of conversation is twofold. On the one hand, of course, you may be more at ease if you understand what's going on around you. On the other hand, if you understand what your doctor is doing and what she's looking for, you may be able to contribute meaningfully to your own exam. After all, you live with yourself and your doctor doesn't. You may have noticed things in yourself that the typical five-minute exam doesn't reveal. In addition, if you're visiting a new doctor for the first time, you'll likely have a far better understanding of your medical history than she will.

All these metaphors are relevant to your use of Norton WinDoctor. As you'll discover throughout this book, Norton SystemWorks is much like your physician because it has been "trained" to work superbly with little or no intervention from you. However, when you do understand what the Norton Utilities are looking for and how they work, you'll be able to step up to the next level. At the same time, you'll gain a remarkable understanding of how your PC itself works, along with a great sense of accomplishment for that understanding. So, while Norton WinDoctor certainly can do a phenomenal job all by itself, let's take a look at the tests WinDoctor puts your PC through and examine how they monitor the safety of your work. Fundamentally, WinDoctor performs three different classes of examinations on your PC: a Windows Registry exam, a Program Integrity exam, and a Shortcut exam. (All these exams are highly customizable, as you'll read later in this chapter.)

Registry Examination

Not many parts of Windows are at once as robust and delicate as the Windows Registry. The Windows Registry is a rather large database consisting of entries, known as Registry keys, that maintain a vast array of configuration data for software as well as hardware on your PC. The Registry also contains vital information about how Windows itself starts up, is configured, and is customized. If more than one person uses your PC, and if you each log on individually and maintain your own customized settings, that information is moved into the Registry for easy access each time a different user logs on. Similarly, if your PC is configured only for yourself, all your preferences—and much more relating to your use of your PC—are maintained in the Registry so that the data is available to any application that requires it. You'll read a good deal more about the Windows Registry in Chapter 14, "Norton Utilities: Heroic Measures and Other Registry Editing." For now, it's just important that you understand the Registry's function in broad terms.

How did all the information in the Registry get into the Registry? Data moves in and out of the Registry on a regular basis as Windows runs, as you install and uninstall software, as you make changes to default settings for software, and so on. In the past, all this information might have been stored in hundreds of files scattered all over your drives. Each of these files was subject to failure, to fragmentation, and to accidental deletion. The

Windows Registry is phenomenally more robust than the old way of doing things in that it cannot be deleted accidentally (under normal working conditions), and because Microsoft has designed it to be relatively fault-tolerant and quite impervious to misconfiguration, viral attacks, and so on.

The delicacy of the Registry, of course, lies in its all-your-eggs-in-one-basket character. If the Registry breaks, it's a Big Deal. Program and hardware configurations can be lost, Plug and Play can turn into scream and stomp, and Windows may simply refuse to even start. The Norton Registry Tracker keeps tabs on every modification that is made to your Registry, as you'll read about in Chapter 13, "Norton Utilities: The Better Part of Valor and Registry Tracker," but Norton WinDoctor catches and eliminates problems that already exist when you first install Norton SystemWorks; this program also keeps your Registry in good health. You're about to learn how this is done.

ActiveX/COM Exams

The first of WinDoctor's default Registry examinations involves a careful check of your Registry's overall integrity. Once this general check is complete, WinDoctor begins its detailed Registry examination by looking at your ActiveX and application component (COM and DCOM) entries. These entries refer to the operation of ActiveX controls throughout your system. ActiveX is a set of technologies that were built upon the foundations established by Dynamic Data Exchange (DDE) and Object Linking and Embedding (OLE) for managing application and Web site components externally. That is, a program you are running may make use of an ActiveX control—say, radio buttons on a Web site or a method for opening Microsoft Access databases from within another application—but that control does not exist within the application itself. Instead, the control is stored in its own file with an .OCX extension (the acronym means OLE Control eXtension) and is thus available to any application or Web site that needs it. After an ActiveX control is installed and registered on your PC, it need not be loaded again. This can save you significant download time while you're moving around the Web.

Further, the re-use of ActiveX controls helps maintain a unified, familiar user interface. When you master how to manipulate a video file on your local PC, you can manipulate any video file you encounter, whether locally or thousands of miles away on an Internet server. However, if the Registry keys specifying configuration and location data of a given ActiveX control become damaged, all applications that call this control seem to break. Windows cannot use what it cannot find. To point, Norton WinDoctor scans through all these entries to verify that the ActiveX component files are present and to determine where they should be on your drives.

Application Paths

Most modern applications store a good deal of data about their internal configuration and operation within the Registry. Among the many keys that a complex program such as Microsoft Word stores in the Registry are the paths to the many external components that Word needs to run properly. As in the case of the ActiveX components described in the previous section, errors or omissions in this part of the Registry can render the entire application—or at least the relevant component, such as the thesaurus or Word's capability of importing clip art—dysfunctional. WinDoctor verifies that every component registered can be found in the drive location specified in the Registry.

Fonts

Back in the days of Windows 3.x, information regarding the various fonts you had installed on your PC was stored in a file named WIN.INI. This "Windows Initialization" file still exists, but all its font-managing functions have been supplanted by the Windows Registry. The Registry keeps track of which font name (as it appears in the font menus of your various applications) is associated with which font description file on disk. The Registry also provides the list of installed fonts to your applications, thereby making all your installed fonts universally available. As you might suspect, serious errors or omissions in this part of the Registry can render some or all of your fonts inaccessible. Cross-mapping in this area can also cause the wrong font to be used when you select a font name through your applications. For example, the improper mapping of the Arial Narrow name could lead to the use of Times New Roman whenever Arial Narrow was selected.

Because TrueType Fonts (TTF) are used for both your onscreen display and for printing, errors here can be pervasive. WinDoctor verifies that each font file is mapped to only one font name and that all the fonts that you think are installed are, in fact, installed. The Registry also keeps track of various default font substitutions. If you open a Microsoft Word document that was created with a font you don't have installed, Word looks to the Registry. If it finds a font substitution guideline there—for example, if Optima is not available, use Arial—then Word makes that substitution, ideally using a font that is as close as possible to the original. WinDoctor also verifies that all such Registry entries are intact and that the installed fonts they point to are installed.

Help

The Windows Registry keeps track of the location of the Microsoft Help Engine and its components. This is actually an independent application that runs whenever you indicate to an application that you wish to see that program's help file. Just as many documents can be opened in Microsoft Word for viewing, so can the standard-format Help file for any application be opened and manipulated using the Windows Help Engine. Of course, if the Help Engine or any of its components cannot be located, then the Help feature of all your applications is disabled. WinDoctor guarantees that all the settings for Help-related functionality are as they should be.

Microsoft Shared

Because so many of us use an array of Microsoft products, the Microsoft Shared folder on the hard drive (usually located at C:\PROGRAM FILES\COMMON FILES\MICROSOFT SHARED\) and the relevant Microsoft Shared component keys in the Windows Registry impact a wide array of the applications we most commonly use. Standard content-proofing tools, such as a spelling and hyphenation checker, exist across the entire Microsoft Office suite. These common components are accessed through keys in the Windows Registry that point to their location and functionality. If you've suddenly lost the capability to correct spelling mistakes or to create simple graphs in both Microsoft Word and Microsoft Excel, chances are very good indeed that something has gone awry between the shared files on your drive and the shared component entries in the Registry. WinDoctor can detect any such inconsistencies.

Run

A set of Registry keys keeps track of what applications you have run most recently and in which order. This information is largely of only administrator value, but WinDoctor verifies that the entries here refer to applications that are actually installed on your PC.

Sound Customization

As you probably already know, Windows was designed to enable you to associate the playing of a given sound file with a given action or event. You may hear the sound of paper being crumpled whenever you empty the Recycle Bin, and so on. If your computer is configured to enable multiple users to log on, each user may have her or his own set of sounds associated to events. Most commonly, users access and modify these associations through the Sound control panel, but these relationships are stored within the Registry. Each time a different user logs on to the PC, that user's personal settings are retrieved (from that user's own set of Registry files) and are copied into the active Registry. If you've ever encountered the error illustrated in Figure 4.1, you have already seen what happens when a discrepancy exists between the Registry entries and the existence or location of sound files on your PC. WinDoctor discovers and repairs this kind of problem at your instruction.

FIGURE 4.1

The association between this event and this sound file has been broken because the sound file is not where it should be.

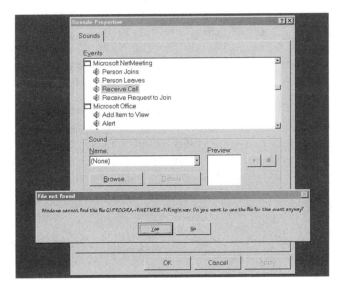

Symantec Shared

One of the nicest aspects of Norton SystemWorks as a whole is its capability of repairing and updating itself with LiveUpdate. LiveUpdate can install updated components, and WinDoctor can verify the integrity of those components. As with Microsoft, Symantec creates a Symantec Shared folder on your hard drive when you install Norton SystemWorks (or when you first install one of the individual Norton utility programs, if you've upgraded to SystemWorks).

As with the Microsoft Office suite, the Norton SystemWorks suite makes use of a variety of redundant components that provide you with a unified interface, regardless of which Norton utility you happen to be working in at any given moment. For instance, LiveUpdate looks and functions the same regardless of the SystemWorks suite components you're updating. The associations between these Symantec Shared files and the various SystemWorks applications are maintained within your Windows Registry. To be sure that Windows is working properly, WinDoctor must make sure that it and the other Norton programs are also all working properly. Scanning this section of your Registry verifies that all is as it should be.

Uninstall

As you've likely seen in the Add/Remove Programs Control Panel, shown in Figure 4.2, most properly behaving Windows 95 and Windows 98 programs place an entry into the Add/Remove list when they are first installed. Some programs, such as the Microsoft Office suite of applications, also use the Add/Remove panel to enable you to add functionality or uninstall unused application components. If you've ever tried to uninstall an application only to be told that the necessary files can't be found to enable uninstalling, you've seen what can happen when these Registry entries no longer accurately match the files and file locations on your hard drive. Norton WinDoctor verifies that the necessary setup and uninstallation files associated with each application are properly identified within the Windows Registry.

Virtual Device Drivers (VxD)

Put most simply, you can generally think of Virtual Device Driver (VxD) files, as being to hardware what ActiveX controls are for software. These are external files, usually stored within the C:\WINDOWS\SYSTEM folder or in a subfolder of that folder, that provide controlled access to a wide array of standard hardware-based features. On most PC's, a virtual device driver exists to manage every type of system resource, such as a display adapter, networking functionality, printer ports, and so on. As with all the various components and their Registry keys, broken associations between what is stored in the Registry and what devices are present in your PC can spell disaster. WinDoctor inspects every virtual device driver key in the Registry and makes sure that it is properly associated with the device it represents, as well as the .VXD file on your disk that contains the device-management routines.

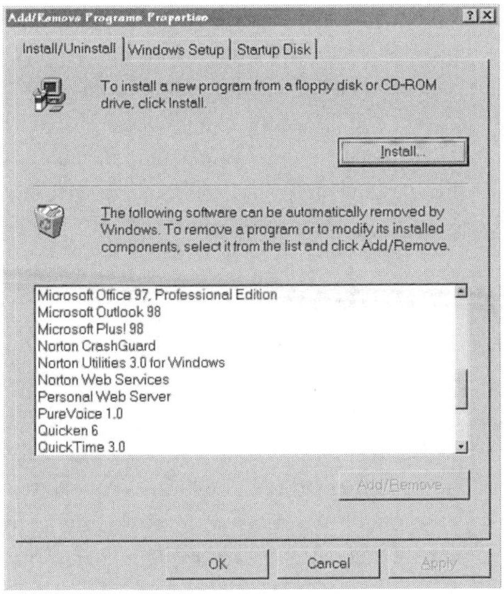

FIGURE 4.2
The Add/Remove Programs Control Panel displays a list of programs that you can uninstall. You also can add or remove installed components for some applications.

TECHNICAL NOTE

> The description here of VxD files is not entirely complete. Although it is true that the majority of virtual device drivers do virtualize hardware functionality for MS-DOS multitasking and related purposes, a VxD may also exist for certain types of software components, such as a TSR. These 32-bit virtual device drivers may emulate the functionality of their related 16-bit software, providing for faster and more stable execution of that functionality within the Windows environment. For our purposes of the discussion of WinDoctor, no relevant difference exists between a hardware-related VxD and a software-related VxD. In either case, WinDoctor verifies that the components with which the VxD is supposed to be related are present.

Program Integrity Examination

After WinDoctor has completed its examination of your Windows Registry—assuming you have not told it to do otherwise—it continues its exam of your PC by looking at the integrity of all your programs. Actually, the Program Integrity exam does go back to your Registry to check two types of entries, but the plurality of this test does not involve the Registry itself. When this test is run, WinDoctor scans your hard drive to verify that all the external components—most of which are found in .DLL files, located within your C:\WINDOWS folder or its subfolders—needed for you to successfully launch and run your programs are present. WinDoctor verifies that entries in your Start menu do, in fact, properly correspond to your installed programs.

A check is also made to see that all the external uninstall files necessary to successfully remove a given program from your PC are present and are found where they are expected.

WinDoctor inspects the integrity of the Windows Desktop, the C:\PROGRAM FILES folder, and its subfolders, to ensure that programs and their related components are found where they are thought to be located. Finally, an inspection of your C:\WINDOWS\SYSTEM folder is made to see that any external components that a program placed here when it was installed are still present. At the same time, WinDoctor checks for extraneous data, as it did when inspecting your Windows Registry, and looks for references to programs or program components that have been uninstalled, relocated, or replaced.

Shortcut Examination

As the last of WinDoctor's primary examinations, every shortcut on your PC is inspected to verify that the application or component to which it refers is located where the shortcut expects to find it. You've probably already experienced invalid shortcuts if you've used Windows for long. You may have even attempted to manually repair a broken shortcut by using the Find Target command found within every shortcut's properties, shown in progress in Figure 4.3. The search Windows performs is time-consuming, and the results often are less than satisfactory. Having already made an extensive analysis of your PC and its installed programs and applets, WinDoctor does not make you wait through such a search for such a dubious return. Instead, WinDoctor analyzes any broken shortcut it encounters and, as you are about to see, repairs this problem whenever the associated program is still located somewhere on your PC. WinDoctor also analyzes your MS-DOS shortcuts, verifying that the settings found in those shortcuts' Program tabs refer to valid files and folders and that the MS-DOS-related devices specified in those shortcuts' Advanced Properties are present and properly configured on your system.

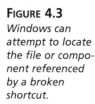

FIGURE 4.3
Windows can attempt to locate the file or component referenced by a broken shortcut.

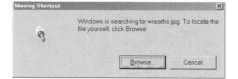

Reviewing the Test Results

Before WinDoctor asks you to look over its findings, it looks over them for you, passing them through an array of (configurable) Analysis Agents. These Agents control a variety of WinDoctor functions and largely determine both what you see reported as errors and what types of solutions WinDoctor recommends with respect to each. The Agents also assist WinDoctor in grouping problems contextually, as discussed in the "Advanced" problem report interface later in this chapter. The Analysis Agents can enable you to ignore certain types of problems that you don't wish to see and can also discourage entry-level users from being presented with repair options that could bring them disaster, such as the opportunity to manually edit the Windows Registry. Specifically, the Analysis

Agents determine the following:

- Whether the user is given the opportunity to manually edit the Registry whenever Registry errors are detected
- Whether WinDoctor should search through the Norton Protected Recycle Bin to determine if files it finds missing were recently deleted (and thereby retrievable)
- Whether WinDoctor should search through the regular Windows Recycle Bin for missing files
- Whether WinDoctor should search all your hard drives for missing files to see if the missing component has been relocated to a different drive
- Whether WinDoctor should detect that a hardware configuration change has caused your drives to be assigned different letters than they previously possessed (enabling WinDoctor to update all such files globally)
- Whether WinDoctor should check to see if folders it thinks are missing are merely located elsewhere on the drive
- Whether WinDoctor should understand that files that appear to be missing from removable drives may only be "missing" because that drive is not present when WinDoctor is run

You can imagine, for example, that it would be tremendously annoying to be informed that a vast array of your files are suddenly missing when, in fact, the drive on which they are located has merely been removed. The configurability of the Analysis Agents, which you'll read about later in this chapter, enables you to screen out those errant errors.

Assuming that you've left all the Agents enabled—which is the default setting—all the checks in the previous list are performed before WinDoctor asks you to review the test results yourself and determine what to do about each problem. Let's look at the various problems WinDoctor can discover and see how each is handled.

> **Caution:** Before you disable any of the Analysis Agents, be sure you know what it is that you are disabling. Additionally, don't forget which Agents you have turned off: You could prevent WinDoctor from alerting you to serious problems with Windows if you do.

Registry Repairs

After WinDoctor determines that one or more problems with keys in your Windows Registry exist, it documents these problems in the WinDoctor Report, as shown in Figure 4.4.

Once detected, Registry errors can be automatically repaired by WinDoctor, using Norton technology to assess what the best way to perform that repair is. Additionally, you can elect to manually repair Registry errors—assuming that Analysis Agent was not disabled—or you can choose to ignore the error for the time being. Depending on the nature of the errors—for example, WinDoctor thinks certain files are missing but you know they are located on a removable drive—ignoring the errors may be the option you desire, until the next time you run WinDoctor and you disable the relevant Analysis Agent. It's much more likely, however, that the errors WinDoctor detects are problems that you'll want to fix immediately, much as you will nearly always want Norton AntiVirus to eradicate any virus it finds on your PC, or Norton Disk Doctor to immediately repair any disk-related damage it encounters.

Figure 4.4
A WinDoctor Errors Report lists problems, including those with Windows Registry keys.

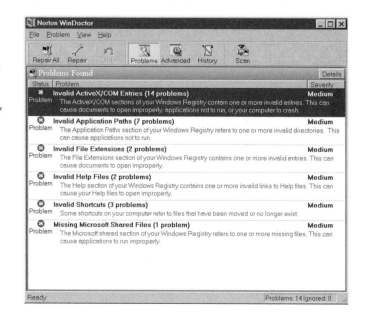

Missing File Search and Rescue

Related to Registry errors, many Registry errors come into existence because files get deleted or moved around on your drives, so missing file errors document applications, DLLs, VxDs, and other components that WinDoctor discovers are not where they should be. For each of these problems, your options are similar to those found with Registry problems. You can let WinDoctor automatically repair the problem as it thinks best, you can do the repair yourself, or you can ignore the problem. With missing files, the type of automatic repair WinDoctor suggests depends largely on what type of file is missing and whether it is entirely missing from your PC or has been found by WinDoctor on your PC in a different location than where it was last reported.

Missing Files

In the case of a missing virtual device driver or DLL application component, WinDoctor's best recommendation may be that you reinstall the application or hardware driver. If you are a power-user and the involved application is one that stores its component files in extractable structures (such as .ZIP files or .CAB files), you may be able to extract the missing file from the application setup disk(s) yourself. (For a brief primer on how to work manually with .CAB files, see the technical note that appears at the end of this section.) On the other hand, if you're not comfortable with this process, or if the application setup files aren't distributed in this manner, you will likely need to reinstall the entire application.

In some specific cases, you may be able to re-run the application's setup program and simply add the missing component. For example, if WinDoctor reports that a .DLL related to Microsoft Office's integrated proofing tools is missing, using the Add/Remove panel to first remove just the proofing tools and then installing them again may quickly solve the problem.

If the missing file is a hardware driver, opening the System Control Panel, selecting the affected device, clicking on its Drivers tab, and then clicking Update Driver may allow you to easily re-load all that device's driver files from its original setup disks (or from the Windows 95 or 98 CD-ROM).

TECHNICAL NOTE

Two ways to extract files from a standard Cabinet (or .CAB) file exist: an easy way and a hard way. For most of the life of Windows 95, the hard way was the only way. This method involves using an MS-DOS based utility known as EXTRACT.EXE (located within C:\WINDOWS) to scan through the cabinet file or files you indicate, searching for a given file and then extracting this file to a location you designate. It's a slow, annoying process. Although WinDoctor tells you the exact name of the file you need to extract and reinstall, it doesn't know which cabinet file that file is located in. Searching through an entire CD-ROM of .CAB files—even though the process can be automated to search all cabinet files in a given folder—takes a good deal of time.

Fortunately, there is a vastly better way. Microsoft has made cabinet files that Windows 98 can open. Just double-click on a .CAB file to view its contents. From there, you can drag-and-drop the replacement files to wherever they need to be. Windows 98 also provides an advanced Find command, available on the Start menu, which (from its Advanced tab) enables you to search for a given file in all the cabinet files located on a given drive—or even your entire PC!

For Windows 95 users, Microsoft provides Microsoft PowerToys, a set of unsupported but freely available tools for the power-user that contains a cabinet file viewer. As of this writing, Microsoft PowerToys can be downloaded from the Web at the following address:

www.microsoft.com/windows/downloads/contents/PowerToys/W95CabView/

As with Windows 98's built-in support, the cabinet viewer enables you to open cabinet files, explore their contents, and drag-and-drop files as you need them. Unlike Windows 98, however, the cabinet viewer PowerToy does not extend the functionality of your Start menu's Find command.

Relocated Files

If WinDoctor determines that a file is not where it was expected but can be found elsewhere on your PC, you're given the option of updating the incorrect reference so that it points to the file's new location. This could be a circumstance in which you might choose to ignore an error if you have intentionally relocated a file temporarily and intend to return it to its original location in the near future. (Understand, of course, that whatever functionality that file provides is disabled until the file is again where it is expected to be, or until the reference is updated.) On the other hand, you may have moved all your customized event sounds from their original folder to the C:\WINDOWS\MEDIA folder and intend them to stay there. In that circumstance, allowing WinDoctor to perform its recommended repair and updating the reference to reflect the sounds' new location is the only way to go.

Files on Removable Drives

The other circumstance in which a file may be errantly reported as missing occurs if it is stored on a removable drive, such as a ZIP or JAZ drive, and that drive isn't present when WinDoctor performs its tests. It's certainly possible that you may not have realized that the involved file was actually stored on the removable drive, in which case you will very likely want WinDoctor to ignore this problem. Doing so enables you to reinsert the removable drive and relocate the involved file or files to one of your permanent hard drives. The next time you run WinDoctor, the program will discover that the file now exists (in whatever location you put it). At that point, you can instruct WinDoctor to update the references to point to the file's new permanent location.

On the other hand, you may be well aware that certain files or applications are found only on removable cartridges and you may want that to remain the case. There are innumerable reasons why this might be so: You may be most comfortable with being able to uninstall a game program or your checkbook program on demand, but be able to access it whenever you want it. Such methodologies are perfectly valid ways of protecting programs and content. WinDoctor, however, has no way of knowing that you've intentionally implemented this technique, so it likely reports numerous errors relating to seemingly broken Registry and file-related references. In such a case, you will want to first tell WinDoctor to ignore this kind of problem, then to go back and deactivate the relevant Analysis Agent so that you're not disturbed with these missing file reports in the future. Of course, certain applications may not behave properly if they make use of components shared with an application that has been ejected, drive and all. For this reason, applications may insist on storing certain files on your C:/ drive or within your C:/WINDOWS folder so that such shared components don't disappear when you purposefully eject the drive on which one of their related applications is installed.

Undoing Repairs

When you enable WinDoctor to repair the problems it detects on your PC, there may be circumstances in which you need to (or want to) undo one or more of those repairs. Fortunately, WinDoctor is as careful about safeguarding your applications and data as is the rest of Norton SystemWorks, and it maintains a configurable repair history file, as shown in Figure 4.5.

FIGURE 4.5

The WinDoctor Repair History Screen lists the most recent actions.

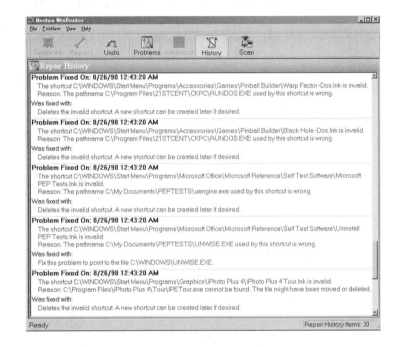

The WinDoctor Repair History documents every repair made by WinDoctor over a given period of time. (You'll learn how to configure WinDoctor's Repair History in the next section.) The report keeps track of the original problem and on what date and time it was repaired. The reason behind the problem—in other words, why the problem was a problem—is also stored in the Repair History, as is the exact method by which the problem was solved. In limited cases, such as the deletion of a broken shortcut, the Repair History also suggests a method for, in effect, repairing the repair. (Of course, you can create a new shortcut at any time you want.) To reverse that particular repair, select any entry in the Repair History (to better safeguard your PC, multiple entries may not be selected for undoing) and then click the Undo button in the toolbar. Because WinDoctor doesn't relocate files (it only updates file references), there's no repair that can't be safely undone (so long as you undo it before WinDoctor's history logs expire, which you'll read about later). You wouldn't want WinDoctor to move a file and then try to move it back to a folder which you've subsequently deleted! If you determine that WinDoctor has made a repair that you later want to Undo, just return to the WinDoctor Repair History and Undo it.

Working with WinDoctor and Configuring Its Examinations

As with many of the Norton Utilities, WinDoctor's primary interface (shown in Figure 4.6) is based on the already familiar Windows Wizard style. That is, you're presented with a variety of options and tasks to select and then you simply click a button labeled Next to move to the next set of options or the next task. To launch WinDoctor, select it from the Norton SystemWorks integrator by clicking Norton Utilities and then clicking WinDoctor on the NU screen. (You can also select it from the Start menu at Programs | Norton SystemWorks | Norton Utilities | Norton WinDoctor, by right-clicking the Norton System Doctor's WinDoctor sensor, or from the Norton System Doctor's Utilities menu.) From this primary screen, you can instruct WinDoctor to either run all its tests, or to enable you to select the tests you want to run. You can also jump directly to the WinDoctor Repair History screen, which you might want to do if you've run WinDoctor specifically to Undo a repair.

Starting the WinDoctor Wizard

Clicking the Next button after selecting the *Perform All Norton WinDoctor Tests* (recommended) option takes you directly into the testing process. We'll look at that in just a moment. Selecting the *Let Me Choose Which Tests to Run* option takes you to the test selection screen, as shown in Figure 4.7. If you intend to run only one or two tests, you'll probably find it easiest to click on the Deselect All button and then select the one or two tests that you want to perform. If you don't want to run a specific test, simply uncheck the box next to that test's description.

Why would you want to select only a few tests? For one thing, if you ran WinDoctor previously and chose to manually repair problems that WinDoctor detected, you may very well want to quickly re-run WinDoctor and verify that the changes you made were proper. (You'll learn how to perform manual repairs in the section entitled "Custom or Manual Repairs," later in this chapter.) In fact, I'd recommend doing precisely that sort of selective testing whenever you've opted to manually edit the Windows Registry. The Registry is fairly self-repairing, but by selecting only the test that relates to your manual changes, you can get nearly immediate verification that all is well. Conversely, you might be aware of difficulties that, for some reason or another, you don't want WinDoctor to report. In such circumstances, deselecting specific tests may provide you with precisely the results you desire. Any tests that you deselect on this page of the WinDoctor Wizard do not appear in the list of tests when WinDoctor actually runs.

FIGURE 4.6
The Norton WinDoctor opening screen enables you to choose which tests to run, or you can choose to display the Repair History.

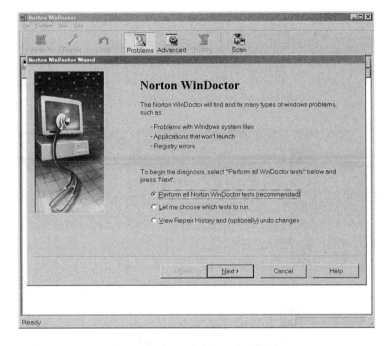

FIGURE 4.7
The WinDoctor Test Selection Panel enables you to choose which individual tests you want to run.

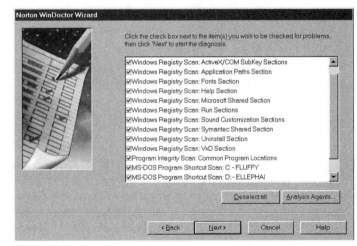

Deactivating Analysis Agents

Just as you may have a desire or need to skip specific WinDoctor tests, you may want to disable one or more of the tools WinDoctor uses to find solutions. As shown in Figure 4.8, the Select Analysis Agents dialog box (accessible by clicking the Analysis Agents button shown in Figure 4.7) enables you to do that. Removing the check from an Agent's box disables that Agent until you re-check the box. If you're not certain what task an Agent performs, you can pass your mouse over its entry to see a somewhat more detailed description pop-up. Of course, you've already read about what each Agent does, but the pop-up help may provide you with a quick refresher. After you select the Agents you wish to disable—or after you re-enable previously deactivated Agents—click OK to save your changes and return to the test selection screen of the WinDoctor Wizard.

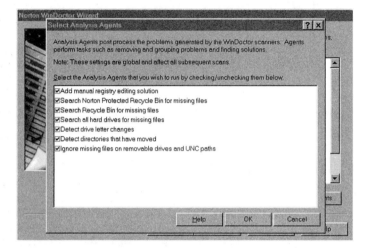

FIGURE 4.8
You can select the solution Analysis Agents you want to run in WinDoctor.

Initiating Testing

After you've determined which tests you want to run and which solution Analysis Agents you want enabled, click Next on the test-select screen to initiate testing. The progress screen displayed during testing is more useful as a status report than for any other purpose. The currently running test is highlighted with a yellow arrow. Completed tests are checked with a blue check mark and the word Done, in the right-most column labeled Status. To stop testing at any time during the process, simply click Stop. This enters the word Skipped into the status column of any incomplete test. If you stop testing, you must click the Back button and restart testing before you can proceed to any repairs. If you know you want to stop testing after a specific test, you must disable the subsequent tests in the test-selection dialog box, discussed previously. You cannot proceed to the Repair process until WinDoctor completes all the tests you instructed it to run in the Wizard.

When testing is complete, WinDoctor prompts you to click Next again. This takes you to a summary screen on which WinDoctor tells you the number of errors that it has detected, as shown in Figure 4.9. If no problems are detected, a similar summary screen—with a cheery green check mark for its graphic—lets you know that everything is well. If problems have been found, clicking Finish exits the WinDoctor Wizard and opens the WinDoctor Report, from which all repairs are initiated. If no problems have been found, clicking Finish quits WinDoctor entirely.

WinDoctor Report and Repair

If you're like most users, problems will indeed be found—at least the first time you run WinDoctor. In that case, you'll be taken to the WinDoctor Report, where all the problems are categorized and summarized for you. It is from here that you also initiate every repair you wish WinDoctor to perform.

Using the WinDoctor Report interface is very straightforward. As you can see in Figure 4.10, a variety of problems are grouped together based on their type and are displayed in the large Problems Found panel. By clicking one of three column headings—Status, Problem, or Severity—you can have WinDoctor Report re-sort the problems based on the category you've clicked. (In this regard, the WinDoctor Report screen works in the same way the standard Windows Explorer does when you are looking at the Details view of a folder's contents.) Notice in the figure that all the problems listed are of Medium severity. This is an indication that these issues may cause significant trouble or inconvenience at some time in the future if they are not repaired. Other levels of severity reported by WinDoctor are Low and High; the latter indicates problems that require immediate attention.

Using The Report Toolbar

At the top of this main Report screen is the toolbar, from which all WinDoctor's primary reporting and repair functions are accessible. Moving from left to right, the first button is the Repair All button. WinDoctor uses its best-recommendation method of repair and attempts to repair every problem it has detected when you click Repair All. Repair All is also available from the WinDoctor Problem menu, at the very top of the window.

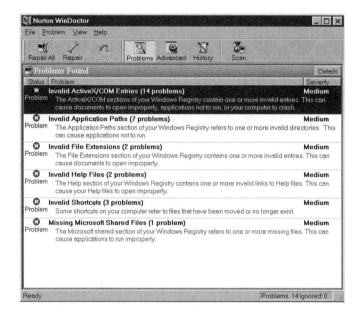

Next to Repair All is the Repair button. When this button is clicked, WinDoctor will ask you if you want to repair manually or have WinDoctor apply its best recommendation method of repair to only the problem selected in the Problems Found panel. The same functionality is available from the Repair Selected Problem entry of the Problem menu.

The next button, Undo, enables you to select a completed repair from the Repair History Report and reverse the action performed by WinDoctor. (You read about the Repair History Report earlier in this chapter, in the section "Undoing Repairs.") Undo functionality is also available from the Problem menu.

The Problems button, selected by default, is grouped with two others, Advanced and History, and determines which of those three types of reports is displayed. The report type may also be selected from the View menu or by pressing Ctrl+P to view Problems, Ctrl+A to view the Advanced report, or Ctrl+H to view the Repair History. The View menu also provides you with a related option: Show Ignored Problems. Problems that you tell WinDoctor you do not wish to repair—or problems that have been detected but for which you have disabled the relevant Analysis Agents—remain visible in the Problems Found display unless you uncheck this option in the View menu.

The Scan button, at the extreme right of the toolbar, resets WinDoctor to its initial wizard screen and starts a new set of examinations. You may wish to use this option after making repairs, to verify that the problems have indeed been fixed. Re-scanning can also be useful if you make manual changes to the Registry and want to verify their integrity and correctness.

Obtaining Problem Details

If the explanation of detected problems is not sufficiently detailed for your taste, you can click the Details button at the extreme right of the WinDoctor Report screen to open the Details panel, as shown in Figure 4.11. Details of the problems that fall under the category selected at the top of the screen are then displayed below. (The Details panel may also be enabled or disabled from the View menu.) With the Details panel open, you can review individual problems, not merely look at them collectively by category, and you can selectively repair those you desire. Using the mouse to grab the bold divider between the Problems Found panel and the Details panel enables you to change the relative size of the two panels, to see more of whichever panel you desire. Scroll bars also enable you to scroll through the panels independently, as necessary.

FIGURE 4.11
The Details panel in this WinDoctor Report Display is enabled.

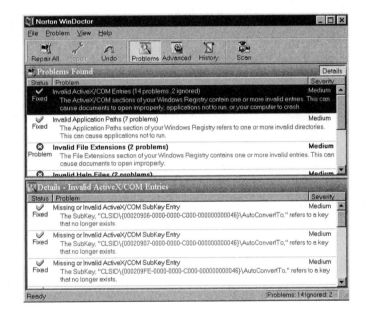

Obtaining an Advanced View

For an even more detailed view of detected difficulties, click the Advanced button in the toolbar or choose Advanced from the View menu. This opens the Advanced view (shown in Figure 4.12), a view that is not unlike the Windows Explorer in its functionality. In the left panel (the Explore panel), problems are sorted by the method you select in the Sort By drop-down box—either Symptoms, Severity, or Scanners. Symptoms and Severity are self-explanatory. Choosing Scanners causes problems to be ordered based on which of the WinDoctor tests discovered them. As in the Windows Explorer, a plus mark next to an item indicates that content is to be displayed that is contextually subordinate to that item. Click the "+" to see the next level down. Once open, the "+" changes to a minus sign, "–", which, when clicked, rolls up the indented subordinate data and changes back into a plus sign. As is also the case in Windows Explorer, double-clicking an entry both selects that entry and opens any immediately subordinate data to that entry.

Selecting Repairs and Repair Methods

Regardless of which view best suits your needs and style, accessing WinDoctor's repair features works the same. In this way, just because you prefer to use the Advanced view does not require that you learn a new set of steps to actually initiate repairs. Double-clicking a repair category (indicated in the WinDoctor report by a red circle containing a white "X," as in Figure 4.12) takes you directly to the Automated Repair options screen for that category's problems. You can also right-click a problem category and choose Repair Selected Problem from the pop-up menu to open the Automated Repair options.

FIGURE 4.12
An Advanced view of WinDoctor's Problem Report displays additional details related to each problem found.

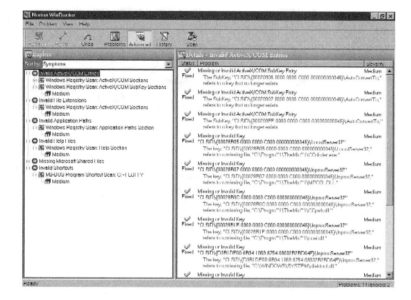

Double-clicking an individual problem or right-clicking the problem and selecting Repair Selected Problem bypasses the Automated options screen. You can also select either a category or a specific problem and click the Repair button in the toolbar to open the Automated options screen. Clicking Repair All completely bypasses all options screens, merely opening a confirmation dialog box. In this confirmation dialog box, click Yes to continue if you want to repair all problems automatically using the best solution possible.

Automatic Repairs

If you choose to Repair All problems found, this section won't apply to you—skip to the section "Reviewing Repair History," and return to this section when the need arises. Otherwise, if you want to have a good understanding of all of WinDoctor's repair options, continue reading.

WinDoctor provides several different options for making repairs. The most straightforward of these is an automatic repair. When you double-click a repair category, WinDoctor opens the Automated Repair dialog box, shown in Figure 4.13. WinDoctor identifies the number of problems relevant to the category you've selected and prompts you to either let it select the repair method for all this category's problems or to specify the repair method for each problem. If you choose to go with WinDoctor's recommended solution, clicking OK performs the repair.

Custom or Manual Repairs

If you want better control over the repair of individual problems, or if you're uncertain that WinDoctor's "best solution" is the best solution for you, then select the Allow me to choose... option and click OK to open the Repair Solutions dialog box, as shown in Figure 4.14.

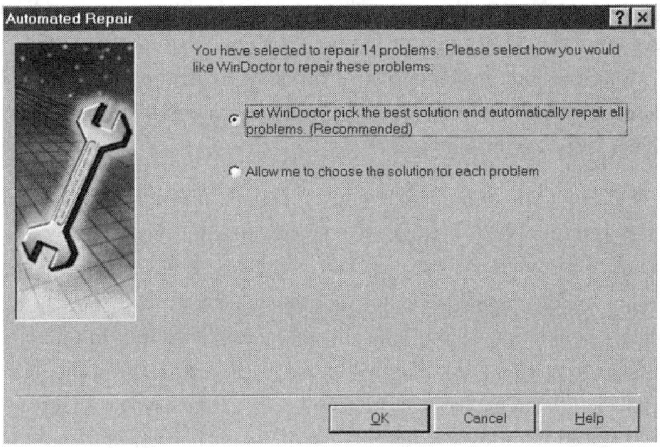

FIGURE 4.13

WinDoctor's Automated Repair dialog box provides you with the option of enabling WinDoctor to repair all problems or choosing your own solutions.

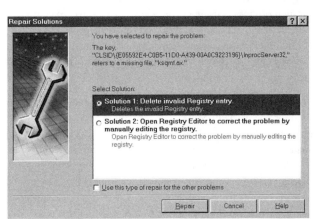

FIGURE 4.14

A sample WinDoctor Repair Solutions dialog box shows two possible solutions to a selected problem.

From here, you'll see a list of two or more different approaches to solving the problem WinDoctor has detected. In some cases, the solutions proposed are as straightforward as those shown in Figure 4.14. In this example, you can either delete the defective Registry key or opt to manually go into the Norton Registry Editor and modify the key yourself.

> **Note:** Be aware that if you have disabled the Analysis Agent that provides for the manual editing of Registry entries, the manual editing option will not be present in this dialog box. In that case, only two options are available to you: allow WinDoctor to modify the Registry itself in whatever manner it suggests or click Cancel to ignore the error.

If you choose to manually edit the Registry, the Norton Registry Editor runs, and its display opens with the defective key selected onscreen. From here you can modify the entry, exit the Norton Registry Editor, and find yourself back in WinDoctor, exactly where you left off. Whichever method you choose to perform the repair, the Status indicator for either that problem or that problem's category—depending on what you repaired—is updated to Fixed after the repair is complete. This lets you know that this problem is no longer a concern.

One thing that you should be aware of is that Norton WinDoctor cannot make modifications to certain objects—Registry entries, missing files, and so on—if those objects are being used by Windows or some other application at the same time. To prevent a crash from occurring when WinDoctor modifies a Registry entry being used by a running application, Windows simply disallows the modification. In that circumstance, you may encounter a message box like that shown in Figure 4.15. In this figure, you see the results when WinDoctor is asked to modify a Registry key that was part of another key being used by Windows at the time. WinDoctor has automatically repaired all those problems it could, but two problems—those that would have violated Windows' protection of the busy Registry key—have failed. At this point, you can either shut down the application or process using the busy key or object, or you can simply ignore the problem. In all likelihood, the next time you run WinDoctor, that key or object will not be busy. (In limited cases, an early repair may also fix a later problem. The later problem—already repaired—may be reported by WinDoctor as one which could not be repaired. Re-scanning in this circumstance will indicate that both problems have been fixed.)

Also, notice that in the Repair Solutions dialog box, after you indicate a custom repair method for one problem, you can choose to use that same method for the repair of all other problems of the same type. With this box checked, subsequent Repair Solutions dialog boxes are bypassed and the customized repairs are performed automatically. Of course, if you have chosen to manually repair the problem, you'll find yourself back in WinDoctor after your repair is complete, looking at the same problem you just fixed. Clicking Cancel prompts you to either continue or stop repairing other problems of the same type. Click Yes to move to the next problem of that type, or click No to stop repairing problems and return to the main Norton WinDoctor Report screen.

FIGURE 4.15
WinDoctor displays a message box when it is unable to complete certain repairs.

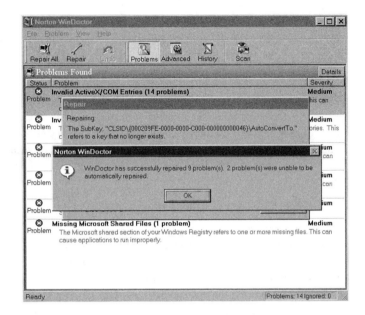

> **Caution:** Manually editing the Windows Registry is serious business. As you've read above, errors in the Registry can render individual applications—or all of Windows—unusable. You can read a good deal more about the Registry (and editing it) in Chapter 14, but Registry editing should not be taken lightly. If you're not sure of what you're doing, enable WinDoctor to perform the Registry modifications for you.

Ignoring Your Problems

As with most problems, those that WinDoctor detects can be ignored—at least until they grow. Some problems, including those involving "missing" files that are actually located on removable cartridges, are safe to ignore and are nearly self-repairing. Other problems can be precursors to major operating system failures and should be addressed immediately upon their discovery. WinDoctor enables you to choose which are which. If you choose to repair a group of problems and then click Cancel when looking at the repair options for one of those problems, that problem is essentially ignored. At that point, WinDoctor prompts you that more problems of the same type exist so that you can repair them. For each such problem, clicking Cancel on the Repair Options dialog box essentially ignores that problem and moves on. (I say *essentially* ignores because choosing to not repair a problem is not the same to WinDoctor as ignoring the problem.) WinDoctor reports a problem that you do not repair each time the program is run, until the problem is repaired. A problem that is actually ignored, however, is placed on the Ignored Problems list and is not displayed again until the problem is removed from the Ignored Problems list, or until the list is cleared in its entirety.

If you are viewing either the Details panel or the Advanced display, as described previously, you can choose to formally ignore a problem by selecting the specific problem and choosing Ignore Selected Problem from the Problem menu. Notice that you cannot formally ignore a class of problems collectively. You must select only individual problems to ignore. You can, however, hold down the Ctrl key and select multiple problems from the detail list, and click Ignore to take care of *those* collectively. Problems that are ignored are placed on the Ignored Problems list, which can be cleared from the View menu by selecting Options and clicking Clear Ignore List. If you don't clear the list, ignored problems remain ignored until you stop ignoring each of them. Clearing the list resets ignored problems and WinDoctor re-detects them the next time it is run. As with the Repair History list, the Ignored Problems list is maintained for all runnings of WinDoctor, not just for the instance in which the ignored problem is detected. Unlike the Repair History list, however, the Ignored Problems list is automatically maintained forever, until it is cleared. Items that appear on the Ignored Problems list automatically include problems detected for which the relevant Solution Analysis Agent was disabled. (To view the ignored problems list, simply verify that Show Ignored Problems is selected in the View menu. Ignored problems are shown in the Problems Found panel with Ignored indicated in the Status column.)

Reviewing the Repair History

To review the WinDoctor Repair History, you can either select that option from the WinDoctor opening screen, or you can run the WinDoctor tests and select the History button from the WinDoctor Report toolbar. Note that if WinDoctor runs and does not detect active problems, you are not given the option to view a WinDoctor Report. In that circumstance, you must open the Repair History from the opening screen.

You've already read in this chapter how the Repair History is used by WinDoctor. Here we'll cover how it can be used by you. If you look back at Figure 4.5, you can see a sample WinDoctor Repair History report. You can scroll through this document, and when you find a problem whose repair you want to undo, select the problem with your mouse and click the Undo button in the toolbar. (You can also Undo a repair by right-clicking the problem in the Repair History and selecting Undo, or by selecting the problem and then choosing Undo Selected Item from the Problem menu at the top of the WinDoctor window.) After you initiate the Undo process, WinDoctor prompts you to verify that you really do want to Undo the repair you've selected. Clicking Yes in the confirmation dialog box undoes the repair and displays a Successful Undo dialog box. The purpose of this dialog box is to merely alert you to the fact that repairs that are undone will be re-detected the next time you run WinDoctor if the circumstances that initially mandated the repair have not changed. (Of course, if they have changed, then the original problem is no longer a problem, and this is the last you'll see of it.) If WinDoctor is unable to Undo the selected repair—for example, if the object to be modified is in use by some other part of Windows or some other application—WinDoctor lets you know that it couldn't reverse that repair.

Configuring the Repair History

As mentioned earlier, the Repair History is configurable. You can access its Options tab in one of two ways. First, while viewing the Repair History Report, right-click any repair and select Options from the pop-up menu to open the History options. Additionally, you can select Options from the View menu at the top of the WinDoctor window. Only three options are available to you on the Repair History tab, as shown in Figure 4.16. You can instruct WinDoctor to maintain your Repair History list forever, or for a given number of days, or until a specified number of individual repairs have been performed. Maintaining the list for seven days is the default.

As you can also see in Figure 4.16, maintaining a very large Repair History file causes WinDoctor to take longer and longer to process the file every time you Undo a repair. The default of seven days may not give you the sense of sufficient time to verify that repairs are reliable and should be made permanent, but neither would it be wise to undo repairs made too far in the past. The configuration of your PC might have changed significantly during that time, and undoing a very old repair might cause other difficulties. Personally, I have my Repair History Report set to clear itself after 14 days.

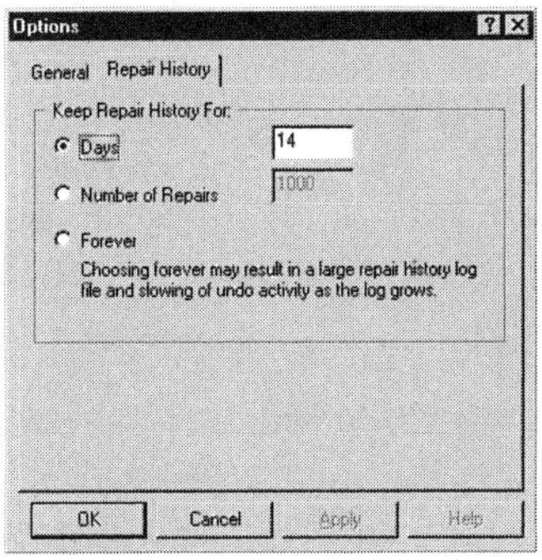

FIGURE 4.16

You can select among three options for maintaining the WinDoctor Report History.

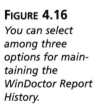

Integration with System Doctor

Norton WinDoctor is integrated with other SystemWorks 2.0 components in a variety of ways. The most obvious of these is the manner in which the WinDoctor sensor within Norton System Doctor causes the WinDoctor tests to run in the background with whatever frequency you specify. As with many other System Doctor sensors, you can configure the WinDoctor sensor to not only detect problems, but to fix them automatically without ever interrupting your work.

Integration with Norton Registry Editor

As you've already read, WinDoctor can not only launch the Norton Registry Editor upon your command, but it does so with the Registry key you were reviewing in WinDoctor, highlighted in the Registry Editor. The Registry is a huge place, and while it might seem a fairly fundamental level of integration, being able to open the Norton Registry Editor to a specific key saves you a tremendous amount of time while manually browsing or searching through the commodious Registry for the one, two, or 40 Registry keys you wish to edit.

Integration with Windows

Finally, Norton WinDoctor is integrated with Windows itself. If you ask to manually modify a shortcut's settings, for example, Norton WinDoctor automatically opens that shortcut's Properties dialog box without ever taking you out of WinDoctor itself. When you've completed whatever modifications you wish to make, you can click the Scan button on the WinDoctor Report screen and immediately re-check your system to verify that your change successfully eliminated the problem.

Norton Utilities: The Connection Doctor Is In

In addition to Norton WinDoctor, the Norton Utilities now includes a powerful communications diagnostic tool. Formerly only available with the purchase of Norton Mobile Essentials—a suite of utilities, now included in the SystemWorks 2.0 Bonus Back, which targets the needs of notebook computer users—Norton Connection Doctor now brings its communications hardware savvy to the Norton Utilities and Norton SystemWorks 2.0.

Norton Connection Doctor

Norton Connection Doctor can help you analyze difficulties in making online connections. The Connection Doctor is launchable from the SystemWorks Integrator by choosing Norton Utilities or by selecting Norton Connection Doctor from the Norton Utilities program group in your Start menu.

The Connection Doctor interface, shown in Figure 5.1, consists of two sets of buttons—along the extreme left and bottom edge of the window—and a test-results display pane. The readout in the pane is divided into various system areas that correspond to the test-selection buttons at the left. Clicking Check All checks computer-, modem-, and dialing-related issues; clicking one of the other three buttons performs tests on that subset.

As Connection Doctor performs its tests, the text box near the bottom of the window keeps you advised with respect to what component is being tested. The electrocardiogram display in the lower-left corner is nothing more than an activity indicator.

FIGURE 5.1

Norton Connection Doctor's startup screen provides the interface for all connectivity-related tests.

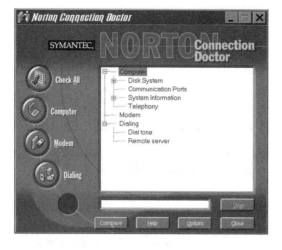

Computer Tests

If you click the Computer button, Norton Connection Doctor performs a survey of your computer hardware and your connectivity-related software settings. (These same tests are the first performed if you click the Check All button.) The results are integrated into the hierarchical display in the Connection Doctor window, as shown in Figure 5.2. Connection Doctor analyzes your disk system (the Windows swap file and your logical drives), your COM ports, your system information, and your telephony-related installations and configurations.

FIGURE 5.2

Norton Connection Doctor's computer analysis checks the integrity of your connectivity-related hardware.

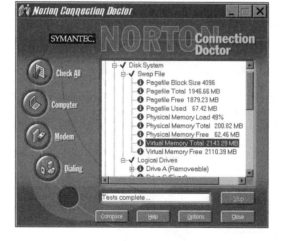

Disk System

Connection Doctor checks the status of your Windows swap file and reports back a variety of statistics with respect to it—its size, what portion of it is being used and what portion is free, what portion of your physical RAM is in use, your total physical RAM and virtual memory, and so on. All this information can be helpful to you or to technical support personnel in troubleshooting different kinds of problems you are having, although the Connection Doctor is designed to help you solve connection-related troubles. Much of this information is similar to what is provided through Norton System Information, another integrated Norton Utilities component of SystemWorks, or by the various sensors of Norton System Doctor, also a Norton Utilities component. System Doctor sensors have to be enabled, however, and the Connection Doctor is always just a few clicks away in the SystemWorks Integrator. Each hard drive will be checked and its space in use and free space reported, as well as its type of FAT.

COM Ports

Norton Connection Doctor identifies all the COM ports enabled on your PC, and the IRQ (interrupt) and the memory IO block for each. Any configuration problems are detected and reported.

If you have a modem properly installed and configured to work on a specific COM port, but Norton Connection Doctor displays an error indicating that your modem can't be found, don't panic. Check these items first:

- If your modem is external, it may be turned off. Turn the external modem on, and run the tests again. If the modem is already on, check that the data cable between it and your PC is connected properly and securely.

- If your modem is a PC-card device, it's likely that the card was not properly recognized when you inserted it. Eject the modem card and reinsert it. Depending on your computer configuration, you may need to restart Windows if the card is still not recognized but has worked properly in the past.

- If your modem is a USB device, check that all connections between the modem, your USB hub, and your PC are made properly and securely.

- If your modem is an internal device, it's possible that the card has come loose from its socket on your PC's motherboard. *Turn your PC off*, open the case carefully, and check to verify that the modem card is properly seated. (If you've never opened your PC before, you may want to obtain the assistance of an experienced friend or associate.)

System Information

The System Information check collects data about all your installed hardware from the Windows Registry. This information is essentially identical to that available to you through the Windows System Control Panel, but Connection Doctor makes it available in one place, along with all other test results. This can be useful in determining which hardware may be available when you are attached to a particular docking station, for instance.

Telephony

Your TAPI configuration and system files are reported here. Reviewing this information can help you quickly identify when antiquated or improper drivers may cause connection troubles. This information can also be useful to technical assistance personnel if you find yourself calling your PC or your modem manufacturer for help.

Modem Tests

Connection Doctor's modem tests check your modem type, its EEPROM revision number, whether a dial tone is currently available on its attached telephone line, and whether the modem supports any of a wide variety of capabilities, including caller ID, distinctive ring response, and voice. If Norton Connection Doctor detects discrepancies that are not exactly "errors," but which may be contributing to connectivity difficulty, you'll see a dialog similar to that in Figure 5.3.

FIGURE 5.3

Norton Connection Doctor has detected configuration inconsistencies with the modem.

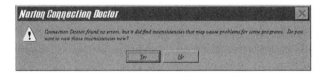

Clicking Yes causes the Connection Doctor readout to scroll and expand as necessary to show you the inconsistencies detected. Although the Connection Doctor's readout cannot be resized, pointing your mouse at any of its data lines causes the entire line to be displayed in a pop-up help-like bar. You can also scroll the readout left and right as necessary. When inconsistencies are detected, you can use this information to reconfigure those characteristics of your modem or your PC, then re-run Connection Doctor's tests to see if they have been successfully eliminated.

The Norton Connection Doctor modem tests can also help you determine whether you should upgrade either your modem's external drivers or its internal software. The revision number information is commonly what you need to know when you go online, for example, to a modem manufacturer's Web site, looking for new support software. You can compare the revision number of your modem with the information you find online. You'll be able to tell if you don't have the latest software stored on your modem itself, or if the manufacturer has released updated drivers for your modem. Keeping up-to-date may be just a click away!

Note: Norton LiveUpdate Pro, part of the Norton Web Services that you'll read about in Chapter 19, "Norton Web Services: Your Current Computer," can also help you automatically locate updated driver software for your modem and any of the other hardware (and software) on your PC.

Dialing Tests

The dialing tests actually check the capability of your modem to successfully connect to a remote server and transmit and receive data. After confirming the presence of a dial tone, Connection Doctor displays the dialog box shown in Figure 5.4, asking you to confirm the location of the remote server to be dialed. Norton Connection Doctor selects Symantec's testing server in Cupertino, California, as the default if you live within the United States. You can select another country and server from the drop-down list if you are not calling from within the U.S..

FIGURE 5.4

You can select the remote server you want to use for Connection Doctor's dial testing.

Keeping Send System Information checked allows Norton Connection Doctor to send a small amount of non-personal data to the remote server, and then receive data back from the remote server. All the while, Connection Doctor listens for a phone line that is inordinately noisy (because of static, for example), negotiation ("handshaking") difficulties, the need for data retransmission, and so on. Any errors encountered are reported within the Connection Doctor display. Certain errors—such as a noisy phone line—may cause the display of a dialog box, alerting you to their existence. After you've noted the issue, dismiss the dialog box.

Comparing Tests

Norton Connection Doctor provides a handy method of comparing the results of one test with the results of another. This allows you to quickly check for improvements if you encounter errors or inconsistencies, make changes, and then re-run testing. At the conclusion of each test, Connection Doctor prompts you to save your test results. You don't need to do this unless you are troubleshooting (outside of storing results for a perfectly working system), in which case you definitely should do so. After making modifications suggested by Connection Doctor or by technical support personnel, you can return to Connection Doctor and re-run your tests. Then, click the Compare button near the lower-left of the Connection Doctor main screen. A dialog box opens consisting of two tabs and a drop-down box. If you've saved more than one test, you can use the drop-down box to select the test against which you want to compare your most recent analysis. The Differences tab shows you anything that has changed between the two tests—it also confirms, somewhat paradoxically, that your modem configuration has not changed, if it indeed has not.

The Previous Results tab redisplays the test results that were obtained by the testing you selected in the drop-down box. This information is presented exactly as in the Connection Doctor main display, organized into a hierarchy, with each line qualified by one of the Connection Doctor results icons, as shown in Figure 5.5.

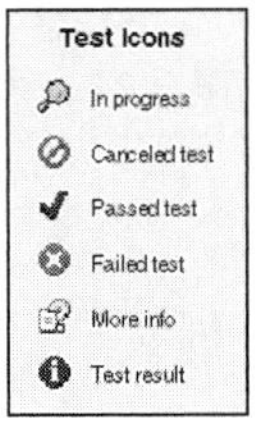

FIGURE 5.5

Norton Connection Doctor uses these icons to display testing results.

Comparing Connection Doctor results can be particularly useful if you are using a mobile computer and you return to a location and suddenly are unable to connect as you have in the past. By checking what has changed between when you ran an earlier Norton Connection Doctor test and the present, you can usually quickly see what system configuration is causing your malfunction.

Putting It Together: Norton System Check

You've already read how Norton System Doctor keeps a continuous watch on vital aspects of your PC. You've also learned that WinDoctor and Connection Doctor can perform detailed but quick tests of your Windows and communications systems, looking for and fixing problems. Norton Utilities 4.0, and therefore Norton SystemWorks 2.0, also includes a new tool that is a bit like a combination of all three—although it is by no means a strict replacement for them.

Norton System Check, or NSC, allows you to perform a speedy, overall check on your entire system. The NSC interface, shown in Figure 5.6, is the same as Norton WinDoctor's interface (with one small addition, which I'll discuss in a moment). As System Check runs its tests, you can watch their progress in the large panel that makes up the right-hand side of the window.

FIGURE 5.6

Norton System Check uses the same familiar interface as Norton WinDoctor.

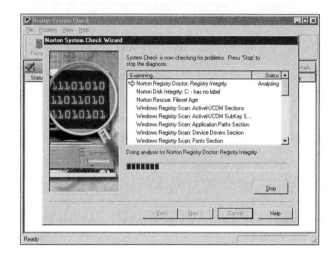

After NSC has completed its tests, the results are displayed in a new window, shown in Figure 5.7, which looks exactly like WinDoctor's results window. The benefit of this similarity should be obvious: After you know how to use one tool, you actually know how to use two!

FIGURE 5.7

Norton System Check uses the same familiar report interface as Norton WinDoctor. (The advanced report is shown here; both it and the basic report are available, as in WinDoctor.)

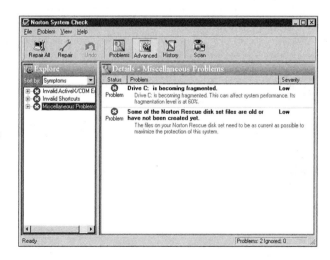

Figure 5.7 also demonstrates what I meant when I said that Norton System Check is a bit like several utilities in one. Notice in the figure that System Check has detected problems with Registry entries and shortcuts—just like WinDoctor—and has also found—just as System Doctor would have found—that one of my drives is fragmented and my Norton Rescue information is out of date. (You'll read about Norton Rescue in Chapter 7, "Norton Utilities: Life Preserver on a (Rescue) Disk.")

> **Note:** Because System Check's Registry tests are identical to those performed by WinDoctor, I won't repeat all the details here; you've probably already read about them at length in Chapter 4, "Norton Utilities: The WinDoctor Is In." If you've not read it already, you'll want to read Chapter 4. It also tells you every-thing you need to know about performing repairs and undoing previous repairs: WinDoctor and System Check work exactly alike.

As when you're using WinDoctor, clicking the various buttons at the top of the Window controls both how problems are displayed and how they are repaired. Click Repair All to allow System Check to use its built-in knowledge base to apply the best solution to all detected problems.

Configuring Norton System Check

Because Norton System Check includes a wide range of tests, it works with you through a simple wizard that allows you to select which tests will be performed. Shown in Figure 5.8, the wizard allows you to select whether disk problems, Windows problems, perfor-mance problems, or periodic maintenance problems exist. To deselect an active test, click to remove the "✔" in its check box. Clicking in the box also activates an inactive test. Of course, performing fewer tests takes less time, but also provides you with a more limited view of your system's status.

This first wizard panel also enables you to undo previously performed repairs. Click the Undo Previous Repairs option button at the bottom of the panel, to activate System Check's undo mode. (For more information on undoing repairs, refer to the "Undoing Repairs" section in Chapter 4.)

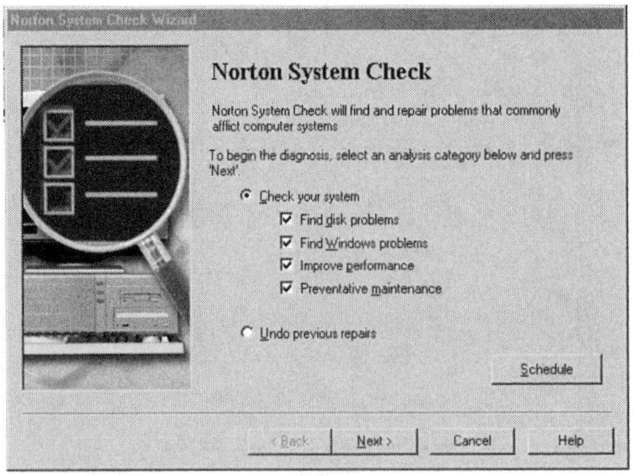

FIGURE 5.8
The Norton System Check Wizard allows you to select which tests are to be performed.

Scheduling Norton System Check

You can also schedule System Check to run and perform its tests automatically on a regular basis. You can't do this with Norton WinDoctor.

> **Note:** As you learned in Chapter 3, "Norton Utilities: The System Doctor Is In," the Norton System Doctor includes a WinDoctor sensor that can launch WinDoctor automatically on an as-needed basis. However, WinDoctor only performs its tests interactively—that is, you have to interrupt what you're doing and attend to the WinDoctor Wizard for its tests to be run. Norton System Check runs all of its tests in a completely non-invasive way. At the same time, you don't need to worry about System Check making unauthorized changes to your system. After its tests run, it generates a report for you, but it won't perform any repairs without your permission.

The System Check scheduler, shown in Figure 5.9, mirrors the test-selection options found in the interactive wizard. You can add and remove check marks here to specify which tests you want run automatically.

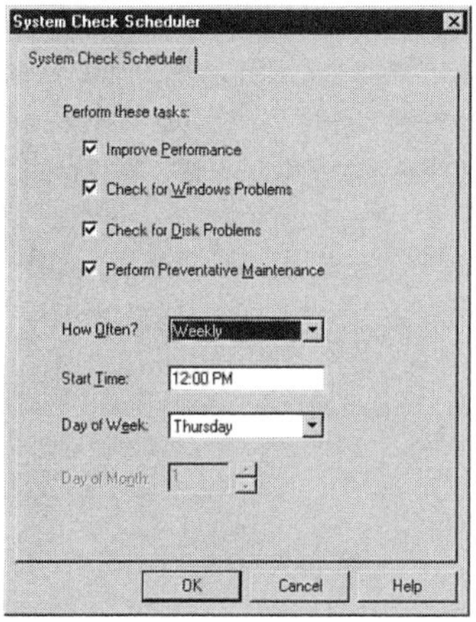

FIGURE 5.9

The Norton System Check scheduler allows you to select which tests will be automatically performed and when they will be performed.

Below the test-selection area is the scheduler. You've seen similarly designed schedulers in Norton System Doctor, and you'll see them again, elsewhere in Norton SystemWorks. Basically, you can specify that the System Check tests are to be run either Daily, Weekly, Monthly, every time Windows starts up, or never (that is, the scheduler is off—there is no automatic operation). For each option, as is relevant, the other areas of the scheduler will become enabled. In this way you can choose when you want tests to be run each day, or on what day of the week (and when) you want weekly tests run, and so on. The settings you select are stored, and System Check performs for you as you've instructed.

> **Caution:** If you schedule System Check to run each time Windows starts, you may discover—particularly on a slower PC—that a great deal of time lapses between when your desktop appears and when you are to be able to begin working. This delay will be even greater if you are also loading Norton System Doctor at startup. My suggestion is that you always allow Norton System Doctor to run at startup, but schedule your Norton System Check tests to run at another time. Of course, if you're using a speedy PC, you may not notice any delay at all.

Be aware that you cannot select System Check to automatically run a few tests at one time and other tests at a different time. When you make changes in the scheduler, your previously scheduled tests are overwritten with your new schedule. If you temporarily disable certain automated tests for a specific reason, don't forget to re-enable them when that reason is no longer pressing.

Total Troubleshooting

Together, Norton System Doctor, Norton WinDoctor, and Norton Connection Doctor provide a complete set of troubleshooting tools for your PC. Anything that isn't configured properly, isn't present but should be, or simply isn't working for any reason is reported to you. This information can save you literally hours of poking around, trying to solve problems blindly. In addition, these tools can provide you with valuable assistance in maximizing the performance of your PC, after everything is working nominally. Norton System Check allows you to run—even automatically—selected key tests that are otherwise performed by the three Norton Doctor utilities. When it comes to the health of your PC, the Norton Doctors are always on-call.

Norton Utilities: Digging Through the Trash with Norton Protection

If there is one single mistake every PC user has made, it's deleting a file he or she didn't want to delete. In fact, the problem is so universal that Norton UnErase was the first utility Peter Norton ever wrote. Being able to get back files that you've accidentally sent into Neverland can not only save you hours of work—it could save your job. Since that first Norton Utility came into existence, it has grown and evolved, keeping well ahead of the dynamism of the PC industry itself. Norton Protection and the UnErase Wizard are two powerful tools that can do far more than the original UnErase. Revolutionary as it was, that DOS program could recover only most deleted files. Used properly, Norton Protection can recover everything—guaranteed.

"Used properly," of course, are the most important words in the paragraph you've just read. The Norton Protected Recycle Bin was automatically installed by the Norton SystemWorks Setup program, unless you installed Norton SystemWorks with the "typical" option or did a custom install and specifically told Setup to not do so. (If you chose that path, read through this chapter and learn what Norton Protection can do for you. I think you'll change your mind and will want to add Norton Protection—or NP, as I'll be calling it—to your collection of active Norton tools.) But even with it installed, you need to know what it does and how to use it before it protects your data effectively.

In the process of learning how to master Norton Protection, you'll learn about what really happens when you delete a file and why sophisticated Norton Protection is needed more than ever. The process of recovering from a mistake starts with preparedness. If you installed Norton Protection, you're prepared. So let's focus on the mistake, and you'll understand how mistakes can be undone. At the same time, you'll learn a little bit about the history of Windows and the Norton Utilities themselves.

Goodbye to Good Data: How Files Are Deleted

The year is 1983. The place is an office. Fannie-Jo User is sitting behind her mahogany desk, working on her IBM PC XT. The green text-only screen shines in her face as she scans over a list of inscrutable filenames, such as 82FRPT0A.123 and 83FRPT0A.DB2. She's just copied all last year's files off her huge 10MB hard drive onto two black, 5.25-inch square, 360KB floppies. Up on the 30th floor, the equipment is the newest available, and life is good. With her files backed up on floppy disk, she goes to erase the old data and types

```
DEL 83*.*
```

at the DOS prompt and presses Enter. A millisecond too late, she realizes that she has just zapped this year's files, while last year's files still grin back at her in that sickening green glow. All the executive's horses and all her technical men inform her that she can't put her files back together again. She can't believe that she can't undo a deletion. But she can't.

Actually, she could, if her technical people had known how. But they didn't, and the first Un-Deletion tool that Microsoft provided with its MS-DOS operating system wasn't available until June 1991. If she'd had the 1982 release of the Norton Utilities, she would have been set, but, as the author of this little story, I didn't let her have them.

What Fannie-Jo didn't know—and what made the Norton Utilities' UnErase tool possible—was that, when you delete a file from your computer's hard drive, you don't actually delete anything. The data in your deleted file isn't touched in any way. What does happen—and what makes it seem like your file has been deleted—is that the first letter of the file's old name is changed in the filename directory from whatever it was into a rarely used ASCII value, hex E5, which happens to signify the Extended ASCII equivalent of the Greek letter sigma. When the operating system reads through the directory entries, it ignores entries that start with the sigma. So, the filename disappears from directory listings; eventually, the operating system re-uses the space occupied by those filename entries, writing over them with new filenames. All through this, however, the data that was your file can remain intact.

The more you use your computer, however, the less likely you'll be able to successfully UnErase a file. Why? Because of another thing that happens when you delete a file: All the clusters used by the file are changed in the File Allocation Table (FAT) from being marked as "in use" to "available." As time passes and you create new files—and as other things happen that you'll read about later—that available space may get used. Then, and only then—when the physical disk locations that formerly held your data have been overwritten with new data—has your file truly been deleted.

How Files Were UnErased

That was the way it worked back in the early 1980s and that's how it works today. The earliest versions of the Norton Utilities UnErase tool were capable of searching for deleted directory entries, used some sophisticated technology to check whether the disk locations to which those entries pointed were still marked as "available" (in other words, had not yet been overwritten), and enabled the user to specify a new first letter for that collection of data's filename. That done, the file was instantly reborn. In 1982, Peter Norton gave personal computers their first phoenix. (Even in the early 1980s, Norton UnErase had more functionality than just that, but for our purposes, that's one major aspect of how it worked.)

The previous paragraph describes the original UnErase process in only the simplest terms, and it includes one very large assumption: that the deleted file was unfragmented. Because all the clusters used by a deleted file are marked as available (set to a numeric value of zero, actually) in the FAT, it was necessary for files to use contiguous clusters if they were to be UnErased reliably. This enabled UnErase to use the starting cluster and file length data in the old directory entry to trace a series of contiguous clusters until an end of file (EOF) marker confirmed that the file length in the directory entry matched the amount of data relocated in "available" clusters on disk. If historic UnErase could not confirm that a contiguous chain of free clusters of the required length was available where the directory entry said the file should have been—in other words, if an in-use cluster interrupted the chain before an EOF was found at the predicted place—UnErase marked the likelihood of recovering the file as "poor." To get a visual sense of all this, take a look at Figure 6.1.

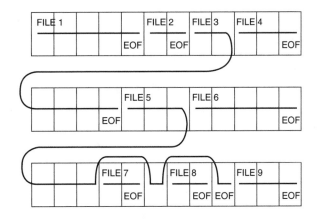

- Files 1, 2, 4, 6, 7, 8, or 9 would be straightforward and easy to unerase unless overwritten.

- Files 3 and 5—especially file 5—would have had a very poor chance of being automatically unerased because of their fragmentation.

Automatic Norton Protection

Although the fundamental process through which files are deleted remains largely unchanged, UnErasing tools have had to become more sophisticated than ever. Why? First of all, because of the fragmentation problem you just read about. Files get fragmented. More problematic, however, is a little thing called your Windows swap file. Briefly put, the Windows swap file is a very large file on disk that Windows uses to create Virtual Memory. As your physical RAM fills with applications and data—and with Windows itself—the Windows memory manager starts swapping data that hasn't been used in a while onto your hard disk. This makes room in physical RAM—which is vastly faster than virtual memory—for more applications, more data, and more Windows. All through the history of Windows 3.1, the swap file made little difference in terms of UnErasing your data because its size never changed, it couldn't be moved around on your drive, and it never behaved dynamically.

All of that changed starting with Windows 95. Windows 9x swap files can not only be relocated on disk, but they grow and shrink dramatically during the course of an extended Windows session. This enables Windows to manage its resources vastly better, provide you with a good deal more Virtual Memory than ever before, and, with the aid of a utility such the Norton Optimization Wizard, keep your swap file defragmented and working at its fastest. However, all that shrinking, growing, and moving means that your deleted files could get overwritten not in a matter of days or weeks (like it was back in the 1980s), but in a matter of a few minutes. Knowing what you now know about how files are deleted, how is it possible that we can UnErase files today *more* reliably than in the past, when every indication is that deleted files are far more endangered than they ever were?

Norton Protection provides an innovative, unobtrusive way of bringing your files back from the dead. It does so by making sure they never really die in the first place, as you're about to see.

Norton Versus Windows

When the Norton Protection Recycle Bin was first installed, it didn't replace the traditional Windows Recycle Bin. The Norton Protection Recycle Bin actually overlays the Windows Recycle Bin, which remains a permanent part of Windows. (You can read more about this near the end of this chapter.) The old Recycle Bin enabled you to restore deleted files by holding them temporarily in a folder on disk. Until you cleared that folder—by "emptying" the Recycle Bin, your files were still very much present on disk and so, of course, were available for restoration.

The problem is that the Windows Recycle Bin to this day protects only a fraction of the files that actually get deleted from your PC. It doesn't protect temporary files. It doesn't protect anything deleted from within Windows programs (except the Explorer and Desktop). It doesn't protect any file that you delete from within MS-DOS, even if you are using a DOS box within Windows. The Windows Recycle Bin also doesn't protect versions of files that get overwritten when you make changes and re-save the file. Norton Protection protects all those files, unless you instruct it to do less.

An Explanation of Norton Protection

Norton Protection dramatically augments the process used by the Windows Recycle Bin by retaining your deleted files on disk in some very different ways. As with the Windows Recycle Bin, Norton Protection reserves a section of disk space and creates a "storage locker" into which deleted files go. In the case of Norton Protection, this storage locker is hidden. The Norton Protection locker can hold up to 1,500 files "per drive", and how long these files remain protected can be configured entirely by you, as you'll read about later in this chapter. As files are moved into Norton Protection—that is, as you delete them—fragmented files get unfragmented. Unlike the Windows Recycle Bin, Norton Protection can—and does—safeguard every file deletion that takes place on your Windows PC.

Norton Protection watches over files that are created and deleted while you're running an MS-DOS program under Windows. These files are usually afforded no protection by other Windows-based file restoration utilities, including the Windows Recycle Bin. Norton Protection keeps track of them and enables you to use the Windows-based UnErase Wizard to get them back. You don't have to work with DOS-based utilities to preserve DOS-based files.

Even the temporary files that Windows applications create while they are running—and automatically delete when you quit—are preserved by Norton Protection. How many times have you decided to not save a file, only to change your mind after the application quit? Norton Protection can help you retrieve work you never saved in the first place. In fact, Norton Protection even preserves earlier versions of a file that you yourself overwrite when you save the file while you work. In this way, if something catastrophic happens to your working file, and if that file gets saved, you can retrieve the previously saved version and pick up as close to where you left off as possible.

Peter and I—and many other writers—have always said that the very best defense against accidental file loss—regardless of what other defenses you have available to you—is backing up your work. In a manner of speaking, Norton Protection provides you with exactly that: Deleted files get copied (backed up, if you will) not to tape, but into Norton Protection, where they can be safety retrieved. You'll obviously want to continue to back up your drives to further safeguard against massive drive failure, although many such failures are repairable by other Norton Utilities, as you'll read throughout this book. But with Norton Protection, you can retrieve a deleted file from backup without ever touching a backup drive.

How Files Are UnErased Today

You'll read about the Norton UnErase Wizard at length in Chapter 15, "Norton Utilities: Getting It Back, Getting It Right: UnErasing and File Compare." We'll look at the Wizard briefly here to acquaint you with how it integrates with Norton Protection.

When you first run the Norton UnErase Wizard (easily done by right-clicking the Norton Protected Recycle Bin and selecting Norton UnErase from the context menu), you can instruct it to check Norton Protection for the list of your 25 most recently deleted files. As you can see in Figure 6.2, the Wizard automatically displays these for your perusal.

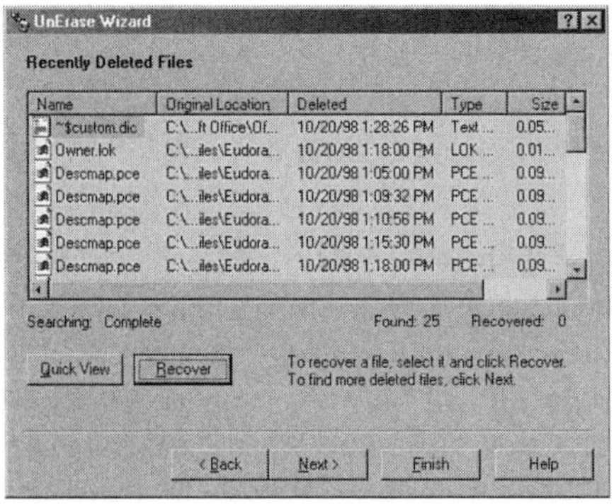

FIGURE 6.2

The UnErase Wizard displays the Norton Protected files that have recently been erased.

You can see in the figure that Norton Protection keeps track of each file's original name, original location on disk, precisely when the file was deleted, the file type, its size, and by what method or application the file was deleted. If you're looking through a large number of files—particularly if you are looking for vital work that was lost and may have been preserved only in an application's temporary files—the deletion time information can be extremely useful. Figure 6.2 shows that temporary files commonly share the same name and the same original location (and obviously, they all share the same file type and "deleted by" data), so telling one file apart from another can be tricky work. Knowing when the file was deleted, especially if you run Norton Protection to recover a file as soon as possible after the work was lost, can make it a lot easier to find what you're seeking.

In the old days, if you were searching through a list of temporary files, the process was much more difficult. You probably would have taken a lot of time to use the Norton Disk Editor to manually look at each file's contents, as you'll read about in Chapter 12, "Norton Utilities: The Laying-On of Hands and Norton Disk Editor." The reason for this was that, in the days before Norton Protection, an UnErased file was reconstructed on disk in the first-available set of contiguous clusters. This meant that UnErasing one file could easily mean writing over another deleted file; UnErasing the wrong file could mean destroying the right file forever. So using the Norton Disk Editor to determine which file was which before you UnErased anything was sometimes vital. It was also a technical, time-consuming operation.

That was then. Now, since Norton Protection maintains a complete copy of these deleted files, it matters much less whether you UnErase the wrong file. Yes, UnErased files may still overwrite previously used clusters. But the files from those clusters are still under Norton Protection, safe from being destroyed. Today's Norton Protection can actually protect you against concerns its own ancestors caused.

> **Note:** Within the Norton UnErase Wizard you can launch a Quick View of any file under Norton Protection, as you can see in Figure 6.2. There may still be circumstances—perhaps you've worked recently on a number of different files and there are many deleted files that were created within a short time—in which you may want to look into a file before restoring it. With the Quick View button, you have the functionality of reviewing a file's contents integrated right into the Wizard itself. You should be aware, however, that this feature makes use of Windows' own Quick Viewers. If these are not installed, this feature is disabled. (You can install the Quick Viewers from the Windows Setup tab in the Add/Remove Programs control panel.)

Additionally, early file-recovery tools never kept track of what application or method was used to delete files. If you used seven different applications—all of which created temporary files with names such as TEMP1.TMP, TEMP2.TMP—and so on, you might have hundreds of files, all with the same name, to search through with the Norton Disk Editor before you found the one you actually needed. Today, you can quickly see what application zapped each file under Norton Protection, and where that file was originally located on disk. By clicking the column headers, such as Name and Original Location, you can even sort your Norton Protected files by that category (see Figure 6.2). Recognizing your temporary Microsoft Word file from your temporary Corel Draw files is a snap.

Why all this discussion about temporary files? When was the last time a temporary file ever did you any good? Consider a scenario: You're working in your home office and the telephone rings. Because you decided to have children, you've also decided to have only one phone. You go into your family telephone vault to answer it. Too late—you later find that you have left your computer to your 7-year old technophile to decide whether a document containing the French word *résumé* is worth saving before quitting Word. "But," you say, "I always save my work. I save constantly while I'm working." To test the veracity of that statement, try this experiment: Tell your child or other highly loved one that, sometime when you are working quietly on your computer, you want them to surprise you by suddenly pulling out your computer's plug from the wall. If the mere thought of that makes you feel ill, you could find that a temporary file will someday save your sanity.

All that said, after you've selected the file you wish to UnErase in the list of deleted files, simply click Recover. The file will be restored to the folder in which it was created. That's all there is to it.

Caution: When you are restoring deleted temporary files, be certain that the relevant application is not running. You're in no danger of over-writing existing work—Norton Protection won't allow that—but you could find that your UnErased temporary file gets deleted along with others by the application. Furthermore, why complicate the issue of restoring a temporary file into a folder containing many other active temporary files?

Additionally, realize that many of your applications will not recognize a temporary file as one that can be directly opened. You may need to change a temporary word-processing file's extension to .DOC, for example, before you are able to manually open the file. I encountered this very problem while recovering a temporary Corel Draw file. The temporary file had an extension that Draw did not recognize. By changing the file extension to Corel Draw's normal .CDR, I was able to double-click the file's icon and open it perfectly. (When you change a file's extension, Windows may give you a warning that doing so can render the file unusable. If you are performing the procedure described here, just confirm to Windows that you know what you're doing by clicking Yes. Also, if you have Windows set to hide file extensions, you cannot change them without first making them visible. To make your file extensions visible, double-click the My Computer icon on your desktop. From the View menu, select Options and click the View tab. Here you can uncheck Hide MS-DOS file extensions for file types that are registered.)

Of course, Norton Protection cares for a good deal more than just your most recently deleted 25 files. If you're recovering a file that you just deleted, the 25 most recent deletions are probably all you'll need to see. The UnErase Wizard provides you full access to all files under Norton Protection, of course, whether there are 25 or 1,200. As you'll read below, you can configure Norton Protection to show you what you want to see when you double-click the Norton Protected Recycle Bin.

Tip: When you're looking for a temporary file saved by Norton Protection, sort the files by date and look for the files saved while you were using the application. If there are many files which meet that criteria, choose the one which is closest in size to the file you were working on. Frequently, the temporary file you want was about the same size and deleted a few minutes before your accident.

Configuration: Getting the (Norton) Protection You Want

If you believe that your data is important, you might agree that Norton Protection is one of the key tools integrated with the Norton Utilities into SystemWorks. For all its importance, however, it's also one of the simplest tools you'll ever configure. All the default settings do a good job of watch-dogging your data. On the other hand, every person is different, and how you use your PC may be vastly different from how I use mine. In this section, you'll learn how to make sure that Norton Protection works for you.

Turning Protection Off for All Drives

Probably the most fundamental issue is whether you use it or not. If you installed the Norton Protection Recycle Bin when you installed the rest of Norton SystemWorks, you may never need to turn it off. But if you want to, you can. By right-clicking the Norton Protection Recycle Bin and selecting Properties, you'll see a context menu from which all Norton Protection can be configured (see Figure 6.3). In some ways, it may remind you of Windows' Recycle Bin properties; in other ways, much is new. Note that if you installed Norton SystemWorks using a "typical" installation, Norton Protection is installed, but is not yet active. To turn it on, right-click on the Norton Protected Recycle Bin, select Properties, switch to the Norton Protection tab and make certain that there is a check mark in the Enable Protection box for each drive you want protected. (Click Apply after enabling each drive, then click OK when you're finished.)

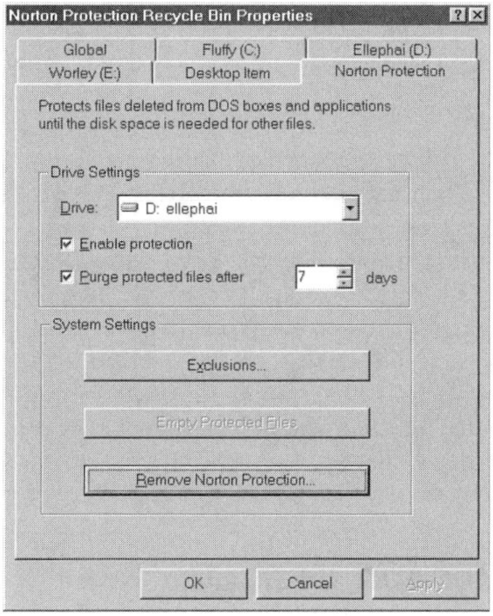

FIGURE 6.3
You can use the Recycle Bin Properties dialog box to configure Norton Protection.

If you want to temporarily disable Norton Protection entirely, click the Norton Protection tab in the Properties dialog box, as shown in Figure 6.3. At the bottom of the Norton Protection tab, you'll see a large button labeled Remove Norton Protection. Click this button. After a confirmation dialog box, Norton Protection is turned off, removed from memory, and does not load automatically the next time you start Windows. Norton Protection remains disabled until you reactivate it. You'll still have the old functionality you used to have with the Windows Recycle Bin. However, all the Windows Recycle Bin's limitations are back as well. If you remove Protection and click OK, you'll see that the Norton Protected Recycle Bin's shield shows a red circle with a slash through it, as at the extreme left of Figure 6.4. This indicates that Protection is disabled and that memory has been released for Windows or other applications to use.

FIGURE 6.4
The three Status Shields of the Norton Protection Recycle Bin protect files at various levels.

The Remove Norton Protection confirmation box mentioned previously has one additional option. Placing a check mark in the Also Empty Protected Files box at the bottom of the dialog box empties your Norton Protection Recycle Bins (one for each currently protected drive). If you do not check the box to indicate you wish files purged, then those files are again protected when Norton Protection is re-enabled. (In the interim, Norton Protected files are moved to the Windows Recycle Bin.) This option has security-related implications, which you'll read about in the discussion of security at the end of this chapter.

Note: Removing Norton Protection from the Norton Protection Recycle Bin's Properties does not remove it from your hard drive. In fact, when you restart Windows, you'll notice that your Recycle Bin still says Norton Protection. This is confusing but normal. Norton Protection reminds you that it remains installed and available to you. (You'll read in a moment how to change both the Recycle Bin icon and label, so you don't have to be reminded if you don't want to be.) As long as the red slashed circle is present in the Norton Protection Recycle Bin's status shield, as in Figure 6.4, Norton Protection neither protects files nor uses any system resources or memory.

Turning Protection Back On

To re-enable Norton Protection at any time, simply right-click the Recycle Bin icon, select Properties from the context menu, and return to the Norton Protection tab.

Enabling protection for any one drive reloads Norton Protection into memory and configures it to load automatically the next time Windows starts. The Recycle Bin status shield resets itself and the red slashed circle disappears.

> **Caution:** Be aware that re-enabling Norton Protection by turning it on for one drive only activates Protection for that drive. If you have multiple drives, you must select each from the Drive Settings drop-down and re-check Enable Protection, then click the Apply button.
>
> Don't accidentally leave one or more of your drives unprotected! (Also, be aware that the Use One Setting for All Drives option on the Global tab has no effect on which drives are covered by Norton Protection.)

Turning Protection Off and On for Selected Drives

If you wish to leave Norton Protection enabled only for selected drives, you can choose to do so. In the Drive Settings section at the top of the Norton Protection tab just discussed, select the drive for which you want Norton Protection disabled (assuming more than one drive is present in your system) and remove the check mark from the Enable Protection box. Until you turn it back on, Norton Protection is disabled on that drive only. If you disable protection for fewer than all drives on your system, the Norton Protected Recycle Bin's (NPRB's) status shield continues to show the status of the drive(s) it is protecting. If no files are being protected, you'll see a gray "N"; if files are being guarded, the "N" turns bright blue, as at the extreme right in Figure 6.4.

While on the subject of the NPRB status shield, I should mention that you'll also see files ("trash") in the Recycle Bin icon, regardless of the status of Norton Protection. Notice in Figure 6.4 that both the inactive and the active-and-protecting bins show files in the basket, while the central icon does not. (You may also see files in the basket, but the NPRB status shield still remains gray.) The reason for this is that, with certain kinds of deletions, files are still protected by Norton Protection but are also placed into the traditional Windows Recycle Bin. You can read about this in the section "Why Some Files Still Go in the Windows Recycle Bin," near the end of this chapter.

To enable Norton Protection from disabled drives, simply select the drive in the Drive Settings drop-down box, then re-check Enable Protection. That drive's Norton Protection is turned back on and remains on the next time Windows starts. You can re-enable multiple drives and then click Apply or OK to accept all your changes. You don't need to click Apply after enabling each drive.

You should notice that when you select a drive in the drop-down box, the Enable Protection check box automatically updates to show you that drive's status. You can quickly check the status of all your drives by clicking your mouse on the Drive down-arrow button, and then using the up- and down-arrow keys on your keyboard to scroll through the drives. As you select each drive, the Enable Protection check box shows you which drives are protected and which are not.

Turning Protection On and Off—File by File

Norton Protection can be turned on and off on a system-wide, drive, or even individual file basis. This is done by creating a list of Exclusions, which Norton Protection uses to identify specific files, types of files, or directories to which it gives no Protection. Because most applications create and delete many files while they are running, protecting all those files can cause your Norton Protected Recycle Bin to reach its maximum capacity—1,500 files protected per drive—very quickly. When the NPRB fills up, the oldest files in it are removed from protection to make room for new files. To avoid losing meaningful files, you don't want to grant protection to the hundreds of little temporary files that you know you'll never use.

But based on our discussion of temporary files, which temporary files do you dare exclude? The designers of Norton Protection have created a default list of exclusions. It's a good start, but it's also probably a list you'll want to edit right from the beginning. Let's take a look at it by right-clicking the NPRB, selecting Properties, and then clicking the Norton Protection tab. At the top of the System Settings area of the tab, you'll find a button labeled Exclusions. Click it and you'll be taken to the Exclusions dialog box shown in Figure 6.5. Here you can see some of the files that the Norton Protection engineers have selected for exclusion by default.

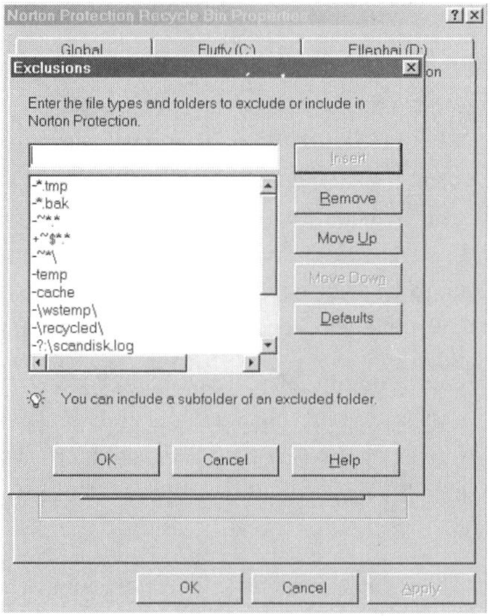

FIGURE 6.5

You can create and modify the Norton Protection exclusion list from this dialog box.

> **Note:** As mentioned previously, the exclusion list is one you'll probably want to edit from the start. You'll notice that, at the top of the list, all files on the system—these exclusions impact all drives unless you select otherwise—that have a .TMP extension are excluded from protection. I personally recommend that you delete this exclusion by selecting it and clicking the Remove button to the right of the exclusion list. You will want to exclude many temporary files, and we'll get to that in just a moment, but excluding all files that use the traditional extension for a temporary file can deprive you of one of Norton Protection's great benefits. You can always add the global exception back if you find that too many files are being pushed through the Norton Protection Recycle Bin.

Although this list is called the exclusion list, it also serves as an inclusion list. Notice in Figure 6.5 that the first three entries in the list begin with a minus sign ("–"), while the fourth entry begins with a plus sign ("+"). This is because you can also use this list to specify files that may meet some of the exclusion rules, but that you don't want excluded. All the entries in the list are evaluated in the order in which they appear. So, a file that meets an exclusion rule found at the top of the list may have its Protection re-instituted by an inclusion rule found at the bottom of the list. Conversely, if you create an inclusion rule early in the list, but files that match it also match an exclusion rule late in the list, those files are excluded from Protection. Let's take a quick look at how this all works. (Incidentally, as you are practicing with these settings, you don't need to worry about endangering files you want to Protect. To restore the default exclusions and inclusions at any time, just click the Defaults button at the right side of the dialog box.)

Creating Exclusions

The format for creating a new exclusion is simple. In the text box at the top of the Exclusions dialog box, type the exclusion symbol, followed by the specifications that name the file or files you want to exclude. (If you want to learn how files are specified, take a look at the technical sidebar, later in this section.) Therefore, if you wanted to exclude every standard JPEG image file that ever appears on your system, you could do so by typing **-*.JPG** in the file descriptor box and clicking the Insert button. Similarly, all word processor documents—or at least, most of them—could be excluded from Protection by entering **-*.DOC** and clicking Insert. (You probably would never want to use either of these exclusions. I've used them here merely for illustrative purposes.)

Each new exclusion is placed at the bottom of the exclusion list, meaning that it takes precedence over all exclusions or inclusions that precede it. To change the order in which exclusions are evaluated, select the exclusion you wish to move, and click either the Move Up or Move Down button at the right side of the dialog box. Again, the higher an entry is in the list, the more vulnerable it is to the fate of all entries that follow it. If you absolutely want to exclude some files from Protection, keep that exclusion last in the list.

To exclude a specific file located in a specific folder, you enter the exclusion symbol followed by the complete path to that file. For example, `-C:\My Documents\Junk\Diary.txt` would remove Norton Protection from a text file named `Diary` located in the `Junk` subfolder of the `My Documents` folder. Any other files in the `Junk` subfolder, and any other files in other directories named `Diary.txt`, will not be excluded.

To exclude a file with a specific name, regardless of where it is found on your system, create a new exclusion with only that file's name. The exclusion `-lrc.doc` would exclude all files named `lrc.doc` from Protection, regardless of the folder or any drive in which they're found.

If you want to exclude an entire folder from Protection, simply create an exclusion with that folder's complete path. You need not use wildcards to specify that all files in the folder should be excluded. This is the default. Therefore, `-C:\Program Files\GMC` excludes all files of any type that are stored in that folder. All files in all subfolders of that folder will also be excluded, so use folder-based exclusions with care. If you do not want to exclude a particular subfolder, you may specifically include it (as described in the next section), making sure that the inclusion is lower in the list than the parent folder's exclusion.

You can also see in Figure 6.5 that specifying a drive letter is optional. If no drive letter is specified, protection is withheld from all files and subfolders found within any folder with the matching name on any drive. (In the figure, for example, all Recycle Bins on the system have been excluded through the `-\recycled\` entry.)

If you forget to type the exclusion symbol, it is added for you automatically.

Creating Inclusions

Inclusions are created in the same manner as exclusions and follow the same rules. The only difference in the process is that you use the inclusion symbol ("+") instead of the exclusion ("–") symbol. Briefly, then, all files in the Windows folder with the extension `.TMP` can be forcibly included by entering `+C:\Windows\*.TMP` and clicking Insert. To forcibly include a specific file, you would use the same structure as this entry: `+C:\Data\MyDiary.DOC`. Including a file with a specific name, regardless of where it is found, can be achieved with the same entry format as `+name.ext`. (There's a subtle difference to be noted here. The exclusion `+name.ext` excludes a file, while the exclusion `+\name.ext` excludes a folder and its subfolders, if any.)

As an example, let's say that you want to exclude protection from all files using the default temporary file extension `.TMP`, except those that may be created in or deleted from the folder you've told your image editing software to use for its temporary files. Early in the exclusion list, you would have an entry such as `-*.TMP`, meaning, "I don't care where you find them, but files with the `TMP` extension are to be excluded." Later in the list, however, you would make an entry like this: `+C:\Program Files\Draw4u\Temp\*.TMP`. When Norton Protection evaluates your exclusion list, it first sees that all

TMP files are to be excluded, but it then modifies that exclusion; the TMP files in the folder you've selected will have protection added back.

As with exclusions, new inclusions are added to the end of the list. An inclusion can be relocated by selecting it and then using the Move Up and Move Down buttons to give it the level of priority you require.

File Descriptors and How SystemWorks Works with Them

If you're not familiar with the Windows way of naming and describing files, options such as the Norton Protection exclusion list can seem daunting. They need not be. A few very basic rules exist for naming files—even in today's world of long file names—and once you've got these in your pocket, you're good to go.

You already know that drives are described by a letter and a colon, with C:, by convention, always being the hard drive from which you boot. (If you boot from a floppy or removable cartridge, that drive is known as A:, and a second floppy drive is known as B:.) The backslash symbol ("\") is used to indicate separations between directories and subfolders on your drives. Therefore, C:\ refers to the root directory on your C: drive, while D:\DATA\YETMORE\STILLMORE refers to the folder STILLMORE, which is located in the folder YETMORE, which is located in the folder DATA, which can be found in the root directory of drive D:.

Every file on your system has a name. In the days of DOS, only eight digits, plus a three-digit file extension (used to indicate the type of file) were allowed. So, 04PNU998.DOC was what filenames looked like in the "8.3" world. Windows 95 and Windows 98, of course, support long filenames, meaning a file's name may now consist of up to 245 characters, including an optional three-digit file extension. Their optional status notwithstanding, almost every file on your Windows 98 system will have an extension. Long filenames may also contain spaces—as well as several symbol characters—which were forbidden in the old days of DOS. Certain symbols remain reserved for particular functions, among which is the backslash. It's still used to separate one folder from another. When you start stringing drive letters, folder names, and filenames together, the amalgam that describes the location of a particular file (or just a particular folder) is called a *path*. In the example on the D: drive in the previous paragraph, a file named LFA Data.DOC would have a complete path of D:\DATA\YETMORE\STILLMORE\LFA Data.DOC.

Symbols other than the backslash are also reserved. Several of these are used as *wildcards*, enabling the user to specify a number of files at once without having to name each separately. The two Windows wildcards are the question mark ("?") and the asterisk ("*"). Norton SystemWorks has added wildcards of its own, which you'll read about presently. The question mark wildcard is used to signify a single character in a file or folder name. So, ?HELLO would be the equivalent of a filename AHELLO, 4HELLO, or PHELLO, but because the question mark represents only one character, the file ANHELLO would not be matched. HELLO.??? would match all files named HELLO with any three-digit extension, but would not match HELLO.12. The asterisk symbol, on the other hand, is used to signify any number of characters. HELLO*, therefore, matches HELLOA, HELLOMY-NAMEISSCOTT, and HELLO.DOC as well. HELLO.* matches any file named HELLO with an extension of any length, including no extension at all.

To these, Norton SystemWorks has added some additional functionality. In the case of the backslash character, a backslash by itself at the end of a path automatically includes all files and all files in all subfolders further down the path. Therefore, for purposes of Norton SystemWorks, C:\Windows\ refers to your Windows folder, all its files, all its subfolders, and all their files. On the other hand, C:\Windows* refers only to those files found in the Windows folder, not those in its subfolders, if any. If you use the backslash at the beginning of a path in lieu of a drive letter, the initial backslash acts as a wildcard for all drives. Therefore, \Windows\ addresses all files and subfolders in any folder named Windows on any disk. If more than one such folder exists, all will be specified. The asterisk has taken on an extended life as well. Two asterisks together after a folder name can be used to refer to all files in that folder and all files in that folder's subfolders. For example, C:\Windows** refers to your Windows folder, all its files, all its subfolders, and all their files.

For purposes of Norton Protection exclusions and inclusions specifically, C:\Windows\ and C:\Windows** mean the same thing. Additionally, while in Windows, C:\Windows and C:\Windows\ generally mean the same thing, they do not in Norton Protection exclusions and inclusions. In this specific context, the first example refers to a file named Windows, located in the root directory of drive C:. The final backslash character in the second example indicates that you are specifying the Windows folder.

Other Norton Protection Settings

Other Norton Protection options are configured from the Properties tab. As you have already read, Norton Protection keeps deleted files for a period of time, after which those files are purged. You can specify that period of time from the Norton Protection tab in Figure 6.3. Purging can be set to occur after as little as 1 day or as many as 999 days. For most users, somewhere between 7 and 14 days is reasonable. Bear in mind that once the Norton Protection Recycle Bin holds 1,500 files for a given drive, the oldest files are purged to make space for new files anyway. If you don't want files purged at all on a time basis, uncheck this setting. Be aware that, as with Enable Protection, the file-purging setting is drive-specific. You can configure each drive in your system to retain files under Norton Protection for a different period of time, based on your needs.

The Desktop Item Properties tab (refer to Figure 6.3) enables you to configure the appearance of the NPRB, as well as determine what you want done when you double-click the NPRB icon. From here you can change the text that is displayed under the

Norton Protection Recycle Bin icon. You can even delete it entirely if you like: Just select the text in the Title box, press the Delete key, and click OK. Only the icon now appears on the desktop. You can also specify whether you want the Norton Protection Status Shield to be displayed. If you do not, unchecking the Show Norton Protection Status box shows only the traditional Windows Recycle Bin icon on your desktop.

At the top of this tab, radio buttons enable you to tell Norton Protection how you want it to behave whenever you double-click on the desktop icon. By default, Norton Protection runs the Norton UnErase Wizard, which you can read about in Chapter 15. The Wizard gives you superb interactive access to all your Norton Protected files. Alternatively, you may prefer the UnErase Wizard to run but automatically default to showing you only the 25 most recently deleted files. The second radio button, moving from the top down, enables that feature. You may also want to have the UnErase Wizard default to showing you all Protected files on all drives. The third radio button enables you do just that. Finally, you may opt to have access to the Norton Protected files only from the Recycle Bin's context menu. Choosing Standard Recycle Bin opens the regular Windows Recycle Bin when you double-click. You can manually access the Norton UnErase Wizard by right-clicking the Bin's desktop icon and selecting UnErase from the context menu.

At times you may want to force the Norton Protected Recycle Bin or the Windows Recycle Bin to purge all files they're protecting before they would otherwise do so. Those two options are also available from the Bin's context menu. Norton Protection advises you on how many files are being protected at the time and asks for your confirmation that you want them all purged.

Caution: The other tabs you see when you select Properties from the Norton Protected Recycle Bin's context menu do not impact Norton Protection. All Norton Protection settings for all drives are set from the Norton Protection tab. The Global tab and the individual drive tab(s) you see continue to perform their traditional role: limiting the size of the standard Windows Recycle Bin. If you leave the Windows Recycle Bin active, some file deletions are placed into it (see the section "Why Some Files Still Go in the Windows Recycle Bin," later in this chapter). If you want Norton Protection to take care of these deletions as well as those it already protects, place a check mark in the box on your Global tab labeled, "Do not move files to the recycle bin. Remove files immediately when deleted." With this setting checked, no files will be placed in the Windows Recycle Bin, but they will still receive Norton Protection. If you do not deactivate the Windows Recycle Bin, files that are placed into it are *not* under Norton Protection. I strongly urge you to place a check mark in this box and disable the standard Windows Recycle Bin.

Integration with Norton System Doctor

As with much of Norton SystemWorks, Norton Protection integrates with a Norton System Doctor sensor, enabling you to keep tabs on all your system statistics and conditions in one place, the System Doctor panel. You read about System Doctor in Chapter 3, "Norton Utilities: The System Doctor Is In." Here, we look at how the Norton Protection Sensor works with Norton Protection itself.

You can add the Norton Protection sensor to your System Doctor panel by selecting Norton Protected Files from the Information entry under System Doctor's Sensors menu. The sensor shows you the number of files under Norton Protection. If you don't like the numeric display, you can select one of the other sensor faces by right-clicking the sensor's face, selecting Properties, and choosing a different display type from the Style tab. You might select an analog display, for example, to show the number of Protected files as a function of the total number of files that can be Protected—1,500. From the Alarm tab, you can instruct the sensor to alert you when the number of files under Norton Protection reaches some threshold you select. By default, you are warned when 1,425 files are being protected. The sensor cannot be configured to fix this issue automatically, but you may want to stop your work and take the time to review all files under Norton Protection to see whether any of them have value to you. If not, simply ignore the sensor's warning and old files will be purged from Norton Protection when the NPRB is full—or when the time period you specified in Norton Protection's own properties expires.

For myself, I leave the Norton Protection sensor active, but I make it hidden. This way, it doesn't increase my System Doctor panel size, but it does remind me to take a quick scan through my Protected files when some of those files are approaching the danger of being purged.

Usually nothing will be waiting around in the NPRB that you will want to recover, but if you have deleted files with the intent to restore them "when you get around to it," the Norton Protection sensor helps remind you that the time is ripe.

Why Some Files Still Go in the Windows Recycle Bin

As you've already read, Norton Protection overlays the traditional Windows Recycle Bin, providing security for files that the Recycle Bin has never protected. The Recycle Bin still exists, however, lurking under Norton Protection unless you disable it. And disable it you should.

The reason for this is that, as long as the Windows Recycle Bin is enabled, files that would generally go into it actually go into it. Those files—files you delete by hand from within the Windows Explorer, or from within a graphic thumbnail viewing application that is Recycle Bin-aware, for example—are not covered by Norton Protection. If you want one straightforward place to look for all your deleted files, you need to let Norton Protection take over and tell the Windows Recycle Bin where to go.

Fortunately, this is easy to do. Right-click the Recycle Bin and select Properties from the context menu. On the Global tab, be certain that the Use one setting for all drives radio button is selected. Then, place a check mark in the box labeled, "Do not move files to the recycle bin. Remove files immediately when deleted." Normally this would mean that your deleted files were toast the moment they are deleted. With Norton Protection installed, however, checking this option *enables* Norton Protection to care for these files as well as all those already under its watchful eye. With the old Recycle Bin disabled, Norton Protection and the Norton UnErase Wizard enable you to use one piece of software to restore deleted files, no matter how they were deleted.

Note: After you disable the Windows Recycle Bin and let Norton Protection take over completely, don't forget to right-click the Bin's icon and select Empty Recycle Bin, if that option is enabled. You won't regain the space being used by the old Recycle Bin until you purge it. Files in the old Recycle Bin immediately come under Norton Protection as soon as the Recycle Bin is disabled and emptied. Norton Protection doesn't take over until you empty the old Recycle Bin for the last time. (After the old Recycle Bin is emptied and disabled, the Empty Recycle Bin option in the Bin's context menu also remains disabled. All restoration and purge functions are controlled through Norton Protection.)

PETER'S PRINCIPLE

Safe Versus Secure

There's no question that Norton Protection and the UnErase Wizard provide significantly enhanced safety for your files. What you erase, you can unerase. It's that simple. But if other people ever have access to your PC, you should pause for a moment to consider the differences between "safety" and "security." If we're talking about your home or your family, the words are sometimes used synonymously. When it comes to deleted files, they are two very different things. Perhaps a better word for security—although it has become a buzzword with its own trappings—might be "privacy." When you use Norton Protection, your safety level increases dramatically; your privacy is another matter.

continues

There are thousands of reasons why people delete files. Your hard disk is full; you deleted the program that created them; you just don't need them anymore. Another reason, of course, is to protect the contents of those files from unauthorized examination. With many of us keeping our financial records, résumés, love letters, and the poetry we wrote in high school on our computers, anyone who has access to your PC could be said to have access to much of your entire life. And you don't have to be anything less than a very morally upstanding citizen to feel that there are parts of your life better kept to yourself. Deleting files is one way to make this happen.

To protect yourself against *accidentally* deleted files and work lost due to system crashes, however, you've invoked a sophisticated technology that makes your erased files UnErasable. Dead files can be resurrected. And old secrets can be shared.

To balance data safety and data privacy, you need to put some thought into how you configure Norton Protection and how you use it with other integrated tools in Norton SystemWorks. You might want to reduce the period of time for which files are retained in your Norton Protection Recycle Bin. You can select a period in which you feel you're given adequate time to recover files you've deleted by accident, but which also purges deleted files you want to stay deleted. You can also create customized sets of exclusion rules for Norton Protection, if a particular type of file or a particular folder on disk contains files you don't want anyone to be able to UnErase easily.

You could try to remember to empty the Norton Protection Recycle Bin whenever you step away from your desk. This solution, however, significantly degrades the safety afforded by Norton Protection, and short-term security can be easily provided other ways. For example, enabling password protection on your Windows screen saver keeps prying eyes and hands away from your desktop for short periods of time. Yes, someone could reboot your PC, and the screen saver password wouldn't help keep them out, but that takes time, makes noise if you have a start-up sound, and is a dead giveaway to you that your property has been tampered with. (Hardware passwords are also available on some PC's and most notebook computers, requiring that a password be entered before a reboot can take place.)

You could also purchase additional software, such as Norton Your Eyes Only, to encrypt your files and deny access to specific directories without an authorized password. Files that are encrypted remain encrypted when they are deleted, so even if such files were UnErased, they would remain useless.

Finally, when you're certain that the files in your Norton Protection Recycle Bin are not files you're going to want again, you can bring out the big guns and use Norton Speed Disk to drive security and privacy to their maximum levels. First, empty the Norton Protection Recycle Bin and the Windows Recycle Bin (if you've left the latter enabled). Then launch Norton Speed Disk from the SystemWorks integrator by selecting Norton Utilities, then Preventative

Maintenance, and finally Speed Disk. With Speed Disk open, click its Properties button and select Options. From the Optimization tab, make sure that Full Optimization is selected and that you have placed a check mark in the box labeled Wipe Free Space. You'll need to select these options for each drive in your system, and you must let Speed Disk fully optimize each drive. The Wipe Free Space option means that, once all files have been unfragmented and clumped together on disk, all the remaining free space is overwritten with the number zero. The endless string of zeros that fills up all the unused space on your drives obliterates whatever was there before. All the other space is over-written by files that you've not deleted. Even with an editor, such as the Norton Disk Editor (which can view a hard drive's contents byte-by-byte), there is nothing to see but zeros when Speed Disk is finished.

This process leaves only one thing left for prying eyes to view: the names of your deleted files. Speed Disk doesn't wipe unused folder entries, and Norton Protection doesn't erase them, even when you empty the NPRB. To delete the names of deleted files, run the Norton UnErase Wizard and select Find Any Recoverable Files Matching Your Criteria. On the next screen, leave the criteria window blank. Continue using the defaults until you get to the page on which the UnErase Wizard asks you to specify the drives you want searched. Select those you want and click Next. (Make sure that Look in subfolders is checked.) When the Wizard's search is complete, scan through the list for any filenames you want obliterated. Select the filename, right-click it, and choose Delete from the context menu that pops up. That folder entry is cleared, and the filename is gone for good.

When you're keeping files around so that you can bring them back on demand, you need to be mindful that other people could bring them back on demand, too. If security is a concern to you, take some time to consider the principles that make safety and security mean such different things when it comes to your data. A variety of tools in Norton SystemWorks can take care of you, however you balance the issues.

Norton Utilities: Life Preserver on a (Rescue) Disk

One of the most important functions of Norton Utilities is the capability of helping you recover your system after a catastrophic failure. The first time you turn on your computer and nothing at all happens, I'm certain you'll agree with me. The Norton Utilities components of Norton SystemWorks provide an array of tools to foresee and prevent devastating problems. Norton Disk Doctor, Norton WinDoctor, Norton System Doctor, Norton Registry Tracker, and Image all work together, doing everything possible to prevent you from having one of "those" days. If you've owned a computer for very long, you almost certainly know precisely what kind of day I mean. In the past, catastrophic failures usually involved hours on hold for technical support people—many of whom seem to have "those" days every day—only to be told eventually that your drive is defective, your data is toast, your life is over.

Enter Rescue Disk, one of the most versatile and valuable components of the Norton SystemWorks safety strategy. Your Norton Rescue Disk may be on a set of regular floppies, on an Iomega ZIP or JAZ drive, or on a combination of the two, depending on which options your PC supports and which hardware you have available, of course. Your Rescue disks contain everything necessary to start up your computer under almost any circumstances, other than a hardware failure.

> **Caution:** If you do power-up your computer and you see nothing whatsoever onscreen, the likelihood is great that you do have a hardware problem. It need not be a disastrous problem, however. Turn to Appendix A for some suggestions.

This chapter introduces you to the features of Norton Rescue Disk, and it guides you through creating, maintaining, and configuring Rescue to provide you with the protection you need.

Caution: If you have already experienced some kind of catastrophic failure and you have *not yet* installed Norton SystemWorks—don't. Turn to Appendix A, "Emergency Recovery Techniques," before doing anything else.

Your Rescue Disks

When created, your Norton Rescue Disks contain everything you need to start up your computer. You can diagnose almost every conceivable disk- and system-related problem. You can then repair those problems without relocating your hard drives, without requiring you to make one of those dreadful technical-support calls, and without having to send your drives and their data in to some frightfully expensive data recovery center. Even if your drive has been reformatted, or if its entire system area—the part of the drive where it maintains its own vital configuration statistics—has been obliterated, Norton Rescue Disks, or NRD, as I'll be calling them, properly created and maintained, are as close to a guarantee of recovery as you'll find anywhere. And NRD is *very* close.

Norton Rescue Disks, depending on your system configuration and hardware, contain a copy of all the files necessary to properly boot your PC, and all the tools necessary to analyze precisely what's wrong. When you first install Norton SystemWorks, you'll be prompted to create a set of Rescue Disks right away—they're that important and that useful. (If you don't perform a Complete Install of Norton SystemWorks, you won't be automatically prompted to create a Rescue Set. Nevertheless, you should do so. You can launch Norton Rescue at any time by selecting it from the Start Menu under Programs | Norton SystemWorks | Norton Utilities | Rescue Disk.) When created, you should plan to keep them very close to your computer, so that it's convenient for you to keep them up-to-date. As you'll read many times elsewhere in this book, antiquated information is sometimes worse than no information at all. Not only can old information add to whatever problems your PC is already experiencing, the false sense of security you'll have if you have Rescue Disks but don't keep them current can lull you into behavior that could make current Rescue Disks all the more important. But we'll get into all those issues later in this chapter. At the moment, let's look at what goes into creating a set of Norton Rescue Disks.

Creating Norton Rescue Disks (NRDs)

As I mentioned above, when you first installed the Norton SystemWorks, you were prompted to create a set of Rescue Disks. I can't stress enough that you should do this, but for the purposes of this discussion, let's assume that you had no blank disks available when you installed Norton SystemWorks, but that you went out immediately after completing the installation and bought yourself some blanks. (You would go out immediately to buy disks, wouldn't you?)

Norton Rescue Disks (NRDs) are created from within Windows only. You can't create them or update them from within DOS, so if you spend a good deal of your time working in DOS, you'll need to plan to start up Windows regularly to keep your disks current. (This advice applies to other Norton recovery utilities as well, such as Image.) The procedure is largely the same for whatever media type you end up using, but what is stored on the Rescue disks is quite different—as you'd probably suspect. A floppy-disk based Rescue set boots your computer only into DOS, and you have access to the full range of Norton SystemWorks' DOS-based Norton Utilities. A ZIP or JAZ Rescue set boots your computer into Windows (either 95 or 98, depending on which you have installed). You'll read more about this later.

If you have only a floppy disk drive available, then floppy disks are your only option. The Norton Rescue Disk will detect that fact when it runs. You won't be presented with options you can't use. If an Iomega ZIP or JAZ drive is present when Norton rescue Disk is launched, NRD will detect that fact, too, and will preferentially select the creation of a ZIP Rescue set. However, you need not choose this option if you have both ZIP and floppy drives present in your system. (For purposes of simplicity, I'm going to continue to refer to ZIP drives; be aware that, unless I let you know otherwise, everything I say about ZIP Rescue sets also applies to Rescue sets created with Iomega JAZ drives.)

> **Note:** Creating a ZIP Rescue set on a PC that has both floppy and ZIP drives will make use of both types of drive. In this configuration, the system boot files will be written to the floppy disk, while all other files will be stored on the ZIP drive. Although this may seem inconvenient, it is a limitation of our PCs' BIOSs, and how they boot, not a restriction of NRD. (An exception to this is the rather unusual hardware configuration of both a ZIP and a floppy drive, with the ZIP drive installed as the primary A: drive, and the floppy installed as a B: drive. In this circumstance, NRD knows that your system can boot from the ZIP drive.)
>
> Finally, if you have only an internal Iomega ZIP drive installed—that is, the ZIP drive serves as your A: drive in lieu of any floppy disk drives—then NRD disables the floppy disk options. NRD also supports the capability to boot from an Iomega ZIP drive on machines for which no floppy drive is present. In such a hardware configuration, the necessary system files are added to your ZIP disk and your computer will have no problem starting up from the removable.

In the plurality of cases, if you are creating a floppy-disk based Rescue set, three blank 1.44MB floppy disks will be required for a basic Rescue set. If you configure Rescue Disk to include additional files in your Rescue set, which you'll learn how to do later in this chapter, you may need to have more floppy disks available.

ZIP Creation

The Norton Rescue Disk program always performs some basic housekeeping functions when it first launches—primarily to locate all the system files that it needs to create your Rescue Disk set. That completed, NRD preselects a Rescue set method, either floppy or ZIP/JAZ. Because in most cases, you'll want to perform your Rescue tasks from within Windows, NRD suggests you create a ZIP rescue set, on which there is sufficient free space to store all the files required to start up Windows fully. As you'll read below, you can also configure your ZIP Rescue Disks so that you start up in Windows Safe Mode, as opposed to Windows' normal operating mode. We'll look at why you might choose that option later. If you do not want to create the type of Rescue Set that NRD recommends, you can simply select the alternate type of set by clicking the other option button, as shown at the top, right of Figure 7.1, in the Choose Rescue Type area. As you can also see in Figure 7.1, NRD has several status areas that keep you apprised of the Rescue set process. Notice also that the PC on which this screen shot was taken did not support booting from the ZIP drive, and so one ZIP cartridge and one floppy disk are required for this Rescue set, which NRD indicates at the center of the window, under the drive panel. To create a standard ZIP Rescue set, simply click Create. If for any reason some of the files that NRD wants to include in its backup set are not present or are not available on your system, the program will let you know. Clicking the Details button on the Unavailable Files Warning dialog box displays the list shown in Figure 7.2. SystemWorks is unable to ocate these files, so they will not be included in the Rescue Set. Clicking the hierarchical plus (+) button next to a filename displays more information, telling you why.

FIGURE 7.1

The Norton ZIP Rescue Disk main display enables you to choose the Rescue type.

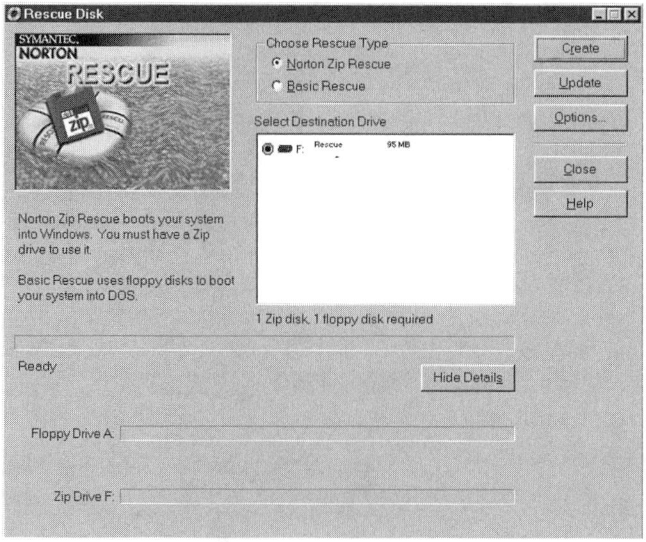

Caution: The Norton Utilities and all of Norton SystemWorks, for that matter, almost never put you in the position of having to make a technical support phone call, but this screen may be the only exception. If certain key files cannot be included in your Rescue set, you will not be able to properly start up and repair your system. If you see a display such as that in Figure 7.2, you might want to quickly jot down the names of these files. When NRD completes creating your Rescue set, you'll be rebooting your computer and testing the set. If your Rescue boot fails, and if you don't know what the files you've listed do, it might be a good time to ring up a computer-savvy friend or, as a last option, Symantec's technical support. Of course, they also can't know the purpose of every file on your PC, and may direct you to your PC manufacturer or to Microsoft for additional help. A Rescue set that won't boot is like a life preserver made of marble.

FIGURE 7.2

Files listed in this dialog box will not be included in your Rescue set.

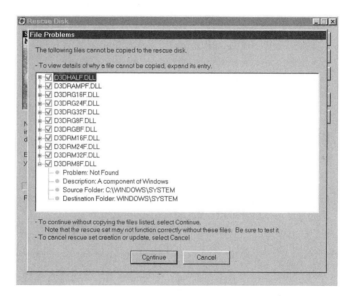

After you review the list of missing or unavailable files—if any—click the Continue button to proceed. NRD prompts you to correctly label the disks you're going to use for your Rescue set, and then to place them in their respective drives. You'll also be given two final warnings: any data on the floppy disks or cartridge that you use for a Rescue set will be deleted, and the final step in creating your Rescue set is to test it—rebooting your computer is required. I suggest that, before you begin creating your Rescue set, you make certain that you've exited from all other applications and that all your data is saved. That done, clicking OK begins the creation process. (NRD alerts you if it doesn't find a disk where it expects to find one.) Figure 7.1 shows the NRD screen with creation details enabled. (The Hide/Show Details button toggles details on and off.) As your Rescue set is made, the progress bars for each disk increments to let you know where you stand. NRD also displays the name of each file as it is added to your Rescue set, although these go past so quickly as to really only serve as another status indicator: if filenames are flashing, creation is in progress.

> **Note:** You can cancel the Rescue set creation process at any time by clicking the Stop button that takes the place of the Create button in the upper-right corner of the Rescue Disk dialog box, after creation has begun. I'm sure it's self-evident that a partially completed Rescue set is about as good as no Rescue set at all. At the same time, no harm will come to your system if you interrupt creation; your Rescue disks just won't work. You can correct that problem at any time by restarting the creation process and letting it finish properly.

After your Rescue set has been completed, NRD lets you know that you should absolutely test the set to make sure it works. Heed this advice. NRD forces you to restart your machine at this point anyway, so you might as well leave your Rescue disk (or disks) in place and enable your PC to restart, using them. You can, of course, eject your Rescue set and click Restart, thereby merely rebooting your PC back to your desktop, but this is *strongly* discouraged. A faulty Rescue set is worthless, and how do you know it works if you don't give it a try? After your Rescue set boots successfully, just click the Cancel button in the Rescue Recovery Wizard, eject your Rescue set and use the Start menu to restart Windows.

If Windows does not properly start when you test your Rescue set, power-down your PC, eject your Rescue set, and reboot Windows. Launch Norton Rescue Disk again and click the Options button after NRD selects Norton ZIP Rescue in the Choose Rescue Type area. From the ZIP Settings tab, choose to have Windows start in Safe Mode rather than Normal Mode by selecting the appropriate option button, as shown in Figure 7.3. Some system configurations are not amenable to being started-up by Rescue Disk in Normal Mode, but all systems should start in Safe Mode. With Safe Mode selected, click OK to return to the Rescue Disk creation display, and re-create your Rescue set. (Use the Create button, not the Update button.)

While certain features of your PC may not be available in Safe Mode—notably, sound cards, your network (depending on your system), and peripherals such as modems and printers—all your hard drives will be available for analysis and repair. After they are repaired, you can restart Windows in its normal operating mode.

FIGURE 7.3

If your ZIP Rescue set refuses to boot, select Safe Mode and re-create the Rescue set.

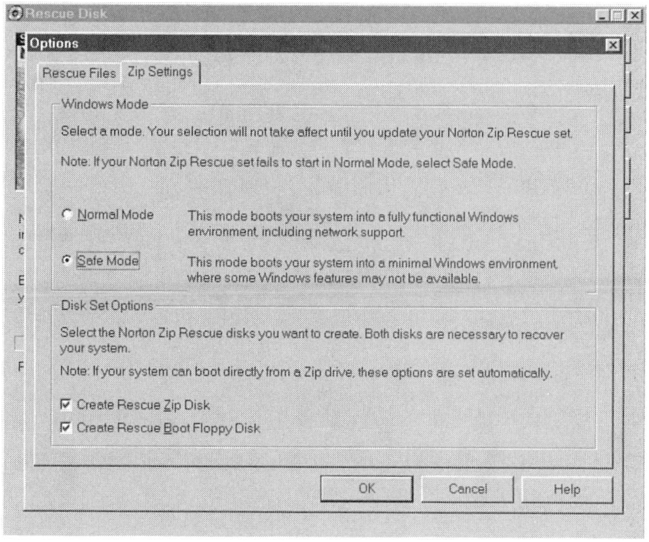

Floppy Creation

Creating a Rescue set based on floppy disks is only slightly different from creating a ZIP Rescue set. Of course, more than one floppy disk is required to store the necessary files, and NRD tells you how many to have available on its main creation screen, as you can see in the middle of Figure 7.4.

FIGURE 7.4

Norton Rescue Disk is ready to create a floppy-based Rescue set.

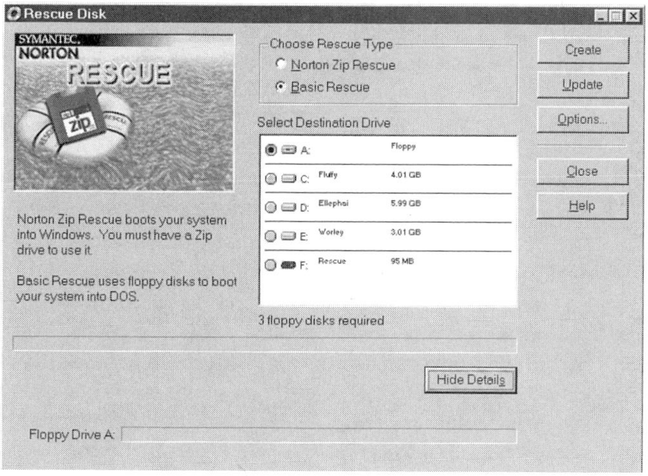

Note: Be aware that, by default, Norton Rescue Disk will quickly format the disks that you use to create a Rescue set. However, I recommend that you change this default behavior so that Norton Rescue performs a full format instead. The reason for this is simple: only a full format checks your disks for bad sectors. If one of your Rescue disks is physically defective, your entire Rescue Set could use rendered useless in your greatest hour of need.

To change Norton Rescue's default format, click the Options button on Norton Rescue's main screen. Then, click the Format Settings tab, and click the Full Format radio button. This setting will help guarantee the reliability of all Norton Rescue Disk sets that you create.

NRD prompts you to insert each floppy disk as it is needed, until the entire Rescue set has been created. When that is complete, Norton Rescue Disk instructs you to place the floppy disk, which you labeled "Basic Rescue Boot Floppy Disk," into drive A: and enable your system to restart, testing the Rescue set. Because there's simply not enough room on a reasonably small set of floppy disks to store the files needed to start Windows, a floppy-disk based Rescue set will only boot into DOS. When this process completes successfully, you'll be prompted either to "Press any key" to begin the Rescue Recovery Wizard or to press Ctrl+C to exit to DOS. Because you are just testing your Rescue set, eject the Rescue boot floppy from its drive and simply press Ctrl+Alt+Delete, to reboot your PC. (This key combination is created by pressing the Ctrl key and the Alt key together and holding them down while you press the Delete key once.)

TECHNICAL NOTE

Although this procedure is not one that I recommend, it is possible to create a basic Rescue disk set that is stored neither on floppies nor a ZIP drive, but in a folder on a local or network hard drive. You do this by selecting the desired drive in the NRD main panel and clicking Create. You are prompted to either type the name or navigate to the folder in which you want your Rescue data stored. The default is a directory named RESCUE, in the root directory of the selected drive. There are two circumstances in which Symantec suggests that Rescue folders can be convenient, but each is flawed, in my opinion.

First, they point out that Rescue data saved in a folder, rather than to a floppy disk or ZIP drive, can be updated automatically. While this is true, it hardly seems useful. The folly of storing your local hard disk Rescue data on one of your local hard disks should be obvious. This is a little bit like locking your car keys in the trunk to make certain that you do not lock the car with them in the ignition. If you store the Rescue data on a network drive, the safety and integrity of your system is now at the mercy of the safety and integrity of another system, as well as itself. Furthermore, to access Rescue data that was stored in a folder, whether on a local or network drive, you still must create a Basic Rescue Boot Floppy, with which to start up the system! The Rescue files can be copied to this floppy on an as-needed basis from any computer that has access to the folder in which they're saved, but the boot disk itself should be one that was created on the damaged computer, before it was damaged. From my perspective, this methodology multiplies both the risk and inconvenience—at least when your PC has crashed, when it really counts—with no meaningful return. Let's face it: it's not all that difficult to click the Create button once a week.

The second purpose for which Rescue folders could be useful is in a networked corporate IT environment, in which Rescue information for every system on the network can be configured to automatically save itself to separate, identifiable folders on the department or company server. This removes the onus of updating Rescue data from the end user and keeps the network administrator in charge of storehousing important Rescue data. This scenario is more feasible than the first, but there are three big problems with it. First, if your server goes, so does all your Rescue data. (Of course, if your server dies, the fate of individual workstations is not likely forefront in your mind, but we'll let that point slide for the moment.) Second, all the problems I mentioned above still apply. A Boot floppy for each workstation is still required, and the Boot floppy must be current. Finally, as much as I appreciate the plight of the overworked systems administrator and her constant struggles to keep on top of end user *faux pas*, this scenario violates one of my principles of responsible computing. End users are already expected to take a certain level of responsibility with respect to their workstations. We expect each individual to save his work, for example, and to be able to locate it when it's needed. We should ideally expect no less of the end user's responsibility towards their Rescue data. Most people thrive in circumstances in which they are called-upon to care for their work. And many people do not take an interest in things for which they are not held responsible. With all vital company data stored on a server anyway—in a properly-designed working environment—there is little danger in making end users accountable for the integrity of their workstations. By educating them about the content and importance of their Rescue Disk data, and giving them the job of maintaining it (and here I mean their workstation, as well as their data), we can also discourage them from participating in risky user behavior—such as loading games and downloading programs from who-knows-where, modifying system configurations, spending company time trying to explore unauthorized areas of their workstation's system, and so on.

Caution: Be aware that the Rescue set created for your PC was created specifically for your PC. This is particularly true for ZIP and JAZ drive based Rescue sets. If you have more than one computer, you need to create a Rescue set for each computer. You should resist the temptation to become Fix-itperson and try to Rescue an associate's crashed computer, using your Rescue disks. Violation of your user agreement aside, it could be an absolute disaster, with incorrect data overwriting a file allocation table or the wrong Windows Registry being restored, forcing you to possibly reinstall Windows and all your software. Never attempt to use a Rescue set in a computer other than the one in which it was created.

Keeping Rescue Current

With your Rescue set properly created, you're well on your way to maintaining a fully recoverable system. The step that takes you all the way is keeping your Rescue set up-to-date. If you enable Norton System Doctor to run at all times with its Rescue sensor enabled, System Doctor will let you know when you should update your Rescue set. By default, System Doctor warns you when a Rescue set is more than five days old. This is a reasonable period of time for a stable, well-functioning system. If you seem to have a lot of problems with your PC, you may want to update your Rescue data more often. The period of time between System Doctor sensor warnings can be set as you like by right-clicking on the Rescue sensor in System Doctor and selecting Properties from the context menu. On the Alarm tab, you can set whatever period of time you require, and the sensor lets you know when that time has passed between Rescue set creation. You can also opt to have the Rescue sensor launch NRD automatically whenever its alarm is triggered. Simply check Fix Automatically on the Alarm tab and click OK.

Be aware that "fix automatically" is a slight misnomer in the case of the Rescue sensor. The sensor does launch NRD automatically when its alarm goes off, but it does not automatically update your Rescue disks. It's unlikely that you keep your Rescue disks in their respective drives—particularly not in the external drive from which you can boot—and you would not want NRD erasing whatever it found on one of your ZIP cartridges, thinking it was updating your Rescue set. Updating, like creating, also requires that you restart your computer, a process for which you doubtless want to retain complete control. For that reason, you still need to click Update when you want NRD to actually update your Rescue disks.

As with Rescue set creation, NRD lets you know whether any files that it wants to include in your Rescue set are missing or unavailable. The same guidelines, with respect to such files, apply to updating as well as creating your Rescue set. When the set is updated, always restart your computer with the set in place, verifying that everything is working properly.

Of course, you can also run the Norton Rescue Disk program at any time by selecting it from the Preventative Maintenance options of Norton Utilities from within the SystemWorks Integrator. (You can also select Programs | Norton SystemWorks | Norton Utilities | Rescue Disk from the Start menu.)

> **Caution:** Although you are, of course, free to create new Rescue disk sets until you are blue in the face or bored, whichever comes first, there is an aspect of the Update button's functionality that you need to remember. Update assumes that you have only one set of Rescue disks. Because of that, when you click Update, Update operates from the assumption that you are updating the last Rescue disk set that you created. You never should use the Update feature when you are maintaining multiple, or different, Rescue Disk sets. In such a case, you should use the Create button to create a new Rescue set each time you want to bring your disks current. In particular, be certain to never use Update if you switch between both floppy-only and ZIP-based Rescue sets.

Looking Inside Rescue

Now that your Rescue set is complete, you probably want to know what it contains, and how to use it when disaster strikes. We'll answer that second question later in the section called, "Rescue Recovery." In this section, you learn what NRD places on your Rescue disks and how you can customize your sets to fit your needs.

Norton ZIP Rescue

You already know that there are major differences between floppy-disk and ZIP Rescue sets. As you read above, floppy disk sets can only boot into DOS, while a ZIP set allows you to boot into Windows. It's obvious, then, that a ZIP set needs to contain all the files necessary for you to start Windows. Indeed, a folder on your ZIP disk called "Windows" contains exactly those files. When NRD is performing its "initialization" tasks at launch, one of the things it's doing is collecting the current set of files required to successfully start your Windows environment. (Incidentally, collecting this list of files can take a very long time on a slow PC. Don't select the ZIP Rescue button just to look around if you don't want to wait for Rescue's initialization task to finish. After it starts, there's no way to cancel it.) You can view this list by first verifying that Norton ZIP Rescue is selected, clicking on the Options button, and then selecting the Rescue Files tab. Click the hierarchical plus "+" button next to the Windows Files entry, and you'll see all the files NRD has selected. Take a look at Figure 7.5 to see an example.

FIGURE 7.5

NRD's list of Rescue files, with Windows files displayed.

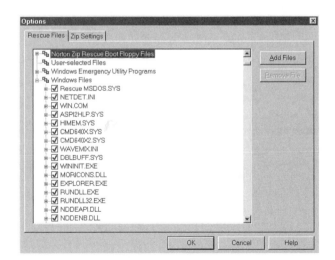

You can see that each filename in the list has a corresponding box with a check mark in it. You can remove a file's check mark by clicking the box, thus deselecting the file from inclusion in your next Rescue set. Be careful! There's certainly nothing wrong with deselecting files you know are not necessary to start Windows. However, if you omit a file from your next Rescue set, be certain that everything works properly when you test-boot from that set. At risk of it sounding like a mantra, a Rescue set that doesn't work is worthless. You can also see in the illustration that each file is part of a hierarchical tree. When you click the plus "+" button next to a file's name, NRD gives you as much information about that file as it can. It lets you know, for example, whether a file is known to be a component of Windows itself, or whether it appears to be a driver or configuration file that is specific to your system. NRD also shows you the size of each file, the folder in which it is located, and the location on your ZIP drive into which it will be placed.

TECHNICAL NOTE

> If you manually omit certain files from inclusion in your Rescue set and then determine that the set is not functional, it will probably be easiest for you to simply re-enable the involved file(s) and re-create your Rescue set. However, if you only omit one or two files, you can record the file's current location and its Rescue set destination and manually move the relevant file(s) onto your Rescue sets.

Figure 7.5 is in grayscale, but NRD will assign a red-bordered check box to any file that is missing or unavailable. Available files all have a blue check box. If you don't want NRD to repeatedly prompt you about files that you know are missing and will not be returning, you can deselect those files from this list and then create a new Rescue Set (rather than updating the set).

While you're looking at Figure 7.5, you'll also notice that three other categories of files exist: Norton ZIP (or Basic) Rescue Boot Floppy Files, User-Selected Files, and Windows Emergency Utility Programs. Each of these categories opens in the same manner as the Windows Files category you just read about (by clicking on the "+"), and you can disable files from these as you require. The Windows Emergency Utility Programs section is where all the Norton SystemWorks components are listed. If your system is able to boot from your ZIP drive, your startup files will simply be labeled "ZIP Boot Startup Files." With a category opened, you can add as well as delete from the files listed. Click the Add Files button on the right side of the dialog box, and simply select the files you desire from the standard Windows Open dialog with which you'll be presented. Shift- and Ctrl-clicking is allowed here, so you can select multiple files to add. All files you select—whatever their type—appear in the User-Selected Files list. After you have added files, if you want to remove them permanently from the Rescue set list, open the User-Selected Files section, select the file, and click the Remove File button. You may disable, but not remove, files from the other three categories.

> **Caution:** Add files to your Rescue sets with some discretion. If your PC is experiencing difficulty and the problem lies in an aspect of its configuration, you could copy the problem to your Rescue set by including a nonessential configuration file. At the same time, although it is very unlikely, if NRD has not identified a file that you do require to successfully boot your computer, such as a processor-enabling or video driver that may otherwise be stored only on your—perhaps damaged—hard drive, that file should be added through this Options dialog box.

When your ZIP Rescue set is created, all Windows files are placed in the Windows folder, and its subfolders, on your Rescue disk. The Norton SystemWorks files are stored in the ZIP disk's root directory. Any files you have manually added are placed in the same folder as their source. Additional empty folders are created by NRD as is necessary. So, for example, if you choose to include EXCLUDE.DAT from C:\PROGRAM FILES\NORTON SYSTEMWORKS\NORTON UTILITIES\REGTRKR on your Rescue set, a folder called PROGRAM FILES will be created in the root of your ZIP drive, with \NORTON SYSTEMWORKS\NORTON UTILITIES\REGTRKR\EXCLUDE.DAT inside it. Boot startup files are also placed in the root directory, even if you are booting from a ZIP Boot Floppy (in which case, they are also placed on the floppy disk). These include three special Norton Rescue files that contain vital, basic information about your PC itself. They are:

- CMOS.DAT, containing the information from your PC's battery-supported CMOS about the types of hard drives installed on your PC, the amount of RAM installed, and other settings required to get your system going between the BIOS and the operating system. This information is particularly important if your CMOS battery has gone dead. Without this data, you might not be able to start your system at all.

- BOOTINFO.DAT, containing all the information normally stored on your hard drives' boot records. This data records both the physical and the software-based, or logical, characteristics of your drives. Loss of this data will definitely prevent your system from booting, but the information stored on your Rescue set can be rewritten back to your drives during a Rescue Recovery (see below).

- PARTINFO.DAT, which keeps track of your drives' partition tables. Damage to this information will also likely prevent your PC from starting, and Rescue can use this file to recreate the partition table on a damaged drive.

Basic (Floppy) Rescue

The floppy, or Basic Rescue set contains those files necessary to boot your PC into DOS successfully, plus the DOS-based versions of the key Norton Utilities programs—Norton Disk Doctor, Rescue, Norton Disk Editor, Unerase, and Unformat. Additionally, the DOS utilities FORMAT, SYS, and FDISK are included, along with CMOS.DAT, BOOTINFO.DAT, and PARTINFO.DAT, as described in the previous section. If you click the Options button with

"Basic Rescue Set" selected, you'll notice that the Windows Files entry is, of course, absent. You can add or delete files from this type of Rescue set as with a Norton ZIP Rescue set, keeping in mind, of course, that if you add too many files, your Rescue set will require additional floppy disks.

As you would likely suspect, it is impossible for the Windows Registry files to be included in a floppy-based Rescue set. Therefore, if you're having system difficulty and you suspect the Registry is the culprit, you will need to restart Windows in Safe Mode and look for a backup of the USER.DAT and SYSTEM.DAT files—commonly saved as USER.BAK and SYSTEM.BAK—which you can use to replace the damaged Registry.

Rescue Recovery

This section introduces you to the basic procedure involved in using the Rescue Recovery Wizard to examine and repair catastrophic damage to your drives. What you won't find here is detailed instructions on how to use each of the different recovery tools that the Rescue Recovery Wizard will launch at your request. That information can be found in the chapter that covers each component. For your quick reference:

Norton SystemWorks Component	Chapter
Rescue	7 (what you're reading now)
Norton AntiVirus 5.0	9
Norton Disk Doctor	11
Norton Disk Editor	12
Norton UnErase	15
Norton UnFormat	16
Norton Diagnostics	20

Depending on whether you're using floppy disks or a Norton ZIP Rescue disk, the Rescue Recovery Wizard provides very different functionality. Because the floppy-based procedure is so straightforward, we'll look at it first. After that, we'll take a look at the sophisticated Rescue Recovery Wizard for Windows.

Recovering with Floppies

The Recovery Wizard supported under DOS is—by necessity—considerably less complex and integrated than is the Windows Recovery Wizard, and its functionality is comparably reduced. When you boot into DOS using your Basic Rescue Boot Diskette, the Wizard runs, performs a fundamental analysis of your hard drives, and informs you of the following:

Rescue restores the data your computer uses to start up and to access hard
disks (CMOS Information, Boot Records, Partition Tables). This data was saved
when you created your Norton Rescue Boot Disk. In the Restore Rescue
Information dialog box (next screen), damaged items are checked. If no items
are checked, Rescue did not detect any damage.

Press Enter to select OK and you will see the Restore Rescue Information screen, shown
in Figure 7.6. If any of the items in the box at the lower-left are checked, verify that the
path described (it is A:\ by default) is the location of your Rescue data files, and click
Restore. If the path is not correct, click New Path, enter the correct path, and then click
OK. Rescue Recovery verifies that the Rescue files are located at the path you specify.
You can then click Restore to repair any checked items.

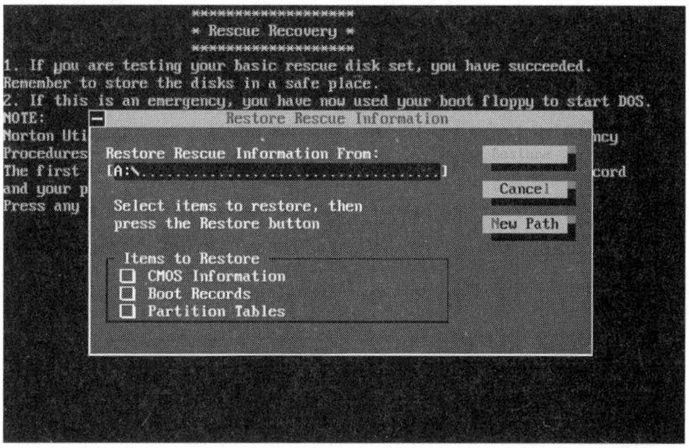

FIGURE 7.6

*Choose which
items you want to
restore in the
DOS-based
Restore Rescue
Information
screen.*

If you're having problems with your PC starting up, but the DOS-Based wizard detects
that none of these three basic areas requires repair, there are several steps you should
take next to inspect your system manually.

Caution: Do not manually check any of the boxes and force a recovery unless
you know very well what you are doing. Rescue Recovery's problem detection is
very reliable, and you could cause new damage or compound any existing damage if you recover over data that is not damaged.

First, click Cancel to exit the Recovery Wizard. If you're certain that you have not accidentally formatted the drive in question—trust me, you'd know—then, when you see the
DOS A:\ prompt, place the floppy disk you labeled "DOS Emergency Utilities Disk #1"
into your floppy drive and type **NDD** to start the DOS-based version of Norton Disk
Doctor. Enable Norton Disk Doctor to run and perform its complete round of tests on

your hard drives, including a normal surface test. If NDD doesn't find any problems, or if NDD's tests fail, you may want to consider the possibility that you have either a loose connector or cable between one of your drives and your PC's motherboard, or you may need to consider mechanical failure. If you or a qualified associate verify that everything seems to be "plugged-in" correctly, but your PC still won't boot, check all the other connections between your PC and its peripherals, and then start up your computer again from the Norton Basic Rescue Boot Disk. (You can read more about safe procedures for checking your hardware in Appendix A, "Emergency Recovery Techniques.") If no problems of any kind are detected, first congratulate yourself that you back up your drives religiously—you do, don't you?—and then it's probably time to explore your hardware-servicing options. If NDD does detect problems, of course, allow it to repair them, and then eject the Emergency Diskette and try booting your system normally.

Recovering from an Accidental Format

If you have accidentally formatted your boot drive, you should use Norton UnFormat, not Norton Disk Doctor to first inspect and repair your drive. You can learn everything you want to know about Norton UnFormat in Chapter 16, "Norton Utilities: The Big "Oops" and Norton UnFormat." The recovery procedure, summarized here, involves three simple steps. First, restart your computer using your Basic Rescue Boot Diskette. Exit from the introduction to the Recovery Wizard by pressing Ctrl+C, as indicated on the startup-screen. When you see the DOS A:\ prompt, insert DOS Emergency Utilities Disk #2 into your floppy drive, type **UNFORMAT** at the prompt, and press Enter. Read the onscreen cautions, and then, assuming you want to continue, follow the prompts to complete the process. When Norton UnFormat has finished, place the DOS Emergency Utilities Disk #1 into your A: drive and type **NDD** to run Norton Disk Doctor on the repaired drive.

Recovering Startup System Files

If Rescue Recovery does not detect problems in the three aspects of your drive that it inspects (CMOS, boot records, and partition table), but you still receive the message No Operating System Found when you start up your PC, chances are very good that your boot drive has an intact boot record, but has lost one or more of its system files. These files, IO.SYS, COMMAND.COM, and MSDOS.SYS are those that the bootstrap loader launches to begin running your Windows operating system. (As a matter of fact, even under Windows 98, these files contain the tiny kernel of DOS that begins to load Windows and then begins to pass operating system control to Windows after the OS is running.)

Recovering from this error is usually quite simple. Boot your computer using the Basic Rescue Boot Diskette, and press Ctrl+C at the greeting message to exit to DOS. At the DOS prompt, type **SYS C:** and press Enter. This is a basic DOS command that copies the system files to the hard drive you've specified, and verifies that the drive's boot record is intact and is marked as bootable. If the procedure is successful, you'll see the message System Files Transferred, and will be returned to the DOS prompt. Eject your Rescue Boot Diskette and restart your PC. If booting continues to be unsuccessful, then boot again with your Rescue Recovery Diskette and run Norton Disk Doctor from DOS Emergency Utilities Disk #1, as above. (You can read much more about the DOS-based Norton Disk Doctor in Chapter 11, "Norton Utilities: The Disk Doctor Is In.")

Recovering Other Files

The DOS-based Rescue disk set also includes Norton UnErase, which you can use to recover accidentally deleted folders and files. Unless the files you have deleted are among those that Windows requires to boot, you should prefer the Windows-based version of UnErase to the DOS version available to you here. If you do need to use the DOS version of UnErase, place DOS Emergency Utilities Disk #2 into your floppy drive, and type **UNERASE** at the DOS A:\ prompt. You can read in depth about using the DOS version of Norton UnErase in Chapter 15, "Norton Utilities: Getting It Back, Getting It Right: UnErasing and File Compare."

Recovering with a Norton ZIP Rescue Disk

If you have the hardware to use an Iomega ZIP or JAZ cartridge for your Norton Rescue set, you will be able to boot your computer into Windows and have the full complement of Windows-based Norton recovery utilities available to you. Boot your PC using your Norton ZIP Rescue Boot Diskette, or boot from your ZIP drive if it is configured as your A: drive. You'll see a customized startup logo with the traveling bar at the bottom—rather reminiscent of the standard Windows startup. As the customized logo tells you, however, launching Windows from your Rescue set may take considerably longer than you're used to experiencing. For example, my 400MHz Pentium II with 128MB of RAM normally boots Windows 98 in about thirty seconds. Using my Rescue Set took more than four minutes. If you have configured your Rescue Set to boot into Windows Safe Mode, your boot time will be even longer (this is a function of Windows, not a limitation of NRD).

When Windows is launched, the Norton Rescue Recovery Wizard runs automatically, as you see in Figure 7.7. Notice also that shortcuts to the primary Norton recovery utilities have been placed on the desktop for easy access. Each of these utilities can be launched by the Wizard, however, as you will see. You should notice and heed the friendly warning on this first Wizard screen, incidentally. Many of your normal applications and system features may not function properly while you are running in Norton Rescue mode. Don't assume you have developed new problems if you try something and it doesn't work; when you reboot Windows traditionally, all should be back to normal. The best advice I can give you is to use Norton Rescue mode exclusively for performing the Rescue operations you require, and then reboot immediately.

FIGURE 7.7

Norton Rescue Recovery's main screen includes the Wizard and desktop icons (on the left side of this screen) to other Norton recovery utilities.

CMOS Tests

Click Next to move on to the first diagnostic page of the Rescue Recovery Wizard. The Rescue Wizard performs a wide variety of tests on your system, the most fundamental of which is the CMOS test, as shown in Figure 7.8. The Norton Rescue Recovery Wizard, *RRW* for short, examines your CMOS data to verify that it matches what is stored in your Rescue set. If it does match, Rescue Recovery Wizard has determined that there is nothing wrong with your CMOS data, you may click Next to move on to the next test. If there is an inconsistency between your "live" CMOS data and that stored on your Rescue set, the Restore button will be enabled. Click the Restore button, respond in the affirmative to the confirmation box, and RRW will re-create your CMOS data. After the process is completed successfully, I recommend clicking Next to continue running through the rest of RRW's system checks. You can, of course, opt to click Cancel and exit the Wizard at any time.

> **Caution:** Before you restore CMOS data, take half a second to mentally verify that your Rescue set is up-to-date and that you haven't added or moved any hard drives since the last Rescue update. If you have, after restoring your CMOS data, you may have to go into your PC's hardware setup screen and manually re-enter the configuration information for the new hardware. Be safe—keep your Rescue set current.

FIGURE 7.8

Norton Rescue Recovery's CMOS diagnosis screen shows any CMOS problems on your system in the Status area. The text at the top of the screen merely explains the function of CMOS.

Viruses

After the Rescue Recovery Wizard has verified that your CMOS data is intact, it runs a careful check of your system, looking for viruses. This scan, provided through integration with Norton AntiVirus (NAV), checks every key aspect of your PC—memory, drive boot records, and partition tables—for viruses that might be preventing your system from starting. Click the Scan button to begin scanning. If NAV detects any virus on your system, it will isolate and eradicate the culprit, as well as restore reliable data from your Rescue files. If no viruses are present, as in Figure 7.9, click Next to continue RRW's examination.

Boot Record

With viruses out of the running, Rescue Recovery Wizard checks the integrity of your drive's boot record. As you've read elsewhere in this book, the boot record maintains configuration data about your drive. If, as in Figure 7.10, nothing has changed in your boot record since the last time your Rescue set was updated, RRW will let you know that this is not a likely candidate for your troublemaker. If there are differences, the Restore button will be enabled. Click the Restore button to copy your boot record data from the Rescue set to your drive. After that process completes successfully, click Next to continue checking your drive for other errors.

FIGURE 7.9
*Norton Rescue
Recovery's virus
detection screen
enables you to
run a scan for
viruses.*

FIGURE 7.10
*Norton Rescue
Recovery's boot
record analysis
screen.*

Partition Tables

Rescue Recovery Wizard will next check the integrity of your drive's partition tables. This table records vital configuration data about your drive. If, as in Figure 7.11, nothing has changed in your partition tables since the last time your Rescue set was updated, RRW will let you know that this is probably not the cause of your problems. If there are differences, the Restore button will be enabled. Click the Restore button to copy your partition data from the Rescue set PARTINFO.DAT file back to your drive. After that process completes successfully, click Next to continue checking your drive for other errors.

FIGURE 7.11

Norton Rescue Recovery's partition table check.

Caution: As you read earlier with respect to restoring CMOS data, you should take half a second to mentally verify that your Rescue set is up-to-date and that you haven't added or moved any hard drives or partitions since the last Rescue update. If you have, after restoring your partition data, you may have to go into FDISK, the DOS partition-maintenance utility, and manually re-enter the configuration information for the new hardware. Trust me when I tell you that the dentist's chair was more fun in 1899 than FDISK is in 1999. Be safe—keep your Rescue set current.

General Disk Damage

With the capability of your drive's configuration structures verified, the possibility still remains that your drive has damage to its FAT, or root directory structures, or to your files themselves. As you can see in Figure 7.12, the Rescue Recovery Wizard will optionally run Norton Disk Doctor for you and check the integrity of your entire drive. As usual, if Norton Disk Doctor detects any problems with your drive, it repairs them for you, unless you instruct it not to do so. After NDD has completed its analysis and repairs, if any were necessary, you'll be returned to the Rescue Recovery Wizard. Click Next to continue.

Figure 7.12

Norton Rescue Recovery's Norton Disk Doctor checks for drive damage.

Deleted Files

After NDD completes its scan and verifies that the file-related structures of your drive are intact, you can safely examine your drive for files that have been accidentally deleted, thereby rendering your PC unstartable or unstable. Click the Run UnErase Wizard button and UnErase looks for and recovers—to the maximum degree possible—files that have been deleted from your C:\WINDOWS folder and its subfolders. The UnErase Wizard uses a filter to accelerate its scan, looking for configuration files of the types shown in Figure 7.13. When UnErase has successfully restored and deleted files, or when it reports that there are no files to recover, click Next to continue the Rescue Recovery Wizard's check.

FIGURE 7.13

Norton Rescue Recovery's UnErase Wizard screen.

Startup Files

Rescue Recovery will next check to see whether your DOS startup files—those that run before Windows starts—have changed since the last time you created or updated your Rescue set. If changes are detected, clicking on the Restore button will copy the files from your Rescue set back to your drive. If RRW detects that there are no startup files missing, the Restore button will not be available and you should just click Next to continue testing your drive.

Windows Registry

In Figure 7.14, you can see Rescue Recovery's Registry Repair. This page of the Wizard allows you to restore the Rescue set copy of your Windows Registry back to your hard disk. There are a couple of things you should consider before you click the Restore button, however. First, all Registry changes of any type made after you updated your Rescue set will be undone. This can include hardware reconfiguration, Windows appearance settings, network permissions, Windows logon passwords, and much more. If you've made significant changes to your Registry between your last Rescue update and when you run the Rescue Recovery Wizard, think long and hard before you click Restore. Of course, if you're running the Rescue Recovery Wizard, and you have made major Registry changes in the recent past, chances are good that you've detected your culprit.

Norton WinDoctor and Registry Tracker only work with the active Registry, which, in this case, is the Registry on your Norton ZIP Rescue disk, not the one you use every day. (This is a function of how Windows works. As a safety precaution, Windows will only actively use the Registry files it finds on the drive from which Windows is starting.) If you are able to start Windows normally, before you restore your Registry, use WinDoctor to look for and repair problems, or use Norton Registry Tracker—assuming you've enabled it to watch your PC in the background—and consider selectively undoing recent Registry changes. If you cannot start Windows, however, and the Rescue Recovery Wizard's tests have shown no problems to this point, chances are very good indeed that your Registry is damaged. Click the Restore button to replace your Registry with the one saved on your Rescue disks. With the Registry either already in good shape, or repaired, click Next to move to the Rescue Recovery Wizard's final page.

FIGURE 7.14

Norton Rescue Recovery's Registry restorer.

Hardware Disasters

This final screen of the Norton Rescue Recovery Wizard, in Figure 7.15, is one that you don't want to arrive at, having previously detected no problems. If you do, it means that you probably have a hardware malfunction somewhere in your PC. If you do reach this point with no other difficulties targeted and resolved, you should turn to Appendix A, "Emergency Recovery Techniques" and read some good suggestions for safely checking your PC's hardware. There's no real reason why you can't perform this kind of examination yourself after you learn some basic guidelines for safe and reliable hardware tinkering. Of course, if you do feel very uncomfortable opening your computer, or if you don't own the workstation involved, it's probably best to check with the right support people before you start looking "under the lid." In any event, this is the final page of the Rescue Recovery Wizard, so click Finish to exit the Wizard and return back to the Norton Rescue desktop.

FIGURE 7.15
Norton Rescue Recovery's hardware failure screen.

Manual Recovery

It isn't terribly likely that you'd work your way entirely through the Norton Rescue Recovery Process and *all* the integrated Norton Utilities without finding problems—but you still have problems. It can happen, however. In those circumstances, it can be possible, and it may be necessary, to manually modify your drive to get it working again properly. This is by no means a beginners' task, but Norton SystemWorks 2.0 provides you with the best tools available for manual drive repair. For this, you need Norton Disk Editor—refer to Chapter 12, "Norton Utilities: The Laying-On of Hands and Norton Disk Editor."

PETER'S PRINCIPLE

There's really nothing more useless than an out-of-date Rescue set. In fact, an old Rescue set can be worse than useless. Having a Rescue set around can lead you to think your system is invulnerable—or, at least, always repairable—and than can lead to incautious behavior, even by the best of us. Personally, my recommendation is to update your Rescue data every evening when you leave your workstation for the night. You can achieve this easily by setting the System Doctor Rescue sensor to automatically launch Rescue once a day, at the time you specify, say, 4:55pm, perhaps. If you keep your Rescue disks handy—particularly if you use a Norton ZIP Rescue set—it won't take you more than a minute each evening to bring everything up-to-date. Your data is well worth sixty seconds.

Norton CrashGuard: When Windows Breaks

Given all of the tools you've already read about and all those that you'll read about later in this book, you might wonder why a product like Norton CrashGuard is even necessary. Don't be fooled: Crashes and freeze-ups are some of the most common sources of danger to your precious data and there's simply no way to prevent all of them. True, the Norton SystemWorks components will do everything possible to keep your PC in tip-top working shape, and System Doctor's sensors will alert you to growing dangers like heavy disk fragmentation or a lack of available system resources. But nothing can completely protect you from all the reasons why crashes occur.

Why Crashes Occur

Crashes occur for hundreds of different reasons. Mechanical failure in one or more of your drives; electrical failure in one or more of the many components of your PC, its motherboard and peripherals; and human error on the part of a programmer or a user may all contribute to crashes. These are several of the reasons why it's simply not possible to prevent all crashes.

Even if there was a reliable way to anticipate hardware difficulties of all types—and there isn't—it would be impossible for any method to somehow scan all of the software on your PC and verify that its programming is flawless. And even if that were possible, much of today's complex software creates a myriad of vital configuration files which are continuously updated as the program runs; incidental corruption of any one of these could cause that software to crash.

Finally, even if software has been crafted with the utmost care to work reliably, there is no way to unequivocally verify that any given program will function perfectly while you're also using any other program. Certainly, there are rules now for the polite behavior of software. But rules are subject to interpretation by programmers and many of us still use older software that was designed before the rules. (You'll read more about this type of software later when I contrast 32-bit and 16-bit crashes.) Trying to fill a computer with different software all guaranteed to work perfectly together would be like trying to fill a cruise ship with people all guaranteed to adore each other's company. Not going to happen in this lifetime.

Nevertheless, the majority of crashes are caused, in technical terms, by one of just a few very common errors. You'll read about these in just a minute. Before you do, let's clear the air for a moment about what a crash is, and contrast it to a freeze-up. You might be asking yourself, "What difference does it make—lost work is lost work, right?" As you'll see, Norton CrashGuard handles crashes and freezes quite differently, and you'll want to understand what CrashGuard is doing so that you won't lose work when a crash *or* a freeze occurs.

What's a Crash?

A crash is what happens when a piece of software violates one of those rules of polite software behavior mentioned previously. These rules are numerous, but they basically address fundamental concerns like:

- Windows controls access to memory; if software needs memory, it must ask Windows.

- Windows controls access to peripherals; if software wants to print or save data, it must ask Windows.

- Software must return control of the system to Windows whenever possible.

- Basic mathematical rules apply; do not, for example, attempt to divide any number by zero.

If a piece of software violates any of these rules, Windows becomes the operating system equivalent of "very annoyed," and takes steps to prevent the disobedient software from harming any other software running at the same time. Without a utility like Norton CrashGuard running, you normally see a dialog giving you some arcane technical information and a single Close button. Your only recourse is to close the software. Of course, you lose any data that you've not previously saved.

Bluescreen Crashes

The real bane of the world of crashes, a bluescreen crash—so called because of the bright blue full-screen background it causes to be displayed—is usually the result of difficulty deep within the operating system. Problems of this type affect Windows itself. As such, they can cascade throughout every piece of software running, wreaking havoc. Worse, some bluescreen crashes reflect serious hardware failures. Either way, the system is knocked into a state of such instability that it's generally unsafe, or impossible to keep running. Fortunately, as you'll read below, Norton CrashGuard can often recover your system from even a bluescreen crash.

What's a Freeze-Up?

A freeze-up is technically quite different from a crash. While crashes occur when Windows detects disallowed software behavior, software may become frozen without ever breaking any of Windows' rules. A piece of software might get stuck in what is commonly known as an infinite loop, in which the same task or set of tasks is repeated forever. (For an example of an infinite loop, turn to the Glossary, look up *Circular Logic*, and follow what it suggests. Please, for the sake of your loved-ones, stop yourself after a few minutes.) A piece of software might also correctly ask Windows for access to some system resource—the printer port, for example—but might incorrectly handle Windows' response to that request. Consequently, the software ends up waiting forever for Windows to respond in accordance with the software's improper design (which will never happen). Windows doesn't know anything is wrong, because it received and responded to a proper request.

Symptoms of a freeze-up are very recognizable. Your mouse pointer may refuse to move on-screen, your keyboard may have no affect on the software, or both. (In fact, it is usually both.) Norton CrashGuard can often resurrect your software from this condition, too. However, because freeze-ups are not easily detectable like full-fledged crashes, recovering a frozen piece of software with Norton CrashGuard is different than recovering from a crash. You'll read about this in depth later in this chapter.

> **Note:** If you're wondering why I keep referring to *software* rather than to *programs* or *applications*, the reason is simple. Crashes and freeze-ups can occur in any aspect of any piece of software that's running. This may, indeed, be an application file, such as WORD.EXE, or it may be an application component, such as a DLL like SOMEDLL.DLL. The offending software may also be a system component itself, such as a VxD like ITSVITAL.VXD. I'm using the more generic term, software, to underscore that any type of software can be the culprit in a crash or freeze-up.

What Is Norton CrashGuard?

Norton CrashGuard is one of the integrated utilities in Norton SystemWorks. As you've already read, Norton CrashGuard can intercept a very wide range of crashes and software freeze-ups, enabling you to save your data reliably and, often, to keep working as though nothing had happened.

CrashGuard is itself a full-fledged utility application, and is comprised of several components. Each component handles a different aspect of either crash interception or crash/freeze recovery. These components are all integrated together through the Crash Monitor. We'll look at each of these components in turn, seeing how each works and how you work with it. Finally, we'll dig into ways in which you can customize Norton CrashGuard's operation.

Crash Interception Tools

Norton CrashGuard's primary set of tools are those which intercept crashes in the first place. These are your scouts, working out in front of the "front line," and returning vital information and recommendations to you. Based on their observations and analyses, you'll be properly armed to deal with the many different types of crashes that may occur. Not only do they inform you know when there is an easy battle ahead, they'll also accurately report in about when the battle is likely lost before it's begun. The Crash Assistant and the Crash Advisor are integrated under the aegis of the Crash Monitor.

Crash Monitor

The Crash Monitor shield is the indicator informing you that Norton CrashGuard is working. Located in the system tray, as shown in Figure 8.1, the Crash Monitor shield is also the means by which you open Norton CrashGuard's configuration options and its online help. Additionally, Crash Monitor is your access-point for FreezeCheck, which you'll read about below.

FIGURE 8.1

The Norton CrashGuard shield in the system tray indicates that your system is actively protected.

Crash Monitor works continuously behind the scenes, watching out for crash-causing activity. When a crash occurs, the Crash Monitor catches the problem before Windows does. Crash Monitor alerts Crash Assistant that a crash has occurred. Consequently, rather than seeing the dreaded Windows crash dialog box, you'll see Crash Assistant's display instead.

Crash Assistant

Crash Assistant, shown in Figure 8.2, is really Norton CrashGuard's primary user interface. Although the options you see here differ depending on the type of crash which has occurred—that's the whole point, as you see—this single Crash Assistant display looks much the same in all circumstances. Once you learn the function of each part of the interface, you'll know how to use the tools it provides for you under any circumstances. As you're reading the following section, it may be helpful to refer occasionally back to Figure 8.2.

Crash Information

The topmost panel in the Crash Assistant dialog box is where you'll find general Crash Information. Here you'll see the name of the piece of software which has crashed. In many cases you'll also see the name of the file which was open and active at the time the crash occurred. If the crashed software is a full-fledged application or a standalone applet (like the Windows Calculator), you'll also see that program's icon at the left side of this display.

Status Indicators

Directly below the Crash Information panel and at the left of Crash Assistant's display is the misleadingly small Program and System area. These two icons will provide you with an immediate, graphical understanding of how severe the crash was. This information is likely vital when you are making decisions about which of the different CrashGuard recovery options you should use. Two different indicators are shown here. The leftmost Program icon indicates the degree to which the crash has likely impacted the crashed program itself. Figure 8.3 shows the four different icons you may see here. Moving from top to bottom, these icons indicate an increasing severity of crash with respect to the crashed program itself. Specifically:

- **Icon #1:** A minor crash has occurred. Crash Assistant has analyzed the crash and has determined that it is very likely that the program can be recovered successfully with no ill effects.

- **Icon #2:** A somewhat-serious crash has occurred. Crash Assistant has determined that you are likely able to recover the program, but you may find that it does not work properly after recovery.

- **Icon #3:** A more serious crash has occurred. This icon lets you know that Crash Assistant is fairly certain that at least one major function of the program will not work properly after recovery. This may be a bit of functionality that you can continue to work without, or it may be that the program ceases to work immediately after recovery because the functionality is somehow vital.

- **Icon #4:** If Crash Assistant displays this icon, you are being warned that not only the specific piece of software, but also all of Windows might be endangered if you attempt to recover and continue working with it.

FIGURE 8.3

The more "broken" the window icon appears to be, the more severely the crash has likely impacted the system.

When you read below about the different crash recovery tools that make up Norton CrashGuard, you'll learn that some tools are more "risky" than others. That is, using some tools is more likely to leave you open to further troubles than are other tools. As Crash Assistant indicates a more-severe type of crash, you should feel increasingly discouraged from using the "riskier" recovery tools in that instance.

The right-hand icon in the Status Indicator area indicates the impact of the crash on the System as a whole. Figure 8.4 shows the two different icons you may see here. The icon labeled 1 indicates that Crash Assistant doesn't detect any conditions that are likely to present any danger to your system as a whole. The icon labeled 2—which looks a little bit like your PC is standing-in for Jimmy Stewart in Alfred Hitchcock's *Vertigo*—indicates that Crash Assistant has determined that this crash has endangered the stability of your entire system.

Figure 8.4

These two icons are the possible System Status Indicators that you may see in Crash Assistant.

—1

—2

You'd probably suspect that Program icon number 4 and System icon number 2 display together a lot, and you'd be right. But you may see these icons in any combination.

> **Caution:** When deciding how you want to handle a crash, of course you need to think first about what you may have lost in the crashed program itself. If what you were working on in the crashed program is vital—or as long as it's more important than anything else you're currently doing on your PC—then you'll want to err on the side of protecting that data, even if it might endanger less-important work on your PC. If you don't stand to lose anything important in the crashed program itself, but you have important data unsaved in other applications, you'll definitely want to err on the side of protecting your system stability until you can recover from the crash and quickly save the data in the other program. You'll read later in the chapter about when to use each different recovery tool, depending on both Program and System conditions.

Crash Advisor

Crash Advisor takes up only a very small amount of space in the Crash Assistant display. However, the Crash Advisor is one of the major components of Norton CrashGuard. Crash Advisor works with Crash Assistant and uses the data behind the System Indicator icons to recommend your best course of action. This saves you most of the guesswork that might have otherwise been involved in selecting how you want to handle each crash. The Crash Advisor may succinctly suggest, for example, that you use VitalSave to safely store your data. Alternately, you might be told that Crash Advisor has determined that your Web browser has crashed, and that you should use QuickReload to try to return to the last Web page you were viewing before the crash. With every crash that occurs, Crash Advisor checks the conditions of your system against these and all of your other CrashGuard recovery options. What you see displayed here on the Crash Assistant's dialog is almost always your best course of action.

SafeOriginal Status

To the right of the Crash Advisor display is the SafeOriginal indicator. The icon and text shown here advises you whether or not you have SafeOriginal enabled. (You'll read about SafeOriginal in more depth later in this chapter.) If SafeOriginal is active, previously saved versions of open files are protected from being overwritten by possibly corrupted data during the crash-recovery process.

Recovery Options Panel

The largest section of the Crash Assistant dialog box indicates the recovery options available to you for this crash. The buttons here are your access points to all of Norton CrashGuard's recovery tools, each of which you'll read about in depth. Depending on the nature of the crash, there are different options here. For example, if Crash Assistant has determined that the crash had nothing to do with your Web browser, the QuickReload option is not displayed. Similarly, since there is no potential for data loss in a crashed Web browser, the VitalSave option is replaced by QuickReload, when relevant. Recovery options may not be displayed at all if Crash Assistant determines that the option is not relevant. For example, if Crash Assistant knows that the crashed program is not capable of saving data (for example, the Solitaire applet), the VitalSave option will likely not be displayed, as in Figure 8.5.

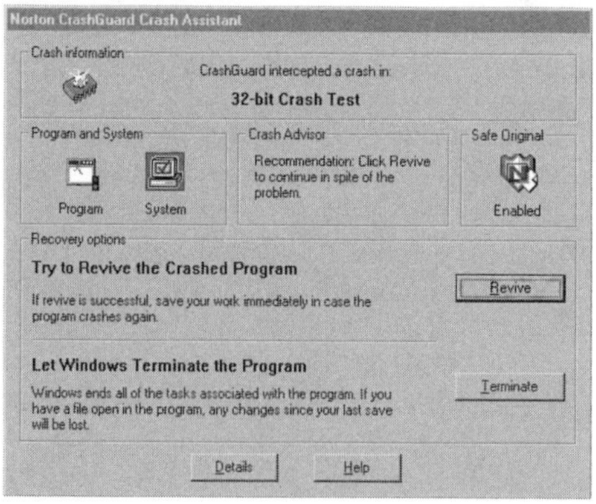

FIGURE 8.5

Crash Assistant knows that the crashed program does not have any data to save, so the VitalSave option is not displayed.

Each of your recovery options is accompanied by a short, standard explanation of what happens, in general, when you select that option. Buttons at the right of this section correspond to each recovery option. Click the button representing the option you wish to try, and that recovery tool is used.

Details and Help

At the bottom of the Crash Assistant window are two buttons which provide you with additional information: the left button (Details) about your current crash, and the right button (Help) about Crash Assistant itself. Clicking the Help button opens the online help for Crash Assistant. From here you can learn more about Crash Assistant itself or you can navigate through the help engine to learn more about the different recovery options (assuming you don't have this book handy to answer those questions for you).

Note: You'll notice that the Help window opens beneath the Crash Assistant window. This is because Crash Assistant's display has a property known as "Always on top." No matter what other windows are open on your PC, the Crash Assistant window opens on top of all of them. Even if you use the traditional Alt+Tab keyboard shortcut to try to move between open applications, Crash Assistant resolutely refuses to let anything stand in front of it. The windows underneath aren't closed or modified in any way, but you do have to move the Crash Assistant window out of the way if you want to view any of them. To move the Crash Assistant window, click in its title bar with your mouse, and, holding the mouse down, drag the window out of the way. Use the same technique to drag the window back into view.

Caution: Depending on the severity of a crash and its impact on your system (refer to the Status Indicators to get a sense of this), using the system resources required to launch the Windows Help engine from Crash Assistant might be disastrous. I strongly urge you to turn to this book or to your printed documentation first if you have questions you need answered while handling a crash.

Clicking the Details button and then clicking the Advanced button will open up a window like that shown in Figure 8.6. In almost no circumstance is this data of any direct use to you. However, if a crash occurs repeatedly, the technical details shown here may be helpful to technical support staff whom you contact about the problem.

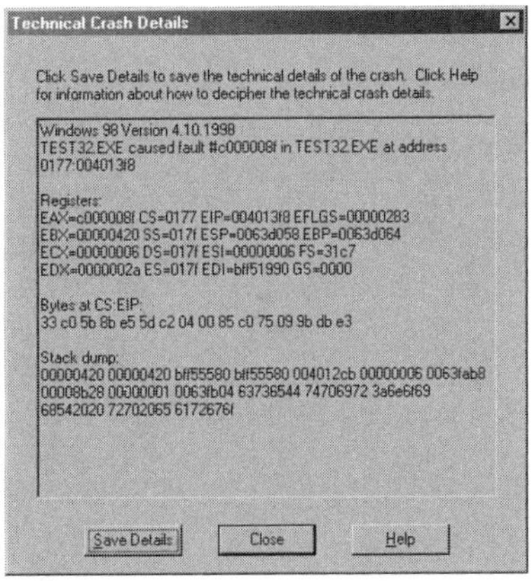

FIGURE 8.6

The Technical Crash Details window provides technical data about the crash, which can be useful to technical support personnel or to programmers.

Note: It's likely self-evident, but it bears mentioning that you should not contact Symantec technical support for assistance in troubleshooting crashes, unless it is a Symantec product which has crashed. You must contact the support personnel who work for the company that made the software or hardware that is causing problems.

Moving from the top of the window, down, you find (a) the name and version of your operating system; (b) the name of the program that crashed, the type of crash, the module or component of the program that actually crashed, and where in memory the crash actually occurred; (c) the contents of all of your processor's registers at the time of the crash; (d) the name of the instruction that the program was trying to perform when the crash occurred; (e) a dump of your processor's stack, showing what was happening in your PC immediately before the crash.

Again, if all but a few pieces of this make no sense to you, don't worry. This data is provided for programmers who are trying to troubleshoot new software they are developing, and for purposes of providing technical support.

After Recovery

If you attempt to recover from a crash and find that the recovery attempt was unsuccessful, don't worry. Crash Assistant is still onscreen, and you can select a different recovery method to try. Of course, in some circumstances, no recovery method is successful, and you'll simply have to quit the program. Most of the time, however, you'll find yourself looking at a screen like that shown in Figure 8.7.

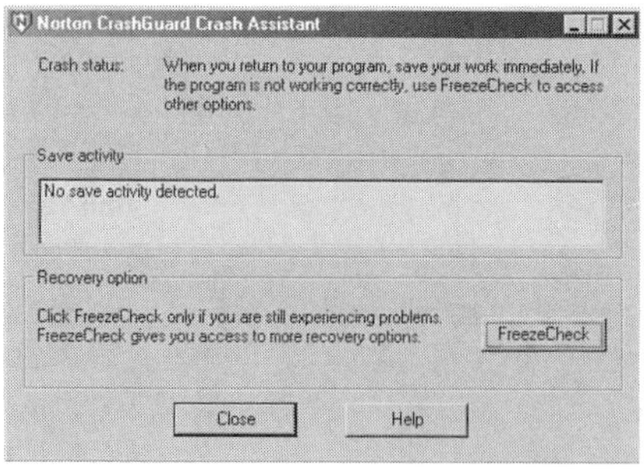

FIGURE 8.7
CrashGuard's Crash Assistant displays additional information and options once crash recovery is complete.

This crash status screen advises you to save your work immediately upon returning to the crashed program. It also indicates, in the Save Activity panel, what steps, if any, have been taken to save your data. The contents of this panel vary, of course, depending on the recovery option you've selected and whether the crashed program has any data to save.

Finally, the Recovery Options panel will provide you with access to CrashGuard's FreezeCheck, so that you can attempt to un-freeze an application which you've recovered but which still seems to not be working.

Caution: Do not attempt to use FreezeCheck if it appears that everything is working normally after crash recovery. Depending on the nature of your system status at the time, using FreezeCheck improperly can actually cause serious crashes—definitely including the dreaded bluescreen crash—from which you may have no recourse but to restart your entire system.

Crash Recovery Tools

CrashGuard's sophisticated crash detection and analysis tools wouldn't be much use to you if you didn't also have tools to help you recover from those crashes. What do you care, after all, if Macrosloth Whatever 99 has caused an invalid page fault, if there's nothing you can do about it? Fortunately, CrashGuard provides no fewer than six new tools designed to help you recover from crashes and freeze-ups. VitalSave, SafeOriginal, Revive, QuickReload, AntiFreeze and FreezeCheck, and Bluescreen Protection give you serious recovery options that protect your work and your system.

We'll look at each of these in turn, starting with the two newest—and arguably, most innovative—tools.

SafeOriginal and VitalSave

SafeOriginal and VitalSave are tools that are new to the latest version of CrashGuard, and they are welcome additions, indeed. These two tools are designed specifically to safeguard the part of your PC that most often can't be restored to life after a serious crash: your data.

SafeOriginal actually works in the background all the time, assuming you leave it enabled. Whenever Crash Monitor identifies that a crash has occurred, SafeOriginal begins to monitor that program. Regardless of what other recovery techniques you select (since SafeOriginal is working all the time, you need do nothing extra to gain its protection), SafeOriginal watches to see whether the crashed application attempts to change any files on disk. If the program does try to write to the disk, either because you've chosen VitalSave directly, or because of activity related to another recovery technique, SafeOriginal intercedes. It makes a write-protected copy of the files the crashed program is trying to modify, and stores these copies safely away in your SafeOriginal folder.

Note: Unless you change the installation defaults for SystemWorks, or CrashGuard's settings, your SafeOriginal folder is located at `C:\Program Files\ Norton CrashGuard\SafeOrig`. (You'll read about how to change the location of the SafeOriginal folder later in this chapter.)

Whenever SafeOriginal makes such a copy, it always creates a standard Windows short-cut to the protected copy in the same folder as the original. If you open the original file and discover that it was corrupted or rendered unusable during the crash, you can double-click on the SafeOriginal shortcut and see whether the saved file is intact. In the past, there used to be considerable danger that saving a file after a minor crash would over-write a perfectly good copy of the file with a corrupted one (thereby destroying perfectly good data). SafeOriginal negates that danger.

If you find that the SafeOriginal copy of a file is your only remaining useful version of your work, you should resave the file to a new location immediately. SafeOriginal auto-matically deletes files from its folder after a certain number of days (which you'll learn how to specify later). You don't want to have to go searching through the Norton Protected Recycle Bin for vital work because you've forgotten to relocate it.

VitalSave also works to directly safeguard your data in a crash. If you select the VitalSafe recovery option (when it is available) CrashGuard sends a command directly to the crashed program, forcing the program (or, at least, trying to force the program) to save your data to disk. (If SafeOriginals is enabled, of course, any existing version of your data files is stored safely away before the open data is written to disk.)

VitalSave works, generally, by telling your crashed program to shutdown. This in turn calls the application's own "save data before quitting" routines. You see a dialog box much like that shown in Figure 8.8, asking you if you want to save data before quitting. (The dialog is different depending on which application has crashed.) You should always say Yes to this question. If the file already exists on disk, it is saved and the program quits. If the file does not yet exist, you see a standard Windows Save As dialog box, in which you need to specify where you want the file saved and what name you want it given.

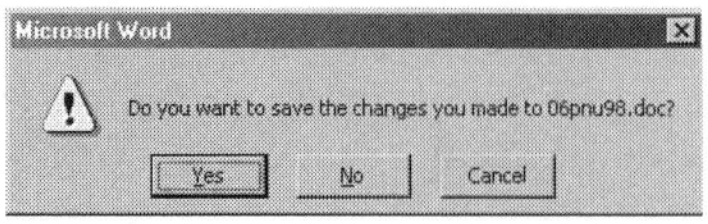

FIGURE 8.8

When you choose to use VitalSave, it causes the crashed program to quit, forcing it to display its own, familiar save routine.

Caution: Navigating around on the disk in the Save As dialog box uses system resources that may be unstable because of the crash. I strongly urge you to save any unsaved data into whatever folder appears by default in the Save As dialog box. If you need to, write down the name of the folder so you can find your data later. It would be foolish to be anal-retentive about saving your data in "just the right spot," if trying to do so causes you to lose your data entirely. Once you restart Windows, you can always move the saved file to where you want it stored.

Revive

The Revive recovery option falls under the category of "higher risk" options that I defined earlier. Using proprietary techniques, CrashGuard attempts to undo the problem that caused the crash and thereby bring the crashed program back to life, as it were. In many cases, this technique is successful. In others, it is not.

Revive is an option which is best suited for use in time-critical circumstances. For example, imagine that you are printing handouts for a company meeting that is just starting. Your page-layout program crashes. You don't need to use VitalSave because the data is already stored on the network server. However, you simply don't have time to restart Windows, log back on to the network, and then start again (if it can be avoided). Using Revive may return you to the program, enabling you to resume printing. Much of the program's functionality may be disabled after a Revive—possibly including the functions you need to continue your task—or the program may work perfectly. Of course, if you haven't yet saved your work, but your needs demand that you try to Revive the crashed application, you should save your data immediately after a successful Revive.

If Revive fails, you may find that the program is frozen. At that point you can try using Crash Assistant's FreezeCheck button (shown in Figure 8.7) to un-freeze and get back to work.

> **Tip:** Only you can judge when your time is too constrained to allow for any option other than Revive. However, if you have unsaved data in your crashed application, let me strongly urge you to use VitalSave and protect that data to the best of your ability. The time it takes to re-launch a failed piece of software (which is often all that is necessary) is negligible to the time involved in re-creating lost work. Even the time needed to restart Windows is nothing in such a comparison. Revive is your best choice when you know your data is safe, but the boss is at your heels, waiting for results.

QuickReload

In all of the shenanigans that go on in the Web browser wars, you rarely hear any party claim that their browser crashes less than the competition—and small wonder. The downside of how easy it is to create good Web pages is that it is also easy to create dismal ones. Error-laden Web code—particularly if Java applets or multimedia plug-ins are involved—can crash your Web browser like pulling the wings off a rock.

If you've just spent five or six hours digging through some company's typically-well-designed online catalogue, looking for their premiere product, only to crash when you finally locate it, "Oh, well…" is probably not your first thought. QuickReload addresses this problem. When Crash Monitor detects that your Web browser has taken a nose-dive, the QuickReload option appears in Crash Assistant's window. Select it, and CrashGuard closes your browser, properly re-starts it, and returns you to the page you last visited. If you crash again when you try to view that page, QuickReload automatically presents you with a list of URLs (Uniform Resource Locators, the method used to identify pages on the Web, usually beginning with http://www.something) you've recently visited. Select one, and QuickReload restarts your browser and takes you there.

Terminate

The final option that you may be presented with by Crash Assistant is to forcibly terminate, or quit the program that has crashed. CrashGuard stops the program immediately, neither making nor enabling for the saving of any unsaved data. Given that this is basically the same option available to you without CrashGuard installed at all, why would you ever select Terminate?

Terminate is most called-for in one very special, very common circumstance. Presume that you've been working for hours on a spreadsheet. Also presume that you've momentarily taken leave of your senses—it happens to us all—and you've not saved any of that work. Suddenly, you realize that you need to retrieve a value from an email message your coworker sent you last night. You run your email client, and it crashes as it's launching.

Consider your options. VitalSave would be useless—indeed, might not even be available—in the case of a crashed program like an email client. Everything is already saved! Revive might work, but as you've already read, Revive can leave your system unstable. Do you want to risk your hours of spreadsheet work on that possibility? (If you're uncertain of the answer to this question, it's "No.") What you need to do is get your precious work saved as quickly and reliably as possible. The best way to achieve that is to just make the crashed program "go away." Terminate does just that. The faulty program closes, and you are able to quickly save your work in the spreadsheet and restart Windows.

Sometimes, however, a crash makes the system unstable in ways that even choosing Terminate can't avoid. What do you do if you Terminate the email client, but can't get your spreadsheet to respond to the mouse or the keyboard? Read on for the answer…

AntiFreeze

Enter Norton AntiFreeze. As you've already read, lack of keyboard or mouse response are symptoms that your application has frozen. Norton AntiFreeze can undo this program in a broad range of circumstances. AntiFreeze, like the remaining recovery techniques you're about to encounter, isn't accessed through the Crash Assistant dialog (with one exception, noted below). This is because a crash and a freeze-up are so different, technically, that Crash Monitor won't necessarily know that one of your applications is frozen. (You've already read about this earlier in the chapter.)

Note: There is one major exception to the statement that AntiFreeze isn't accessed through the Crash Assistant. If you have just used the Assistant to recover from an actual crash, you'll see the display shown previously in Figure 8.7, from which you can click the FreezeCheck button and start the freeze-recovery process.

FreezeCheck

You can launch FreezeCheck by double-clicking on the CrashGuard shield in the system tray, or by selecting Programs, Norton CrashGuard, Norton FreezeCheck from your Start menu. FreezeCheck is also available from the main CrashGuard menu, shown in Figure 8.9. (The main CrashGuard menu is found at Programs, Norton CrashGuard, Norton CrashGuard in your Start menu, but if you're using your Start menu to access FreezeCheck, you might as well access it directly, as suggested earlier.

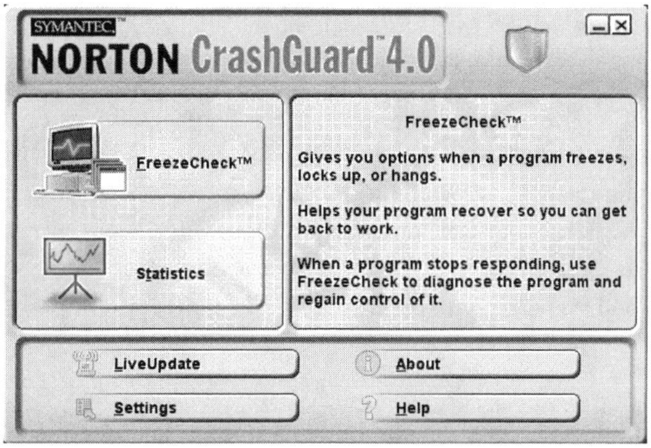

FIGURE 8.9
The Main CrashGuard screen provides access to FreezeCheck as well as other CrashGuard tools and features.

The FreezeCheck display, shown in Figure 8.10, provides you with a list of all open applications. You should ignore anything in the list other than the application that appears to be frozen. The caution note you read earlier bears repeating here:

Caution: Do not attempt to use FreezeCheck on an application that appears to be working normally. Depending on the nature of your system status, using FreezeCheck improperly can actually cause serious problems.

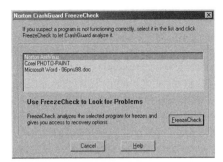

To apply AntiFreeze to a frozen program, select its name in the list, and click the
FreezeCheck button. CrashGuard analyzes the program you've chosen and displays the
results of its analysis. In most cases, you are told that the frozen program appears to be
"busy." A program or application is busy when it is waiting for some condition to be satisfied, for example, for Windows to inform it that a file's data has been saved properly. If
the program is waiting for some condition which is never satisfied, and thus is frozen,
you want CrashGuard to interrupt the busy program, thereby thawing it out, as it were.

FreezeCheck gives you recovery options very like those given by the Crash Assistant. A
new option, AntiFreeze, is always present. In some circumstances, FreezeCheck also
enables you to opt to use VitalSave or QuickReload to attempt to undo the condition
causing the freeze-up. If the program is frozen, you almost always want to select
AntiFreeze. If AntiFreeze is successful, you should immediately save any unsaved work
and quit and restart the program (or Windows itself, particularly if you've also just recovered from a crash).

> **Caution:** Whenever you experience a crash or a freeze-up, remember that it's
> because something has gone wrong. When one thing goes wrong, more wrong
> things are usually sure to follow. You should expect further difficulties whenev-
> er you recover from a crash or a freeze-up and take steps to avoid those prob-
> lems. The best way to do this, when possible, is to make sure your work is saved,
> and restart Windows.

Remember that FreezeCheck is available to you on-demand, not only when you've
encountered an actual freeze-up. If, for example, you use AntiFreeze to try to recover a
frozen program, but then cannot save your work, re-launch FreezeCheck. This time, try
using the VitalSave recovery option. The crashed program almost always quits, of course,
but in doing so, it probably provides you with the chance to save your data.

Bluescreen Crash Protection

If you experience a bluescreen crash, you discover that CrashGuard has added some
options to the bluescreen that you've not seen in the past. Traditionally, a bluescreen

crash advises you that—well, basically—your computer is messed-up pretty badly, and suggests you press the spacebar to try to continue (which never works) or press Ctrl+Alt+Del to reboot your system (which only works sometimes; bluescreen crashes can be so severe that your PC may not even respond to the three-fingered salute).

With CrashGuard's protection, you are given the opportunity to choose Yes if you wish to have CrashGuard attempt to recover your system from the fault and return you to Windows, or choose No if you don't want CrashGuard to try. (Selecting No reboots your system immediately.) If you select Yes and return to Windows successfully, you should immediately save any work that is not yet saved, and restart Windows.

> **Caution:** It is not always necessary to do so, but after any successful crash recovery, I recommend you restart Windows. Certainly, after any crash recovery that is not successful, you should restart, even if CrashGuard doesn't give you any indication that a restart is required.

Close Program Enhancement

By default, Norton CrashGuard provides enhancements to Windows traditional Close Program dialog (shown in Figure 8.11, and accessed by pressing Ctrl+Alt+Del). With enhancement-enabled (you'll learn how to disable it in a moment), CrashGuard adds AntiFreeze and FreezeCheck buttons to every Close Program screen. In this way, you can quickly obtain access to AntiFreeze or FreezeCheck. This may be useful if, for example, the Explorer itself is frozen and you can't use your mouse on the system tray icon or use the keyboard to open the Start menu. Your keyboard often resumes working in a Close Program dialog box when it's frozen everywhere else. From here you can select the frozen application, click AntiFreeze, and ideally, get right back to work!

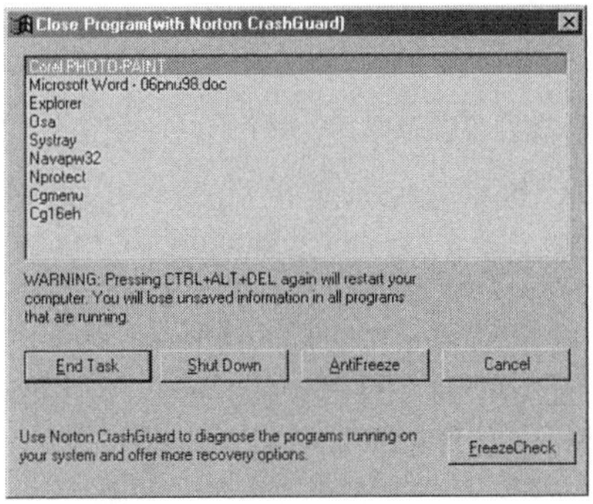

FIGURE 8.11
CrashGuard enhances Windows' Close Program dialog box.

Other CrashGuard Tools

In addition to its crash detection and recovery tools, Norton CrashGuard provides a statistical display and log that can be particularly useful to programmers and technical support personnel who are trying to understand why crashes are occurring. You can access the Statistics dialog box through the main CrashGuard menu, by selecting Programs | Norton CrashGuard | Norton CrashGuard from your Start menu.

Crash Statistics

The Statistics dialog, shown in Figure 8.12, displays a summary of all crashes and freeze-ups that CrashGuard has encountered. The first column shows the name of the application that crashed. In the case of complex applications, clicking on the hierarchical plus sign "+" button to the left of the program's name opens a list of different program sub-modules that have crashed. Moving to the right, the Type column keeps track of whether it was a 32-bit or a 16-bit application which bit the dust; the Crashes column records how many times each application or module has crashed; and the Freezes column shows the number of times each has been unfrozen.

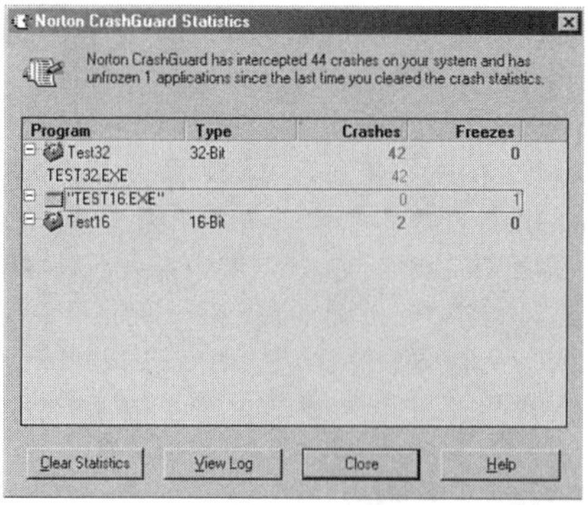

FIGURE 8.12
CrashGuard's Statistics dialog box provides a summary of crashes and the number of programs which have been unfrozen.

Crash Log Information

The View Log button, at the bottom of the Statistics dialog, opens CrashGuard's technical log of crash information. The log is stored in a file named CGStats.CG, which can be opened and read by any text editor. A bit of a sample log is shown in Figure 8.13. This data, along with that found in the crash details dialog box (about which you've already read) can further help troubleshoot problems.

> **Tip:** If you habitually encounter crashes, and find yourself calling technical support for the offending application, be sure to let them know that you have Norton CrashGuard installed and running. The information in the Statistics dialog box and the crash log may contribute significantly to their ability to rectify your troubles.

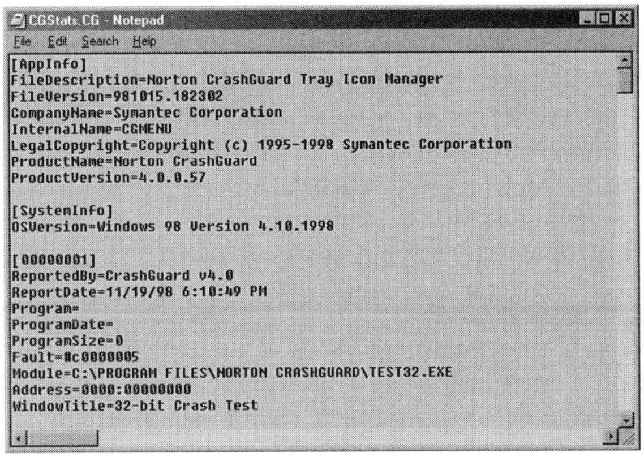

FIGURE 8.13
CrashGuard's crash log contains additional information about crashes encountered by Crash Monitor.

Customizing Norton CrashGuard

Norton CrashGuard is an elegantly designed tool. It works tremendously well without your intervention, and most users obtain the best results from CrashGuard's default settings. Nevertheless, there are a few modifiable options that you might find useful. CrashGuard's settings are most easily accessed by right-clicking on the CrashGuard shield in the system tray and selecting Settings from the context menu. You can also click the Settings button on CrashGuard's main display after launching it by choosing Programs, Norton CrashGuard, Norton CrashGuard from your Start menu. CrashGuard's settings dialog is shown in Figure 8.14. As with other standard Windows settings tabs, you can click Apply to immediately activate modifications, click OK to accept changes you've made and close the entire Settings window, or Cancel to discard all changes you've made (unless you've clicked Apply) and close the window.

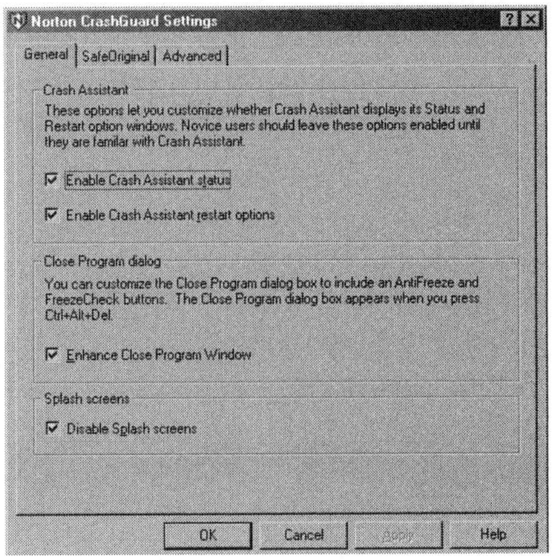

FIGURE 8.14
CrashGuard's Settings dialog box provides access to three tabs on which CG's functions can be customized.

The General Tab

On the Setting's General tab, shown in Figure 8.14, you can enable or disable certain fundamental CrashGuard functionality. Remember, of course, that tools you turn off won't be available to you if you encounter a crash. The top panel, labeled Crash Assistant, enables you to select whether Crash Assistant displays its status window after a crash recovery, and whether it shows you options to restart Windows. Unless you are a software engineer who is testing a program, I strongly recommend that you leave these two features enabled at all times.

Beneath the Crash Assistant settings is the Close Program enhancement option. When checked, this option instructs CrashGuard to add FreezeCheck and AntiFreeze buttons to your standard Close Programs dialogs (as you read about previously).

Finally, the Disable Splash Screens option, when checked, suppresses the "CrashGuard is Protecting You" display that you see every time Windows restarts. Unless you find this screen to be somehow reassuring, I recommend that most users disable it. You can tell that CrashGuard is working by looking for the CrashGuard shield in your system tray. Disabling the splash screen will carve a second or two off of the time it takes you to reach your desktop when you start Windows.

The SafeOriginal Tab

The SafeOriginal tab, shown in Figure 8.15, enables you to configure how SafeOriginal handles data. SafeOriginal can be disabled—an option I urge you strongly to not even consider—by removing the check in the Enable SafeOriginal box. If you find that you don't want SafeOriginal to create shortcuts for the files it protects—a matter of convenience, not a major change in SafeOriginal's functionality—then unchecking the Create shortcuts option turns shortcuts off.

Below these two options you can see the full path SafeOriginal uses for storing the files it protects. You can click in this text box and change the path manually, or you can click the Browse button and easily navigate around until you find the folder into which you want SafeOriginal files stored. Click OK in the folder navigation window and the new path is shown in the SafeOriginals tab.

Finally, you can specify the number of days after which you want SafeOriginal to delete the files it stores in the SafeOriginal folder. By default, deletion is set to seven days. This means that SafeOriginal never deletes files from your SafeOriginal folder. You can type any number up to 999 in this box, or use the arrow buttons to scroll up and down to the number of days you want specified. To delete files from your SafeOriginals folder immediately, click the Delete Now button.

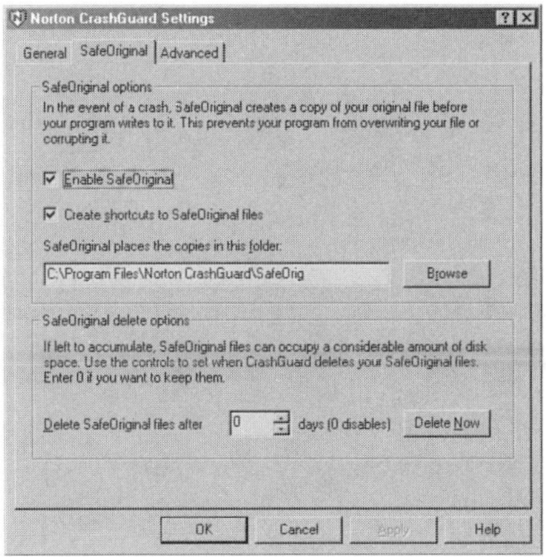

FIGURE **8.15**

The SafeOriginal tab enables you to select how SafeOriginal works and where it stores your files.

The Advanced Tab

The Advanced tab, shown in Figure 8.16, allows you to enable or disable the three major types of protection provided by CrashGuard. If you do not wish CrashGuard to try to help you recover from 32-bit, 16-bit, or bluescreen crashes, you can uncheck the relevant option on this tab and turn that class of protection off. The only circumstances in which you might want to do this are extremely rare and technical, and have no relevance to 99.999% of users. Unless you know precisely what you're doing and why, don't disable any of Norton CrashGuard's protection.

The Advanced tab also enables you to generate crashes of a variety of types so that you can see how CrashGuard handles them. There are 18 different types of 32-bit crashes and three types of 16-bit crashes that can be created here. Click either the Generate 32-bit crash button or the Generate 16-bit crash button on the Advanced tab, select the type of crash you wish to simulate, and click Test Crash.

Caution: The reason CrashGuard responds to a test crash exactly like a real crash is because test crashes are real crashes. For this reason, you should never test crashes with any other application running—certainly not with any unsaved data at risk.

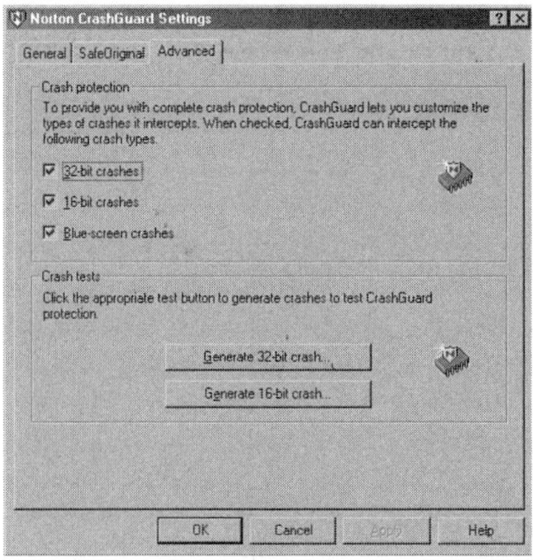

FIGURE 8.16

The Advanced tab enables you to enable or disable CrashGuard protection and to perform test crashes.

Keeping CrashGuard Current

Like other Norton SystemWorks components, you can keep CrashGuard up-to-date by using LiveUpdate to download updates from Symantec. LiveUpdate for CrashGuard is available directly from the main CrashGuard screen (choose Programs | Norton CrashGuard | Norton CrashGuard from your Start menu) but it is more conveniently available from the LiveUpdate button on your Norton SystemWorks Integrator, which you've read about already in this book. For detailed information about LiveUpdate, refer to Chapter 19, "Norton Web Services: Your Current Computer."

Norton AntiVirus: Infection Protection

Norton AntiVirus, an integrated Norton SystemWorks component, provides extensive, advanced protection against viral infection of your PC. The threat of viruses has been variously sensationalized and marginalized by the press, but the danger is real. Norton AntiVirus will, however, all but eliminate that danger entirely if you use it wisely. This chapter will tell you everything you need to know about doing just that. If you'd like a broader understanding of viruses themselves and some of the issues you may encounter in dealing with the viral threat—particularly if you are a network administrator—check out Appendix E, "A Virus Primer."

The Norton AntiVirus Main Screen

The Norton AntiVirus main screen is a small, uncluttered interface. Like a watch, running this program is "wind and forget," which is an advantage. Good antivirus software should be unobtrusive. Once you've set up Norton AntiVirus to your liking, you'll seldom be bothered again, especially if you use scheduled scanning and LiveUpdate (Symantec's automated online program for receiving software upgrades). Additionally, many people use Norton AntiVirus without adjusting the default settings at all.

The Norton AntiVirus main screen's central feature is single-click scanning (see Figure 9.1). If you have reason to believe a virus is afoot, simply click Scan Now. The Drives list on the left side of the screen indicates which drives will be scanned. To scan a drive, click its check box.

FIGURE 9.1

The Norton AntiVirus Main Screen is small and uncluttered.

A Few Words About Auto-Protect

Manually running a scan is far from your only mode of protection. Norton AntiVirus Auto-Protect is always running in the background.

The main screen displays Auto-Protect status. When Auto-Protect is on, Norton AntiVirus is constantly monitoring your computer for virus-like behavior. NAV Auto-Protect not only uses virus signatures, but also a combination of the best methods for detecting virus-like behavior.

Sometimes, though, installing programs will cause virus alerts. Some examples are large suites or applications that alter system files, and associate themselves with many other executables. For this reason, Norton AntiVirus enables you to turn Auto-Protect off by clicking the Disable button on the main screen.

Note: If you've turned off Auto-Protect to install a particularly large or complex program, check to make sure its enabled again, after you restart your computer.

The Norton AntiVirus Toolbar

You have access to all Norton AntiVirus' tools from the toolbar. Click one of the five toolbar buttons at the top of the screen to open a feature.

Note: The only feature not directly available from this main screen is the Scheduler, which is accessed by clicking its icon on the System Tray at the lower-right corner of your desktop. Scheduling unattended Virus Scans and LiveUpdates is an integral component of your antivirus strategy, and will be discussed in following sections.

We'll explore each toolbar button in due course. The menus, by the way, provide very little access that is not available through the toolbar. You'll learn how to use the Scan menu to scan only those folders and drives you think are essential. Beyond that, we'll deal very little with the menus.

The Norton AntiVirus main screen is always a double-click away. It resides minimized in the System Tray at the lower-right of the screen, next to the Task Scheduler icon (see Figure 9.2).

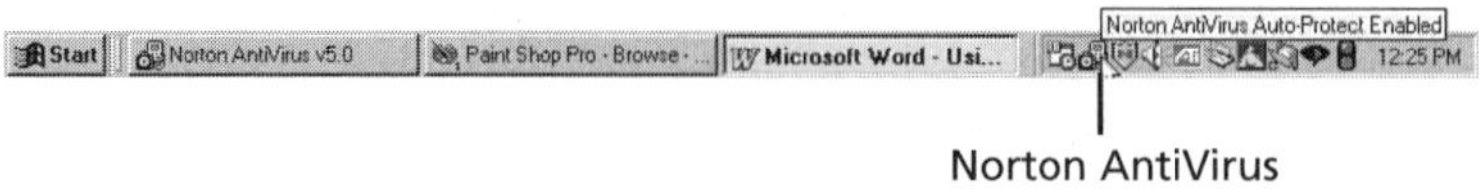

Norton AntiVirus

FIGURE 9.2
The Norton AntiVirus main screen is always a double-click away, at the lower-right of your screen.

The toolbar buttons always remain on the main screen. Hold your mouse momentarily over any button for a tooltip describing the button's action. You cannot remove or hide the interface toolbar buttons. Likewise, the Quarantine notice, which reminds you how many files are currently in Quarantine, and the Auto-Protect button are not removable. (Quarantine is Norton AntiVirus' utility for isolating potentially harmful files. You'll then be prompted to upload those files to Symantec's special facility for evaluating possible viruses.)

If you've used Norton AntiVirus in previous versions, perhaps back when features where largely controlled by DOS commands, you may be happy to know that all your favorite DOS switches will still work. (DOS switches are typed commands that activate certain Norton AntiVirus features. If you activate Norton AntiVirus in a DOS environment, type **NAVDX** at the DOS prompt, and a list of DOS switches for Norton AntiVirus will appear. You can check out the DOS switches in a DOS window, but you cannot execute them unless you reboot in DOS.)

Memory and Boot Scan

When you boot up your computer, Norton AntiVirus scans your memory, Master Boot Records, and Boot Records for viruses. That's because there are many viruses that try to write data to your boot records, and Master Boot Record. Although damage from this type of virus can generally be repaired by booting with Norton Emergency Disks, the virus' action makes your hard drive data unavailable, until it's fixed. Norton AntiVirus' automatic scanning at startup prevents this infection from taking place. You can, if you wish, disable Boot Scanning as part of the installation process.

> **Note:** If you have more than one hard drive, you'll have two boot records, but only one Master Boot Record. When your computer boots up, it may not detect the boot record of the second hard drive (depending on how the boot sequence is configured). In such a case, manually run a Master and Boot Scan when booting up your computer is complete. This will ensure that your additional hard drives' boot records are scanned as well.

Not only Boot viruses try to become "resident" upon startup. Many others will install themselves this way, allowing the virus to mastermind all kinds of destructive activities, arranging either a gradual chipping away at your data, or setting the stage for a major attack. Again, Norton AntiVirus' Memory and Boot Scan prevents this type of virus from getting a foothold.

Not just at startup, but any time you initiate a scan, Memory and Boot Scan will take place first. This is a necessity, because if a virus exists in memory, you cannot trust your antivirus software to behave properly. If a virus is found in memory, you'll be instructed to boot from your floppy disk (which resets memory and then bypasses any infected memory region). The floppy disk virus scanner is able to remove the virus from memory, and proceed to disinfect the rest of your system.

Understanding the Startup Scan

The Startup Scan is a fundamental virus prevention technique. Directions to carry it out are placed in your AUTOEXEC.BAT file. Here is some information about how it's implemented:

- The executable file for the Startup Scan is NAVDX.EXE, found in the C:\PROGRAM FILES\NORTON SYSTEMWORKS\NORTON ANTIVIRUS folder (unless you specified another location for Norton AntiVirus' files).

- NAVDX.EXE is referenced in your AUTOEXEC.BAT file (C:\PROGRA~1\NORTON~1\NOR-TON~2\NAVDX.EXE /STARTUP) and is run very early in the startup process.

Please note that the Startup Scan is different than the Manual Scan, which you initiate by clicking the Scan Now button on the Norton AntiVirus main interface. It's also not to be confused with a Scheduled Scan, which is set up with the Windows 98 Task Scheduler, or Norton's own Scheduler, when running Windows 95.

> **Note:** Since the Virus Scanner is invoked before Windows begins to load its drivers, long filenames in the Startup Scan path will be truncated to their DOS versions.

Auto-Protect

By default your computer is protected from viruses by Auto-Protect, which launches at startup. Auto-protect works two ways:

- Scans all program files that are run, open, copied, created, or downloaded (see Figure 9.3). When you access a file in your day-to-day computing activity, Auto-Protect examines it and sees if it bears signs of contact with known viruses. As you use your computer, Auto-Protect scours your files for virus signatures.

- Monitors your computer for virus-like activity, such as calls to rewrite executable files or format the hard drive.

This dual technique protects you from known viruses (by scanning for virus signatures) and unknown viruses (by watching for virus-like behavior anywhere on your computer).

Some antivirus products slow down your computer when running in the background. Older antivirus software could be fairly intrusive. Since executable files and program files of all types must jump through this additional hoop in order to run, a lag in perfor-

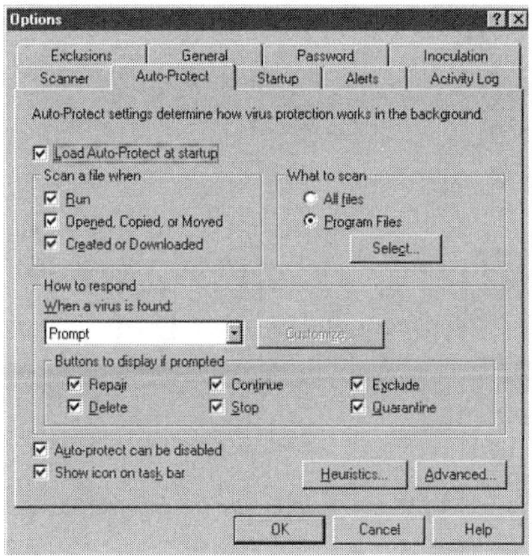

FIGURE 9.3

The Auto-Protect Options tab enables you to specify which files should be monitored.

mance would not be surprising. Using Norton AntiVirus on a Pentium 100, 133 laptop, 300 and 350MHz and a Pentium II 400MHz computer, however, I did not notice any per-

Tip: Using Norton AntiVirus' options, you can specify the type of files, and the type of activities that will trigger scanning by Auto-Protect.

formance drain while running Auto-Protect.

Adjusting Auto-Protect Sensitivity

Some legitimate activities might trigger Auto-Protect to issue a virus alert, especially those involving Word or Excel macros. Happily, you need not totally disable Auto-Protect when faced with false alerts. Norton AntiVirus allows you to adjust the sensitivity of its detection technology. Here's how it's done:

1. On the Norton AntiVirus main screen, click the Options button in the toolbar, and choose the Auto-Protect tab. The Auto-Protect Options panel opens.
2. Click the Heuristics button, and a slider appears (see Figure 9.4).
3. Drag the slider to the left to decrease the sensitivity to virus-like activity. This carries a risk of allowing a virus to slip through undetected, although minor movements to the slider are nothing to fear.
4. Moving the slider to the right makes Norton AntiVirus more sensitive to virus-like changes, and may increase the likelihood of false alerts.

Later, you'll learn how to fully customize Auto-Protect, allowing you to specify added security where needed, based on your computing habits, and not monitor areas as closely that you deem less of a risk.

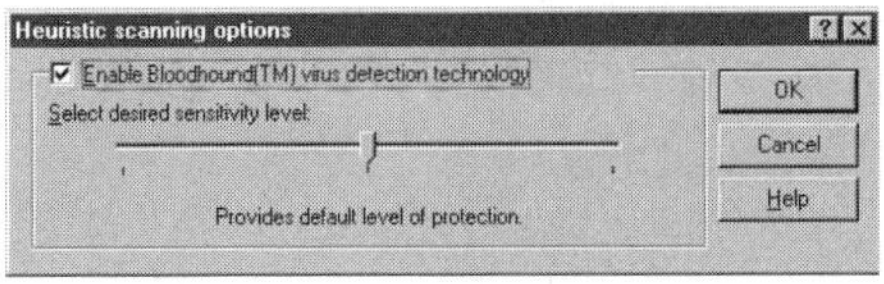

FIGURE 9.4
*Use the Heuristics
slider to alter how
sensitive the fea-
ture is.*

Updating Virus Information

The first order of business after installation is to run LiveUpdate. That's because even your AntiVirus Rescue Disks need the newest virus signatures and other updates to be of the most value to you. Also, the scanner will be more effective using the most recent data.

For downloading new data, LiveUpdate will use the connection type you choose, or search for one automatically. Most often, it's best to connect to the Internet first, and then select Find Device Automatically. For a broader understanding of LiveUpdate and the other Norton Web Services, refer to Chapter 19, "Norton Web Services: Your Current Computer."

Since the installation program automatically opens the LiveUpdate Wizard, just click Next after verifying your Internet connection. LiveUpdate will commence. If you do not have an established Internet connection through Windows Dial-Up Networking, or if you connect via an online service, you will likely want to select Via Modem, and make a short telephone call directly to the LiveUpdate server.

Downloading New Definitions

LiveUpdate indicates its progress in making a connection, and contacting the server. Once the download actually begins, a blue bar at the lower right indicates download and installation progress. This process may take a few seconds or a few minutes.

Scanning with the Newest Virus Definitions

After Norton AntiVirus downloads the update, the virus list is updated without you having to do anything else. The program reports new virus signatures that have been added. The next time you scan, you'll be doing so with the most recent set of virus signatures. Please note that, although it's a good idea to have the most recent virus lists to work with, many of the most virulent and prevalent viruses have been with us for quite some time. Don't neglect scanning just because you've not been able to download the newest virus update.

> **Tip:** In the future, to obtain a LiveUpdate, you may use the Task Scheduler, or click LiveUpdate on the Norton AntiVirus main screen.

Creating a Set of Norton AntiVirus Rescue Disks

As mentioned previously, there are three things you should do after installing. The second task is the creation of a set of Norton AntiVirus Rescue Disks (see Figure 9.5). To create them, you'll need three blank floppy disks. Just follow the onscreen directions and you'll have three disks, labeled as follows:

1. Norton Rescue Boot Disk

2. Norton AntiVirus Program Disk

3. Norton AntiVirus Definition Disk

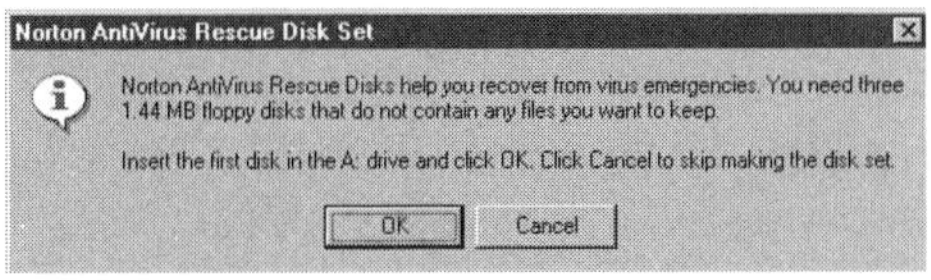

FIGURE 9.5

Norton AntiVirus guides you through the creation of three Rescue Disks.

Note: If you are going to use a Norton Zip Rescue set for your Norton SystemWorks Rescue Disks (refer to Chapter 7, "Norton Utilities: Life Preserver on a (Rescue) Disk"), you need not create a set of AntiVirus Rescue Disks. Norton AntiVirus and the latest virus definitions will be included on your Zip Rescue Disk. However, if you use floppy disks for your Norton Basic Rescue set, you must create an additional three-floppy set of AntiVirus Rescue Disks to be covered in the case of virus difficulties. A Norton Basic Rescue set contains no protection against viruses other than the ability to restore your boot record. While this may solve booting problems in the short term, you could re-infect your system easily. For this reason, I strongly suggest using Zip disks for your Norton Rescue set, or taking the time to create and maintain an additional AntiVirus Rescue Disk set.

Caution: It's very important that you remember to write-protect each floppy after the Rescue Disk is finished writing data to it. It's quite possible for an AntiVirus Rescue Disk to get contaminated by a virus. Since you know these disks will be sent right into the line of fire, make sure you write-protect them.

To begin creating your AntiVirus Rescue Disk set, select Programs | Norton | AntiVirus Rescue Disk from the Start menu. The NAV Rescue Disk program first asks if you want to do a Quick or Full format on each floppy disk before writing data on them. Quick format is faster, but Full format guarantees that your disks will be error-free (at least at the time you create them). After answering this question, just follow the prompts onscreen to create the disks.

The Rescue Boot Disk

The NAV Rescue Disk Program moves through the process asking you for each blank disk as needed (see Figure 9.6). The first disk to be created is the Norton Rescue Boot Disk. This tool will start your computer if a virus has overwritten a boot sector or Master Boot Record. It will start the computer, check the memory, boot sector, and MBR for viruses, and prompt you in due course for the other two disks containing "search and kill" data for removing viruses.

FIGURE 9.6

*You'll be prompt-
ed when to insert
each blank disk.*

For Viruses Only

It's important to point out that the Norton AntiVirus Rescue Boot Disk will not allow you to use your computer for anything else other than eliminating viruses. Booting from this disk does not provide access to an array of troubleshooting tools, other than those directly related to getting rid of viruses. If need be, you can format your drive (only as a last resort), but the Norton AntiVirus Rescue Boot Disk does not have the same function-ality as the Windows 98 or Windows 95 Startup disks.

This can be an important distinction because you may run the Norton AntiVirus Rescue Disks as directed and realize you don't have a virus. Some other malfunction, then, is causing your problem. At that point, I'd highly recommend that you reboot from your Norton Rescue Zip or Basic Rescue set. That will give you access to other key Norton SystemWorks programs which enable you to scan drives for file errors, reinstall your operating system, and look for Registry and configuration errors that could easily do as much damage as a virus.

Testing Your NAV Rescue Disk

The NAV Rescue Boot Disk has a Test file for making sure your disk will actually do what it's supposed to do in times of crises. To test it, simply open a DOS window, put the NAV Rescue Boot disk in drive A:, log on to drive A:, type the word **TEST**, and press Enter. The program will tell you if this disk can restart your system or not.

Caution: You'll have to make a new set of NAV Rescue Disks when you make a major change to your system, such as add or partition a hard drive, add a Zip drive, change a CD-ROM drive to DVD, or change operating systems. Failing to do this will restore your computer's configuration to its condition before you up-graded your system. Such a problem requires meticulous dedication to repair. So remember to make new NAV Rescue Disks any time you upgrade your computer.

The Norton AntiVirus Program Disk

The second NAV Rescue Disk is the Norton AntiVirus Program Disk, which scans your computer for viruses. Please note that the first disk, the NAV Rescue Boot Disk, will prompt you for this disk when needed.

The NAV program will load, which scans your entire hard drive for viruses. When the program is executed in such a manner, the program will run from the floppy disks executable file, but will search the Norton AntiVirus folder of drive C: to find the most recent virus definitions.

Setting Scanning Options with the NAV Program Disk

Even when scanning from the NAV Program Disk floppy, you do not have to check every single folder or file, if you'd rather be more specific. Rather then endure a prolonged scan, after inserting the NAV Program Disk into the drive, type **NAVDX /?**. A set of switches will appear giving you control over the extent of the Norton AntiVirus search.

If Your Hard Drive Disappears

Some viruses encrypt or relocate the partition table of your hard drive, and then reside in memory, so when you boot up normally, the virus takes control and tells your operating system where the "real" partition is. Thus, you can run your computer, and all the while the virus is spreading its effects, day after day, getting ready for the Payload (the attack). So, your partition table is not really where it should be, but the virus boots up in memory, and right away, locates it for you, so you can run your computer—until Payload day, of course.

However, when you boot up from a clean floppy, the virus is not loaded into memory, but your partition table is still corrupted by the virus. Without the virus in memory to tell the computer where to find the partition table, you will not see your hard drive when you boot up with a virus-free floppy disk. Nonetheless, your hard drive and its data are still "there," and all Norton AntiVirus has to do is repair the corrupted partition table (and, of course, eliminate the virus). So when you boot up with a Norton AntiVirus Rescue Disk and do not see your hard drive, just let the program make its repairs, and all will be well.

The AntiVirus Definition Disk

The third Norton AntiVirus Rescue Disk is the Norton AntiVirus Definition Disk. You cannot use it unless prompted for it by one of the other two disks. This disk contains the newest virus signature data, and supplements the NAV Program Disk with additional virus definitions that could not fit onto the NAV Program Disk floppy.

After creating these three disks, store them in a safe place, and at least every couple of months, create another set, just in case these "go bad" or become outdated.

Using Your Norton AntiVirus Rescue Disks

You would use your Norton AntiVirus Rescue disks when your computer cannot boot up and when you have reason to believe the cause is a virus. Here are some examples:

- Your computer suddenly won't boot.
- Other computers you know of have been exhibiting problems on that same day.
- Booting problems occur preceded by bizarre screen messages ("Counterwailing!" "You're an MWDF!").

If your computer begins to display odd messages at startup, or odd color sequences, should you interrupt the booting? Yes, you should. Turn off the computer, insert the first Norton AntiVirus Rescue Disk, and boot from it. Do, by all means, make sure your disk is write-protected.

Not all startup problems are caused by a virus. For example, hardware upgrades like video cards or additional hard drives can cause your computer to "hang" at startup. If you just installed a major hardware component and you have trouble booting, don't think "virus" first. First, think about jumpers on your hard drive. Improperly set jumpers on a new modem can also cause "hanging" at booting.

Sometimes, changing operating systems can cause booting problems. In such cases, resolve those problems first, before worrying about a virus. Boot problems attended by lots of hard drive "seek" noise probably have to do with a failing hard drive, or if you do not hear your hard drive cycling at all, then, unfortunately, you need look no farther than that obvious (and expensive) problem.

Scanning for Viruses

The third task you should perform after installing Norton SystemWorks—or after adding Norton AntiVirus if you didn't install it when you installed the rest of SystemWorks—is a complete virus scan. Here's how.

After installing Norton AntiVirus and using LiveUpdate, launch Norton AntiVirus from the Norton SystemWorks integrator and make sure that all of your local hard drives are checked in the Drives pane. Click Scan Now and NAV will then automatically scan all the program files on all drives for viruses (see Figure 9.7). Later, you can configure many aspects of how scanning behaves, but initially it's good to allow Norton AntiVirus to have its way with your computer, and scan what it deems necessary.

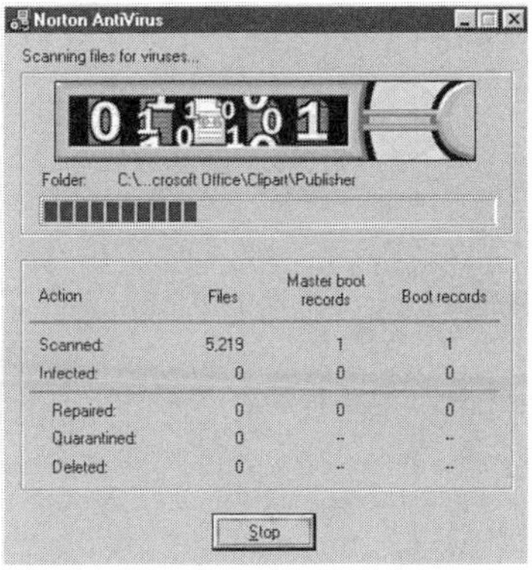

FIGURE 9.7

Norton AntiVirus indicates scanning progress and reports how many files have been scanned so far.

Note: As well as program files, Norton AntiVirus by default scans all archived files (such as Zip and Mime), Word documents, and Excel spreadsheets.

For all later scanning sessions, you can specify your own preferences. To control options for NAV scanning, click the Options toolbar button on the Norton AntiVirus main screen, and choose the Scanner tab. As shown in Figure 9.8, you'll see two groupings of options—What to scan and How to respond.

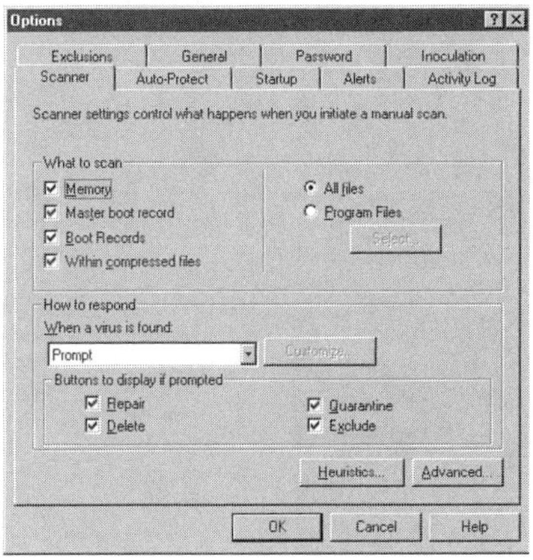

FIGURE 9.8

Change what files are scanned and how to respond to an alert with this panel of options.

Scanning Settings

There's never a reason, really, to make many changes to the left side of the What to scan panel. It's always advisable to scan memory, the Master Boot Record, and the Boot Record, as part of your scanning routine. These are key areas of infection for about half of all known viruses.

You can reduce scanning time significantly by unchecking Within compressed files. Doing so would leave ZIP, ARC, and other archived files unscanned. However, if you've recently zipped lots of files, or obtained a zipped file from a potentially unknown source, you should scan compressed files the next time you scan.

> **Caution:** Norton AntiVirus does not scan compressed files within compressed files. That means if you zipped together a collection of zipped files, nothing below that first level of compression will be scanned. For example, Java .CLASS files are often stored in compressed volumes, and must remain that way. If you download and scan a compressed Java applet or program, that second layer of compressed Java .CLASS files will not be scanned. Bear in mind, however, that NAV Auto-Protect will most likely catch any suspicious activity caused by a virus lurking down inside such doubly compressed Java files.

Choosing What Files to Scan

On the right side of the What to scan panel on the Scanners tab, you can choose to scan all files on your computer, or only program files. Please note that when you choose to scan only program files, Norton AntiVirus by default scans many types of files containing executable code, such as DOC, DOT, and CLA file types. Scanning only program files, then, does not limit antivirus scanning to COM or EXE files alone.

When you click the Program Files option, a Select button becomes available. Click it, and you can view, add, and remove types of files scanned by Norton AntiVirus (see Figure 9.9). To add a file type to the list of scanned files, click the New button, and in the window that appears, type in a file extension. You need not add a preceding period when typing it in. NAV adds it for you.

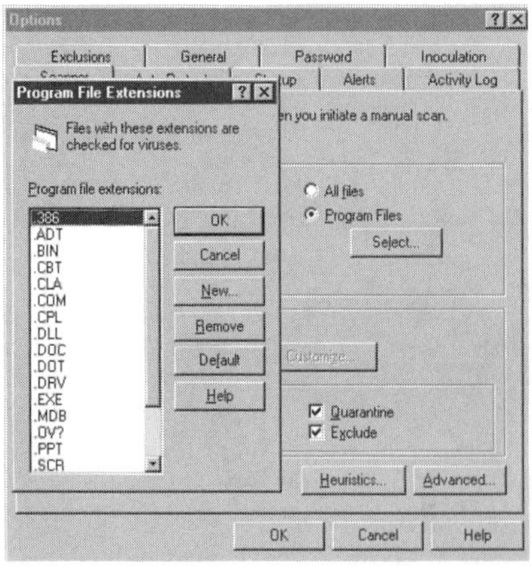

FIGURE 9.9
Add a file type to a group of files to be scanned.

Including Other Files

While Norton AntiVirus is careful to add the most common executable code-bearing files to this list, you may want to add others. Here is an example:

- Few database file types are included. Databases contain powerful executable code, and could represent the next frontier for virus creators. For that reason, if you work a great deal in Access or other database applications, you may want to add DB, DBF, and common ODBC database types to the scanning list.

Setting Up a Custom Virus Response

Scroll down the How to respond drop-down menu, and choose Custom Virus Response. The Customize button becomes available. Click it, and you'll see you can set specific response types to three virus threats: viruses in general, Macro viruses, and boot record viruses (see Figure 9.10).

FIGURE 9.10

Create a Custom Virus Response with this dialog box.

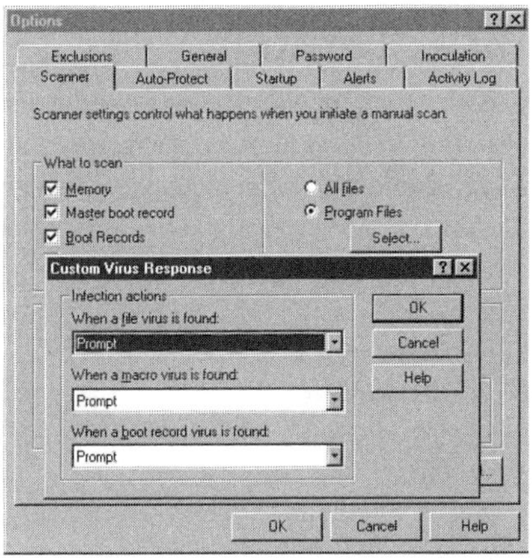

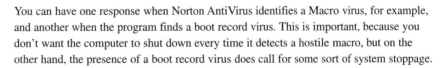

You can have one response when Norton AntiVirus identifies a Macro virus, for example, and another when the program finds a boot record virus. This is important, because you don't want the computer to shut down every time it detects a hostile macro, but on the other hand, the presence of a boot record virus does call for some sort of system stoppage.

Having a flexible response mechanism is a good idea. Your response options are: Prompt, Notify Only, Repair Automatically, Delete Automatically, Shutdown Computer, and Quarantine Automatically.

One response warranting a brief comment is Notify Only. Select this response, and a notice appears informing you that a virus alert has occurred. You'll not be offered a set of options for fixing the problem.

Setting Bloodhound Heuristics Sensitivity

Still working with the Scanner tab of the Options menu, click the Heuristics button, and you can adjust how sensitive Norton AntiVirus is to virus-like behavior (refer to Figure 9.4). At its most sensitive setting, many Word and Excel macros could trigger a virus alert, because they would appear to be opening automatically—unless you have them configured to ask permission before launching—and closing programs and changing file sizes, which could resemble virus behavior in some situations. Diminishing sensitivity too far, however, could allow subtle virus-like activity to go undetected.

Understand, though, that Bloodhound Heuristics doesn't identify and destroy known viruses. Heuristics is the science (and art) of detecting activity that could be virus-like, isolating the file that seemed to break certain rules of behavior, and telling you what just happened. When you scan for viruses, Norton AntiVirus looks at your files and compares their code to telltale code fragments of a known list of viruses. Bloodhound Heuristics will tell you when some activity is the sort of thing a virus might do.

Advanced Scanner Settings

On the Scanner tab of the Options menu, click the Advanced button at the bottom left. A dialog box appears, enabling you to allow network scanning, or to stop a virus scanning in mid-session, as shown in Figure 9.11. (If you uncheck the Allow scanning to be stopped check box, you'll later find that clicking the Stop button during a scanning session has no effect.)

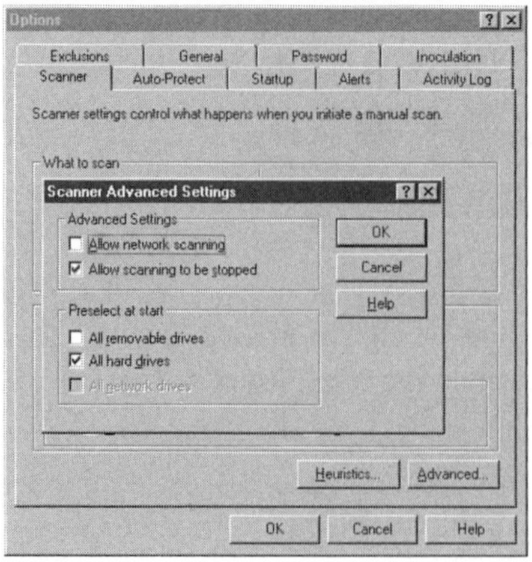

FIGURE 9.11

Scanning settings for network and other advanced options are available on the Advanced dialog box.

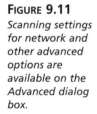

To determine what drives should be scanned when a scanning session begins, check one of the Preselect at start options. Here, the word "start" does not refer to scanning that occurs when you start your computer, but rather, determines what drives should be scanned by default during any scanning session, Manual or Scheduled.

A Virus Alert Stops Your Computer

Using the default settings, whether virus scanning has identified a virus, or Bloodhound Heuristics has detected a virus-like event, your computer's initial response will be the same. It will stop its operations. Printing jobs will pause, but usually, not be knocked out of queue. If you are downloading a file, downloading may pause, and the interruption may or may not disconnect you, depending on many factors. Most often, though, you will not be disconnected from the Internet just because a virus is detected.

However, your computer will stop, your mouse probably will not work, and you cannot use any key combination to "get around" the virus alert to deal with it later. You'll have to deal with the prompt right then and there. This is something to keep in mind when setting up your Bloodhound Heuristics Sensitivity settings. (Of course, if you've truly got a virus, stopping short is precisely what you want to do!)

While scanning, if you specify that Norton AntiVirus should simply repair or delete infected files, your computer will not stop. Norton AntiVirus will fix the problem according to your preferences and move on.

Scheduling AntiVirus Actions

After you've installed Norton AntiVirus, you're ready to integrate Norton AntiVirus into your regular computing life. We've already discussed some basics about how to set scanning file preferences, and, as you know, Auto-Protect will always run in the background unless you turn it off. Now you'll learn about scan-scheduling options. First, scheduling LiveUpdates will be discussed, followed by scheduling AntiVirus scanning.

Scheduling a LiveUpdate

When you install Norton AntiVirus on a computer with Windows 98 loaded, the program integrates LiveUpdate with the Windows 98 Task Scheduler. Rather than set up a separate scheduler, NAV works with the one already installed with your operating system. Let's review how Windows 98 Task Scheduler works. (Please note that LiveUpdate Pro, a Symantec service for locating all kinds of software patches for dozens of different programs and devices, is not used for downloading AntiVirus definitions. Make sure you are using LiveUpdate for this service, not LiveUpdate Pro.)

By clicking on the Task Scheduler icon at the lower-right of the screen (see Figure 9.12), you can see how Norton AntiVirus has already chosen scheduling options, both for obtaining a LiveUpdate, and for your next automatic virus scan. If you are happy with the program's scheduling choices, you need not do anything other than make sure your computer and modem connection are up and running at the scheduled time.

FIGURE **9.12**

The Task Scheduler is automatically loaded and appears at the lower-right of the screen.

By default, Windows 98 places Task Scheduler in the System Tray, at the bottom-right of the screen, as shown in Figure 9.15. This feature enables you to run any executable file at any time. You can schedule regular activities, like defragmenting your hard dive on a certain day every month, or even vary scheduled actions from week to week or month to month. Norton AntiVirus uses Task Scheduler to automatically schedule LiveUpdates and scan your computer for viruses.

To view the scheduled times Norton AntiVirus has chosen for LiveUpdates and AntiVirus scanning, do the following:

1. Double-click the Task Scheduler icon in the System Tray, at the bottom-right of the screen. The Scheduled Tasks dialog box appears, as shown in Figure 9.16.

2. Locate both tasks in the list, and read when they are scheduled.

3. To view both the date and time set up for these tasks, you may have to use the mouse to widen the Schedule column.

Rescheduling LiveUpdates and Virus Scans

If you'd like to set up a different time and date for Norton's automated antivirus events, double-click on either event as it appears in the Scheduled Tasks list, and the Task Scheduler for that task appears (see Figure 9.13). You'll notice three tabs: Task, Schedule, and Settings.

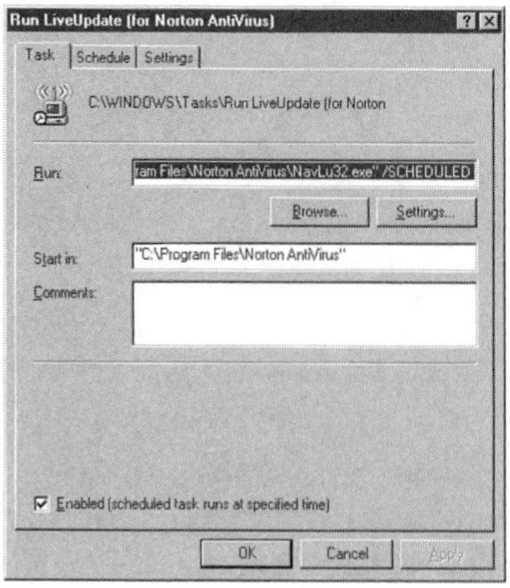

FIGURE **9.13**

Set a new schedule for any event by double-clicking on it, and its own scheduler will appear.

The Task tab simply identifies the executable file that will run at the scheduled time. You need not concern yourself with this tab, because Norton AntiVirus has already identified which tasks should occur. We'll take a closer look at the Schedule tab (see Figure 9.14), which enables you to set up precise timing of a scheduled event.

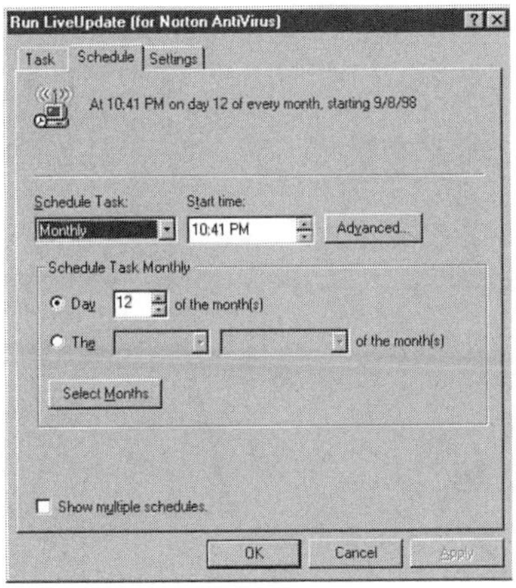

FIGURE 9.14
The Schedule tab lets you set up precise timing of events.

Click the Schedule Task drop-down menu of the Schedule tab to set up how regularly your event should occur. You can choose Monthly, Weekly, Once, At System Startup, At Logon, or When idle.

This is a convenient set of choices. For example, you can specify that a LiveUpdate should occur when you are not doing anything else (When idle), instead of trying to guess ahead of time exactly when your computer will have a free moment. Here are some important Scheduling Option features:

- If you specify When idle, a number dial appears for determining how many minutes the computer should be idle before this task takes place.

- The Start time lets you choose what time the event should occur. If you have specified When idle, At System Startup, or At Logon, the Start time option will not be available.

- Use the Schedule Task Monthly settings for either choosing a day of the month for this event, or a particular day (or days) of the week. These options will change depending on your choice of a Monthly or Weekly scheduled event.

- Some Schedule Task Monthly settings offer an Advanced button, allowing you to choose start and end dates for this task, and determining how often the task should repeat within the given date and time settings. These options won't have much bearing on regularly scheduled LiveUpdates and Virus Scans.

The Settings tab enables you to delete a scheduled task once it's finished (which has no relevance for us here), and set various power management options, such as postponing the task if the computer is on battery power at the scheduled time.

Setting Up Multiple Schedules

Still working with the Schedule tab of the Schedule Task dialog box, click the Show multiple schedules check box to set up more than one schedule for an event (see Figure 9.15). For example, choose one schedule for periods of heavy computer use, one for regular use, and one for when you are out of town.

FIGURE **9.15**

*You can set up
more than one
schedule for an
event.*

Just click the New button to create a new schedule setting. This will appear with the list of other schedules you've set up for this task. Then click the drop-down schedule menu and choose one from the list, and that schedule will govern when this event occurs.

Setting Up a LiveUpdate Connection

The simplest way to download the newest virus definitions with LiveUpdate is to already have your Internet connection open before starting the update. However, it's rather pointless to schedule an unattended LiveUpdate if you are required to be on hand to log on when the time arrives.

If you have a standard Dial-Up Networking connection, LiveUpdate will dial it for you in your absence. When you open LiveUpdate by clicking LiveUpdate on the Norton AntiVirus main screen (or from the Norton SystemWorks Integrator), you'll notice the program has already selected a connection method, and will open it automatically.

To choose a specific type of server connection and bypass LiveUpdate's Automatic Detection, click the LiveUpdate opening screen's drop-down menu labeled "How do you want to connect to a LiveUpdate server?" You can choose a server connection type from the list.

> **Caution:** LiveUpdate cannot open an America Online connection unattended. If you want to use AOL to create an Internet connection for a scheduled LiveUpdate you must use Auto AOL to set up a time for logging on to AOL in your absence, and make that time correspond with your scheduled LiveUpdate.

If you have several Dial-Up Networking connections, and you want to specify which one LiveUpdate should use, do the following:

1. Select LiveUpdate from the Norton AntiVirus main screen, and click the Options button at the bottom. The LiveUpdate Properties dialog box appears, with three tabs.

2. Click the Internet tab (see Figure 9.16). In the Modem Connection area, you'll see a drop-down menu labeled "Use this Dial-Up Networking Connection."

3. Click this drop-down menu to choose which connection LiveUpdate should use. You'll also notice that many network connection properties can be managed from this dialog box, saving you from having to hunt through your Accessories/ Communications menu to make preference changes.

4. Just like accessing this menu through the Windows Connection Wizard, click the Properties button to change the number dialed, network protocols, and other server settings.

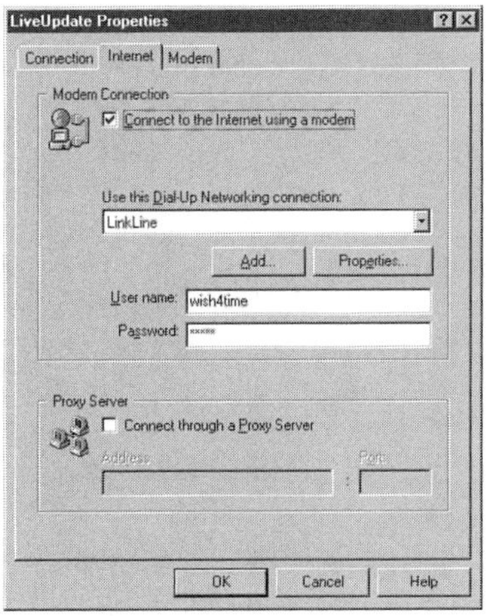

FIGURE 9.16

The Internet tab lets you set up a specific Dial-Up Networking connection.

> **Tip:** If you plan to set up a LiveUpdate to run in your absence, make sure you store your User Name and Password with your dial-up settings.

Scheduling an AntiVirus Scan

Scheduling an AntiVirus Scan works the same way as setting up LiveUpdate schedule preferences. You can accept Norton AntiVirus' defaults, or open Task Scheduler, click Virus Scan as it appears in the list, and select the Schedule tab, as outlined above. From here, make changes to the schedule settings, as discussed with LiveUpdate scheduling.

Keep Your Computer On

In scheduling an AntiVirus scanning session, you do not have to worry about dial-up preferences or Internet connections. However, your computer must be turned on for a scheduled event to occur. If you computer is turned off when a scheduled LiveUpdate or AntiVirus scan is to have occurred, all is not lost. When you turn on your computer again, you'll be given the opportunity to perform the task immediately, delete the task, or reschedule it later.

Choosing Automatic Repair

If you allow Norton AntiVirus to repair a file infected with a virus while scanning, you'll not even know of any changes to your computer until you read the Scanning Results summary at the end of the process. (Or, you can read the Activity Log later.)

Allowing Norton AntiVirus to automatically repair files is necessary for running unattended scans. If you are not at your computer to indicate a response to a virus detection, then your computer will remain inactive and the screen will display the message until you return. This defeats the purpose of an automatic, or unattended scan. Therefore, if you plan to allow Norton AntiVirus to scan for viruses while you are away, use the When a Virus is Found menu of the Scanning tab to select an automatic response. The Scanning tab appears when you click the Options button on the Norton AntiVirus main screen.

Determining Norton AntiVirus' Response to Virus Alerts

By default, Norton enables you to determine how to respond to a virus alert. You will be prompted when a virus or possible virus is detected or identified, and be given the following choices:

- **Repair the file**. This is not always successful, but if it is, then you don't have to reinstall the infected file from your source disks. It's usually worth a try.

- **Delete the file.** When Norton AntiVirus says a file is free of infection, it is free. You need not delete a file to be 100 percent sure it's uninfected. However, if you suspect the infected file is so damaged by the virus that it's more than likely unusable, save yourself some time by just deleting it.

Note: Deleting an infected file is not the same as ridding your computer of that virus. The virus may have infected other files. Deleting and disinfecting are two different processes.

- **Quarantine the file.** This places the file in Norton AntiVirus' Quarantine area, a section of your hard drive where Norton can safely store possibly infected files until you determine what to do with them.

- **Exclude the file from any further scanning.** Use this option to mark a file that you know is virus-free, but because of its nature, it keeps triggering virus alerts. For example, favorite Word macros that keep tripping virus warnings can be excluded from scanning, using this feature. As dangerous as excluding certain files is, it's far safer than simply reducing the sensitivity of Norton AntiVirus Bloodhound Heuristics to achieve the same end. Exclude files that you know are safe, rather than diminish Norton AntiVirus' ability to detect infected files in general.

You can Exclude files in a more elegant manner by using the Exclude tab, which appears when you click Options on the Norton AntiVirus main screen.

Selecting Folders or Files for Scanning

Although it's advisable to scan all your drives and folders for viruses, you can limit scanning to a particular drive, folder, path or even individual file, if you like. This is fine if you have a habit of storing all new files in one particular folder, especially new downloads. For example, at the end of your computing day, rather than scan your entire drive, you may want to scan only the newest files you've downloaded or received from colleagues. Here's how to use the Scan menu, at the top-left of the Norton AntiVirus main screen.

To limit your scan to a particular drive, folder, or path, click Scan on the menu of the Norton AntiVirus main screen (at the upper left). A drop-down menu appears with four scanning options, and the Exit command (see Figure 9.17).

FIGURE 9.17

The Scan menu is available from the Norton AntiVirus main screen.

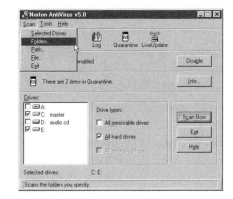

- The Selected Drives option merely scans the drives you've chosen in the main window of the Norton AntiVirus screen.

- Click Folders, and an Explorer-like Browse menu appears. Click a plus sign to expand your view of any drive or folder you want to see. Continue clicking plus signs until you've found the subfolder you want to scan. Placing a check next to a folder marks it for scanning. You can place a check by more than one folder, checking any combination of folders you like for scanning.

- Select Path from the Scan menu, and you can type in a particular path for scanning. A check box appears for scanning subfolders of the path you chose. However, there's no Browse button to make choosing a path easier. You have to type it in exactly.

- Click File from the Scan menu, and a File menu appears for choosing a particular file to scan. This is redundant, because you can scan any file on your computer from any location by right-clicking on it and choosing Scan with Norton AntiVirus from the shortcut menu that appears. You certainly don't need to open the Norton AntiVirus program and dig through a menu to scan a single file.

The ability to scan any set of folders you like is a great convenience. Rather than scan your entire hard drive, you can scan only those folders that received new files recently, perhaps a download directory or an Inbox.

Saving Customized Scan Settings for Later Use

If there are several folders you want to regularly scan, perhaps scanning them with certain options enabled, for example, zipped files only, or only files with particular file extensions, you need to employ DOS command switches. You cannot use the Norton AntiVirus Windows interface to save customized scanning options of the type just mentioned and apply them later.

To save a particular scanning set of options, for example, including only certain folders and file types in a scan, do the following:

- Open Windows Notepad, and type a command line that follows the syntax of the example below:

```
NAVW32 C:\ZENITH\*.CLA C:\NADIR\*.MDB
```

- In this example, the scanner will scan two specific paths, one is the ZENITH folder, and the other is the NADIR folder.

- In the first folder, only CLA files will be scanned. In the second folder, only MDB files will be scanned. This is another example of Norton AntiVirus' DOS command switches.

What you've done in the above example, then, is typed the scanning executable file (NAVW32) followed by command switches that modify its behavior, confining the scan to only certain folders and file types.

Now you can save this Notepad file as an executable file and create a Desktop shortcut for it. That way you can start this customized scan anytime you wish. Here's how it's done:

1. Save your Notepad file as MyScan.BAT, taking care not to save it as a TXT file.

   You may choose a name that is more descriptive rather than MyScan, but make sure you include the BAT file extension.

2. Make sure you save the file in the same folder as your Norton AntiVirus files.

   Your Notepad file is now saved as an executable batch file in your NAV folder. All you need to do now is create a path to access it conveniently from a Windows Desktop shortcut. Let's continue.

3. Right-click on your desktop and select New Shortcut. In the dialog box that appears, click Browse. The Browse dialog box appears.

4. Locate your Norton AntiVirus files, and find the MyScan.BAT file.

5. Click the MyScan.BAT file once, and then click the Open button. The file now appears in the Shortcut dialog box, ready to save.

6. Click Save, and the shortcut will appear on the desktop. Click it anytime to execute your customized scanning options, scanning only the folders and file types that you've selected.

Pausing, Aborting, and Background Scanning

Stopping a virus scan does no harm. No parsing or moving of data occurs. Therefore, it's perfectly OK to stop your virus scan and get to work quickly if you need to. Please note that if you scan using the Windows interface (by clicking the Scan Now button on the Norton AntiVirus main screen) you cannot resume scanning where you left off. Clicking the Stop button causes the Scan Results screen to appear, displaying the number of files scanned and viruses found.

If you want to scan with the options of pausing and resuming scanning, do the following:

1. Open a DOS window.

2. Type C:\PROGRA~1\NORTON~1\NORTON~2. This opens the Norton AntiVirus folder in a DOS shell, enabling you to use keyboard options that are not available from the Windows interface.

3. Type NAVDX to view the command switch options and then type GO, as the screen instructs, pressing any key to continue.

4. When you want to pause scanning, press your keyboard's Pause button. To resume scanning, press any key. The scanning program will start where it left off.

The Norton AntiVirus Scanner is not like a defragmenting program, where every time you write to a file, the utility must start again from scratch. Norton AntiVirus scanning will push onward, regardless of disk activity. Testing on a Pentium 133MHz, and a Pentium 400MHZ, I've noticed that scanning for viruses in the background while working does not seem to slow down common workday tasks.

To abort scanning while running a DOS shell, press Ctrl+C, then close the DOS window.

Manual Scanning Options

When you run a virus scanning session in DOS, you can specify what should be scanned. Using DOS command switches, direct the scanner to scan only files in a certain folder, only compressed files, for example, or to prompt before taking action against a possibly infected file. You can also set Bloodhound Heuristic sensitivity with DOS command switches as well. Every scanning option available from the Windows interface (and then some) is available by using DOS command switches executed in a DOS shell.

Examining the Virus Log

If you run unattended NAV scans, you'll want a way of knowing what the results were. Sometimes, onscreen virus scanning results windows are closed before you have a chance to read if anything was found. It's important, then, to have a record of any virus activity that was dealt with while you were away.

You can open Norton AntiVirus' Activity Log right from the main screen. It keeps an ongoing record of scans, when they were done, and what the results were. The results will be maintained in this log until you clear them. To open this log, click the Log button on the Norton AntiVirus main screen. The Activity Log appears (see Figure 9.18). The number of entries appears at the upper left. Scroll down to view all Norton AntiVirus activity that has occurred since you last cleared the log.

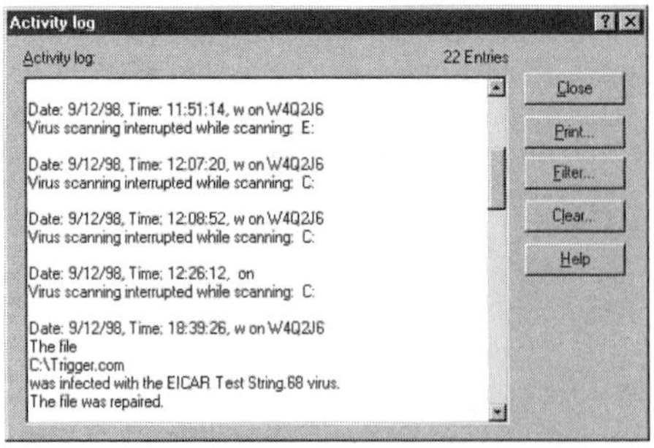

FIGURE 9.18
The Norton AntiVirus Activity Log displays the results of scans and other program actions.

You can print the log file, but oddly, you cannot save the log as a TXT file, or copy a portion of it with your mouse to the Windows Clipboard, for pasting into a word processing program. It is saved automatically as ACTIVITIES.LOG. this file can be found in the Norton AntiVirus folder, and will open in any text viewer.

If the log is too long to conveniently locate a particular date or incident you want to view, do the following:

1. Click the Filter button. The Activity Log Filter appears (see Figure 9.19).

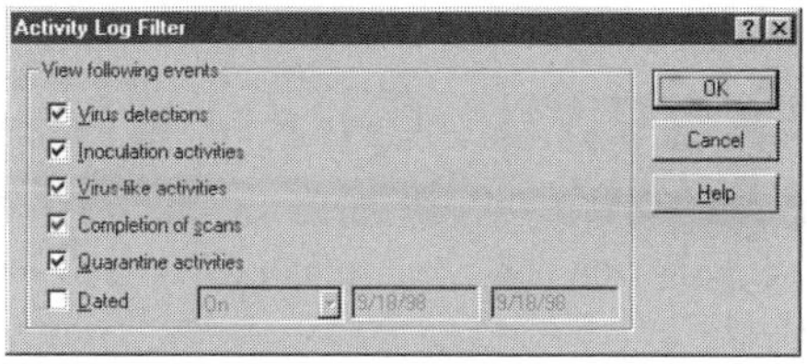

FIGURE 9.19

Filter the Activity Log to include only those events you care to see reported.

2. Remove the check next to the type of information you do not want to appear in the Log window. For example, if you are interested only in viewing virus alerts or virus-like activity, remove the check next to Completion of Scans and Inoculation Activities.

3. Use the Date Filter to limit your search to a particular time frame, if you like.

4. When you're done adjusting the settings, click OK to close the dialog box.

The Filter feature only limits what data is viewed in the log. You've done nothing to change how much data is recorded. By default, every potential virus event will be recorded in the Virus Log.

To change the data recorded in the log, perhaps making it less unwieldy to keep track of, do the following:

1. Click Options on the Norton AntiVirus main screen, and select the Activity Log tab (see Figure 9.20).

Remove the check next to any event you do not want recorded by the Log.

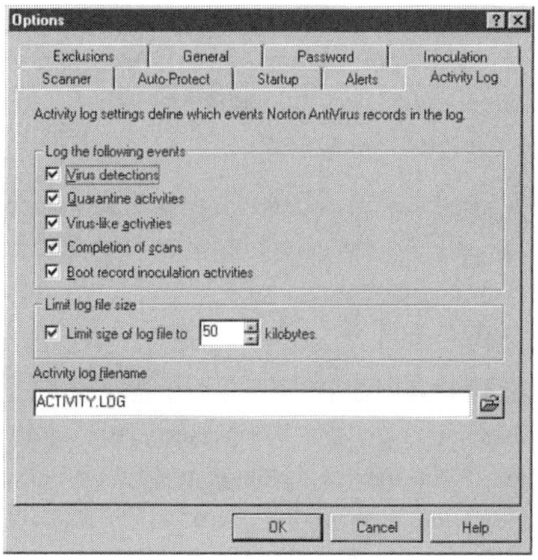

FIGURE 9.20

The Activity Log tab lets you change what data is recorded by the Log.

3. If you like, you can change the Limit Log Size number (in KB), to not allow the `ACTIVITIES.LOG` file to grow beyond a certain size.

4. To save the Log file under a different name or new location, make any changes you like in the Activity Log Filename field.

Norton AntiVirus Quarantine

Norton AntiVirus' Quarantine feature is an interesting thing. It helps occupy the space between a strange-acting file you don't want running lose, and a file that is most certainly a virus and should be killed. Not every file on your computer that makes a call to other executables should be sent to the gallows. On the other hand, you don't want to wait around for a file to show its malicious colors, and find out the truth the hard way. Norton AntiVirus Quarantine enables you to isolate a suspicious file on your computer, keeping the rest of your files out of harm's way, while you determine if it is a virus or not. In this effort, you have all of Symantec's antivirus research department behind you, literally.

Part of a Team Effort

When Norton AntiVirus quarantines a file, you can send it, via the Internet, to SARC with a single mouse-click. (SARC, Symantec's Antivirus Research Center, is where viruses are studied and where fixes are created to combat them.) Once you've submitted a suspicious file to SARC, they'll get back to you within two weeks, either with a fix to eliminate the virus, or with word that the file is safe.

This arrangement is good for everyone, and here's why. In times past, viruses were mostly created at, around, or near academic institutions. While you were off studying for your first big job at a computer firm, your lab partner could be down the hall cooking up a new virus. This proximity had a beneficial side effect: Viral contaminants spend a good deal of time in a localized environment before sprouting in Uncle Joe's computer in Peoria. Virus researchers, who also functioned in largely academic environments, had time to program a fix for a virus before they had to worry about bad news all over the country. Antivirus personnel could think like epidemiologists, localizing an outbreak before the virus became prevalent everywhere.

That was before macro viruses, which popped up in people's workplaces and homes, and were not particularly associated with academic institutions. Also, as computer interconnectivity grew, the notion of quietly isolating a virus before it could strike everywhere became old-fashioned. The ease with which Macro viruses could be created was staggering.

Antivirus Researchers had to assume, then, that non-experts might be the first to come in contact with certain viruses or virus-like files. Researchers could not count on having first crack at a virus, then make a fix available to the public before damage became prevalent. Normal computer users needed the tools to isolate a virus before their files were damaged, setting that dangerous file aside and upload it to Virus Researchers, where they could devise a fix, and make that available to the world at large.

How Quarantine Works

The Quarantine feature, therefore, makes you an integral part of Norton's Antivirus research and treatment efforts. When you quarantine and send a file to SARC for identification, you might be doing the world a big favor.

When Norton AntiVirus detects a virus, or virus-like activity, one of your choices will be to quarantine the file. When you quarantine a file, three things immediately happen:

- The file is separated from others on your hard drive. Quarantine does not leave the file where it once was; the file is physically relocated.
- A backup copy of the possibly infected file is made and stored in a backup folder in the Quarantine area.
- Neither of these files can be used or executed. Your computer is out of harm's way.

Once your file is quarantined, there are four courses of action to choose from:

- You can have Norton AntiVirus attempt to repair it. If it can be repaired, the file will then be returned to its original location.
- If the file cannot be repaired, Norton AntiVirus will suggest deletion. If you already are pretty sure the file is not usable, delete the file without trying to repair it, but you may want to give Norton AntiVirus a chance at it first.
- The file can be sent to SARC for examination. You'll be advised via email or phone within seven days regarding what to do with the file.
- You can, although this is highly ill-advised, restore the unrepaired filed to its original location.

A visit to the Quarantine area is not in your future if you simply let Norton AntiVirus attempt to repair or delete infected files. But if you decide a middle ground is needed for a file that may not be dangerous after all, then Quarantine is the answer. If you do quarantine a file, of course, you'll have to open the Quarantine screen to determine its fate.

When you've authorized Norton AntiVirus to quarantine a file, click the Quarantine button on the main program screen, and the Quarantine screen appears.

You'll see Explorer-like windows with folders on the left and files within the folders on the right. The three folders on the right contain quarantined files, backups, or files that have been sent to SARC for examination.

Click the Quarantined Items folder on the left, and any files you've quarantined will appear on the right. This list can get quite long, if quarantine is your usual first course of action against viruses.

Click Backup Items, and all the files Norton AntiVirus has made backups of will appear on the right. The program not only makes backups of quarantines, but any file manipulated by Norton AntiVirus. All files identified as possibly infected, whether a repair was successful or not, will appear in this backup area.

The Resurrected File

Before Norton AntiVirus does anything to a file, it creates a copy in a backup folder of the Quarantine Area. Any changes the program makes to a file can be undone, in a sense, by restoring the backup of the file that Norton AntiVirus had an issue with. This can be helpful if, for example, Norton AntiVirus detects a virus-infected file, tries to repair it, and cannot. Alas, the file must be deleted. Then soon afterward, Norton AntiVirus distributes a fix for that particular virus. After downloading new virus definitions via LiveUpdate, go ahead and try again to repair the infected backup copy with the newly updated definitions. You may get your file back, after all.

Click Items Submitted to SARC, and on the right will appear any file you've sent to Symantec to be examined.

Examining a Quarantined File's Properties

Still working with the Quarantine main screen, double-click on any file on the right side of the screen, and its Properties panel appears (see Figure 9.21). You'll see two tabs: General and Client Info.

- The General tab tells you the filename, size, submission status (have you sent it to SARC yet?), and quarantine date. The General tab also has a Recommendation area. Here, Norton AntiVirus advises you on what to do with this file.
- The Client Info tab tells you the computer user's name, computer name, and domain. This information is more relevant in a networked environment.

You need to know how to look up information about a file as explained here, because you'll not be able to access a Quarantined file any other way.

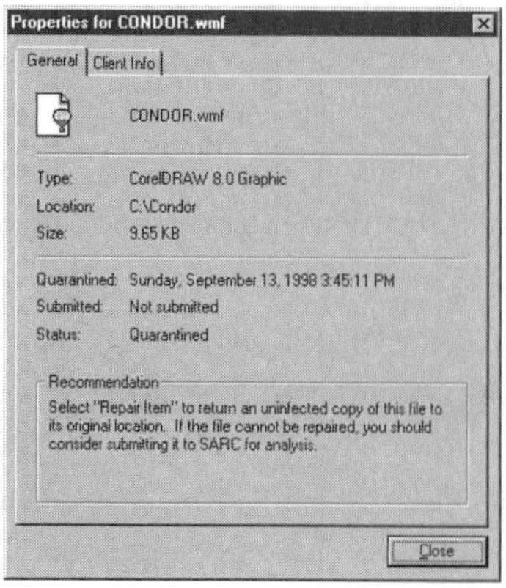

Figure 9.21

While a file is in Quarantine, you can view its properties.

Viewing the Quarantined File List

If you only have a few files in this Quarantine list, it's not much trouble to scroll through them and find one that might offer a clue about where a virus came from, or the type of files initially infected by a virus.

However, if Norton AntiVirus finds that many of your files have been contaminated and you opt to quarantine them, rather than attempt a repair right then and there, then your Quarantine list can grow very long. You'll need some way of viewing files you think are most important in accessing what is going on in your computer.

Changing Your View of Quarantined Files

To change how files are arranged in this list, right-click on any file on the right side of the screen, and choose Arrange Icons. Arrange the files using any of the six criteria listed for viewing order. For example, you can view them by Location, helping determine which programs of yours were hit hardest by this virus, or by Virus Type, which would indicate if more than one virus were to blame.

Working with Files in Quarantine

The toolbar at the top of the Quarantine screen enables you to repair files (see Figure 9.22), and if the repair is successful, the file can be restored to its original location. If not successful, it can be deleted, using the same toolbar. Just click once to select any file on the right side of the screen, and click the toolbar icon to carry out a particular task.

FIGURE 9.22

The Quarantine screen has a toolbar offering various file options.

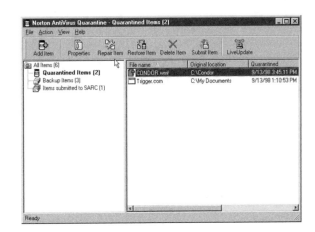

Here are some tasks carried out using the Quarantine toolbar:

- While selecting a file, click the Restore button at the top of the screen, and that file will be returned to its location, whether it has been repaired or not. Understand, though, that this is very unadvisable. You should allow Norton AntiVirus to give a file a clean bill of health before restoring it.

- You can add a file to Quarantine, even if it has not been directed there by Norton AntiVirus. Just click the Add Item icon on the Quarantine toolbar (top of the screen, and to the left). A Browse menu appears, enabling you to search your hard drive and select any file you wish to quarantine. Remember that doing so will make this file unavailable to you for use.

- To delete a file, just click the Delete Item button on the toolbar, and it will be gone. Remember, you do have a backup as well. An unrepairable file, as well as its backup, should be considered potentially dangerous to your system, and ought to be deleted.

Sending a File to SARC

The Symantec Antivirus Research Center will examine and report back to you on any file, letting you know if the file is infected with a virus and making recommendations. It might then refer you to the LiveUpdate features, to download a virus signature for destroying the virus.

To submit a file to SARC, do the following:

1. Click a file for sending on the right side of the Quarantine window.

2. Next, click the Submit Item icon, on the toolbar. You'll see a screen introducing SARC's *Scan and Deliver* service. Click Next to continue the submission process.

3. The next few screens will ask you to supply your name, email address, and phone information, and verify the file you want to send. Click Next to continue.

4. You'll then be asked to describe the problem and specify if you want Symantec to try to strip text and other salvageable data from the file (see Figure 9.23).

FIGURE 9.23
Be prepared to describe the problem the file caused.

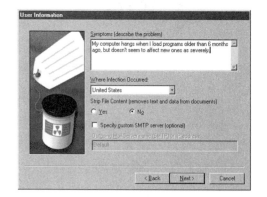

5. After confirming the accuracy of your contact information, click Next one final time to submit the file. Have your Internet connection open beforehand.

6. A blue bar appears, indicating upload progress. When finished, a confirmation screen appears, indicating that you'll receive a response within two business weeks regarding your file.

Once a file is uploaded to SARC, it's best just to leave the file alone until the results are reported. You'll receive an email with a confirmation number and some follow-up data in about two days.

> **Tip:** Some files will be rejected for submission to SARC, even before you get very far in the process. Most often, the reason will be that the file is infected by a known virus and there is no reason to submit it.

Using the Virus List

The Virus List, available from the Norton AntiVirus main screen, provides basic information about all known viruses. Once a virus is identified on your computer, it can be helpful (after all is repaired) to read a little about what nearly attacked your computer. Currently, the entire list is over 11,000 entries long, and would not make for inspiring reading without some sort of lead. If you want to learn a little about a virus, its type, and how and where it attacks, use this list to look it up. Each virus reference contains only a sentence or two. (For a primer on viruses in general, take a look at Appendix E.)

Scroll down the Virus List, arranged alphabetically, to locate an entry, and double-click on it to view its properties (see Figure 9.24).

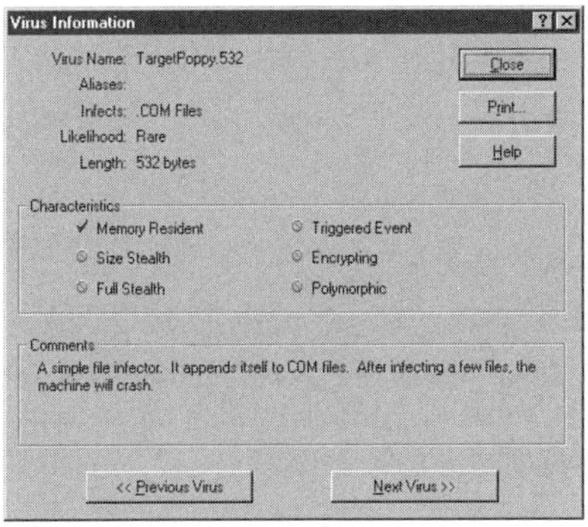

FIGURE 9.24
Double-click on any virus in the list to view its properties.

To narrow the list so it includes only certain types of viruses, making your search easier, click the Display drop-down menu. This is helpful if you know the type of virus you are looking for, such as Boot, Program, or Common Viruses.

A Speedy Virus Search

The fastest way to look up a virus is to click any name, and just start typing it (regardless of the name you clicked on, type any name you like). The name you are typing will appear in a small field window next to the list. The list will automatically scroll to the name you are typing, if the virus exists. You can be sure, though, that if Norton AntiVirus has reported an infection by a particular virus, then it will certainly be found in the Virus List. The Virus List is updated every time you run a LiveUpdate.

More Detailed Virus Information

If you'd like to learn more, check out the Symantec Virus Research Center's Virus Encyclopedia (`http://www.symantec.com/avcenter/vinfodb.html`). Here, you can look up any virus alphabetically, and obtain detailed information.

Also, point any search engine to seek the phrase "types of viruses," and you'll find plenty of detailed descriptions.

Customizing Norton AntiVirus Preferences

You can control many Norton AntiVirus features, personalizing your virus protection to meet your own needs. Click the Options button on the Norton AntiVirus main screen to reveal nine tabs for adjusting Norton AntiVirus settings.

> **Caution:** Take care in making changes to Norton AntiVirus defaults. Too much tinkering, and you could end up with far less antivirus protection than you may need.

We've already explored the Scanner tab, specifying the types of files Norton AntiVirus should scan, and how to deal with a possible virus, when an alert is triggered. You learned about changing Activity Log preferences earlier, as well.

We've also briefly discussed Auto-Protect, which constantly monitors your system for virus-like activity. Now you'll learn about Auto-Protect options in more detail. After discussing Auto-Protect, you'll learn all the ways you can customize Norton AntiVirus.

Auto-Protect Day to Day

Use the Auto-Protect Options tab to specify if a file should be scanned when it is run, created, moved, copied, or any of the above (see Figure 9.25). Auto-Protect Options let you determine how to respond to a virus, enabling the program to repair any possibly infected file without consulting you first, or prompting you before Norton AntiVirus makes any change whatsoever to your files.

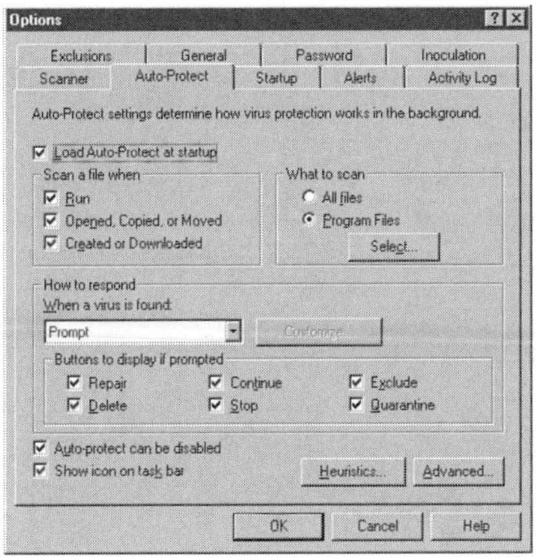

FIGURE 9.25

Set Auto-Protect options from its own Options tab.

Like the scanning options you are able to set, Auto-Protect can monitor all the files on your computer, or only program files. Remove the check next to Load Auto-Protect at Startup if you don't want antivirus protection when you boot up. This, however, is highly unadvisable, since many viruses become resident and infect boot sectors at startup.

Use the When a Virus is Found drop-down menu to automatically repair or quarantine an infected file, rather than prompt you for an action. There are many options here. For example, Norton AntiVirus can merely notify you that a virus was found, delete the infected file without further ado, or Quarantine the file only if the program cannot repair it.

Startup Options

The Startup tab enables you to remove certain file types from the list of those scanned at startup. As mentioned, this is highly unadvisable. If your computer reports an error when trying to scan for viruses at startup, it's best to try to fix that error, rather than simply go without this vital protection. See the section, "Troubleshooting Common Norton AntiVirus Errors," later in this chapter.

Besides allowing you to bypass scanning certain file types on startup, the Startup tab also enables you to specify bypass keys as shown in Figure 9.46. Use these keys to occasionally bypass Virus scanning at startup, should you ever need to.

Alert Options

The Alerts tab governs these four settings:

- Add a message to Norton AntiVirus onscreen Virus Alert (see Figure 9.26).

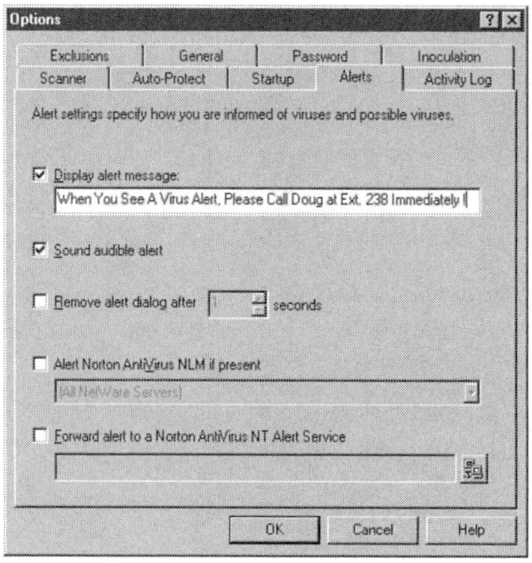

FIGURE 9.26
Alert options enable you to customize what the screen says when a virus alert occurs.

- Add or remove the audible alert (the Windows Exclamation sound if you have a sound card, or a beep if you don't).
- Specify that the Alert dialog, with its choices for actions, should be removed after a certain amount of seconds. This last option should be used with caution, because if a virus alert occurred during an unattended scan, you'll have no way of knowing why your computer "just stopped," if the onscreen Alert dialog is not there.
- Automatically broadcast virus alerts to a Norton AntiVirus Network Alert service, if you are working with one.

Exclude Options

Exclude is a powerful set of options to be used sparingly. It enables you to specify certain files to be excluded from triggering alerts because of certain behavior. Figure 9.27 shows the default files Norton AntiVirus excludes from certain behavior triggers. As you can see, most Microsoft Office application startup files are granted some sort of exclusion.

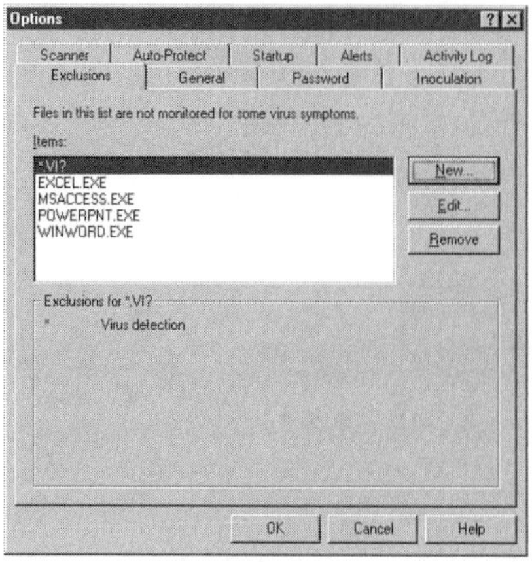

FIGURE 9.27
The Exclusions tab lets you specify what file types to exclude from Virus scans.

Please note that this exclusion does not necessarily mean you are allowing certain files to go undetected for viruses. Rather, you can allow some programs to write to other programs or change DOS read-only attributes, or other types of behavior that would normally send the virus police to your door.

Looking at the Exclusions panel in Figure 9.27, notice that when you click on a file, the lower part of the panel displays the type of behavior that is excluded from checking. You can add files to this exclusion list, perhaps a favorite Word macro of yours that is always tripping the panic wire. If you are sure the file is not hostile, just add it to the exclusions list, and use the check boxes to specify the type of behavior that you'll accept from this file (see Figure 9.28).

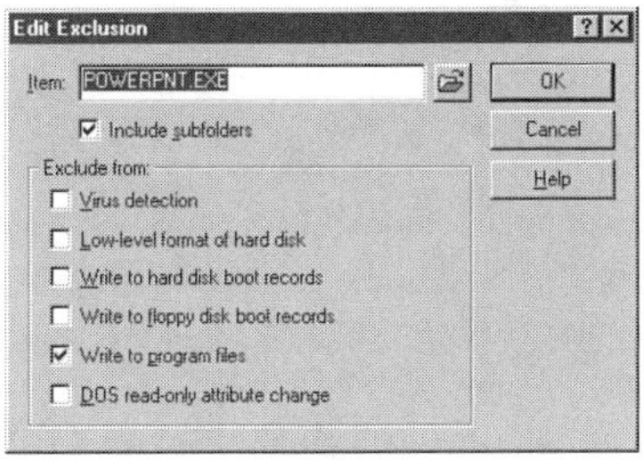

FIGURE 9.28

Use these check boxes to specify what type of behavior is enabled for these chosen file types.

Look closely at the check box selections. As you can see, Norton AntiVirus is giving you a powerful excluder here. You can allow certain files to low-level format your hard drive or write to disk boot records. Be careful in granting such permission.

> **Caution:** Norton AntiVirus already allows your operating system files to perform such tasks. Donít use the Exclude feature liberally. You may be too generous by granting many files the power to alter your system.

Double-click on any of the default files in the exclusion list. You'll see a screen appear for adding or removing allowable behaviors. Norton AntiVirus only allows these excluded files to write to program files (a check appears by that entry, indicating such behavior is acceptable). No other exclusions are needed.

Inoculation Options

Before you learn about Inoculation options, we'll discuss how Inoculate works.

When a virus infects critical boot sector areas of your hard drive, your data is unavailable. To prevent this, Norton AntiVirus records boot sector and partition table information, and if a virus tries to write to those areas, the program can immediately detect a change and repair the problem. This process is called inoculation. Norton AntiVirus includes other vital startup information in this Inoculation Record as well. Thus, when a file tries to write to one of these critical areas, Norton AntiVirus knows what to do.

However, there are many benign activities that can trigger an inoculation alert. After all, Norton AntiVirus is not sure if a virus is trying to alter your boot record, or some legitimate activity is afoot. For example, changing operating systems, installing software that reconfigures your startup files and installing hardware could each cause Norton AntiVirus to generate unnecessary alarms. For this reason, the Inoculation tab enables you to specify how to respond to events that trigger an inoculation alert.

How to Respond to an Inoculation Alert

Two of the options you can select are straightforward enough: Stop and Continue. Stop enables you to stop the computer operation taking place at the time the inoculation alert occurred. This gives you free moments to figure out what to do. Since your computer already pauses because of the inoculation alert, the Stop option is not applicable.

Click Continue to go on your merry way, without making any changes to your files whatsoever. Continue could also be called "Ignore."

It's important, though, that you understand the difference between the other two options: Repair and Inoculate. Let's back up first and examine what triggers an inoculation alert.

Repair or Inoculate?

After Norton AntiVirus records boot record information and other startup files, your computer is inoculated against boot sector viruses. Norton AntiVirus can quickly restore correct boot sector and startup information, should a virus tamper with those files. When a program changes your startup or boot record information for legitimate reasons, Norton AntiVirus will issue an inoculation alert, letting you know that a program has made such alterations. If you just installed a new operating system, a major software suite or perhaps a new hard drive, you will of course know that a legitimate program made changes to the boot records and startup files.

The two active choices the inoculation alert presents you with are used for very different purposes: Inoculate and Repair. Here's the rule:

- When a program has made legitimate changes to your files, select Inoculate when an alert appears.
- When an unknown or unplanned change has triggered the alert, perhaps a virus or malicious program of some sort, the correct response would be Repair.

Choosing Repair will restore your boot information to what it was before the change occurred. Choosing Inoculate updates the Inoculation Record to reflect the new operating system or hardware you installed. For this reason, I think it might be a little clearer to think of the Inoculation option as though it were labeled Update Inoculation.

Remember, though, that when making legitimate changes to your system that involves altering to the boot records or startup files, an Inoculation Alert will be triggered nonetheless.

Caution: If you were to install new hardware or a new operating system, thus triggering an inoculation alert, choosing Repair would be dangerous. Doing so will undo important changes made to your startup files by the new software or hardware.

The Inoculation tab enables you to determine what should happen after an inoculation alert. Use the drop-down menu to either be prompted to respond to the alert, or to simply notify you that an inoculation alert has occurred.

The Inoculation path field enables you to change the folder where the Inoculation Records are stored. By default, this information is stored in the \NCDTREE folder.

Password Options

The Password tab of the Options menu enables you to assign passwords to any or all of Norton AntiVirus' user-initiated functions (see Figure 9.29). By default, there is no password assigned to any Norton AntiVirus user action. Using this tab, check the Password Protect box, and Password options will no longer appear gray.

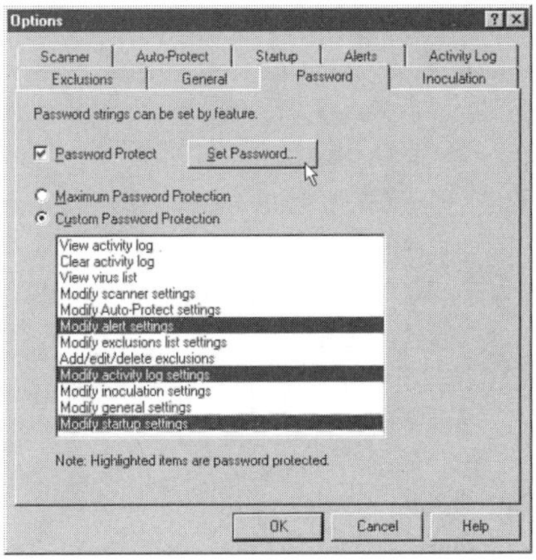

FIGURE 9.29

You can assign passwords to any critical Norton AntiVirus action, and some non-critical ones, as well.

You'll notice two options for determining what actions passwords should be assigned to:

- The Maximum Password Protection option disallows any user-initiated activity without a password.
- The Custom Password Protection option assigns a password to activities of your choosing, perhaps Modify Alert Settings and Modify Startup Settings. This would allow other users to perform some tasks, but none that are system-critical.

Please note that when choosing multiple actions for password protection in this list, you do not have to press the Ctrl key at the same time. Just click as many tasks as you want to protect with a password.

Troubleshooting Common Norton AntiVirus Errors

What follows is some general help for broad classifications of errors that may occur when using Norton AntiVirus.

Cannot Find a File or Files

If your computer reports that it cannot find Norton AntiVirus scanning files at startup, it could be because you loaded Norton AntiVirus on an external drive or partition that does not load its drivers until after Norton AntiVirus tries to scan. The command to scan for viruses is placed early in the startup process. Some secondary drives may not have been loaded yet.

If you installed Norton AntiVirus on that secondary drive, your AUTOEXEC.BAT file will try to locate the files to begin the virus scan, but will not be able to. That's because the drive on which they reside has yet to be loaded. To fix this, reinstall Norton AntiVirus on your C: drive.

Startup Errors

If you've installed Norton AntiVirus and then encounter an error when starting your computer, the solution greatly depends on your operating system. Symantec offers many types of troubleshooting assistance, and the answers you receive will be specific to the version of Windows (or even DOS) that you are running.

For example, to solve one particular Windows 95 and 98 startup error, the Symantec Troubleshooting instructions would require you to add a specific line to your CONFIG.SYS file (a common fix is to add DEVICE=HIMEM.SYS /M:1), as well as your AUTOEXEC.BAT file (SET DOS16M=2). This solution eliminates one particular memory addressing problem at startup. However, Windows 3.1, Window 95, 98, and NT often each require different solutions for these types of problems.

Visiting the Symantec Troubleshooting Page

If you experience Norton AntiVirus errors, visit *Symantec's Norton AntiVirus Troubleshooting* Web page at www.symantec.com/techsupp/nav.html. Helpful fix-its are always being added to Norton AntiVirus' online collection of tips and answers. Many provide solutions to troubles installing the newest version of Norton AntiVirus over an older one, specific video cards that need coaxing to display virus alerts, and the need to free up specific memory page addresses so Norton AntiVirus can work properly. The Frequently Asked Questions and Knowledge Base sections are particularly helpful and clearly organized.

You can, of course, call Symantec Tech Support. The numbers and hours of support are located at the back of the manual.

Peter Norton

Norton Utilities: More Than a Mirror, an Image

You've already begun to see how thoroughly Norton SystemWorks has integrated all of the components of the Norton Utilities. System Doctor monitors the health of nearly every aspect of your PC, helping you prevent problems from occurring and solving them when they do. But many of the key features of the various utilities are aided in their duties by a powerful tool you might not have even noticed—a tool, nevertheless, that you can really benefit from understanding. That tool is called Image.

With the help of Image, and the data it stores in files known reasonably enough as Image files, severe damage to your disks can be prevented, and even undone. Knowing how Image works and how it can be configured to work for you can mean the difference between disaster and security.

The Changing Image

The functioning of Image is rather straightforward, although there are a number of different ways in which the Image files are eventually used. For the purposes of this discussion, assume you have Image configured with its default settings (you'll read later in this chapter about how to modify those settings to best suit your needs and desires).

In fact, Image creates a set of three Image files, into which different but equally vital data is stored. These files will, by default, reside in the root directory of each Imaged drive. The files—IMAGE.DAT, IMAGE.IDX, and IMAGE.BAK—work with each other and the rest of the Norton Utilities to provide the highest possible level of drive security. Whenever Image runs, all three files are updated to ensure that no incompatibilities exist between them. With the Norton System Doctor Image Sensor enabled, the status of your Image files is monitored, and the files are updated automatically whenever the data is more than one day old.

Image File Contents

What exactly, then, is stored in the Image files? Each time Image runs, a copy of your drive's boot record, file allocation tables, and root directory is copied to the IMAGE.DAT file. At the same time, any old Image data is copied into the IMAGE.BAK, or backup, file. This way, if you allow a damaged disk to be re-imaged, you can still retrieve the valid information from the backup file. Finally, the IMAGE.IDX file records the location of the other two Image files, so that the Norton Utilities can locate your Image files even if your drive's FAT or root directory have been damaged. The IMAGE.IDX file is always stored at the very end of the disk, so that Rescue Recovery can locate it, even if the file allocation table has been obliterated.

Each piece of data in your image file is important. The boot record contains absolutely vital information about your drive. Even a drive that never starts up or "boots" your computer has a boot record. Every physical drive has its own Master Boot Record, which keeps track of how the drive has been partitioned into one or more logical volumes. This information, known as the partition table, is responsible for keeping track of the fact that, for example, your 6GB-capacity physical drive has been partitioned into two 3GB logical drives. If this information is lost, the logical drives on the damaged physical disk will become useless. Additionally, each physical drive's Master Boot Record contains information telling your computer's BIOS (basic input-output system) which partition—known as the active partition—has the operating system stored on it.

In addition to each physical drive's Master Boot Record, each logical drive contains its own boot record. Just as the Master Boot Record keeps track of how the physical disk is configured, at the most all-encompassing level, each logical drive's boot record contains a computer-readable description of how that logical drive has been formatted. Among the pieces of information stored here are the number of physical platters that exist inside your hard drive, how many tracks are on each platter, how many sectors exist within each track—as well as the total number of sectors on the disk—and the number of sectors that together form a cluster. You'll read more about all of these structures in Chapter 12, "Norton Utilities: The Laying-On of Hands and Norton Disk Editor." These pieces of information can vary from operating system to operating system, and incorrect data in a drive's boot record will render the drive inoperable. If the logical drive has been configured as a bootable drive—for example, a drive that has been set up to function as C:/ under Windows 95 or 98—that drive's boot record will also contain a very small piece of code. This code is known as the bootstrap loader, and it is a very tiny program that tells your PC how to begin loading the operating system off the bootable drive. If you'd like to know more about exactly what takes place each time your PC boots, take a look at the following technical note.

Image stores a duplicate copy of each Imaged drive's boot record in that drive's Image file, guarding against a number of serious data threats which you'll read about in a moment.

The process through which your PC starts up and makes itself ready for you to work with is commonly referred to as booting. The term is believed to have originated in the antique notion of "pulling oneself up by one's own bootstraps"—that is, achieving one's goals entirely through one's own talents, skills, and efforts. It certainly applies to what a PC does when it is first powered-up.

On every PC's motherboard resides a chip—or set of chips—known as the ROM BIOS (read-only memory, basic input-output system). In most cases today, the expression "ROM" is somewhat of a misnomer, because most BIOS chips are now capable of being written to, allowing the motherboard manufacturer to support new features or fix bugs in the original BIOS itself. In general, the BIOS is the hardware-based program responsible for controlling all of the different components inside your PC. Along with another part of the motherboard—the CMOS (complementary metal-oxide semiconductor)—the BIOS keeps track of what ports exist on your PC, what types and configurations of hard drive exist, and what resources are available to service the needs of these and all other components. Most modern BIOSs are known as Plug-and-Play BIOSs, which means they are now capable of detecting Plug-and-Play compatible cards and devices and allocating resources to each of them well before the operating system ever loads. This system is far from foolproof, as anyone who has installed a new device into a PC will tell you, but under ideal circumstances, the Plug-and-Play BIOS sets the stage for a Plug-and-Play compliant operating system, like Windows 98, to be entirely self-configuring.

What is really interesting about the BIOS, for the purposes of this discussion, is a small piece of code, known reasonably enough as the boot program. When power is applied to your PC, the system has enough intelligence—just enough—to locate the boot program in the BIOS and start it running. The boot program is responsible for checking the status of a variety of devices, including the Power-On Self-Test, or POST, of which we users see only the quick run-through system memory. The POST enables the PC to verify that all of its most basic components are present and functioning properly. Having completed successfully, the boot program proceeds to carry out a user-configurable instruction. In general, your PC is probably set up to look for a disk in your primary floppy drive, and boot from it if one is present. This configuration allows you to start your PC from the floppy if your primary hard drive has failed. If no floppy drive is present—or if the user has configured the PC to not look for floppy drives—the boot program then identifies the Master Boot Record on the physical hard disk which appears first on the IDE bus. As you read earlier, the Master Boot Record identifies which partition of the drive contains a bootable operating system and directs the boot process to look at that bootable partition's own boot record for the bootstrap loader. The bootstrap loader begins the process of loading your OS—Windows 95, Windows 98, Windows NT, whatever the case may be—and the process finally completes, with you being presented with your familiar desktop.

In addition to a drive's boot record, Image also stores a copy of that drive's file allocation tables. You will read more about the file allocation tables, or FATs, in Chapter 12, which discusses Norton Disk Editor. Briefly, the file allocation tables are responsible for maintaining the location of every part of every file on your drive. When the operating system wants to retrieve a file from disk, it looks to the FAT to determine where on the drive—that is, in which cluster—that file begins. The OS continues to follow the FAT through a structure known as a cluster chain, identifying where each next cluster's worth of data is located. Finally, the operating system will encounter an End-Of-File marker in the FAT, telling it that the entire file has been located and read into memory. As you might imagine, and as you will read about in Chapter 15, regarding the Norton Optimization Wizard and Speed Disk, errors in your drive's FAT can make your data just as inaccessible as errors in your drive's boot record. Without the FAT, your hard drives are just endless, nested rings of magnetically recorded pulses—gibberish. Imagine looking through a room containing thousands of filing cabinets, with no guide as to how the files have been placed in those cabinets, and you've got a pretty good sense of what your hard drive is like without its FAT.

Finally, Image records a copy of your hard drive's root directory. The root directory consists of all files or folders that can be described accurately by placing their name directly after the drive's identifying letter; that is, `c:\` describes the root directory of drive `c:`, and `C:\COMMAND.COM` refers to a file in the root directory, while `C:\WINDOWS\` refers to a folder which exists off the root. Take a look at Figure 10.1 for a graphic representation of this structure.

Figure 10.1

The root directory consists of all your top-most files and folders, with all subfolders branching away from it.

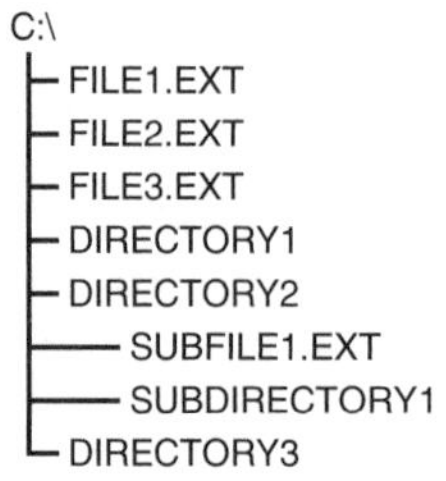

```
C:\
 ├─ FILE1.EXT
 ├─ FILE2.EXT
 ├─ FILE3.EXT
 ├─ DIRECTORY1
 ├─ DIRECTORY2
 │    ──── SUBFILE1.EXT
 │    ──── SUBDIRECTORY1
 └─ DIRECTORY3
```

All items which directly connect with C:\ (FILE1.EXT, FILE2.EXT, FILE3.EXT, DIRECTORY1, DIRECTORY2, and DIRECTORY3) are in the root directory. SUBFILE1.EXT and SUBDIRECTORY1 are not in the root directory, but are in its subdirectory, DIRECTORY2.

The content stored in the root directory is vital to maintaining the operating system's awareness of the logical structure you have set up on your drives. The folders you or your applications create contain the names, sizes, and locations of every file, or subfolder, contained within that folder (along with some other data, as well). All of the long filenames you create within Windows 95 or 98 are also maintained within folder entries in, or branching away from, your root directory. Damage to the root directory can render every piece of data on your drives inaccessible.

Keep Your Image File Current

As you probably intuitively sense, given the highly sensitive nature of the data stored within your Image files, it is vital that the files be kept up-to-date. To illustrate this, consider the implications of an antiquated Image file. You'll be learning in a moment how various pieces of the Norton Utilities and SystemWorks actually use Image files. For now, just consider that the Image files can help restore accidentally deleted folders. On Monday, you Image your hard drive and then begin reorganizing your files. You create a number of new folders in which to place them, and you also install a number of new programs, each of which creates one or more of its own folders. Life is wonderful until Thursday evening, when something causes damage to your root directory, and all of your folders and files vanish. Yes, your Image files will help you restore the drive—but only to the condition the drive was in when the Image files were created. For this reason, it's of the utmost importance to keep your Image files as current as possible. Fortunately, Norton SystemWorks can automate the entire process for you.

Configuring Image

Configuring Image is amazingly straightforward and after Image is properly configured, its operation is something you'll never notice again until you are thanking the program for existing after you have a massive drive failure. But, like performing backups, the easiest tasks are often the easiest tasks to ignore until it's far too late. I'd recommend you read this section while sitting at your computer, and that you configure Image as you read how to do just that. Unless your needs or your drive configuration changes, you'll never have to do this task again if you do it now.

Image really consists of two pieces, the Image program itself, and the Image Sensor in Norton System Doctor. When you first installed Norton SystemWorks, Norton System Doctor was installed and activated, but the Image sensor for your C: drive was not enabled. The Disk Health sensor, which you read about in Chapter 3, "Norton Utilities: The System Doctor Is In," and which is enabled within System Doctor by default, includes the Image tests in its arsenal. However, you will likely want to re-verify your Image data more frequently than you will want to perform the other Disk Health tests. For this reason, I recommend that you enable the Image sensor in addition to the Disk Health Sensor. If you have more than one drive on your PC, I strongly urge you to configure the Image sensor for all drives. To reactivate the Image sensor for your primary drive, click on the Sensors menu in Norton System Doctor.

> **Note:** If System Doctor is not running, you may launch it by selecting Programs | Norton Utilities | Norton System Doctor from your Start menu, or by double-clicking on the Norton SystemWorks icon on your desktop, and then selecting Norton Utilities | Preventative Maintenance | Norton System Doctor.

You've already read in Chapter 3 about all of the different sensors available to System Doctor, so here, you can simply select the Disks menu entry, and then select Image from the bottom of the pop-up menu. The sensor will appear and add itself to your System Doctor panel, as in Figure 10.2.

FIGURE 10.2
The Norton System Doctor Panel with Image Sensor enabled.

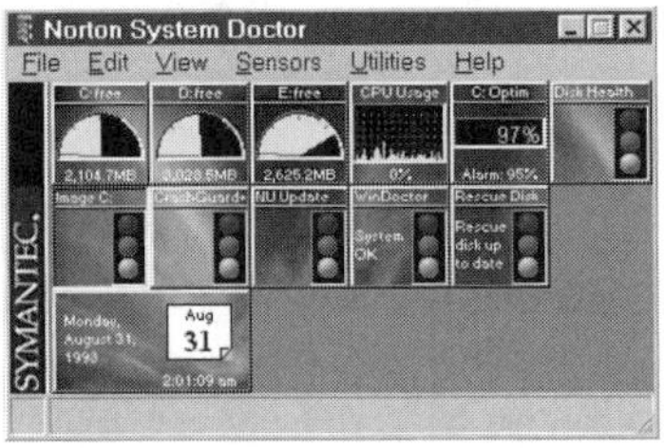

Drive Tab Settings

Right-click on the Image sensor's face and select Properties from the context menu. As with all of the System Doctor sensors, what appears is a dialog box containing a number of standard Windows "tabs." The most important of these is the Drive tab. I say this is the most important tab because the settings here determine which drives are Imaged and which are not. By default, Image configures itself to monitor only your C: drive, as you can see if you bring the Drive tab to the front. Within the drive panel you will be able to identify all non-removable drives on your system; the radio button next to a drive, as in Figure 10.3, indicates only that drive's Image data is being monitored. Despite the fact that this is the default setting, there is almost no reason to ever leave the Image sensor configured in this manner. Imaging is a quick process which, as you are about to see, can take place entirely in the background. You might, from time to time, want to check on a specific drive's Image data; selecting Monitor a Particular Drive and clicking that drive's radio button allows you to do exactly that. However, all of your data is too valuable to risk to anything less than optimal protection, particularly when the "cost" is so little. I recommend you click on the Monitor All Local Drives radio button and leave the Image sensor configured in that manner at all times.

Alarm Tab Settings

The next most important of these configuration tabs is the Alarm tab. It determines the standard for timeliness against which your Image files are checked, and whether or not they are kept up-to-date automatically. As you can see in Figure 10.4, I recommend that you never allow your Image files to become more than one hour old. You can specify any time frame, even weeks, here on the Alarm tab, but your Image files will not be refreshed until the time you specify has passed. Maintaining your files once an hour is reasonable during periods of normal use. If you are making a large number of changes to your PC's drives, you may want Image to refresh its files rather more frequently. I personally recommend you don't set a time shorter than about 15 minutes, however, because if a problem occurs, but remains concealed for, say, half an hour, both the current Image file and the backup file will have been overwritten and may contain the damaged data, not the condition of the drive before the failure occurred. For help on how to recover from Imaging a damaged drive, see the technical note in the next section.

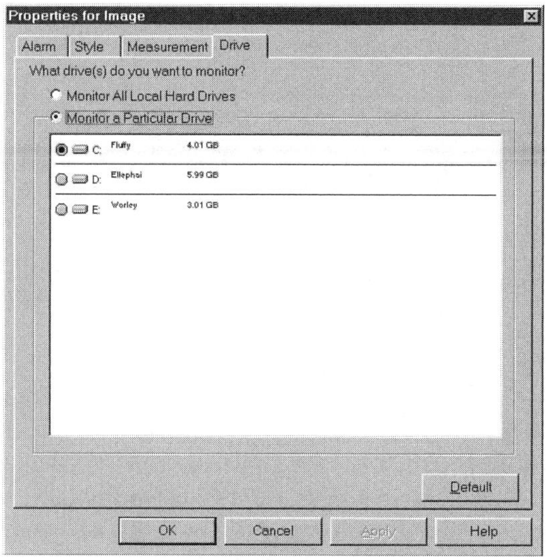

FIGURE 10.3

Only C:\ *on this system is being monitored.*

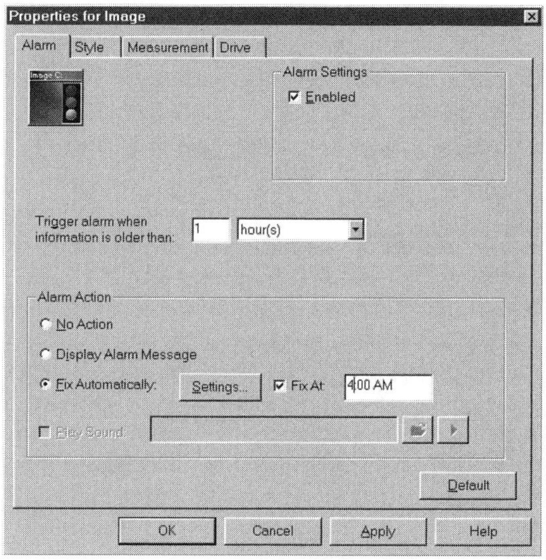

FIGURE 10.4

Image's Alarm tab enables you to specify how often an alarm is triggered and the alarm action.

As the figure also shows, I strongly recommend that you configure the Sensor to automatically fix out-of-date Image files. After you click the Fix Automatically radio button, you should click on the Settings button and verify that every drive in the list has a check mark in the box next to its letter. It may seem that this feature is redundant. You told the sensor to monitor all of your drives, now you have to tell it which drives to update. But this feature allows you to only have certain drives updated, even though all drives are being watched. Why would you care? If you are capturing audio or video to one of your drives and that drive's operation is interrupted so that its Image files can be refreshed, you will very likely lose data. By unchecking that drive's letter in the Fix list, you can keep on top of that drive's Image files without losing control over when those files are modified. Alternatively, you can place a check mark next to all of your drives, but click the Fix At checkbox and specify a time when you know you'll never be working. Image will watch your files, but will only update them—if necessary—at the time you specify.

Of course, the Alarm tab also gives you the ability to merely be alerted when one of your drive's Image files are outdated, but why bother? Most of us are looking for more and more ways in which our PC can automate the little annoying tasks that seem to fill our days. If you've enabled the sensor, and you know you will want your Image files kept up to date, you might as well allow System Doctor to do the task for you. Finally, as with other System Doctor sensors, you can specify a custom sound to be played when the Image sensor detects outdated Image files. Again, however, why allow your work—or that important conference call—to be interrupted by Mortimer Mouse's evil laugh when you can just let System Doctor take care of the entire problem?

Measurement Tab Settings

Finally, look at the Measurement tab. This setting determines how often the sensor checks to see whether your Image files are older than the time-frame you set on the Alarm tab. Of course, the setting here will normally be less than the setting on the Alarm tab, so that if, for example, your PC is turned off for 24 hours, within some short span of time after turning it back on, you'll have your Image files checked for timeliness—perhaps against a one-hour alarm setting—and they will be updated right away. Because the amount of computing power required by this sensor is almost nil, I would recommend a setting of either one or two minutes. In this way, not much time passes after you power up your PC before your Image files are checked.

TECHINCAL NOTE

Do not run Image on a damaged drive. If you determine that you have just Imaged a damaged drive, or if you discover damage shortly after the last time you know your drive was Imaged, you should correct the problem immediately. Damaged data within your Image files can lead to errant repair and more headaches than you ever would have had to endure. Furthermore, recovering from Imaging a damaged drive is very easy. Because your Image files are saved on your hard drive as read-only files, you need to first eliminate this file attribute before you can proceed. To do so, open up My Computer, and select the damaged drive. Locate the IMAGE.DAT and IMAGE.BAK files in that drive's root directory and right-click on them. Select Properties from the context menu and remove the check box from the Read-Only setting. Click OK to close the file properties. (If you choose to access and delete the file through the Windows

Explorer rather than through My Computer, it is not necessary to first uncheck the read-only setting.)

Having successfully done so, delete the IMAGE.DAT file from your hard drive. This is the file that contains the damaged information, and there is no reason to keep it anywhere on your system. Then, rename IMAGE.BAK as IMAGE.DAT, thereby replacing the deleted Image file with the data from the pre-failure backup file. Finally, you should run Norton Disk Doctor to check the drive and repair whatever damage caused the problem with your Image files.

Customizing the Image Program Itself

The final aspect of configuring Image involves configuring the Image program itself. To run Image, right-click the System Doctor Image sensor and select Open Image from the context menu, or select Norton Utilities | Preventative Maintenance | Image from the Norton SystemWorks Integrator. Here, you should verify that there is a check mark in the Create Image Backup File check box, at the left side of the dialog box, as in Figure 10.5.

Tip: Although you are given the flexibility of disabling the creation of backup Image files, this is not recommended. The files are very small, and their value to you could be many times greater than the amount of disk space they require.

Figure 10.5
You can use the Image Utility's main screen to select which drives you want to image.

Notice in the main drive panel that the Image Utility enables you to Image both floppy and removable drives—a feature absent from the sensor, because this kind of disk is most likely to change repeatedly over the course of using your PC. It could be disastrous for the Image sensor to save a backup copy of ZIP Drive "QQY-4's" data into the IMAGE.BAK file of ZIP drive "QQY-5," so Norton SystemWorks protects your removable drives by disallowing automatic checking on them. Here in the Image Utility, however, you may manually Image any drive, or select multiple drives and click Image to Image them all. If you make extensive use of removable drives, like Iomega ZIPs, I do recommend that you run the Image utility and create or refresh Image files on each of them.

Your data is worth it. The main panel will also show you the last date on which each drive in your system was Imaged. You may, of course, choose to disable the Image sensor in Norton System Doctor and perform only manual Imaging based on the dates you see here, keeping in mind that, if the Disk Health sensor is enabled, it will continue to perform Image testing.

The Options button on the main Image panel opens a single-tab dialog box, in which you can specify that one or more of your drives should be Imaged every time Windows starts. These startup Imagings will function in addition to, not as a replacement of, the settings you configure for the Image sensor in System Doctor. Each time Windows starts, your Image files for each selected drive will be immediately updated. I recommend this plan of action highly. Allowing Image to run at startup will not delay your access to the desktop at all, and it is a superb way to keep your Image files up-to-date. Notice that here, too, you may indicate that you do, or do not, want any old Image files saved as backups when each drive's startup Image is taken.

With the Image utility configured to run automatically at startup, and the System Doctor Image sensor configured to keep a watchful eye on the timeliness of your Image files, you are guaranteed very strong protection against a number of data-threatening ills, as you'll read in the next section.

> **Caution:** There are two rather unique circumstances in which you may not want Image to run immediately upon startup. If you live in an area that is particularly susceptible to power surges—say, from lightning storms, or older wiring in your home—it is possible for a power surge to damage one or more of your drives. If you enable startup Imaging, the damaged drive will be Imaged when the power turns on again and Windows reboots. This could overwrite the previous Image data which would have otherwise enabled you to entirely recover from the power-surge damage. A partial solution to this problem, of course, is to be certain that backup creation is always enabled, so that, in a worst-case, the previous Image data will likely still be intact. Of course, the very best solution to this problem is to be certain your PC and all its peripherals are connected to your electrical and telephone lines through a highly rated power-surge protector or uninterrupted power supply (UPS). A surge protector will keep power spikes from ever reaching your PC, and a UPS will keep your PC on even when the lights go out.
>
> Additionally, if you know your PC is not very stable—if you are experiencing a large number of crashes which require you to reboot, for example—you should not enable startup Imaging because the crash that forced you to restart could have also damaged your drives, or left files in a precarious condition. If you are testing software, or find that you crash regularly, do not enable startup Imaging. At the same time, this kind of system difficulty can be an indication of serious problems with one or more applications or with the Windows Registry. You should first be certain that Norton CrashGuard is fully enabled to protect yourself and your data from most types of crashing. (You can read about Norton

CrashGuard in Chapter 8, "Norton CrashGuard: When Windows Breaks.")
Additionally, run Norton WinDoctor and allow it to perform a thorough test of
your entire PC. In all likelihood, problems will exist, and WinDoctor will be able
to repair them. You can read about WinDoctor in Chapter 4, "Norton Utilities:
The WinDoctor Is In."

Integration with SystemWorks

The presence of Image files on your hard drive alone, of course, wouldn't do anything to
secure and maintain the safety of your precious data without an array of integrated support utilities and applications that make use of those Image files. Fortunately,
SystemWorks provides exactly that. You just finished reading about how Image and
System Doctor work together to create and maintain those Image files. Understanding
how those files are used by the rest of the Norton Utilities and SystemWorks will give
you a firm grasp of why the Image files are so important.

Norton UnErase Wizard

The Norton UnErase Wizard is an integrated part of the Norton Utilities that are able
to—working with Norton Protection and Image—retrieve files and folders which were
accidentally or mistakenly deleted. How it works is very straightforward. While Norton
Protection keeps a hidden copy of the files you delete—something you read about in
Chapter 6, "Norton Utilities: Digging Through the Trash with Norton Protection," certain
types of operating system or drive failures can cause you to lose files and folders you
never actually deleted. The Norton UnErase Wizard will access your Image files to locate
these kinds of "destroyed" files and folders and enable you to recover them. The Norton
UnErase Wizard will also make use of the FAT data stored in your Image files while it is
looking for deleted files not found under Norton Protection's protection. In this way, files
that were deleted longer ago than the maximum protection time in Norton Protection can
be re-located and, perhaps, retrieved more readily than otherwise. You can read all about
the Norton UnErase Wizard in Chapter 15, "Norton Utilities: Getting it Back, Getting it
Right: UnErasing and File Compare."

UnFormat

Norton Image serves an incredibly important role in repairing what could possibly be the
most severe damage that can happen to your drives—accidental formatting. Although
Windows 98 makes it impossible to format your c: drive from within Windows, your
other drives are not so protected. Even with Windows 98's internal protection, if you
spend any time in DOS—or if an associate or your children boot into DOS to play
games, for example—there are still ways for your drives to get zapped. As you'll read
about in Chapter 16, "Norton Utilities: The Big "Oops" and Norton UnFormat," when a
hard drive is formatted, its data areas aren't actually erased. Similar to when you delete a
file, only the hard drive's FAT is zapped. By using your IMAGE.IDX file to locate where

your IMAGE.DAT file's data was stored, UnFormat can retrieve that Image data and reconstruct your entire drive and its directory structure. In essence, Image makes it possible to UnFormat your drive in less time than it took to accidentally format it in the first place.

Speed Disk

The integration of Norton Speed Disk and Image works in the opposite direction from Norton UnErase Wizard and UnFormat. Rather than using your Image files to aid in the optimization of your drives, Speed Disk takes the initiative of running Image and updating your Image files after every completed optimization. The benefit of this should be obvious. Speed Disk may have relocated every single file on a drive if the drive was severely fragmented, or if you just completed running Speed Disk for the first time. Under such circumstances, using an out-dated Image file would be a disaster! Let's suppose, for example, that you have just run Speed Disk for the first time, and it did not—although it does, this is just an hypothetical example—update your Image files. Your young son comes in, starts up your PC in DOS, and formats your drive rather than installing his game properly. If your old Image files were used to reconstruct the drive, the reconstructed FAT would point to where your files used to be, not where they are now that Speed Disk has optimized the drive. Not good. To avoid such nightmares, Speed Disk updates your Image files—assuming they exist—upon completing an optimization. In this way, your FATs are continually updated while Speed Disk is working (which you can read about in Chapter 17) and your emergency restore data—your Image files—are brought up to date as soon afterwards as is relevant (in other words, immediately). If you have never used Image and your Image files don't yet exist, Speed Disk will not create them. Speed Disk will only update them. If you want to take advantage of this automatic updating, you must use both Speed Disk and Image.

PETER'S PRINCIPLE

Don't Burn Your FAT

Our society seems bent on barraging us with endless demands that we do all we can to avoid eating fat, juxtaposed on endless claims that there are good kinds of fat, which we should be sure to eat regularly. Fortunately, when it comes to your PC, there's only one kind of FAT, and it's good. Like the lumpy stuff we add to our body mass at the holidays, however, it's how you use your PC's FAT that makes the difference in your lifestyle.

Although your PC already maintains a duplicate FAT, there's no question that FATs get damaged. If you've ever had an application crash Windows—and who hasn't—you may have noticed that when Windows reboots and ScanDisk or Norton Disk Doctor runs, ScanDisk or Norton Disk Doctor identifies "lost clusters." Lost clusters means FAT damage. By using Image, you'll be maintaining yet another emergency backup FAT—as well as a backup of other vital disk particulars. There are also a number of things you can do to keep your FAT healthy in the first place.

First, configure Norton Disk Doctor to run every time you start up Windows to verify the integrity of your disks—both the data areas where your files are kept and the system areas where the boot record and FAT are stored.

Second, run Speed Disk daily to keep your drives as unfragmented as possible. The more fragmented a file is, the more likely it is that an error will occur in the reading or writing of that file. Such errors commonly manifest themselves as "crossed clusters," meaning that one cluster becomes assigned to two different files, effectively damaging both files.

Additionally, configure Norton System Doctor to update the WinDoctor sensor quite regularly. WinDoctor will verify that your PC's setup—your Windows Registry, in particular—is in tip-top shape. Registry mishaps and a wide variety of other "under the hood" problems are a major cause of Windows crashes, which, in turn, are a major cause of lost clusters and other FAT-related difficulties.

Keep CrashGuard running and watching out for crashes, too, so that when one of your applications crashes, CrashGuard can extract your data and save it into a proper file, closing the temporary files then can lead to FAT difficulties.

With your entire PC maintained at its healthiest, and Image providing emergency backup copies of your drive's configuration data, your PC will be the most reliable it has ever been.

Peter Norton

PART III

Recovery

Norton Utilities: The Disk Doctor Is In

It's likely that no single part of your computer causes you more stress than the hard disks, and with good reason. As one of the very few system components with moving parts, hard disks are susceptible to wear and tear and transport dangers in many ways that your RAM chips and your motherboard are not. Additionally, as the only part of your system responsible for maintaining vast quantities of your data, possibly forever, any risk to your hard disk can easily be more important to you than whether or not your main processor has just overheated. The problems you can fix with money—like buying a new motherboard—are always more tolerable than the problems you must fix through labor—like rewriting that sure-hit screenplay from scratch.

Unfortunately, contrary to what you might expect, the regular daily use of your computer does more than anything else to put your data in jeopardy. Inherent in the writing of new data to your hard disks is the potential for disaster. Much more than you might think is happening when you save a file. And, as you'll see, an error anywhere along the way can avalanche on you.

Fortunately, many of the most common sorts of difficulties to be encountered with our hard disks are quite repairable, without ever opening up your computer and—if you want it that way—without your even needing to know what's really going on. The fact that you're reading this book, however, implies that you do, in fact, want to keep on top of how your system works. As we go on, you'll see that this understanding will enable you to better prevent problems, not merely respond to them once they're in your face.

Norton Disk Doctor was designed to give you the ability to repair hard disk difficulties and stay on the lookout for problems before they manifest as lost data. Like a real physician, Disk Doctor can help you with the computer equivalent of a simple flu or a life-threatening malady. Also like a human physician, the expertise is built-in to Disk Doctor, giving you the option of just letting it do its work, or of letting Disk Doctor assist you through your own, better understanding of why your hard disk is "sick" in the first place.

Human metaphors aside, Norton Disk Doctor can scan for and correct a wider range of disk related problems than any other tool available to you. Norton Disk Doctor (NDD) can examine not only your data, but also the structures keeping your data accessible and the physical characteristics of your hard drive itself.

Additionally, Norton Disk Doctor is integrated into the rest of the Norton SystemWorks suite to further enhance the safety of their operation and the reliability of your computer as a whole. For example, the Disk Health sensor in Norton System Doctor runs in the background, checking for the most common kinds of problems NDD can repair. If the Health Sensor shows a yellow or red light, double-click on it to get an explanation of the detected problem and an opportunity to run NDD—or whichever part of SystemWorks is best suited to the particular problem. Working in the other direction, Norton Speed Disk can automatically launch NDD if it encounters an unexpected error of almost any kind. This, on top of the many internal safety checks that Speed Disk itself performs, can make the process of optimizing your hard disk almost worry-free.

Norton System Doctor is discussed in Chapter 3, "Norton Utilities: The System Doctor Is In," and Norton Speed Disk is discussed in detail in Chapter 17, "Norton Utilities: Getting It Together with Norton Optimization Wizard, Speed Disk, and Speed Start."

> **Caution:** If you have turned to this chapter first because you are experiencing trouble with your computer right now, look first at Appendix A, "Emergency Recovery Techniques," for suggestions on how to solve your immediate problem.

Detecting and Repairing Problems

First, you should know that certain types of disk errors cannot, in fact, be repaired by Norton Disk Doctor. If you have a disk that has been accidentally formatted or that you suspect is severely damaged, Norton Disk Doctor won't make anything worse, nor will it necessarily improve matters. In such a case you should use your Rescue Disk and its associated components—Rescue, UnFormat, and so on—to rebuild the damaged disk from the ground up. Having completed that process first, use NDD to verify all of the drive's data structures and its physical integrity. (Rescue is discussed at length in Chapter 7, "Norton Utilities: Life Preserver on a (Rescue) Disk" and UnFormat and Image are detailed in Chapter 10, "Norton Utilities: More Than a Mirror, an Image.")

Additionally, if you have lost data by accidentally deleting it, Norton Protection and the UnErase Wizard are your keys to recovery, not Norton Disk Doctor. Again, NDD will not exacerbate existing disk problems, nor make deleted files suddenly inaccessible to UnErase, but neither will it bring them back in most circumstances. You'll see one or two exceptions to this later in this chapter. Knowing which recovery tool to use is your first major step towards success. (A good deal more information on this specific issue—knowing when to use which utility—can be found in Appendix A.)

Norton Protection and the UnErase Wizard are covered in Chapters 6, "Norton Utilities: Digging Through the Trash with Norton Protection" and 13, "Norton Utilities: Getting It Back, Getting It Right: UnErasing and File Compare."

Finally, it is vital that your hard disk characteristics—which are stored in your motherboard's CMOS—are set properly before you attempt to use NDD. If you suspect that your CMOS battery has failed, or if you have other reasons to believe that your CMOS hard disk parameters have been compromised, you should use Norton Rescue first to properly restore those parameters before using Norton Disk Doctor to verify the integrity of your data.

That being said, what, actually, does Norton Disk Doctor do? Plenty. Norton Disk Doctor makes thorough checks of all parts of your disks, both system and data areas, to safeguard—and, if necessary, repair—your disk's integrity. We'll look at NDD's examination of your hard disk in the same order that NDD does.

The Master Boot Record

When a hard disk is initially partitioned—either into one partition or many—the first sector of that drive is reserved for system information that, collectively, is known as the Master Boot Record. This Master Boot Record contains information about how the drive has been partitioned, where each of those partitions is physically located on the drive, and which of those partitions is the active, or bootable, partition. This information leads your computer's BIOS to the active partition's own, individual Boot Record. The individual Boot Record stores specific information about how that partition has been formatted and instructions on how the BIOS should proceed to begin loading that partition's operating system.

TECHNICAL NOTE

> Since floppy disks cannot be partitioned, no partitioning information is recorded. Thus, if both a "Master Boot Record" and a "Boot Record" existed on a floppy disk (and they don't), they would contain the same data. For this reason, the terms "Master Boot Record" and "Boot Record" are interchangeable for floppies and some of the large-capacity removable disks.

Norton Disk Doctor is able to check the integrity of the data stored in the Master Boot Record and verify that it is useable. Were it not, your computer would have no way of knowing any of the fundamental characteristics of your hard disk that enable its use.

If the Master Boot Record appears to contain invalid information, NDD will so advise you. Chances are very good that if your Master Boot Record has been damaged, your hard disk is no longer functioning anyway. You should, at this point, cancel the operation of Norton Disk Doctor (simply press Esc and confirm that you want to cancel) and use Rescue Disk techniques to recover the data from the Master Boot Record (see Chapter 7). After that operation is complete, run NDD to check for any additional problems.

The Partition Table

Located within the Master Boot Record is the drive's Partition Table and Extended Partition Table. Contained within it are the locations of the separate partitions on your hard disk. (Even if your hard disk contains only one partition, its location is stored within the Master Boot Record as well as within that partition's individual Boot Record, which you'll read about later in this chapter.) This information tells the hard drive where to physically place the drive's read/write heads and begin reading to continue to boot the active partition. If any of this data is damaged, your hard disk is likely non-functional. The Extended Partition Table also contains information about logical drives which may be defined within each partition, and whether each of these is bootable.

Caution: If you see a message while running the Windows version of NDD, informing you that there are no partitions on your drive, you should immediately exit Windows, and then run the command-line version of NDD on emergency disk #1, using the /REBUILD switch:

`A:\NDD /REBUILD`

When Disk Doctor again encounters the damaged Partition Table, it will ask you to allow it to search for lost partitions. Press Enter to confirm. For each partition NDD locates it will ask if you want to recreate the partition information. Click Yes to recreate the partition or No to abort the process. Norton Disk Doctor will also give you the opportunity to store "Undo" data to a floppy disk. You should always avail yourself of this option when repairing fundamental disk structures like Partition Tables, Boot Records, or, corrupted FATs.

Boot Records within Partitions

As noted previously, each partition on your hard drive contains one or more Boot Records—one for each logical drive defined within the partition. These boot records include information about the size of each logical disk, with which operating system it is to be used, and where that operating system's startup files can be found. (Much more technical information on a drive's structures can be found in Chapter 12, "Norton Utilities: The Laying-On of Hands and Norton Disk Editor.") It is possible for Norton Disk Doctor to repair the boot records of individual logical drives. As mentioned above, you should always create an Undo disk when performing this kind of repair.

CMOS

Not actually part of your hard disk at all, your computer's CMOS chip (it stands for Complementary Metal-Oxide Semiconductor… impress your friends!) stores a variety of information about your system, including how much memory your computer has, how many disk drives are installed in your computer and their physical characteristics, and all the rest of the information you see when you examine your system's Hardware Setup (usually accessible by pressing a key or keys early in the power-up process). The purpose of this chip is to maintain all this vital information while your computer is off, and even if it is unplugged. A Lithium battery on the motherboard provides permanent power to this chip (and also to your system's clock). Disk Doctor will check to verify that the information it finds stored on your hard disk is in compliance with the information stored in your CMOS.

If the information does not match, two main possibilities exist. First, your CMOS information may be corrupted, most commonly because your motherboard battery has died (life expectancy is supposed to be greater than 5 years, but mileage may vary). If you are having difficulty accessing your hard drives (or, indeed, booting your computer at all) this is likely the problem. You should consult your computer system's manual to determine what kind of battery is required and whether or not it is user-replaceable. If it is not, consult with your hardware manufacturer or an authorized hardware repair center.

Less commonly, there are hardware configurations which are not what is frequently termed "100% IBM-compatible," and these configurations can report invalid information to Disk Doctor because of those incompatibilities. Such problems exist almost exclusively on computers more than 10 years old. If Disk Doctor reports that there seems to be a problem with your CMOS but you have not had any difficulties in accessing your hard disks, it's likely that your system has such an incompatibility. To avoid having NDD repeatedly report errors based on this sort of issue, you should use the NDD Advanced Settings to simply turn the CMOS test off. Click on the Options button on the Disk Doctor opening screen, and then select the Advanced tab. Place a check in the Skip CMOS Tests box and click OK.

> **Note:** If you find that you have this sort of incompatibility, it is possible that you will encounter others. You will find information about configuring NDD for these other issues later in this chapter, in the "Configuring Norton Disk Doctor" section.

FATs

After verifying the integrity of your hard disk's boot records and partition tables, NDD proceeds to perform several tests which relate to a logical drive's FAT, or File Allocation Tables. These tables maintain the vital data needed to keep track of which parts of a drive are in use and which parts are free, in addition to where all of your files are located. In Windows 95 and 98, long filename information (specifically, where and how in a drive's directory the long filenames are maintained) is also stored within the FAT. If any of this information becomes corrupted, it can quickly become impossible to access your files or the operating system itself (since the operating system is stored in files, too).

FAT32

> The actual structure and content of the FAT32 FATs is dramatically different from those found on older, smaller, FAT16 drives, and there are differences in the boot records of FAT32 drives, as well. You'll find a technical discussion about the relevant issues in Chapter 12, which covers the Norton Disk Editor. However, Norton Disk Doctor is able to safely examine and repair both FAT16 and FAT32 structures.

FAT Comparison

There are two copies of the FAT on every logical drive, even floppy disks. Norton Disk Doctor first checks to make sure that both copies of the FAT are exactly the same. If there is a discrepancy, NDD can repair the damaged FAT by using the information found within the backup copy.

Media Descriptor Byte Comparison

Located in the FAT is a single byte of data known as the media descriptor byte. This is a copy of information that is also stored in your logical drive's boot record, indicating whether a disk is a hard drive or one of several types of floppy disk. If the information in the FAT's copy does not match that of the boot record, Disk Doctor will repair the errant FAT data before proceeding.

Cluster Checks

The logical structures in which files are stored are known as clusters. After comparing the two copies of the FAT and checking the media descriptor byte, NDD then verifies that every cluster the FAT indicates is in use is actually related to a specific file on the disk. (The FAT also records information about the folders on your disk, but for purposes of our discussion here, we'll think of the information about each folder as though it were stored in a file like any other.) If Disk Doctor finds that the FAT says a cluster is being used and it, in fact, isn't, Disk Doctor will tell you that it has found lost clusters—probably the most common error you will see from NDD. Clusters become detached from actual files in a number of ways, the most common of which is a system crash. Among other things, a program may create temporary files while it is running, and these files are not deleted when a crash occurs. The space occupied by those files may remain marked "in use" in the FAT, even though the files are gone. Other system mishaps make it possible for the information about actual user (or OS) files to be lost, leaving those parts of the drive marked as "in use," but making them inaccessible.

Norton Disk Doctor gives you the opportunity to repair the lost cluster problem in one of two ways—or three, if you count your option to ignore the problem entirely. Most simply, NDD can modify the FAT to indicate that those used clusters are not actually being used. This has the effect of "deleting" the lost data and making that drive space available again for future use.

Alternatively, NDD will create new file structure entries in the FAT, one for each chain of lost cluster information, effectively creating new files. (These files will have names like `FILE0000._DD` and will be saved for you in the root directory of the drive you're checking.) You can examine the contents of these files at your leisure using Norton Disk Editor or, in some cases, the Windows Notepad, to see if they contain important information. If they do, you can, of course, re-save them to a more appropriate location and delete the `._DD` (Disk Doctor) files from your root directory.

Part of Norton Disk Doctor's cluster tests is a verification that each used cluster is reported as belonging to only one file. If NDD finds that the FAT reports a cluster is being used by two different files, NDD will tell you that your disk contains cross-linked files. Cross-linked files are troublesome because, by definition, their presence indicates that all of the involved files are corrupted (whether they seem to open properly or not). Always create an "Undo" disk when repairing cross-linked files. Norton Disk Doctor will make the most intelligent repair that it can, but this repair may be wrong. In such a case, undo NDD's changes and use Norton Disk Editor to manually repair the problem. (Norton Disk Editor is discussed in Chapter 10.)

You may find your greatest success in repairing cross-linked files by combining NDD's automatic repair with some manual techniques as well. Run NDD and write down the names of all cross-linked files it identifies, but do not yet allow Disk Doctor to repair those files. Then, quit NDD, and, using the Windows Explorer, manually locate those files and move them to another drive. Re-run Norton Disk Doctor and, this time, let it perform the repairs. By copying the files to another drive, you will be creating non-linked versions of those files (because even though the original data is cross-linked, the new files will occupy non-crossed areas of the different drive's FAT). If NDD's automatic repair is unsatisfactory, you may find that you are better able to access the data in those files by working with the new copies you've made. Of course, in either case, some data will likely be lost—such is the perilous nature of cross-linking. However, this two-pronged approach may minimize your risk and maximize your chances.

Directory Tests

Disk Doctor will next check the integrity of the disk's directory, or folder hierarchy, and can repair invalid or corrupted entries by reconstructing information from the second copy of the FAT. NDD will also check the size of each file on disk as it is reported in the FAT and the disk's directory structure and make similar repairs. This is known as a file allocation error. If the first and second FATs agree on the file's length, NDD will repair the invalid information in the directory structure. If the two FATs do not match, NDD will repair the invalid FAT.

At this point, Disk Doctor will also check for files saved with invalid dates or times. In general, these sorts of errors are of no significance, but can be confusing to the user. In the case of some older, copy-protected software, a hidden file may exist which has an intentionally invalid date. This file is checked each time the software is run to try to make certain that you have a legal installation. If you allow NDD to change the date of this sort of file, the software may no longer function. If you know you have software of this type on your system, you may wish to treat this circumstance as an incompatibility between your system and NDD and permanently deactivate date and time testing on the Advanced Options tab (discussed later in this chapter). If you do not permanently disable this test, NDD will automatically change invalid dates and times during any Auto-Repair session.

Long Filename Tests

Finally, Disk Doctor will check through the portion of the FAT that is responsible for maintaining the links between Windows 95 and 98 long filenames and the 8.3 DOS-compatible filenames for each file. If this information becomes damaged, some or all of your long filenames will be useless. When Norton Disk Doctor encounters "lost" long filenames, it reports the error and will give you the option of deleting them or attempting to re-attach them to their 8.3 filename equivalents. For example, the long filename C:\Norton Books Data.DOC might have the 8.3 equivalent of C:\Norton-1.DOC. If these two names became detached, NDD would put them back together again (with apologies to Humpty Dumpty).

Compressed Disks

If you use Disk Doctor to examine DriveSpace-compressed disks—either hard disks or floppy disks—NDD performs an extra set of tests relating to the integrity of the compression. When you are testing uncompressed volumes, you will see the international symbol for "No" indicating that the tests have been automatically skipped (see Figure 11.1).

FIGURE 11.1
NDD is analyzing an uncompressed drive.

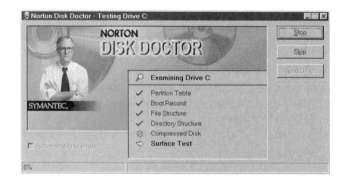

In order to understand why Norton Disk Doctor operates the way it does with respect to compressed drives, it's necessary to understand a little bit about how DriveSpace creates those drives. This is also examined in more depth in Chapter 12, which discusses Norton Disk Editor. In fact, a compressed drive is a single, huge file on your hard disk, into which all your files and their data are placed. The traditional FATs still exist on the hard drive, which is called the host drive for the compressed drive, but those FATs point only to this single, composite file. At the beginning of this compressed volume file or CVF, is yet another set of FATs that keep track of, among other things, the same information the traditional FATs maintain for an uncompressed drive.

Simply put, Norton Disk Doctor performs its normal tests on the host drive's FAT, making certain that the information defining the compressed volume file is intact. NDD then looks inside the CVF—which you see as a compressed drive—and repeats the same FAT tests against the compressed FATs stored there. Norton Disk Doctor then performs additional specialized tests which further watchdog your data inside the CVF. In this way, the integrity of the compression file, as well as the integrity of all of your files inside the compression file, can be verified and maintained.

FAT32

> Windows does not allow FAT32-formatted drives to host compressed volume files.

Surface Testing

The final test performed by Norton Disk Doctor examines the physical integrity of your disk itself, checking for anomalies which could easily endanger your files and their data. Which surface tests NDD actually performs is determined by whether you have selected Normal Test or Thorough Test on the Surface Test tab within Options. (Normal testing is the default.)

Normal Test

With surface testing set to the Normal Test setting, Norton Disk Doctor will sequentially read every cluster of data from your hard disk to verify that all of your data can, in fact, be read. If NDD encounters a read error, you will be notified. Read errors encountered during the surface test may indicate specific physical defects on your hard drive. Alternatively, they may indicate areas of your hard drive in which the drive formatting information—the magnetic indicators of where tracks, sectors, and clusters are located and how they are divided—may have faded. This latter problem generally occurs only on hard disks approaching five years in age or greater, as a marked amount of time must pass before this type of fading occurs. (This sort of difficulty was mentioned in Chapter 1, "When Bad Things Happen to Good Computers.")

When NDD encounters a cluster that cannot be reliably read from disk, NDD checks the FAT to see if the cluster is currently in use. If not, NDD marks the cluster as "Bad" in the FAT, guaranteeing that data will not be stored there in the future. This setting further prevents other utilities, like Norton Speed Disk, from moving data to the unreliable cluster during optimizing. If the errant cluster is assigned to a file, NDD will attempt to read the entire file and move as much data from the defective cluster as possible to a more reliable location on the disk, updating the FAT to reflect the change. If this process fails, you may be able to manually retrieve and reconstruct the file using Norton Disk Editor. If the process is successful, NDD will mark the unreliable cluster as "Bad."

Thorough Test

The thorough surface test uses a different set of instructions (BIOS calls) to check the integrity of your disks at a deeper hardware level. NDD's behavior when an error is detected is the same as during a normal test. Unreliable clusters are marked as bad in the drive's FAT with active files being moved off of the questionable clusters whenever possible.

Windows' Interruption of Disk Doctor

Norton Disk Doctor is capable of checking your disks in the background while you continue to work. However, you should know that if any program other than NDD—including the operating system itself—writes to the drive being checked while NDD is working, NDD will begin the examination of that drive over from the beginning. The reason for this is simple: Writing to the disk involves making modifications to not just the file storage area of the disk, but also to the FAT. Further, if a drive is already malfunctioning, otherwise benign disk changes (like saving a file in your word processor) can create or contribute to disk-based problems. To compensate for this possibility, Norton Disk Doctor goes back to verify that the disk-write has not generated an error condition on part of the drive that was already checked.

As you can likely imagine, if you or Windows makes numerous writes to a drive while NDD is running, NDD will seem to take forever as the examination begins over and over again. There are several solutions to this possibility. First, of course, don't try to run Norton Disk Doctor minimized while you are working in another program. Second, configure NDD to run automatically every time you start Windows (this will be explained later in the chapter), and simply let NDD complete its checks before you begin work. (There are drawbacks to this method of course, including the time you have to wait before starting to do any actual work, and the fact that drivers or programs Windows loads when it starts may make writes to drives, even if your computer is unattended.) Finally, you can run NDD from the DOS Mode command line (as discussed toward the end of this chapter) so you know nothing is running that might interrupt Disk Doctor's examination.

Undoing Disk Doctor Repairs

Undoing repairs made in a previous session of Disk Doctor testing is much the same experience from within Windows as from the command-line version of the program. After clicking the Undo button, you'll see a warning advising you that you should be certain your disk is free of errors before performing an Undo. If it is not, Undo may wreak havoc with your data, certainly making it annoying—at best—to repair. After dismissing the warning, you'll be asked to specify the drive to which the Undo information was saved. Unless you have more than one floppy disk drive, you will see only drive A: in this list. Select the drive, make sure the proper disk is in place, and click OK.

Norton Disk Doctor stores Undo data in a file named NDDUNDO.DAT, which must be in the disk's root directory. Assuming the file is on the disk you've selected (you'll get a File Not Found error if it's not), Disk Doctor will examine the file's contents and report the date and time at which the Undo file was created. Verify, to the best of your ability, that this is the correct Undo file and click OK. Using the information stored within the file, Disk Doctor will undo all of the repairs made during the specified session. An Undo is not, itself, Undoable, so do be certain that you want to Undo before you do.

> **Caution:** You should dismiss any thought of maintaining multiple Undo disks (that is, disks from multiple runnings of Norton Disk Doctor), thinking that you can go back a week from now and safely Undo Disk Doctor changes. Indeed, you should really only ever Undo NDD changes immediately after NDD makes repairs, and you determine right away that the repairs were not what you wanted. The reason for this is that the Undo file contains details of the drive's FAT prior to Disk Doctor's repair efforts. If you run NDD on Monday, use your computer for a few days, and then attempt to Undo NDD's changes on Thursday, you will lose or damage—at least, temporarily—the files you created or modified between Monday and Thursday when NDD replaces your current FAT with the FAT stored in the Undo file. You may be able to then run NDD again and recover those files, or you may not be able to retrieve them except by manually looking for them with Norton Disk Editor and UnErase. Save yourself a good deal of grief: If you have questions about the wisdom of NDD repairs, explore the relevant disk extensively and immediately after quitting Disk Doctor. If your concerns are justified, immediately Undo the NDD changes.

Configuring Norton Disk Doctor

It's extremely easy to set Norton Disk Doctor to work the way you want it to work. A variety of options have been well organized using the familiar Windows 95 tabs with context-sensitive help available for each item on each tab. The most obvious of your available options are found on the NDD startup screen itself, as shown in Figure 11.2. From here, you can select which drives you wish Disk Doctor to examine from a list of all of your available drives, including floppy drives. (Read-only drives such as CD-ROM drives will not be listed.) Simply select the drives you want NDD to examine. Additionally, you can choose to allow NDD to automatically repair any errors it encounters without either notifying you of them (until NDD generates a final report) or asking for your permission. Selecting this check box enables automatic repairing, and this setting overrules any other setting you have selected on the General Options tab.

If at any time you want more information about what you see on the NDD screen, clicking the Help button launches the Norton Help engine. Once the engine is running, you can click the Help Topics tab to access information on any of the integrated Norton SystemWorks, including NDD. Additionally, the Dictionary tab gives you access to a wide-ranging computer glossary. Just begin typing the term you want defined and, if it's in the dictionary, the list will jump as you type. Double-click the term when you locate it in the list to see its definition.

General Options

Clicking on the Options button on the NDD startup screen opens the Options screen to the General tab, shown in Figure 11.3. As you probably already know, clicking any of the other tabs will bring that tab and its options to the front. At any point while you're making modifications to NDD options, you can click OK to accept all of the options you've set or Cancel to ignore all changes you made since opening the Options dialog box.

The General Options tab enables you to specify that Disk Doctor will (or won't) run automatically every time you start Windows. If you do select automatic operation, you'll need to look down at the drive list and place a check mark next to each drive you want automatically tested. Notice that placing a check mark next to a drive does not enable automatic repairing, only automatic checking.

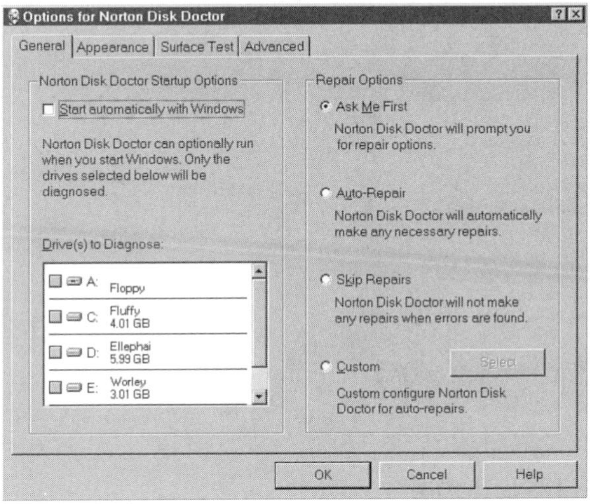

FIGURE 11.3

*The options on
the General tab
of Disk Doctor
broadly configure
how NDD per-
forms its tests.*

Prompted Repair

You can also select which repair methodology you want NDD to use as its default (unless you enable automatic repairing on the NDD startup screen). This setting will apply to both manually-started and automatic testing. If you leave the Ask Me First radio button selected, Norton Disk Doctor will stop its testing and will ask for your permission to correct every error it encounters. At the first such juncture, you will be asked if you want to create an Undo disk. If you do so, all subsequent error-correction you approve is added to the undo information. If you decline to create an Undo disk, you will be asked again at the next error NDD encounters, and so on.

Auto-Repair

If you select the Auto-Repair radio button, Disk Doctor will work in automatic or unattended mode. During this operation, NDD will examine all of the disks you've selected and automatically repair any errors it encounters without asking for any input from you. Several other decisions are made for you during an Auto-Repair session.

- No Undo disk will be created.
- Lost clusters will automatically be saved as files in the root directory of the tested drive.
- An attempt will be made to repair and save cross-linked files.
- Detached long filenames will be reconnected to their 8.3 counterparts, if possible.
- A surface test is performed if surface-testing is enabled.

When an Auto-Repair session is complete you will be shown the standard NDD Test Results screen, regardless of whether any errors were found (see Figure 11.4).

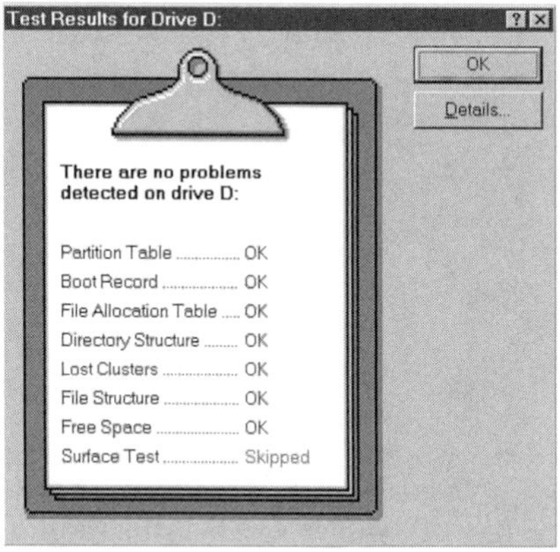

FIGURE **11.4**
*The Disk Doctor
Test Results
screen indicates
any difficulties
encountered and
problems repaired
by NDD.*

Make No Repairs

If you select the Skip Repairs option on the General tab, Norton Disk Doctor will check all of the selected drives for errors and will generate a final report of those errors, but it will not make any changes to your disks. This setting can be useful in circumstances when you fear a disk may contain errors that must be repaired with Rescue, not Disk Doctor. It can also be helpful if you want to diagnose a large number of drives and then selectively re-run NDD on only those drives in need of repair. In organizations where employees are expected to periodically check their own disks for errors but are not permitted to repair those errors, this option can be used to generate an error report for submission to the hardware administrator.

Customized Repair Settings

If you select the Custom radio button on the General tab, the Select button next to it will be enabled, allowing you to specify customized settings for each type of error NDD might encounter (see Figure 11.5).

The following options appear on the custom settings screen:

- File allocation tables
- Directory structures
- Compression structures
- Surface errors
- Partition tables
- Boot records

For each of these options, you can instruct Disk Doctor to either notify you when it encounters an error of that type, to automatically repair any such errors without notifying you or asking for permission, or to make no repairs of that type. (As above, if repairs are skipped, their existence is still included in the final report.)

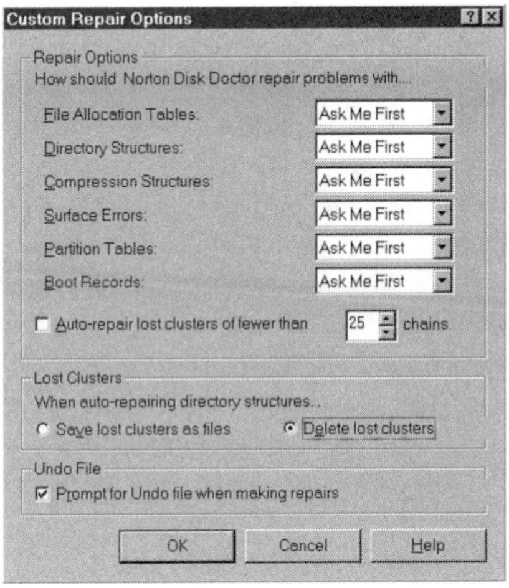

FIGURE 11.5

The Disk Doctor Custom Repair Settings allow you to fine-tune how NDD performs.

Additionally, you can limit the number of lost cluster chains NDD will save to the root directory as files. If you suspect that a drive is rife with lost clusters, you could quickly end up with a hundred or more files in the root directory of your drive. By setting Disk Doctor to repair, for example, no more than 20 lost cluster chains, you will cause NDD to automatically save (or discard) the first 20 such chains to your disk as files and to ask you before saving (or discarding) additional chains. If you leave this box unchecked, NDD will automatically attempt to repair all of the lost cluster chains it encounters, based on the setting you have selected in the Lost Clusters area.

The Lost Clusters setting simply tells NDD to either save or delete lost clusters that it encountered during any session in which lost clusters are to be auto-repaired. (Bear in mind that all settings on this screen are ignored if you have anything other than Custom selected from the General Options tab.) If you are certain that you have had no data vanish into lost clusters, you can save yourself the trouble of deleting all of the lost cluster files from your root directory by telling NDD to not create them in the first place. Clusters which NDD detects as lost will be marked as unused without asking you for further permission. If you suspect that meaningful data may be scattered about or lost, then you should leave this option set for saving lost cluster chains so you can examine them later.

Finally, this custom screen allows you to instruct NDD to never ask you about creating an Undo file while it is making repairs. In general, it is safest to leave this box checked even if your drives appear to be functioning perfectly. If you have any reason to suspect that serious errors may be present, you should always have NDD create an Undo disk. This option might be unchecked, however, on a networked computer to avoid confusing users who are authorized to run Disk Doctor but who do not have access to floppy drives. Unless you really know what you're doing and what condition your drives are in, unchecking this option may be anything from unnecessary to foolhardy.

Appearance Options

With the Appearance tab, you have the potential for maximizing performance, annoyance, and personnel control in one location. What more could anyone ask? The Appearance options enable you to de-activate the small window of animation that runs while Disk Doctor is examining drives (see Figure 11.6). On very slow computers or systems with very little memory, turning the animation off can enhance NDD's performance. If your monitor is set to 256 or fewer colors, this option is not available. (The animation requires a high-color display, so with a low-color setting, the animation is always inactive.) You can additionally instruct Disk Doctor to play a piece of music while it runs. Any MIDI or WAV file on any available drive can be selected from a standard Open dialog box in Windows 95 by clicking on the folder icon in this setting. Once a file is selected, you can listen to it to make sure it's the right file by clicking the speaker icon.

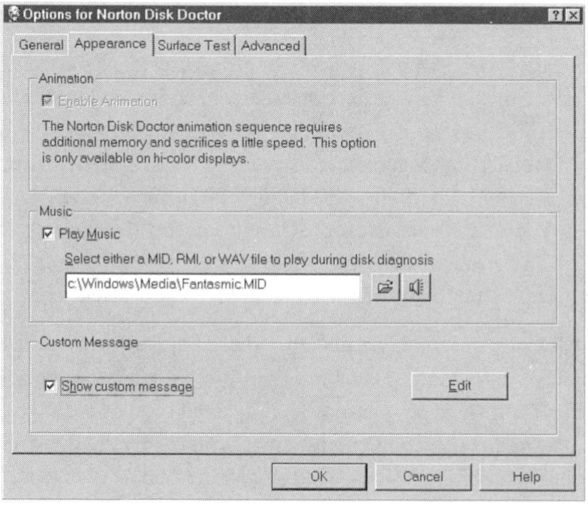

FIGURE 11.6

The options on the Appearance tab of Disk Doctor enable you to configure what you see onscreen while NDD runs.

Lest you should fear running Disk Doctor in peace and quiet, be assured: If the music or sound you select plays for less time than it takes Disk Doctor to run, the file will be played over and over until NDD is done. (Children will quickly discover that a short WAV sound, like Windows' default "Ding," will play about a zillion times during one run of Disk Doctor.) If you're a parent or a teacher, you may want to be certain you know how to disable this option if someone else turns it on. As you would expect, unchecking the Play Music option disables the file selection and speaker buttons. The most recently used sound or music file will remain chosen, however, ready to be enabled at a moment's notice. To clear the File Selection box, check the Play Music box, select the name of the music file with the mouse, and press the Backspace key on your keyboard. Then, uncheck the Play Music box.

Far less likely to cause a nervous breakdown is the Custom Message option at the bottom of the Appearance tab. Place a check mark in this box and the Edit button is enabled. Click the Edit button to open up the Custom Message screen (shown in Figure 11.7), where you can enter a message to be displayed—instead of Disk Doctor's normal error messages—whenever an error is encountered.

FIGURE 11.7

The Custom Message box enables you to create a personalized message which will be displayed if errors are encountered.

This option can be useful, as above, in situations where a lab technician or system administrator wants to be notified of errors, whether or not Disk Doctor repairs those errors. With the Custom Message box enabled, a message such as the one you saw in Figure 11.7 will be displayed if NDD encounters errors. Such a message may help prevent a beginning-level user from working on a damaged system, possibly making matters worse. Of course, compliance with whatever message you create is beyond what even Disk Doctor can guarantee.

Surface Test Options

The Surface Test tab shown in Figure 11.8 determines whether—and what type of—physical surface testing will be performed by NDD. The settings will apply to all selected drives; you cannot automatically perform a thorough test on one drive, a normal test on another, and no test at all on a third. If you wish that degree of control over surface tests on individual drives, you must manually run NDD, changing the settings on this tab each time. Incidentally, the Norton System Doctor Surface Sensor (which is discussed in detail in Chapter 3) performs only the "Normal" type of surface test.

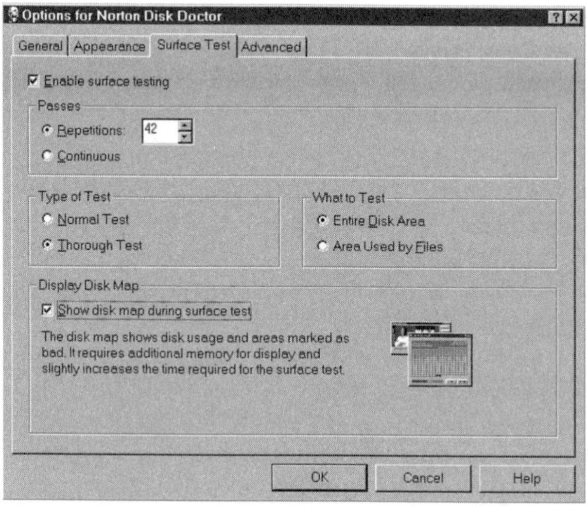

FIGURE 11.8

The Disk Doctor surface test options enable you to configure how NDD's surface testing is performed.

Chief among the surface test options is, of course, the Enable Surface Testing check box. Disabled, all of the other options on this screen are made inaccessible and Disk Doctor will not perform a surface scan of any drive until you return to this options screen and re-check the box. With surface testing enabled, you can instruct NDD to perform the surface test continuously (as you might want to do if, for example, you are responsible for burning in drives on a new system) or for any number of times that you preselect (between 1 and 999). If you suspect that a drive is having surface-related problems intermittently, you may want to have Disk Doctor perform the surface test 3 or 4 times, just to be certain. As with continuous testing, some corporations may specifically require that a fixed number of surface tests be performed before a drive is made available for employee or network use. That sort of selection can be made here, allowing NDD to do its work unattended.

This screen also enables you to select whether you want the Normal or the Thorough level of surface testing to be performed. As stated previously in this chapter, the Normal testing setting tells Disk Doctor to read every cluster of data from your drives to verify that the data can be read accurately. Thorough testing reads each cluster of data at a lower, hardware level, ensuring that read operations can be performed reliably.

Because of the amount of time involved in performing a surface test of large drives, you may wish to only look for surface errors on portions of the drive which are already occupied by your files. The What to Test setting allows you to make this distinction. With Area Used by Files chosen, areas of free space (in other words, unused clusters) are not checked during a surface scan. Although this can dramatically reduce the time a surface scan takes on a large drive—particularly one that is mostly empty—there are strong reasons to avoid using this sort of test exclusively. One of the things you want Disk Doctor to do for you, ideally, is protect your data from ever encountering damaged or weakened areas of your drive. In so doing, you don't merely recover from data loss, you prevent it.

> **Tip:** When an NDD surface test only checks used portions of the disk, any new data that you save to the disk is vulnerable until the next time you run a surface test. When you consider the value of your data and the fact that Disk Doctor can run in the background—and that you can also perform surface tests with the Norton System Doctor Surface Sensor which operates only in the slack time when you're not using your CPU anyway—use of the Area Used by Files option seems generally ill-advised. Depending on the level of protection you feel you need, however, you may want to perform a surface test of used disk areas daily and a complete disk scan only once a week. The What to Test options make that possible.

Finally, the Display Disk Map option determines whether you see the standard NDD screen or a drive map (similar to the one available through Norton Speed Disk) while a surface test is performed. Unlike the standard NDD screen which shows only the percentage of surface test complete, the drive map screen will give you an estimate of how long the surface test will take, the amount of time it has already taken, a numeric indication of what sector of the drive is being tested at any given moment, and a graphical display of used, unused, and bad areas of the disk (see Figure 11.9). As with Speed Disk, a surface test performed with the drive map screen enabled takes somewhat longer than the same test performed with less feedback to you. Depending on the size of your disks, the time difference may be anywhere from negligible to very significant.

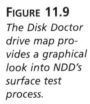

FIGURE 11.9
The Disk Doctor drive map provides a graphical look into NDD's surface test process.

Advanced Options

The options on the Advanced tab, shown in Figure 11.10, aren't truly so much "advanced" options as they are options most users won't ever need to fiddle with. It is here that you are able to deactivate specific NDD tests to compensate for incompatibilities between your hardware and Disk Doctor. Generally, a "100% IBM-compatible" computer will also be 100 percent NDD-compatible, and almost all new computers are 100 percent compatible. However, incompatible systems certainly exist and hardware added to otherwise compatible systems (a hard drive cache controller, for example) may not, themselves, be 100 percent compatible.

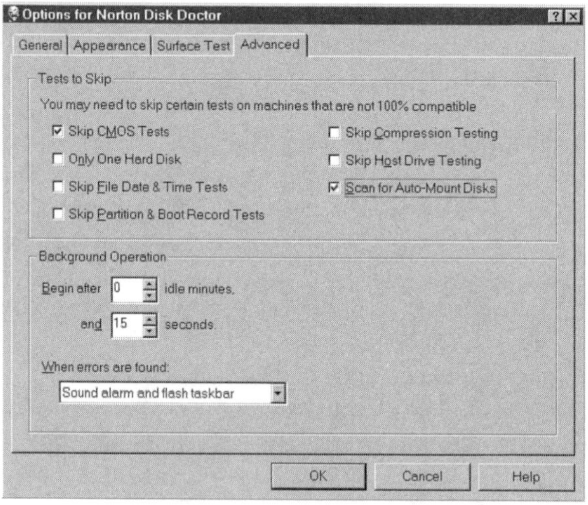

FIGURE **11.10**

The Disk Doctor advanced options provide special "tweaks" to handle uncommon hardware incompatibilities.

Tests which can be selectively skipped are:

- CMOS tests
- Date and time tests
- Partition and boot record tests
- Compressed-drive tests
- Host-drive tests

Of course, remember that skipping tests means you will no longer benefit from NDD's ability to detect errors in these areas. Unless you are quite certain you have a compatibility problem, skipping tests is not advised. In addition, you may configure Disk Doctor to ignore errant reports from your hardware indicating you have several hard disks when you only have one, and to automatically mount any compressed drive NDD encounters on removable media (like a floppy disk or an Iomega ZIP drive).

The Background Operation options determine how Norton Disk Doctor behaves when you run it minimized. Unlike the Norton System Doctor Surface Sensor, which automatically runs little-by-little in the few seconds of slack time that appear while you use your computer, Norton Disk Doctor only performs its tests during more extended periods of idle time. How much idle time must pass before NDD begins its testing (or returns to a test in progress) can be set here. You may want NDD to start up again after only a few seconds of idle time, or you may only want it to run after several minutes of idle time, while you are likely away from your desk. In addition, you can tell NDD how to behave when it is both minimized and encounters an error. You may choose to have NDD open up a report window (the default) or you may wish to be notified only by hearing a short alarm, seeing the Windows taskbar flash, or both. If you have NDD set to Auto-Repair, the notification you select will occur and NDD will continue with its testing. If you have NDD set to ask for confirmation before making any repairs, the minimized Disk Doctor will notify you that it has encountered an error (by whatever method you've selected from this Options tab) and will then wait for you to restore the NDD window to its normal size and confirm or decline the repair.

The Command-Line Norton Disk Doctor

If you have a completely inaccessible drive (and, obviously, if it's your startup drive) you won't always be able to get the Windows version of Disk Doctor running to repair the problems. Additionally, certain repairs cannot be made from within the Windows environment—Windows "protects" you from potentially disastrous types of disk modification, even if those changes are actually repairs. For that reason, Norton Disk Doctor has been included in the suite of command-line (formerly known as DOS) utilities. These utilities were placed on your hard disk when you installed the Norton SystemWorks, but they are easier to access from the Norton Emergency Disks or your Rescue disks. This dual placement also enables you to run the command-line utilities if the drive on which the Norton SystemWorks are installed is damaged. None of these utilities can be run from within a Windows MS-DOS box. If you try to run these utilities in that condition, you will see the error screen in Figure 11.11.

To run the command-line version of NDD, you must boot your computer using either Norton Emergency Disk #1, the Basic Rescue Boot Disk that you created after installing Norton SystemWorks, or else you must access the Windows startup menu (by immediately pressing F8 when you see the words Starting Windows 95 appear) and select Command-prompt only or Safe mode command prompt. You may also restart your computer in MS-DOS mode by selecting Shutdown from the Start menu, and choosing Restart in MS-DOS mode from the Shutdown options.

FIGURE **11.11**
*Command-line
Utilities cannot
run in a multi-
tasking environ-
ment (such as
Windows 95).*

Assuming you have booted using the Norton Emergency Disk #1, you will find yourself
looking at the prompt for drive A:, which is the name of the floppy drive from which
you've booted. If you have booted from the Basic Rescue Boot Disk, press Ctrl+C when
prompted to return to DOS. Insert Norton Emergency Disk #1 into your floppy drive.
(Command-line NDD is located on that disk.) If you boot into command-prompt mode
using the Windows startup menu, you will see the prompt for drive C:.

> **Note:** If your C: drive is damaged in a number of ways, attempting to boot
> through the Windows startup menu will likely fail, giving you one of several
> possible errors. In this circumstance, you will need to boot from diskette.

Whether you have booted from disk or into command-line mode, you run the Norton
Disk Doctor program by typing **NDD** at the drive prompt, and then pressing Enter. (This
assumes you are using traditional disks, and not a Norton ZIP Rescue disk. If you are
using the latter, boot your computer using the Norton ZIP Rescue floppy—or directly
with the Norton ZIP Rescue disk, if your ZIP drive is your only "floppy" drive—and
follow the onscreen prompts.)

Once started, the command-line utility is much like the Windows-based utility, with a
few exceptions. From the main screen, you can select to diagnose a disk, perform a surface test, Undo changes that NDD made during a previous session (either in Windows or
command-line mode) or change options for the command-line version of NDD. Changes
made within the command-line version of NDD do not impact the Windows version, and
vice versa.

In terms of its actual operation, the differences between diagnosing a disk within
Windows or at the command-line are largely cosmetic. One significant difference is that
as soon as you select Diagnose a Disk, the command-line version of NDD will ask you if
you have lost access to a partition that you were previously able to access (assuming that

NDD has detected what it suspects to be a damaged partition table). If you answer Yes to this question, NDD will attempt to rebuild and repair the damaged structures before running any other tests. This sort of repair, as previously mentioned, cannot be made from within Windows. If you wish, you can start the command-line version of NDD in this mode directly by including the /REBUILD switch at the command prompt, as shown below:

```
A:\NDD /REBUILD
```

If the partition rebuild process is successful—or, of course, if your partitions are all accessible and you tell Disk Doctor to not run the partition rebuild test—NDD proceeds with the same tests at the command-line that its big brother performs under Windows, generating a printable report when the process is complete.

FAT32

> Do not use the /REBUILD switch if you are working with FAT32 drives! The DOS version of Norton Disk Doctor is only able to detect and rebuild standard DOS partitions. In general, you should really only use the Windows version of NDD on FAT32 drives.

The options available to you under the command-line version of NDD are almost entirely the same as those under Windows. You can exclude specific tests based on apparent hardware incompatibilities; you can perform different types of surface tests; you can create a customized error message with a small variety of different text attributes (reversed text, boldface, underscore, and normal); and you can tell NDD how to behave during Auto-Repair sessions.

Tragically, you cannot play a music or sound file while the command-line version of Norton Disk Doctor is working.

The report generated by command-line NDD contains the same information as does that created under Windows, except that the Windows-generated report includes an estimate of what percentage of the files on the disk are fragmented.

The Next Step

Regardless of which version of Norton Disk Doctor you use, there may be times when you need to be more aggressive in your attempts to resurrect deceased data. Norton Disk Doctor can repair a tremendous number of disk-related problems, certainly all of the ones you are most likely to encounter. However, the nature of certain difficulties— cross-linked files, for example—can require you to lift the hood, as it were, and get your fingernails dirty. Norton Disk Editor is one of the best and most powerful tools on the market to help you do just that, and will be covered in Chapter 12.

Regular Doctoring

Nothing that can go wrong with your computer can go as wrong as your hard disks. Nothing that breaks, burns out, or gets soaked with coffee can cause you to lose your important data on the same scale as can disk errors. I'm very pleased to have been able, back in 1982, to begin reducing the danger posed by those all-too-common drive failures. Of course, as drives have become increasingly sophisticated, certain types of problems cannot be monitored and detected by the hardware itself. You'll read about drives with the new SMART sensor technology, for example, in other chapters of this book. However, as I'm sure you know, the more capable our technology becomes, the more we demand from it. Those new demands cause us to create increasingly complex systems, and with that complexity comes an array of new ways our technology can fail us. We've updated Norton Disk Doctor more times than I can count to keep up with—or even ahead of, I'm pleased to say—the cascade of technology.

You'll read elsewhere in this book about other parts of Norton SystemWorks that provide support for Disk Doctor. The System Doctor's Disk Integrity, Surface, and SMART sensors can watch your system while you work, checking continuously—but not intrusively—for problems as they begin to develop. If you like, you can have these sensors run Disk Doctor automatically as soon as they discover difficulties.

Just as you would take your healthy child to the physician for an annual health check-up, Disk Doctor will provide the same sort of preventive protection for your disks and the precious data they contain.

Peter Norton

Norton Utilities: The Laying-On of Hands and Norton Disk Editor

This chapter will acquaint you with Norton Disk Editor, one of the DOS-based programs that is part of the Norton Utilities and has been integrated into Norton SystemWorks. Norton Disk Editor, or *NDE*, runs under DOS because it enables you to directly view and modify your drives, their structure, and the data they hold. Many of these changes would be prohibited under Windows; there, access to fundamental disk structures is reserved exclusively for the operating system. In early versions of the Norton Utilities for Windows, nearly all major disk-repair operations had to be performed under DOS because of Windows' "protection" against low-level drive manipulation. Now, as mentioned in this book, most types of drive repair—even the repair of catastrophic damage—can be performed from within Windows if you create and boot from Norton Iomega ZIP Rescue Disks. For some things, however, there's still no alternative to DOS.

In DOS, the interface tools available are much more primitive than under Windows. Depending on your system's configuration, your mouse may not work at all under DOS. In all likelihood, it won't.

If you're familiar with working in DOS, this isn't news to you, and you're likely already as comfortable as you'll ever be there. If you're not used to DOS, the transition from Windows to DOS can seem like the difference between living in a luxury hotel or a one-room apartment. When you order dinner in the apartment, you may get it a little faster, but that's about the only advantage. Within the Norton Disk Editor's DOS-based environment, every program option is accessible through a keyboard shortcut. By default, these keyboard shortcuts follow the pattern of holding down the Alt key or the Ctrl key, depending on the command, and then pressing the highlighted letter of the command you wish to execute.

In some instances, these keyboard shortcuts will navigate you quickly through Norton Disk Editor's menus; in others, they will immediately perform a command. This much is very like Windows, although you won't have the mouse to fall back on. Also like Windows, in Norton Disk Editor's DOS-based environment you can often use the Tab key to move the focus—the indicator showing you which button or item is selected for use. With the focus on a given button or item, you can activate that item by pressing the Spacebar or the Enter key. Similarly, you can use the arrow keys to select items from lists, or use the Page Down key to display a drop-down list and see its options.

Caution: All of that introductory material aside, please understand that Norton Disk Editor is a power-user's tool. You can do untold damage—and even irreparable damage—to your drives and your data if you are not closely familiar with the technical aspects of disk and file structures like FATs, directory entries, boot records, and cluster chains. If you don't have that knowledge under your belt yet, do not take Norton Disk Editor out of its default read-only mode. In this operating mode you can examine and learn about your disks to your heart's content, but you cannot easily change anything. And changing nothing is the best advice to take until you know exactly what you are doing. Be warned, however, to avoid using the Disk Editor's cut and paste tools. Confoundingly, these will still write to the disk, even in read-only mode.

Note: If you would like to get up-to-speed on these disk-related issues, a great book is the eighth edition of *Peter Norton's Inside the PC* (Sams 1999). Chapters 9 and 10 of *Inside the PC* give a great introduction to much of what you'll want to know before you start manually editing disks, and you can work along with the Norton Disk Editor as you read.

It really is not possible to over-emphasize the admonition to keep Norton Disk Editor in read-only mode until you need to—and are prepared to—do otherwise. That said, let's examine how Norton Disk Editor works and what tools it makes available to you. All of this discussion will be from the perspective of working inside read-only mode. Only the most arcane of disk-related problems can be repaired only from within Norton Disk Editor rather than through one of the other Norton Utilities or Norton SystemWorks components. Discussion of affecting those repairs can be found in Appendix A, "Emergency Recovery Techniques." Appendix A assumes you are familiar with using Norton Disk Editor.

Using the Norton Disk Editor

The Norton Disk Editor is an MS-DOS only program, but it can be run in a DOS-box under Windows. To do so, open an MS-DOS box by selecting MS-DOS Prompt from your Start menu, under Programs. At the prompt, type CD C:\Program Files\Norton SystemWorks\Norton Utilities and press Enter. Then, type DISKEDIT and press Enter. You will receive several warnings that Norton Disk Editor may not be reliable in this mode, but it will run in a limited fashion. In practice, what's actually happening is that the Disk Editor is not coordinating with other multi-tasked operations, so you may end up with different results than you expect if you write to the disk in this mode. This isn't a flaw in Disk Editor so much as just a fact of life when you force this kind of multitasking.

> **Caution:** I strongly recommend that you never run Disk Editor while simultaneously running Windows. The results may be unpredictable at best, disastrous at worst.

You can also launch the Norton Disk Editor from within Windows by choosing Run from the Start menu, typing C:\Program Files\Norton SystemWorks\Norton Utilities\DISKEDIT in the Open box, and clicking OK. (You can also click the Browse button and navigate to DiskEdit, within the Norton Utilities subfolder of your Norton SystemWorks folder, under Program Files—unless you installed it elsewhere.) If you launch Norton Disk Editor from the Run menu, you will receive a confirmation dialog like that in Figure 12.1. If you confirm that you want NDE to run, Windows will be shut-down and your system restarted in DOS mode. When you quit Norton Disk Editor, Windows will be restarted.

FIGURE 12.1
Windows will be shut down if you launch Norton Disk Editor from within it.

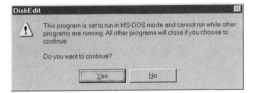

You can also launch Norton Disk Editor from either the Norton Emergency Disks which came with Norton SystemWorks or from a Norton Basic Rescue disk set. If you are starting with an Emergency Disk, boot your PC with Emergency Disk #1 in the floppy drive. You'll eventually see a small menu program which you can use to launch any of the four primary Norton DOS-based tools. Select Diskedit from the menu and press Enter. Optionally, you may add additional parameters to the menu's command-line by typing them after selecting Diskedit from the menu. For example, Norton Disk Editor will default to reading the drive on which it is itself stored, unless you specify otherwise. To do so, you might enter C: after Diskedit in the menu, before pressing Enter. You can also have Norton Disk Editor launch and automatically display a particular folder or file by adding the path to the menu's command line. For example, you might type C:\Windows\WIN.INI to have Norton Disk Editor open and directly display the disk cluster in which your WIN.INI file begins. If you enter /? after Diskedit in the menu, you will be shown a complete list of all of the various command-line parameters available to you. We'll discuss these throughout the chapter.

When Norton Disk Editor launches into its default operation (that is, if you launch it without using any command-line switches), you will first see a reminder that the program is running in read-only mode, as in Figure 12.2. This warning also indicates that, should you wish to change to read/write mode, you can do so without leaving the program. The NDE Tools menu contains a Configuration entry from which you can toggle between enabling and disabling writing to the disk. You can also launch NDE into read/write mode by typing the /W switch to the command-line after Diskedit.

Figure 12.2

This menu is a reminder that Norton Disk Editor is in read-only mode, with brief instructions on how to change to read/write mode.

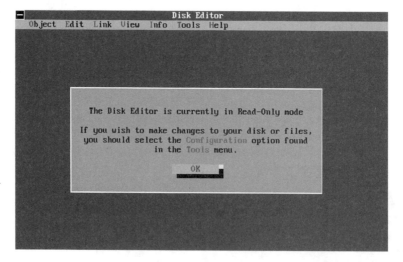

Once you press Enter to acknowledge the operating-mode notice, NDE will perform a preliminary scan of the disk and its structures. During this scan, you will be notified if any fundamental disk errors exist. Unless you have already exhausted other repair possibilities, when NDE reports trouble with a drive, you should immediately quit the Norton Disk Editor and run Norton Disk Doctor—which is one of the other DOS-based utilities available from the Emergency disk's menu—to repair any damage which it can repair. If you already know that Norton Disk Doctor cannot fix the problems NDE has identified, you can choose to ignore NDE's warning. With the warning ignored or no problems found, you'll find yourself looking at Norton Disk Editor's primary screen, as in Figure 12.3. By default, NDE will display the Root Directory of the selected drive in "View as

Directory" mode. NDE provides several special viewing modes which become automatically active when you view relevant disk structures. You'll learn about these when we discuss the View menu. With NDE's launch and preliminary scan completed, you're ready to work.

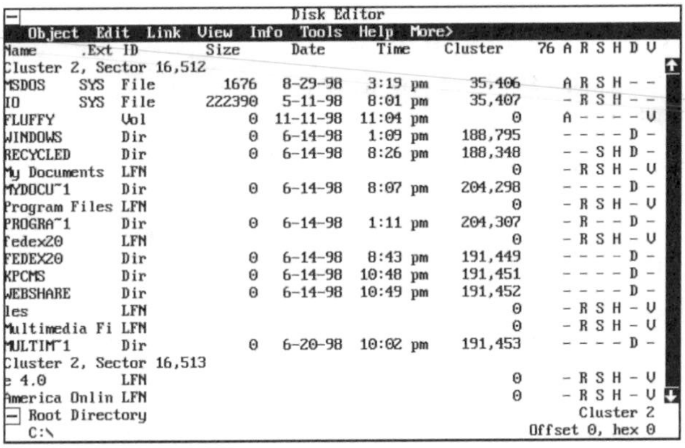

FIGURE 12.3

Norton Disk Editor's opening edit screen shows the root directory of the selected drive.

```
─┤                          Disk Editor                          ├
   Object  Edit  Link  View  Info  Tools  Help  More>
  Name     .Ext ID    Size    Date      Time    Cluster   76 A R S H D U
 Cluster 2, Sector 16,512                                                ▲
 MSDOS    SYS File     1676   8-29-98   3:19 pm    35,406     A R S H - -
 IO       SYS File   222390   5-11-98   8:01 pm    35,407     - R S H - -
 FLUFFY       Vol         0  11-11-98  11:04 pm         0     A - - - - U
 WINDOWS      Dir         0   6-14-98   1:09 pm   188,795     - - - - D -
 RECYCLED     Dir         0   6-14-98   8:26 pm   188,348     - - S H D -
 My Documents LFN                                       0     - R S H - U
 MYDOCU~1     Dir         0   6-14-98   8:07 pm   204,298     - - - - D -
 Program Files LFN                                      0     - R S H - U
 PROGRA~1     Dir         0   6-14-98   1:11 pm   204,307     - R - - D -
 Fedex20      LFN                                       0     - R S H - U
 FEDEX20      Dir         0   6-14-98   8:43 pm   191,449     - - - - D -
 KPCMS        Dir         0   6-14-98  10:48 pm   191,451     - - - - D -
 WEBSHARE     Dir         0   6-14-98  10:49 pm   191,452     - - - - D -
 les          LFN                                       0     - R S H - U
 Multimedia Fi LFN                                      0     - R S H - U
 MULTIM~1     Dir         0   6-20-98  10:02 pm   191,453     - - - - D -
 Cluster 2, Sector 16,513
 : 4.0        LFN                                       0     - R S H - U
 America Onlin LFN                                      0     - R S H - U ▼
 ─┤ Root Directory                               Cluster 2
    C:\                                           Offset 0, hex 0
```

TECHNICAL NOTE

> If you have experienced severe damage to disk system areas, you may want to bypass the NDE preliminary scan and open the Editor directly into "physical sector" mode, which enables you to look at the raw data as it is laid-out in the drive's physical sectors, with no structuring or formatting of any kind. To launch Norton Disk Editor in this "Maintenance Mode," append the /M switch to the command-line when running NDE.

The Norton Disk Editor Interface

Norton Disk Editor provides a menu-based environment in which to work. NDE does support the use of a mouse, but you must have real-mode mouse drivers on your boot disk and have them properly enabled through your AUTOEXEC.BAT and CONFIG.SYS files.

With or without a mouse, all of NDE's tools are available to you through its menus and dialogs which will open based on menu items you select. We'll look through each menu item to help acquaint you with the entire interface.

The Object Menu

Serving as the equivalent of a File menu for NDE, the Object menu is where you retrieve areas of the disk into memory for editing. All items in the Object menu—other than one item, which gives you access to the Clipboard—have direct keyboard shortcuts. Once you have these memorized, you'll not need to use the drop-down menu to select the items you need. Keyboard shortcuts (indicated onscreen by a single letter highlighted in each command or menu option) are included in the following discussions in parentheses after an item's name.

The Big Three Commands

First among the Object menu's items are Drive (Alt+D), Directory (Alt+R), and File (Alt+F). By default, the Drive item enables you to select which of the logical drives on your PC you wish to edit. Once you invoke the Drive dialog, however, you can choose to view physical disks, rather than logical drives, by pressing Alt+P while the Drive dialog is open. This will be of particular use to you if you need to edit a drive on which the Partition Table or Master Boot Record have been damaged. Such damage could hide the existence of logical drives until it is repaired. As you'll read later, NDE will also enable you to copy an entire disk partition to another physical drive so you can work with its original host drive without ever endangering the partition's contents.

TECHNICAL NOTE

Examining a physical drive is a way to enter Maintenance Mode without leaving Norton Disk Editor and re-launching it with the /M switch on the command-line. By definition, if you are working outside of a drive's logical partitions, you are bypassing DOS, so physical sector mode is automatically enabled and the view is switched to hexadecimal, as in Figure 12.4. You still have the option of viewing physical sector data through one of NDE's formatting viewers, but you will see garbage if you are not examining the type of structure which corresponds to the viewer you've chosen. Notice in Figure 12.4, the different sector number from that shown in Figure 12.3. This is indicative of the change from viewing logical structures on a logical drive to viewing physical structures on a physical drive. The difference between the two sector numbers shown is accounted for by the physical sectors used at the beginning of the physical drive for, among other things, the partition table.

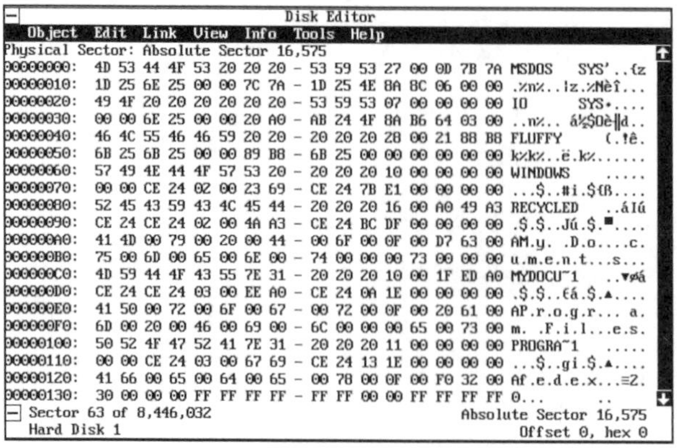

FIGURE 12.4

Norton Disk Editor displays the same data as in Figure 12.3, but in "Maintenance Mode."

Selecting the Directory item from the Object menu shows you a hierarchical tree of all directories on the selected drive, as shown in Figure 12.5. This tree is viewable only as fully-expanded; there are no hierarchical plus "+" and minus "-" buttons to open and close directories as there are in Windows. You can, however, quickly navigate through the Directory tree by typing letters on your keyboard. These letters will automatically appear in the Speed Search box, and the directory tree will jump automatically to the best match. This search is limited inasmuch as it performs exclusively from left to right. So typing PAPER will find the directory whose name begins with those five letters. If you have a directory named "Papers," adding S to the above entry will jump you to the second directory. You cannot, however, type PERS and hope to be taken to the "Papers" directory. If a directory named "Persons" exists, typing **PERS** would take you there instead. Another limitation of Speed Search is that, if you have two directories of the same name on a drive—perhaps a /USERS/MIKE/ directory and a /ADMIN/MIKE/ directory, Speed Search will only take you to whichever MIKE directory appears first on the drive. If you type a letter and it refuses to appear in the Speed Search box, that means no directory matching such a search string exists. So, if you type HAPP but the "y" of "HAPPY" refuses to display, you know that you've found a directory which matches "HAPP," but there are no HAPPY directories on your drive. You can press Backspace to delete the last-entered letter from the Speed Search box.

FIGURE 12.5

NDE's Change Directory command enables you to dynamically search for directories using either DOS-style or long filenames.

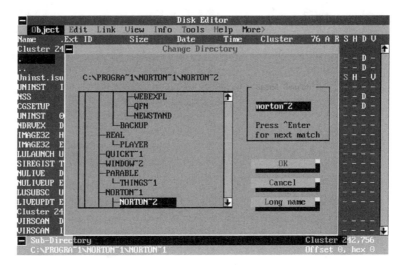

You can use your arrow keys to move up and down, browsing through the Directory tree manually. You can also press Alt+L to enable viewing directory names as Long File Names (for directories with long names). This can be particularly useful if you're trying to determine whether you want to select NORTON~1, NORTON~2, and so on. NORTON~1 might become Norton SystemWorks, for example, and NORTON~2, Norton Utilities. You can turn long filenames back off by pressing Alt+D, for "DOS Names." Once you have located and highlighted the directory in which you wish to work, pressing Enter loads that directory into the Editor. Figure 12.5 shows an open Directory tree with Speed Search being used.

Selecting the File item from the Object menu opens up a dialog which roughly simulates Windows' own "Open File" dialog.

Here, unfortunately, you cannot view long filenames. One of the most difficult aspects of this dialog—because it's not documented anywhere—is changing from one drive to another. In reality, it's very simple. Press Alt+V to activate the drive box, then press PgDn to drop the list of logical drives. With the drive box dropped, you can either type the letter of the drive you wish to select, or you can use the arrow keys to scroll through the list. The Directories and Files boxes will automatically update if you change drives as soon as you press Tab or Alt+key away from the Drives box. You can use keyboard short-cuts or the Tab key to move between the various boxes. You don't need to select OK after finding the file you want; pressing Enter with its name selected will load that file into the Editor. Figure 12.6 shows the Select File dialog.

FIGURE 12.6

Use the Select File dialog box to choose the drive, directory, and file you want to load into Disk Editor.

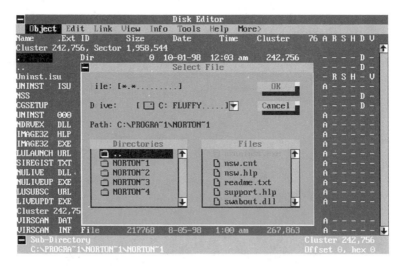

Disk Structures

You may find that examining your drives based on the high-level structures discussed in the previous section doesn't give you access to what you want.

The Object menu provides seven alternatives. The Cluster menu item (Alt+C) enables you to specify the number of any single cluster on disk which you want loaded into the Editor. With that cluster loaded as a starting point, you can scroll down the Editor to view contiguous clusters. The Sector (Alt+S) menu item, similarly, enables you to select any logical sector from the active logical drive for editing. You may find such manually created groupings useful if you, for example, want to select an entire File Allocation Table and work with it as a single unit, across clusters.

The Object menu's Physical Sector (Alt+P) item works a bit differently. Again, by choosing to view a physical disk structure you will be dropped into "Maintenance Mode" after the Select Physical Sector Range dialog box is closed (see Figure 12.7). Here you may indicate the cylinder, side, and sector you wish to view, or you may enter a specific sector number at the bottom of the dialog box. If you are troubleshooting the possibility of physical damage on one of your drive's platters, being able to specify platter side, cylinder, and sector can be very useful.

FIGURE 12.7

The Sector Range dialog box enables you to select a physical sector for editing.

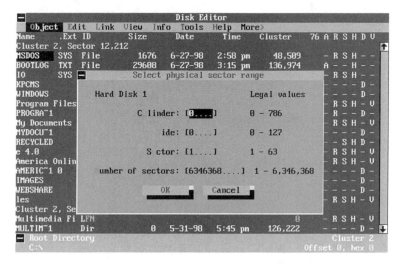

An Object menu item which is available only in Maintenance Mode—that is, when examining a physical, not logical, drive—is Partition Table (Alt+A). Choosing Partition Table displays the partition table for the active physical disk, as shown in Figure 12.8. The partition table display indicates the size and physical disk location of every partition on the active disk. It also indicates whether each partition is bootable or not. If the partition format is known, that information also appears. In read/write mode, all data on the partition table screen is editable. You can forcibly change a partition's size or repair damage that has made a formerly-bootable partition non-bootable.

The partition table display is also a good opportunity to see one of Norton Disk Editor's important features. NDE has been designed so that whatever data is selected by the cursor in one view will remain selected in a different view. For example, in Figure 12.8, the first partition's boot byte is highlighted. You can see its location on disk by looking at the lower-right corner of the status bar. Cylinder, platter side, sector, and sector offset are shown, the latter in decimal and hexadecimal. If you use the View menu—which you'll read about in the next paragraph—and switch to a standard Hex view, as in Figure 12.9, the boot byte remains highlighted (notice that the status bar reports the same data as before). This consistency will be a great help to you as you find yourself switching between views to perform a variety of editing tasks. This function is also a good educational tool that can broaden your understanding of where data is physically stored on your disks.

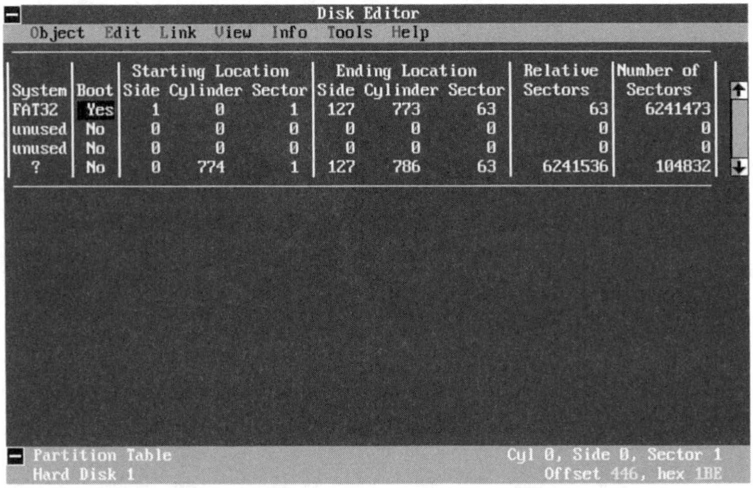

Figure 12.8

You can edit a physical drive's partition table with NDE.

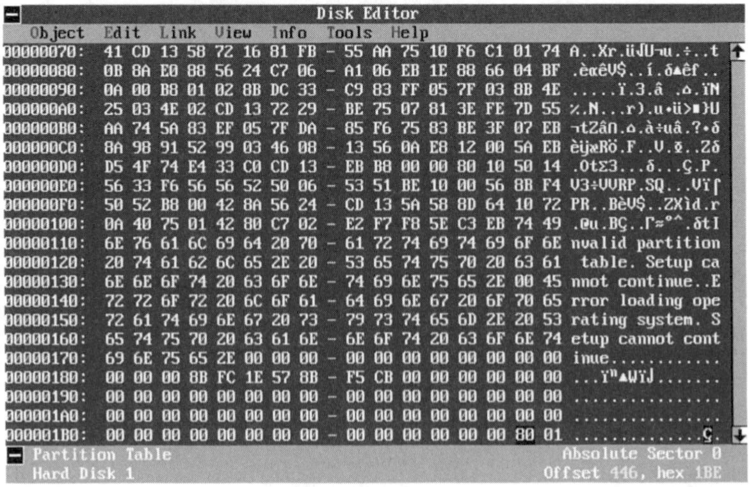

Figure 12.9

Editing a physical drive's partition table with NDE.

TECHNICAL NOTE

> Remember that changing the bootable entry in a partition table from "no" to "yes" will toggle the drive's "boot byte"—located at offset 1BEh from the beginning of absolute sector zero on the physical drive—but you will not be able to boot if the boot record of the logical drive contained in that partition is also damaged. If you change a partition from non-bootable back to bootable, but still receive errors at boot time, you probably have boot record damage, which needs to be repaired. You can, of course, attempt to do this manually, but Norton Disk Doctor and your Norton Rescue set and Image were designed for just that sort of problem. (Of course, for a partition to be bootable, it must also be a primary partition and its logical drive must also contain the relevant system files.)

In read-only mode, pressing Enter while highlighting any item on a primary partition's horizontal row will display the Boot Record data for that partition, as in Figure 12.10. (Pressing Enter while highlighting any item on an Extended partition's horizontal row will display the Extended partition's partition table, where one or more logical drives in that partition are managed. Pressing Enter again while highlighting one of these logical drives will show that drive's Boot Record.) You can also view a logical drive's boot record by selecting Boot Record (Alt+B) from the Object menu. If the data within a logical drive's boot record becomes damaged—if, for example, an invalid value is stored in the "Sectors Per Track" entry—that entire logical volume could be rendered inaccessible. Norton Disk Doctor will repair these kinds of problems, but you can—if you are a more advanced technician—also explore and repair them yourself with NDE.

FIGURE 12.10

You can use Disk Editor to view a partition's boot record data.

```
┌─────────────────────────── Disk Editor ────────────────────────────┐
│ Object  Edit  Link  View  Info  Tools  Help                          │
│            Description        Boot Record Data    DOS Reports         │
│ Physical Sector: Cyl 0, Side 1, Sector 1                             │
│                   OEM ID: MSWIN4.1                                    │
│            Bytes per sector: 512                  512                 │
│          Sectors per cluster: 8                   8                   │
│   Reserved sectors at beginning: 32               32                  │
│                 FAT Copies: 2                     2                   │
│                  Reserved: 0                                          │
│                  Reserved: (Unused)                                   │
│        Media descriptor byte: F8 Hex                                  │
│            Sectors per FAT: 0                     6090                │
│          Sectors per track: 63                                        │
│                    Sides: 128                                         │
│        Special hidden sectors: 63                                     │
│   Big total number of sectors: (Unused)                               │
│         Big Sectors Per Fat: 6090                 6090                │
│        Number of active Fats: 0                                       │
│                  Reserved: (Unused)                                   │
│                  Mirrored: Yes                                        │
│                  Reserved: (Unused)                                   │
│      File System Ver (major): 0                                       │
│ Boot Record                              Cyl 0, Side 1, Sector 1     │
│ Drive C:                                      Offset 3, hex 3         │
└─────────────────────────────────────────────────────────────────────┘
```

As with partition tables and boot records, a logical drive's file allocation table and its backup are both editable from within Norton Disk Editor. To view or edit the active logical drive's primary FAT, press Alt+F1. Press Alt+F2 if you want to display the backup FAT. While you are moving through the FAT, all FAT entries pertaining to a specific file will turn red while the selection cursor is resting on any of those entries. The name of the file belonging to the selected entry and its red companions will appear at the bottom of the screen in the status bar, as in Figure 12.11.

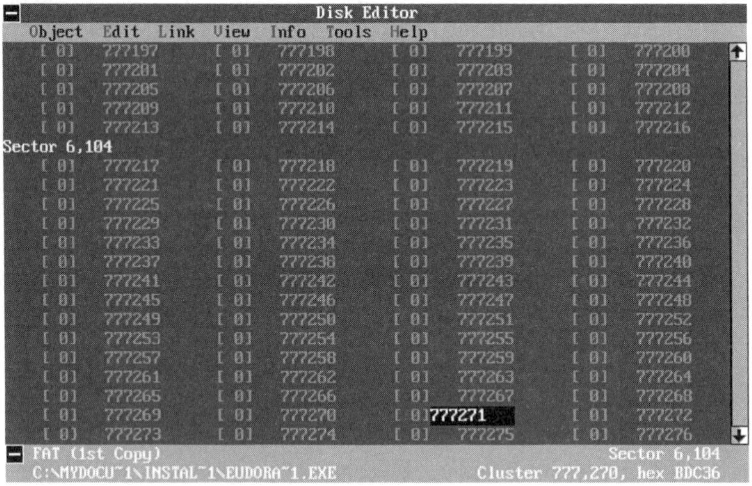

FIGURE 12.11
NDE views FAT (FAT32, actually) entries for the file EUDORA~1.EXE.

Caution: Norton Rescue can use your Image data to restore a damaged FAT back to health, but manually modifying the file allocation table's entries is definitely a job for experts. It is easier to reconstruct a partial file using Norton UnErase's manual mode than with the Norton Disk Editor, and Norton Disk Doctor will repair any discrepancies which arise between the two FATs. Norton Disk Editor can, nevertheless, be a great tool to use in read-only mode if you're studying and trying to understand exactly how the File Allocation Tables work.

Cut and Paste

The Norton Disk Editor supports a rudimentary cut-and-paste ability accessible through the Mark and Copy commands in the NDE Edit menu, which is examined in the next section. The Clipboard item in the Object menu eanbles you to view data you have copied after marking. There is no direct keyboard shortcut for viewing the Clipboard. It is accessible by pressing Alt+O to open the Object menu and then pressing C, for Clipboard. To close the Clipboard view, you must select another object to view from the Object menu. (Incidentally, the Clipboard is capable of holding a maximum of 4K of data).

Exploring Memory with a Disk Explorer

The final entry in the Norton Disk Editor's Object menu, other than Exit, is Memory
Dump (Alt+M). While NDE will not allow you to make changes to the data in active
memory, you can view the contents of a memory range which you specify and then
mark, copy, and paste that data to disk, if need be. This can be a useful tool for programmers who want to capture areas of memory used by their software for troubleshooting
purposes. As with the Clipboard, viewing a Memory Dump is disabled by selecting
another object to view from the Object menu.

The Edit Menu

The Norton Disk Editor's Edit menu, displayed in Figure 12.12, gives you Windows-like
control over a number of modification-oriented tools. You can Mark (Ctrl+B) a range of
data or a directory entry while viewing it in one location and Copy (Ctrl+C) it to the
Clipboard for Pasting (Ctrl+V) elsewhere, even to another drive. The default for pasting
data is different from what you may be used to: paste normally overwrites existing data.
That is, if you have a 32-byte string of data stored on the Clipboard and you paste it to a
disk using the normal Paste command, the 32 bytes of Clipboard data will replace the
32 bytes of data which exists in the area in which you perform the paste. For disk editing, this is often precisely what you want, because you'll be performing a manual edit to
repair bad data. You don't want your bad data merely moved out of the way. You also
have the option of filling a particular range of bytes on disk with a specific single value.

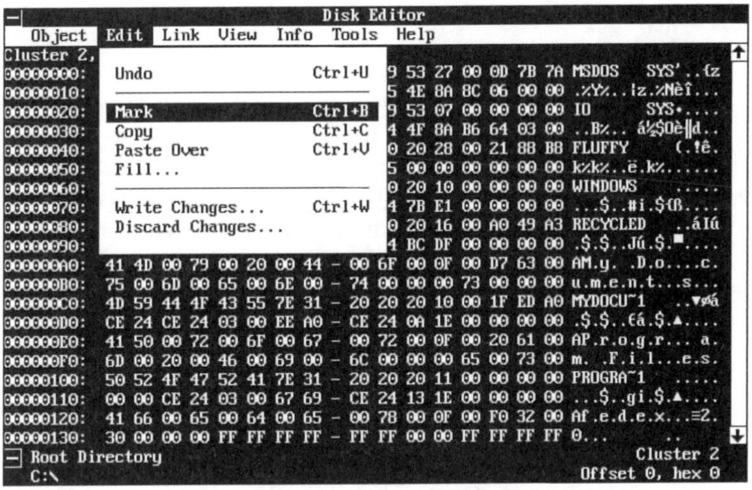

FIGURE 12.12

*The NDE Edit
menu gives access
to the Disk
Editor's modifica-
tion features.*

Activate Mark mode by selecting it from the Edit menu, then use the arrow keys to mark
the block over which you want to fill. Select the Fill command from the Edit menu—
there is no keyboard shortcut—and a small dialog box will open into which you may

type the value you want filled into the marked location. With this dialog box open, you may also use the arrow keys to scroll through the characters (and their respective values) which can be filled. Select OK or press Enter when you have the desired fill value selected, and each byte in the marked range will be set to that value.

> **Caution:** When you're marking areas of the disk for filling, be certain you mark both the start and end of the block you wish to modify. If you do not, Fill will automatically mark to the end of the selected sector or cluster (depending on what mode you're using). This could overwrite data you don't intend to change. And remember: a Fill operation is *not* undoable!

The most-recent modification which you have made can be Undone through use of the Undo (Ctrl+U) command, with one significant exception. Undo does not work across sectors. That is, if you make a modification which spans a sector edge by even one byte, that entire modification will be permanent. Undo will not be available. So long as you modify less than one disk sector at a time, Undo will reverse your modifications, replacing them with the values previously found on disk. Only one level of Undo is provided, so you must undo any given modification before you perform another.

> **Caution:** Remember—a Fill operation is an exception to the rule. A Fill *cannot be undone.*

In addition to the Undo command, Norton Disk Editor will display a confirmation dialog box whenever you have modified an area of disk and try to move to another disk location or view a different object. If you wish to keep your modification, selecting Write will write those changes to disk. Selecting Discard will throw your changes away, leaving the disk untouched. The drive's actual contents are not physically modified until you Write those changes to disk. Until then, modifications are in the Editor's memory only. If you wish to manually Write (Ctrl+W) or Discard changes, you can do so by selecting the appropriate command from the Edit menu. (There is no keyboard shortcut for Discarding modifications.)

> **Tip:** Although there is no specific keyboard shortcut for discarding changes, you can discard changes by scrolling the cursor past the end or beginning of a sector. You'll see a confirmation dialog box, advising you that you need to save or discard your changes before continuing to a new sector. Simply select Discard, and your changes are thrown away.

The Link Menu

The Link menu enables you to quickly jump from one bit of data on one part of a disk to a related bit of data, elsewhere on the disk. Link enables you to quickly move from a file's directory entry to the file's contents. You can move instantly from a subdirectory back to its parent, or to the area of the FAT showing that subdirectory's physical location on disk. (Recall that a subdirectory's contents are maintained in special subdirectory files which are maintained in the FAT and can become fragmented just like any other file.) You can jump from a physical drive's partition table to the boot record of a selected partition, and so on. All of these links are bi-directional, of course, so you can jump from a file's contents back to its directory entry or to the FAT, and so on. The four primary Link menu commands—File (Ctrl+F), Directory (Ctrl+D), FAT (Ctrl+T), and Partition (no keyboard shortcut)—will automatically enable and disable, depending on what type of data is selected in the Editor window. It would be meaningless, for example, to link from a Partition Table to a cluster chain in the FAT. In which FAT? On which partition? And where in the FAT? Therefore, if you find that a Link tool is not available, look into the status bar at the lower-left of the screen to verify what type of object you are viewing. Chances are good that you aren't where you think you are.

The Link menu also enables you to create a link between two split Editor windows—a useful technique you'll read about in the next section. With windows linked, moving the cursor in one window moves the cursor to relevant data in the second window. With this technique you can, for example, view a directory, then split the window, link to the directory's cluster chain in the FAT, and then link the two windows, so moving through the cluster chain will scroll the directory, or contrariwise. Window linking is toggled through the Link menu—there is no keyboard shortcut. Window linking will, of course, automatically disable if you unsplit the Editor window.

The View Menu

The View menu enables you to look at a variety of disk-based data in a variety of ways. And, unlike the Link menu, when looking at a certain bit of data with a certain viewer makes no sense, NDE won't stop you. This may seem illogical, but after discussing each viewer, the reason for this becomes clear. Nine different viewers are available from within NDE. Also, the View menu's Window commands give you powerful control over what you see onscreen, and how you see it.

The Viewers

By default, Norton Disk Editor is configured to do its best to analyze what type of data you are viewing in the Editor window. It uses this analysis to select one of nine different built-in viewing tools which format the raw disk-based data into meaningful, human-readable content. (This configuration—Disk Editor selecting the best viewer automatically—is the default, but it can be deactivated from the Tools menu, as you will read later in this chapter.) Look for a moment at Figure 12.13. Here you can see the DOS boot record for a hard drive. Now look at the accompanying Figure 12.14. Here, you're looking at precisely the same data, but you're viewing it as raw hexadecimal code. Note that the OEM ID which you see in Figure 12.12—MSWIN4.1 (or Windows 98)—will remain highlighted in the Hex view if it is highlighted in the Boot Record view.

Figure 12.13
A DOS boot record, viewed as a boot record.

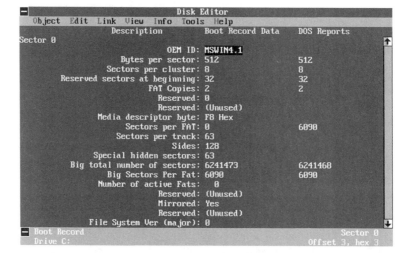

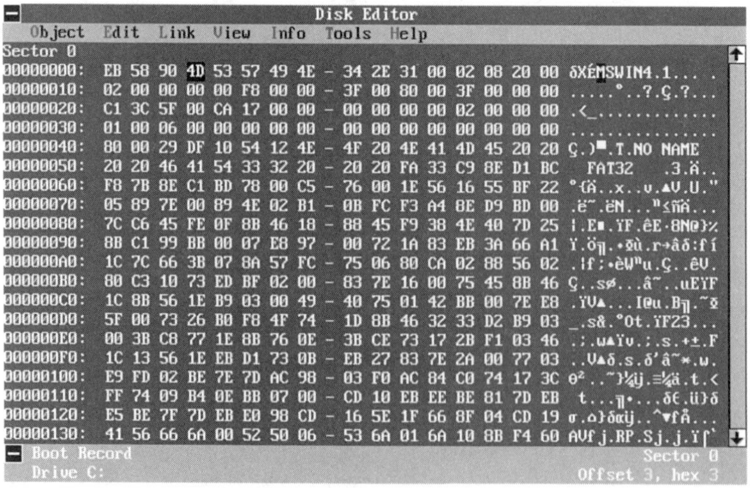

Figure 12.14
The same DOS boot record, viewed as hexadecimal code (with ASCII text equivalents at the extreme right).

Obviously, if you're looking for the OEM ID for the operating system installed in a particular partition, you can see this information much more clearly by looking at the boot record as a boot record and not simply as raw data. Because this is true about a number of logical and physical disk structures, the Norton Disk Editor comes with its own intelligence, enabling it to break up the raw code into its components and display those components to you clearly. Here's another brief example: Figure 12.15 shows the partition table of a physical disk. Norton Disk Editor has organized all of the table's data so that you can easily read—or edit—it. Each partition's system type, whether it's bootable, and so on, are all sorted out into an easily-used table. Figure 12.16 shows the same data, viewed as hex code.

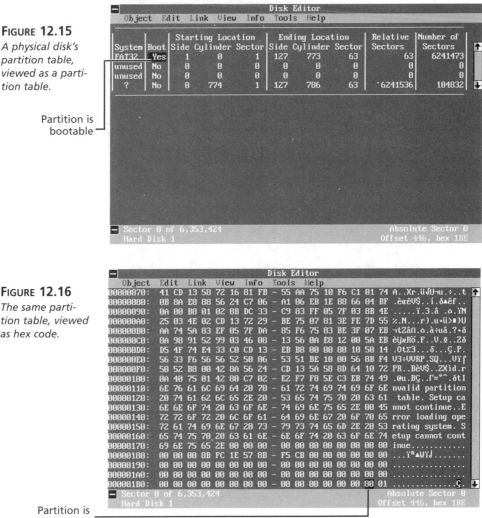

FIGURE 12.15

A physical disk's partition table, viewed as a partition table.

Partition is bootable

FIGURE 12.16

The same partition table, viewed as hex code.

Partition is bootable

In Figure 12.15, you can see that the selected partition is bootable. In Figure 12.16, you can see precisely the same information, but if you don't know that 80h at sector offset 1BEh means that a partition is bootable, you may no know what to do with this bit of data. Norton Disk Editor knows. NDE has intelligence about most standard disk structures, including those on non-DOS partitions, like PCIX, CP/M, XENIX, HPFS, and many others long lost to history. Why this matters is because Norton Disk Editor, being able to understand structures on those disparate formats of partition, can help you recover data lost in those partitions, even on a 15-year-old CP/M disk.

It is for this reason that NDE includes all of the nine viewers it does. The more ways you can view an area of disk, the better the likelihood that you'll be able to successfully accomplish whatever it is you launched Norton Disk Editor to achieve. If you're using Norton Disk Editor, for example, to look through a selection of UnErased partial files in the hope of recovering vital data, you might find the process very frustrating if all you had to look at was a Hex display, as in Figure 12.17.

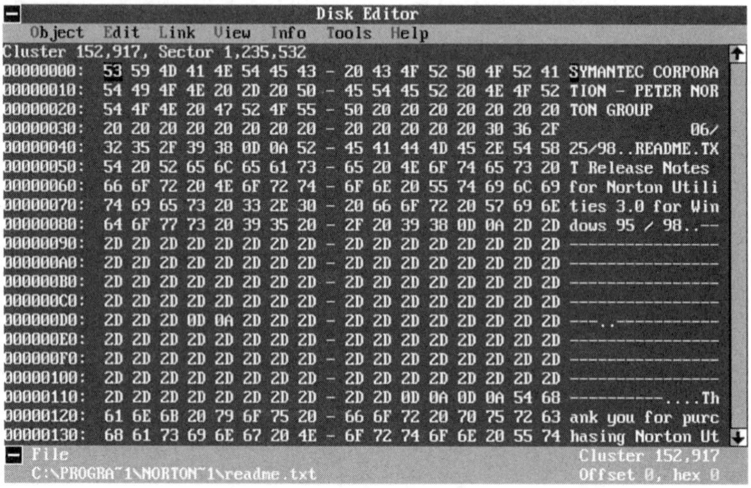

FIGURE 12.17

Viewing an area of disk as raw hexadecimal code.

Compare the Hex view with the text view of the same part of the disk, in Figure 12.18. What a difference! Not only is it much more obvious what you're looking at, the text display is infinitely more efficient than the hex display for viewing this kind of data. Notice how little of the text file appears onscreen in Figure 12.17. In order to determine whether this bit of data is what you want, you might have to scroll through screen after screen of verbose hex code. All the while, you'd probably be watching the text column at the right anyway. And consider the benefit of the text view in Figure 12.18 when it comes time to marking some of this data and copying it into a new file! This text file is occupying 115 sectors; NDE displays about half of one sector per screen in hex view. In text view, between one-and-a-half and two sectors are shown per screen. You'll have a lot less scrolling to do while you're marking text if you mark it in text view. (Of course, depending on the formatting and structure of your text file—particularly if it isn't a true text file, but is a formatted word processor document containing text, like a .DOC file— you may find using either the hex view *or* the text view to be more clear.)

FIGURE 12.18

Viewing the same README.TXT file using the text viewer.

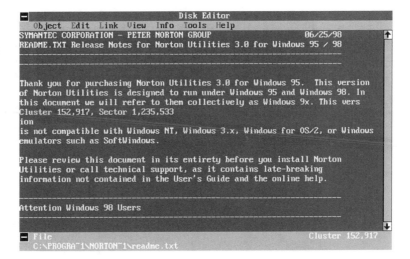

On the other hand, of course, you may want to add characters to a file that are not readily available from the keyboard—DOS line-drawing characters, for example. If you know the hexadecimal equivalent for the ASCII line character you wish to use, you can very easily open the file, switch to the hex view, type the character's hex code in the proper place, look at the text column to verify you work, save, and you're done.

Sometimes, of course, a certain view won't make sense for certain data. Figure 12.19 shows the effect of viewing a directory as if it were a drive's boot record. Even if you know next to nothing about boot records, you can compare this display with the one shown in Figure 12.13, and sense that you're probably looking at garbage. There is no OEM ID, and the File System ID in Figure 12.19 is made up of seemingly random characters. When you look down in the status bar at the lower-left corner and recall that you're viewing a subdirectory, all this nonsense suddenly makes sense.

So why does NDE enable you to view data in inappropriate ways? Two reasons. First, for all of its intelligence, Norton Disk Editor's default viewer may not be the one you want to use. Once the user has established that NDE did not select the preferred viewer for a particular bit of data, NDE has no way of knowing what you want to do, so it makes all viewers available to you. Additionally, think back to the discussion of the Edit menu. Recall that you can mark whole areas of disk, copy them, and then write them elsewhere. Imagine the circumstance in which you are encountering intermittent failures when you try to read a particular directory. You suspect that the magnetic structure markings on that part of the disk have weakened with age. Using Norton Disk Editor, you can view that part of the disk, mark and copy the directory to another, unused location, update the directory's FAT entries to reflect the new location, and, in essence, save the directory from the fading disk. (There are much better ways to solve this same sort of problem, and Norton Disk Doctor repairs such concerns automatically when you perform a surface scan. Nevertheless, as a hypothetical situation, it works for our purposes here.)

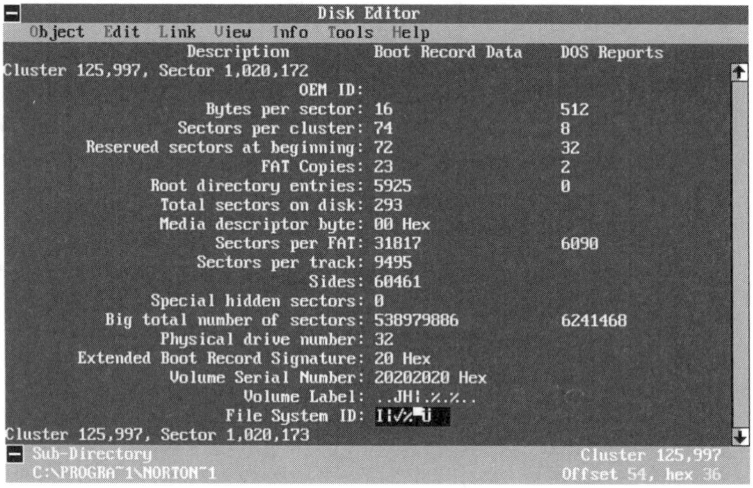

FIGURE **12.19**
*Subdirectories
make very poor
boot records.*

```
┌─                      Disk Editor                                     ─┐
│ Object  Edit  Link  View  Info  Tools  Help                           │
│               Description         Boot Record Data    DOS Reports      │
│ Cluster 125,997, Sector 1,020,172                                    ↑ │
│                    OEM ID:                                            ▓ │
│             Bytes per sector:  16                     512             ▓ │
│          Sectors per cluster:  74                     8               ▓ │
│   Reserved sectors at beginning: 72                   32              ▓ │
│                 FAT Copies:  23                       2               ▓ │
│        Root directory entries:  5925                  0               ▓ │
│          Total sectors on disk:  293                                  ▓ │
│        Media descriptor byte:  00 Hex                                 ▓ │
│             Sectors per FAT:  31817                   6090            ▓ │
│          Sectors per track:  9495                                     ▓ │
│                      Sides:  60461                                    ▓ │
│         Special hidden sectors:  0                                    ▓ │
│      Big total number of sectors:  538979886          6241468         ▓ │
│          Physical drive number:  32                                   ▓ │
│   Extended Boot Record Signature:  20 Hex                             ▓ │
│        Volume Serial Number:  20202020 Hex                            ▓ │
│                Volume Label:  ..JH!.%.%..                             ▓ │
│              File System ID:  I¦√%█U                                  ▓ │
│ Cluster 125,997, Sector 1,020,173                                    ↓ │
│ ─ Sub-Directory                              Cluster 125,997          │
│   C:\PROGRA~1\NORTON~1                        Offset 54, hex 36        │
└──────────────────────────────────────────────────────────────────────┘
```

Now, once you've pasted the directory to its new location, you go back to DOS, examine the directory, and see only garbage. Obviously, something went wrong. Returning to Norton Disk Editor, you view the directory's new location with the Directory viewer. You know that every directory must start with the dot and double-dot (".", "..") entries, but your new directory doesn't. Obviously, you missed some data when you marked and moved the directory. You can go back with NDE, re-mark and move the directory, and be thankful for this ability to re-check your work.

Directory Viewer Formatting

You've already seen that each viewer has its own formatting style. While it is generally clear what a viewer is showing you when you are using the best viewer for a specific piece of data, the Directory Viewer provides a good deal more data about directory and file entries than will fit on the screen. For this reason, while you are in Directory view, you will notice a new menu, More>, has been added to the menu bar, following the Help menu. When the More> menu is present, pressing Alt+> on your keyboard will cause the entire display—except for the first column, the file and directory names—to scroll to the left. There are a total of three screens available, and the <More (Alt+<) menu will also appear if you are looking at anything other than the first horizontal screen. These two additional screens provide, among other information, the creation time and date for each directory entry, when the file or directory was last accessed, and whether a file's DOS 8.3 filename and its Windows long filename are properly attached to each other. (This last item is a problem easily repaired by Norton Disk Doctor.)

Arcane Viewers

Just as NDE has intelligence for dealing with antiquated types of disks and data, so too are the viewers designed for maximum flexibility in this regard. Among the nine viewers available, you'll find FAT(12), FAT(16), and Boot Record(16) (along with their 32-bit equivalents). A 12-bit FAT is used, to this day, on floppy disks. Before MS-DOS 3.3, all file allocation tables were 12-bit tables; this was expanded to 16-bit to allow support for ever-larger drives. Sixteen-bit FATs and Boot Records are still widespread, too, and if you haven't updated old hard drives on your system to FAT32, it is these viewers you'll want to use to view those structures with clarity.

Window Control

In addition to providing these various ways to control how you display data in the Editor window, the View menu gives you a good deal of control over the window itself. You will recall from the section on the Link menu, that you can split the Editor window into two panes. You can also synchronize those panes to view the same data—or related data, or entirely other data, such as a location to which you intend to paste data copied out of the other pane—in different ways. A Split window may be created by selecting that item from the View menu or by pressing Shift+F5. Figure 12.20 shows one example of this in action. Here you can see one of the Norton Utilities' "read me" file's contents in the upper panel and its directory entry in the lower panel. With the two panels linked, you can scroll through the directory entries and the upper panel will jump to display the contents of each file you highlight in the lower panel.

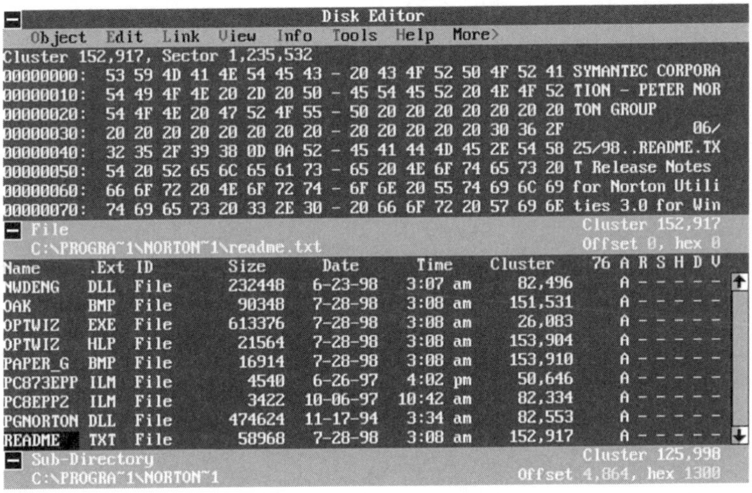

Figure 12.20

You can view the contents of a file and the file's directory entry simultaneously through split, linked windows.

The steps for creating linked windows are these: First, using a single window, view one of the two pieces of data you want to show in the split windows. With that piece of data selected, press Shift+F5 to split the window. By default, you will now see the window split horizontally, and two copies of the same data—one in each pane. You can move the cursor between panes by selecting Switch Windows (Shift+F8) from the View menu. Next, select the Link command you wish. The active panel will update to show the linked data. Finally, to synchronize scrolling between the two panes, choose Window from the Link menu. The two panes will remain linked until you turn the link off.

Indeed, even if you use the Unsplit Window (Shift+F5 toggles between split and unsplit) command, if you re-split the window, the former link will remain active.

There are times when you won't want the windows linked. If you are moving data from one area of disk to another—or even from one drive to another... you can view a different drive in each split panel, if you wish—you will likely have need for neither linked data nor linked windows. There will also be times when you'll want to keep the windows split, but an equal split won't best suit your needs. The View menu provides two items, Grow Window (Shift+F6) and Shrink Window (Shift+F7) which increase or decrease the size of the active pane (the pane in which the cursor is found) one line at a time. You might be copying data off a damaged hard disk to a floppy disk, for example. You want to keep the window split for maximum convenience, but you have no need to devote half the screen to the floppy drive's display while you are marking and copying data from the hard drive. You can shrink either panel down to as few as two lines, then increase its size on demand.

The Info Menu

The four items in the Norton Disk Editor Info menu provide you with background data about the currently selected Object, the active Drive, the area of disk occupied by the current Object, and any errors which were encountered by NDE when it performed its initial scan of the active drive. If no errors were encountered, the Error Info entry will not be available.

Figure 12.21 illustrates the Info screen for a directory. Whether you are viewing a directory, a file, a FAT, or a boot record, the object's info screen will also show you the drive letter on which the object appears, the capacity of that drive, and the type of drive—either hard disk or floppy disk. In the Selected Object box you can quickly review the full DOS path to the object you've selected, as well as its DOS attributes (such as whether it is a directory, a system file, hidden, archive bit set, and so on). You will also be shown the date and time the object was last modified, and both its starting cluster number and the number of the physical sector in which that cluster begins. Finally, the size of the object in terms of both bytes and clusters used is shown, along with the number of fragments in which the object is split.

Note: Fragmentation data from these windows may be a bit confusing at first. What, precisely, is one fragment? To answer that meaningfully, I need to point out that the real misnomer here is "fragment." An object which is on disk in one fragment is actually an unfragmented object, with all of its contents located in one contiguous cluster chain. Thus, the term "fragment" is being used to refer to contiguous clusters in which one and only one file's data is stored (whether the fragment contains the entire file or only a portion of it). An object using two fragments, contrastingly, is precisely what it sounds like it would be: an object that is stored in two cluster chains which are not contiguous. The confusion arises because we normally think of a fragment as being a part of the whole. In this case, one fragment refers to the whole.

Figure 12.21

The Info display for a directory.

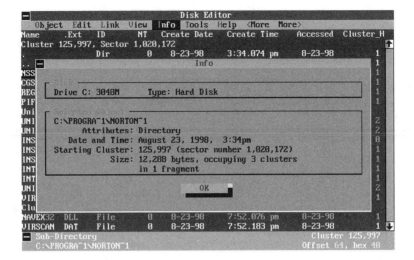

With either a directory or file selected, you can use the Map of Object command from the Info menu to see, graphically, where a file appears on disk. In Figure 12.22, for example, you can see the drive map for a file which is part of Norton SystemWorks. You'll notice that the letter "F" is used within the map to show disk areas where the file is located. In this example, the file selected is fragmented, so there are two noncontiguous "F" marks on the map. These two fragments are separated both by partially free space and by the contents of other files. If I ran Norton Speed Disk on this drive and reshot the screen image, the two "F" marks would be together. The resolution of the drive map is limited by the size of a DOS-based display and is set by the capacity of the drive on which the object occurs. On this large drive, each block in the map represents 1,343 clusters! On a much smaller drive, a floppy drive, for example, each block might represent as few as three or five clusters. You can view a much higher-resolution disk map through Norton Speed Disk.

The Info menu's display of information about the active drive is always the same, regardless of what sub-drive object you have selected. You'll again be shown the letter, capacity, and type of the active disk, along with both its logical and physical characteristics. Much of this information—bytes per sector, sectors per cluster, FAT type, and so on— you will recognize from the drive's boot record.

The Tools Menu

Norton Disk Editor's Tools menu is where a number of NDE's manual editing-oriented tools for power-users are found, as well as configuration properties for the entire program. Because you should understand the disk objects upon which these tools work before you start using them, the discussion here will deal exclusively with how to use these tools. Incidentally, many of the tools on this menu will be unavailable while you have NDE set to read-only mode. Others will become active only when you are viewing appropriate objects. The Tools menu is shown in Figure 12.23.

FIGURE 12.22

The drive map for one file, showing clusters used by the file and clusters free and in-use surrounding the file.

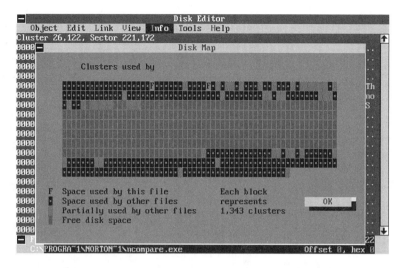

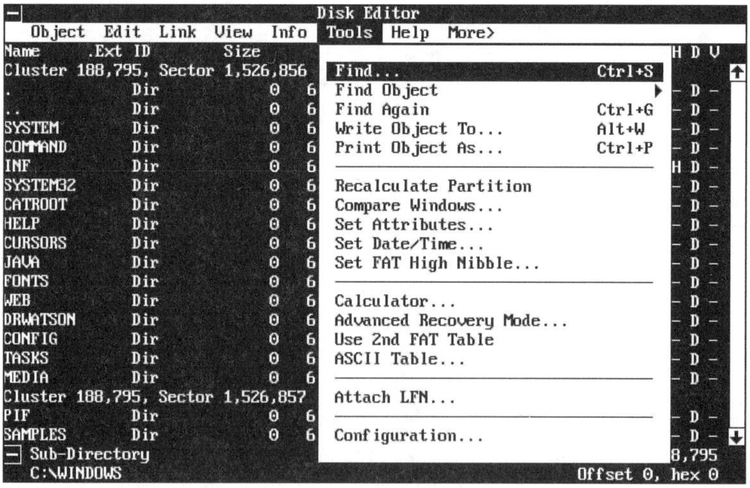

FIGURE 12.23

NDE's Tools menu provides you with a wide variety of search, replace, and reference tools.

Find Tools

At the top of the Tools menu are three related Find commands. The third of these, Find Again (Ctrl+G) is obvious inasmuch as it simply performs again the last Find you executed. In this way, you can continue searching for specific content without having to re-specify what that content is.

The primary Find tool (Ctrl+S) enables you to search through the current object (file or directory, a group of sectors or clusters, or a system area of a drive) for some string of data which you can specify in either ASCII or hexadecimal. You can choose to perform a case-sensitive or case-insensitive search, and you can, if you choose, begin the search starting a specific number of bytes—known in jargonland as the *offset*—after the beginning of the sector in which the current object is located. As soon as a match to your search string is found, the match is displayed, and the search stops. Use Find Again (Ctrl+G) to resume the search from where it left off.

When the Norton Disk Editor has searched through the entire selected object for your string and has found all matches—or none—you will be told that no more matches have been found.

The Find Object entry expands into a small pop-up menu from which you can select either Partition/Boot Record, FAT, or Subdirectory. With the disk viewed by physical sectors, or with all clusters selected on the current logical drive, these Find sub-commands will search for data which has a structure and content matching that required for either a partition table, a boot record, a file allocation table, or a subdirectory. You may recall the previous example in which a subdirectory was relocated on disk. If you had temporarily exported the subdirectory to a blank floppy disk, you could use this Find command to scan through the entire floppy quickly and re-locate your exported data. You can also use this command to locate data that is somehow intact but not found where the operating system or BIOS expects to find it. Such data can be relocated to its proper place using the Mark, Copy, and Paste techniques previously discussed when you read about the Edit menu.

Writing Object Tools

The Write Object To (Alt+W) command causes a copy of the currently-selected file or range of data to be written either to another location on disk, or to another disk entirely. If you are manually reconstructing data from a deleted file, for example, this command enables you to write that data to a new file from which it can be accessed normally. You can also use the Write Object To command to forcibly replace a drive's defective Primary FAT with the backup FAT (after verifying that the backup FAT is intact, of course).

When you first invoke Write Object To, you'll be asked to which device or structure you want the data written. You'll also be reminded of the amount of data currently selected.

If you choose to write data to a range of sectors on disk, as in Figure 12.24, Norton Disk Editor will remind you which areas of disk are generally used for certain types of system-related data. This would be a useful reminder in the case of replacing a damaged FAT. Finally, if you choose to write data to physical drive sectors, you will need to specify the cylinder, platter side, and sector into which you want the first bit of the data to be placed.

Caution: If you invoke Write Object To with no data marked or copied, Norton Disk Editor will assume you want to copy the entire drive. You should also be aware that data will be truncated if you attempt to write data to a disk or an area of disk insufficient to contain it.

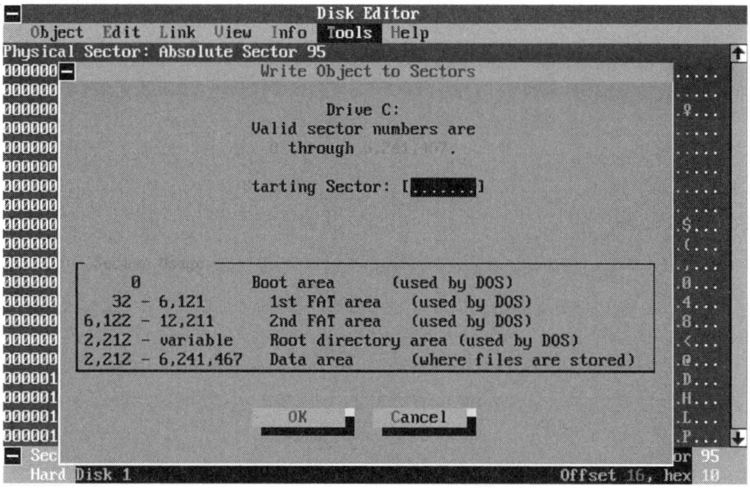

Figure 12.24

Figure 12.24
Writing an object to specific drive sectors, showing reminders of where key system (DOS) structures are located.

```
                              Disk Editor
    Object   Edit   Link   View   Info  [Tools] Help
Physical Sector: Absolute Sector 95
000000                  Write Object to Sectors
000000
000000                      Drive C:
000000               Valid sector numbers are
000000                      through     .
000000
000000                  tarting Sector: [       ]
000000
000000
000000
000000
000000        0              Boot area      (used by DOS)
000000     32 - 6,121        1st FAT area   (used by DOS)
000000   6,122 - 12,211      2nd FAT area   (used by DOS)
000000   2,212 - variable    Root directory area (used by DOS)
000000   2,212 - 6,241,467   Data area      (where files are stored)
000001
000001
000001                OK              Cancel
000001
  Sec                                                         or  95
  Hard Disk 1                                    Offset 16, hex  10
```

Caution: A Write Object To command is not undoable. Be extremely careful whenever writing data to anything other than a file. Writing directly to clusters, sectors, or physical sectors will replace any data currently located on those parts of the disk. Anything that was previously stored in those clusters—your tax return, pictures of your cat, hate mail, whatever—is gone forever.

Printing Tools

The Print Object As (Ctrl+P) tool enables you to print the current object—a directory entry, a file, raw data, whatever—either to a printer or to a text-format file on disk. If you choose to print to a file, you must manually enter the complete path, including drive letter, of the file you wish created, otherwise Norton Disk Editor will create the file in its own directory (or on its own disk, if the disk is not write-protected).

As with viewing objects onscreen, you may select from a variety of formats in which to view the data you've selected. You can print data as hex, with the traditional ASCII text view to the right of the hexadecimal. You may also print any selected data or object as a directory tree, a file allocation table, an interpreted boot record, or an interpreted partition table. Just as with viewing onscreen, Norton Disk Editor will do its best to fit your chosen data or object into the structure required by each viewer, but if you print the contents of a Windows video AVI file as if it were a file allocation table, the printout will be sheer nonsense. Printing is made available because a good many people find it easier to analyze printed data than data displayed onscreen.

Tip: Before you print data from NDE, be aware of what object you've selected. You'll use up a great number of trees if you accidentally send the entire content of a 3.4GB hard disk to your laser printer!

Partition Reconstruction

The Recalculate Partition command (there is no keyboard shortcut) enables a disk-repair specialist to verify direct modifications made to a manually-edited partition table. The command is available only when you are using the partition table viewer—viewing an actual partition table—with a given partition marked. If your partition table becomes damaged, you can enter what data you are fairly certain of about it—its type, the drive's hardware configuration data from your PC's hardware CMOS setup, and so on—and Norton Disk Editor will attempt to calculate all of the values of which you are uncertain. As you are adding information back into the partition table, simply leave as zero (0) any value you don't know. When you select Recalculate Partition from the Tools menu, NDE will fill in all of the blanks it can, based on the data you have supplied.

> **Caution:** Manually editing partition data is a marvelous way to make whole gigabytes of data inaccessible in a matter of seconds. Before you make any changes to a partition table, be certain you know exactly what you are doing. Many types of partition-table damage can be easily and much more safely reconstructed from your Norton Rescue set and Image data.

Comparing Split Windows

In a process not unlike that performed by Norton File Compare, which you'll read about in Chapter 15, "Norton Utilities: Getting It Back, Getting It Right: UnErasing and File Compare," Norton Disk Editor enables you to compare the contents of two split windows without leaving the Editor. This Compare Windows tool can easily identify discrepancies between two supposedly-identical files on disk, or between your primary and backup file allocation tables. When you compare windows, the comparison begins at the beginning of the data line in which the cursor is located when you invoked the command. The first discrepancy encountered will be highlighted by the cursor. To continue searching for more discrepancies, select Compare Windows again from the Tools menu. If no differences are found, Norton Disk Editor will let you know that, too.

Setting Tools

The Tools menu also provides three ways to easily set certain object-related characteristics. The Set Attributes command enables you to set the DOS file attributes for a selected file or a set of files. You must be exploring a directory and using the Directory view for this command to be available. If you want to change the attributes for a single file, the easiest way to do so is to simply tab over to that file's attributes—located on the right side of the first horizontal screen in the directory view (refer to Figure 12.3). From left-to-right, these attributes reflect the Archive, Read-only, Hidden, System, Volume, and Directory bits, respectively.

To set attributes for a range of files, first mark the files in Directory view. Invoke the Set Attributes command from the Tools menu. You'll see a dialog box like that shown in Figure 12.25. Use the spacebar to switch between the three attribute-setting indicators, then press Enter to accept your changes. Your modifications will display in the directory viewer.

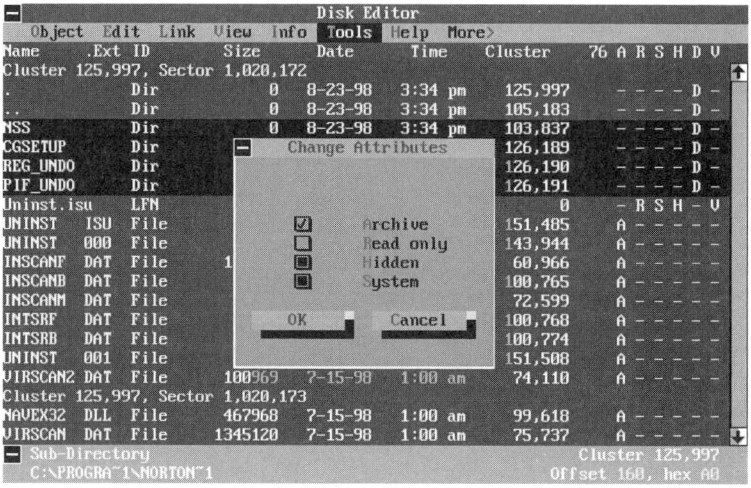

Figure 12.25

In the Change Attributes dialog box, a checkmark causes the selected attribute to be set. A solid white rectangle indicates that the current status of the selected attribute will not be changed. A clear space causes the selected attribute to be cleared.

The Set Date/Time command on the Tools menu works in a very similar manner. With a range of files selected in Directory view, you can change the modification time and date, the creation time and date, and the last access date for a set of files. This procedure is commonly done by software manufacturers before sending their final product out for duplication. By giving every file related to the product the same time and date, it gives a "clean" look to the product when the user examines the installed-product's directory. Although Norton Disk Doctor will find and repair problems with invalid times and dates, you can also use this Norton Disk Editor command to manually modify such values.

Finally, the Set FAT High Nibble command, only active while you are viewing a FAT32 file allocation table, sets or clears bit 28, 29, 30, and/or 31 from a given cluster or set of marked clusters in the FAT. These bits are reserved for future use, as of this writing, but expert users can use them to identify FAT32 clusters in a way that they can easily search for at a later time. When this book went to press, setting or clearing these bits had no effect on any aspect of file- or operating-system actions whatsoever.

Miscellaneous Tools

The remainder of the Tools menu is comprised of a set of miscellaneous commands which may be useful in a number of circumstances.

The Calculator displays a graphically-simulated calculator onscreen. This calculator can be made to function on binary, decimal, or hexadecimal numbers, and can convert any of those bases into any other of those bases. Three special keys are present to provide functionality that is of particular use to disk editors (the people, not the programs). Selecting the 2comp button will convert the number currently displayed into its twos-complement for the performance of binary operations. The Swap button swaps low and high bytes of the currently displayed hexadecimal number. Finally, the tilde, ~, button causes the currently-displayed binary number to be inverted. That is, for example, 10101010 would be changed to 01010101.

Advanced Recovery Mode enables you to create a temporary, virtual disk to aid in the repair of a damaged logical drive. In brief, Advanced Recovery Mode enables you to simulate the existence of normal disk structures like file allocation tables, directory entries, and boot records when those actual structures have been damaged. Such damage would normally force you to perform any manual recovery in Maintenance (or physical sector) Mode. It's not much fun. The Advanced Recovery Mode configuration screen, shown in Figure 12.26, requires that you specify as much information about the damaged drive as you possibly can. Norton Disk Editor will verify most of your entries to make certain they are valid with respect to each other. Some of this data is information normally stored in CMOS. Other parts of it are found variously in the disk's partition table—like the physical values and settings for the damaged drive's partition—or in the logical disk's boot record—like the partition parameters.

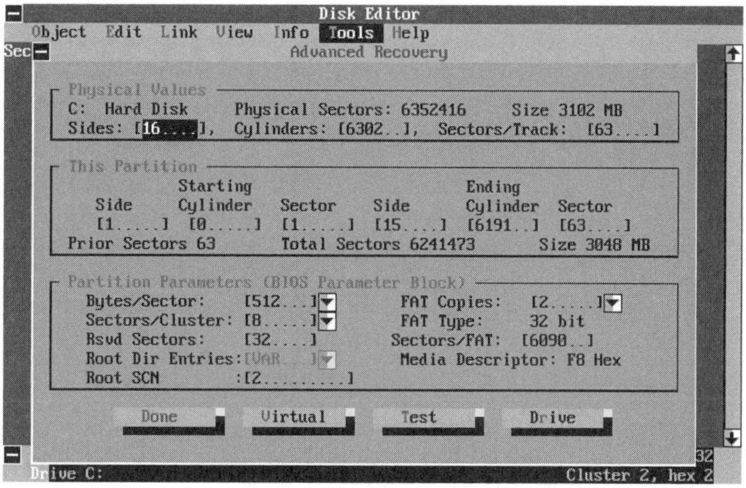

FIGURE 12.26

Enabling and configuring Advanced Recovery Mode enables you to work with a damaged disk as through its vital structures were intact.

Once you have entered the values you believe are correct, press Alt+T to check the validity of what you've entered. Norton Disk Editor will identify invalid entries and enables you to see variances between what you have entered and what NDE believes to be the correct values. With all of your data entered and checked as valid, press Alt+V to virtualize the disk. Norton Disk Editor will re-scan the damaged drive, using the parameters for the virtual disk, and will attempt to reconstruct the boot record, file allocation tables, and directories. If the virtualized data looks correct in the Editor, you can split the window, view the various damaged structures of the damaged disk in one window and the virtualized disk in the other, and copy the virtualized values back to the physical disk, thus repairing it. In this way, data that is entirely inaccessible through any other means may still be recovered. Selecting any other object to view from the NDE Object menu will de-virtualize the disk.

Note: This sort of catastrophic drive damage is precisely the type of thing that your Norton Rescue set and Image data can reconstruct painlessly. If you don't have a current Rescue set or Image data, however, but you do have the values needed to properly create a virtual disk, this method is a very reliable way of replacing erased or fatally damaged drive structures.

You have read above about marking and copying the backup version of the file allocation table and replacing a damaged FAT with that backup. The Tools menu's Use 2nd FAT Table command and the Write Object To command will let you do precisely that in two steps, rather than moving all of that data manually. Select the Use 2nd FAT command and NDE will re-scan your active drive, replacing its primary FAT *in memory* with the backup. (Of course, before you do this, you should verify that your backup FAT is not also damaged. Norton Disk Doctor can also detect damaged FAT data and use your Norton Image data to automatically repair it.) Then, select the Write Object To command and write the 2nd FAT over the primary FAT, thus repairing it.

The ASCII Table command simply enables you to view a display of the 255 different ASCII values and their hexadecimal and decimal equivalents. This can be a useful reference if you are manually entering hexadecimal data into a file because the characters you require are not directly accessible via keyboard.

Finally, the Attach LFN command enables you to reconnect a Windows 95 or Windows 98 long filename to a file's DOS 8.3 filename. Normally this kind of repair is most easily performed through Norton Disk Doctor—which will fix these problems automatically— but you can perform them manually from within NDE. While viewing a long filename entry in a Directory view, invoke this command to see a dialog box showing the selected long filename and its DOS equivalent. If you wish to reconnect the two names, press Alt+Y to accept the dialog's confirmation.

Configuring Norton Disk Editor

The Norton Disk Editor configuration screen, shown in Figure 12.27, enables you to set the most basic of performance properties for the entire program. Read-Only mode can be enabled and disabled from here by pressing Alt+R. If you find that you want Norton Disk Editor to perform faster, you can elect to not have the status bar at the bottom of the screen update. To toggle between an active and inactive status bar, press Alt+Q. If you don't want NDE to analyze objects as you load them from the Object menu and select the viewer it feels is best for that object, you can deactivate viewer selection by pressing Alt+A. With automatic viewer selection disabled, new objects will be viewed using the most recently-used viewer. With the Quick Links option enabled—the default setting— pressing Enter while looking at a filename in a directory automatically opens that file's contents. To disable this feature, press Alt+L.

Caution: If you disable Read-Only mode here, you may want to exit this screen
by selecting OK, rather than Save. Selecting OK will disable Read-Only mode for
this session of Disk Editor. Selecting Save will make Write-Enabled mode the
default for all future Disk Editor sessions (until you turn Read-Only mode back
on at this screen and select Save again). Unless you're an experienced disk editor, I would urge you to leave Read-Only mode as the default.

FIGURE 12.27

*Configuration
options for
Norton Disk
Editor enable you
to turn Read-Only
mode on and off
and select a vari-
ety of other
customizable
features.*

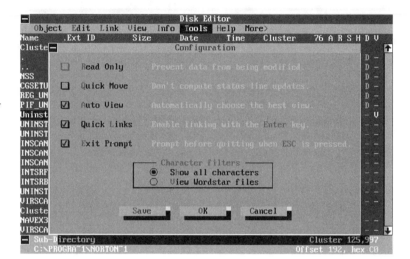

My personal favorite configuration option is Exit Prompt (Alt+E). If you have spent any
time working in manual mode with the DOS-based version of Norton UnErase, you will
see how beneficial the NDE Exit Prompt setting is. With Exit Prompt checked, you will
receive a confirmation that you wish to quit if you press the Esc key at a time when
doing so would normally quit the program. Until you are very familiar with the DOS
keyboard-based environment—and, frankly, even after you are—it's very easy to find
yourself looking at a display and thinking that you can make the display vanish and show
you the previous display simply by pressing Esc. In many instances, this is exactly how
the software works. At other times, however, there is nothing to "Escape" from, and Exit
Prompt disabled, Norton Disk Editor will quit immediately. If you're in the middle of a
long manual repair, that can be frustrating at best, disastrous at worst.

Finally, the Character Filters configuration enables you to either see all characters of all
types or to mask-off certain character data. This masking-off is enabled by selecting the
View WordStar Files radio button. It's very unlikely that you have any antiquated
WordStar files on your drives today, but some other types of files—some databases and
older spreadsheets, in particular—can also be viewed more easily if you enable character
masking.

Using Norton System Information for Daily Disk Viewing

Norton Disk Editor is an amazingly powerful tool in the hands of a disk-repair expert. Disk repair can, and does, cost hundreds or thousands of dollars, and having the knowledge and skill to perform repairs can be invaluable. Most of us have neither the knowledge nor the skill, however, to change a severely-damaged drive into a perfectly healthy one. For us, the three primary Norton SystemWorks protection and repair utilities— Norton Disk Doctor, Norton Rescue, and Norton Image—automatically perform most of the repairs that, only a year or three ago, would have been either impossible or unaffordable.

Even using Norton Disk Editor to view a disk may be a threatening procedure for a lot of today's users. Many people have never even seen a DOS screen, much less ever used a DOS program. An expert disk-manipulating tool like Norton Disk Editor is probably not what you want to run to teach yourself to be comfortable in DOS. For this reason, and others, Norton SystemWorks includes a Windows-based analysis tool known as System Information. You can launch it from the SystemWorks Integrator by selecting Norton Utilities, Troubleshoot, System Information. Much of the disk-related information which is accessible for viewing through Norton Disk Editor can also be seen through System Information, often in a more straightforward, familiar graphical manner. You'll read about System Information in detail in Chapter 20, "Norton Utilities: Checking Your Own Nametag—System Info and Norton Diagnostics," but you may want to consider using System Information's Drive tab and its Details button to investigate your disks if using NDE gives you the jitters.

PETER'S PRINCIPLE

The Path to Power User

The road to becoming a power-user can be long and arduous. In fact, an argument can be made that today, becoming a power-user—in the sense in which that term first evolved—is simply impossible. Fifteen years ago, even 10 years ago, you could know it all. From sectors to serial ports, volume labels to video display adapters, there was little-enough diversity that knowing all of the "basics" meant knowing everything. Today, knowing the basics means less than ever before. The knowledge itself hasn't lost its value, but the amount of total PC-related knowledge out there has been exploding logarithmically. Relative to today's "everything," the basics are basic indeed.

And yet, some of the basics are still a vital part of becoming a power-user in whichever branch of PC-knowledge you might now choose to be a power-user. A fundamental understanding of how your PC—its processor, its memory, and its drives—work continues to form the core of most "power-user" knowledge. Because of this, tools like Norton Disk Editor and System Information continue to be as useful and important today as they were 5 and 10 years ago. From a purely educational perspective, Norton Disk Editor can add a face, if you will, to the body of reading you may find yourself doing about disks in a college or even a high-school computing course. For many people, myself included, having a visual image of a thing makes that thing so much more tangible. Understandable. Somehow actually seeing a file allocation table can make it easier to understand how lost clusters show up peppered across your disks, and why and how files become fragmented.

Even today, these are not white-tower concepts; they are problems that each of us encounters in the normal use of our personal computer or workstation, and they can seriously threaten the data we spend, really, our whole lives creating.

Many times, too, when the abstract becomes tangible, it also becomes less threatening. When you understand how files are saved, you'll irrationally fear losing them less, but you'll also be motivated to take proactive steps to prevent their loss. When you understand how old DOS 8.3 filenames and wildcards work, you'll be less-inclined to freeze when you encounter an antiquated program that doesn't support long filenames. Overcoming the fear of your PC—fears felt by the majority of new users, and bred in an absence of knowledge about how your PC works, what you can and cannot do to harm it, and how you can best care after it and your data—is truly the first step on the path to power-user.

Norton Utilities: The Better Part of Valor and Registry Tracker

While it's true that most people who have a little experience with the Registry would rather do, well, almost anything rather than work with it, it's both possible and useful to understand the broad sense of what goes on inside the two Windows 95 files, SYSTEM.DAT and USER.DAT, or the three Windows 98 files, SYSTEM.DAT, USER.DAT, and HWINFO.DAT, that comprise it. The contents of these files keep track of nearly every aspect of your PC, and they're updated continually while you work. You'll learn a good deal about the technical aspects of the Registry in the following chapter, "Norton Utilities: Heroic Measures and Other Registry Editing," as you read about using the Norton Registry Editor. This chapter explores a different Norton tool that, perhaps ironically, could prevent you from ever needing to dig into the Registry in the first place. This tool is called Norton Registry Tracker.

The Norton Registry Tracker—or, NRT, as I'll be calling it, enables you to keep track of all changes to your Windows Registry—and to a variety of setup and .INI files as well. Not conceptually unlike Norton Image, which you read about in Chapter 8, "Norton Utilities: More Than a Mirror, An Image," NRT enables you to capture a copy of your Registry and setup files as they are at a particular moment. Unlike Image, however, the Norton Registry Tracker grants you the ability to interactively review those files, observe changes that have been made to them since the last time those files were tracked, and integrate them with other parts of Norton SystemWorks and Windows to manually modify those changes.

Recovering from the Brink of Disaster

As you read in Chapter 4, "Norton Utilities: The WinDoctor Is In," the Windows Registry is a mighty, robust database. As you've also read, when the Registry breaks, so does everything else. There's no question that Registry files are very self-repairing, often simply ignoring incomplete or errant Registry key entries. But how does the Registry always know when an entry is incomplete or wrong? It doesn't. When invalid entries look valid, the Registry uses invalid data, and the results can be disastrous. In the most minor of cases, Registry problems can trigger intermittent crashing, making you better acquainted with Norton CrashGuard than you ever hoped to be. At the other extreme, Registry damage can render your PC useless, can damage your data or your drives (depending on how the Registry error manifests itself), and can easily turn "one of those days" into "one of those weeks."

If you're an average user, you will probably find that WinDoctor can catch and repair the majority of your Registry-related problems. If you install and uninstall a lot of software, if you download ActiveX components from Web sites, if you test any unreleased or "beta" software, or if you just enjoy poking around and really being in control of your PC, NRT will be a very valuable tool.

Of course, just how valuable it is to you is a direct function of whether and how you use it. As with Norton System Doctor, the Norton Registry Tracker uses very few system resources and can be configured to automatically run in the background every time Windows starts, as you'll read about later in this chapter. As you've already discovered, combining the tools of Norton SystemWorks provides your PC and your data with the maximum security.

NRT Snapshots

Norton Registry Tracker works by making copies—essentially taking *snapshots*—of the Registry and other configuration files you specify. By comparing one snapshot with another, NRT shows you what has changed and enables you to undo those changes. Several different types of snapshots exist, and you use them together to obtain the results you want. To launch NRT, select it from the Norton SystemWorks Integrator under Norton Utilities or from the Start menu at Programs | Norton Utilities | Registry Tracker. If you want NRT to run automatically every time you boot, select Settings from NRT's Options menu and, on the Automatic Tracking tab, place a check mark in the box labeled Start Automatically With Windows. Whenever NRT is first run, it takes a snapshot.

If this is the first snapshot to be taken of this PC, this becomes the foundation upon which all future snapshots are based. If other snapshots already exist on your hard drive, then NRT automatically compares its startup snapshot with the previous snapshot. If differences exist, or if this is the first snapshot on this PC, NRT labels the snapshot as an "Activation Snapshot." As NRT continues to run in the background while you work, it takes a new snapshot every time an item that is being tracked—such as the Windows Registry—is modified. Such snapshots don't have a formal, standard name, but they're labeled with the name of the applet or application that prompted the modification.

Finally, manual snapshots can be taken whenever you desire, and these can be labeled as you choose. If you're installing a piece of software or are trying out a variety of system settings, taking a manual snapshot before you begin enables you to painlessly undo

whatever changes you make. To take a manual snapshot, simply choose New Snapshot
from Norton Registry Tracker's File menu. You can see examples of each of these snapshots in Figure 13.1, which shows the NRT Snapshot log.

FIGURE 13.1

*The Norton
Registry Tracker
displays all stored
snapshots here in
its Snapshot log.*

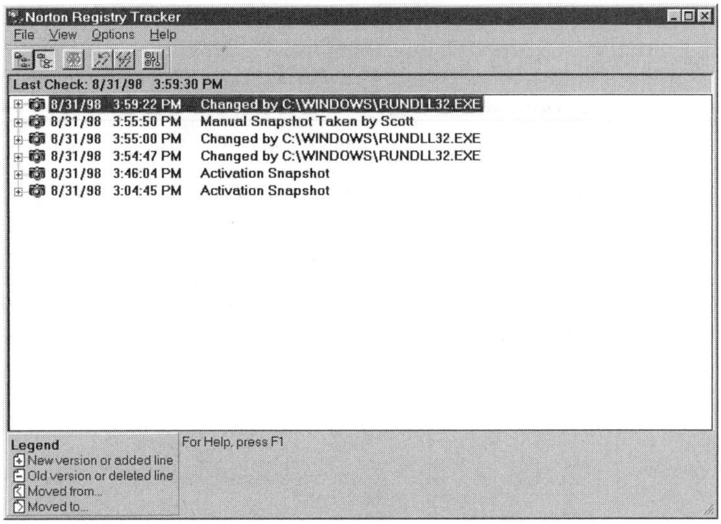

Snapshots are always organized in reverse chronological order, with the most recent
snapshot at the top of the screen. You'll notice in the figure that each snapshot entry
looks rather like a folder entry in the Windows Explorer: The plus ("+") symbols are present, indicating that snapshot information is kept in a hierarchy that you can open at will.
We'll look at that feature in a moment. What you see in Figure 13.1 is known as the
Snapshot view; that is, the changes to your system have been organized chronologically
under the snapshot that first noticed the change. Figure 13.2 shows a dramatically different view, the File view, accessed by selecting By File from the NRT View menu.

Within the File view, changes to your files are organized by which files have been
changed. The snapshots recording each of those changes remain in chronological order
under each file heading. The Snapshot view is the most useful view to use if you're trying to determine what has just happened to your computer. The File view, on the other
hand, will be most useful when you know what change has occurred and you want to
undo or explore a specific change. Let's look at two contrasting examples, both of which
will also acquaint you with NRT's powerful recovery features: Restore and QuickFix.

A Snapshot View Example

Imagine that you're working at home one evening on some graphic design work and you
step away from your PC to get some refreshment. When you come back into your office,
you discover that the Control Panel is open and the color of everything on the screen has

changed—including the carefully selected colors of your own work. Everything seems blotchy, your icons are huge and jaggy, your desktop photograph of your kids looks like a Seurat, and there's a noticeable flicker to your monitor. Dead silence in the brightly decorated room down the hall identifies the culprit, but you're more concerned about your PC and your work. You have Norton Registry Tracker running in the background, so you click its icon in the System Tray and look at the Snapshot view. Sure enough, modifications were made to C:\WINDOWS\WIN.INI. Clicking on the plus sign next to the most recent snapshot, and then again on the plus sign next to WIN.INI, as in Figure 13.3, you breathe a sigh of relief. You can see clearly that the only things changed relate to someone—wonder who—playing around in the Display control panel. Your color depth has been dropped, large icons have been turned on, and your Windows appearance scheme has been "customized." Nothing serious, this time.

FIGURE 13.2
NRT's Snapshot log is viewed by modified file rather than by chronological snapshot.

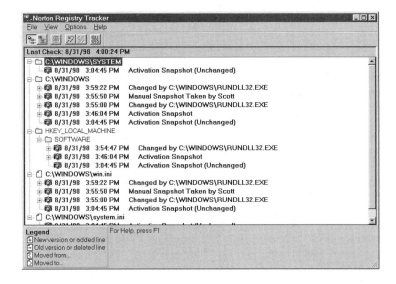

You could always go back to the Control Panel and manually undo all those changes, or you can just let Norton Registry Tracker do the work for you. With the relevant snapshot selected in the Snapshot view pane, click the Restore button in the toolbar, or select Restore from the NRT File menu. If multiple snapshots exist, a confirmation dialog box will ask you to verify that you want to restore the settings that existed before or after that snapshot was taken. Because you are looking at the modified data, select Before and click OK. Suddenly, Windows is back to normal. (In some cases, you may need to reboot to actually see the reversion.) You get on with your work. Time elapsed: about a minute.

Even if you looked at NRT's most recent snapshot and didn't understand the changes it showed you, you could still Restore your PC to its prior condition with a high sense of security. If your PC had crashed, you'd be looking at a Norton CrashGuard screen and working with its tools to recover your work. That wasn't the case here, but it was a very good bet that whatever had changed could be easily undone.

Of course, you do always save your work before stepping away from your desk, don't you?

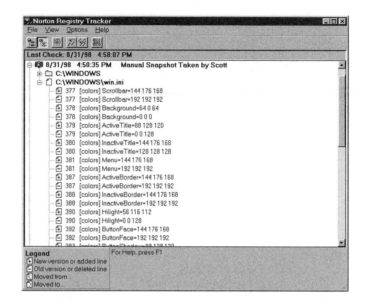

A File View Example

On the other hand, you might have just been installing the world's greatest new widget processing software, and the Setup program might have frozen halfway through. You're able to delete the program's folders and its configuration files from your hard drive, but Windows keeps crashing. It's reasonable to assume that the install program made changes to your Registry that are corrupting other aspects of Windows. Opening NRT in File view mode, as in Figure 13.4, enables you to zero in directly on modifications made to your Registry keys. You'll be able to identify the changes made by the install program because those changes will be labeled with that program's name. You can see an example of this in Figure 13.4, in which RUNDLL32.EXE (located in your Windows folder) modified Registry subkeys under the HKEY_LOCAL_MACHINE\SOFTWARE key. Clicking the change's plus ("+") button opens up the change so you can see exactly what's causing the trouble. From there, you might want to launch Norton Registry Editor and correct the change yourself (refer to the next chapter). Or, more likely, you'll simply want to undo what was done.

Right-clicking a Registry change in either Snapshot or File view brings up a menu from which you can select Restore. You can also select data with your mouse, then click on the Restore button in the toolbar, or choose Restore from NRT's File menu, as in snapshot view. (You must use either the toolbar or the menu item to restore a change to a non-Registry file.) Confirm that you want to change the current data to match either the data saved immediately before or after the snapshot you're looking at and click OK.

Then you're done. When some time has passed between when you believe the errant data came into existence and when you hope to correct the problem—particularly if you know which system or configuration file was impacted—File view is the way to go.

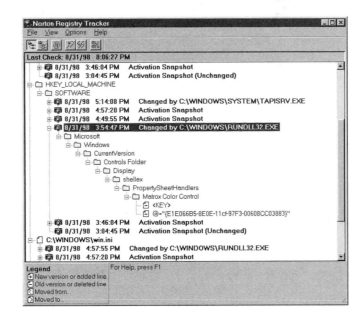

Regardless of which view of the Snapshot log you select, you may find that Norton Registry Tracker is monitoring changes of a type that doesn't interest you. For example, you may indeed want to keep watch over your WIN.INI file, but you might not care a whit about changes that involve only the selection of a different color scheme or screen saver and so on. While you are exploring tracked changes, as in Figure 13.4, you can right-click an individual change and exclude that property from future tracking by selecting Exclude in the pop-up menu. Exclusions can be created for Registry keys, subkeys, or external configuration files; all are managed through their related settings tab, accessible from the NRT Options menu. You'll read more about all these configurations, as well as how to manage your exclusions, later in this chapter.

Comparing Files

Of course, even when you know which file has been modified, you might not want to simply undo modifications without understanding them. What's more, if many modifications have been made, it would be very useful to just see those modifications alone, where you can study them properly. Norton Registry Tracker includes a tool that enables you to do just that. Norton File Compare—which you'll read more about in Chapter 15, "Norton Utilities: Getting It Back, Getting It Right: UnErasing and File Compare"—is integrated with Norton Registry Tracker, allowing you to identify a modified file within the Tracker and immediately launch Norton File Compare and examine precisely what has changed in a neat, isolated interface.

Figure 13.5 shows two versions of the WIN.INI configuration file, which were accessed directly by clicking the Compare button in the NRT toolbar. (Comparison functionality is also available by selecting Compare from NRT's File menu.) Here, Norton File Compare displays only those entries in the WIN.INI file that have been changed. When you open Norton File Compare from within NRT, you are asked to specify whether you want to compare the file you've selected with its previous version—that is, the version that existed prior to the changes Norton Registry Tracker is reporting—or with the current version running on your PC. If you've chosen to go back in NRT and look at the file before it was modified, then you'll want to compare it with the current version so you can identify settings changes that are currently impacting Windows.

FIGURE 13.5

Norton File Compare can be used to examine an old and new WIN.INI file.

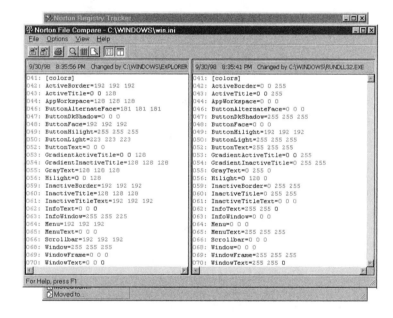

From within Norton File Compare, you can launch the Windows Notepad to edit whichever version of any system configuration (.INI) file you choose. Note, however, that using the Notepad to edit Registry entries actually edits only an exported text-file version of the relevant keys. To edit the Registry directly, you must use Norton Registry Editor, as you'll read in the next chapter. If you use such a tool to edit the Registry, you must import your changes back into the active Registry, using Norton Registry Editor.

Configuring Norton Registry Tracker

Norton Registry Tracker is highly configurable and can be made to track precisely what you want it to track. It can also be made to display its tracking data in the manner you select. From the NRT Options menu, selecting Settings opens a dialog box containing six standard-issue Windows "tabs," each of which contains related settings for an aspect of NRT's functionality.

Automatic Tracking Tab Settings

The first of these is the Automatic Tracking tab, shown in Figure 13.6, which determines when—and if—Norton Registry Tracker runs automatically and for how long snapshots should be archived. Earlier in this chapter, I suggested that you enable NRT to run in the background every time Windows starts. You can enable this feature by placing a check mark in the Start automatically with Windows box here on the Automatic Tracking tab. (Because NRT does use system resources and can cause slow machines to run sluggishly, and because the Norton people know you want to maintain control over exactly what's happening inside your PC, automatic launching is disabled by default.)

The Automatic Tracking tab also enables you to specify that snapshots should be automatically deleted after some number of days. It's a good idea to keep this setting enabled and set to a period of no more than two weeks. Undoing Registry and setup file changes over longer periods of time can have cascading effects on the workings of Windows. While it is certainly possible to go back a month and change your Registry and setup files so that they look precisely as they did a month ago, consider how many modifications are made to the Registry in a month—modifications that would be lost in an instant. To safeguard against such horrors, NRT eliminates truly antiquated snapshots from its archives. Having a large number of snapshots archived may also compound your search for specific changes, particularly in File view. Of course, each change retains its time and date stamp, but if you're looking through a month of snapshots, it could still take you a month of Sundays to identify the particular changes that interest you.

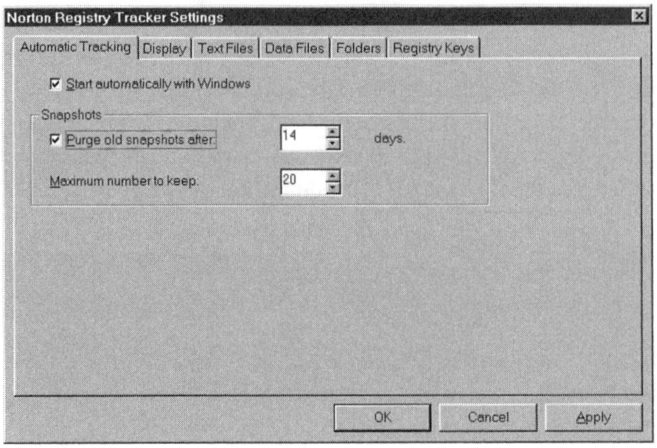

FIGURE 13.6

Norton Registry Tracker contains these Automatic Tracking settings.

You can turn off time-based purging. You cannot, however, tell NRT to store an infinite number of snapshots. When the number of NRT snapshots reaches the quantity you've selected as the Maximum Number of Snapshots to Save, old snapshots are purged to make room for new. Valid entries here range from as few as 10 to as many as 1,000. As mentioned previously, remember that a large number of snapshots can confound your search for specific system modifications. Maintaining a large archive of hundreds of snapshots also increases the time NRT requires to sort and display them for you.

 Efficiency and safety together dictate that you maintain somewhere in the neighborhood of between 20 and 100 snapshots. Of course, if you are working on a system config-uration project that is making continuous changes to system files, you may want to temporarily alter your archival limitations to reflect those special circumstances.

Display Tab Settings

The next settings tab, Display (shown in Figure 13.7), controls the manner in which Norton Registry Tracker displays its snapshot data. By default, NRT tracks the Registry and a small subset of your PC's system files. In each snapshot, however, it shows you only those tracked files that have changed. By deselecting the Show Only Changed Files in Snapshot View check box, Norton Registry Tracker includes the names of all tracked files in each snapshot, regardless of whether a given file was modified or not.

FIGURE 13.7

Norton Registry Tracker includes these Display options.

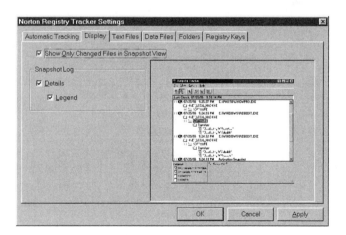

If you deselect the option to display problem details here, Norton Registry Tracker shows only the names of files and Registry keys that have been modified—it does not show the actual modified data. Compare the Snapshot log display in Figure 13.4 with that shown in Figure 13.8, with "Details" disabled. Notice that the hierarchical plus ("+") buttons stop in the latter view with the name of the Registry subkey or the system file that was modified.

Restoration functionality is not impacted by disabling details; you can still right-click a subkey or filename and restore the previous set of values. With Details off, you're simply not shown—or bothered with, depending on your perspective—the changes being made. If your sole interest in Norton Registry Tracker is to aid in the immediate recovery from catastrophic system modifications, turning Details off certainly tidies up NRT's Snapshot display. If you leave Details enabled, you then have the option of leaving the Legend on for reference, or you can free up a good deal of screen space by turning it off. The Legend merely reminds you of the basic symbols NRT uses to indicate new data added to the Registry or setup files (a blue plus symbol on a document), data changed or removed (a reddish minus symbol on a document), or data relocated (gray arrows on document backgrounds). After you understand Norton Registry Tracker's symbols, there's little reason to leave the Legend enabled.

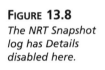

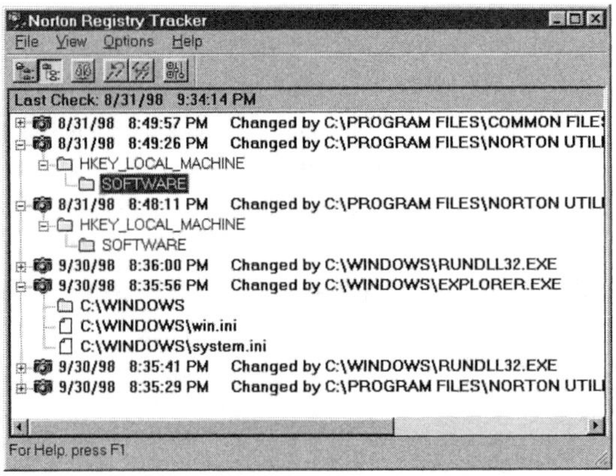

FIGURE 13.8
The NRT Snapshot log has Details disabled here.

Text Files Tab Settings

The remaining four tabs make up the heart of Norton Registry Tracker because they determine which files and which parts of the Windows Registry are monitored. You can even specify that all files located within certain folders should be tracked. First, let's look at how the myriad text-based configuration files on your PC can be monitored, by examining the Text Files tab shown in Figure 13.9.

As the figure shows, text-based configuration files—most of which are located within your C:\WINDOWS folder, or a subfolder of it, and most of which have the .INI file extension—that Norton Registry Tracker monitors are listed in this panel. Adding files to this list is simply a matter of clicking the Add button and selecting the file you want to add from a standard Open dialog box. This dialog box also supports Ctrl-clicking, that is, holding down the Ctrl key and clicking multiple files to select them. If you use this method, clicking OK adds all those files to the tracking list. Using Ctrl-clicking makes it very easy to add a large number of files to your tracking list. However, if you want to add an entire folder's worth of files, you will find it much easier to use the Folders tab, which you'll read about later. Removing a file is just as simple: Select the filename in the list, and click Remove. To safeguard your settings against accidental global changes, Ctrl-clicking is not supported within the tab for purposes of removing entries.

FIGURE 13.9

Monitor text-based configuration files on the NRT Text Files setting tab.

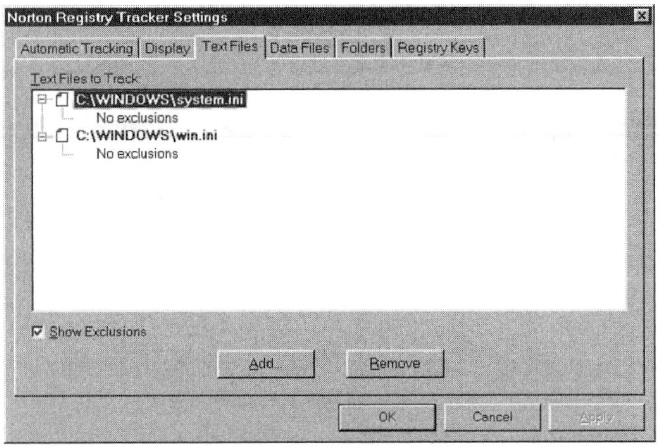

Notice also that this tab has a check box to enable you to show exclusions. With this box checked, standard Windows plus "+" hierarchical buttons appear next to each file entry, as in Figure 13.9. Clicking a plus button reveals any properties stored within that file that have been excluded from tracking. (You read about excluding properties earlier in this chapter.) It is from this tab that you remove exclusions so that the related properties will again be tracked by NRT. Simply select the exclusion you wish to delete and click Remove. Of course, as in Figure 13.9, if a file has no exclusions associated with it, NRT will let you know that, too.

TECHNICAL NOTE

While the method mentioned here is the standard, integrated way to manage your exclusions, manual editing of your exclusions is also possible. The Norton Registry Tracker records all exclusions you specify into an .INI file, located in the Registry Tracker folder within the Norton Utilities folder on your hard drive. This file, called EXCLUDE.INI, is an ordinary text file and can be edited within any Windows text file editor, such as the Windows Notepad. If you wish to exclude a large number of settings from, say, your WIN.INI file's tracking, you will probably discover that the fastest way of doing that is opening your WIN.INI file in the text editor of your choice and then copying the names of the properties you wish to exclude manually into EXCLUDE.INI.

The format for exclusion is very simple, although it is easiest to begin working manually with exclusions if you create one exclusion from within NRT and then open EXCLUDE.INI to see the format. Basically, the name of each file with excluded content—including its complete path and drive letter—is used as

continues

a section header within EXCLUDE.INI. The section header under which the excluded property is found in the original file must also be included, as in this example:

```
[C:\Windows\WIN.INI Colors]
```

This line specifies that properties for exclusion follow that are to be found inside the [Colors] section of WIN.INI. A separate section header inside EXCLUDE.INI must be created for each section in the original configuration file that contains properties to be excluded, although multiple properties from the same section may be listed together, one on each line. In the case of excluding entire files, the complete path to that file's location, excluding the filename, forms the section header within EXCLUDE.INI. For example, to exclude a file located within your root directory on C:, the following line shows the proper and complete section header:

```
[C:\]
```

Immediately after the section header may be listed the filename or names, one per line, that are to be excluded.

One caveat: The first time you open EXCLUDE.INI, you'll notice that the Windows swap file is the first exclusion on the list. Because your swap file is modified thousands of times during an average Windows session, never remove the Windows swap file exclusion from EXCLUDE.INI.

Data Files Tab Settings

The Data Files tab, next in line after the Text Files tab, functions largely in the same way as the Text Files tab, but this one contains no option to view exclusions. This is because Data Files, unlike text files, are almost always comprised of binary data, which cannot be read by humans. Norton Registry Tracker watches over these files to let you know if and when they are modified, but it generally does not show you the modifications. This is based on the fact that every data file is designed internally differently from every other data file, and because the contents would just be an endless stream of hexadecimal numbers.

In general, because you cannot directly review the changes made to these files, and because every file is set up differently, it would be meaningless to allow you to exclude certain types of changes to these files. As with text files, selecting a filename in this list and clicking Remove deletes the file from NRT's future snapshots.

Folders Tab Settings

The Folders tab works in precisely the same manner as the Text Files tab, with one difference: You click Add to select an entire folder's worth of system and configuration files at a time. The Add Folder dialog box displays only folders and resembles the Windows Explorer's traditional use of the hierarchical plus ("+") and minus ("–") buttons, as you can see in Figure 13.10.

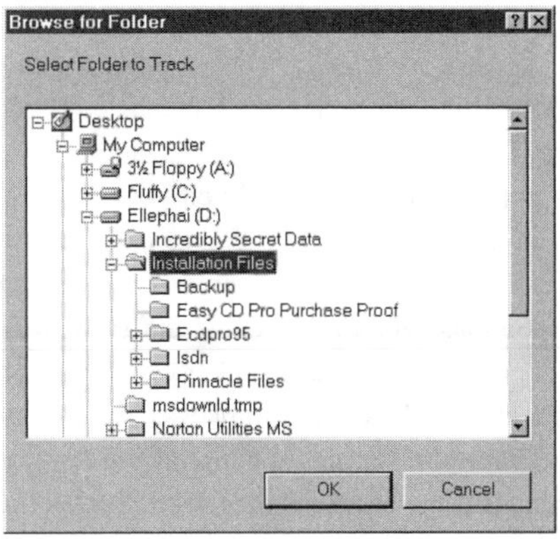

Figure 13.10
*Norton Registry
Tracker's folder
selection dialog
box displays only
folders.*

Figure 13.10
*Norton Registry
Tracker's folder
selection dialog
box displays only
folders.*

By default, the Add Folders dialog box opens to your Windows folder because this is
where most of your configuration files are stored. You can freely select any folder on any
drive, and changes to any files within that folder will be tracked. Notice that the option
to show or hide exclusions is again present. After NRT has tracked that changes have
occurred within a folder, you can click the affected file in the NRT Snapshot log and
exclude it from future tracking. Excluded files are listed here, and you can also manage
your exclusions here by selecting an excluded item and clicking Remove to return it to
NRT's tracking list.

Registry Keys Tab Settings

Finally, the Registry Keys tab, shown in Figure 13.11, determines which keys Norton
Registry Tracker will track. You can see here that NRT is capable of tracking two of the
Registry's six primary HKEYs, HKEY_LOCAL_MACHINE, and HKEY_USERS.
Within each of those HKEYs are literally hundreds of keys and subkeys that together
manage your PC's hardware configuration and your own software configurations. NRT
can track changes to all of them.

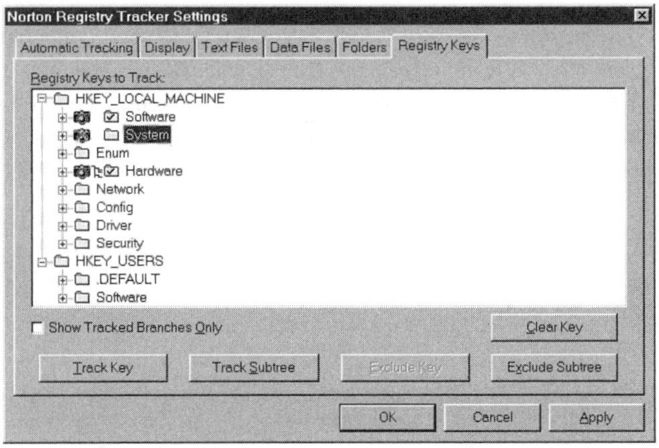

Figure 13.11
*Determine which
Registry keys
should be tracked
on the Norton
Registry Tracker's
Registry Keys set-
tings.*

As you see in Figure 13.11, NRT shows all the keys under each of the major HKEYs, regardless of whether those keys are tracked. You have the option of simplifying the display by viewing only tracked keys; checking the box labeled Show Tracked Branches Only enables this feature. The first time you open this tab, however, it's most likely that you will be adding keys to NRT's list of tracked items, so you'll want to make sure that check box is empty and all keys are displayed. You can use the hierarchical plus ("+") symbols to open branches of the Registry's tree until you locate a key you wish to track. Selecting that key with the mouse and then clicking the Track Key button tracks that key and its properties. It does not, however, track subkeys of that key or their properties. To do so, select the relevant key and click Track Subkeys. The button naming may seem a bit confusing; saying that you want to track subkeys also tracks the primary key. (For example, it would be redundant to specifically track both HKEY_LOCAL_MACHINE\ Software\Microsoft and HKEY_LOCAL_MACHINE, because the latter is automatically tracked when you indicate you want to track the former.)

When a key and its subkeys are being tracked, you must click Clear Key to disable all tracking, and then click Track Key if you decide you wish to track only the primary key. Clicking Clear Key at any time resets that key's status entirely, whether the key is being tracked or excluded from snapshots. As you can see in Figure 13.11, tracked key's folder icons are marked with a check mark. Keys for which subkey tracking is enabled (as with the Hardware key in Figure 13.11) are marked both with the tracking check mark and with a series of short lines that resemble a tree hierarchy between the NRT Snapshot icon and the key's folder icon. Keys that have been cleared and that are not marked specifically for tracking or exclusion appear as unchecked folders, as with the Enum key shown in Figure 13.11.

If you wish to exclude a key from tracking, you select it on this tab and click either Exclude Key or Exclude Subkeys, depending on the degree of exclusion you desire. As with the System key in Figure 13.11, excluded keys are identified by a large red "X" placed through the Norton Registry Tracker Snapshot icon. (As with tracking, a key marked for subkey exclusion also shows the small hierarchy symbol between the NRT icon and the key's folder icon.)

After the Norton Registry Tracker is configured to your liking, tracking is—or can be— an entirely automatic process. Of course, you can always initiate a manual snapshot whenever you like, but as with the rest of the Norton SystemWorks "data butlers," Norton Registry Tracker does its job by maintaining a delightfully low profile until you need it.

All Your Eggs in One Basket

It's probably no surprise that I strongly recommend that you keep the Registry Tracker running in the background while you work. No other single place on your PC stores more vital information than the Windows Registry. When you combine Registry tracking with configuration file tracking, the Registry Tracker really takes on a new dimension, enabling you to monitor and even reverse changes that have been made in almost any of your computer's primary configuration warehouses.

One of the Tracker's features that is probably most under-utilized is the capability it gives you to manually take a snapshot at will. If you allow Norton System Doctor to continuously monitor your PC with its WinDoctor and Disk Health sensors, your disks will be kept in tip-top shape. Each time WinDoctor runs, finds, and repairs errors, the Registry Tracker takes a snapshot. But I suggest you periodically take manual snapshots when WinDoctor has just run and has found no errors. In this way, you'll be regularly updating your baseline snapshot at a time when you know your system has just been checked and has passed with flying colors. If your PC has been working satisfactorily and is configured as you like it, this may also be a great time to erase your old snapshots—just select Reset Snapshot Log from the Options menu inside the Registry Tracker— and start tracking again from scratch.

This is rather like getting into the good habit of throwing away the Undo files that you may have Norton Disk Doctor create when it runs. After you verify that no Undo is necessary, it's best to destroy the Undo file so that it doesn't get accidentally used later, wreaking havoc on your drives. By resetting the Snapshot log when you know all lights are green, you're giving yourself the same kind of protection against accidents.

As you continue reading into the next chapter and learn about using the Norton Registry Editor, I urge you to keep the Registry Tracker running in the background. While it is true that the Norton Registry Editor has an Undo feature if your changes prove undesirable, you'll find it ever so much easier to simply Undo your changes through the Registry Tracker. It's a powerful maintenance tool, whether you're busy being a power-user or are just changing the way Windows looks.

Norton Utilities: Heroic Measures and Other Registry Editing

Norton Registry Editor is a Windows-based application designed to enable expert users to make modifications to both local and networked Windows Registry files and certain Windows configuration files. Broadly considered superior to Microsoft's REGEDIT tool, Norton Registry Editor provides action tracking, undo, advanced find capabilities, and close integration with Norton Registry Tracker—none of which are provided by REGEDIT. Norton Registry Editor (NRE) provides a methodology for backing up selected branches of the Registry and importing new keys from external sources. NRE enables you to bookmark commonly visited keys so that you can jump to them instantly. Furthermore, Norton Registry Editor can be run in a read-only mode, making it a truly safe environment for budding Registry aficionados to explore and learn about this powerful but complex database.

For the most part, although this chapter describes that read-only mode, what you find here assumes that you're already familiar with the Windows Registry, Registry keys, and the database organization. You won't find an exhaustive tutorial about the world of HKEYs and CLSIDs here, although those concepts are described in the context of getting the most out of Norton Registry Editor.

> **Caution:** Editing the Windows Registry is serious business. If you are an inexperienced user, you can quickly render Windows unstartable. Although the Registry has some self-repair tricks, anyone who has worked with the Registry can tell you that relying on these tricks is truly demonstrating the humor inherent in faith. Norton Registry Tracker and Norton Rescue—particularly Norton Zip Rescue—can do a tremendous job of helping you recover from Registry damage, but there's little as frustrating as hours of repair work made necessary by carelessness. By all means, explore and understand the Registry if you will, but edit only when you're certain of what you are doing. The vast majority of changes that can be made to the Registry can be made by far safer means—through Control Panels, application preferences menus, and so on.

Read-Only Mode

Without question, the first aspect of Norton Registry Editor with which you should be familiar is read-only mode. As with Read Mode in the Norton Disk Editor (see Chapter 10, "Norton Utilities: The Laying-On of Hands and Norton Disk Editor"), read-only mode enables you to putter and explore and learn all about the Registry without ever putting the Registry's contents at risk. When read-only mode is enabled, it remains enabled—even if you quit NRE and re-launch it—until you intentionally turn it off again. There is no keyboard switch through which to enable or disable read-only mode at launch.

To start NRE, select it from the SystemWorks Integrator under Norton Utilities, or find it on your Start menu under Programs I Norton Utilities I Norton Registry Editor. To enable or disable read-only mode, click the Registry menu and select Read Only from the bottom of the menu. Norton Registry Editor's default display appears, as shown in Figure 14.1. A check mark appears beside the Read Only menu item to indicate that read-only mode is enabled and that editing is disallowed. The words Read Only appear at the lower-right of the status bar when that mode is active.

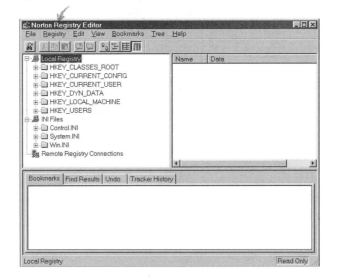

FIGURE 14.1

Norton Registry Editor provides a simple-to-use interface.

The Norton Registry Editor Interface

If you are familiar with Microsoft's free Registry-editing concoction, REGEDIT, you've already noticed that Norton Registry Editor (shown in Figure 14.1) provides a more sophisticated editing environment. In addition to the several tools that are unique to NRE, the application is widely considered to be significantly more robust than REGEDIT. The presence of an Undo feature certainly makes NRE more tolerant.

As with REGEDIT, Norton Registry Editor provides two primary panes for displaying Registry and selected .INI file content. The hierarchical tree in the left pane displays Registry keys and subkeys. Key values appear in the right pane. Double-clicking a value enables you to modify it, so long as read-only mode is not enabled. At the bottom of the NRE screen, a status bar displays the name of the key being browsed.

For the most part, similarities with REGEDIT end there. REGEDIT has its uses, as do the other Microsoft applets, but Norton Registry Editor is to REGEDIT as Microsoft Word is to WordPad.

The Tab Panel

The most visually obvious difference between NRE and REGEDIT is the panel at the bottom of the NRE screen, which contains four Windows-type tabs—labeled Bookmarks, Find Results, Undo, and Tracker History. These tabs serve as your window on much of NRE's additional functionality, as you'll read later. Each tab displays a different class of content and has a different set of actions that can be performed upon that content. Let's take a look at each tab and its related functionality.

> **Note:** You can use standard grab-and-drag techniques to resize the three panels within the Norton Registry Editor display. Click the mouse on the bold divider between the two top panels or the upper and lower panels to change the size to fit your needs. The entire lower panel can be hidden by shrinking it to the bottom of the window. Clicking and dragging the bold gray line above the status bar restores the panel. Resize functionality is also available from the View menu. In an admirable nod to accessibility, after selecting Resize Pane Horizontal or Resize Pane Vertical from the menu, the keyboard has been designed to enable resizing. Arrow keys select a new pane size; Enter accepts the new configuration.

The Bookmarks Tab

Unlike any other Registry modification tool available at the time of this writing, NRE provides the capability of creating and retrieving bookmarks within the Registry itself. These bookmarks function in a way that's similar to hyperlinks in a Web document. In fact, if you like the Web analogy, consider the Bookmarks tab to be a Web document in one frame, and the hierarchical Registry pane to be another Web document. Bookmark entries in the Bookmark tab are like HTML labels for content within the Registry "page."

Analogies aside, the Bookmark feature enables you to select Registry keys that you visit commonly or that you wish to edit, then review the impact of those changes and perhaps return and quickly re-edit. Figure 14.2 shows the NRE window with several bookmarks created. (Bookmarks are created by selecting the key you wish to bookmark and then selecting Bookmark This from the NRE Bookmarks menu.) You can see in the figure that three bookmarks have been created: two within HKEY_CURRENT_USER and one within HKEY_LOCAL_MACHINE. Bookmarks retain their place in the Registry hierarchy, so you can quickly collapse or expand bookmarks based on their handle key. Notice that the final bookmark represents the major key Hardware directly within the handle key (HKEY) LOCAL_MACHINE. The first bookmark, which leads to a subkey containing the value for default application event sounds, demonstrates how NRE maintains key hierarchy by displaying the entire path to the marked subkey: AppEvents\EventLabels\.Default. This hierarchical maintenance is important; imagine looking at a list of bookmarks, all entitled only .Default.

FIGURE 14.2
Bookmarks are expanded on this NRE Bookmark display.

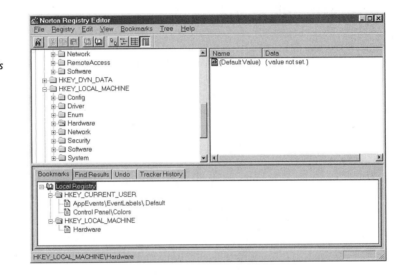

Double-clicking a bookmark automatically scrolls and, as necessary, expands the Registry tree to display the marked key as the active key. The same functionality is available in a context menu by right-clicking the bookmark and selecting Go to Bookmark. Also notice in the figure that bookmarked keys have a small red dot added to their folder icon in the Registry tree. This serves as a very handy reference to what is bookmarked as you're scrolling through the tree manually.

If you export or print Registry keys from NRE, these bookmark reminders will be included. Bookmarks will not appear within REGEDIT, although the last bookmarks used are maintained from one NRE session to the next.

You can create as many bookmarks as you like; their usefulness is limited only by your ability to scroll through the Bookmark tab and quickly locate the mark you want. You can also create multiple sets of bookmarks, which can be loaded on demand. If you're working on a variety of Registry-related tasks, you may want to maintain a specific set of bookmarks for each of those tasks. Similarly, if you're supervising Registries for several networked computers, you can generate bookmarks specific to a given workstation and load those bookmarks when you connect to that workstation's Registry (you'll read about this later in the chapter). To save the currently selected bookmarks to a file, choose Bookmarks | Save Bookmarks from the menu. To retrieve saved bookmarks in a later session, choose Bookmarks | Load Bookmarks from the menu. (Loading bookmarks from a Registry other than the one you're viewing won't cause any harm—but, of course, they won't work, either.)

> **Tip:** Because bookmarks do not actually modify the Registry, they can be created even while in read-only mode.

To prevent accidental deletion of bookmarks, selecting a mark in the Bookmark tab and pressing the Delete key has no effect. Bookmarks can be deleted by choosing Remove from the selected mark's context menu or from the NRE main Bookmarks menu.

> **Caution:** No confirmation appears before a bookmark is removed. Likewise, the creation or deletion of bookmarks is not tracked by the NRE Undo tab or Norton Registry Tracker. After you remove a bookmark, you must relocate its key and create a new bookmark if you change your mind about the deletion.

Shortcuts—A Partial Alternative to Bookmarks

In addition to creating bookmarks, you can create shortcuts to keys. These shortcuts appear not in the Bookmarks tab but in the main Registry tree itself, alphabetized by their names (which you can specify). To create a shortcut, select the key to which you want a shortcut, and choose Make Shortcut from the key's context menu (right-click). You can also select Make Shortcut from NRE's main Edit menu. Figure 14.3 shows a shortcut called "HandoffPriorities#1," with the Registry tree expanded to show the key to which the shortcut points.

Note that you can give a shortcut any name you like when you create it. A default name is chosen but also highlighted for editing; simply type a new name to replace the default. Once created, however, a shortcut cannot be renamed. You must remove the shortcut, create a new one, and give the new shortcut the name you want to use if you want to change a shortcut's name. To remove a shortcut, you can simply select it and press the Delete key. You can also choose Remove Shortcut from the shortcut's context menu or from NRE's main Edit menu.

Shortcuts function differently from bookmarks. If you double-click a shortcut, the shortcut itself opens, displaying any subkeys of the target key and any key values. Changes made to the shortcut also change the target key without opening it within the tree. Shortcuts are great because they enable you to work within the one editor pane, but they cannot be saved externally like bookmarks. The most recently used shortcuts are maintained from one NRE session to the next, however. As with bookmarks, shortcuts do not actually change the Registry, and they can be created while in read-only mode.

Figure 14.3
This shortcut was created for the HandoffPriorities subkey.

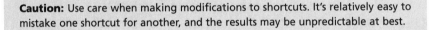

> **Caution:** Use care when making modifications to shortcuts. It's relatively easy to mistake one shortcut for another, and the results may be unpredictable at best.

The Find Results Tab

The second of NRE's four tabs provides the functionality for Norton Registry Editor's sophisticated Find command. A search for Registry keys or key values can be initiated from the main NRE Edit menu, from the context menu of any key (right-click), or by pressing Ctrl+F. When selected, Find opens a two-tab dialog box similar to that shown in Figure 14.4. The What & Where tab enables you to enter the data that you want to search for, and then select the search's target.

Had NRE been connected to a remote Registry when this figure was captured, remote Registry connections would have also appeared in the displayed drop-down menu. As you can see, you can perform a search of far more than just the Registry from within Norton Registry Editor. Any other .INI files that you had connected to NRE—you'll read about how to do this later—also would have appeared in the Find Where list.

Notice that the Find What box is a drop-down list. All searches performed earlier in that NRE session can be quickly selected from here; they need not be manually re-entered.

The Advanced search tab, shown in Figure 14.5, provides access to all NRE's extended search capabilities. Notice first that the default is to search all branches of the Registry (or of whatever file or remote connection is selected in the What & Where tab). This is the default even if you invoke the Find command from a given key's context menu. If

you wish to search within a specific key, you must select the Selected Branch radio button and enter the key's name. (If you have selected Find from a key's context menu, that
key's name automatically appears in the Selected Branch box.) For the sake of simplicity,
you can quickly choose a handle key as the search target by selecting its radio button.
(Notice that this search shortcut is not provided for HKEY_CURRENT_CONFIG or
HKEY_DYN_DATA, which you will likely never manually edit.)

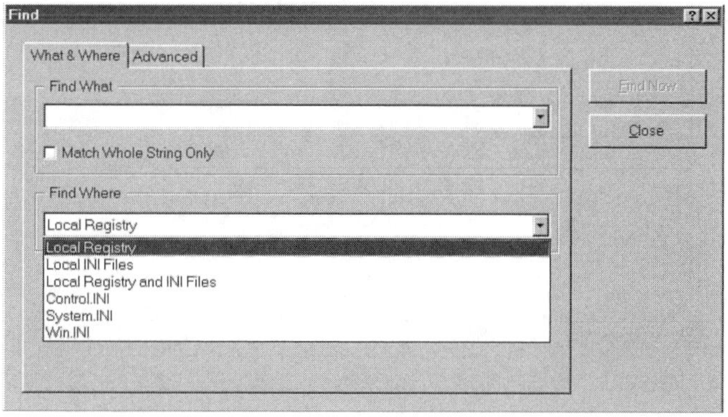

FIGURE 14.4

*Use NRE's Find
What & Where
tab to enter data
that you want to
search for, and
choose where the
data is located.*

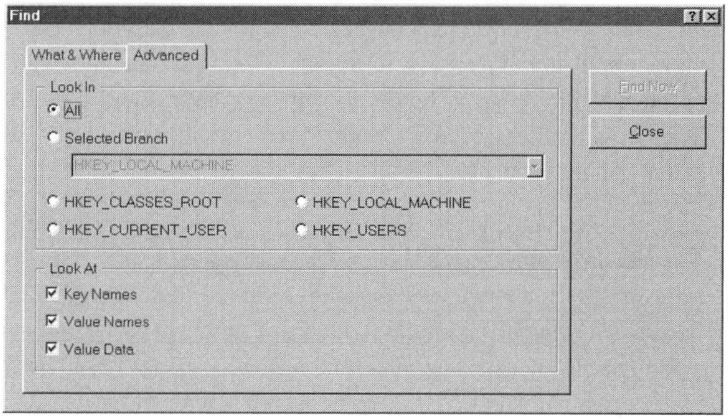

FIGURE 14.5

*NRE's Advanced
find tab provides
additional search
options.*

At the bottom of the Advanced tab (as in a regular REGEDIT find), you can select
whether you want search results to include Key Names, Value Names, Value Data, or any
combination thereof. With your search string entered in the What & Where tab, and with
your target defined in the Advanced tab, click Find Now to perform the search. (Bear in
mind that you need not visit the Advanced tab for each search you perform. By default,
NRE performs the most inclusive search, checking the entire Registry for all three types
of data—Key Names, Value Names, and Value Data.) Figure 14.6 shows the results of
searching the entire Registry for my first name.

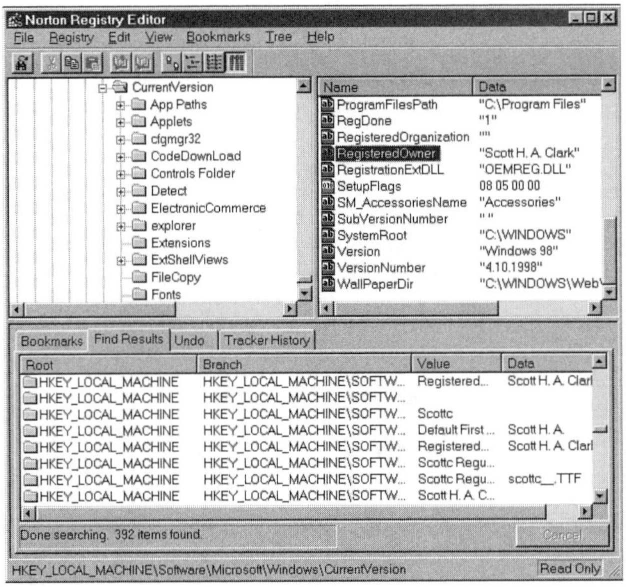

FIGURE **14.6**

NRE's Find Results showing the first match and all other matches.

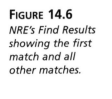

You can immediately see the power of NRE's searching tool. In REGEDIT, searching for my name would have found the same 392 results, but I would have had to step through those results one at a time, selecting Find Next over and over until I arrived at the key I wanted. Norton Registry Editor does display the first match in the upper panes, opening the tree as is necessary to do so. But NRE also displays all matches in the Find Results tab in the bottom pane.

Find Results functions just like temporary bookmarks: Double-click to open the target key and display the matched data. The results are organized first by handle key and then subkeys. For quick reference, matches located within key values also display the matching value in the two right-most columns. You still have the option of scrolling through search results by choosing Find Next or Find Previous from NRE's main Edit menu, but never again will you have to step through hundreds of matches to search for a specific key or value entry.

Searching the entire Registry may take some time. If you wish to cancel a search in progress, you can click the Cancel button at the lower-right corner of the Find Results tab or select Cancel Search from the main NRE Edit menu.

Find and Replace

The Find and Replace capability is provided through the familiar two-tab interface. This is similar to a simple search except that a box is provided on the What & Where tab for you to enter a replacement string. A Replace can be started at any time, so long as read-only mode is inactive. Select Find | Replace from any key's context menu, select Replace from the main NRE Edit menu, or press Ctrl+R. After the replacement has begun, NRE stops at each match it encounters by default, asking you to confirm the replacement. You can leave this active if you want to be certain you don't replace a value or key name unknowingly. You can also instruct NRE to stop pestering you for confirmations by removing the check from the box labeled Confirm on the first confirmation dialog box you see. Selecting Yes, of course, confirms a replacement, while selecting No prevents the selected key from being modified. In either case, the search-and-replace process continues after each match is found, unless you click Cancel in a confirmation dialog box.

The Undo Tab

Having just discussed the possibility of making global replacements throughout your Registry, it seems appropriate that we come next to the Undo tab, as seen in Figure 14.7. Norton Registry Editor provides infinite Undos, enabling you to reverse changes all the way back to when you launched this session of NRE. (Changes made in previous sessions are not undoable through NRE, although you may be able to undo them if you are also using Norton Registry Tracker.) All changes made to the Registry during the current session appear in the Undo tab, whether they reflect the creation of new keys, the deletion of a key, modification of a value, and so on. Whatever action was taken is displayed in the left column of the Undo tab, while the name of the key or value upon which the action was performed appears in the right column. The most recently made edit always appears at the bottom of the list. You can see an example of this in Figure 14.7.

FIGURE 14.7
The NRE Undo tab shows Registry modifications tracked.

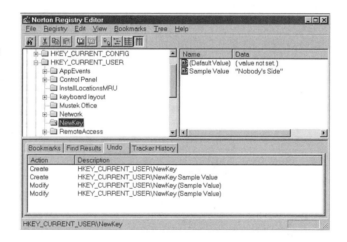

In Figure 14.7, you can see that a new key was added under the handle key CURRENT_USER, that it was given a value, and that the value was modified. To undo the most recently performed action, simply right-click anywhere in the Undo tab and select Undo from the context menu. You can also select Undo from the main NRE Edit menu or press Ctrl+Z. Actions that are reversed disappear from the Undo tab and are not automatically "re-doable." In this manner, you can quickly reverse a Registry modification made in error.

> **Caution:** In some versions of Norton Registry Editor, an error occurs in the context-sensitive pop-up help for the Undo tab. The errant help indicates that you can select a specific entry in the Undo list—even if it is not the last entry in the list—right-click it, and select Undo This from a context menu to undo a specific edit. This functionality is not present. Selecting Undo always undoes the last modification. Selective undo is available through Norton Registry Tracker, as you will read in later sections and in Chapter 13, "Norton Utilities: The Better Part of Valor and Registry Tracker."

The Tracker History Tab

The last of the four NRE tabs displays any modification history that exists for the selected key, as shown in Figure 14.8. If Norton Registry Tracker is not active, a Launch Registry Tracker button is enabled at the bottom-right of the Tracker History tab. As with creating a backup of your Registry before you begin any editing, launching Norton Registry Tracker is a superb idea. Unlike the Undo tab, however, Norton Registry Tracker enables you to undo any modification made to the Registry at any time, whether it was the most recent modification or not. Also unlike Undo, the Norton Registry Tracker records modifications made to the tracked items in the Registry from any source, not just those made within Norton Registry Editor. (For information on using Norton Registry Tracker, refer to Chapter 13.)

FIGURE 14.8

The Tracker History tab shows a key which was modified before the last NRT snapshot was taken.

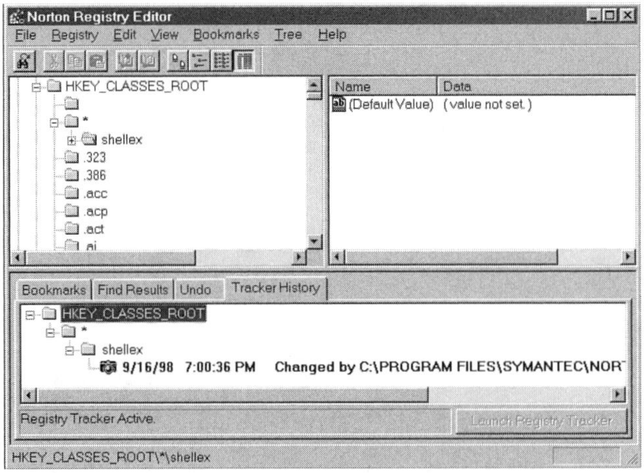

For a detailed discussion of Norton Registry Tracker, and for information on enabling and disabling the selective tracking of keys and .INI file contents, refer to Chapter 13.

The Toolbar

Microsoft REGEDIT does not provide a toolbar as part of its fundamental interface, but Norton Registry Editor does. From the toolbar, you can initiate a search, perform Clipboard-related actions, add and remove bookmarks, and change to one of the various views provided by NRE. We'll explore those views next.

Selectable Views

Norton Registry Editor provides four different views: List, Report, Large Icon, and Small Icon. For most uses, the default Report view will be the most useful to you—if you're used to using REGEDIT, it is also the view that most resembles REGEDIT's interface. Switching to another view affects only the right-hand or Value pane, not the Registry tree display.

Selecting a Large Icon view presents the values of any key as file icons. The name of each value appears beneath it, but the value itself is not displayed.

Small Icon view and List view are approximately the same view, with small icons presented in rows and listed items presented in columns, much like the alternative display modes within Windows Explorer. Each value is represented by a small icon, and the name of the value (but not the value itself) is displayed.

Report view—NRE's default—displays both the value name and the actual value, along with a small icon indicating the value type. Figure 14.9 shows a sample of each type of icon in the Value pane of the selected key. Each icon is labeled in accordance with its type. String, Extended String, and MultiString data are represented in the Data column directly. Numeric data is always represented as a 32-bit DWORD value, although it can be entered as binary, hexadecimal, or decimal form. Binary data is always displayed in its hexadecimal equivalent.

FIGURE 14.9
Icon types are shown in the Value pane.

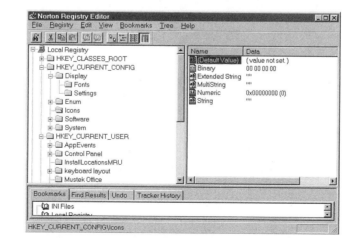

Registry Editing

Having looked at the fundamental interface provided by Norton Registry Editor, this chapter concludes with a discussion of how editing actually takes place. You'll learn about the various methods for entering and modifying keys and data, importing and exporting keys and values, and changing the list of initialization files connected to Norton Registry Editor. Finally, you learn how to connect to remote Registries across a network.

Backing Up the Registry

Before you begin making changes to your Registry, however, it's always well-advised to create a backup, just in case something catastrophic happens. From within Norton Registry Editor, making a complete backup of your Registry couldn't be simpler. From the File menu, simply select Backup Entire Registry, specify a destination—be certain that the destination drive contains sufficient free space to hold the Registry backup—and click OK. As you can see in Figure 14.10, NRE displays a window showing the progress of the backup. On a slow computer, this can take some time. Clicking Cancel at any time aborts the entire backup. Delightfully, the backup is performed in its own process and can be minimized, enabling you to do other work with Norton Registry Editor while the backup continues in the background.

Another way to safeguard your Registry contents before performing any manual editing is to update your Norton Zip Rescue set immediately before launching NRE. Setting your Zip Rescue to completely restore a Registry damaged during editing is a snap.

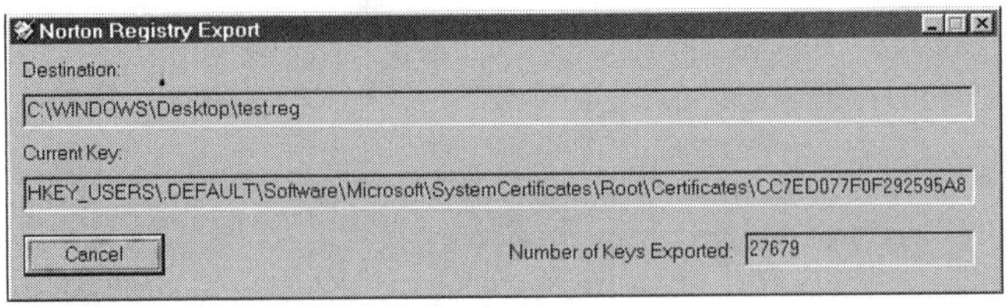

FIGURE 14.10

NRE backs up the entire Registry.

Modifying Registry Keys

New keys can be added to the Registry at any location and at any time. Be aware, however, that any modifications to existing keys—even the addition of meaningless subkeys—may impair whatever functionality is registered within that key. Always back up your Registry before making any changes.

To add a key to the Registry, simply right-click the key (or handle key under which you want the new key to be located) and select New | Key from the context menu. You can also select New | Key from the main NRE Edit menu. The new key is given a default name, which will also be selected. Simply begin typing to rename it. You can rename a key at any later time by selecting Rename from the key's context menu. (Recall that you cannot rename a shortcut, but you can rename a key.)

Deleting a Registry Key is even simpler. Simply select the key, press the Delete key, and confirm the removal. You can also select Delete from the key's context menu or from the main NRE Edit menu. The key, along with all its subkeys and values, vanishes. (Of course, you can always immediately undo this deletion, or selectively undo it in Norton Registry Tracker, if the Tracker is running while you edit.)

Modifying Keys (and Values) by Importation

You can easily add multiple keys to the Registry through the use of .REG files. These .REG files are created by exporting the Registry—or, more commonly, selected branches of the Registry—to a file on disk. These files are text files that can also be edited and also manipulated within Norton File Compare. In fact, Norton Registry Tracker's capability of providing Registry comparison functionality—which you read about in the previous chapter—is done through .REG files.

One of the great benefits of .REG files is that they enable a system administrator to quickly make many modifications to the Registries of many workstations without having to manually enter those keys and values on each machine. As you'll read later, the administrator can make these changes on every workstation without ever leaving his or her own. By creating the keys and values to be imported in one workstation's Registry and exporting that branch to a .REG file, the administrator can import those keys to other Registries at will. The keys will be added to each Registry as they are imported. To import a .REG file, simply choose Import Registry File from the main NRE File menu. Specify the .REG file, click OK, and the keys and values become an active part of whatever Registry is being edited.

One of the strengths—or limitations, depending on your perspective— of Microsoft's REGEDIT applet is the fact that the process of importing Registry data only adds content to the Registry. REGEDIT does not allow imported data to overwrite any existing values or delete existing values. Norton Registry Editor does not have these restrictions. It provides a method for performing those two tasks, although you should make any such choices with great care. To instruct an imported .REG file to modify existing Registry data, use the following techniques:

- To delete a specific Registry key, as well as all its subkeys and values, place the name of that key in the .REG file to be imported, with a tilde ("~") before the key's name:

  ~[HKEY_CURRENT_USER\CustomKey]

  This command deletes everything under the CustomKey key upon importation.

- To delete all the values under a specific Registry key—including those within its subkeys—without destroying the key or its subkeys themselves, enter that key's name in the .REG file to be imported, with a minus sign ("–") before the key's name:

  -[HKEY_CURRENT_USER\CustomKey]

- To delete a specific key's value, place a tilde ("~") in the .REG file in place of that value's data:

```
[HKEY_CURRENT_USER\CustomKey]
"ThisKey"=~
```

These two lines together would delete the value ThisKey from the key HKEY_CUR-RENT_USER\CustomKey.

- To modify an existing value, simply use the previous notation to delete the existing value, followed immediately by a new value for that value:

```
[HKEY_CURRENT_USER\CustomKey]
"ThisKey"=~
"ThisKey"="Sounds Like I'm Stuttering"
```

None of this functionality is provided by Microsoft REGEDIT, and it's relatively easy to understand why. When applications create Registry entries during their setup process, they normally use .REG file scripts that are essentially processed by REGEDIT. It would be highly undesirable to allow one program to delete or modify the Registry entries of another, perhaps rival, program. For that reason, the capability simply does not exist without Norton Registry Editor. (Incidentally, .REG files containing special NRE notation still work with REGEDIT, but all the special notation is ignored; existing keys are neither deleted nor modified, but new keys are added.)

Manually Modifying Values

Just as keys can be entered, deleted, or changed by hand, so can key values. A new value of any of the five types—numerical, binary, string, extended string, or multistring—can be entered into any selected key by choosing New from the key's context menu or from the main NRE Edit menu. The new value is given a default name that also can be selected for editing. Simply type to replace the default. (As with keys, values can be renamed at any time by selecting Rename from the value's context menu or from the main NRE Edit menu.)

After a key exists—whether it's a new key or an existing one—its value can be modified by double-clicking the value's name. A dialog box such as that shown in Figure 14.11 opens, into which the new value can be typed. In this figure, you can see the modification box for a binary value named ConfigFlags. Note that binary data is entered in hexadecimal form and that the ASCII equivalent for each entered hexadecimal byte appears to the right of the hex values. (In this case, the values are all zero, so NRE displays placeholding periods. Had the hex values been 50 45 54 45 52, you would have seen the name PETER to their right.)

String values, including special extended strings and multistrings, are entered directly as text. These are commonly used to store the path to an application or an application component, or to provide an embedded structure into which programmers can place a variety of often private data. Note that the Norton Registry Editor automatically adds quotation marks around string values; you should not enter them yourself. Note also that Microsoft REGEDIT enables you to view extended strings and multistrings only in hex form; NRE displays them as editable text. Numeric values are stored in the 32-bit DWORD format and can be entered in hexadecimal, decimal, or binary form. The entry method is selected through the use of radio buttons on the Modify Value dialog box.

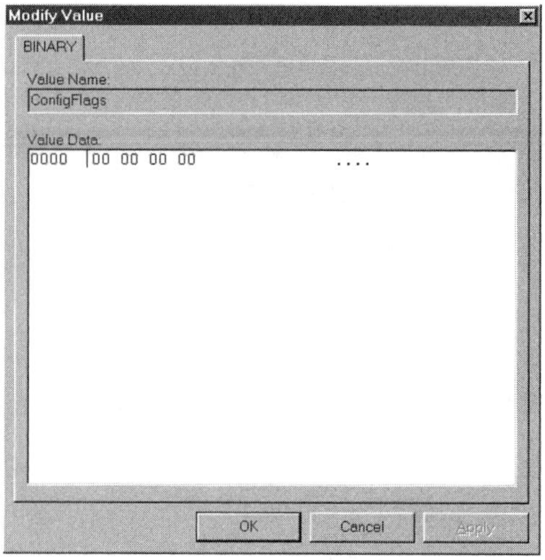

FIGURE 14.11

This Modify Value dialog box shows the data for a sample, binary value.

Deleting values is also easy. Select the value and press Delete, or select Delete from the key's context menu or the main NRE Edit menu. After you respond to the confirmation, the value disappears.

Working with .INI Files

As with Registry files and their keys, the entries within .INI configuration files can be edited using the Norton Registry Editor. Bookmarking within these files is also enabled from within NRE, exactly as it is with Registry files. Look at Figure 14.12 to see an example of SYSTEM.INI being edited within NRE. In the figure, you can see that all the different sections of the .INI file—sections normally viewed like this [SectionName]—are represented as folders within Norton Registry Editor. Because .INI files are flat as opposed to hierarchical, you'll never see any subfolders within folders in an NRE display of an .INI file. Still, the folder metaphor remains useful. The separate configuration entries—each delineated in the .INI file by a carriage return—are represented as values within the right-hand NRE pane. All .INI values are string values because .INI files are fundamentally regular text files. Even numeric data is entered as a string; it's up to the operating system or the application related to the .INI file to properly interpret these values as numbers, application paths, or anything else.

Notice in Figure 14.12 that a bookmark has been set for the drivers32 section of SYSTEM.INI. Bookmark functionality is the same for .INI files as for Registry files: Double-click the bookmark to cause the tree to jump and expand as necessary to show the marked section. Shortcuts cannot be created within .INI files.

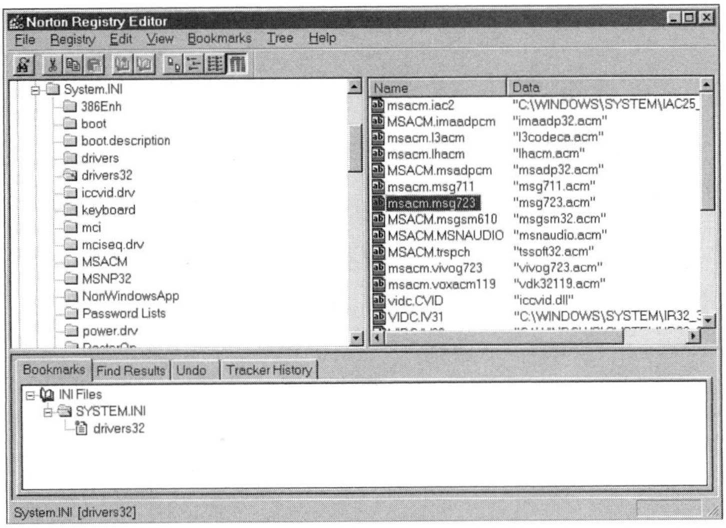

FIGURE **14.12**

*Use Norton
Registry Editor to
edit* SYSTEM.INI.

Creating New .INI Files from NRE

New .INI files can easily be created from within Norton Registry Editor by selecting
Create New INI File from the main NRE File menu. You'll be asked to specify a name
and location for the file. From that point forward, you can use the New | Key command
to add sections—in the left pane, just as if you were adding Registry keys—or New |
String to add values within those sections—in the right pane, just as if you were adding
Registry values. Note that after you create an .INI file using NRE, that file is considered
"loaded" into NRE and is located at the bottom of the left pane. Unless you unload it, the
file is included in the list of .INI files each time you run Norton Registry Editor. You
also don't have to save an .INI file created with NRE. As with Registry modifications,
NRE writes changes to disk after each change is made.

Unloading .INI Files

To remove an .INI file from NRE's display, you must unload it. To do so, select Unload
INI File from the main NRE File menu. A small dialog box opens, displaying the names
of all .INI files that can be unloaded. Shift-clicking and Ctrl-clicking are supported in
this dialog box. Select the .INI file(s) you want unloaded from NRE, and click OK.
Unloading .INI files does not delete them from disk; it simply removes them from the
NRE display. The .INI Files can be reloaded at any time by selecting Load INI File from
NRE's main File menu.

> **Note:** WIN.INI, CONTROL.INI, and SYSTEM.INI are considered base .INI files and
> cannot be unloaded.

Working with Remote Registries

As you've already read, Norton Registry Editor enables system administrators to review
and modify the Windows Registry of any workstation on the network. This enables one
individual to quickly check the status of an entire workgroup's Registries without leaving
his or her office. The network administrator can also use NRE to load remote Registries,
import .REG files into them, making necessary modifications and deletions, and having
those changes instantly present on the remote machine.

> **Note:** Working with remote Registries is enabled only for workstations on
> which Windows Remote Administration has been enabled by the network
> administrator.

To begin working with a remote Registry, select Connect Remote Registry from the main
NRE Registry menu, or right-click Remote Registry Connections at the bottom of the
Registry tree display and choose Connect Remote Registry from the context menu. You
can either type the name of a workstation or you can click Browse to view all workstations to which you have access. You can also connect to multiple remote Registries at
once; each connection appears at the bottom of the Registry tree display, under Remote
Registry Connections. In this way, you can quickly modify a number of Registries without having to stop and connect to each between modifications.

The actual manipulation of a remote Registry is no different from the manipulation of
the local Registry. Modifications take place immediately—unless the network goes
down, of course—and changes are as reversible as before.

> **Caution:** Norton Registry Tracker does not track modifications made to remote
> Registries, so you cannot rely on NRT's Undo capability when making remote
> changes. If you wish to enable Norton Registry Tracking protection for changes
> made to workstation Registries, you must run NRT and NRE locally and make
> the modifications directly on each workstation.

When you're finished working with a remote Registry, select Disconnect Network
Registry from the main NRE Registry menu.

Printing Registry Data

Printing your entire Registry is known to be a fantastic way to convince your coworkers
that you're nuts: It can easily take hundreds of pages to print out an entire Registry. Just
printing my current Control Panel settings would have taken 28 pages (had I not stopped
the print job).

It can be very useful to print selected Registry branches, however, and NRE enables you to do this. (It also enables you to print the whole thing, but why would you?) By default, NRE prints the Registry from your currently selected key inward. Simply select the relevant key, then choose Print from the NRE File menu. The key, all its subkeys, and all their values will print. (You can also export the entire Registry to a .REG file, then open and edit it in any text processor, cutting out the keys you donít wish to print.) Such printouts are handy for studying Registry settings away from the PC. However, your Registry contents should be treated as sensitive information. Names of files you recently accessed, hardware installed in your PC, software serial numbers with which someone could illegally install software for which you paid good money—any number of reasons exist for why it simply might not be in your best interest to have endless reams of printer paper floating around. For that reason, and for conservation's sake, be selective about printing Registry data, and dispose of it properly. The trees will thank you.

Peter Norton

Norton Utilities: Getting It Back, Getting It Right: UnErasing and File Compare

Back in Chapter 6, "Norton Utilities: Digging Through the Trash with Norton Protection," you first read about Norton Protection. Norton Protection is the integrated Norton Utilities component of SystemWorks that tracks and cares for the files which are deleted from your system—whether by you, your applications, or Windows itself—and maintains them as resurrectable. Because Norton Protection is a key weapon in your arsenal of protection and problem-prevention tools, I talked about it back in the Protection and Prevention section of this book (Part I).

If you configure Norton Protection in the way I suggested in Chapter 6, it will replace your Windows Recycle Bin, taking over that desktop tool's functionality and adding its own dramatically-increased level of protection to your PC. You probably remember that when you delete a file in Windows, it traditionally goes into the Recycle Bin and stays there until either the Bin is full, or you empty it. While a file is in the Recycle Bin, it can easily be restored, as if it had never been deleted. Sounds nice. But the Windows Recycle Bin provides *no* protection for just as many, or more, files than it does protect. Until you add Norton Protection, files deleted by applications like temporary files, files you delete from within a DOS box, and working-versions of files which you save over are all gone for good. Norton Protection catches all of those deletions, and more. When the day comes and you really *need* one of those files, Norton Protection will have saved it for you. (Nevermind the fact that, far too often, files under Windows simply *disappear*; in many of those occasions, Norton Protection and Norton Unerase will know where to find them.)

The fact of the matter is, however, that keeping track of your deleted files is only half the story. It's wonderful to know that your files don't really get deleted when you delete them, but that knowledge only becomes useful when you know how to get them back once they're gone. This is where the Norton UnErase Wizard comes into the equation. The UnErase Wizard exists in both a Windows-based and DOS-based form, and you'll learn all you need to know about both forms in this chapter. Depending on the circumstances under which you've lost—or want to retrieve—files, you could find yourself using either tool.

Tip: It may seem self-evident, but you'd be surprised how many users fail to remember that the best way to prevent accidental deletion of files is to not delete files until you're absolutely certain that you'll never need them again. As a matter of policy, I *never* delete *any* correspondence files, no matter how old. Given the increasing size and decreasing cost of hard disks, you should really endeavor to resist those anal-retentive urges to delete everything you've not touched in a month. When I do delete files—unless they're files that never had any value in the first place—I always create a long-term backup of the file on CD-Rewritable first.

But what do you do if you want to get a file back, not because you've lost the original, but because you've made changes to a file, don't like the changes, and wish you could just undo-them? Norton File Compare will allow you to make side-by-side comparisons of two files, allowing you to interactively undo settings you have changed, quickly import whole sections of one file into another, even compare two HTML files for trouble-shooting World Wide Web site design. You encountered Norton File Compare for the briefest moment in Chapter 13, "Norton Utilities: The Better Part of Valor and Registry Tracker," when you were learning about Norton Registry Tracker, but all of the details and the ways to master its use are to be found in this chapter. So, let's take a look at the Norton UnErase Wizard first, and then move on to manipulating those files with Norton File Compare, once they've been recovered.

Note: You'll find lots of uses for Norton File Compare that have nothing to do with UnErased files. But there are a wealth of benefits that File Compare brings to the party when you do need to get down and dirty with files you've recovered. It works so well with much of what you may be doing someday with Norton UnErase that I've grouped them together in this chapter.

The Norton UnErase Wizard

The Norton UnErase Wizard takes responsibility for reliably restoring the files which Norton Protection has been safeguarding on your behalf. As you'll see, it also does a lot more. The UnErase Wizard can help you search for files which were deleted even before Norton SystemWorks was installed. UnErase Wizard also puts some very powerful tools at your disposal, allowing you to easily indicate that you want to see only a subset of deleted files which match a criteria you specify. This can dramatically speed up your search for important, but deleted, content.

At its most fundamental level, the UnErase Wizard will do all of the work for you. You can directly select that it show you the last 25 files you deleted or that it show you all files which Norton Protection has safeguarded. We'll look at those two options first, then explore how you can create criteria against which your drives will be searched for lost

data. Finally, before exploring Norton File Compare, we'll look at the DOS-based
version of the Norton UnErase Wizard and how it works and differs from its Windows-
based cousin.

Recovering from a Sudden Deletion

For the majority of us, Norton UnErase will be used most often immediately after we've
deleted a file. Most of us will eventually have the experience of selecting a file in the
Explorer and pressing Delete, only to realize that we're still staring at the file we *wanted*
to erase, and the file that's now gone was our schedule of income tax deductions. Other
times, the deletion may be less obvious. You could be working in your word processor of
choice and select all the text in the file, delete the text, then save file before you realize
what you've done. (Don't laugh; I've done it myself. It usually happens around three in
the morning.)

In either of these possibly-disastrous circumstances, the Norton UnErase Wizard should
be the first tool you turn to as soon as you realize a mistake has been made. If you are
working in an application, you need not exit before running the UnErase Wizard,
although there may occasionally be reasons to do so, which you'll read about later. To
start the UnErase Wizard, just go to your Start menu, and select Programs | Norton
Utilities | UnErase Wizard. Alternately, you can double-click on the Norton SystemWorks
Integrator icon on your desktop. From the Integrator, select Norton Utilities, then select
Find and Fix Problems, and finally choose UnErase Wizard. You can also configure the
Norton Protected Recycle Bin to simply run the UnErase Wizard when you double-click
on it. The Wizard's opening screen is shown in Figure 15.1, below.

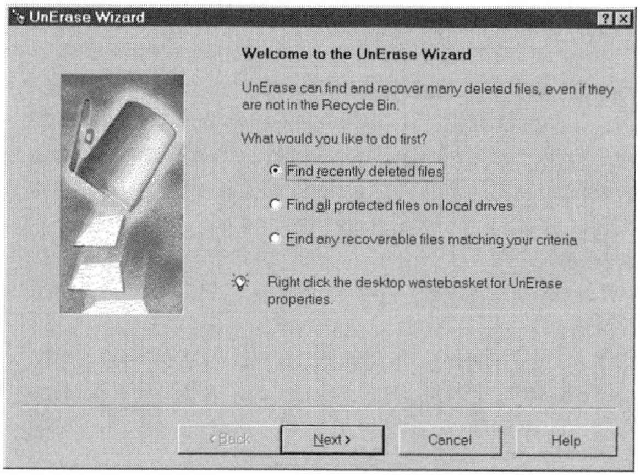

FIGURE 15.1

*The first screen of
the Norton
UnErase Wizard
lets you select
how the Wizard
will perform for
the remainder
of this recovery
session.*

By default, the UnErase Wizard opens with Find Recently Deleted Files selected. If
you've run the UnErase Wizard immediately after a problem has occurred, this will be
the option that solves your troubles most quickly. Click on the Next button at the bottom
of the Wizard to continue. The UnErase Wizard will quickly scan through all of your

Norton Protection files and will display the 25 files which were most recently Protected (that is, deleted). Figure 15.2 shows the display the UnErase Wizard will provide.

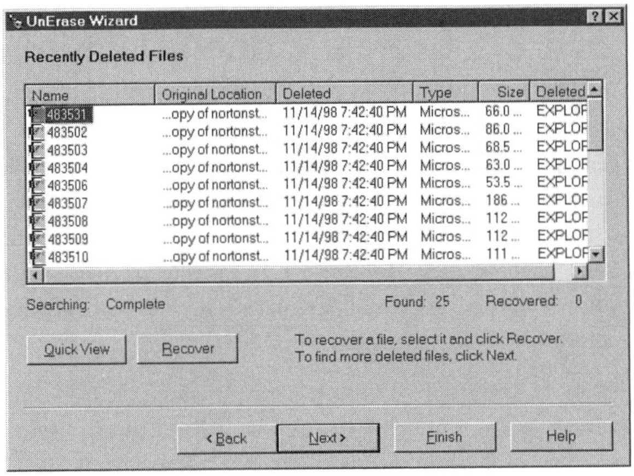

FIGURE 15.2

The Norton UnErase Wizard will quickly scan Norton Protection for the 25 most-recently deleted files and display them here. This is also the default display after double-clicking the Norton Protected Recycle Bin (unless you change the default).

While the UnErase Wizard is searching, its search status will display in the Results pane, just above the QuickView button, at the left of the figure. If you have other applications running while the UnErase Wizard is scanning, some of those applications may write to the disk, even if they are operating in the background. In order to provide you with the most current list of 25 deleted files, the UnErase Wizard will restart its search after each such disk write—just in case one of those writes was deleting a file. You'll see the message, Restarting due to Disk Write, in this circumstance. If the UnErase Wizard encounters a number of writes while it has yet to complete its search, it will pop up a warning dialog box, alerting you that there is a large amount of disk activity, and that it has had to restart many times. You can either select to cancel the search, or to have UnErase Wizard keep trying to complete its scan. For the most part, you'll want to stop the UnErase Wizard's scan if you receive such a message, and shut-down other applications which are running. You should preferentially shut down any apps which you know write to the disk regularly, perhaps creating automated backups or checking your drives for integrity.

Note: Although I generally recommend you leave it running all the time, the Norton System Doctor can sometimes be a culprit in these instances. If System Doctor is open, and no other applications are running, try closing System Doctor temporarily until you have completed UnErasing files.

In Figure 15.2, you can see that the UnErase Wizard has retrieved information from Norton Protection about when a file was deleted, what its file type is, where it was originally located on the disk, its size, how it was deleted, and of course, it's name. In fact, two of those items—the file sizes and their manner of deletion—are not shown in Figure 15.2. The size of the UnErase Wizard's window is not itself resizable, but the columns in this display are. In Figure 15.3, you'll see the various columns resized to show you all of the data maintained by Norton Protection.

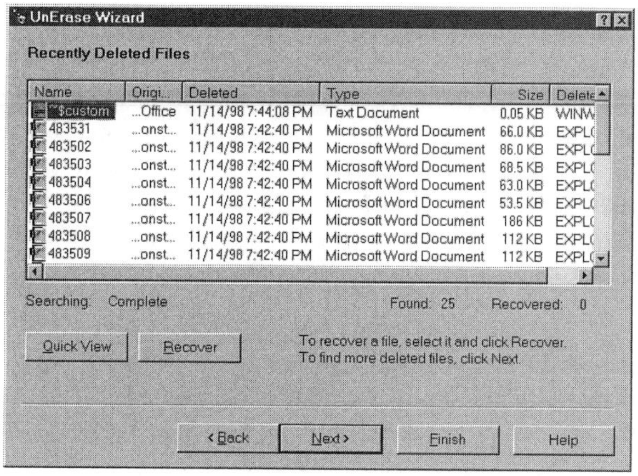

Figure 15.3

Columns in the UnErase Wizard can be dragged to size so you can see the data you wish to see.

The Wizard will display a scrollbar at the bottom of its Results window (as in Figure 15.2) when all columns don't fit onscreen, but it will usually be easier to just resize the columns. Any column that doesn't have data you are interested in can be squeezed down to almost nothing. This saves you the annoyance of scrolling back and forth horizontally.

Organizing the Display

Each column has a heading, indicating what information will appear below. By clicking on a heading, you cause the entire list to be re-sorted, based on that category. This is very much like viewing files in a Windows 95 or Windows 98 My Computer window, with the view type set to Details. By re-organizing the files, you can quickly focus on the category that you feel will get you the quickest results. For example, if you've just deleted a file because you didn't select what you thought you had selected, you might not even know the name of the file you just zapped. Sorting by the Deleted column will place the most-recently deleted file right at the top of the list. Chances are very good that it will be the file you're seeking. On the other hand, if you've intentionally deleted a file and then changed your mind, sorting by Name will let you find that file right away. If you're working in an application and it suddenly quits on you, you may be able to recover a good deal of your work from temporary files that application opened while it was running and deleted when it suddenly quit. In this case, sorting based on the Deleted By category will let you find the files deleted by the crashed app while it was crashing down.

Other information about deleted files is available for display on demand. Right-click anywhere in the Results panel, except on a file's name, and a context menu will pop up.

From this panel you can add or delete columns from the results display by adding or
removing check marks from each category's entry in the menu. You might find it useful,
for example, to view the date and time on which a deleted file was originally created, or
when it was last accessed. You can add this information to the Results display through
this context menu.

Once you've got the files organized by the method best suited to your needs, you'll click
on the name of the file you want to recover. The Results pane in this UnErase Wizard
display supports both Shift+clicking and Ctrl+clicking, so you can recover a number of
files all at once. In the past, recovering multiple files at one time could be dangerous
because each recovered file could write over the precious disk space occupied by another
file which was lower on your recovery list. Norton Protection has eliminated that problem entirely by maintaining an actual copy of each deleted file on disk. None of these
can be overwritten accidentally while you're busy UnErasing.

> **Note:** With the Results pane sorted to your tastes, you may want to review
> additional information about the files shown before recovering any of them.
> You can view Protected files without ever leaving the UnErase Wizard, as you'll
> see in the next section. You can right-click on any file's name and select
> Properties in the context menu which will pop up in order to see a wide selec-
> tion of data including a file's type, attributes, when it was created and deleted,
> its recoverability, and so forth. All of the data which can be displayed in the
> Results pane's columns is collected together for each file in this Properties dis-
> play. Reviewing what you find here may be a more convenient way to see that
> you are recovering the correct file.

Checking a Deleted File's Contents

If a number of files in the Recover pane appear to be strong possibilities for the file
you're looking for—for example, 10 of the 25 most recently deleted files could all be
Microsoft Word temporary files—then you may be uncertain as to which is the file that
will best meet your needs. You don't need to recover all of the suspects, interrogate them
individually, and then delete the unneeded files again. The UnErase Wizard provides a
QuickView button, located in the lower-left of the display, from which you can launch a
QuickView of any file in the Results pane. Select a file that you want to review without
actually restoring, then click the QuickView button. The Norton UnErase Wizard will
integrate with your installed Windows 95 or Windows 98 QuickViewers, allowing you to
very rapidly scan through a number of "possibles," looking for precisely what you're
missing.

Note: Notice that I said that the UnErase Wizard integrates with your installed Windows 95 or 98 QuickViewers. This means that, if you don't have any QuickViewers installed, you'll get a message like the one you see in Figure 15.4. In such a circumstance, you'll need to recover all of the files which may be what you need, and then look through them manually. You may also see a dialog indicating that no QuickViewer exists for the file type you have selected. You'll be offered the opportunity to look at the file with the default viewer. This is little more than a text editor, but it may provide you with exactly what you need. There's little harm in trying the default viewer before you decide you'll need to review the files after recovering them.

If your QuickViewers are not installed, you can quickly install them, usually without needing to reboot. Place your Windows 98 CD in the drive and open the Windows Setup tab of the Add/Remove Programs Control Panel (located in your Start menu under Settings | Control Panel). Select the Accessories entry in the list box and click the Details button. Scroll down to Quick View and place a check mark in the box, then click OK twice. Windows will install the viewers from the CD-ROM and enable them.

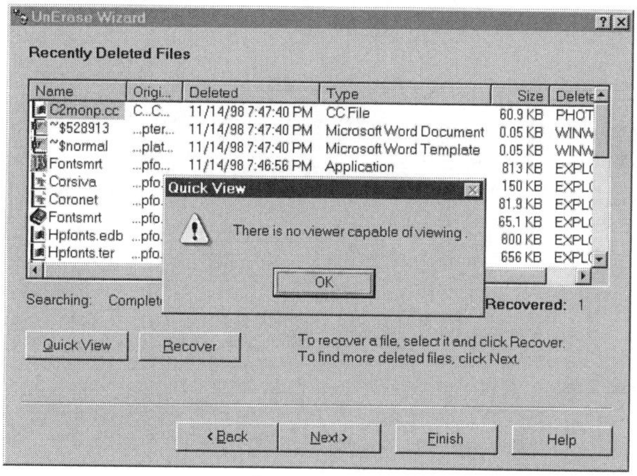

FIGURE 15.4

A message like this one indicates that no QuickViewers are installed on this PC, so you will not be able to review files before recovering them.

Recovering Files

With files sorted and reviewed as need be, and the file or files you actually want to UnErase located, recovering the deleted information couldn't be simpler. Select the file(s) in the Results pane and click the Recover button. UnErase will recover the file back to the original location from which it was deleted. (This is one reason that the UnErase Wizard lets you know where a file was before it was erased; you'll want to know that information so you can immediately find your UnErased files.) If you glance back to Figure 15.3, you'll see at the right-hand size of the Wizard is an indicator labeled, Recovered:. Each time you recover a file, this indicator will increment. When a file is recovered, its name and other information are removed from the file list. Keep track of the location to which a file is recovered or you may have difficulty locating it. If you have located precisely the file or files you need, you can click Finish to quit the UnErase Wizard.

Recovering a File to a Different Location

As you've just read, the UnErase Wizard's default is to recover files to their original locations on disk. There are several reasons why you might want the Wizard to behave differently in this regard, and you can make it do so, on a file-by-file basis. First, you may be attempting to recover multiple versions of the same file—perhaps versions of a letter which you saved-over several times while writing it. Each of these files will have the same filename, and UnErase would prompt you to overwrite one of the files with its successor. Obviously, if you're recovering two files, the last thing you want to do is delete one of them again! Select the file or files you want to recover to an alternative location. Right-click on one of the selected files' name, and a context-menu will pop up. Select Recover To in the context menu. The UnErase Wizard will display a dialog box like that shown in Figure 15.5. You can use the hierarchical plus "+" buttons to expand the display to show the drive or folder—or even the remote machine on the network—to which you want the file recovered. Click OK, and the recovery will be performed.

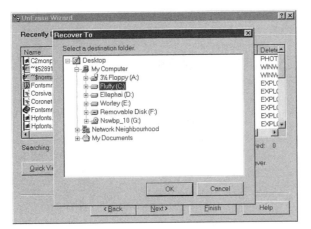

FIGURE 15.5

You can select an alternative recovery location on the local machine, or on the network.

Norton UnErase Wizard will also not allow you to recover over files which are in use. This includes system files like the Registry and initialization files, as well as files being used by open applications. Such files can be recovered, but only by using the Recover To option in the context menu, and recovering the file to a different location.

> **Caution:** An obvious implication of the discussion of recovering same-named files, is that you must recover such files one at a time, saving them to different locations. You can send multiple files to an alternate location using Recover To, but UnErase will still prompt you to overwrite files with the same name.

Possible Problems with Recovery

If you have not been able to locate your deleted file within this list of 25 files, there are two options available to you from within the UnErase Wizard. You can go back to the first panel of the Wizard and select a different display option, or you can click Next and move on to a more interactive search. We'll look at both of those options in the next two sections.

If you *have* located the exact file you need, there is really only one major problem to be on guard for during a recovery, and that problem is illustrated in Figure 15.6. The UnErase Wizard will not recover a file to disk if that disk has been modified—that is, written to—after the UnErase Wizard completed its file search. There are a number of reasons for this, and they are all really designed to protect your valuable data, not to cause you problems. First, if a drive has been modified, that modification may not have been something so benign as a file being properly saved. It's possible that you're using the UnErase Wizard because a drive-related failure has zapped your work. The UnErase Wizard has no way of knowing the difference, but it does know very well that recovering a file onto a possibly-damaged disk could be disastrous. The recovery process would take that file out of Norton Protection, but storing it on a damaged part of the disk could make the file unusable. You'd go from having a perfectly-safe file made inaccessible, perhaps forever, by the very tool you used to recover it. There may be nothing as hateful as a software utility that actually *causes* damage. Therefore, UnErase Wizard won't write files back to a disk that may be unstable, as evinced by its having been modified.

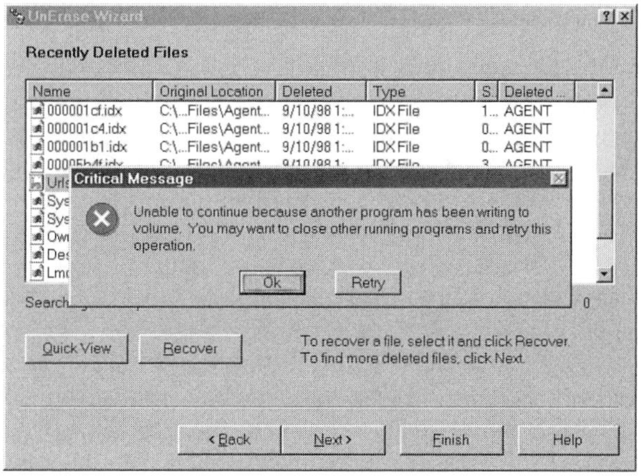

FIGURE 15.6

UnErase will not write back to the disk if the disk has been modified after UnErase completed its search for deleted files.

Alternatively, the problem could be more benign, but no less troublesome. Let's face it: some applications are really stupid. They create temporary files with names like TEMP1.TMP, TEMP2.TMP, and so on. (Sophisticated applications create temporary files with randomly-generated filenames like 01934623.TMP.) If you happen to be trying to recover such an application's temporary file while that application is running, recovery could attempt to write the deleted file into a folder in which a file of the same name already exists. Rather than even beginning to risk such problems, the UnErase Wizard will simply not write a recovered file back to a drive that's been modified.

Regardless of the cause, the solution is quite simple. Click the Back button on the UnErase Wizard's Results display panel, and then click Next again. This will cause UnErase to perform a new scan. Since you've already done the work of selecting the file or files you want to recover, simply click on their names and Recover them after the UnErase Wizard's scan is complete. If you receive the warning in Figure 15.6 again, be certain that you have quit all applications other than the UnErase Wizard, then perform a new scan.

As an alternative to performing a new scan, you can use the techniques described in the previous section to try recovering the file to a drive other than the one in which it was originally located.

Delayed and Interactive Recoveries

While you'll probably find that the UnErase Wizard's list of 25 recently deleted files meets your needs 95% of the time, there are certainly going to be occasional exceptions to this rule of thumb. What do you do, for example, if you need to recover more than 25 files? How do you recover a file that you deleted a few days ago? Finally, what do you do if, for a number of possible reasons you'll read about, you need to take a more involved role in recovering what you've lost?

Reviewing All of the Norton Protected Files

It's one thing if you accidentally delete a file. It's another thing if you accidentally delete a folder containing many—possibly hundreds of—files. Fortunately, the UnErase Wizard can easily handle either problem. It may also be the case that you intentionally deleted a file three or four days ago, have done a lot of work in the meantime, and only now have decided you want that old file back. UnErase Wizard to the rescue!

In these cases, rather than viewing the default display of 25 files, you'll want to select the Wizard's second option: viewing all protected files on the drive. Choose that radio button and then click Next to continue. Depending on how recently you have emptied your Norton Protected Recycle Bin, this UnErase Wizard could detect hundreds of files—up to a maximum of 1,500 per drive. (This scan checks every drive in your system for which Norton Protection is enabled.) If you're recovering a deleted folder, you will definitely want to sort the files listed by their original location. This will place all of the files from each folder together. Use either Ctrl+clicking or Shift+clicking to select all of the files you want to recover, then click the Recover button. Norton UnErase Wizard will integrate with your saved Norton Image data (if it is available) and will reconstruct the folder precisely as it was before the deletion. The deleted folder itself will be re-created, and all of its files placed back where they belong. (The absence of Image data in no way prevents Norton Protected files from being recovered.)

Recovering a file deleted a few days ago is similarly best performed by reviewing all Protected files. Once the Norton UnErase Wizard has completed its scan, you'll probably want to sort the Results pane by filename. That done, you can scroll down the alphabetic list, select the file or files you want, and click Recover. If you are recovering an old version of a file, and the new version has the same filename as the old, recall that you'll want to right-click on the file's name and select Recover To, so that you can keep the new file intact.

Interactive Recovery

Norton Protection will watch over your files for a period of time which you specify. The default is seven days, a reasonable time frame for most users. After that time expires—or if you delete more than 1,500 files per drive during that time, or if the drive becomes more than 90% full—Norton Protection will begin purging your oldest deleted files from its storehouse. This makes room for newly deleted files and prevents all of your drives' free space from being used by files which, most of the time, you deleted because you wanted them gone. If a file has been purged out of Norton Protection, that does not mean, necessarily, that the file is gone forever. You can use the interactive techniques described in this section to scan your drives for files which Norton Protection is not safeguarding. (These may also be files that you deleted before Norton Protection was installed.)

> **Caution:** If you have not installed Norton Protection and you need to UnErase files, *do not* install Norton Protection! The recovery software could over-write those files as it installs. Instead, shut-down Windows and boot your computer using either your Norton Rescue disk set or Norton Emergency Disk #1, which came with Norton SystemWorks. Then use the DOS-based version of the UnErase Wizard which you'll read about later in this chapter. For additional information refer to Appendix A.

You can begin an interactive recovery session in two ways. First, you can select the third radio button on the Norton UnErase Wizard's opening screen—find any recoverable files matching your criteria. When you click Next, you'll be taken directly into interactive mode. Alternatively, you can try using one of the two other recovery methods discussed above—viewing the 25 most recently deleted files or viewing all Norton Protected files—and, if that method is unsuccessful, click the Next button on the UnErase Wizard's Recovery Panel, rather than clicking Finish as you do after a successful recovery.

Figure 15.7 shows the first of the interactive recovery panels.

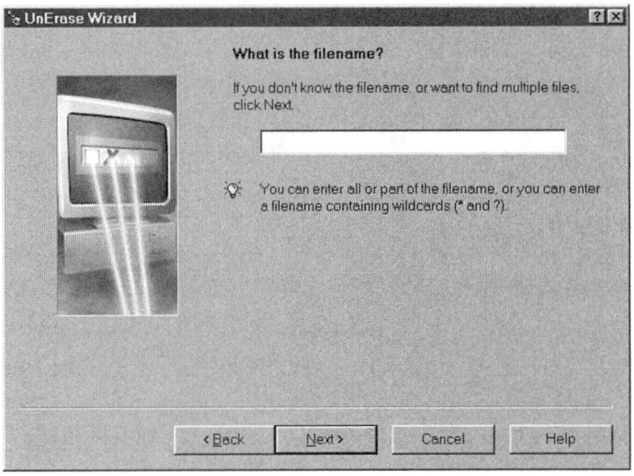

FIGURE 15.7

*Step one of inter-
active recovery is
identifying file
names or wild-
cards to use in
the search.*

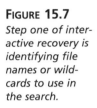

Searching by File Name

The first interactive screen asks you to indicate the name of the file you wish to recover. If
you know the file's exact name, of course, enter it here. If you know only a portion of the
file's name, you should still enter it here, but be mindful of the possibility that you may
obtain better results by specifying no filename than only a partial name. It is an issue with
which you'll have to experiment on a case-by-case basis. Finally, you can use wildcards
here to specify a range of filename possibilities. For example, entering **DESOLE.*** will
instruct the UnErase Wizard to look for filenames with any extension that begin with
"DESOLE". Click Next to move on to the next step in the interactive recovery.

> **Note:** You need not specify *.* in this panel to indicate you wish to search for
> any filename. Searching for any filename is the default.

Searching by File Type

As you can see in Figure 15.8, the second piece of information which the UnErase
Wizard will solicit from you during an interactive recovery is the file type. If you don't
know what the file type is, or if you've used wildcards already in the previous panel to
indicate files of *any* type, just click Next, to continue. On the other hand, you may have
deleted a number of files of the same type—say a series of JPEG images—and so you
have specified no filename guidelines in the previous panel, but you would select JPEG
images from this list. Additionally, more advanced users will recognize that this list of
file types comes directly from your Windows Registry. All file types which have been
registered on your system will be in this list. That can be useful because, in many cases,
one registered file type can speak for files with a number of different file extensions.
(Using the JPEG example from above, it is not uncommon for JPEG-compatible files to
have file extensions such as JPG, JPEG, JG, IMG, and so forth.) By specifying the file type

on this panel, rather than a specific file extension in the previous filename panel, you can search for all files of a given *type*, regardless of their filename extension.

Shift+clicking and Ctrl+clicking is supported in the list of file types, so you can easily scroll through the list selecting a variety of types for which to search. You may, for instance, be looking for an image file, but have no idea in what format the file was saved. It could be a JPG file, or a GIF file, or a CDR, or a… well, you get the idea. Ctrl+clicking a variety of image-related file types here will widen the UnErase Wizard's search on your behalf. In this way, you can search for disparate kinds of files in a single search.

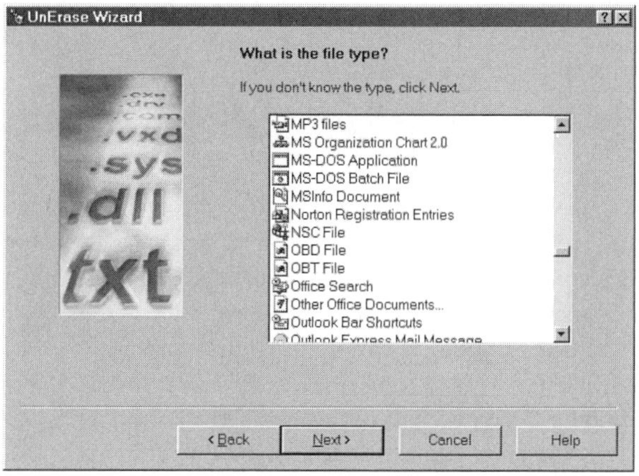

FIGURE 15.8

Step two of interactive recovery involves selecting a file type to search for, if it is known.

Searching by File Contents

The third panel in the interactive version of the Norton UnErase Wizard is one of the most powerful. The reason for this is that this panel allows you to scan your entire PC for a file which *contains* certain information which you specify. Of course, the type of data you can specify here is only text, so if you are looking for an image file, a file containing a waveform, or MIDI instructions—any kind of binary data—then you should simply skip over this panel by clicking Next. If, on the other hand, you are trying to retrieve a file containing text (and for most of us, most of the files we create do contain text—comprising letters, memos, spreadsheets, reports, and so on) then this panel can be your lifesaver.

You may have been thinking, earlier in this chapter, that all of the discussion of file types, original folders, and so on, is wonderful if you're a power-user and are on top of that sort of thing. You may have conceived of the possibility that you need to retrieve a deleted file, but you don't know anything about the file other than what was in it. No fear. This panel allows even a novice user to get power-user results from Norton UnErase. Figure 15.9 shows the contents panel.

FIGURE 15.9

The third power-ful step in interactive recovery allows you to search based on what was in the file.

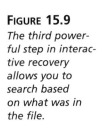

Notice in the figure that this panel consists of a box into which you can type or paste text, and two radio buttons. When the box is empty, the two radio buttons are not available. (I placed a blank space in the box before taking the screen shot used in Figure 15.9.) As soon as you begin typing something in the box, the two radio buttons become active. What you type in the box will likely influence which radio button you select, and contrariwise. The text box itself is relatively simple. Whatever you type into this box will be used in the UnErase Wizard's final scan. The Wizard will search your drives for the text which you enter—using the method you select by choosing a radio button—and will report back to you the existence of any recoverable files on any drive which contain the text you've entered here. Of course, any specifications which you have selected on the two previous Wizard panels will also be applied to the final scan.

You can also paste text into the specification box. Use any application that allows you to place text on the Clipboard, and copy that text. Then, switch to or launch the UnErase Wizard, click your mouse in the box, and press Ctrl+V to paste. You can also right-click on the box and select Paste from the context-menu which will pop up. (Paste will not be available on the menu unless there is text stored on the Windows Clipboard.) Wildcards cannot be used here, per se, but the Norton UnErase Wizard will automatically search for word fragments, so wildcards are unnecessary. Let's look at a few quick examples.

Perhaps the file you're looking for is a letter to your mother. You always start such letters with "Dear Mom," and you know you've only got one mother, so files which contain "Mom" are probably letters to her. You enter **Mom** into this box. Assuming for the sake of simplicity that you haven't pre-selected any other search criteria, the UnErase Wizard would search your drive or drives looking through all of the drive's free space for an occurrence of the word, "Mom." If the UnErase Wizard locates that text, it will then check back with the drive's File Allocation Table to see if the disk space on which that text appears is part of a complete *cluster chain*—in simpler terms, the file in which that text originally was placed is still complete, even though it is using space marked as "free." If it is, UnErase Wizard will retrieve that file's name from its old folder entry and will list that filename in its Results pane. There, you can select the filename, click Recover, give the filename a new first letter, and you're done.

> You may remember from reading about Norton Protection earlier in this book that when a file is erased, the first letter of it's name is set to a value which Windows uses to identify folder entries for deleted files. When such a file is recovered without the help of Norton Protection, you need to replace that first character with a new letter. Depending on the type of file and its purpose, the character you choose may or may not need to be the same as the file's original first letter. With application documents, it won't matter. With system configuration files or similar files, the recovered files will likely not work unless you replace the missing letter with its original.

That's a best-case scenario. Of course, there are a number of possible wrinkles to this scenario, including the possibility that many files will be found which match your content specifications. In that case, you can use the QuickView button to view the files before recovering them, or you can recover them all and then look through the contents. If too many files are found which match your criteria, however, you will probably want to rethink those criteria and perform a new scan. To do that, just click the Back button, modify the contents panel, and try again.

For example, perhaps over fifty deleted but recoverable files are found which contain, "Mom." Give some more thought to the contents of the specific letter for which you're searching. Did it contain a date? Did you use other proper names or less-common words in the letter? Perhaps you talked about your recent vacation to Paris. In such a case, you would add the word "Paris" to the specification box, and—since you're trying to limit your results, not expand them—you'll click the second radio button. This tells UnErase Wizard that you only want to see files which contain *both* the word "Mom" and the word "Paris." (For the record, this text is not case sensitive. "Paris," or "paris" would find occurrences of both.) When you complete this search, unless you've written a lot of bragging letters to your mother about the City of Lights, you may only see the one file—the correct file—in the Results pane. Recover it, and you're done.

What if you are fairly, but not entirely, certain of the contents of the file you need? Searching with the first radio button on the contents panel selected can really help you there. "Must contain at least one word," means that you can enter several words which you *think* might occur within your deleted file, and UnErase Wizard will return a list of any files which contain *any* of those words.

Searching by Drive

The fourth panel of the interactive mode of UnErase Wizard allows you to specify whether you want to search your entire PC, a specific local drive, or even a network drive. (Be advised that a network drive search will take considerably longer than a local

search and may use significant network resources. Such searches are probably best performed locally on the server in which the drive is installed, or locally on the remote
workstation containing the drive.) You can use the hierarchical plus "+" buttons to
expand the listing of drives to also show folders. Placing a check mark in a specific folder will limit UnErase Wizard to reporting only those files whose original folder entries
were in the folder you select. Placing a check mark in selected drives will allow you to
search several, but not require you to search all—of your local drives.

Searching Unused Space

Finally, if all of the preceding techniques have failed, you can click Next yet again and
have Norton UnErase scan all currently unused disk space for the string of text you
entered earlier in the "What Words Are In the File" panel (see above in the section
"Searching by File Contents.") This is an exceptionally slow technique and, frankly, one
that is traditionally unsuccessful. However, if you are desperately seeking a text file that
you've been unable to locate through the Wizard's other methods, this is a valid final step
to take.

When Recovery Fails

Unfortunately, by the time you find yourself using the interactive recovery process to look
for files which are not under Norton Protection, you are fighting a battle against time.
Files which are not Protected exist on your drives only so long as the areas of the drive in
which they formerly resided—which is marked as free space after a file is deleted—
remains unused by another file. If even one cluster of a deleted file is being used by
another file, the UnErase Wizard will not report that file as recoverable. UnErase Wizard
does not normally display unrecoverable files, but you can enable this by right-clicking
anywhere in the Results pane—except on a file's name—and enabling Show Unrecoverable Files in the context menu. (In this way, you can check to see, for example, if the
name of the file you've been trying to locate appears in the Unrecoverable list.)

If you try to recover an unrecoverable file, the UnErase Wizard will let you know that the
file is no longer available because at least some of the disk space it occupied is now being
used by another file. You may, in fact, be able to recover it manually by turning the clusters of it which remain intact into a new text file, using manual mode of the DOS-based
UnErase Wizard. This is discussed in the following section. Manual file recovery—in fact,
it's re-creation, not recovery—is truly a last resort. The likelihood that you will recover
significant useable information from a partial file is commonly quite small. Nevertheless,
there may indeed be times when something is infinitely better than nothing, and the DOS-
based UnErase Wizard can help make "something" attainable.

Recovering Files Through DOS

The DOS-based version of Norton UnErase is located on Emergency Disk #2 which
came with Norton SystemWorks. It can also be found in your Norton Rescue Disk Set,
and in the Norton Utilities folder on your hard drive, under the name UNERASE.EXE. The

DOS version of UnErase cannot run within a Windows DOS box. You will need to either boot into DOS using Norton Emergency Disk #1, or using a Norton Basic Rescue Set of disks. Assuming you do boot with the Norton Emergency Disk #1, you will boot into DOS with a small menu program from which you can select UNERASE. If you look in the right panel of this menu, you'll see that you can specify a filename for which you want UNERASE to search, simply by typing it after UNERASE's name at the bottom of the menu. It is unlikely that you will have occasion to do this, as such searches will likely seem more pleasant from within Windows. If you're having drive- or Windows-related problems, however, and your first priority is rescuing a deleted file with a known name, you can do so from here. You can also specify a drive letter in this menu, and Norton UnErase will launch by looking at the disk on which it is contained, if you don't.

The DOS-based version of Norton UnErase will also very likely not support your mouse. You can change that fact if you have a real-mode mouse driver which you load through your boot disk's CONFIG.SYS and AUTOEXEC.BAT files. Every screen command has a keyboard equivalent, however, highlighted in red. These are all Alt+key commands, much as in Windows. For example, to display the File menu, you would press Alt+F. (Incidentally, once any menu is displayed, you can scroll to the other menus using the arrow keys. Pressing Esc will close any open menus, but be careful: pressing Esc twice will quit the utility.)

The DOS-based UnErase Wizard will open by displaying the results of a quick analysis it makes of your Norton Protection data, if any is available on its default drive. If you have not yet specified the drive you want UnErase to work with, you can do so by pressing Alt+F to drop the File menu, and then pressing D to Change Drives. As you will see in the File menu display, you can also sidestep the menu and merely press Alt+D to bring up the Change Drives dialog box. Any files which UnErase locates under Protection on your selected drive can be quickly viewed by pressing Alt+V, for View. You can obtain more information about any entry you see in the UnErase window by pressing Alt+I. The Information display shows when a file was deleted, its size and type, the number of the cluster on which it begins on disk, how many clusters it requires for its length, and a prognosis: the likelihood of recovering the file successfully. The DOS-based UnErase Wizard gives you a little more information on this last category, rating recovery of files as "good," "average," or "poor." "Poor" generally means that trying to recover the file will be a waste of your time, but you may be inclined to try, nevertheless.

With its initial scan complete, Norton UnErase will show you the folder tree of the entire drive you've selected. If you know the folder in which your deleted file used to exist, you can use the arrow keys to scroll to it and open it by pressing Enter. Navigating into subfolders is done through the same process. Select the folder you want to view, then press Enter. To move back up the folder tree, highlight the double-dot (. .) folder entry and press Enter. Once you are looking at a folder, UnErase will only show you deleted files unless you tell it to do otherwise, as you'll see in a moment. If there is nothing in a folder's entry but the double dot (. .) folder entry, then no files were found associated with that folder. If you do find the file you need, and its prognosis is good, press Alt+U to UnErase the file. If you wish to UnErase the file to a different location, you can do so by selecting the file, then selecting UnErase To from the File menu. You'll be presented with a box into which you can either manually type a destination path or navigate through the drives and folders semi-graphically. Press Alt+O to select OK and accept the destination you've chosen.

Modifying the Search

The DOS-based UnErase tool allows you to modify its search for files in a few different ways, all of which are accessible by pressing Alt+S, and selecting options from the Search menu. The Search For Data Types option allows you to search for specific types of data which are found in older, proprietary formats. This option will open a menu which will allow you to search for Normal Text, Lotus 1-2-3 and Symphony, or dBASE files. The Search for Text option is similar to a content search in the Windows UnErase Wizard, but it is more rudimentary. You can enter a search string and select whether you want case to matter in the search or not. You cannot, however, specify that you want to see files which contain *any* rather than *all* of your search terms. You will have to perform multiple searches to obtain that functionality under DOS. DOS UnErase will only display files which contain *all* of the text you specify.

The For Lost Names option performs a drive search looking for folders which have been deleted. If you are unable to locate the file you require, performing a For Lost Names search will display filenames found within those deleted folders. If you find the filename you want after a For Lost Names search, and its prognosis is good, you can simply press Alt+U and UnErase it like any other file. In this way, a deleted folder does not make a recoverable file unrecoverable. (As you have already read, however, you will normally want to perform all but manual recoveries through Windows. Manual recovery is discussed below.) While any search is in progress, you can press Esc to stop it, and then select Continue Search from the Search menu if you wish to do so at a later time.

Finally, the Set Search Range option allows you to tell UnErase to only look at certain clusters—which you specify by number—for your lost file. This can reduce the time it will take to perform a text-search of your drive. How would you know which clusters to include? If the file you're looking for has a prognosis that makes it suitable only for manual recovery, you will likely still be able to select its name in the display and press Alt+I to learn on which cluster the file began. You can use that cluster's number as a starting-point in your later work to manually recover the parts of the file—if any—which are still intact.

Display Options

The DOS-based UnErase does not let you click on a column's heading to sort the file list, but you can still sort by a number of criteria by selecting a sort method from the Options menu (Alt+O). From here, sorting by filename, extension, time of creation, size, prognosis and, sometimes, by folder, is possible. You can also enable a display of nondeleted files by selecting Include Non-Erased Files from the bottom of this menu. If you're very used to long filenames and are having difficulty figuring out whether you want to search in a folder named ELLEPH~1, ELLEPH~2, or ELLEPH~5, turning this option on will let you see the files that are active in each folder. This may help you figure out what you're looking at. At the same time, viewing both erased and non-erased files will make the display cluttered and less clear.

A Manual UnErase: Clusters Last Stand

If some of a file's former clusters are being used by an existing file, that file would normally be considered unrecoverable. If your life is on the line, however, it may be worthwhile to attempt to manually recover whatever parts of that file may be available.

> **Caution:** Recovering partial files is truly for experts. In attempting to recover fragments of a file, you could damage perfectly-good existing files and—whether you damage files or not—cause yourself a lot of grief.

The process begins by selecting the poor-prognosis file in the folder display, then choosing Manual UnErase from the File menu. (If you cannot find the file's folder entry, you can create a new file using the Create File option on the File menu, or by pressing Alt+M to bypass the menu. However, without having a folder entry from which to work, you will know neither where the original file started on disk, nor how many clusters it formerly used. The likelihood of a successful recovery under these conditions is very nearly zero.) You will first be asked to specify a new first letter for the file's name. Press the single letter you wish to use.

Assuming that a folder entry was available to you, the Manual UnErase screen will show you the file's new name, its special attributes, if any, the date of its creation, the time of its creation, and its former size. You'll also find the First Cluster and Clusters Needed information which you may have previously reviewed from the file's Info box. The Clusters Found entry at the bottom-left will increment as you manually add clusters back into the file. Theoretically, when "Clusters Found" equals "Clusters Needed," your file is complete. *Theoretically.*

You begin adding clusters to the file by pressing Alt+A (Add Cluster). From here, at the Add Clusters menu, you have several options. "All Clusters" will allow you to add all of the clusters that Norton UnErase thinks most likely once belonged to this file. Basically, Norton UnErase will look for contiguous (unfragmented) clusters which follow immediately after clusters being used by another file. If UnErase can locate the same number of unused contiguous clusters as were required by the file, your manual recovery may be complete. When you return to the Manual UnErase window, press Alt+F to review the contents of the clusters UnErase has selected. If you've had the good fortune of capturing most of your lost data into the file, count yourself fortunate, press Esc to close the viewer, and press Alt+S to save your recovered file.

If you view the file and its contents seem correct, but seem to be jumbled, you can select a cluster number in the Manual UnErase window by highlighting it and pressing the spacebar to mark it as selected. Your keyboard's arrow keys will allow you to move the cluster towards the beginning or end of the file, as seems to be necessary. With the cluster moved, press the spacebar again to deselect the file, and view it again. If reorganizing the clusters unjumbled your contents, you're done! (Don't forget to save your work by pressing Alt+S.) You can also delete clusters from the Manual UnErase window by selecting them with the spacebar and pressing Alt+R.

If you view your new file and it's garbage, however, you may want to return to the Add Clusters menu and try other options.

Search and Browse

From the Add Clusters window, you can begin a searching and browsing process in an attempt to locate more of your lost file. Selecting Data Search will open a dialog box into which you can type either normal text or a string of hexadecimal numbers. The latter may be useful to you if you are trying to locate a binary file containing a particular bit of code or a digital signature. As earlier, you can select to ignore upper- versus lowercase issues if you choose. You can also specify that you want your search to begin a specific number of sectors after the disk location where the file originally began. Press Alt+F to execute your search. If your specified text is located within a cluster, the UnErase viewer will display that cluster in ASCII format. Press Alt+H if you wish to view it as hexadecimal code. If the located cluster belongs to your lost file, pressing Alt+A will add this cluster to the file you are reconstructing. If the cluster does not appear to belong to your file, or if you have added the cluster, pressing Alt+F will find the next occurrence of your search string.

As long as the search continues to locate your specified text, you can continue in this manner, adding the most-likely clusters to your file as they are found. When you've finished, pressing Alt+D will return you to the Manual UnErase window. Here you should compare "Clusters Found" to "Clusters Needed" to see if you have—perhaps—found your entire file. As above, you can press Alt+F (View File) to view the reconstructed file, and Alt+S (Save File) to save it to disk, if all seems well.

If searching does not provide acceptable results, you may wish to try manually browsing your drive for recognizable content. To do so, press Alt+B (Browse) at the Manual Add window. The drive viewer will open again, and as before, you can choose to view only ASCII codes, or a combination of hexadecimal and ASCII. Using the Next, Prev, and Go To buttons, you can move around on your drive, browsing for content that belongs in your lost file. Once a movement button has been selected, pressing the spacebar will select that button again, so you can quickly jump forward or backwards without having to press Alt+N (Next) and Alt+P (Previous), over and over. As you find the correct content, pressing Alt+A (Add Cluster) will add that cluster to the chain you are rebuilding. When you feel that you have located all of your file's data—or all of it that remains— press Alt+D to return to the Manual UnErase window and view the file.

Other Manual Tools

Those are the basic tools provided to enable you to manually UnErase fragments of an otherwise unrecoverable file. It is an arduous task than can be extremely time-consuming and frustrating to even the most experienced user. There are two other resources at your disposal which may assist you in the process. One is found on the Manual UnErase window itself: View Map. Pressing Alt+M will show you a simulated map of the area of disk occupied by the file you are attempting to recover. By seeing where the various pieces of your lost file are located on disk, you may be better able to piece the file back together. The map will indicate clusters you have added back to the file, clusters being used by other non-erased files, as well as free and mostly-free disk space.

One of the most useful things that the disk map can show you is whether or not the beginning of your lost file is followed immediately by non-erased files. If this is so, then there is little doubt that the lost file was fragmented before it was deleted. Manually recovering a fragmented file is not impossible, but the process may give you cause to learn whether your health insurance covers psychiatric care. You could easily be bouncing back and forth across the entire disk, searching or, heaven forbid, browsing for relevant clusters. It is no exaggeration to say that, even if all clusters of a highly-fragmented file are available, it could take you longer to locate them and reconstruct the file than it would take you to recreate the file from scratch. Of course, that may simply not be an option, in which case Norton UnErase is the best tool for the job.

Related to the disk map is another resource: the ability to add clusters by name. Accessed from the Add Cluster window inside the Manual UnErase window, "Cluster Number" allows you to enter a starting and ending cluster which you want added to your recovering file. The disk map can help give you insight into which clusters may contain some of your fragmented file's lost data, and it *may* be quicker to enter a range of clusters here and then view the clusters' contents from the Manual UnErase window.

> **Note:** While adding clusters, you may notice that you will not be allowed to add any clusters which are already allocated to files. This is Norton UnErase's very sensible way of protecting you from manually creating cross-linked files.

Final Thoughts on Norton UnErase

There really is very little question that the Norton UnErase Wizard and its manual-recovery DOS-based cousin are simply the best tools available to you to do the job of recovering lost files. There's also no question that finding yourself in the position of having to try to manually UnErase a file to save your career is a dreadful position in which to be. If ever there was proof that discretion is indeed the better part of valor, it is a realization of the time and stress than can be involved in manually reconstructing a file which could have been preserved intact by proper use of Norton Protection and a good backup scheme.

Norton File Compare

Moving back to the brighter side of things, let's assume for the remainder of this chapter that you have been using Norton Protection and that any deleted files you need are still under its care. This isn't an unrealistic scenario if you've read Chapter 6, "Norton Utilities: Digging Through the Trash with Norton Protection," and have configured Norton Protection to suit your needs. Even so, working with recovered files—particularly if you have the need to compare them to existing files—can be a tiresome task.

Norton File Compare takes a lot of the work out of the process by presenting you with a highly-configurable two-panel display in which you can quickly compare two files, and cut and paste their contents as you might require. You can selectively undo changes which you find have been made, all from within the same window. Norton File Compare is accessible under the Find and Fix Problems category of Norton Utilities, inside the Norton SystemWorks Integrator. You can also launch it by choosing Programs | Norton Utilities | Norton File Compare from the Start menu.

> **Note:** Norton File Compare is only available if you've performed a Complete install of Norton SystemWorks as we recommended. If you've performed a Typical install, you must go back and do a complete reinstallation in order to gain access to NFC.

As soon as Norton File Compare launches, it will prompt you to select the two files you want to compare. Once you do so, Norton File Compare, or *NFC*, will display the two side-by-side. Because NFC is so highly configurable, we're going to explore it on a menu-by-menu basis so you don't miss any of the wrinkles available to you.

NFC File Menu

The File menu of NFC gives you access to a variety of fundamental tools as well as, of course, allowing you to select which files you want to compare. You can see the NFC File menu in Figure 15.10. The Open Left Pane and Open Right Pane options repeat the respective dialog boxes which you encountered when you first launched NFC. If, while you are working, you choose to change one or both of the files you're comparing, you can do so from these menu options. This functionality is also provided in the toolbar, by clicking the left-most and second left-most icons to open a new file in the left or right pane, respectively. From the File menu you can also manually update the display in the two panes by selecting Refresh Both Panes. This can be particularly useful after you've made changes to the files, as you will see below.

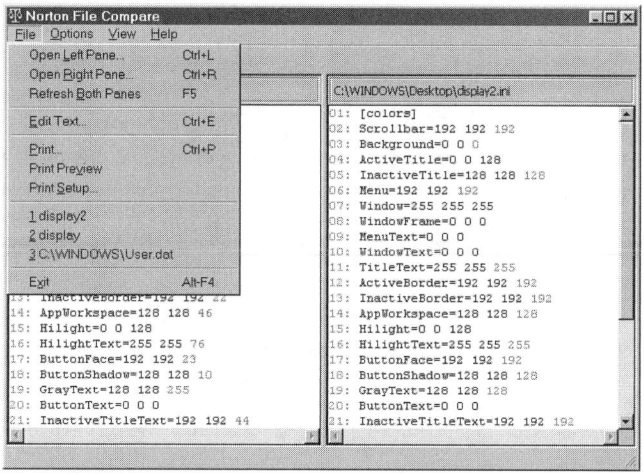

FIGURE 15.10
The Norton File Compare utility running with its File menu displayed.

Caution: Norton File Compare is capable of opening text-based files, such as those with TXT, DOC, or INI file extensions. You should not try to open application or system files (such as those with EXE or DLL file extensions) using Norton File Compare.

Editing Files

In addition to the automated "undo changes" functionality which you'll read about in a few moments, NFC allows you to open your default Windows editor and make changes, additions, or deletions to one or both of the files you're comparing. The File menu's Edit Text selection will display a dialog box from which you can choose whether you wish to edit the file in the left or right pane. Norton File Compare remains active while you are editing, and when your changes are complete, you can save the file, return to NFC, and select the Refresh Both Panes option, as mentioned above. This will reload both files from disk and re-compare them, so you can see the impact of your modifications immediately.

Editing is also available by clicking the Edit button on the toolbar. This button resembles a sheet of paper with a pen laid across it.

Note: While you are comparing files, you'll notice a number of things about how the twin panes function. First, you'll see that they are linked so that they scroll together. This can be particularly handy when you're scanning for differences between two large files. Second, you'll also likely notice that NFC will do its best to keep the files in sync, line-for-line. This means that if, for example, you have two versions of the same file, but one version has some extra blank lines in it, NFC will automatically add blank lines into the pane of the file with which you're making the comparison, so that the content will continue to line-up. NFC doesn't actually add blank lines to the second file; this is only a change made in the way that the file is displayed so that you can more easily compare it with the file in the other pane.

Printing Files

The display synchronization you just read about in the above note extends to the way in which NFC behaves when you choose to Print from the File menu. NFC will print one full page from the file in the left pane, followed by one full page from the file in the right pane. This alternation will continue until both files are printed. If you have line numbers enabled—which you'll read about in a moment—line numbers will print, as you see them in the onscreen display. Additionally, if you have a color printer, NFC will print differences between the two files in the different color you select. NFC's default is red. When you wish to review how files will look before printing, you should use the Print Preview menu item. This functions much the same way as the Print Preview in Microsoft Word, with which you may be familiar. You can zoom in and out of the preview, see the two files side-by-side or one at a time, and so on.

With as much functionality as NFC has available, you may wonder why you'd ever want or need to print out your files. In some ways, you'd be right. But, sometimes it's easier to get a feel for "the big picture" on paper than it is onscreen. Some people just prefer reviewing technical data on paper, also. So, the ability to print is there when and if you need it.

Print functionality is also available from the Print button on the toolbar; the button has the icon of a small printer on it.

NFC Options Menu

The Options menu gives you access to all of the configuration settings for NFC. Foremost among these is the Settings item at the top of the menu. Selecting it opens up a dialog box containing two standard Windows properties tabs. From the Comparison tab, you can configure three primary aspects in how Norton File Compare determines whether one file is different from another and whether those differences are important to you. You can see the Comparison tab in Figure 15.11.

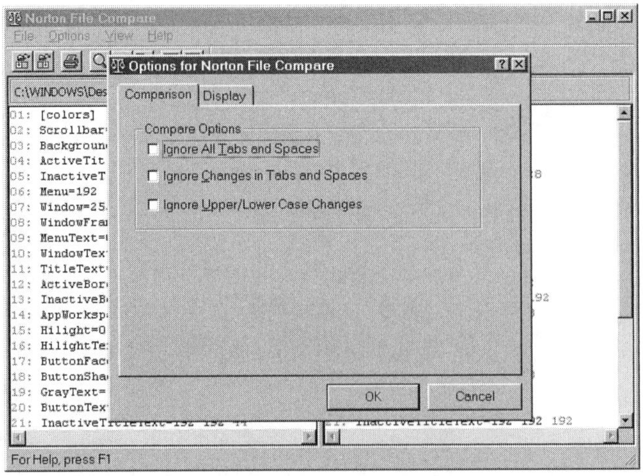

FIGURE 15.11
Norton File Compare's comparison options allow you to select certain types of file differences to ignore.

Choosing to Ignore All Tabs and Spaces will instruct Norton File Compare to pay attention exclusively to characters in the two files, not whitespace. With this setting enabled, an INI file entry like

```
123 456 789
```

in one file will be treated as being the same as 123456789 in the other file. Depending on what type of file you are editing, ignoring whitespace can either make differences more obvious, or it can mask them. If the proper settings for this file require spaces to separate three sets of three numbers, the absence of those spaces in the second file could be the reason that you are experiencing whatever difficulty may have led you to run Norton File Compare in the first place. With spaces ignored, that difference will not be highlighted in the difference color, and you might miss it.

If you choose to Ignore Changes in Tabs and Spaces, then adding or deleting whitespace from one of the files will not be registered as a difference between it and the other file you are viewing. For example, changing the entry

```
User: Scott H-A Clark
```

in one file to

```
User: Scott H-A        Clark
```

would be registered as a difference between the files, unless this option was enabled. Whether there is one space or fifty between the "A" and the "C" is not a "difference" in such a circumstance. However, this option applies only to whitespace that exists in the two files when the option is enabled. Therefore, if you change the entry

```
User: Lorifromalabama
```

in one file to

```
User: Lori from alabama
```

even with this option enabled, the addition of whitespace where no whitespace previously existed will still be registered as a difference between the two files. Enabling this option can allow you to edit one or both of the files and add additional whitespace to make the file contents more legible without creating the appearance of many new differences between the files' meaningful content.

Finally, you have the option to Ignore Upper/Lower Case Changes. If you need both files to say "Peter Norton," but it doesn't matter to you whether they say "peter norton," "PETER NORTON," or some mind-boggling combination of the two, then enabling this option will make all such occurrences of "Peter Norton" the same.

The Display Tab

With the Comparison tab in this Settings dialog is the Display tab. From here, you can configure how files appear both onscreen and when they are printed from within Norton File Compare. From the Display tab, you can select whether NFC's Comparison Statistics window is displayed or hidden. This small window, shown in Figure 15.12, along with the Display tab itself, will provide a summary of differences between the two files. As you make changes to the files, this display will update, indicating you've either added or removed differences.

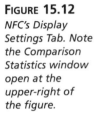

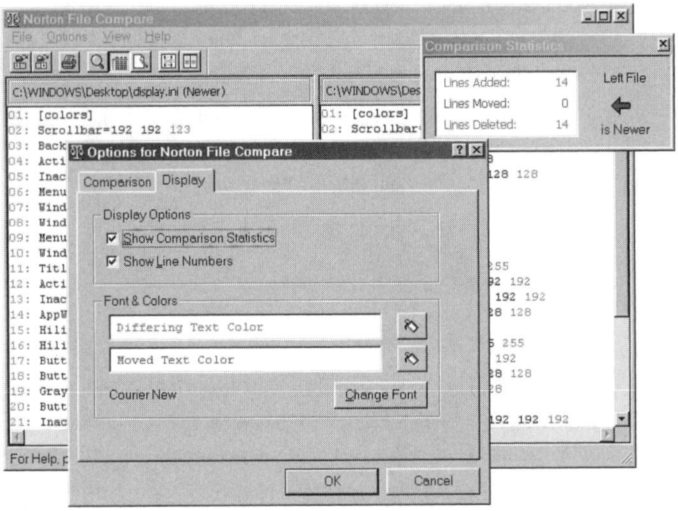

FIGURE 15.12

NFC's Display Settings Tab. Note the Comparison Statistics window open at the upper-right of the figure.

The Display tab also allows you to set whether line numbers will be added to the file displays and to any file printouts. As you can probably imagine, just as the presence of line numbers makes analyzing poetry much simpler, so too is it far easier to compare differences between two large files with line numbers enabled. Finally, the Display tab gives you access to standard Windows color- and font-selection dialogs, so you can customize the display to look, as well as function, in the way that best suits your tastes and your needs. Text which does not differ between the two files will always be displayed in black, but you can customize the colors in which both differing and relocated text are displayed and, on a color printer, printed. (If you select your colors carefully, you will be able to see different shades of gray on a laser or black-only inkjet printer, as well.)

Before you change the font of the display, give some thought to why the designers of Norton File Compare selected Courier New as the default. Courier New is one of what are known as "monospaced" fonts. That is, fonts in which ever letter, number, or character uses the same amount of horizontal line space as every other character. This feature can be very useful indeed when making comparative analyses of two files, particularly if numbers are involved. Look at the following example:

```
123,489,145,268,890,658,463
965,457,902,105,302,235,667
```

123,489,145,268,890,658,463
965,457,902,105,302,235,667

Notice how much easier it would be to perform arithmetic on the first two lines of numbers. In the third and fourth lines, above, even though the numbers are displayed in the same font, the varying width of the numbers means that they still do not line up properly. Carrying the two takes on a whole new dimension when you have to carry it half-way across the page! And consider trying to compare two sets of numbers like this to see in which places they were the same. For the first two lines, you can drop a ruler down on the page and quickly move right across the line. With the second set of numbers, you'll move far more slowly, probably losing your place at least once.

So a monospaced font has the effect of standardizing a display, making it very easy to read, and making one part of the complete display—say, a file in the Norton File Compare left panel—easy to visually compare with another part of the display—say, a file in the right panel. Nevertheless, if you absolutely cannot stand to work in Courier, or if you have another monospaced font installed which you prefer, you can make such changes here.

Search Options

Following the Settings item in the Options menu is the Search item, from which you can initiate a search for similar text, dissimilar text, or text which you specify. Let me explain. A "matching block" search and a "non-matching block" search are essentially the same search, but they return opposite results. If, for example, you want to jump in the two files from wherever you are viewing at a given moment to the next large block of text which contains no differences, performing a "matching block" search will yield that result. Whether you search up or search down in the Search dialog, the synchronized displays will jump to the next set of lines in the two files which are exactly the same. Contrastingly, a "non-matching block" search will skip through the files, ignoring all of the content that isn't different, and displaying the next—again, either moving up or down in the files, as you like—line or group of lines which does contain a variance. These two searches are a marvelous way to skip through particularly large files, locating similarities or dissimilarities in accordance with your needs. Additionally, you may have occasion to search for a string of text in the files. Once you select a text search on the Search dialog, you can enter in text for which you want to search. You can also specify whether or not you consider case important. When you search up or down, Norton File Compare will jump to the next location in which your search text is found, if it is present. Text searches are particularly useful when you are trying to locate a specific, known change between two large files.

Search functionality is also available from the Search icon on the toolbar (it looks like a magnifying glass).

Undoing Changes Between the Two Files

The next item on the Options menu, Undo Selected Changes is one of Norton File Compare's most powerful tools. If you have recently installed a piece of software or hardware which has modified configuration settings on your PC—and you want some of those modifications undone—you can simply load the current configuration file into one panel and the backup of the pre-modification configuration file into the other panel. Using the search methods described in the previous section, locate the changes in the new file which you want reversed, and highlight them with your mouse. Then select Undo Selected Changes from the Options menu. A window will open in front of Norton File Compare's two-panel display in which you'll be able to review what the current file will look like once the changes you've selected are undone. Lines which will be modified by the Undo process will be highlighted in the "differences" color you selected from the Display Settings tab, described above. If you like the look of the final file, click Save to replace the current file with the edited version. If you want the opportunity to review the file again before overwriting the current configuration file, selecting Save As from the confirmation display will let you assign a new filename and saving location to the modified file.

It's very likely that configuration file changes won't take effect until the next time you boot Windows. Additionally, if you are editing Windows Registry keys and have opened Norton File Compare through its integration with the Norton Registry Tracker (described in Chapter 13), then you will need to import your changes from the Registry editing file back into the Registry itself *and* reboot before your changes will become active.

Exclusions and Editing Exclusions

These two final Options menu entries are part of Norton File Compare's integration with the Norton Registry Tracker. As you read in Chapter 13, the Registry Tracker allows you to dynamically watch for changes to your Windows Registry and configuration files. You can also export Registry keys to Norton File Compare (from Norton Registry Editor) to see precisely how they differ from earlier versions of the same keys. There will be times, however, when you will not want Norton Registry Tracker to monitor modifications in certain configuration files or certain Registry keys—perhaps because you know you are making a series of system modifications over time, and you don't want these changes that you *know* about distracting from the clarity of the Registry Tracker's display. In other words, you may not be interested in your changes, but you may be very interested in changes caused by your changes. Selecting Registry keys in the Norton File Compare display and choosing Exclude will add those keys to your Norton Registry Tracker exclusion list for all future scans until the exclusions are removed. You can additionally add or delete Registry Tracker exclusions without ever leaving Norton File Compare by selecting Edit Exclusions from NFC's Options menu.

NFC View Menu

Finally, the Norton File Compare View menu gives you quick control over the appearance of the NFC utility. The simplest View options are the three settings at the bottom of the menu. Selecting each item toggles a check mark on or off, indicating that view item's status. Removing the check mark from Toolbar, for example, will remove the small row of toolbar buttons from the Norton File Compare window. If you are comparing two large files or using a small monitor—or both—you may want to reserve as much screen "real estate" for your file contents as possible. In a similar way, disabling the Status Bar turns off the band at the bottom of the file comparison panels, retrieving that space for file comparison.

The third option on the View menu, Statistics, is used to enable or disable the Comparison Statistics panel which you saw in Figure 15.12. This feature can also be toggled on and off by pressing Ctrl+S. Since the Comparison Statistics appear in their own, free-floating window, you can maximize the Norton File Compare panel to use all available screen space and then use the keyboard to toggle the Statistics display on and off as you require. You can also drag the Statistics window to a corner of the screen and leave it open, out of the way. This window has a characteristic known as "stay on top," which means that you can work in the underlying Norton File Compare window without having the large NFC window occlude the small Statistics display. (Of course, the small window *will* occlude whatever is beneath it in the larger NFC window, which is why you may want to use the keyboard to toggle statistics on and off as you need them.)

Statistics can also be toggled on or off from the Statistics button on the toolbar. This button has an icon that somewhat resembles a spreadsheet.

Viewing in INI Mode

Moving back up to the top of the View menu, you'll find the INI Mode entry. INI Mode functionality is also available from the INI Mode button on the toolbar; it's the second-right-most button on the panel. You can see the impact of INI Mode if you compare the display in Figure 15.13 with the visible right-hand panel of the display in Figure 15.10.

With INI Mode disabled, configuration file entries are displayed in the order in which they appear in the files, with precisely the same whitespace—or lack thereof—as is present in their files. With INI Mode enabled, as in Figure 15.13, all configuration file entries are grouped together under the section heads, and whitespace is added into the display to differentiate one section from another. Within each section, entries are alphabetized so that it is much easier to locate a particular entry. It's very difficult to show the scale of benefits INI Mode provides within book illustrations. However, if you want to see a dramatic example, launch Norton File Compare and, in the left pane, open your current WIN.INI file. In the right pane, open your WIN.BAK file, both of which should be located within your Windows folder. With INI Mode disabled, you will likely see dramatically different spacing between the two panes, as Norton File Compare tries to keep as many similar entries aligned as possible by adding blank lines as necessary.

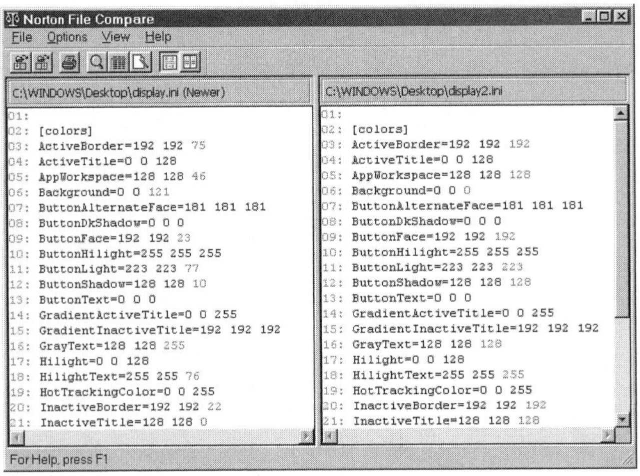

FIGURE 15.13

FIGURE **15.13**

*Norton File
Compare with
configuration file
entries grouped
under their sec-
tion headings and
alphabetized.*

Differences Mode

Regardless of what kind of files you're viewing, whether configuration files, sets of
Registry key entries, or even letters to a friend, Norton File Compare's Differences
Mode, located on the View menu and also available from the right-most button on the
toolbar, can really help the differences between two files stand out. It does this, as you
might suspect, by hiding all file content *except* differences.

Compare, for a moment, Figure 15.13 and Figure 15.14. Both displays show INI Mode
active, but in Figure 15.14, Differences Mode has been turned on as well. Although differences between the two files are highlighted in red in both displays—difficult to see in
a greyscale book, I know—even with the entries alphabetized by INI Mode, everything
still runs together. After all, you're using Norton File Compare, presumably, to find differences between two files. And while it can certainly be useful to look at both similarities and differences, Differences Mode allows you to really hone in on the ways in which
two files are not the same.

Differences Mode can make selecting changes for Undoing remarkably easy. You can
turn Differences Mode on and select contiguous sets of changes, even if those changes
are separated by wide areas of similar text. You can do the same thing with Differences
Mode off, but it's a lot easier to see what you're doing and what you've selected when
you're looking at a more concise display. Editing Windows Registry keys can be a complex and tricky business with a good deal of data exported by Norton Registry Tracker
for viewing, even if you only export selected keys. Differences Mode will temporarily
hide all of the "noise," let you see what you need to do, and get you back to more pro-
ductive tasks.

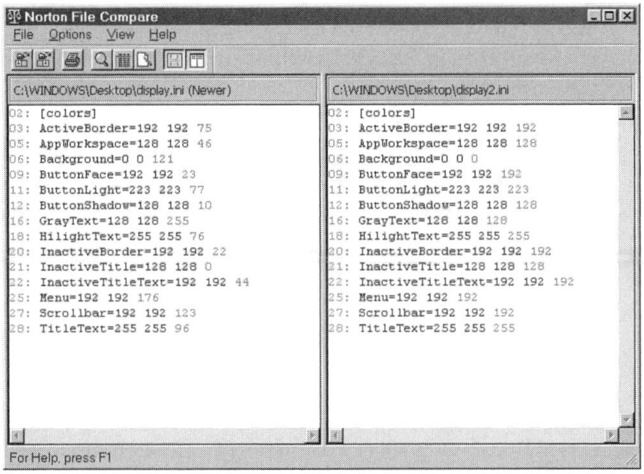

FIGURE 15.14

The same display shown in Figure 15.13, with Differences Mode enabled.

PETER'S PRINCIPLE

Norton "Don'tErase"

When it comes to the issue of deleting files, I'm often amazed by how obsessive people can be about purging old files from their drives. Fifteen years ago, when a large drive was 5MB, I suppose a lot of us got into the habit of maintaining precious disk space by getting rid of old files as soon as we no longer needed them. Old habits die hard, but, as anyone who has lost vital work knows, this is a good habit to put behind you.

Given the capacity—and moreover, the economy—of today's hard drives, there's somewhere between little and no reason to continuously sweep through your folders in search of files you've not used in 48 hours. Backups are a great thing, and Norton Protection really does provide total protection against accidental or undesirable deletion for the period of time you desire. But the most convenient way to access an old deleted file is to not delete it in the first place. Perhaps a wonderful new utility would be Norton "Don'tErase," a small pop up that would ask, "Are you sure you don't have enough disk space to keep that file for a little longer?" whenever we went to erase a file.

People commonly respond to admonitions to not delete their historic files with complaints about simplicity. They say that it's too hard to find current files amongst all of the old files. This is why subfolders exist. Create archival subfolders into which you move files as they become "Two Weeks," "One Month," and "One Year" old. This keeps your current set of documents compact and concise without sacrificing the safety of data which—who knows—you may be desperate for two months down the road. Moving files according to date couldn't be easier: Open the Windows Explorer and select Details from the View menu. Then, click the header of the Modified column to sort the entire folder by date. From there, just click and drag files into their archival folders.

Simplicity is also one of the reasons that Long File Names exist. If you use LFN's to give your files meaningful names, then even if your archived files are divided

continues

into different folders based on their age—or their content... however you like—they remain easily searchable using the Windows Find utility located on the Start menu.

The fact is, the vast majority of people I've talked to who have been burned by needing files that they had intentionally deleted, all confessed that they didn't really need to delete the file when they did. It was just "in the way," and "taking up space." Space is valuable. But sometimes the most valuable space around is the space you use.

Norton Utilities: The Big "Oops" and Norton UnFormat

If you're reading this chapter because all your files are gone, you're probably experiencing a bit of anxiety at the moment and not in the mood for lengthy discussion. Perhaps, then, the next few paragraphs will tell you everything you need to know, and in a few minutes from now, all those folder icons will again be lining up on your screen. And never will they have looked so nice. What follows is a quick bit of information that might tell you right off the bat if UnFormat is your answer, and how much is involved in implementing it. So let me cut to the chase:

- If you've just tried to access a drive, either a hard drive or a floppy, and found all its files and folders are missing, realize that several situations are present with that symptom—and most are repairable. (Your hands can stop shaking now.) Norton UnFormat is often the tool of choice for fixing such a problem.

- Formatting your hard drive does not erase all your files. It reinitializes the system area of that drive, but the data files are still there. If you accidentally change the size of a partition using FDISK and then do not precisely change it back, or if you perform a CMOS Set-Up low-level format, you will indeed burn down the barn, but the FORMAT command does not.

- UnFormat is used to restore missing or corrupt information from your disk's boot record, File Allocation Table, and root directory. This information is overwritten when you format your hard drive or floppy, or it could be corrupted as a result of a virus. Other culprits could be impending hard drive failure; an incident that causes system files to become scrambled, such as plugging in a peripheral device while your computer is on; or sudden termination of electrical power.

- UnFormat does not only restore disks that have been accidentally formatted, but it should be considered a possible solution any time your hard drive or floppy appears empty for unknown reasons.

> **Note:** If a virus is considered a possible culprit, use Norton AntiVirus first. It, too, maintains a record of your boot files and can resurrect an "empty" hard drive or floppy by restoring a saved version of your boot files, or a portion of them. Refer to Chapter 9, "Norton AntiVirus: Infection Protection" for more information.

Dynamic Drive Overlays and UnFormat

Before we rebuild a formatted drive step by step, I have one very important warning to anyone whose hard drive boots with a Dynamic Drive Overlay, such as E-Z Drive or OnTrack's Disk Manager. (You might be one of those people without knowing it, so read on.)

For a few years now, software programs have been available to allow owners of older computers to use extra-large hard drives without having to become experts in DOS partition commands first. These programs install from a floppy disk and are often called Dynamic Drive Overlays.

Your computer may be running one of these if you purchased a large hard drive and were told you had to install it with a floppy disk that came with the drive. This issue applies specifically to computers not capable of using hard drives larger than 512 MB, and it also applies to pre-plug-and-play configurations.

The problem is this: If your hard drive uses a Dynamic Drive Overlay, the boot information will not be where UnFormat expects to find it. The Dynamic Drive Overlay installs itself in that first sector and moves the real boot sector and file table information elsewhere. For your hard drive to work, the Dynamic Drive Overlay must load first. But when you boot from a Norton Rescue Disk floppy, the Dynamic Drive Overlay is not loaded. The trouble is that UnFormat still tries to access that hard drive anyway. The results could be irreversible, catastrophic data loss.

If you think you might be running with a Dynamic Drive Overlay, do the following before booting with a floppy:

1. Start the computer as normal, without a floppy.

2. Momentarily, the screen will display a message, instructing you how to boot with a floppy. Often, you'll be told to press a certain key combination (such as Alt+A),

which pauses the computer and allows you to insert a bootable floppy. Your mouse will not be active. Read the screen carefully to see the keystroke sequence you'll be required to press.

3. After pausing the computer as prompted, insert your Norton Basic Rescue Disk and press any key to continue (unless a special key is assigned for this). (Refer to Chapter 7, "Norton Utilities: Life Preserver on a (Rescue) Disk," for detailed instructions on how to create Norton Rescue Disk sets.)

The screen displays the "insert floppy now" message only after the Dynamic Drive Overlay is safely loaded. After this procedure, you're home-free. The Dynamic Drive Overlay is now poised to reroute any directions regarding boot sector information appropriately, and you can continue booting with your floppy, using UnFormat as normal. Do not attempt to reboot from your hard drive; you must boot with your floppy disk at this time.

How UnFormat Works

UnFormat works by reading your missing boot information from a file called IMAGE.DAT, the creation and maintenance of which you read about in Chapter 10, "Norton Utilities: More Than a Mirror, an Image." For maximum protection, you should configure Norton SystemWorks to refresh your Image data every time you start Windows, if not more often. If UnFormat can locate this IMAGE.DAT file, then your chances of full recovery are very good. That's because UnFormat has a complete blueprint from which to work in rebuilding your data.

Other utilities create *disk mirrors*, or *drive images*, thereby taking a snapshot of your boot records. In the absence of a Norton Utilities IMAGE.DAT file, Norton UnFormat can often read these files, restoring at least a portion of your missing data. When using mirroring files created by other utilities as a blueprint, UnFormat can sometimes restore the files, but the folder names are lost.

The result of using UnFormat is a slew of numerically named folders. You'll then have to look at the files inside those folders, figure out what the folders used to be called, and rename them. But even that task is much better than having to install everything from scratch or, of course, losing valuable data forever.

When You Would Use UnFormat

Troubleshooting is best done systematically, starting with the most simple possible solutions, and perhaps running Norton Disk Doctor first to find out what went wrong with your computer. However, several situations warrant jumping straight to UnFormat, without spending much time seeking other solutions first:

- If you formatted your hard drive accidentally, or if you formatted it without knowing what the procedure would do.

  It's easy to format the wrong drive accidentally if, for example, you've installed a new hard drive and your operating system did not "bump up" the drive lettering system the way you thought it should. Perhaps a partitioning program skipped letters, so you accidentally formatted a drive with data on it rather than the brand new one. Portable ZIP drives sometimes play fast and lose with such a process, causing your hard drive to "bump" to a new letter while the ZIP occupies a lower one. You can think you are formatting your ZIP drive but then, sadly, find out otherwise.

- If, after a sudden power outage, you turn on your computer and receive a `Drive Not Found` error.

- If you are plugging in a printer, mouse, or joystick in a port and you suddenly hear unpleasant noises and a system reboot. When the dust settles, your files appear to be gone.

- If you have an old hard drive and you know it's wheezing along, taking longer and longer to access data. You spend more time repairing cross-linked files each week. Then, finally, you boot up one morning and your computer cannot find your drive.

- If you accidentally formatted a floppy disk or ZIP disk, then realized it contained data you really needed.

- In special circumstances when Norton Disk Doctor detects several dozen errors, it may be easier—and more successful, ultimately—to use UnFormat rather than Norton Disk Doctor to repair the damage. This determination is best made by a power-user. Fortunately, such situations are exceedingly rare.

Situations in Which UnFormat Is Not the Answer

The right tool for the right job was never a more apt cliché than when considering the safety of your data. That's likely why you bought Norton SystemWorks and didn't just download some shareware disk-fix. You now have many tools from which to choose, and some instances do not call for UnFormat:

- If you think the damage may be due to a virus, use Norton AntiVirus first (refer to Chapter 9, which discusses AntiVirus at length).

  Both Norton AntiVirus and UnFormat take their own snapshots of your boot sector files and restore from them. Norton AntiVirus, of course, destroys the virus first before restoring your boot record, File Allocation Tables, and such. However, at times Norton AntiVirus can destroy the virus but not fully restore the files as they were. UnFormat might be called upon to finish the job started by Norton AntiVirus.

- If you see the message `Operating System Not Found` when booting, this is not a disk-formatting problem. To repair this, boot from your Norton Emergency Disk (from the set of three disks that you created when you first set up the program). Then when booting is finished, ensure that the `C:` drive is your familiar `C:` drive, replace the boot disk with Emergency Utilities Disk #1, and type **SYS C:**. Then reboot as normal.

- If you've used FDISK to remove the primary partition of your hard drive, your files are indeed gone. (In limited circumstances, attempting to recover your primary partition by using Norton Rescue may be successful. Refer to Chapter 7 for detailed information about Norton Rescue.)

- If you've gone into CMOS and performed a low-level format, your files are irretrievable.

- If you boot up and do not hear your hard drive cycling at all, or if you hear it cycle, shudder, and stop, then it's time to go shopping. Think of it as an opportunity for growth, and be thankful that you maintain such a comprehensive backup scheme. (You do, don't you?)

- Errors very late in the booting process, such as General Protection Faults just as Windows is about to finish loading are more indicative of Registry errors, driver incompatibility, or corrupted software. Leave UnFormat out of that equation. In this case, you may need to boot up without allowing Windows to attempt to load drivers that may be conflicting with others. This process is detailed after the next point.

- If your computer "hangs" during booting (as in, it just won't move past a certain point), this problem probably has nothing to do with your hard drive. Rather, Windows is trying to load a start-up command and is unable to. To fix this, refer to the procedure that follows.

If your computer starts loading and, at a certain point, just won't load anymore, try the following:

1. Reboot again, and when the screen reads `Starting Windows 98` (or `Starting Windows 95`), press the F8 key.

2. You'll be given a set of numbered options. Select `Step By Step Confirmation`.

3. You'll be prompted before Windows loads every line of your CONFIG.SYS or AUTOEXEC.BAT file. The purpose of this is to empower you to skip loading a problem driver, or to command that Windows cannot execute for some reason. Such a bottleneck can prevent Windows from executing the rest of your startup commands, even if the rest are all fine.

4. Watch to see which command is the last to appear before your system "hangs." Then reboot, repeating the procedure. When the computer prompts you to load or skip the command that hung the last time, tell Windows to skip it and not load it. (If the file is a vital system component, you may have other difficulties to work through. A file may be corrupted. Start by running Norton Disk Doctor to verify the integrity of it and all your other files.)

5. Finally, after Windows opens, select Run from the Start menu and type **SYSEDIT**. Your system files open. Locate the line that references the driver causing the problem. Type **REM** in front of that line. That way, the next time Windows boots, it will not attempt to load that driver or command from your startup files.

Unformatting Your Hard Drive

If, after reading the preceding sections, you've determined that you need to use the UnFormat utility to restore your hard drive, follow these steps. Refer to the following section, if you need to unformat a floppy disk.

To UnFormat your hard drive, perform these actions:

1. To begin, reboot from your Norton Rescue Boot Disk or Norton Emergency Disk #1. If you made a Norton ZIP Rescue set, you'll be booted into Windows. UnFormat does not work in Windows; it must be run in DOS. So it's floppy time.

2. If you've booted with the Norton Emergency Disk #1, skip to step 4. Otherwise, when the Rescue disk is finished booting, press Ctrl+C to abort the Rescue process. When asked if you want to Terminate the Batch Job, press **Y** for Yes. The A: command prompt appears.

3. Replace the current floppy disk with the DOS Emergency Utilities Disk #2. This is the third floppy you made when you created your Norton Rescue Disk set.

4. Type **UNFORMAT**, followed by the letter of the drive you want to unformat.

5. You'll see a screen asking if you used IMAGE or MIRROR to save recovery information for your drive. If you don't know for sure, answer Yes, which simply sends UnFormat on its way, looking for such a file. If none is found, UnFormat continues without it.

   UnFormat issues warnings if any data is found on this newly formatted disk. It's important to note that any data you put on this hard drive since your IMAGE.DAT file was last updated will probably be lost—or at least hard to locate (saved in a cryptically named folder). Any data placed on this drive since it was formatted accidentally will definitely be gone after using UnFormat. (In the case of a floppy diskette, data written to the floppy after an accidental format will likely destroy much of what was previously on the disk. Repairing with UnFormat in this circumstance will likely fail. The data is gone.)

After warning you about files that may be lost, UnFormat sets out to locate IMAGE or MIRROR information to use as its blueprint for restoring system files (see Figure 16.1). Remember, UnFormat does not have to rebuild all your files; it merely has to restore information about their location.

FIGURE 16.1

While UnFormat looks for IMAGE information, the screen appears like this.

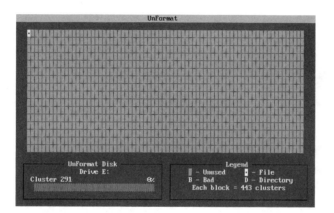

6. If UnFormat finds multiple IMAGE.DAT files from which to restore, you'll be informed (see Figure 16.2). You must choose the version of IMAGE.DAT with which to work.

Caution: If this is not your startup drive and you've been living with it in its impaired, newly formatted state for a day or two, you may have had a new IMAGE.DAT file created in the process. (You'll be warned about this, as shown in Figure 16.3.) This is not the IMAGE.DAT file you want to use. You want the one that mirrored your hard drive when it was full and working well. You want to work with the "pre-format" version of IMAGE.DAT. For this reason, do not reflexively choose the most recent version of IMAGE.DAT to restore. Think back to the date right before this problem occurred, and restore an IMAGE.DAT file from as close to that date as possible. If only newer, after-the-event versions of IMAGE.DAT files are available, see if perhaps you have an older version on a backed-up media, such as a ZIP drive or tape drive. This older one may be better to use in restoring.

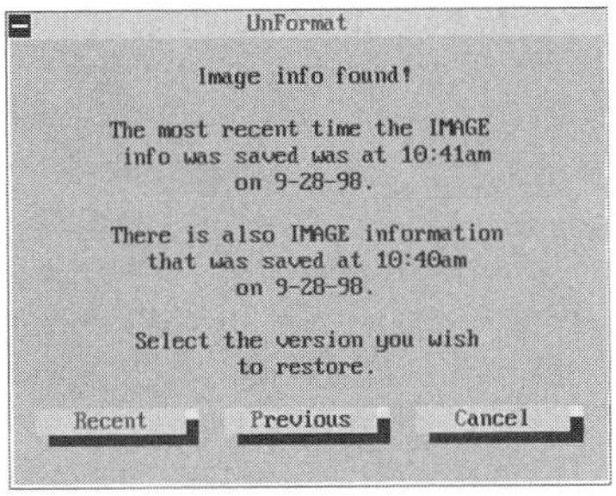

FIGURE 16.2

When UnFormat finds an IMAGE.DAT *file, you'll be asked which one to restore.*

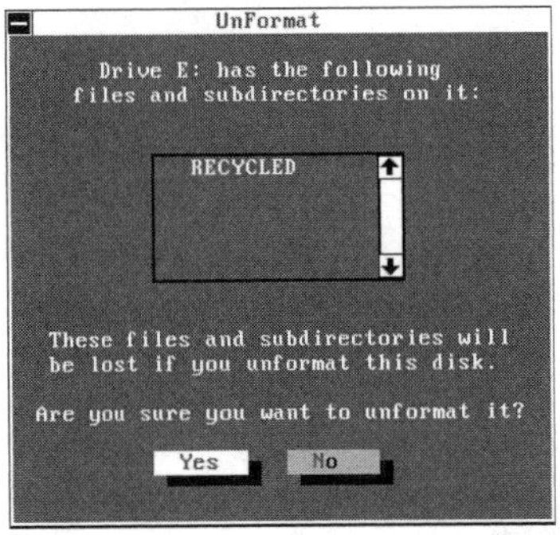

FIGURE 16.3

UnFormat warns that the program may overwrite any changes since the last IMAGE information was saved.

If UnFormat does not find IMAGE.DAT or MIRROR.FIL files from which to restore, it still tries to restore what it can. Be prepared for anonymously named folders and some missing files. In this case, the restore will probably only be partial.

7. You'll be given the choice between a Full or Partial Restore. If you attempt Full Restore, and it turns out that Full Restore is not possible, UnFormat will not automatically attempt a Partial Restore. You'd have to repeat the above steps, and this time around, chose Partial. Therefore, if you have the time, go ahead and let UnFormat attempt a full restore. If none is possible, begin UnFormat again, and this time, select Partial. You may also want to choose Partial Restore if you want UnFormat to hunt around for even a handful of files that may be salvageable, and not simply report back that a Full Restore is out of the question. In a partial restore, all the files that were in your boot directory may be missing. The folders may be quite intact, but individual files will probably be gone.

Note: UnFormat does not restore data files. It uses data from the IMAGE.DAT file, if possible, to reconstruct address information that tells your computer where to find your files. UnErase actually restores data files to their previous locations (or other locations you specify, as you can read about in Chapter 15, "Norton Utilities: Getting It Back, Getting It Right: UnErasing and File Compare").

UnFormat does not take long if `IMAGE.DAT` or `MIRROR.FIL` data is present. Usually within a minute after determining the type of restore you want, you'll see a message indicating UnFormat has done its job. If recovery data is not present, however, UnFormat will manually reconstruct the disk. This requires a detailed scan of the entire partition and may take several hours for a large disk. Using Norton Image can save you time in many ways! Once the `UnFormat has completed its work` message is displayed, the job is not quite done. UnFormat tries its best to bring your drive up to speed, but a visit to Norton Disk Doctor is a must. You'll be prompted to allow the computer to reboot, again, from Norton Emergency Disk #1. Place your Norton Emergency Disk #1 in the floppy drive, and confirm that you want to reboot.

8. When you boot with the Emergency Boot Disk #1, you'll see a menu of Norton options. You can either use the menu to select Norton Disk Doctor from the list of choices, or just type **NDD**, followed by the letter of the drive you just unformatted. (For example, **NDD C:**. Don't forget the space before the drive letter and the colon after it.) Typing **NDD** starts the DOS version of Norton Disk Doctor. Doing the necessary clean-up after unformatting a disk is best carried out in the DOS environment, without trying to load the Windows GUI in all its complexity.

   You'll have to select which set of NDD options to run. If you suspect your hard drive may be failing, or if you think it may have bad sectors, be sure to run a Surface Test as well as the standard set of Diagnose Disk tests.

9. After running Norton Disk Doctor, boot normally in Windows. As mentioned, you might need to do a little detective work to determine what files were rescued and where they are now. Immediately after booting into Windows, Disk Doctor may prompt you for permission to fix errors that are evident only when all your system files are loaded. After that final pass, the files that were restored should be working well.

Unformatting a Floppy Disk

Unformatting a floppy disk still requires that you restart your computer in DOS mode. The commands are similar to what is described in the preceding section, except that very few people create `IMAGE.DAT` information for floppy disks. Thus, your chances of 100 percent recovery are usually not high. Unless you've saved `IMAGE.DAT` information for the floppy disk you want to UnFormat, files saved in the root directory of your floppy disk aren't retrievable. Files that were saved in folders on your floppy disk often are retrievable, but the folder names will be lost. They'll have numeric sequential titles instead, as shown in the first figure in this chapter.

One important factor in successfully unformatting a formatted floppy is the amount of data you've put on the floppy after reformatting it. The magic of unformatting a formatted floppy is possible because formatting does not truly erase data. However, saving large amounts of new data on a floppy indeed erases the old files irrevocably.

The bottom line? If you've done little to your floppy other than format it, then your chances of unformatting the floppy and restoring your data are quite high unless the data was saved in the root folder.

Here's how to UnFormat a floppy disk you accidentally formatted:

1. Restart your computer in DOS mode, and then place the floppy disk in the floppy drive.

2. Switch to the folder with your Norton SystemWorks files, taking care to use the DOS names for those folders (usually C:\PROGRA~1\NORTON~1\NORTON~1\). If for some reason, your Norton SystemWorks files are not available on drive C:, then restart your computer in MS-DOS mode, insert your Norton Emergency Utilities Disk #2, and continue with step 3.

3. Type **UNFORMAT A:**. (If you've invoked UnFormat from drive A:, you might be wondering how you are going to stop UnFormat from unformatting itself. Read the next step, and you'll see.)

4. You'll be prompted to specify that drive A: is the drive you want to UnFormat, and you will be informed of any files that will be lost as a result of unformatting. Note that any files currently on the floppy will be erased as a result of unformatting. Saving any new files to another medium will not decrease your chances of retrieving the original data. If you've invoked UnFormat from drive A:, then when you see this confirmation Are you sure you want to Unformat Drive A:?, remove the Norton Utilities disk you've used to load UnFormat, and replace it with the disk you want to unformat.

5. UnFormat will ask if there is IMAGE or MIRROR data available for this floppy. If so, then 100 percent recovery is indeed possible. If not, then you can still probably retrieve some data, but the folder names will be gone, as will any files in the root folder of the floppy.

6. If you specify that UnFormat should take some time to search your floppy drive for information that will help restore the files, the entire floppy drive will be scoured to locate such files. This adds a few minutes to the UnFormat process.

7. Whether UnFormat ultimately locates the IMAGE or MIRROR data or not, the program attempts to UnFormat your floppy drive, if you give it permission to do so.

   UnFormat moves through each sector of your floppy drive, looking for and restoring folders and files. This process usually takes 3–10 minutes.

UnFormat reports how successful it has been in unformatting and restoring files to that floppy disk. If 100 percent restoration was not possible, UnFormat directs you to use Norton UnErase to retrieve files that you may have sent to the Recycle Bin from that floppy. If you deleted files before formatting your floppy, then UnErase can help retrieve them.

PART IV

Optimization and Customization

Norton Utilities: Getting It Together with Norton Optimization Wizard, Speed Disk, and SpeedStart

If you've been reading this book from the beginning, you've already come to understand the myriad things that can "go wrong" with your computer. This chapter, the first in this part on "Optimizing and Customizing" your PC, introduces the aspects of Norton SystemWorks that hone your PC productivity to a fine edge.

Norton SystemWorks includes three very special tools that dramatically increase the speed at which your PC performs file-related tasks: the Norton Optimization Wizard, Norton Speed Disk and Norton SpeedStart. Used properly with the Norton System Doctor, these tools keep your drives in tip-top shape and can significantly decrease the time you spend waiting for your PC to respond when you open a file or launch an application. As you see, these same tools also contribute significantly to the overall health and safety of your PC's drives and the data they contain.

WINDOWS 98

> If you have just installed the Norton SystemWorks under Windows 98 and rebooted your computer for the first time, you may have encountered a dialog box indicating that, under Windows 98, Speed Disk performs all of the benefits that are provided separately by Speed Disk and SpeedStart, under Windows 95. If you're using Windows 98, as you read the discussions of SpeedStart, below, remember that Speed Disk is handling all of the same issues.

Fragmentation Contemplation

Of all of the disk-related circumstances that can impact your daily productivity, none is perhaps as all-pervasive as fragmentation. Simply put, *fragmentation* means that when your PC attempted to save a file, it was not possible to store all of that file's data in consecutive locations on the disk. So, the operating system "fragmented" the file, saving its pieces in the next-best available location.

You may remember from earlier chapters that the platters inside your hard disk have been formatted into logical structures which the operating system—either Windows 95 or Windows 98—uses to store and retrieve your data and applications. At the lowest level, these structures are known as *sectors*, and there can be tens of millions of them on a single hard disk. To better manage this ungainly number of locations on your disks, the operating system gathers sectors together into groups or allocation units, known as *clusters*. One cluster is the smallest portion of a disk that the operating system can address. How much data can fit into a cluster—and, indeed, how much data can fit into a sector—is a function of the operating system under which the drive was formatted, and the partition's size. Read the following technical sidebar if you'd like to learn more about this issue. If you're having difficulty visualizing all of this "sectors and clusters" stuff, take a look at Figure 17.1, below.

FIGURE 17.1

Simplified view of a hard disk, showing sectors and clusters.

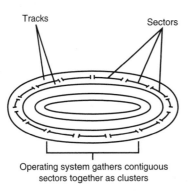

Tracks   Sectors

Operating system gathers contiguous
sectors together as clusters

TECHNICAL NOTE

The size of clusters on a hard disk has a direct correspondence to the total capacity of the disk—or, more accurately, the logical disk. A hard drive may have a total theoretical capacity of many gigabytes, but that drive can be partitioned into multiple logical disks, which the operating system treats as though they were actually separate drives. It is the size of each of these logical disks that determines the size of cluster used for that particular logical disk. A DOS 16-bit FAT limits the allowable partition size of a hard disk to 2GB, so a 4GB drive, for example, must be partitioned into two logical drives in order for it to be used. Each logical drive has a capacity slightly less than the FAT 2GB maximum.

For drives with capacities over one gigabyte, like almost all drives today, DOS uses a cluster size of 32KB, meaning that the smallest addressable space on the disk is 32KB. A direct consequence of this is that any file which is smaller than 32KB, still uses up 32KB of space when it is saved. (The reasons for this are now part of history. A "16-bit FAT" is called that because it uses numbers which are 16 bits long to keep track of drive clusters. This limits the total number of clusters that can exist on a hard drive to 65,535, the largest number which fits into 16 bits. As a drive's capacity increases, the maximum number of clusters remains the same, so the size of each cluster must be increased to compensate.)

> With Windows 95 OSR2, however—and in Windows 98 from the start—Microsoft introduced FAT32, a new 32-bit addressing scheme for keeping track of drive clusters on larger drives. With 32 bits available, the maximum number of clusters increases to a whopping 4,294,967,295! As a consequence, it's no longer necessary to sacrifice so much of your disk space to a mathematical limitation. Under FAT32, drives of greater than 260MB and less than 8GB capacity have a cluster size of a delightfully economical 4KB. Between 8GB and 16GB, cluster size is doubled to 8KB. A 16GB to 32GB drive uses a cluster size of 16KB, and only a massive drive of greater than 32GB capacity requires the use of 32KB clusters. (FAT32 supports drives of capacities less than 512MB, but you are not given the opportunity to enable FAT32 on drives which are that small.)

You may also remember from Chapter 12, "Norton Utilities: The Laying-On Of Hands and Norton Disk Editor," that data is stored in these clusters. The locations used by each file—also known as the file's *cluster chain*—are stored within the FAT (file allocation table). It is by looking up the locations referenced in the FAT that the operating system locates and retrieves your data on demand. Under optimal circumstances, a file's data is saved contiguously. That is, the operating system is able to begin storing a file in a given cluster, and then continue storing data in the sequentially next cluster, and the next, and so on, until the entire file is on disk. Normal day-to-day use of your computer, however, quickly leaves "optimal" circumstances by the wayside. Take a look at Figure 17.2 to see how this can happen.

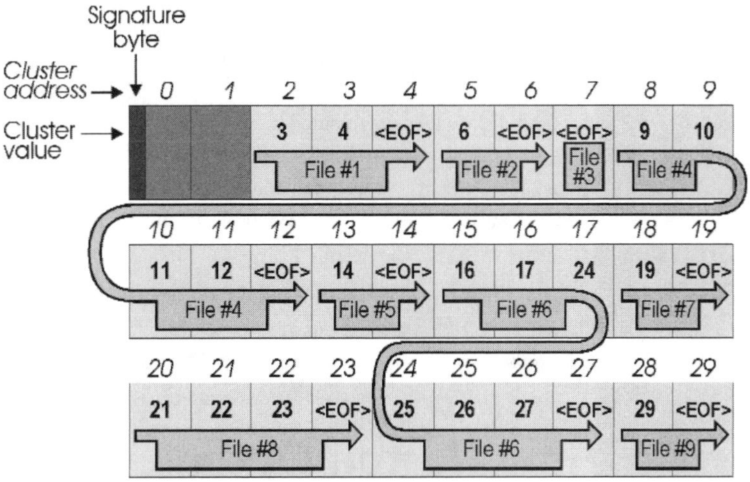

FIGURE 17.2

A schematic FAT with unfragmented and fragmented files.

How Fragmentation Occurs

Figure 17.2 is a simplified schematic for a File Allocation Table. In the circumstances shown in the figure, through the normal use of the PC, our hypothetical user saved six files to the hard disk. In the figure they're numbered one through six. When file 6 was first saved, it was an unfragmented file, using only the clusters numbered 15, 16, and 17, in the figure. Files 7 and 8 were then saved, which were stored immediately after the original file 6. However, suppose later, file 6 had a significant amount of data added to it. This time, when the operating system goes to re-save the file, it cannot use contiguous space without over-writing files 7 and 8. To solve this problem, the new file 6 is fragmented into two pieces, and the second of the two pieces is stored immediately after file 8 on the disk. The operating system stores the beginning location of the second half of file 6 in the FAT, so that the next time the user opens the file, the operating system knows to which cluster the read/write heads must jump in order to read the entire file. If, as in the figure, our user then creates another file—file 9—it is stored in the first free cluster available after the second half of file 6.

The example illustrated in Figure 17.2 is quite simplified, and demonstrates only a simple fragmenting. As you might guess, if the user opens and adds to file 6 again, perhaps as the user adds new customers to the company database, the additional length of file 6 has to be stored after file 9, and so on, as free clusters are available on the hard disk. A few months of opening, saving, deleting, and modifying files can lead to a severely fragmented hard disk. The more fragmented a file is, the more the hard disk's read/write heads have to chatter back and forth to retrieve or store it. Not only does fragmentation put a great deal of wear-and-tear on your hard drive's mechanics, the time it takes for the read/write heads to make all of those moves can become quite noticeable. Keep in mind that Windows reads and writes a large number of files while you are working, and most major applications also create temporary files as you use them. If all of the free space on your hard disk is very fragmented, then all of these files are also fragmented, and you'll notice a significant, ever-increasing performance degradation. Together with the Norton Optimization Wizard, Speed Disk can undo fragmentation, not just of your files, but also Windows' swap file—something Windows itself can't do.

> **Note:** Fragmentation can also make the recovery of deleted files far less reliable than otherwise, as you read in Chapter 15, "Norton Utilities: Getting It Back, Getting It Right: UnErasing and File Compare."

How Norton Optimization Wizard Works

Norton Optimization Wizard performs some very special tasks, which can contribute tremendously to the efficiency of your PC's operation. Unlike even Microsoft's own

Disk Defragmenter, Norton Optimization Wizard, or NOW, can analyze and optimize your Windows swap file. It can optimize the entries within your Windows Registry. It can also automatically run Norton Speed Disk and optimize your entire PC system, all through a simple wizard interface.

As you probably know, as you use your computer—particularly as you install and uninstall applications—data is added to and removed from the Registry continuously. It's quite common for space that is freed-up in the Registry to not be made available for other use, and so the Registry grows. Of course, as the Registry gets ever larger, it takes ever longer for the operating system to navigate through it. NOW analyzes your Windows Registry, detects this "slack" space, and removes it. Furthermore, NOW can sort through the data that it finds in the Registry and can optimize that data so that it is positioned for maximum performance. As you read in Chapter 3, "Norton Utilities: The System Doctor Is In," you can use Norton WinDoctor to analyze your Registry and delete data that no longer has any relevance to your PC. The Norton Optimization Wizard works with these WinDoctor corrections to give you the most streamlined Registry possible.

Norton Optimization Wizard also sets your Windows swap file in order. As you can read in greater detail in the technical sidebar below, Windows 95 and 98 use this file to provide *virtual memory* services to your PC. As you use your computer, the size of this file can change dramatically, providing you with more or less virtual memory on a needs basis. Because the swap file is a file like any other, it, too, can get fragmented. More so than any other single file, however, the fragmentation of your swap file can slow your PC down to a crawl. Norton Optimization Wizard analyzes your swap file and determines its optimal size. NOW also makes an analysis of your drives and determines which drive is your fastest performer. NOW then resets the swap file to its optimal size, relocates the swap file, if necessary, onto your fastest drive, and automatically runs Norton Speed Disk to unfragment the swap file itself, and all of your other files as well.

TECHNICAL NOTE

Virtual memory is a way that Windows can appear to provide you with far more memory than the physical RAM installed in your computer. Windows does this by creating a file on disk—the swap file—which it uses to temporarily store data on an as-needed basis. When is it needed? As your physical RAM fills with the applications and data that you are using at any given moment, Windows can determine that some of the data in your physical RAM will not be used in the immediate future. It stores this data in the swap file, essentially "extending" the amount of RAM your computer appears to have available. Once the data is stored in the swap file—that is, in virtual memory—the space it used in physical RAM can be made available for other immediate uses.

When your application—or Windows itself—needs to use the data that has been "swapped" out of memory and onto disk, the virtual memory manager portion of the operating system quickly retrieves that data from the swap file, returning it to physical RAM, simultaneously "swapping" other non-essential data out of RAM, onto the disk. As Windows is performing all of these tasks, it

continues

does so with a sensitivity to the amount of free space on your hard disk, as well as the fact that it takes longer to search for data in a huge file than in a small file. Consequently, Windows changes the size of the swap file dynamically in an attempt to balance your immediate memory needs, your need for disk space, and its own data-retrieval limitations. At the same time, of course, the applications you run store data to your disks.

As with any other file, the Windows swap file can become severely fragmented. In fact, because its size changes so frequently, without external aid, it is likely that your swap file is very fragmented indeed. The integration of Norton Optimization Wizard and Norton Speed Disk can rectify this problem, creating an ideally-sized swap file and defragmenting it forever. Additionally, Norton Optimization Wizard will guarantee, by properly optimizing your swap file once and for all, that you never encounter the serious problems than can occur when the system runs out of swap file space. In such a circumstance, crashing is very common, and system instability can lead to data loss even if you don't actually crash.

How Speed Disk Works

Put briefly, Speed Disk analyzes your drives and reorganizes your files so that they are no longer fragmented. It sounds simple enough, but the task is actually quite delicate. All that moving around of your data could lead to disaster if Speed Disk loses track of which data belonged with which files. Fortunately, Speed Disk has no such difficulties. The first question, in fact, isn't whether Speed Disk is ready for your drives; it's whether your drives are ready for Speed Disk.

Integrity Scan

When Speed Disk first runs, it briefly analyzes the FAT of your primary hard drive, and uses this analysis to provide you with the dialog box in which that drive's percentage of fragmentation is reported. This test is repeated for each drive you select to unfragment or *optimize*. When you tell Speed Disk to begin optimizing, it first performs an integrity scan to verify that the condition of your drive is within a range of parameters for safely relocating all of your precious data. As you will read below, Speed Disk has been designed so that even a power failure while Speed Disk is moving files around won't cause you to lose data, but safety is what Norton SystemWorks is all about, really, and Speed Disk takes no chances.

FAT Analysis

Speed Disk then analyzes the FAT on the drive you've selected to optimize. This analysis is very like the one performed by Norton Disk Doctor and it can detect a wide variety of problems that could threaten the safety of your data during optimization. First, Speed Disk checks the integrity of the FAT itself. As you've read elsewhere, the FAT actually

consists of two FAT tables—an original and a backup. Speed Disk will check to see that
the two tables match, as they should. A variance between the two means that one of them
has inaccurately recorded where a file's data is located. It could be disastrous to use the
errant FAT's data when Speed Disk starts moving files around. If a variance is discovered
between the two copies of the FAT, Speed Disk will stop and immediately suggest that
you run Norton Disk Doctor to fully analyze and correct the problem. Speed Disk won't
actually begin optimizing until the drive is problem-free.

Having verified that the two copies of the FAT match, Speed Disk begins an extensive
analysis of the FAT's content. The first step in this check is a verification that your drive
does not contain any lost clusters, that is, clusters which are in use but are marked as
available in the FAT. As above, if such discrepancies exist, Speed Disk automatically
suggests you run Norton Disk Doctor, enabling you to correct the problems before
proceeding.

Defragmenting Operations

The real work of Speed Disk begins when all of these underlying analyses are complete.
At that point, Speed Disk begins to systematically work its way through the FAT, detecting the disk locations where every file is stored, and moving files around so that every
file's contents fall within contiguous clusters. This is a process that you can watch happening on the Speed Disk disk map. You'll read more about the disk map and the entire
Speed Disk interface, below.

The first files that Speed Disk concerns itself with are your applications. Speed Disk will
analyze which applications you use most frequently and will use this information to reorganize your applications and their supporting files into a physical configuration that
means the quickest running of your apps from that point forward.

Having determined the order in which your application-related files will need to be
placed on disk, Speed Disk next optimizes your directory and subdirectory—or folder—
structure. As you read in Chapter 12, under Windows 95 and 98, the information about
your folders is stored in files like any other. While these files are relatively small and not
subject to severe fragmentation themselves, you will discover that you can move much
quicker from folder to folder in Windows once Speed Disk places all of these "folder
files" together. As you would likely expect, it is far quicker for Windows to display the
contents of a folder if it does not have to move the drive's read/write heads far to access
that data. In addition to moving the folder files together, Speed Disk will relocate them at
the beginning of your drive, when their access is further optimized.

As it is reorganizing your folder structure, Speed Disk can and will also reorganize the
file entries in those folders in accordance with settings which you can customize thoroughly, as you will read about shortly. While this re-ordering may be of use to you in
certain circumstances, it is largely of historical interest. Under DOS, filenames are displayed in the order in which they appear in each folder, unless you specified otherwise.

By using Speed Disk to place the folder entries in your preferred order, you could obtain your ideally-styled file listing, by using the DOS DIR command, every time.

With directories and folder entries sorted, Speed Disk will optimize the swap file, and then begin the job of working on your application and data files. As you will read about below, Speed Disk is extremely customizable, and you can truly make it work how you want it to work. Regardless of most of the options that you select, however, Speed Disk works with your files in the following manner. As it begins to unfragment a given file, Speed Disk rechecks the file's integrity to verify that, from the start to the end of the file, all appears to be in order. (If, at any point in the process, Speed Disk encounters an error, it will automatically stop work, and will suggest you run Norton Disk Doctor to repair the problem. More on this later.) Speed Disk then checks the size of the file against a number of factors—available locations on disk, predetermined issues of where application-related files need to be placed, and so on—and determines where on disk the file will fit in its defragmented form. On some hard drives, it may be necessary for Speed Disk to temporarily store a number of files at the end of the disk, while it works on other files. You can see the effect of this in Figure 17.3. Speed Disk moves these files into their proper, final places as it continues to work.

FIGURE 17.3
Speed Disk has moved several files out of the way so that it can best optimize the overall disk.

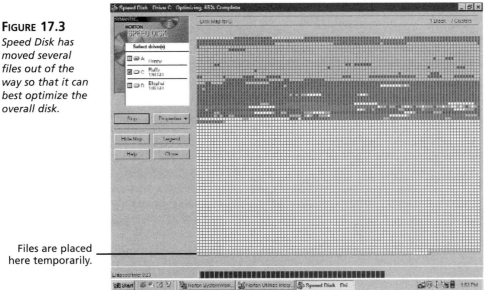

Files are placed here temporarily.

Speed Disk then reads a number of clusters of the file into memory, and copies those clusters to their new locations. When the last cluster in memory is successfully written, Speed Disk modifies the FAT to indicate that the file now starts at its new location. In this way, the file remains usable even if there were to be a power failure while Speed Disk is running. With each successful write operation, Speed Disk updates your drive's

FAT, maintaining file accessibility and integrity throughout the entire process. These steps are repeated until the entire file has been defragmented, and Speed Disk then moves on to the next file. All of this takes place in accordance with the options you configure, as you'll read about next.

> **Note:** You can have Speed Disk doubly verify that every cluster of data has been successfully written to disk by enabling the Verify feature. This tells Speed Disk to read the newly written cluster back from disk and compare it with the cluster contents Speed Disk has in memory. If this process is successful, Speed Disk continues on to the next cluster. If the process fails, Speed Disk undoes its last changes to the FAT—since the file's data is still in its original location, this makes the file whole again—and then stops and urges you to run the relevant part of Norton SystemWorks to address the error. The following sections discuss how to configure Speed Disk to work this way and about how Speed Disk handles errors.

The Speed Disk Interface and Configuration

There are several ways to run Speed Disk, but the easiest of these is to launch it from the SystemWorks Integrator, an icon which was placed on your desktop when Norton SystemWorks was installed. From the SystemWorks Integrator (accessible through the Norton SystemWorks icon on your desktop), click on Norton Utilities, then click on the Improve Performance icon, and finally, click on Speed Disk. You can also access Speed Disk from the Start menu, under Programs | Norton Utilities | Speed Disk. Finally, if you are displaying the Disk Integrity sensor inside System Doctor, you can right-click on the sensor and select Open Speed Disk from the control menu.

Like most of SystemWorks, Speed Disk's interface is straightforward to navigate, but its easy-to-use design hides great sophistication. As with any application—and make no mistake, utility programs are applications, like your word processor or spreadsheet—the key to getting the most out of Speed Disk is to understand how the interface works and what each of its tabs, buttons, and checkboxes can do for you.

When you first run Speed Disk, you'll see a screen that is very much like that in Figure 17.4. It consists of two large panels and a status bar at the bottom of the window. The left panel consists of the buttons that control Speed Disk and give you access to its configuration options. The right panel consists of a graphical map on which Speed Disk displays the status of your disk and its files. As Speed Disk runs, this map panel is continuously updated, so you can see precisely how your files are being relocated.

FIGURE **17.4**

Speed Disk's start-up screen showing its two operative panels and status bar.

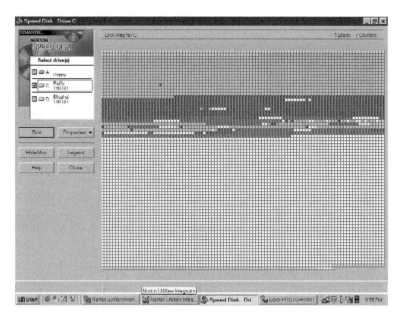

Immediately upon running, Speed Disk begins to check the fragmentation of your primary hard drive. When this check is complete, you'll see a dialog box pop up in front of the main interface, like the one you see in Figure 17.5.

FIGURE **17.5**

Speed Disk displays fragmentation check results in a dialog box like this one.

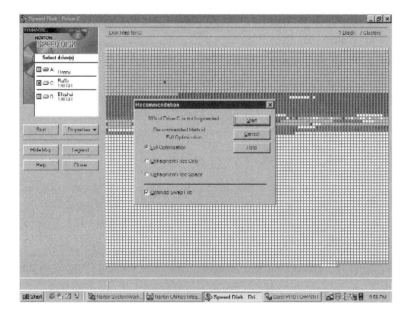

From here you can immediately click Cancel, if, for example, you wish to unfragment a drive other than your primary drive. The Start button may be unavailable if Speed Disk detects that the drive is not fragmented. You can force Speed Disk to perform an optimization, however, by clicking one of the three radio buttons next to the type of optimization you want performed. When one of the radio buttons is selected, the Start button will become available.

Assuming you don't click Cancel—or that you do so, but then select another drive to unfragment—you can instruct Speed Disk to begin one of three types of optimization: a full defragment, a defragment of files but not free space, or a defragment of free space but not files. With each option, you have the additional choice of allowing Speed Disk to optimize your Windows swap file. Optimization of the swap file is the default, and there is almost no circumstance under which you would need, or want, Speed Disk to leave the swap file alone. However, should you wish to do so, unchecking this box turns swap file optimization off. As you would expect, clicking the Start button begins the optimization you have selected, while clicking Help launches the Norton Help engine. Assuming you instruct Speed Disk to perform its recommended defragment of your primary disk, the Recommendation dialog box closes, revealing the main interface.

TECHNICAL NOTE

You've already read about performing a full defragmenting of your drives. Why would you ever want to defragment only your files or, of all things, your unused space? There are a number of reasons. The most obvious of these is speed. A partial defragmenting takes less time than a full one, although it may be decidedly less efficient as well. On the other hand, if you are working with a few files that you know are severely fragmented, defragmenting files only may be a quick solution for you. Of course, if the files are very large, you need a good deal of free space available on your drive, or a files-only optimization will not change those files at all. (This is because, without gathering a large clump of free space together, or taking the time to move many files back and forth, huge files cannot be defragmented. If you've chosen the files-only option, Speed Disk assumes that time is a major factor to you, and thus avoids using more lengthy defragmenting techniques.)

If you're about to install a large piece of software, or if you have some other need for a large clump of free space—for example, if you are running under FAT16 and are about to create a compressed volume on the drive—defragmenting the free space can be a quick way to address those goals. Bear in mind that files are not defragmented, even if they are relocated, during a space-only optimization.

Speed Disk Controls

The first button on the main panel is the Hide Map button (refer to Figure 17.4). On an older or particularly slow computer, the map display can add time to your optimization. If you don't care to watch the process, clicking Hide Map returns you to a reduced Speed Disk screen, as shown in Figure 17.6.

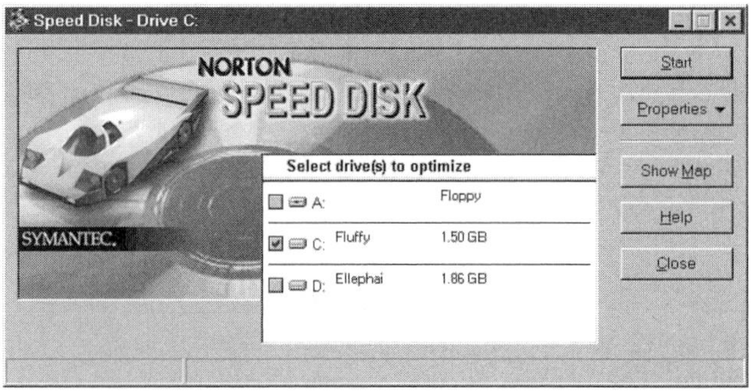

Figure 17.6
Compact view reduces Speed Disk's desktop footprint.

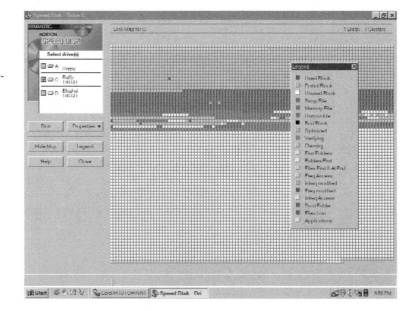

Next to the Hide Map button is the Legend button. (Assuming, of course, you didn't hide the map; if you did, click the Show Map button to return to the full Speed Disk display.) Clicking Legend opens a window from which you can customize any of the colors used in the Speed Disk map display, as shown in Figure 17.7. If your eyes are not particularly sensitive to certain tones, for example, this customizable feature can provide you with some accessibility you wouldn't otherwise have. Of course, if you simply loathe one of the default colors, you can make that change here, too. Double-click on the color box that you want to modify to open the standard Windows color picker. Select a new color—or define your own—and click OK to save the change. Your custom color settings will be retained until you change them again.

Figure 17.7
The Speed Disk Legend window provides additional information about what is shown in the drive map.

The Start button here, as on the Recommendation dialog (refer to Figure 17.5), begins to optimize the drive that you've selected in the small area just above all of the buttons. If you try it, you find that only one drive can be selected at a time, and as you select each drive, Speed Disk automatically runs its fragmentation analysis on that drive, reporting the percentage of fragmented files, and displaying new recommendations for that drive. The Select Drive panel also shows you the capacity of each drive, as you can see in Figure 17.7.

While Speed Disk is optimizing a drive, the Start button changes into a Stop button. Notice that this is a Stop button, not a pause switch. Clicking Stop causes Speed Disk to complete any task that is in progress, then display an Interrupted By User dialog box. Click OK to dismiss the dialog. Clicking Start, of course, restarts the process.

Finally, clicking either the Close button in the main panel or the Windows Close button in the upper-right of the Speed Disk window quits Speed Disk. If you click Close while Speed Disk is running, it completes any task that is pending, and then quits.

The Disk Map "Buttons"

Not exactly buttons in the conventional sense, the entire Speed Disk drive map is a detailed, clickable grid. Clicking at any point in the grid displays a small window of information about the area of the disk represented by where you clicked. An example is shown in Figure 17.8.

FIGURE 17.8

The Map Block Detail shows cluster numbers, the files using those clusters, and the status of those files.

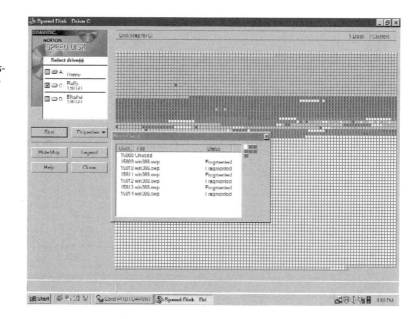

By default, the Block Detail window opens at a very small size. You can point your mouse at a corner of the window and click and drag the window to a larger size. You can also relocate the window, like any other. The colored boxes at the right of the Block Detail screen just serve as a graphic representation of how disk space is being used in the area where you clicked the mouse on the map. These colors are the same as those used in the map and are changed if you customize the map colors. At the left of this display is a columnar table showing the sequential cluster numbers in this part of the drive, the names of the files that occupy those clusters—or if the cluster is unused, the file column shows "Unused"—and whether or not the file is currently fragmented or has been optimized. The columns in this display are resizable. If the default column width is insufficient to display the information you're interested in, clicking on the vertical bar separating the column headers changes the mouse cursor into a resizing tool, enabling you to click and drag the column to the width you desire. (Click on the right-hand edge of the column you wish to resize.) Another neat trick to try: put your mouse pointer on the divider between two column headings and double-click. Both columns expand to display the longest item in each column.

> **Tip:** A particularly interesting—although sometimes difficult to see—feature of the Block Detail window is the fact that clicking on a used cluster in the Block Detail table causes all of the clusters used by that file to be highlighted in the map display. This way, you can see exactly how any given file is spread across your disk.

Obtaining Detailed Fragmentation Reports

Notice that the Properties button, to the right of the Start button on the main panel, has a small downward-pointing arrow at its extreme right. As you likely suspect, if you click on the Properties button, a menu drops open. From here, you can make configuration changes to Speed Disk or to see detailed information about any drive which Speed Disk has scanned for fragmentation. If you have stopped Speed Disk's initial fragmentation scan on a drive, this option is disabled. Click on the drive again in the Select Drive panel, to enable Speed Disk to complete its preliminary analysis, and then click the Properties button again. The Fragmentation Report button is available. A sample Fragmentation Report is shown in Figure 17.9.

Each Fragmentation Report shows a directory tree on the left, and list of every file in the selected folder on the right. Clicking on a folder in the left panel displays its contents at the right. For each file, the degree to which that file is fragmented is expressed as a percentage. The drive shown in Figure 17.9 is optimized so each file is showing zero percent fragmentation (or 100 percent optimized). The Frags column, moving to the right, shows the number of fragments of which each file is comprised. Again, this drive has just been unfragmented, and so every file is using one fragment—that is, every file is using one contiguous area of the disk. (This isn't a fragment, per se, it's the entire file. But it makes more sense to refer to a contiguous file as being one fragment than showing unfragmented files as having zero fragments, and the next-most fragmented files showing two.) A very large, very fragmented file might show 10, 30, or over 100 fragments. The final column displays the number of clusters being used by each file. This bit of information tells you how many clusters needs to be read and written by Speed Disk before the entire file is contiguous. The columns in this display are also resizable. If the default column width is insufficient to display the information you're interested in, clicking on the vertical bar separating the column headers changes the mouse cursor into a resizing tool, allowing you to click and drag the column to the width you desire. (Click on the right-hand edge of the column you wish to resize.)

FIGURE 17.9

A Fragmentation Report shows the percentage of fragmentation for each file (in the right-hand panel) in the currently selected directory (in the left-hand panel).

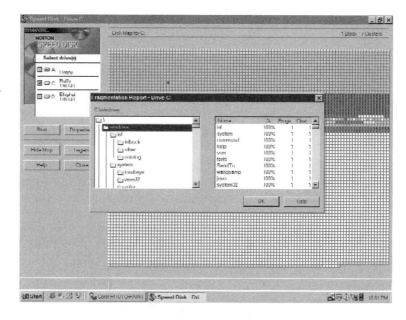

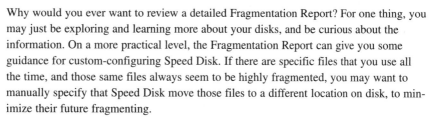

Why would you ever want to review a detailed Fragmentation Report? For one thing, you may just be exploring and learning more about your disks, and be curious about the information. On a more practical level, the Fragmentation Report can give you some guidance for custom-configuring Speed Disk. If there are specific files that you use all the time, and those same files always seem to be highly fragmented, you may want to manually specify that Speed Disk move those files to a different location on disk, to minimize their future fragmenting.

Customizing the Optimizer

The other option available to you under the Properties button's menu is—surprise!—Options. Selecting this opens up three deceptively simple-looking tabs, from which you can adjust almost every important aspect of Speed Disk's function. You can set defaults for how Speed Disk optimizes each of your drives, change the appearance of the Speed Disk map, set how Speed Disk can operate in the background, and annoy your friends and coworkers. What more could anyone want? Let's start by looking at the Optimization tab, which Speed Disk displays by default.

Optimization Settings

You'll notice right away, as in Figure 17.10, that the settings available to you on the Optimization tab closely resemble those found on the Recommendation dialog box. There are other options here, as well, but the big four—full, file, or space optimization, with or without swap file optimization—seem primary. Much is different here from the Recommendation dialog, however. Notice that you can select a drive in the drop-down box at the top of the tab. By selecting a drive from the list here and then selecting a type of optimization, you can tell Speed Disk to perform that type of optimization on that selected drive, just as on the Recommendation dialog box. However, if you set an optimization type for a drive and then click the Save button, that optimization is always used with that drive until you specify otherwise. For example, if you save your settings here for drive D and then select drive D from the Recommendation tab, the settings you save here are used on drive D.

If you have a number of drives that you will always want optimized differently, you can select them one at a time from the drop-down box, choose the type of optimization you want, click Save, and not have to worry about the issue again.

> **Note:** Notice that a bold line separates the optimization types from the checkbox which determines whether the swap file is optimized. This is because the Optimize Swap File option is either on or off for all drives. When checked, Speed Disk will optimize any swap file it encounters, regardless of on which drive it is located and regardless of which optimization method you select. (This issue is not one that will impact you unless you have your PC configured for multibooting different versions of Windows.)

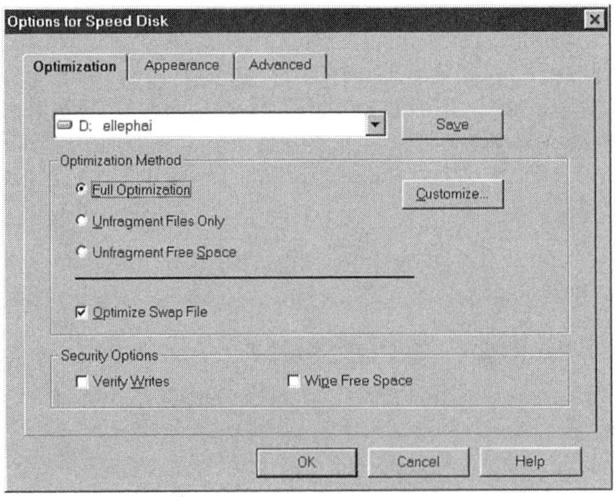

FIGURE 17.10

The Speed Disk Optimization tab enables you to configure how each drive in your system is optimized.

Beneath the Optimization Method section of this tab is a Security Options section, which consists of two check boxes. The Verify Writes check box, when checked, enables the verification of writing that you read about earlier in this chapter. Speed Disk reads back every cluster that it writes to disk and checks that data against the data in the original cluster. Any variance between the two could mean a serious disk problem. Because of that, Speed Disk stops when it encounters any such errors and encourages you to run the relevant part of Norton SystemWorks—with this kind of error, it most often is Norton Disk Doctor—to repair the underlying disk problem.

The other security option available here is Wipe Free Space. If selected, this process occurs after Speed Disk has completed its optimization of the drive. You can read more about how this option impacts the security of your data—and this tiger, like most, is both beautiful and has teeth—later in this chapter. What this option does is instruct Speed Disk to write an endless string of zeros to every unused cluster on the drive, once it has completed its optimization. This option is applicable to all optimization types. You could, for example, unfragment only free space, and then wipe that space. As with the Optimization Methods, clicking the Save button makes the security options you select the default for the drive shown in the drop-down box.

Completely Custom Optimizations

There's one button on the Optimization tab that we haven't yet explored: the Customize button. It enables you to customize how full optimizations are performed on the drive you previously selected from the drop-down box. (Notice that the button is disabled if you do not have the Full Optimization radio button selected.) Clicking on Customize takes you to one of the most complex-looking screens you'll find anywhere in Norton SystemWorks. Don't be dismayed. It's a lot more straight-forward than it looks. We'll look at each tab in order; you may find it extremely useful to be running Speed Disk and looking at this screen while you read. Much of what follows in this section is most useful to advanced users who want to "tweak" the last bit of speed out of their systems; for the rest of us, Speed Disk's defaults work superbly.

The Customize Full Optimization dialog box is divided vertically into two panels. To the left are all of the tabs on which you can set the custom options you desire. To the right is a graphical display of what your disk layout looks like when Speed Disk completes the custom optimization that you define here. Look at the default settings in Figure 17.11. By default, files which are frequently accessed—but rarely or never modified (for example, application components or Windows system DLL files)—are stored at the beginning of the disk, where they can be most rapidly read.

These files are followed by files and folders which do not meet any of the other specific criteria you're about to read about. After that set of "generic" files and folders, by default, come files which are accessed somewhat frequently, and are modified only occasionally. (An example of this type of file is support files for applications you use regularly, but not daily.) These are followed by files that Speed Disk detects are modified with some frequency or regularity, like your personal calendar or journal files, perhaps. Next come any files that you specifically tell Speed Disk to place last, which you're about to learn how to do—and why you would. Finally, free space and infrequently used files round off the list. As you make changes to the settings on the tabs at the left of the graphical display, you'll be able to immediately see how your modifications impact the final layout of your disk.

FIGURE 17.11

Customize Full Optimization enables you to configure how files will be relocated during full optimizations. The default is shown in the figure.

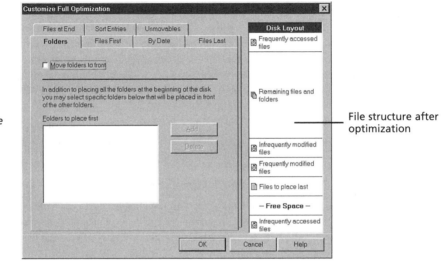

File structure after optimization

Let's start by looking at the Folders tab. To quickly see how the graphical display updates to reflect changes you make, click on the Move folders to front check box at the top of the tab. Notice that a new entry, Folders, appears in color at the top of the display. Notice also that the area that previously said "Remaining Files and Folders" now says only "Remaining Files." If you optimize a disk with these settings, all of the folders on the disk and the filename lists that they contain are placed first, the speediest place on your disk. If you spend a lot of time navigating through your folders, this may be a very good option for you to use.

> **Note:** You should understand that these settings change where your files are physically located on your drives, but they will not change how your files appear to be located when you browse your drives using the Windows Explorer or My Computer. The only noticeable change based on moving your files around in Speed Disk is that your system may operate more swiftly.

Beneath the Move Folders to Front check box you can see a blank area, with an Add and Delete button immediately to the right. Clicking on Add opens a standard Windows folder-navigation box, from which you can select folders that you want moved in front of all the other folders. If you are constantly retrieving files from and saving them to your My Documents folder, for example, you may want to add it to this list of top-priority folders. Double-click on a folder to open it. Once a folder is opened, you must click OK to add that folder to the list. If the folder you add contains subfolders, that folder and all of its subfolders come before the others.

Why does placing files at the beginning of the disk speed their access? The reason is that, as you know, every time a file is requested by you or one of your applications, the drive's read/write heads must travel back to the very beginning of the disk to read the FAT and determine where on the disk the file begins. Once the file's starting location has been found, the heads travel to that location. Even if the heads were already resting on the relevant file's starting location, they must still travel to the FAT and back before the file is actually accessed. Logically, the shorter the distance the drive heads have to travel to get back to the start of the file, the sooner they can begin doing the job you've asked of them.

The Files First tab has much the same sort of configuration as on the Folders tab. Here you can click on the Open Folder icon and specify individual files—files you often read from but rarely change, like program files or Windows support files and DLLs, for example—that you want placed at the beginning of the drive. You might also have a large read-only database file, say, another company's catalogue of special-order items—that you refer to often, but never change yourself, except when you replace the entire file with a new catalogue. You'll notice that Folders First has priority over Files First, so if you enable both options, your selected files are placed immediately after your folders.

The Files at End tab works in exactly the opposite way as the Files First tab, but for the same underlying reasons. These are the files that Speed Disk knows you very rarely access. Files that you almost never use are not files that need to be available at a microsecond's notice—if at all—and so Speed Disk sequesters them away where they won't hinder access to your important data.

The Files Last tab sounds like it should be the opposite of Files First, but it's actually quite different. Notice that Speed Disk has already entered a number of filenames—wildcards, mostly—into this list. Files in your Recycle Bin, your temporary Internet files, and so on, are accessed so regularly and changed so frequently that they are the most-commonly fragmented of files. At the same time, regular modification means that their severe fragmentation could be a real hindrance to your productivity. Speed Disk places these files immediately before your drive's free space, so that there is plenty of room for them to expand into and contract from, minimizing their tendency to fragment.

The Unmovables tab sounds like it should grant you access to some secret world of PC fortitude, but it simply enables you to specify files that you don't want Speed Disk to touch. There are quite a few reasons why you might add files to this category, although most of them are leftovers from a history that's happily behind us. Most commonly, files that need not be moved are files that are associated with vertical-market or copy-protected software. This is because one of the most common copy-protection schemes involved placing certain files in specific places on disk, or, at the least, recording where certain files were placed when the program was installed. Each time the program ran, it checked to verify that those files were in exactly the same location. If they weren't, the program assumed that you had copied the files from someone else's computer—stealing the software—and it would refuse to run. So, if you know that you have copy-protected software on your computer, it's probably a very good idea to specify that program's files here.

Caution: If you specify files in the Unmovables tab, then launch your copy-protected application and find that it no longer runs, it is likely you weren't aware of all of the files that it installed, and so didn't specify them all in the Unmovables list. There is no "undo" feature for Speed Disk, so here are some suggestions, none of them perfect:

- Contact the manufacturer of the software, explain to them the circumstances under which their software stopped working, and ask them for their recommendation. They should be able to verify that you are a valid owner of their product and be willing to speak to you somewhat candidly about their copy-protection.
- Uninstall and reinstall the software onto a different drive, and then do not use Speed Disk on that drive. (This option has serious limitations, and may be unsuccessful if, for example, the copy-protected program only places its special file(s) on your primary hard drive.)

Notice that, on the Unmovables tab, you can also specify that all files of certain types—Read-Only, Hidden, or System files—never be moved. These settings impact only the drive you have selected from the Optimization drop-down box, and are not global. By checking one or a combination of these file attributes, you can instruct Speed Disk to never move files for which those attributes are set. For example, checking Hidden and System guarantees that Speed Disk never moves any invisible system files on that drive.

All four of these file-related tabs—Files First, Files Last, Files at End, and Unmovables—support the use of filename wildcards. A brief review of wildcards is found in the technical sidebar, below. By using wildcards, you can easily specify, for example, that all files ending in a certain extension are globally treated in the manner you desire. You can also use wildcards, as you see Speed Disk has already done on the Files Last tab, to specify the treatment of all files within selected folders. In this manner, you can tell Speed Disk to always place My Documents in a particular location on disk, for example.

Filename wildcards have been with us since the earliest days of DOS. They allow the specification of a group of files with some common filename characteristics, like all files whose names begin with MIKE or all files with the extension, .DOC. Norton Speed Disk supports the use of two traditional DOS wildcards, plus one of its own.

The asterisk * wildcard is used to represent any number of characters, and can thus indicate that all files with any extension which also begin with MIKE (expressed as MIKE*.*), or all documents which begin with MIKE (expressed as MIKE*.DOC), or all JPEG image files (expressed as *.JPG), or all files in the active folder (expressed as *.*, meaning literally, any number of any characters, with any file extension of any length).

The question-mark ? wildcard is used to represent exactly one character. If you wanted to tell Speed Disk to never move any file with a special, two-character file extension, you would enter *.?? into Speed Disk's Unmovables tab. The presence of the two question marks tells Speed Disk that only two characters may appear after the file extension dot in the case of relevant files. So, Speed Disk would move MIKETODD.HEY, but would never move MIKETODD.YO or MIKE-TODD.HI. Similarly, you might save all of your marketing work with the beginning of MK, always followed by a six-digit date, such as MK980824.DOC. On the other hand, you might also save your novel about your cat's life with MK, followed by a one- or two-digit chapter number. The specification MK??????.DOC would tell Speed Disk how to handle only your marketing files. Files with names like MK01.DOC or MK329.DOC would not meet the requirement of exactly six characters.

Speed Disk also enables you to use the wildcard expression, **, which is not a conventional DOS-originated wildcard. To Speed Disk, however, this means that you wish to specify all files in the active folder, plus all subfolders and their contents, as well. For example, C:\DOCS** tells Speed Disk how to treat all files in the C:\DOCS folder, as well as all files in all subfolders of C:\DOCS.

The By Date tab eanbles you to instruct Speed Disk to relocate files based on time-related criteria. For example, you might want Speed Disk to place all files that you have used in the last week together at the beginning of the drive. By checking Sort files by last access date, and clicking the Week radio button, you've told Speed Disk that files should be in chronological order, and files which you've accessed in the last week should go first on the disk. (Unless, as you have read, you have already specified Folders First.) The settings on the By Date tab impact Speed Disk's analysis of what is a frequently and an infrequently used file. Selecting the proper radio button to group files by Quarter, for example, tells Speed Disk that any file which you have not used in the last three months qualifies as an infrequently used file, and is placed at the end of the drive.

Finally, the Sort Entries tab enables you to have Speed Disk resort the filename entries in each folder in the order you specify. This feature is of no use to Windows, but if you commonly shell out to DOS to use the DIR command, having Speed Disk sort filenames while it optimizes can free you from having to specify those annoying sorting command-line switches to the DIR command. (As you've already read, DIR displays filenames in the order in which they appear in the folder unless you tell it to behave otherwise.)

Having set the custom features to your liking, you can review the areas in which you have made changes by looking at the graphical display, as in Figure 17.12. Areas which are impacted by your specifications are highlighted in color.

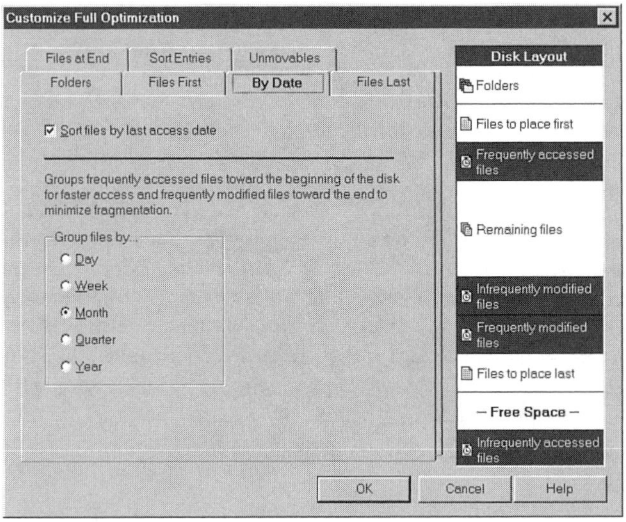

Figure 17.12

Speed Disk's Customize Full Optimization dialog box enables you to significantly change how Speed Disk optimizes files, as shown here.

Appearance Settings

Once you have told Speed Disk precisely how you want it to go about the technical aspects of its operation, you can use the Appearance tab to tell it how you want it to look and, if you're so inclined, sound.

At the top of this tab is a setting which enables you to alter the appearance of Speed Disk's map. As you prefer, you can have Speed Disk show you blocks representing each cluster, as in Figure 17.13, or you can look not at individual clusters but file fragments, by selecting the Bar radio button. Looking at individual clusters with Speed Disk maximized can make it easier to accurately click on a section of the drive when you're interested in a Block Detail, which you read about earlier in this chapter. Looking at the map in bar mode can make it easier to not get vertigo from the display.

> **Note:** Unless your monitor is reasonably large and your resolution set reasonably high, you may not be able to see the difference between the Block and Bar settings on the Speed Disk map. Maximize the Speed Disk window to get the maximum benefit from changing the appearance of the map.

You can additionally instruct Disk Doctor to play a piece of music while it runs. Any MIDI or WAV file on any available drive can be selected from the standard Windows Open dialog box by clicking on the folder icon in this setting. Once a file is selected, you can listen to it to make sure it's the right file by clicking the speaker icon.

If you hate running Speed Disk in peace and quiet, be assured: If the music or sound you select plays for less time than it takes Speed Disk to optimize your drive, the file is played over and over until NDD is done. (Children quickly discover that a short WAV sound, like Windows' default "Ding," plays about a zillion times during one optimization.) If you're a parent or a teacher, you may want to be certain you know how to disable this option if someone else turns it on. As you would expect, unchecking the Play Music option disables the file selection and speaker buttons. The most-recently-used sound or music file remains chosen, however, ready to be enabled at a moment's notice, as in Figure 17.13. To clear the file selection box, check the Play Music box, select the name of the music file with the mouse, and press the Backspace key on your keyboard. Uncheck the Play Music box.

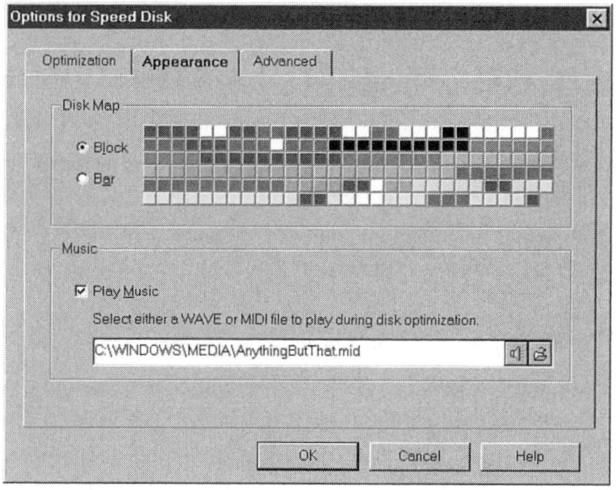

FIGURE 17.13
The Appearance Tab enables you to modify how Speed Disk's Disk Map looks and whether Speed Disk operates silently or with a musical background.

Advanced Settings

Compared to the custom settings for a full optimization, the options on the Advanced tab may not seem very advanced, but they control a vital aspect of how Speed Disk operates in the background. Since disk activity while Speed Disk is running could feasibly re-fragment part of the drive that Speed Disk has already optimized, Speed Disk restarts itself after any disk write occurs. You can see this happen if you watch Speed Disk's status bar closely. The words, "Write detected," briefly flash, and Speed Disk starts over, re-optimizing your folders. This is a key part of the technology used by Speed Disk to keep your data safe at all times during an optimization. Of course, all of that stopping and restarting can significantly impact the performance of your PC.

If you have Speed Disk minimized, you can use the settings on the Advanced tab to restrict Speed Disk from repeatedly restarting while you are typing or using the mouse in a foreground application. Not unlike a screen saver, you can tell Speed Disk that it should work on optimizing your drives only until it detects that another program has written to the drive. Rather than restarting, Speed Disk waits until after you haven't performed any foreground tasks—like typing a letter, or actively using any application, for that matter—for a specific period of time. When that time has passed, Speed Disk resumes the optimization. In this way, Speed Disk optimizes your drive as it can, while inconveniencing you as little as possible.

Additionally, you can enable Speed Disk's Watch Communications Ports feature, if you want Speed Disk to stop optimizing whenever your COM ports are in use. Speed Disk could cause incompatibilities with certain types of communication software if the software is trying to store incoming data to disk while Speed Disk is optimizing. Checking this box enables Speed Disk to stop when it detects a disk write, as normal, but prevents it from restarting until there is no COM port activity for the time period you specify. Speed Disk safeguards not only the data on your drive, but the data that is only just arriving.

Integration with SystemWorks

You've already read, above and in other chapters, some of the ways that the many components in Norton SystemWorks work together to maximize the reliability and performance of your PC. Norton Speed Disk is no different. It is integrated in ways enabling it to provide you with immediate solutions to errors, as well as enabling other parts of SystemWorks to call it into operation automatically on a needs basis.

Norton System Doctor

Speed Disk and Norton System Doctor work together through the Disk Optimization sensor, which you read about in detail in Chapter 3. This sensor watches your disks in the background, so long as System Doctor is running. It analyzes the level of fragmentation on each drive for which you have it enabled, and can alert you when any drive's percentage of fragmentation is greater than a limit which you set. If you activate Fix Automatically in the sensor's properties, the sensor displays the same options tabs for configuring Speed Disk which you've just read about. Set the configuration you want, click OK, and the sensor runs Speed Disk in the background whenever disk fragmentation is above your specified level. Automatic fixing disables the sensor's alarm feature; Speed Disk is merely run in minimized mode. An animated icon appears in your system tray, showing the work is in progress. Moving your mouse pointer over the tray icon displays the optimizing percentage complete. Double-clicking on the tray icon maximizes Speed Disk.

> **Caution:** When configured for automatic optimization, the settings you specify in the sensor's Speed Disk Options dialog box—accessed by clicking the Settings button next to Fix Automatically in the sensor's properties—override any other settings you have saved in Speed Disk for that drive. Before you enable automatic defragmenting, be certain you have specified the methodology you desire for the relevant drive!

Image

Image, which you read about in Chapter 10, "Norton Utilities: More Than a Mirror, an Image," is an integrated part of SystemWorks which stores an image, as you would expect, of your drives' FATs, boot records, and root directories. This file is used by several of the Norton SystemWorks recovery tools to repair a severely-damaged drive. Speed Disk instructs Image to take a new snapshot at the completion of every drive optimization, ensuring that your Image recovery data is always up-to-date.

Norton Disk Doctor

As you read about in Chapter 11, "Norton Utilities: The Disk Doctor Is In," Speed Disk automatically runs Disk Doctor whenever an error is encountered during a drive optimization. Disk Doctor analyzes the drive and repairs the damage before Speed Disk continues.

Norton SpeedStart

Norton SpeedStart is a small utility that works in the background under Windows 95 to optimize and accelerate your application launching. As you start each application for the first time after loading Norton SystemWorks, SpeedStart monitors the many tasks that must be performed to successfully load and run the program. It uses this information to optimize all future launches of that program—acceleration of up to 50 percent is not uncommon. The reasons why this is possible involve proprietary Norton technology, but the benefit to us as users is no secret.

SpeedStart provides maximum benefits when used in conjunction with Speed Disk and the Norton Optimization Wizard. Enabling NOW to resize, and Speed Disk to optimize your Windows swap file can dramatically reduce the amount of disk activity involved in launching apps. SpeedStart can make use of this optimized swap file in conjunction with its own acceleration technology, driving your PC to its maximum potential.

There is no need to do anything to launch SpeedStart or configure any settings with respect to it. If you enable SpeedStart to install with the rest of Norton SystemWorks, it is always present, working in the background (using only 60K of memory for itself).

SpeedStart is automatically disabled under Windows 98. The first time you reboot your PC into Windows 98 after installing Norton SystemWorks, you may see a dialog box like the one shown in Figure 17.14. This is because Speed Disk itself gathers all of the necessary application-launching data together and uses this to help determine how your applications and their support files are physically optimized on your drives.

Figure 17.14

SpeedStart is disabled under Windows 98.

Using Speed Disk to Enhance System Security: Wiping Free Space

Earlier in this chapter, you read about Speed Disk's two security features. One of these, Wipe Free Space, can indeed provide significant security benefits to you. These benefits do come with their own cost, however.

In Chapter 6, "Norton Utilities: Digging Through the Trash with Norton Protection," I explained that, when files are deleted from your disks, they are not, in fact, deleted. All that really happens is that Windows makes changes to the drive's FAT, indicating that the clusters used by that file are now available. Windows also changes the first letter of the deleted file's name to a question mark, but it is the changes to the cluster table which are of concern to us here. Once the cluster table entries are marked as available, the file's data remains as it ever was until another file is written over the deleted file's clusters. The implications of this are likely obvious to you. With the data still very much intact, anyone with sufficient UnErase technology could bring the file back from the grave, as it were. Additionally, even with no UnErase software, any simple disk editing tool would eanble someone to scan your disk and read any data that interests them. The costs of such espionage, to your business or your life, could be incalculable, depending, of course, on what data you place on your computer in the first place.

After optimizing your drive, Speed Disk can go a long way to foiling this kind of skullduggery by writing an endless string of zeros to every cluster of free space. Although the security standards of certain governmental agencies require free space be wiped several times, the single-pass wipe which Speed Disk performs effectively obliterates any data which was left behind from old files. Anyone using a disk editing tool would see nothing in your free space but the number zero, repeated enough to fill each cluster. No corporate plans, no personal finance data, no rendezvous appointments.

The cost to this, however, is that the writing of all those zeros makes retrieving the file through an UnErase process, like Norton Protection, impossible. The UnErase program may be able to locate the deleted filename—although this itself is unlikely once Speed Disk has finished with the drive—but none of the data remains to be retrieved. If you're a company spy, this is bad news because there's nothing for you to get your hands on. If you're the PC's owner with a file you validly want to UnErase, this is a tragedy. Once you run Speed Disk with free space wiping, any deleted files are gone.

Unless, of course—you knew there would be a saving grace—Norton Protection is enabled and the deleted file is still under NP's care. Running with its default settings, Norton Protection actually moves deleted files to a hidden area on the disk and keeps them there for seven days. Files older than seven days—or whatever other number of days you select—are automatically deleted. Files are also automatically deleted from NP's hidden area if the drive runs out of free space. Speed Disk optimizes the files under Norton Protection's care just like any other files on disk. They are hidden, but they are still very much present. If you have Speed Disk wipe free space, files in the hidden NP area remain intact. Only by emptying the Norton Protection area first and then running Speed Disk with "Wipe Free Space" enabled do you truly obliterate all of your deleted data. Working together, Norton Protection and Speed Disk can provide maximum security for your data, whether it's deleted or not.

PETER'S PRINCIPLE

Optimal Optimizing

No matter which processor you select for your PC, or how much memory you install, no one I've ever met has ever owned a sufficiently-fast computer. Of course, this is a people problem, not a technical problem per se, but there are a number of technical things you can do to squeeze the very last bit of performance from your hardware. One of the best of these is keeping your files, especially your Windows swap file, optimized.

Like any tool, however, Speed Disk is only useful when it's used, and it's only really useful when it's used regularly. The optimization scheme I recommend is really straightforward, and my experience is that it works very well. First, make certain that you keep Norton System Doctor running whenever you're using your PC. As you know, you can minimize it if you don't want to have the panel open on your desktop. Second, enable a Drive Optimization sensor for each drive on your computer. If you have an unusually large number of drives, be certain that the sensor is enabled for your C: drive as well as any other drive on which your Windows swap file might be located. The default fragmentation level (usually around 92 percent, depending on your drive) is a very reasonable setting. You can increase or decrease this to fit your desires, but setting the sensor too low runs Speed Disk so infrequently that you might as well just disable the sensor entirely. I also recommend that you configure the sensor to run Speed Disk automatically, performing full optimizations. This minimizes distractions to you, since Speed Disk runs in the background in lieu of the sensor's

continues

alarm going off. This also enables optimization to occur on a truly as-needed basis. (You can also set the sensor to optimize the disk only at times when you know you won't be working.)

Finally, I would suggest you explore the results of instructing Speed Disk to place all of your application and application-support files at the beginning of your disk. You can do this from the Files First tab under customizing a full optimization. The simplest way to do this is to enter *.EXE and *.DLL in the Files First tab. With your application-related files as close to the FAT as possible, and as close to each other as possible, you can really diminish the time you spend watching the hourglass.

Norton Utilities: More Room for Your Stuff—Norton CleanSweep, Space Wizard, and WipeInfo

Norton SystemWorks 2.0 comes with two powerful tools you can use to keep all your hard drives properly managed and free from useless files. Unfortunately, filling your drives up with useless files is easier than it ever was in the past. When you connect to the Internet—particularly the World Wide Web—data is downloaded to your PC and stored in your Internet cache for every page you view. This can be useful if you're going to be revisiting those same pages again; your browser can quickly download the page contents from your hard drive, rather than pulling it all off the Web again. On the other hand, if you're not revisiting pages often, these files just proliferate in your cache as your free space dwindles. Applications, too, are notorious for spreading their files all over your drives and filling your Windows Registry with entries. When you uninstall an application, all the files are supposed to get removed, but you probably already know that doesn't always happen. Furthermore, as you use applications, many of them create temporary files. These files are supposed to get deleted when you exit the program. But if the program or Windows crashes, those temporary files stay on your drives (and all programs aren't as good about deleting temporary files as they should be, even when no crash has occurred).

In this chapter, we'll look at two SystemWorks components—Norton CleanSweep and the Space Wizard—to see how they can be used to make more room for your stuff. Finally, at the end of this chapter, Peter Norton talks about WipeInfo, a small utility that provides security for your deleted files.

Norton CleanSweep Integrator

Norton CleanSweep is one of the new components of SystemWorks, added to the release of version 2.0. In fact, Norton CleanSweep is much more than one utility; it's an entire sub-suite of utilities designed to help you keep your hard disks organized, and to maintain and regain free drive space.

Because CleanSweep has been carefully arranged into a set of wizards accessed through a tab-based integrator, we'll take a look at these wizards in order. This will make it easy for you to follow along online as you read, if you so choose.

Norton CleanSweep can be launched from the SystemWorks Integrator by clicking its name in the left-hand panel. You can also open it from the Start menu by selecting Programs | Norton CleanSweep | Norton CleanSweep. Once launched, you'll see the CleanSweep Integrator, shown in Figure 18.1. The Integrator consists of seven standard Windows tabs through which all CleanSweep features are available. These tabs, labeled Program, Cleanup, Internet Sweep, Restore, View, Registry, and Options, keep CleanSweep's many functions organized in a logical manner. We'll look at each in turn.

FIGURE 18.1

Norton CleanSweep Integrator provides quick access to every CleanSweep function.

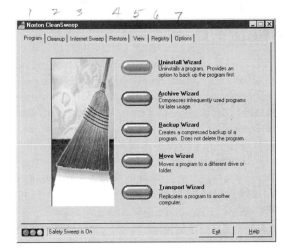

The first time you run Norton CleanSweep, you are told that it needs to rebuild its database. This is a collection of data regarding the programs on your PC which CleanSweep will maintain and use to provide you with better drive cleaning down the road. If you don't let CleanSweep perform this first-run database function, the program quits, advising you that the database must be rebuilt before you can do anything else. So just click Yes, and we'll move on to exploring Norton CleanSweep in depth.

CleanSweep Programs Tab

Much of the time when you use Norton CleanSweep, you'll be working with the Program tab. Here you'll find the five major CleanSweep utilities that do the major work of removing applications you're no longer using. If you've ever uninstalled a program, you know that most of the time, even professional uninstallation tools don't usually remove all the files and support documents that are associated with the program you're removing. And what good does that do you? You hardly need to keep a bunch of dedicated support files around if you've deleted the only program that uses them.

Additionally, the capabilities of uninstallers are limited. For the most part, they just uninstall. What should you do, then, if you need hard disk space but aren't absolutely sure you'll never use a program again—that is, you aren't sure you want to delete it forever? What should you do if you need space on a specific drive, you have plenty of space on another drive, but the full drive contains mostly huge applications. You're not using a Macintosh, so you know you can't just easily move a program from one drive to another and expect it to work; or can you? Finally, what should you do if you're switching over to a new computer and you can't reinstall some of your programs because your dog ate the CD-ROMs, or something? The CleanSweep Program tab has tools to cover you in each of these cases.

Uninstall Wizard

The Uninstall Wizard can quickly step you through the process of removing an application completely from your hard drives. When you want to regain hard disk space and you know you'll never want to use certain programs again—or you know that you'll be willing to reinstall them if you ever change your mind—then the Uninstall Wizard is the tool for you. To start the wizard, just click the silver button next to its name in the Norton CleanSweep Integrator.

When the wizard opens, as in Figure 18.2, you are asked to locate the program you want to uninstall.

FIGURE 18.2

The Uninstall Wizard opens to allow you to remove entire applications. Here, you're asked to locate the short-cut to the pro-gram you want to uninstall.

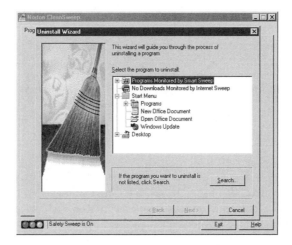

Notice at the top of the window are two entries, Programs Monitored by Smart Sweep and No Downloads Monitored by Internet Sweep. We'll look at these two special entries later when we cover Smart Sweep and Internet Sweep. (And, of course, if programs or downloads have been monitored, this screen won't say "no.") For now, just notice that what follows beneath them is a standard listing of your Start Menu, followed by an entry for your desktop.

The standard way to tell the Uninstall Wizard which application you want to remove is to select it from here. You navigate into your Start menu (or display the contents of your desktop, if you have it cluttered with shortcuts to your most frequently used programs) and you click the shortcut to the relevant program. If you want to remove a program or application which does not have an entry in your Start menu (or a shortcut on your desktop), you can click the Search button at the right of the window. The Uninstall Wizard performs a search of your drive(s), similar to what you see in Figure 18.3.

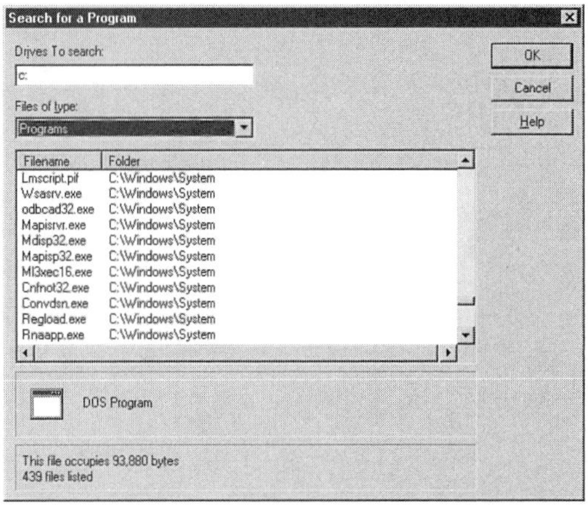

FIGURE 18.3

The Uninstall Wizard searches your drives for programs.

Note: This search window can search for all programs (including files with COM, EXE, BAT, CMD, and PIF extensions), Windows programs only, DOS programs only, or Dynamic Link Libraries (DLLs) only. Just choose the option you need from the Files of Type drop-down list near the upper-left of the dialog box.

From here, if not from the previous screen in the wizard, you can select the program you want to delete.

After you've selected the application you're going to remove, the wizard analyzes it, looking for all the files that are related to it. If you have selected a complex application, this analysis process can take several minutes, even on a fast computer. After the analysis has begun, there is no way to stop it in progress.

When the analysis has finished, the wizard asks if you want to back up the program you're deleting. This means that a compressed copy of the software will be stored in a location you choose so that you can quickly restore it, should you decide to do so in the future. Backing up is highly recommended, unless you're certain that you'll never be using the program again. If you instruct the wizard to make a backup, it prompts you to specify a backup location.

With a backup location selected, you can choose whether you want to confirm the deletion of each item or not. In this case, an "item" refers to a single file or Registry entry. Keep in mind that for any given application there could be well over a hundred files and entries involved. That's a lot of clicking Yes buttons over and over to confirm the removal of each. By default, the Uninstall Wizard assumes you don't need to confirm each item's deletion, but you can click the Yes option button for if you want to do so.

> **Note:** If you have CleanSweep's Safety Sweep feature enabled, you will not be asked if you want to make a backup. A backup is always created. You'll learn how to change this setting later in the chapter.

Finally, the Uninstall Wizard gives you the opportunity to review the files that have been selected for removal. A sample review screen is shown in Figure 18.4.

Figure 18.4

The Uninstall Wizard allows you to review, alter, or even run files that have been selected for deletion before any changes are actually made to your drives.

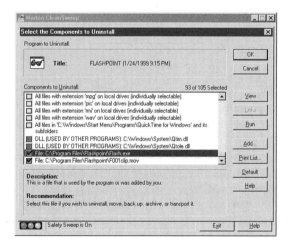

> **Caution:** It's always a good idea to review the files that CleanSweep has selected for removal. Programs sometimes include external links to files that are used by several other programs (programs you aren't uninstalling) and on occasion, CleanSweep may include these files for removal.

Files to be deleted are shown with a check mark in the left-most column next to their category. Whenever a single file is named in this list, you can click the View button to see its contents before proceeding. Selecting the "Main Program File" line in this list activates the Link button. Click Link and you are shown other programs that use this file, if any, and other files that are used by this program (DLLs, for example). To delete files or configuration entries that you know are associated with the program that is to be deleted, just click the Add button. You'll be able to browse and select files or specify the section in your WIN.INI file which you want included in this removal. The Print List button sends a complete file list to either your printer or a file on disk. Finally, the Default button undoes any changes you've made manually here. When all is well, click OK to return to the Uninstall Wizard, then click Finish to begin the removal.

> **Caution:** If you have Safety Sweep enabled, you may find that some files in the removal list are left unchecked and are marked with a Yellow square in the leftmost column. These are files that Safety Sweep does not feel are safe to delete—either because they are used by other programs or because they were created after Safety Sweep finished monitoring a program's installation (more on this later). You cannot force the Uninstall Wizard to remove files that are flagged yellow. This is to protect you from deleting files that could cause other applications—or Windows itself—to fail. You'll learn how to change the Safety Sweep setting later in this chapter. Incidentally, occasionally a file will be coded blue—this means that CleanSweep is not able to analyze and assign a safety level to the file, for whatever reason. Blue coded files—like red files—can never be removed through CleanSweep.

When the deletion and backup is complete, the Uninstall Wizard gives you the option of viewing or printing a summary, or simply exiting. Exiting returns you to the Norton CleanSweep Integrator.

Archive Wizard

After you know how to work with the Uninstall Wizard, you know most of what you need to use the four other Program tab wizards as well. Indeed, the Archive Wizard and the Uninstall Wizard perform precisely the same task, except that the Archive Wizard assumes you want to make a backup (that is, an archive) of the program you're uninstalling, whereas the Uninstall Wizard gives you the option of backing up or not. Both remove the application from its installed location. If you want to create a compressed backup of an application but do not want to uninstall it, you should use the Backup Wizard, which you'll read about next.

> **Note:** With Safety Sweep enabled, the Uninstall Wizard always creates a backup.

Backup Wizard

The Backup Wizard uses the same interface you've already seen with respect to the Uninstall and Archive Wizards. In all respects except one, its function is the same, but it's

this one difference that makes all the difference. The Backup Wizard doesn't delete anything. Instead, it gathers together all the selected program's files and configuration settings and creates a compressed backup of these. You can then move this all-in-one backup file to another drive or store it on a backup tape. If you ever have difficulties with corrupted program files—perhaps from a software upgrade that doesn't work or doesn't finish properly—you can restore this backup and have your program is working perfectly
again in much less time than it would have taken you to reinstall. Additionally, because
the Backup Wizard includes all your personal customizations and configuration options
in the backup file, the restored program will work precisely as you want it to work, not
the way it works when it's installed from scratch.

> **Caution:** You should not use the Backup Wizard to create compressed versions
> of applications for restoring to another PC. Backups created by the Backup
> Wizard (or the Uninstall or Archive Wizard, for that matter) should be restored
> only to the PC from which they were originally made. Doing otherwise could
> render the application—or even Windows—unusable. To move a program from
> one drive to another or from one PC to another, use the Move or Transport
> Wizard, respectively. You'll read about them next.

Move Wizard

What could be more frustrating? You've got gigabytes to spare on your D: drive, but the
application you're installing insists it needs a few gigabytes free on your C: drive and
only your C: drive. What to do? Simple. Move some installed applications from C: to D:
until you have enough space. "Yes, simple. Right." you say. But despite Windows'
deserved reputation as being unfriendly to program relocation, the Move Wizard makes
moving applications a breeze.

Here's the inside story: When you install an application, the support files it uses are
stored in a variety of places on your disks. Library files like DLLs might be stored in
your C:\Windows\System directory, other support files might be placed in C:\Program
Files\SomeMaker\Shared, and still others in C:\Program Files\Program Name\, and so
on. The locations of all these files are usually hard-wired, that is, fixed. So long as the
files are where they are installed, everything works. If files are missing or moved—
sometimes if even one file out of fifty is missing—the entire application might refuse to
launch, or might crash on you unexpectedly, endangering your work and your blood
pressure.

Although it's true that these file locations—we'll call them *associations*—are fixed,
they're not fixed in stone. With the right technical know-how, they can be changed.
Unfortunately, doing this by hand would age most of us unduly; missing even one association could still be disastrous.

The Norton Move Wizard takes care of these problems for you. Select the program you want to move, select the location to which you want it moved, and it moves. The Move Wizard interface is fundamentally the same as the Uninstall, Archive, and Backup Wizards. The only real difference is shown in Figure 18.5, where you see the Move Wizard asking for the location to which the program should be relocated. You can type in a full path here, or you can click the button at the right of the text box—it has an ellipsis on it—and browse your disks to the new location. If you specify a folder that doesn't yet exist, the wizard asks you to verify that you want it created before changes are made to your drives.

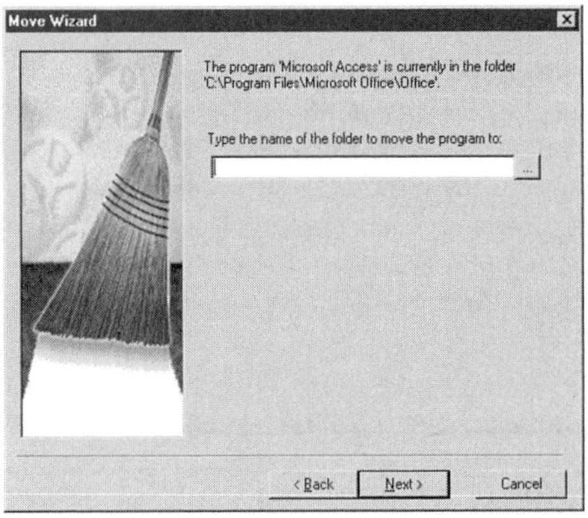

FIGURE 18.5

The Move Wizard prompts you to enter a location to which the selected program will be moved.

The Move Wizard relocates all the program files to the location you select, and it updates all the program's existing associations so that you'll be able to run the application from its new location, just as if it had originally been installed there.

Transport Wizard

What the Move Wizard does for moving applications between folders or drives, the Transport Wizard does for moving applications between PCs. The Transport Wizard enables you to remove an entire application from one PC, store all its files and configuration settings in a special, compressed file, and then expand that file on another PC. You can store the compressed transport file on floppy disks (the Transport Wizard prompts you for multiple disks, as needed) or to any other kind of drive, including removable and network drives.

As with all of the previous wizards, the program is analyzed and then sent to the location you've selected. Be aware that the Transport Wizard deletes the program from its original location. You can either physically take the media containing the transport file to the new PC or, if you've stored the transport file on a network server, you can access the server from the new PC. Run Norton CleanSweep on the new PC, and use the Restore Wizard (which you'll read about later in this chapter) to expand the transport file back into a usable program.

> **Caution:** As I mentioned previously, transport files created by the Transport
> Wizard are designed to be expanded and installed onto a PC other than the one
> from which they were originally created. Backups or archives created by those
> wizards should only be restored to their original PC and, ideally, to their original
> locations on that PC.

CleanSweep Cleanup Tab

The second of the CleanSweep Integrator tabs, Cleanup, provides access to five utilities
that can quickly remove unnecessary files from your PC. These utilities differ from those
found on the Program tab in that the purpose here is to work with individual files—or
types of files—to free hard disk space. If you want to remove whole applications at once,
use the Program tab utilities.

Duplicate File Finder

The Duplicate File Finder is a spiffy tool that does exactly what its name says: It searches your PC for duplicate copies of files. The Duplicate File Finder interface, shown in
Figure 18.6, automatically opens to display files on your drives that have the same name
and size. Thus, in this mode, two files named PICTURE.JPG which are both 64KB are
considered possible duplicates, but two files named IMAGE.JPG which are of different
sizes are not considered duplicates.

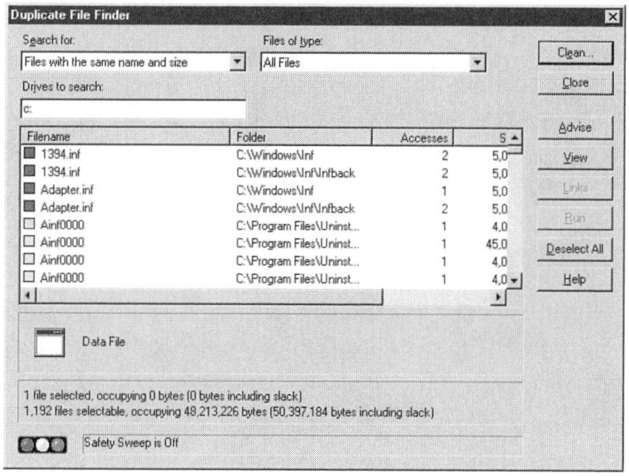

FIGURE 18.6

*The Duplicate File
Finder defaults to
a display of files
that have the
same name and
size.*

To change the criteria by which files are suspected of being duplicates, use your mouse
to open the Search For menu in the upper-left corner of the window. Here you can
instruct the file finder to use one of these rules for determining if files are duplicates:

- Files have the same name
- Files have the same name and size
- Files have the same name, size, date, and time

Changing the selection rule in the Search For box automatically causes the File Finder to re-scan your drives.

To search for drives other than those being used by default, click in the Drives to Search box, just under the Search For menu. A small window opens in which you can check the drives you want to include and uncheck those you want to exclude.

The Files of Type list enables you to specify whether you want to search for Programs, Dynamic Link Library files, or a custom file type that you can manually enter.

The large panel in the middle of the window displays files that the File Finder thinks are likely duplicates. Files are color-coded in the left-most column: Green files can always be safely removed without causing problems to your system; yellow files may be in use by one or more programs; red files are vital to your system and, even if they are duplicates, cannot be deleted. (If Safety Sweep is on, yellow-coded files cannot be deleted either, and blue files can never be deleted). Use your mouse to scroll down the list of probable duplicates, and click in the left-most column to place a check next to those you want removed. You may remove all copies of a duplicate file, but be certain that's what you want to do before you do it.

If you're uncertain whether you want to remove a file, two tools are available to help. First, with the file selected, click the Advise button at the right-hand side of the window. CleanSweep opens a display showing you vital statistics about the selected file. Information such as when the file was last changed, when it was last accessed, and so forth may help you determine which of two or more files should be saved and which are unused duplicates. Your second tool here is the View button. With a file selected, clicking View launches the Windows QuickViewer, enabling you to view the file contents. If no QuickViewer is installed for the type of file you've selected, you may try using the default viewers. If you don't have Windows QuickView installed (it's part of Windows, but it is an optional part), you can't use the View feature. Selecting an application file-name in the list enables the Links and Run buttons. Click Links to see a list of any programs that use this file, or any files that are used by this program. Click Run to launch the selected program. The Duplicate File Finder continues running the background.

With the duplicates you want to remove selected, click the Clean button at the top-right of the Window. The screen shown in Figure 18.7 opens, presenting you with options essentially like those you have already seen on the main Program tab of the CleanSweep Integrator.

You can delete the duplicates. You can delete and archive them. You can back them up without deleting them. You can move them to another folder or drive. You can create a transport file and transport them to another PC entirely. Each of these options works like its Program-tab namesake. Follow the instructions onscreen and click Finish when you're done. This returns you to the CleanSweep Integrator.

Figure 18.7
You can work with duplicate files in any of these ways— reminiscent of the Program tab in the CleanSweep Integrator.

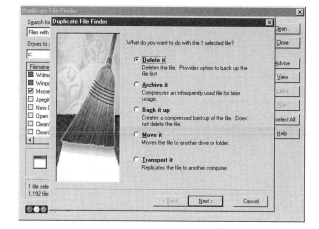

2B **Redundant DLL Finder**

This specialized tool looks for duplicate DLL and VBX files on the drives you select. Its interface is essentially the same as that of the Duplicate File Finder, except that, because you're not looking for programs, the Run button is absent here. Unlike the Duplicate File Finder, the redundant DLL Finder checks the version numbers of files it suspects to be duplicates. This technique is far more accurate than relying on filenames or dates. You might have two copies of D3X.DLL on your PC, both with the same date, but one might be version 1.0 and one might be version 6.3. The DLL Finder displays this version information in its central window so that you can make more informed decisions about which files are actually duplicates. The Redundant DLL Finder also automatically selects files for action that it knows to be duplicates that are safe to remove. You can, of course, always click and uncheck these preselected files. Again, when you click Clean, you are given the standard five options for how to deal with the files you've selected. When the process is complete, you are returned to the CleanSweep Integrator.

2C **Unused File Type Finder**

The Unused File Type Finder, shown in Figure 18.8, searches your drives for files of types that are commonly removable. This is a rather extensive list of file types, all of which are displayed in the drop-down menu at the top-left of the window. Here, too, you can see how many of each type of file have been found, the amount of disk space they are using (this is also the amount of space you'll regain if you delete all files of this type) and the safety levels associated with the found files. As you've read, green files are not vital to the working of your programs or Windows. Although these may contain your important data, they can otherwise be removed without causing applications or Windows to crash. Yellow files are known to be associated with at least one application. Red files are vital to Windows and cannot be removed.

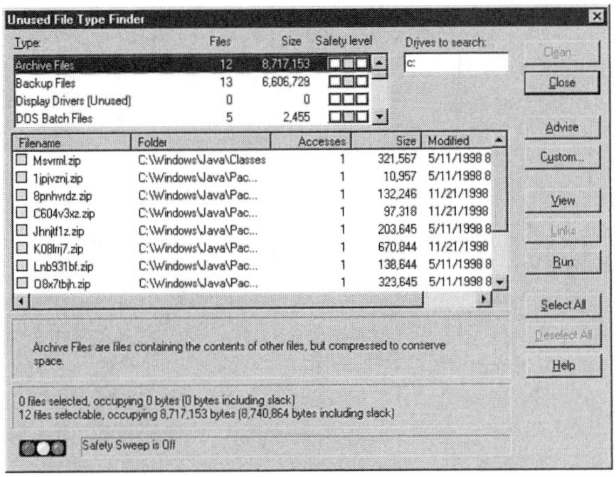

FIGURE 18.8

*The Unused File
Type Finder
searches your dri-
ves for files that
are commonly—
though not
always—unused
and taking up
space on your
drives.*

As you look through this list of commonly unused files, do so carefully. Included here
are all the ZIP files, multimedia files (pictures, sounds, and movies), DOS batch files,
and text files on every drive you've selected for searching. All of them. No files are automatically selected for deletion here, but you'll nevertheless want to work with this list
carefully. If there are files of a type that are not automatically gathered here that you
want to include, click the Custom button at the right of the window to enter new file
types for searching. As with the Duplicate File Finder, you can obtain advice on files,
you can view or run files, as applicable, and you can see the associations that exist
between program files in the list and other files on your drives. Click in the left-most column to select or deselect files for action, then click Clean to see the standard five action
options. I personally recommend that you not delete files when you're working with this
finder. It's a bit too easy to include, for example, a Help file which, unbeknownst to you,
your favorite game won't run without.

To see the possibly unused files of each type, scroll through the Type list in the upper-left
corner of the window and click to select the file type you want displayed below. In this
way, you don't have a list of potentially thousands of files through which you need to
search. You can focus on only those types of files you want to remove. Thus, for example, if you know you don't want to ever delete ZIP archives, you need not pay attention
to the files listed under that type.

Select the files on which you want to act as in the other finders, then click Clean and
choose your action type. When the process is complete, you are returned to the
CleanSweep Integrator.

Low File Usage Finder

If caution was advised when using the Unused File Type Finder, it's mandatory here. The
Low File Usage Finder searches your drives for files that haven't been accessed or
opened in some time. These can be files of any type. As with the Duplicate File Finder,

after the scan is complete, you can click the Files of Type drop-down list and specify that
you only want to see certain types of files included in the list, but All Files is the default.

> **Caution:** For the Low File Usage display to have any meaning, you need to
> understand that the Finder relies on your file usage database (that's the data-
> base that CleanSweep forced you to let it create the first time you ran the pro-
> gram) for information about when you last used files. For this database to be
> properly maintained, you must leave CleanSweep's Usage Watch feature
> enabled. (You'll read more about Usage Watch later in this chapter.) If you dis-
> able Usage Watch, your database won't be current, and this Finder's analysis of
> which files haven't been recently used will be inaccurate.

As with the other cleanup finders, you can view, run, or check links to any files listed in
the Finder window. When you click Clean, the five action options are displayed, and you
can dispose of the files you've selected.

Orphan Finder

The Orphan Finder is rather unique. Orphans are files that have been wrongfully left on
your drives when you uninstalled the programs that created them in the first place. In
other cases, orphans are files that exist on disk but have a length of zero—in other
words, they're empty. The Orphan Finder is a great way to get rid of all the shortcuts left
on your system when a program was uninstalled and didn't clean up after itself properly.

Here, as in the Unused File Type Finder, a scrollable list in the upper-left corner of the
window gives you organized access to the different types of possible orphans on your
drives. To see the files gathered under each orphan type, just click the name of the type
in this list. As in the other finders, select the files you want to act upon, click Clean,
select your action type, and you're done.

I strongly recommend archiving files you want to remove, rather than simply deleting
them. It's much easier to restore a file from a CleanSweep archive than it is to reinstall an
entire application because you deleted one file that turned out to be vital. This is especially true of files listed under the Orphaned DLLs type. Although it may seem to the Finder
that none of these DLLs are being used, that's because no programs have registered that
they are using them in the Windows Registry or other configuration files. So doing is considered good programming practice, but it's not ubiquitous. A DLL file that is not registered as the property of any applications may, nevertheless, be used by several.

Internet Sweep Tab

The CleanSweep Integrator's Internet Sweep tab gives you access to five tools that are
designed to get rid of useless files stored on your PC while you were working online.
You have already read in this chapter how some of these files find their way to your PC.

The World Wide Web, especially, is the primary culprit for storing thousands of files on your drives, and you may never use these files again! (Of course, alternatively, you may.) These Internet Sweep tools can help you delete Internet-related files that you know are just wasting space.

Internet Uninstall

The Internet Uninstall tool works, essentially, exactly like the Uninstall tool on the Program tab. As you've read, previously, you select the program you want to uninstall, determine whether you want to create a backup of the program or not, and let the uninstaller do its work. Like the Program tab's Uninstall Wizard, the Internet Uninstall Wizard can easily remove ActiveX files that have been downloaded to your PC and monitored by CleanSweep's Internet Sweep tool (which you'll learn about later in this chapter). For detailed instructions on using the Uninstaller, refer to the previous section entitled "Uninstall Wizard."

Internet Cache Cleanup

The Internet Cache Cleanup tool allows you to quickly throw away all the temporary files that are stored on your PC while you're browsing the World Wide Web. You might not know it, but every picture you view on every Web page you visit is actually stored on your hard drive. The same is true for every multimedia object (sound files, for example) and even the HTML code of the Web pages themselves. These files are stored on your drive—it's usually called storing them *locally*—because your hard drives work a lot faster than your modem. If you visit a Web page and then visit it again shortly thereafter, the page's contents can be loaded from your cache, rather than from the Internet. This dramatically increases the speed at which you can revisit pages and it also diminishes the bandwidth being used by the sum of all Web browsers.

If you don't periodically clean out your cache, however, it can waste a lot of drive space. The Internet Cache Cleanup tool zeros out the cache, throwing away all of its contents. You're not given the option of making a backup of the cache—in all truth, there is almost no situation in which you need to do this anyway. However, deleted cache files are stored under Norton Protection, if Norton Protection is enabled. (For more information on Norton Protection, refer to Chapter 6, "Norton Utilities: Digging Through the Trash with Norton Protection.")

The Internet Cache Cleanup tool couldn't be simpler. It analyses the size of your cache, and then displays the cache statistics for your review. A single Clean button enables you to delete the entire cache contents. If you browse the Web regularly, you should clean out your cache regularly as well.

TECHNICAL NOTE

You have total control over the maximum size to which your Internet cache can grow. You can set this size through your the Internet icon in the Control Panel window. Open your Control Panel by selecting Settings | Control Panel from your Start menu. Alternatively, if you have a shortcut for the Internet on your desktop, right-click it and select Properties.

When the Control Panel window opens, double-click the Internet icon. Windows maintains most of your Internet-related settings here. In this instance, we're interested in the Settings button within the Temporary Internet Files section in the middle of the tab. (If you don't see this section, make sure you are looking at the Control Panel's General tab.) Click Settings to display, among other settings, a sliding bar that lets you indicate the maximum size to which you want your cache to grow. After your cache reaches the size you select, the oldest files in it will be deleted to make room for new entries.

Slide the slider with your mouse to the maximum cache size you want, and then just click OK. Click OK again to close the Control Panel and you're done.

Cookie Cleanup

The Cookie Cleanup tool allows you to delete cookie files from your drives. *Cookies* are small files that Web sites store on your PC so, among other things, your identity can be remembered between visits to that page. For example, you might visit a page that greets you by name. It knows your name because, at some point, you visited the site, told it your name, perhaps through registering, and the site then stored your information on your PC in a cookie file. When you visit the site again, it looks on your drive to see if its cookie file is present. If it is, it can "remember" you and your preferences.

However, cookie files tend to proliferate too, and can eventually take up a sizable amount of drive space. There's no reason for you to retain cookies for Web sites you never intend to visit again, and so Cookie Cleanup lets you select and delete these files. (Cookies have special dispensation within your Internet Temporary Files folder and are not automatically deleted when you empty the cache.) The interface for this cleanup tool is essentially the same one you've been seeing through this chapter. You can review the URL that is associated with each cookie file on your PC. You'll find these listed in the URL column at the right of the main window. For those cookies you know you'll never need—or those you know you don't want saved—just click in the left-most column to select files and then click Clean. As elsewhere, you can click the Advise button and obtain more information about working with this type of file, or you can click View and view its contents directly. Unless you are unsure about whether you should keep a cookie file or not, there's rarely any reason to create a backup of those you select for deletion. Just zap em and get on with your life.

Plug-In Cleanup and ActiveX Cleanup

These two tools perform almost the same function and use an interface that is similar to the one you've been seeing throughout this chapter. These tools search your drives for plug-ins and ActiveX controls that were stored on your PC while you browsed the World Wide Web. Plug-ins and ActiveX controls are actually small Web-based programs that may perform a variety of tasks, from playing music or other sounds to maintaining a stock ticker onscreen while you chat online with your broker. (Incidentally, the Web-based chat feature is also probably a plug-in or an ActiveX control.)

These cleanup tools locate and list the plug-ins and ActiveX controls they find, and you can select and clean those files that you have no interest in keeping or using again. If you delete a plug-in and then visit a Web site that uses it, one of two things may happen. Depending on your Internet security settings (you can set these through your Internet Control Panel) the plug-in will either download and install itself automatically, or you may be asked if you want to download and install the plug-in. In either instance, there is little harm in deleting plug-ins or ActiveX controls, only to discover that you need them again. All you lose is a little downloading time. Of course, if you're thinking of deleting a large ActiveX control (or plug-in) you may want to Archive it, and save what could be a long re-download.

Restore Tab

The Restore tab in the CleanSweep Integrator enables you to perform one function: You can restore applications that you've either archived, backed-up, or transported. The Restore process is, basically, the reverse of the archiving or backup process. You locate the program you want to restore, select where you want it restored, and restore it. Let's see how it actually works.

Open the Restore Wizard by clicking its button on the Restore tab in the CleanSweep Integrator. Figure 18.9 shows you that the Restore Wizard always displays the most recently created backup or archive, asking you if this is what you want to restore. If it is, just leave the Yes option button selected and click Next to proceed. If this isn't what you want to restore, click the No, Let Me Select Another Item option button, and then click Next.

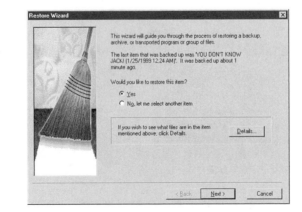

FIGURE 18.9

For convenience, the Restore Wizard always asks if you want to restore the application you most-recently archived.

Assuming you've selected No, the Restore Wizard scans your default backup folder and
presents you with a list of all archive, backup, or transport files found in that folder. (By
default, backups are stored in `C:\Program Files\Norton SystemWorks\Norton
CleanSweep\Backup\`). If the program you want to restore is in this list, just select it and
then click Next to continue. If it's not, or if you're transporting a program to a new PC,
you'll need to click the browse button at the bottom of the window, as shown in Figure
18.10, and select the location of the archive, backup, or transport file you want to use.

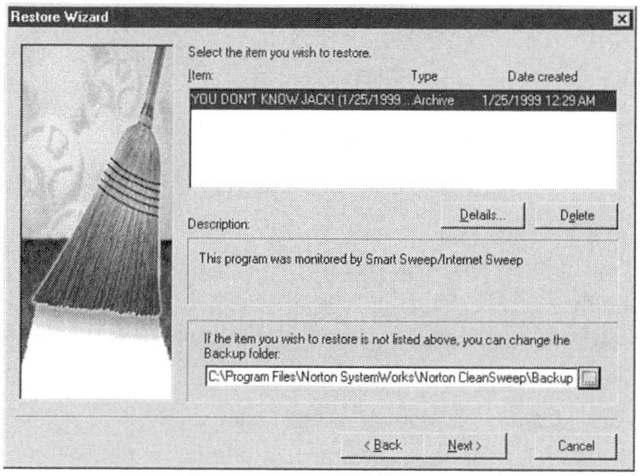

FIGURE 18.10

*If the program
you want to
restore isn't in this
list, click the
browse button—
it's labeled with
an ellipsis, near
the lower-right of
the window—and
navigate to where
the file is stored.*

Note: If you need more information about an archive, backup, or transport file
before you proceed with the restore, clicking the Details button displays the
contents of the selected file. (Incidentally, the only practical way to get more
information about backup or archive files is through this window. Files are
stored on disk with cryptic filenames that in no way reflect their contents.)

After you've successfully located the file you want to use for the restore process, the
wizard asks if you want to restore some or all of the files in the archive or backup. If this
is a program you're transporting to a new PC, you'll always want to restore all the files.
If you don't the application likely won't work. On the other hand, if you've deleted and
archived a selection of image files, you may only want to restore a selected image for a
specific purpose. If you click the Only the Files Selected Below option button as in
Figure 18.11, the list window will be enabled and you can click to remove check marks
from any files you don't want restored.

Tip: If you only want to restore one or two files from a large archive, click the
Deselect All button and then you only have to click once or twice to select the
files you want to use, rather than clicking hundreds of times to deselect the files
you don't.

FIGURE 18.11

You can restore all or only a selected few files from an archive, backup, or transport file.

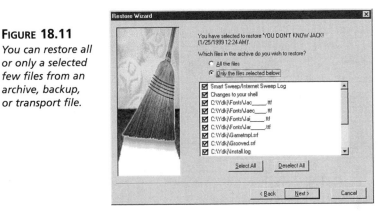

After selecting the files you want to restore, the Restore Wizard asks how you want to handle files that already exist on your drive but have the same name and location as some of the files in the archive, backup, or transport file. You have the options of overwriting only older files, overwriting all extant files, or not overwriting any files. You also have the option of confirming on a file-by-file basis each overwrite operation (assuming you haven't chosen to turn overwriting off, of course).

The Restore Wizard next asks whether you want files restored to their original locations or to new locations. In the case of a transport file, the wizard knows that you're not restoring to the original location, but it creates folders of the same names and in the same locations, as needed, so it can restore all files into locations that are similar to those from which they were originally transported. In general, it's always a good idea to restore files to their original location. However, you can tell the wizard No, in which case it asks you to specify both the folder to which you want files restored and, in the case of a program that you've archived or transported, the name of the group in the Start Menu in which you want the restored or transported program's shortcut placed. You can either type new data directly into the wizard, or you can click the browse buttons (labeled with ellipses) and select an existing location.

Finally, the Restore Wizard gives you one last chance to review what will be restored, and where, and how. To see this information, click the View button you'll see on the last panel of the wizard. Alternatively, if you don't need to review your choices, just click Finish to proceed with the restore.

When the restore process is complete, the wizard recommends that you delete the program's archive, backup, or transfer file. If you've only restored selected information, you'll probably want to ignore the wizard's recommendation and keep the archive. On the other hand, if you've just transported a program from one PC to another, delete the archive to regain the space on your transfer media.

Caution: It's a violation of Federal law to transport applications to more computers than the number for which you own end-user licenses. Please, don't steal software.

View Tab

The CleanSweep Integrator's View tab lets you review three different features of your PC. View Master Log allows you to see every function that has been performed by any part of CleanSweep. This list can be printed, or can be saved to a file for editing and printing later. View Savings opens a window in which is shown the cumulative amount of disk space regained by using the various CleanSweep tools. Disk space is broken out by tool, so you can see how much free space is the result of using the Uninstall Wizard, how much has been made available through your use of the Unused File Type Finder, and so on. You can also see the amount of drive space that is being used by all the backup or archive files you've created. Finally, View Folder Usage shows, as in Figure 18.12, the amount of space being used by each folder or subfolder on the drive you select. The View Folder Usage display also shows, in the right-most column, what percentage of files within each folder have actually ever been used. This information can be particularly useful if you're trying to determine what files you can delete or archive to obtain more free space.

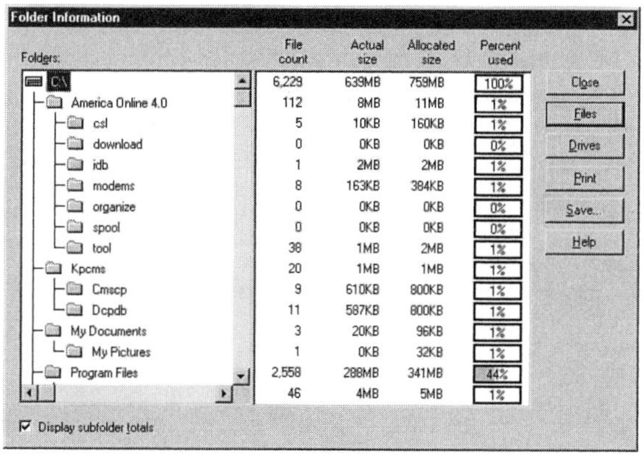

FIGURE 18.12

View Folder Usage graphically shows how much disk space, in megabytes, each folder takes.

Note: As with the Low File Usage Finder, the indication of what percentage of files in folders have been used is reliant on the continuous operation of CleanSweep's Usage Watch feature. If you turn Usage Watch off, it may erroneously appear that the files in a folder have not been used.

Registry Tab

The CleanSweep Integrator's Registry tab gives you access to two tools which can help keep your Registry neat and compact. Some of the functionality of these tools is duplicated by WinDoctor, one of the integrated utilities within the Norton Utilities, so you can choose the tool with the interface and feature-set you prefer. (You can read about WinDoctor in depth in Chapter 4, "Norton Utilities: The WinDoctor Is In.")

> **Caution:** Editing your Windows Registry is a job best left to power users and other experienced people. Errant changes you make to your Registry may cause applications—or indeed, Windows itself—to function improperly or not at all. Before you begin editing your Registry, be sure you're confident and comfortable with the task.

Registry Genie

The Registry Genie, shown in Figure 18.13, provides similar functionality to the Norton Registry Editor, which you read about in depth in Chapter 14, "Norton Utilities: Heroic Measures and Other Registry Editing." Both tools are provided within Norton SystemWorks so that users who are experienced with one or the other need not adjust their working methods or learn a different interface to perform the same tasks. Similarly, new users can review both utilities and decide in which environment they are more comfortable. Because their features and functions are so similar, I'll just discuss their differences here. For a detailed discussion of Registry Editing, in general, you can also refer to Chapter 14.

FIGURE 18.13

The CleanSweep Registry Genie looks at functions almost identically as the Norton Registry Editor.

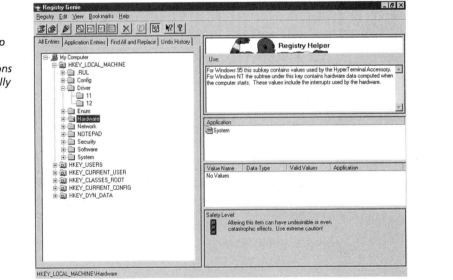

You can see in Figure 18.13 that the Registry Genie displays the contents of your
Windows Registry in the same hierarchical manner as does every other Registry-editing
tool available. However, the Registry Genie provides two areas of information which
may be useful to less-experienced Registry editors. (Nevertheless, Registry editing is a
task best left to experts).

First, in the upper-right corner of the window, you'll find the Use field. As you scroll or
click through the Registry's hierarchy, this field provides you with plain-English explanations of what the select key or value means. Users who are trying to learn more about the
Windows Registry may find these explanations useful. Of course, an explanation won't
be available for every key; many keys are dedicated to the specific software or hardware
which created them. However, you can still learn a lot about how your Registry works by
expanding the hierarchy in the left-hand panel and scrolling through it, reading the explanations that do exist.

Also helpful is the Safety Level panel, at the bottom-right of the window. This panel displays graphically and in text the degree of caution that should be used in modifying the
selected key or value. As in the case shown in Figure 18.13, modifications to certain keys
can have devastating effect on Windows or your installed applications.

Personally, I prefer Norton Registry Editor for my own work. It has a somewhat larger
feature set and I think experienced Registry editors will find that its interface is more
sophisticated and elegant than is CleanSweep's Registry Genie. Although the Norton
Registry Editor doesn't provide the key explanations that the Registry Genie does, an
argument can be made that you shouldn't be editing the Registry if you don't already
know what the keys you plan to edit actually do. Furthermore, despite what the Registry
Genie's Safety Level display may tell you, extreme caution should always be used when
you're editing your Windows Registry. Additionally, while the Registry Genie's Use
explanations may be useful to beginners, Registry Genie does not support a read-only
mode. This means that there's no way to protect yourself against accidental changes to
your Registry file from within the Registry Genie. Norton Registry Editor does provide
this protection.

Registry Sweep

CleanSweep's Registry Sweep is a much safer tool than is the Registry Genie. Of course,
it also provides functionality on a far more limited scale. Registry Sweep analyzes your
Windows Registry—a process that may take a few minutes—looking for Registry entries
that are invalid. The Search Results screen, shown in Figure 18.14, is, again, much the
same as the interface you've seen throughout this chapter.

This window shows all the invalid Registry entries that have been detected by Registry
Sweep. An invalid key refers to a file or program that is no longer present on disk. Some
keys will be labeled with red flags, indicating that although the keys are invalid, they are
still associated with installed applications. These keys cannot be deleted. Other invalid
keys may be checked for action and then cleaned up, just as can files using the cleanup

tools about which you've already read. When you are removing Registry entries, I strongly urge you to back up the keys you've selected. This way, you can restore any keys that prove themselves to be vital, however unlikely this may be.

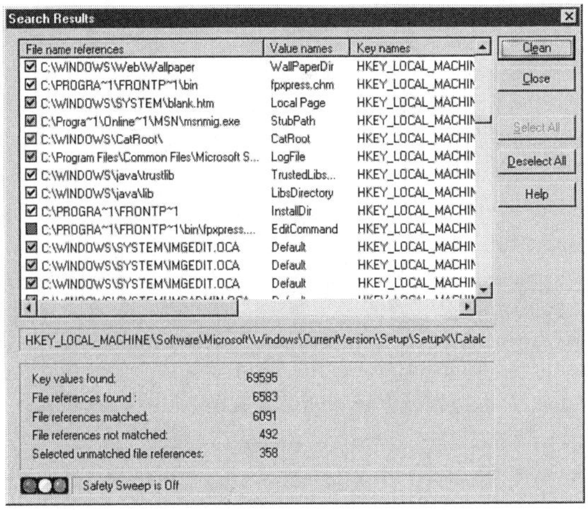

Figure 18.14
Registry Sweep displays the invalid Registry keys which it has found.

Note: Norton WinDoctor can also clean invalid entries from your Windows Registry, along with performing other functions that can increase the performance and reliability of your system. You can read about WinDoctor in Chapter 4.

Options Tab

The CleanSweep Integrator's Options tab lets you configure CleanSweep's operation and also lets you run LiveUpdate to look for new versions of CleanSweep on Symantec's server. You've already read, in Chapter 2, "Norton SystemWorks Integrator: Putting It Together," that SystemWorks 2.0 supports using LiveUpdate to find and install updates to all your SystemWorks components at once. For this reason, I suggest that you always use the LiveUpdate button within the SystemWorks Integrator when you want to run LiveUpdate. That said, you can always run LiveUpdate from here, within the CleanSweep Integrator, and update just CleanSweep if you so choose.

Options Tab: Usage Watch Tab

If you click the Configure CleanSweep button on the Options tab, you'll see the window shown in Figure 18.15. Here, CleanSweep options have been organized onto five standard Windows tabs through which you can control how CleanSweep works.

The first of these tabs controls the Usage Watch feature. Usage Watch is the tool that maintains CleanSweep's usage database—the table of files you've used since CleanSweep was installed. To get the most out of several of CleanSweep's utilities, Usage Watch should be left on, and set to load upon startup.

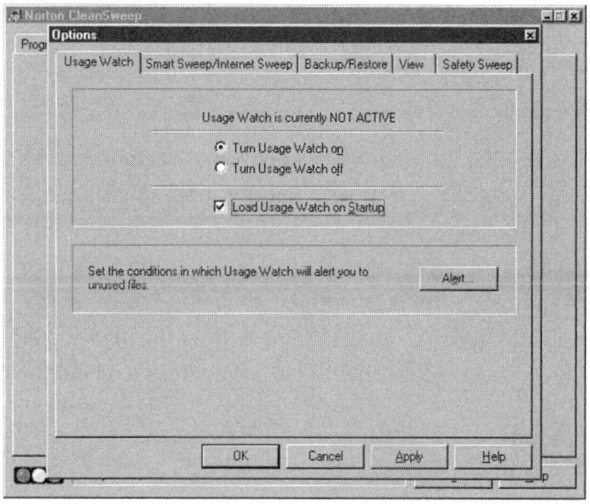

FIGURE 18.15

Usage Watch settings control whether file use is tracked by CleanSweep.

Usage Watch can also be configured to watch for files that have not been used for some period of time. To enable this feature, click the Alerts button shown on the window in Figure 18.15. The smaller Alert dialog box shown in Figure 18.16 opens.

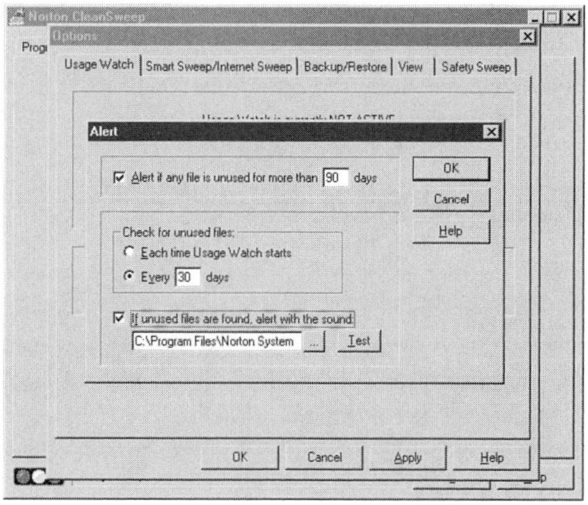

FIGURE 18.16

Usage Watch can alert you when files remain unused for some period of time.

Place a check mark in the Alert If Any File Is Unused for More Than *xx* Days box by clicking with your mouse. Then, set the number of days against which you want file usage compared. You can also specify whether you want file usage checked every time Usage Watch starts, or only after a period of time—which you can also set—passes. Finally, place a check mark in the If Unused Files Are Found, Alert with the Sound check box to help draw your attention to Usage Watch's warnings.

Why should you care if files remain unused? Well, if you're concerned about maximizing your free disk space, you may want to remove or archive files that you don't use very often (or at all). Usage Watch can automate the task of determining which files go unused, and, therefore, which files may be safely deleted.

Smart Sweep/Internet Sweep Tab

As you've read to this point in the chapter, you've encountered Smart Sweep and Internet Sweep already. Smart Sweep is the portion of CleanSweep that can monitor the installation of new software on your PC. When you monitor an installation, you guarantee that the program can later be completely uninstalled. Every change to your PC that is made by the installation software is recorded. When you run the Uninstall Wizard, all of these changes have to be undone—making a backup of the involved files, if you so choose—to return your PC to the condition it was in before you installed the new software.

Smart Sweep can also monitor changes made to your PC at any time. To enable this feature, just right-click the Smart Sweep icon in your system tray and select Start Logging from the pop-up menu. Until you right-click the Smart Sweep icon again and select Stop Logging from its context menu, every change made to your PC is recorded in a log file. The information in this file can be useful if you're trying to reproduce the conditions that cause a particular error, or if you want to monitor someone else who is using your PC.

Internet Sweep, as its name implies, performs a function similar to Smart Sweep, but with respect to the plug-ins and ActiveX controls which are downloaded to and installed on your PC while you browse the World Wide Web.

The Smart Sweep/Internet Sweep tab, shown in Figure 18.17, allows you to configure how and whether these two utilities are enabled.

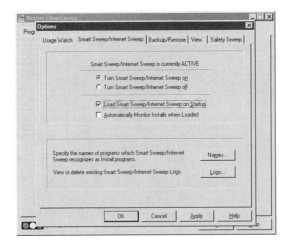

FIGURE 18.17

The Smart Sweep/Internet Sweep tab controls whether the installation of software on your PC is monitored or not.

Normally, either Sweep utility asks for your permission before it begins to monitor the installation of a piece of software. You can change this default and cause automatic monitoring to occur by checking the Automatically Monitor Installs when Loaded check box. You can also determine which programs Smart Sweep will recognize as installers by clicking the Names button. This opens a small dialog box to which you can Add and from which you can Delete the names that are commonly given to software installation programs. If these two "Sweepers" can't tell that a running program is an installer, they won't know that they should be monitoring its progress. For that reason, you should use care when deleting entries from this list.

Finally, you can click the Logs button to review or delete installations that you've previously monitored with either Smart Sweep or Internet Sweep. If you determine, for example, that you'll never want to remove a given installed program, you can delete it from this list. This, in turn, removes it from the various windows you've seen earlier in the chapter where programs monitored by either Sweep utility are displayed for uninstallation or archiving, and so on.

Backup/Restore Tab

From the Backup/Restore tab, you can change how all the CleanSweep tools work with backup files and how restores are performed. You can change the default backup folder to a new location and be alerted by CleanSweep whenever a backup has been around for longer than a period of time which you can select. (In this way, you can be reminded to delete backup files that you don't intend to ever use.)

The Backup/Restore tab also lets you determine whether the Uninstall Wizard will prompt you to confirm the deletion of each file and whether the Restore Wizard asks for your permission to overwrite existing files during a restore.

View Tab

The View tab lets you select the name and location of CleanSweep's default logging file.

Safety Sweep Tab

The Safety Sweep tab, shown in Figure 18.18, lets you select whether yellow-labeled files, identified as possibly safe to remove, can be selected for action in any of the CleanSweep utilities. If you leave Safety Sweep on, only green-labeled files can be deleted and both red- and yellow-labeled files cannot be removed. Additionally, if Safety Sweep is on, the Uninstall Wizard and the Archive Wizard perform precisely the same function because backups are mandatory within the Uninstall Wizard. By default, Safety Sweep is on.

Additionally, this tab allows you to choose whether CleanSweep performs a fast or a detailed analysis of your PC when you use any of the CleanSweep removal tools. With Fast Analysis off, CleanSweep takes longer to verify that all components of programs will be removed, even if a program's installation was not monitored by Smart Sweep. However, turning Fast Analysis off can be extremely useful. Here's an example: you install a program and track it with Smart Sweep. Later, you install an upgrade to that program. Finally, you want to uninstall that program. If you turn Fast Analysis off, CleanSweep re-analyzes the entire program, guaranteeing that everything—including the software update you installed—is properly removed.

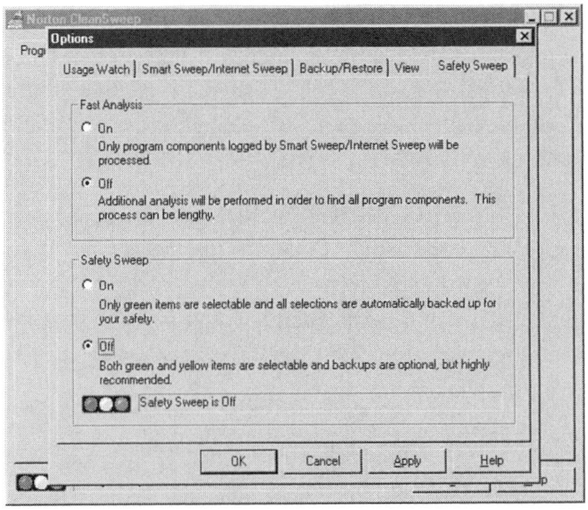

FIGURE **18.18**

The Safety Sweep tab controls whether yellow-labeled "possibly safe" files can be deleted or whether they are protected from deletion.

Norton CleanSweep is really a suite within a suite. It's a complete set of utilities dedicated to maximizing your free space and keeping your PC well-organized. Norton SystemWorks provides another tool which you may want to use to perform some of these functions. We'll look at it in the remainder of this chapter.

The Space Wizard

Norton Space Wizard is a Norton Utilities component that can help you retrieve valuable hard drive space from useless or antiquated files and applications. You can run the Space Wizard at any time you choose; you can also use the Disk Space sensor to integrate Space Wizard's functionality with Norton System Doctor, reminding you to run the Space Wizard when drive space drops below some minimal level that you set.

When run, the Space Wizard makes an analysis of the files on your drive, based on parameters that you can configure, as you'll read about later in this chapter. The Space Wizard then gives you the option of either deleting files that match your criteria, or compressing and archiving them so that they remain available but use less drive space. The Space Wizard comes preset with two distinct default criteria for opening free space. We'll look at the defaults before digging into how you can configure Space Wizard to work the way you want.

Performing an Express Search for More Free Space

Chances are good that, until you want to take the time to configure the Norton Space Wizard to your own working style and needs, you'll be using the Express Search method for locating files on your disks that could be safely erased to give you space. Performing an Express Search is the Space Wizard's default—when you run the utility, Express is

preselected for you on the wizard's first screen. You need only click Next to begin. In an
Express Search, the Space Wizard first scans the drive you've selected, checking for
errors or problems. This scan is something like a mini-Norton Disk Doctor scan,
although it verifies only the integrity of your File Allocation Table. If you suspect you
have any form of serious drive damage, always run Norton Disk Doctor before using
Space Wizard. If Space Wizard detects any FAT-related difficulties, it reports these and
gives you the option of repairing them by running Norton Disk Doctor from within the
Space Wizard. (Alternatively, you can quit the Space Wizard; it won't run on a drive with
an unrepaired FAT.)

After checking for any type of FAT-related problems, the Space Wizard Express Search
looks through your Recycle Bin, through Norton Protection, and through Windows folders that are common homes for temporary files. If there are files in your Recycle Bin,
you are prompted to delete them. Finally, Norton Space Wizard displays a results panel,
like the one shown in Figure 18.19.

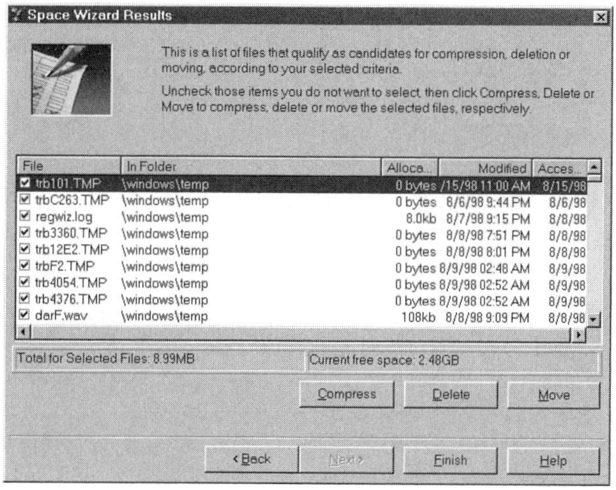

FIGURE 18.19

*The Space Wizard
Results dialog box
displays results
from an Express
Scan of a hard
drive.*

As you can see in the figure, the results panel is similar to many you'll encounter when
using the various Norton Utilities and Norton SystemWorks components. A pane at the
top displays a list of files that Space Wizard believes can be safely deleted. (In the case
of an Express Scan, these will be exclusively temporary files and files that have not been
emptied from the Recycle Bin.) This display is divided into five columns. As usual,
clicking the name of the column in its header sorts the display by that category. By
default, the display is sorted by the folders in which candidate files are found. This
enables you to quickly scan folder names and ignore files that exist in folders you may
may already know are removable. Space Wizard also defaults to enabling removal for all
files it locates in an Express Search. If you agree with Space Wizard's analysis, you
don't need to do anything additional before acting on that analysis. If you want to

exclude a file from any action, you can click its name, which automatically toggles the selection check mark. Click the file's name again to re-check it. The Space Wizard does not support either Ctrl+clicking or Shift+clicking; if you want to exclude multiple files for security you need to click each file.

Right-clicking in the results pane opens a context menu. From here, you can choose to select all files (this is the default selection, but you may have unselected several files and then changed your mind). You can also invert whatever is currently selected, making it unselected and making what is unselected selected again. Use this command to deselect all files in the default list. You can then go back and manually add the files upon which you want to act.

If you're uncertain about a file's contents, the context menu gives you access to your standard installed Windows 95 or Windows 98 Quick Viewers. Right-click a file's name and select Quick View from the context menu to rapidly check a file, verifying whether it is safe to delete.

> **Note:** In most cases, no default viewer is installed for viewing temporary files. Some of these files can't be read by the default text viewer. However, when Space Wizard asks if you want to try the default viewer, saying Yes may enable you to see at least some of the data contained in the file. If the file cannot be read by the default viewer, or if the file is an active temporary file—that is, a temporary file that is in use—Space Wizard displays an appropriate message to so advise you.

Below the files pane (refer to Figure 18.18), Space Wizard indicates the total size of the selected files. This is the amount of free space you will gain if you delete all the selected files. As you check and uncheck files in the results pane, this free space amount is updated to reflect your changes. To the right, you can see the total capacity of the drive that has been scanned. Beneath these two status displays, you'll find buttons that enable you to compress, delete, or move the selected files.

Compressing Files

Clicking the Compress button causes the Space Wizard to prompt you for a filename and a storage location. You'll see a standard Windows Save As dialog box, through which you can navigate to the location where you want the compressed files to be saved. By default, the Space Wizard opens your My Documents folder. After you enter the filename for your compressed files, the Space Wizard creates a standard-format ZIP file at the location you've selected and compresses all checked (selected) files into that ZIP file. When the ZIP file has been successfully created, the original files are deleted from your drive. If you are using Windows 98 configured to use Compressed Folders as the default handler for ZIP files, you can double-click these Space Wizard-created files to open them and work with them directly in the Explorer. If you are using Windows 95, or

Windows 98 without Compressed Folders active, you must obtain a program—many are available for downloading as shareware from the Internet or an online service—that enables you to open and manipulate ZIP files. (A simple file decompressor, SWUNZIP.EXE, was also installed in your Norton Utilities folder.)

> **Caution:** If you choose to compress files on a drive with little free space, the compression may fail. This is because, in order to compress a file, there must be room for the original file and the compressed file on disk, at least temporarily. When compressions fail, it can be exceedingly difficult to determine what portion was successful and what portion was unsuccessful. Save yourself an unnecessary call to technical support—when you compress files, compress them to a different drive than the original whenever possible. After they are compressed, move them back to the original drive if you desire.

Deleting Files

If you click the Delete button, the selected files are deleted from disk, except in one circumstance. If you have Norton Protection enabled, files you delete using the Space Wizard are under Norton Protection (unless they are on your Norton Protection exclusion list, in which case, they will not be protected). In this way, you can change your mind about a deletion, even after you exit the Space Wizard. To truly remove files and recover free space, you must empty the Norton Protected Recycle Bin or, at the least, open the Norton Protected Recycle Bin, right-click the filenames deleted by Space Wizard, and select Delete from the context menu. This removes the selected files from Norton Protection immediately, without requiring you to empty the entire bin. (Click the header of the Deleted By column to quickly locate files deleted by Space Wizard.)

Moving Files

If you want to neither compress nor delete the files that Norton Space Wizard has selected, you have the option of moving them to another location, thereby still regaining their space on their current drive. Click the Move button, and select the location where you want the files relocated. At the bottom of the screen from which you'll select a new file location, you'll see a Preserve Paths check box . If you check this box, each moved file's current path is recreated, starting with the destination folder you select. For example, let's say you choose to move a file with the current path C:\WINDOWS\TEMP\BU.TMP to your E: drive, placing it in a root-directory folder named BACKUP. With Preserve Paths checked, Space Wizard creates E:\BACKUP\WINDOWS\TEMP and places BU.TMP into it. In this way, that location has been preserved for you, should you ever need to move a file back to its original location. (Of course, all the folders leading to your moved files will be empty, unless other moved files fall into them.) If you do not select Preserve Paths, all files are moved to the folder and drive you select. After they're successfully stored in their new home, the originals are deleted.

As you perform any of the three actions, the Space Wizard result pane is updated, showing only those files on which you performed no action. If you want to leave these files as they are, click Finish to quit the Space Wizard.

Performing a Comprehensive Configured Search

As an alternative to an Express Search, Norton Space Wizard performs a comprehensive scan that looks for files that meet any criteria you specify. (To begin a comprehensive search, change the selected option on the Space Wizard's first screen from the default [Express] to Comprehensive. To continue, click Next.) As with an Express Search, the Space Wizard asks you to select the drive to be searched and then makes a preliminary check for FAT errors. Assuming no errors are found, the Comprehensive Search begins with folders with names such as TEMP, CACHE, or TEMPORARY and files with extensions such as TMP. Unlike an Express Search, which looks only through preselected temporary locations, the Comprehensive Search looks through your entire directory tree.

> **Caution:** If you have a folder in your My Documents folder (or anywhere else on disk called TEMP) into which you place valuable files that you want to assign permanent homes later, you should remember that Space Wizard includes all those files in a comprehensive search. If you don't want to have to manually deselect such files every time you use the Space Wizard, give your temporary file folders a different name, such as TO BE RELOCATED, or GOOD STUFF, and so on.

When the entire drive has been scanned, Speed Wizard displays the first of its Comprehensive Search results screens, which you can see in Figure 18.20.

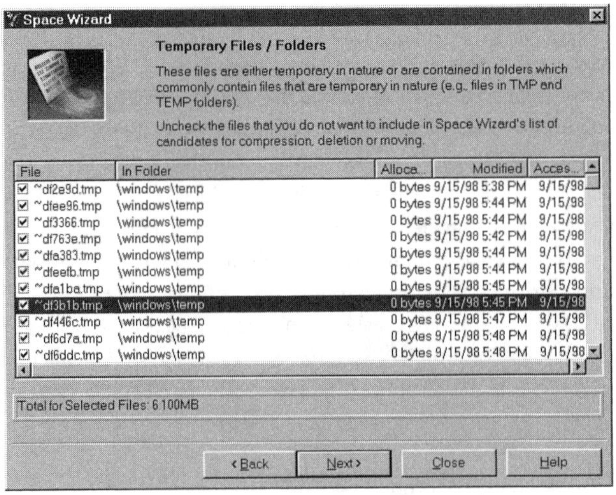

FIGURE 18.20
This dialog box displays the temporary files and folders located by a comprehensive search.

This panel looks much like the one displayed after an Express Search, except that the action buttons (Compress, Delete, and Move) are missing. A Comprehensive Search is an interactive, multistage process. After you select files upon which you want to act from Space Wizard's various context-oriented panels, you are given a final file list, on which you can selectively perform whatever actions you like. As with the Express Search panel, right-clicking opens a context menu from which you can select all files or invert the current selection. Also, as before, clicking a filename toggles its selection from on to off and back. The amount of free space to be regained by deleting these temporary files is shown to the left, beneath the results pane.

Commonly Removable Files and Folders

After you have selected the temporary files you think you want the Space Wizard to act upon, Space Wizard searches for what it calls "commonly discardable files and folders." These are files and folders that meet either the Space Wizard's default criteria or criteria that you specify. After files matching the default criteria have been selected and displayed, you can right-click the results pane, opening a context menu. This menu contains two items not found in menus you've seen earlier in this chapter: configure files and configure folders. Figure 18.21 shows the result of selecting either of those two items from the context menu. (The figure is a composite; you cannot configure both files and folders at the same moment.)

FIGURE 18.21
This composite image shows Space Wizard's method for configuring files and folders for selection.

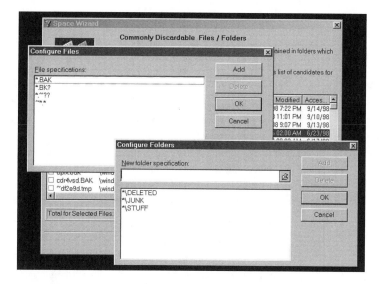

These two boxes work in the same way as others you've already encountered in this book. By selecting an entry in one of the panes and clicking Delete, you remove that criterion from Comprehensive Searches for removable files. By clicking Add, you'll be able to use the Configure Files pane to select any file type from the displayed list of registered file types, or you can use the Configure Folders pane to select folders. In the case of the

Configure Folders pane, the Add button does not become active until you have either typed in or, using the folder icon, navigated to the folder you want to add. After you've entered or located the folder, click Add to place it on the list. Notice in the Configure Folders pane that some folders have been entered using the somewhat unique `*\foldername` format. This format specifies that any folder with the name *foldername*, located anywhere on the drive (the asterisk represents any number of folders or subfolders) are included in the Comprehensive Search. If you want to select a specific folder, you can do so.

Unlike the Temporary Files results, the default for the Commonly Removable files results is to not act upon any of the files found. The reason for this is simple enough: Temporary files are, by definition, supposed to be removed by the applications that created them when those applications quit. If Space Wizard locates temporary files, they are usually orphans. Such files will never again be used automatically and can almost always be safely deleted.

On the other hand, just because a file has been placed in a "commonly removable" folder doesn't mean that you want it deleted, nor that every file of a commonly deletable file type will be one you want zapped. It's for this reason that the Comprehensive Search is configurable. The next time you run the search, your modifications will be preserved. If a large number of files are being selected for deletion and you know you would never want to get rid of them, you can change the criteria on which the Comprehensive Search works, making the process more efficient for all your later searches.

As you select files by clicking their names, the space indicator at the bottom of the panel increments, showing you the amount of space you'll regain if you delete all the selected files.

Unused Files

The next of the Space Wizard's Comprehensive Search panes prompts you to specify some period of time after which, if a file has not been accessed, it may be removed. You can select this time frame as a function of days, weeks, months, or years. Six months is the default. When you click Next, Space Wizard scans the drive for files that have neither been read nor written to since the period of time you selected. Another results panel is displayed, from which you can add files to Space Wizard's final results pane (the default is that files are unselected).

> **Caution:** Be advised that many vital system and application files may not have been accessed since the application—or, indeed, since Windows was installed. This doesn't necessarily mean that you won't ever need those files, although a file that hasn't even been accessed in several years is certainly a good candidate for deletion. Use caution when selecting old files in your Windows folder, and stay mindful of Norton Protection so that you can get the files back if you realize they are necessary.

Large Files

Space Wizard next prompts you to select some file size, over which you may want to consider whether a file is removable. Be careful! Space Wizard is intelligent enough to exclude application files themselves (EXE files, for example) from this list, but many applications—particularly high-end, graphics-editing applications—create and use support files that can be well over 2MB or even 10MB in length. High-quality sound (WAV) and video (AVI) files are also commonly large, and application help (HLP) files also may be quite sizable. The default for this panel is, as before, to not include any files in the final results display. Add files from this list that you know you never use.

> **Caution:** It's considered bad form, but there are some applications that will not run if any of their support files—even help files—are missing. So, if you know all there is to know about your latest Contempt Processor Application and choose to delete its huge help file, be sure to run the application after Space Wizard closes. If it seems to be misbehaving, you can restore its files from Norton Protection.

Duplicate Files

The Space Wizard defaults to not searching for duplicates, even in a Comprehensive Search, because this is a time-consuming process. As the wizard itself explains, the Space Wizard checks your hard drive for files that have the same date, time, and size, even if their filenames differ. The wizard then analyzes all such matching files to determine whether they are true duplicates or whether they coincidentally appear to be. When duplicate analysis is complete—it takes three minutes on my 4.0GB hard drive installed in a Pentium II 400, but it can easily take half an hour or more on a large drive installed in a slow computer—Space Wizard displays another results panel. Confirmed duplicates are grouped. Unlike other results panels, this display cannot be sorted. Files appear in the order in which the Space Wizard determines they are actual duplicates.

As with other results panes, you can check files upon which you want to act, but you can select to act upon only one of each pair of duplicates. When one file in a pair is checked, its twin is disabled so it cannot be selected. This helps protect you against deleting every copy of a file that you later determine is necessary. Of course, all deletions are available under Norton Protection if it is enabled. You should also be alert to the fact that just because a file is a duplicate, that doesn't mean that both files aren't being used. Applications are not always the smartest things known to mankind. Just because you already have 65 copies of USELESS.DAT on your drive doesn't mean that Widgetmaker 3.0 won't install a new copy. Your system may also be capable of only using the copy that it installs in the location at which it installs—applications are supposed to use the Windows Registry for keeping this kind of common duplicate to a minimum, but do people listen? Seriously, when you are deleting duplicates, be mindful of what you're deleting—and keep an eye on your Norton Protection file expiration time so that you have the chance to verify that a deleted duplicate was really unnecessary.

Taking Action

The search for duplicate files completes the Comprehensive Drive Search. Space Wizard then displays a results panel similar to the one shown in Figure 18.19. You can select and deselect files manually or using the context menu, and you can perform any of the three available actions—compress, delete, or move—on any subset of files that you choose. Just because files are present in this final display does not mean you have to act on them. Clicking the Finish button exits the Space Wizard, with all untouched files intact on your hard drive.

PETER'S PRINCIPLE

Deleted File Security

Deleting files is all well and good, and there are certainly times when increasing the amount of free space on your drives is your primary concern. But what do you do to address instances in which your concerns over security are right up there with your need for space? You have already read about Norton Protection and Norton UnErase, so you know that deleted files can often be retrieved. What can be retrieved can be viewed (and, sometimes, even what cannot be retrieved can still be viewed). How can you guarantee that the files you remove are gone forever?

Norton WipeInfo, part of the Norton Utilities 4.0, can help lay your security fears to rest. WipeInfo can erase files such that they can never be retrieved and it can overwrite free space so that previously deleted data can never be viewed.

You already know that files aren't actually removed from your disks when you delete them. Even if you have Norton Protection disabled, the data once contained in your deleted files remains on disk until it is overwritten. This usually only happens when new files are eventually created and use previously allocated space. As its name implies, WipeInfo allows you to overwrite data on demand—wiping the slate clean, as it were.

One word of warning before I talk about how to use WipeInfo. The entire purpose of WipeInfo is to guarantee that deleted files are irretrievable. WipeInfo does its job so well, it even meets Department of Defense specifications for deleted file security. Be certain of which files and folders you wipe. When they're gone, they're gone.

There are three ways to use WipeInfo. First, a WipeInfo icon was placed on your desktop when you installed SystemWorks 2.0. Drag any files you like onto the WipeInfo icon and they will be deleted. They will not be placed into Norton Protection. Additionally, the space which they previously occupied will be immediately overwritten by meaningless numbers, obliterating forever what was once there.

You can also use the WipeInfo Wizard—which you can launch from the Norton Utilities Integrator, under the "Preventative Maintenance" category—to remove files or even entire folders, wiping the space which they previously occupied. Whenever possible, WipeInfo will even overwrite the directory entries for these files, so no one can ever know where they were stored on disk or what they were named. It's as if these files and folders never existed.

Finally, you can use the WipeInfo Wizard to overwrite all existing free space on your drives. This allows you to guarantee the security of files which you deleted either without using WipeInfo directly (for example, files you deleted with CleanSweep), or that you deleted before Norton SystemWorks 2.0 and WipeInfo were installed.

Wiping free space does not overwrite any files that are under Norton Protection (because these files are still taking space on disk), so if you want to truly wipe the space occupied by all deleted files, make sure you empty the Norton Protected Recycle Bin before using WipeInfo. Wiping free space also does not overwrite backup or archive files you've created with Norton CleanSweep, so if you want those overwritten, you need to either wipe them directly with WipeInfo or else delete them before using WipeInfo to wipe free space.

Norton CleanSweep and WipeInfo are the perfect pair. Together they can guarantee that you maintain as much free space as possible and that, when you delete a file, it's safely out of reach.

Norton Web Services: Your Current Computer

Norton Web Services, in conjunction with LiveUpdate and LiveUpdate Pro, provide you with the ability to keep your Norton SystemWorks software current. Via a telephone line or through an Internet connection, LiveUpdate will analyze all of the SystemWorks components on your PC—from the utility applications themselves to the virus definitions used by Norton AntiVirus. LiveUpdate can then automatically download and install any updates as they become available. This is truly a vital part of your total protection and problem-prevention toolbox. Outdated virus definitions can leave your system susceptible to new infections—although Norton AntiVirus's proprietary heuristic technology can significantly compensate for that danger. As new software and Windows itself evolves, incompatibilities can arise that might hamper the proper operation of some of your Norton SystemWorks components. LiveUpdate can put a stop to all of that. LiveUpdate is a feature included in the cost of your purchase of Norton SystemWorks and requires only a phone line and modem; an Internet connection is supported but not required.

Norton Web Services is a subscription-based Web site (a six-month free subscription is included with Norton SystemWorks) through which you have access to LiveUpdate Pro. This amazing tool will scan your entire PC for all installed software, and then scan Symantec's software database, looking for available updates, bug fixes, demo software, hardware drivers, and even freeware and shareware able to enhance the software you're already using. You can selectively download any of these components to keep all of your installed software, not just SystemWorks, up-to-date. Norton Web Services does require access to the Internet through an Internet service provider (ISP) or online service (like America Online).

LiveUpdate

The first time you launch Norton SystemWorks, you'll encounter Norton LiveUpdate because you'll be prompted to go online and check for any available updates to your SystemWorks package. You need not have an Internet or online service account to use LiveUpdate. All you need is a phone line and modem. You can launch LiveUpdate at any time from the SystemWorks Integrator, as shown in Figure 19.1. Clicking the LiveUpdate button at the lower-left corner of the Integrator opens the LiveUpdate menu. From here, you can choose to update any or all parts of Norton SystemWorks. Selecting any item from the LiveUpdate menu launches the LiveUpdate Wizard, which will step you through the updating process the first time. After you're certain your LiveUpdate connection is working properly, you can use the Norton AntiVirus scheduler to configure LiveUpdate for automatic updating. You'll read about this later in the chapter.

FIGURE 19.1
LiveUpdate is launched from the Norton SystemWorks Integrator.

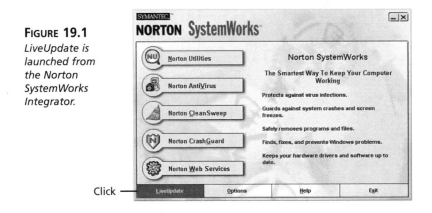

After the LiveUpdate Wizard is launched, you'll first be asked what kind of connection you want to make with the Symantec LiveUpdate server. The Wizard panel shown in Figure 19.2 gives you three options: direct modem connection, an Internet connection, or allowing the software to select one of the two connection methods for you. If you choose auto-select, the software checks to see whether you have an Internet account configured within your Windows Dial-Up Networking. If you do, LiveUpdate will use that Internet connection for your updates so you are not charged for a toll-call. If no Internet dial-up connection is found, the software will select the direct modem method.

FIGURE 19.2
In the first step of the wizard, you select the connection device for LiveUpdates.

TECHINCAL NOTE

If you have the good fortune of having a continuous connection to the Internet, LiveUpdate will automatically detect that connection. If you do not want to use it, for some reason, you can still choose to make a direct modem connection with the LiveUpdate server.

In contrast, if you are using America Online as your online service/Internet connection, you should manually select the Internet option for your LiveUpdate connection. You will then need to log on to America Online (or any other online service that provides Internet access but does not use the standard Windows Dial-Up Networking for a connection) before beginning a LiveUpdate session.

With a connection choice made—or letting the software decide for you—click Next, and the LiveUpdate Wizard will immediately initiate that connection. If you have selected the modem method, you'll see a small dialog box advising you that a toll call will be made to Eugene, Oregon, in the United States of America, where the LiveUpdate Server is located. You have the opportunity to cancel the connection if you do not want to place this call. LiveUpdate will use the Windows dialing properties set in your Modems control panel. If you're not familiar with these, check out the following technical note.

TECHINCAL NOTE

LiveUpdate uses your modem's default dialing properties to make a direct connection to the LiveUpdate server. Normally, these properties are set immediately after your modem is installed, but yours may not be configured correctly if someone else installed your modem. If your modem appears to be working properly already, chances are good that your settings are fine, but the next few paragraphs will instruct you on how to check.

Open your Modems Control Panel by selecting Settings | Control Panel from the Start menu, and double-clicking the Modems icon. You'll want to click the Dialing Properties button to open the properties screen. Verify that your area code is entered properly, as well as any special codes you know you need to connect to an outside line. If you are used to dialing "9" for example, and then waiting for another dial-tone before continuing, you'll want to enter the 9 followed by a comma. The comma tells the modem to wait briefly before dialing more numbers. Other settings regarding call-waiting and using a calling card may be made here as well. Click OK when everything is correct, then click OK again to close the Modems Control Panel. You're set!

LiveUpdate will either dial directly or will connect to the Internet via your Dial-Up Networking (DUN) connection. (Depending on what settings you have set for DUN, you may need to enter your account name or password and click Connect.) Via either method, LiveUpdate will connect to the LiveUpdate server and will check for updates to the program you've chosen. You can see this process in Figure 19.3.

If updates are found to be available, they will download automatically.

FIGURE 19.3
*LiveUpdate
searches for new
software on the
server.*

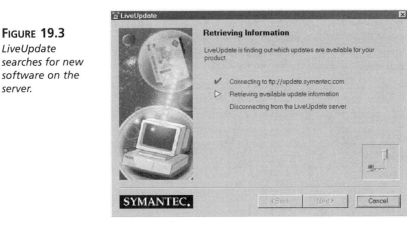

When the update has been successfully downloaded, LiveUpdate will install it for you automatically. This may take a few seconds or a few minutes depending on the size and nature of the update and the speed of your computer. After this is done, you'll see a screen similar to that shown for updating Norton AntiVirus, in Figure 19.4. New virus definitions were available, and they have been downloaded and properly installed within NAV. Had this been an update added to Norton Utilities, for example, you would have been advised that the software on your PC has been update-appended to the latest available version. If you have connected to LiveUpdate via the Internet, you'll be asked if you want to remain online or if you want to disconnect. You may also see a message indicating that you should reboot your computer. You need not reboot at that point, but you won't be able to use any of the updated products until you do so.

> **Tip:** LiveUpdate should be run monthly, if for no other reason than keeping
> your virus definitions current. You need not attend to the updating by hand,
> however; LiveUpdate can be configured to do all of its work automatically.

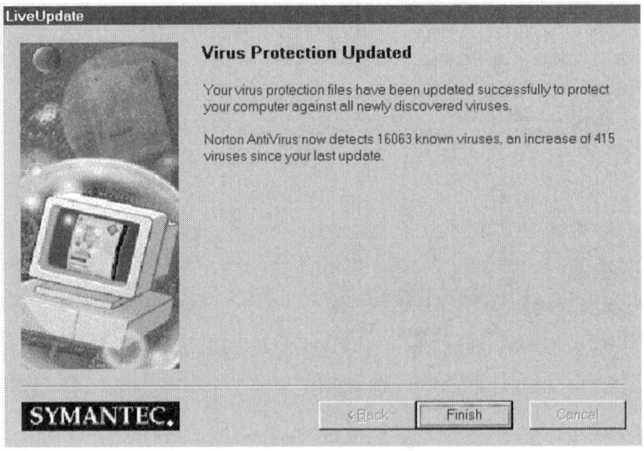

FIGURE 19.4
*Software, NAV in
this case, has been
successfully updat-
ed and all en-
hancements are
active. (In certain
cases, rebooting
may be necessary
first.)*

Virus Protection Updated

Your virus protection files have been updated successfully to protect
your computer against all newly discovered viruses.

Norton AntiVirus now detects 16063 known viruses, an increase of 415
viruses since your last update.

SYMANTEC.   < Back   Finish   Cancel

Configuring LiveUpdate for Automatic Downloads

After completing the first successful LiveUpdate session, the LiveUpdate scheduler will enable you to configure LiveUpdate to update Norton AntiVirus definitions and software automatically. You will be shown the panel in Figure 19.5. You can select the date and time each month that you want LiveUpdate to check for new software. In general, it's best to have this occur at some time when your computer will be on, of course, but when you won't be working. I leave my computer on continuously and schedule the updates to occur at 4 a.m. Monthly updating is usually more than adequate, but you can have LiveUpdate run twice a month, if you place a check mark in the appropriate box on this panel. If you like surprises, you can have LiveUpdate run itself at a randomly selected time—this time will always fall within normal working hours. You can also ask to have LiveUpdate launch but ask your permission to connect each time. Of course, if your Dial-Up Networking is not configured to auto-connect, or if you connect to the Internet via an online service, LiveUpdate will not be able to connect without your attention anyway. If you have LiveUpdate set to use your modem to dial directly, so long as the line is free, updates will be automatic.

If you don't want LiveUpdate to prompt you after each LiveUpdate with regards to automatic scheduling, place a check mark in the box at the very bottom of the panel. LiveUpdate will never again ask you about automatic scheduling. (Automatically performed updates do not "wait" for you to acknowledge the schedule screen.)

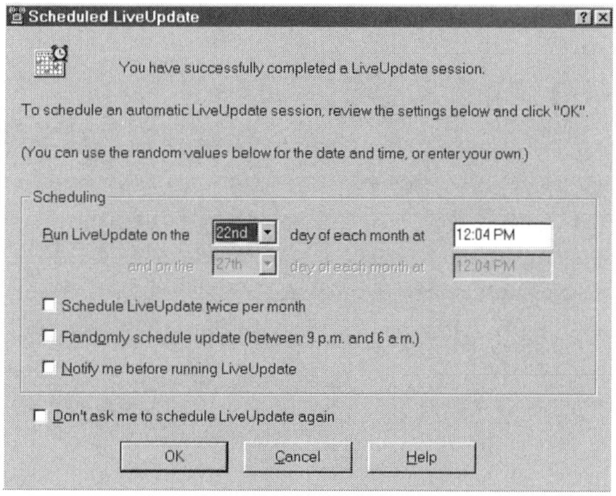

FIGURE 19.5
Use the LiveUpdate Scheduler to specify when LiveUpdate should be run.

The LiveUpdate Control Panel

With LiveUpdate installed, you'll find a new Windows Control Panel has also been installed, called LiveUpdate. (To access your control panels, select Settings | Control Panel from the Start menu.) From here, you can change your selection for how LiveUpdate connects to the LiveUpdate server. You can also reconfigure your Internet or modem connections to specify a different Dial-Up Networking connection, to enter in your Dial-Up Networking account name and password, or to select a different modem. The account name and password are for LiveUpdate's use only. After you are connected to the Internet, of course, anyone at your workstation would have access to your Internet account, as is always the case.

Moreover, LiveUpdate is capable of updating itself through this Control Panel. If you click the Update Now button, a LiveUpdate session will begin using your normal preferences, and LiveUpdate will verify that it is as current as possible (see Figure 19.6).

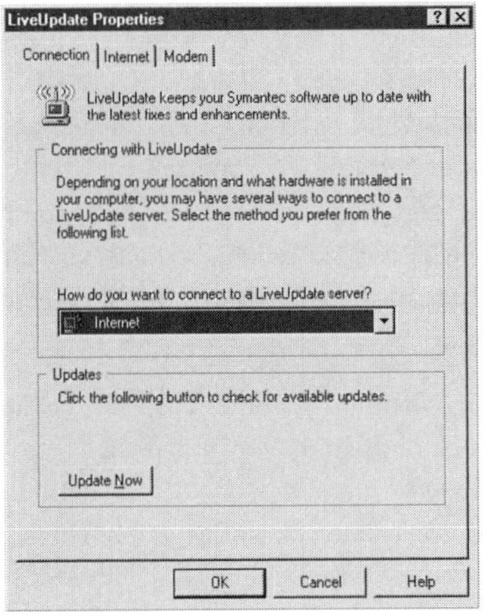

FIGURE 19.6

The LiveUpdate Control Panel—a new Windows control panel that is installed with Norton SystemWorks— enables you to quickly modify how LiveUpdate works with your hardware and even lets you update LiveUpdate itself.

Norton Web Services

Norton Web Services, accessed through Symantec's Web site, gives you access to tools that can keep not only your Symantec and Norton software up-to-date, but much of the software on your entire PC. Norton Web Services also gives you access to a range of software support options, information, and articles related to PC performance, data safety and security, and utility software in general. A six-month free subscription to Norton Web Services is included in your purchase of Norton SystemWorks. After six months pass—six months from the first time you use NWS, that is—you can elect to re-subscribe on a monthly or annual basis. You can find Norton Web Services on the World Wide Web at the following URL: `http://www.nortonweb.com`. If you have Windows Dial-Up Networking configured to automatically log you on to the Internet (or if you have already logged on to an online service providing your Internet access) you can also launch Norton Web Services directly by selecting Programs | Norton Web Services | Norton Web Services from your Start menu. The main NWS screen, as of this writing, is shown in Figure 19.7, although there's no question that it will be changing regularly. The primary tool found within Norton Web Services, as of this writing, is LiveUpdate Pro, a dramatically enhanced version of LiveUpdate. We'll look at LiveUpdate Pro first, then see how to subscribe to Norton Web Services.

FIGURE **19.7**

Use the Norton Web Services home page to access LiveUpdate Pro.

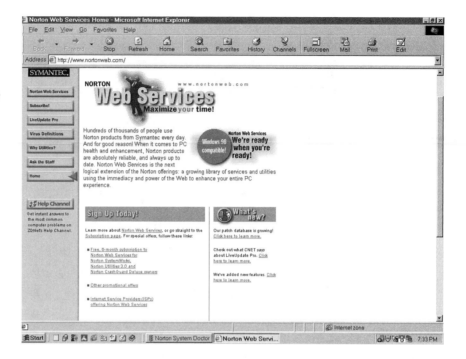

Note: If you do not choose to subscribe to Norton Web Services after your free subscription period expires, you can continue to use the standard version of LiveUpdate to keep your Symantec software current. You do not lose access to your free LiveUpdate updates simply because you do not choose to pay for Norton Web Services. Indeed, LiveUpdate Pro—the version which is part of Norton Web Services—requires your interaction to run. Even if you do subscribe to Norton Web Services, you should allow the standard version of LiveUpdate to keep your Norton SystemWorks software automatically current.

LiveUpdate Pro

Each time you run LiveUpdate Pro (after logging in to Norton Web Services and clicking the Run LiveUpdate Pro button), it will check to see if any updates exist for itself. If such updates are found, LiveUpdate Pro will download and install them automatically, as shown in Figure 19.8. With its own software made as current as possible, LiveUpdate Pro will continue running, looking for updates to other software on your PC. (You'll see a progress indicator as LiveUpdate Pro checks its status on your PC against its status on the server. It's very unlikely that you would ever want to cancel the update mid-stream, but you might want to know in advance that the only way to do so is to shut down your Web browser.)

FIGURE 19.8

LiveUpdate Pro, unlike LiveUpdate, updates itself automatically on an as-needed basis, each time you use it.

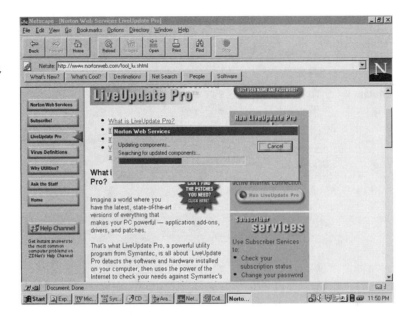

Selecting Software to Download

With its own update complete—if one was necessary—LiveUpdate Pro will make a quick scan of your Windows Registry and your hard disk directories to find software you have installed. Because some software is not as "neat" as it should be when uninstalled, LiveUpdate Pro may find updates available for software that you removed from your system long ago. You can choose to ignore these updates, of course, or you might want to download them if you think you're likely to reinstall the software at a later time. With your system checked, LiveUpdate Pro will display a screen like the one you see in Figure 19.9. This is the main LiveUpdate Pro screen, and most of your installations and downloads can be done from here. (In rare cases, you may be required to register a particular update online. These must usually be downloaded and then manually installed by you, but LiveUpdate Pro will let you know when that's the case.)

The screen is divided into three tabs, two panels, and a set of buttons, as you can see in Figure 19.9. The tabs allow you to select which kind of updates you want to see listed. The Software tab refers to an update for applications you've installed, and can be anything from word processors to games. In fact, you can see a game listed in the updates available in Figure 19.9. Available options on the Hardware Drivers tab refer to just that—software which supports hardware you have installed on your PC. From time to time, hardware manufacturers make modifications to this supporting software to provide you with new functionality. A recent widely publicized example of that is the V.90 compatibility updates for most brands of 56K and X2 modems. The software is downloaded to your PC and installed—either somewhere in your Windows folder or into a chip on the hardware itself—and the new functionality is immediately present. Finally, the Freeware/Shareware tab shows you a broad set of software that can enhance software you already have installed on your PC.

FIGURE 19.9

LiveUpdate Pro's main display of available updates.

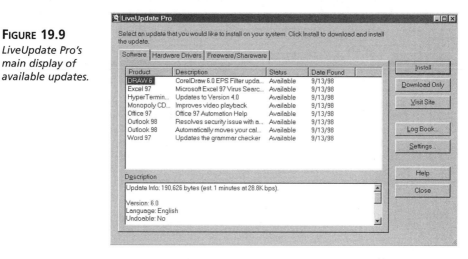

This freeware or shareware may be from the major product's manufacturer, or from one of that manufacturer's official development partners. Figure 19.10 shows a sample Freeware/Shareware screen.

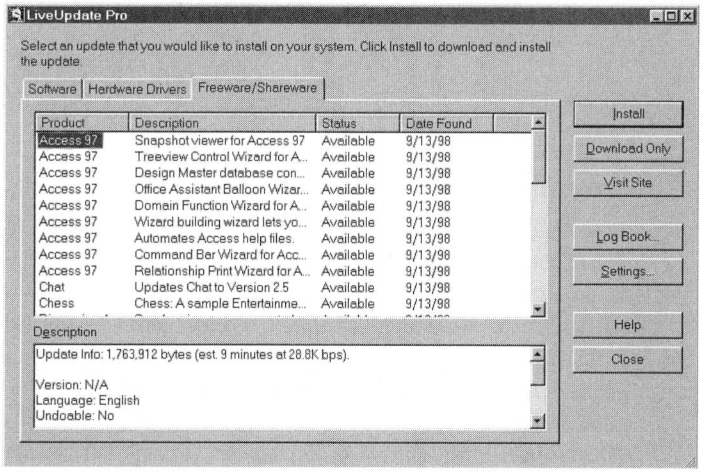

FIGURE 19.10

Freeware and Shareware available through LiveUpdate Pro.

Regardless of which tab you've selected, choosing and downloading or installing software works the same. If you look back at Figure 19.9, you will see that an update to CorelDraw 6 is selected in the top panel. You select an update by clicking your mouse on the name of its main product or by moving the focus to the panel and using your arrow keys. As you select an update, the lower panel will show you some selected information about that update. An example of this type of information follows:

```
Update Info: 1,122,407 bytes (est. 6 minutes at 28.8K bps).

Version: 2.0
Language: English
Undoable: No
Use to detect and remove the Laroux virus from your computer. This virus
attaches a module named "Laroux" to Excel worksheets. This is a non-
destructive virus, and is the first to infect Excel worksheets. This patch
can also update earlier versions of Excel. See the file "We1280.doc" for more
information.
Released: 05/30/1997


Found in: C:\Program Files\Microsoft Office\Office.
Update URL: ftp://ftp.microsoft.com/Softlib/MSLFILES/WE1280.EXE.
```

> **Tip:** Use the scrollbar at the right of the Description pane to read all of the available information about the selected update.

This gives you just about everything you could want to know about the update: How big it is, how long it will take to download, whether the update can be removed after it's installed, what the update does, where it will be installed, and where on the Web it's located. With an update selected, LiveUpdate Pro's buttons become active. You can choose to download and install an update, download it only, or visit the Web site on which the update can be found.

Download Versus Install

If you find an update you want, you don't have to install it immediately. If you click Install, then LiveUpdate Pro will download the software, install it for you, and let you know anything special you may need to know about the update—for example, that you need to reboot your computer before it will take effect. Figure 19.11 shows an installation in progress. If you stop an install, its name will usually continue to appear in the available updates list. In a few rare cases, however, LUP will think you installed software which, in fact, you cancelled. Simply rescanning your computer will correct this. After an install (or a download, for that matter) completes, its name will be deleted from the list.

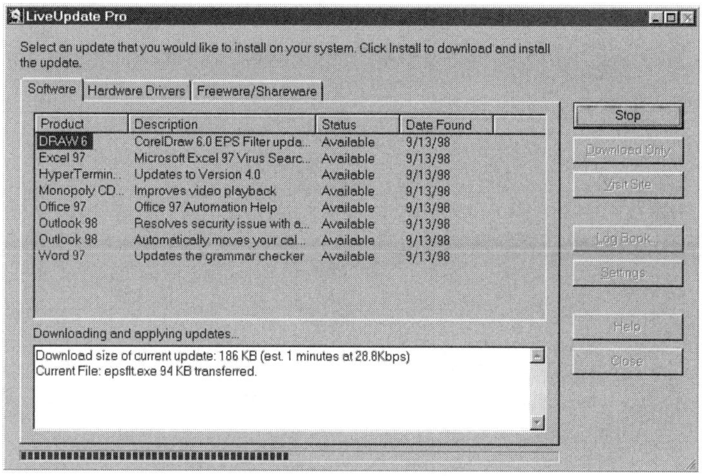

FIGURE 19.11

A LiveUpdate Pro install in progress.

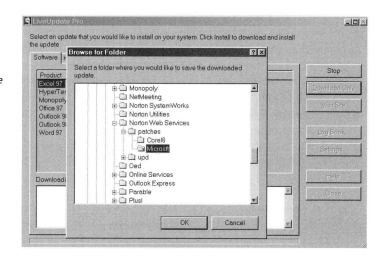

If you click Download Only instead of Install, however, LiveUpdate Pro will ask you where you want the update saved—the default will be a folder inside the Norton Web Services folder, as shown in Figure 19.12. The update or patch will download to the location you specify and you'll be able to open that folder and install the patch at a later time, whenever you choose to do so. (Additionally, if you allow updates to be stored in the default location, LiveUpdate Pro will be able to locate them and access them in the future, should you ever need to reinstall the update. You won't have to download them again.)

FIGURE 19.12

Selecting a destination for downloading an update or patch.

Undoable Installations and Otherwise

Previously, I mentioned that some updates are undoable and some are not. For certain types of system enhancements or software repairs (bug fixes), the producer of the patch doesn't feel that the software should be run without the patch, and so provides no way for you to uninstall the patch. You can always uninstall the software entirely and then reinstall it, of course, effectively returning your system to its pre-patch state.

There are also those updates or software installations that are undoable, either by LiveUpdate Pro, by hand, or both. In most cases, major undoable updates will create a new entry in your Add/Remove Programs control panel through which you can select and manually delete them from your system at any time you want. In a few cases, they may only create an entry in their Start menu folder that will be named something like, "Uninstall Wowbanger," which will remove the software when manually chosen. In the case of all undoable upgrades—however major or minor—you can click on the LiveUpdate Pro Logbook button and have LiveUpdate Pro automatically uninstall undoable updates.

Visiting Web Sites

With an update selected, you can click the Visit Site button and LiveUpdate Pro will open a new Web browser window into which it will open the site corresponding to the selected update. You may find configuration tips or additional guidelines about how to best use the update or new software. You may also find information—particularly in the case of shareware—about how to register the program if you like it and, perhaps, receive an enhanced version offering additional functionality.

The Installation Log

Clicking on the Log Book button opens LiveUpdate Pro's record of all installations and downloads you've performed. All successful downloads and installations will appear in the log, as when the install was performed and which product feature—either LiveUpdate Pro or the standard LiveUpdate—did the downloading or installing. If you're aware of problems existing with a certain piece of software, and you download the patch but continue to have problems some weeks or months later, you can check back here to verify that the patch was, in fact, successfully installed. If you have more than one computer, the log can be useful to help you remember whether you installed a given update on each machine.

Other Interface Tricks

The available updates panel supports right-clicking, which will open a context menu. If an update is selected when you right-click, you will be able to choose to Install, Download, or Visit Web Site for the selected update from the context menu. You can also select to view the Log Book from the context menu.

It may sometime happen that an update is available for a piece of software you own, but you may not want to install or download that update. You may not even want to see it displayed in the available updates list each time LiveUpdate Pro runs. With an update selected, choosing Hide from the context menu will remove that update from the available list. You can select Show from the context menu at any time you want, to display all hidden updates in a window, from which you can select to un-hide them individually. Being able to hide certain updates can help to keep the available display neat and tidy.

Finally, the context menu gives you the ability to Rescan your entire PC, looking for installed software and hardware. LiveUpdate Pro will then re-check Symantec's update database to see if additional patches or updates are available.

Configuring LiveUpdate Pro

The Settings button will open two configurations tabs for LiveUpdate Pro, shown in Figure 19.13. When you use LiveUpdate Pro to install software, a copy of the downloaded update files remains in a folder inside your Norton Web Services folder. This enables you to reinstall the update should you ever need to completely uninstall and reinstall the main application. The LiveUpdate Pro tab enables you to configure how frequently you want those update files deleted, if at all. You also have the option of clicking the Remove Now button, thereby deleting all of the installed updates immediately. (Software you have downloaded but not installed will also be deleted.) LiveUpdate Pro's Norton Web Services tab allows you to enter your Norton Web Services user name and password so that you will not be prompted for them each time you run LiveUpdate Pro. When you first subscribe to Norton Web Services, you are given the option of storing this information automatically. If you choose not to do so, you can return here and input your user name and password at any time.

FIGURE 19.13

You can change the configuration options for LiveUpdate Pro.

Subscribing to Norton Web Services

As a purchaser of Norton SystemWorks—or, indeed, if you purchase the standalone versions of either the Norton Utilities or Norton CrashGuard—you are entitled to a free six-month subscription to Norton Web Services and to LiveUpdate Pro. In the box with the software is a card on which is printed a unique Norton Web Services serial number. Launch Norton Web Services by selecting it from your Start menu (Programs | Norton Web Services | Norton Web Services) and click the Subscribe button you'll see near the upper-left corner of the Web page. (Refer to Figure 19.7, if needed.)

The Norton Web Services site will tell you a little bit about what is available to you, which you'll have already read about in this chapter. You'll find a button to select if you have a free subscription—which you do—and another to choose if you want to begin a paid subscription. Use your free subscription first and, when it expires, you'll find a Continue My Subscription option on the Norton Web Services page. Assuming you choose to begin your free subscription, Norton Web Services will ask you for some basic information about yourself and for the serial number that is on the card in your software's box. You'll have to select a user name and a password, which will help identify you to Norton Web Services each time you check the site. If you desire—and you might as well—you can have Norton Web Services automatically store your password and user name in the configuration settings you read about, above. (Don't worry; your password is never displayed as anything other than asterisks. Nevertheless, you should choose a Norton Web Services password that is not the same as any password you use to log on to the Internet, to an online service, or your ATM PIN.)

All of that done, Norton Web Services will welcome you, advise you when your subscription expires, and then immediately begin the process of updating its own software on your PC. When that is complete, you'll be able to choose a button labeled Run LiveUpdate Pro, and you're set!

Requesting Software

Norton Web Services (NWS) changes regularly, and the Symantec database of updates, demos, and shareware is growing fast. If you find, however, that there's a piece of software or a patch that you want but isn't offered by Norton Web Services, you can click the button labeled Can't find the Patches You Need? on the NWS Web site and ask for the software. Your message will be sent directly to the team responsible for maintaining Norton Web Services. In this way, all of your fellow users can benefit from something you know that Symantec may not. And you can benefit from others doing the same.

Norton Utilities: Checking Your Own Nametag—System Info and Norton Diagnostics

System Information, together with the DOS-based Norton Diagnostics, provide information about every aspect of your computer. These two tools are informative only—they don't provide elaborate solutions to problems or fix things that don't work. System Information and Norton Diagnostics tell you if something works or not. They tell you how fast it runs, how well it runs. If something is broken, they do not tell you why, but the information they provide can be a tremendous service to you or to support personnel when it comes time to troubleshoot those problems.

Norton System Information (NSI) is a Windows application, run by clicking the Utilities menu in System Doctor and choosing Troubleshooting, then System Information. You can also launch it from the Norton SystemWorks Integrator by selecting Norton Utilities, then Troubleshooting, then System Information. Upon launching, NSI runs a basic system test and displays the results on your screen (see Figure 20.1). If all you need to know is who made your BIOS chip and when, or what build of Windows you are running, for example, then this simple introductory test may be as far as you need to go. However, opening System Information reveals nine standard Windows tabs. Each tab tests various aspects of your computer's performance in great detail. (Your tabs may be spaced differently onscreen than what you see in the figures here.)

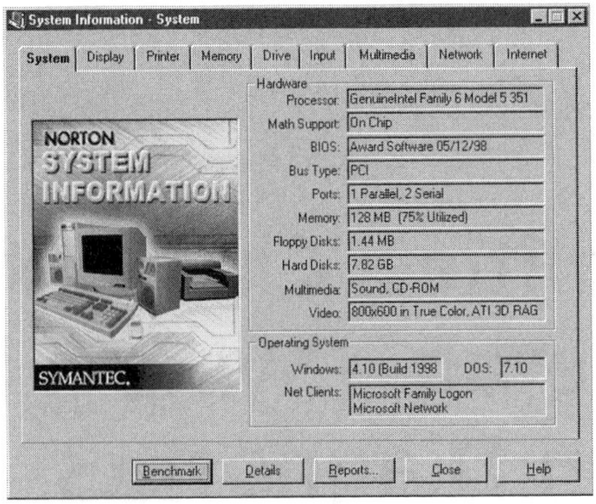

FIGURE 20.1

By the time the main System Information screen appears, it has already run a quick system test.

System Information Versus Norton Diagnostics

Before we explore System Information in great detail, let's go over the difference between the results obtained from DOS-based Norton Diagnostics tests, and what you can glean from System Information. Then we'll delve into System Information thoroughly, and finally, tackle Norton Diagnostics in earnest.

Norton Diagnostics, run from a command line while your computer is in MS-DOS mode, tests the fundamental electronics of your system. It checks the raw physical integrity of components, such as baud speed of serial ports, hard drive revolutions per second, RAM quality and such. The tests resemble those that an engineer would perform before giving the final OK to a piece of hardware. (In fact, one of the reports is titled *Burn In*.) You might run Norton Diagnostics if, for example, you've noticed an error in your printer port's functioning, and have ruled out every possible software conflict. There's no choice left but to investigate the possibility of true port failure. Norton Diagnostics can perform the full series of tests that will allow you to proclaim that your LPT1: is indeed dead in the water.

Windows-based tests are performed above thick software overlays, not directly upon fundamental electronics. If you want to send the computer back to the store and say "I know it's not the software. The RAM itself is faulty," for example, you'd have to run Norton Diagnostics to be sure of yourself.

Norton System Information, on the other hand, tests hardware and components, but is more a tool for checking performance in real-world situations. It would test, for example, not only the raw speed of your CDROM drive, but rather, how it ranks in exceeding MPC-2 (Multimedia PC-2, an industry standard for minimal specifications for a multimedia-capable PC) recommendations. And, while System Information can test your video card's use of raw color data in various modes, it's better used to test efficiency at displaying 3D, AVI or MPEG movies, that is, stuff you're likely to do in real life.

When Would You Run System Information?

Of course, System Information provides a helpful profile of your computer that can come in handy in many ways. Here are some specific instances:

- If your computer displays system-wide error messages that are beyond your ability to troubleshoot. The technician asks you to print out a detailed system report before taking it in.

- A very important application keeps causing a General Protection Fault, or Invalid Page Fault and you want to find out exactly what other application keeps wanting to share the same system resource, thus triggering the error.

- You need to know what WINSOCK.DLL file you are using, and are you using more than one?

- You are endlessly curious about your computer. System Information's Technical Support Report prints out at over 500 pages. Curiosity might not kill the cat, but it will surely fell a few trees. Remember the sage words of John Muir, who observed that Mother Nature can save great trees from disasters, but she cannot save them from foolishness.

Working with System Information

As mentioned, when you first start System Information, a single screen displays basic info, such as the number of ports, hard drive size, processor type and speed, and even verifies the presence of a Math Coprocessor. To display more detail about any reading (see Figure 20.2), right-click on any field, and click "What's This?"

However, the power of System Information lies in the tabs underneath. Before we walk through them one by one, you need to know a little about *Benchmark* testing.

FIGURE 20.2

Right-clicking on any field and selecting "What's This?" reveals a brief description of a test's results.

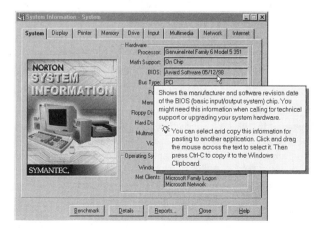

Benchmarks and Testing Standards

Computer enthusiasts are a competitive lot, and nothing is more disheartening than to be stuck with a machine that can't quite cut it. There are a number of ways to test your computer's performance. One is to simply do your work, and if your computer is hampering your production, then do something to bring it up to speed. Another is to test your computer by a set of standardized routines, and see by the numbers how your computer compares to others.

Benchmarks are a set of such tests. They'll record how accurately and quickly your hard drive can open files, the speed with which your video card renders an image, and how fast your coprocessor can calculate sums with a database.

Experts differ, though, on whether its best to test your computer's performance in a situation that would simulate a work-a-day computing situation (two Word documents open, paste an Excel spreadsheet, a game running in the background), or if it's more fair to test simple component speed and efficiency. Thus, there is disagreement on the value of some benchmark numbers, and there are a variety of Benchmark tests available. For example, Ziff-Davis' WinBench tests raw system performance, while Winstone tests application performance.

Hoping to touch all bases and satisfy everyone, Norton's Benchmark tests are very comprehensive. There are three, actually—a System, Hard Drive, and Multimedia Benchmark test. Each are run separately, and are described below:

- System Benchmark reports the speed of your CPU, memory, and motherboard, compared to other computers. It's available from a button on System Information's front panel.

- Drive Benchmark measures your hard drive speed, with and without the advantage of a disk cache, accessed through a the Benchmark button on the Drive tab.

- The Multimedia Benchmark tests your system's conformity to MPC Level 2 specifications. Be aware, though, that MPC-2 standards are rather dated, and it's essential that your system exceeds MPC-2 specifications by a factor of ten or better, in order to run the newest graphic-intensive software. You can run your Multimedia Benchmark with and without MMX. Depending on the difference in speed, you can determine if its worth extra money to purchase MMX-enhanced tools. Multimedia benchmarking is available through the Benchmark button on the Multimedia tab.

Note: Although Multimedia Benchmark tests your system's ability to meet or exceed MPC-2 standards, you won't be able to run applications with specific multimedia needs unless you have the necessary drivers. These may include RealAudio, MP3 and MPEG players, Active Movie, and QuickTime for Windows. Multimedia Benchmark tests raw hardware capacity, but does not check or confirm the presence of popular multimedia "players" and drivers.

Testing Each System with System Information

Each tab represents a set of components. Both your mouse and keyboard are covered in the Input tab. Your Sound Card and CD-ROM are tested under the Multimedia tab. Internet and Network are each given their own tab.

Simply clicking a tab launches a basic test of that particular system. When the tests are completed, the tab contents appear. You'll see the test results are organized under Windows Explorer-style headings. When clicking through these headings, your goal is to locate the information you want to know, and not get bogged down in details that are not helpful to you at the moment. Here's how exploring the headings works:

Click the plus sign next to any heading to reveal specific results (see Figure 20.3). Click the plus sign next to a subheading if you like, drilling down to as much detail as interests you. Drilling down into some submenus will open their own window of details. This arrangement is preferable to filling the screen with a laundry list of random results. Click a minus sign to close that list, and view only the data one hierarchy above that level.

FIGURE 20.3

A plus sign indicates more detail is available below a heading.

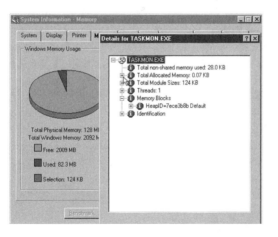

A descriptive icon appears next to any heading. Some icons indicate a particular file or information line. Here's what some of the icons mean:

- The letter *I* indicates *information*: one line's worth of diagnostic data.
- A check next to a feature means that your device passed the test.
- The International "No" sign means the feature did not pass that particular test. It could also mean the feature is not present in your hardware.

Some tabs have a Details or a Benchmark button at the bottom for further testing. Clicking Details opens a new window of information about any particular feature. We'll explore Benchmarks momentarily.

Walking Through the Tabs

Let's look at each tab, and find out what System Information tests and reports. We've already discussed the System tab that appears when you first invoke NSI. Following sections cover the eight remaining System Information tabs. At times, Device Manager covers ground similar to what you'll see here.

> **Note:** To open the Windows Device Manager, click the System Icon in Control Panel. Then select the Device Manager tab. Double-click on any component's icon in the list to learn more about it.

The Display Tab

The Display tab combines both the video card and monitor into one list of features (see Figure 20.4). You'll learn mainly about the type of imaging and accuracy your video card is capable of. Information from this tab helps you determine if your video card is capable of high-end video performance, sharp graphics that won't take too long to render, and support for advanced gaming features. If your video card fails in too many of the basic tests displayed in this panel, the card may not be up to running complex graphics applications, or 3D games that require lots of video firepower.

FIGURE 20.4

The Display tab combines both video adapter and monitor into one set of tests.

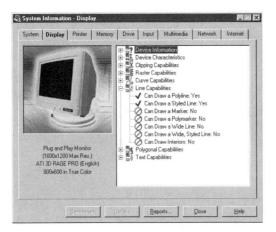

The Windows Device Manager runs a similar set of tests, if your video card supports them, and provides more details about the driver files required by the video card. You'll also get a bit more specific Memory Page Address info about your video card from Device Manager. Device Manager does contain a separate tab for your monitor, whereas Norton System Information combines these features on one tab.

Regarding your monitor, neither System Information nor Device Manager confirm or refute a manufacturer's claims about dot pitch size, flicker, or refresh rate. These features are good to learn about, because a favorable flicker and refresh rate rating means your monitor can reduce eye fatigue and create more accurate screen images. Some monitors and video cards come with programs that allow you to test your monitor's refresh rate and flicker amount.

The Printer Tab

The Printer tab tests your printer's ability to render accurate graphics and text on paper (see Figure 20.5). Again, too many International "No" symbols next to features indicates that high-end images are not possible with your printer. However, most computer users do not purchase printers for producing magazines or razor-lined architectural drawings. These tests hold your printer up to a fairly high standard, and thus, few of the most popular inkjet and inexpensive laser printers will do well in these tests. Not to worry, though, because popular graphic and desktop publishing software is attuned to the shortcomings of consumer-level printer types. Poor ratings here does not mean your printed output will look bad. It may not be magazine-quality, however.

FIGURE 20.5
The Printer tab holds your printer up to a very high set of standards.

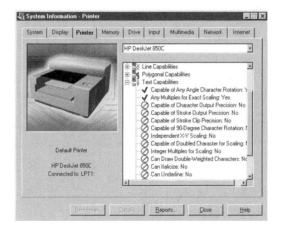

Lots of very specific printer information is only available from your printer's Properties menu—not only print quality settings, but spool output and data type settings, as well. These features allow you to trade off print quality for speed, and their significance is not covered in System Information's printer profile. (Please note that your printer's Properties menu may not look exactly as the above, since every printer's menus are configured a little differently.)

Note: To access a Printer's Properties, click Printers from the Settings icon in the Window's Start menu, and right-click on any printer. Select Properties from the shortcut menu. The Properties menu will appear.

The Memory Tab

The Memory tab serves a very helpful function. It tells you all the programs that are open on your computer at the moment, including all the .DLL files, shared programs and routines, and all the tiny executables that, piece by piece, chip away at your available memory for running programs. (Please note that, in order for .DLL files to appear, you must check the Display Libraries button at the bottom of the Memory tab.)

> A .DLL file is an executable module that is called up by any application you are running. You yourself almost never open a .DLL file. DLL stands for *Dynamic Link Library*. Thus, it is used by more than one application. It is "looked up" as needed, to perform a particular, common task. Popular .DLL files, such as VBRUN400.DLL are necessary for certain applications to run. Sadly, many programs install their own version of a .DLL file and erase a previous version without warning. Because of minor differences in programming, applications depending on *previous* versions of that same .DLL file may not run. System Information's Memory tab can be helpful in identifying which .DLLs are running at a particular time, which helps you determine which duplicate is safe to erase, if any. Windows 98 helps control this problem of applications erasing and reinstalling common system files.

On the Memory tab, the left side of the screen shows a pie chart, displaying Windows total physical memory, and the amount of memory currently in use. This number is different than Window's Device Manager's "System Resources." (Click the System icon in Control Panel, then select Device Manager, and choose the Performance tab.) Device Manager's System Resources reports the amount of available memory as a percentage, including Windows dynamic swap file and running DLLs (which are treated as part of the swap file, incidentally) as part of the picture. Norton's System Information Memory tab tells you how much physical RAM is in use at the moment, as well as swap file size. The right side of the screen shows a list of all currently open programs, devices, and other executables.

Shared Resources and Memory Usage

One of the amazing facts of modern computing life is how much is on when nothing's on. Before you even open an application, your available resources can be knocked down to 60% or less. The usual culprits are small programs that open when Windows starts, for the sake of availability. Microsoft Fast Find, Office Start, applets that control video driver features, personal information managers, and programs that run in the background organizing all your graphics files—each of these contributes to a memory drain before you open an application. Additionally, startup applications—that is applications that run every time you boot Windows, such as Norton CrashGuard or Norton System Monitor— also use resources of their own. System Information's Memory tab tells you the name of each open program or device, as well as its size and type. Click on an item on the right side of the screen once, and the pie chart to the left reflects how much memory is used by the selected program, appearing as a red "slice of pie." Double-click on any item in the Memory tab list, and you'll learn more about each program's allocated and non-shared memory, total blocks used, page and address thread ID, and Parent Process. (Some applications use so little memory, that you'd not notice a change in the pie chart.) Knowing this data can be helpful when you have to track down which two applications are conflicting with each other.

> **Caution:** You might think that none of the open programs are very large in and of themselves. Added together, however, these little components can exact a serious toll on performance. In some circumstances they can even contribute to memory-related errors.

Using Memory Details Information

Click on the Details button in the Memory tab for a look at the specific file types responsible for current memory usage. Click the plus sign next to the General Information heading to learn about available physical memory, largest block size, swap file utilization, and 16-bit availability. The 16-bit applications cannot use dynamic memory as efficiently as 32-bit applications, so if you use a good deal of older 16-bit programs, this number can be important.

If you need to identify which Dynamic Link Library (.DLL) or Virtual Device Drivers (.VXD) are associated with certain programs, open the program you want to learn about, then click the 32-bit Library and Dynamic Device Driver headings of the Details window in the Memory tab, and see what files are currently in use. The reason why such detective work may be necessary is that many applications share these files, and even run different versions of the same file. Tracking down which one is causing an error is hard because you have to know which file is running, and when. Figure 20.6 shows many totally unrelated applications all using the same .DLL file, GDI32.DLL, which provides key user-interface support. The Memory tab can help sort out a problem, should a conflict arise between these programs. For the memory allocation enthusiast, much helpful information is here about any .DLL's specific usage count and Module ID.

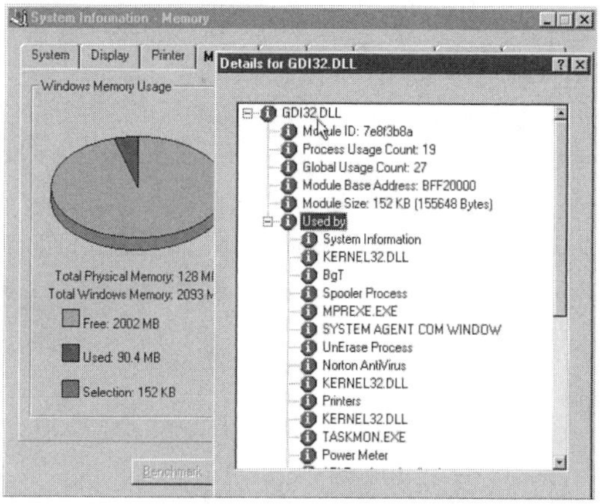

FIGURE 20.6

DLL files are shared by Windows applications, and can be a source of conflict and Invalid Page Fault errors.

The Drive Tab

The Drive tab shows the contents of each hard drive, while a pie chart to the left displays total drive and remaining free space (see Figure 20.7.) To see what percentage of hard drive space any folder uses, click a folder on the right, and it will appear in red as a percentage of the total pie area (unless the percentage is too small to be visible). Notice, too, that if you select a file or folder, the Selection heading under the pie chart will show you the size of the selected object. You'll also see how much disk space has been allocated for that object, and what percentage of that allocated space is not currently in use. This percentage is known as the slack space used by the file. You may remember that slack space is disk space that is being used by a file but which does not contain any of the file's content. (If you select a folder here on the Drive tab, you will be shown the amount of allocated space for all files in that folder, as well as the percentage of that total allocated space that is slack.) For a detailed discussion of this issue, refer back to Chapter 3, "Norton Utilities: The System Doctor Is In," and read the section which discusses System Doctor's Disk Slack Space sensor.

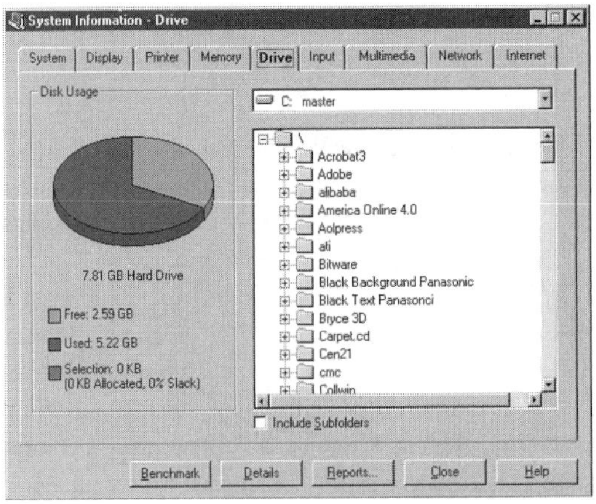

FIGURE 20.7
The System Information Drive tab shows data on available and used hard drive space.

The Hard Drive Benchmark

This test lets you compare your drive's current performance to its best ever performance (see Figure 20.8). Click the Benchmark button and then the Logical Drive button to measure your hard drive's speed with the aid of disk caching. Click the Physical Drive button to test your drive's raw speed performance. Higher numbers are better.

The Logical Drive test more accurately indicates how your drive performs on a daily basis. To learn more details about the results, right-click on any of the resulting bar graphs, and click "What's This?" You'll learn a few more details about the significance of the test.

FIGURE 20.8
The hard drive benchmark tests your drive against its own best-ever performance.

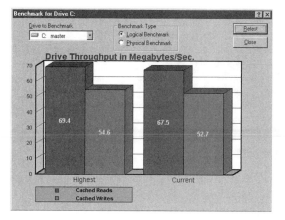

When Other Resources are Needed

To update a drive's driver (if required), change its DMA settings, or alter its status to "Removable," you'll have to open Device Manager, from Control Panel. System Information does not give information on these features. Norton Diagnostics also tests a drive's revolutions per second, using a slightly different methodology than is used by System Information.

The Input Tab

To display raw specifications about your mouse and keyboard, click the Input tab. Details about input devices, such as styluses connected to your serial port, will not show up on the System Information tab, but trackballs will. Trackballs hard-wired to your laptop may not display here, but a USB mouse will. System Information's ability to display hardware details depends greatly on the driver used by the device.

Depending on your mouse driver, System Information may not tell you if the mouse is serial or PS/2, but will inform you if the buttons have been reversed to accommodate left-hand usage. Specific driver information about your mouse, calibration, and alternate pointer settings are only available from the Windows Control Panel.

The Multimedia Tab

The Multimedia tab may provide the most useful information to the average computer user, specifically someone who wants to know if their system is capable of running the newest multimedia applications (see Figure 20.9). Its disappointing to spend money on a program, find out it runs like molasses on your computer, then have to choose either to go without, or to upgrade.

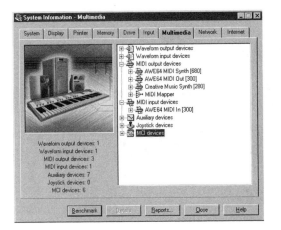

At first blush, the Multimedia tab outlines your CD-ROM and sound card configuration the same way Device Manager does. It lists .WAV and MIDI input and output devices, Joystick settings, and evaluates the compatibility of your CD-ROM drive with popular multimedia file types. Click Benchmark, though, and you'll see how your computer performs in a large variety of multimedia environments. It evaluates MPEG, AVI, 3-D, Imaging, Audio Mixing, and CD-ROM playback speed and rendering quality. High marks on these tests assure you that you won't be left at the starting gate when trying to run demanding multimedia applications. Multimedia Benchmark is one of System Information's most attractive features. When running Multimedia Benchmark, have your Norton SystemWorks CD handy, since you must provide it for the test to complete successfully.

The Network Tab

The Network tab provides information about your server, volumes, groups and users set up on your network. You'll see detailed information about remote folders, hierarchy names and auxiliary network-wide components, such as printers and fax machines.

The Internet tab provides detailed information about various WINSOCK.DLL files on your computer, information that is otherwise hard to view in one dialog box (see Figure 20.10). This is important, because different Internet connections you employ may use different Winsock routines, and this duplication can cause errors. To fix them, you might need to eliminate or update a particular WINSOCK.DLL, and knowing which one is causing the problem can be difficult, unless you know which application it is associated with. System Information's Internet tab provides such details.

Please note that to facilitate viewing of different WINSOCK.DLL versions, the Internet tab provides a drop-down menu, as shown in the Figure 20.10. Click a version in the menu to view its details. Also, the Filename and Description field do not provide enough space to view the entire line of information. To view the entire line, place your mouse inside the field and drag to the right.

Click the Details button to view dial-up parameters, recent successful connections, Winsock output data, and IP and Gateway information as well.

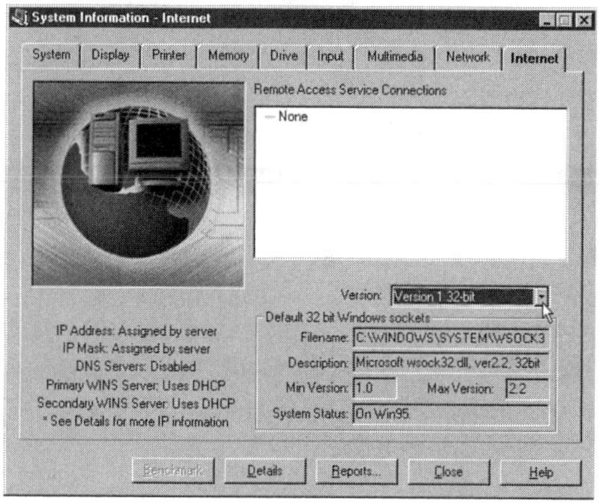

FIGURE 20.10
Click the Version drop-down menu on the Internet tab to view information about the WINSOCK.DLL files used by various programs.

Caution: If someone drills deeply enough into the Dial-Up Phonebook Entries heading, *they can view your logon password.* You may, therefore, want to set up a password from the Control Panel, so not just anyone can run System Information.

System Information Reports

System Information Reports let you determine how much detail you want to include. Ranging from the behemoth Technical Support Report (which includes the entire Registry printout, and thus, tops the 500 page mark), to the simple Current Tab report (which reproduces what you see on your screen in text form), you yourself get to decide how much of this information needs to be kept around for later. The Reports button is always available at the bottom of any tab. Click it to open a dialog box with various report options.

Before we look at what each report and Reports button does, I want to point out two features:

- You need not print your report to hardcopy. All Report Destination options are revealed after clicking the Print button. That means you actually click the Print button when you plan to save the report on your hard drive, but not print it.

- System Information's Print feature lets you save only the information you need. You can select a print option to save as minimal or as comprehensive a report as you wish. Otherwise, it is saved in the SystemWorks folder of your hard drive.

Here's how reports work:

At the bottom of the System Information screen, click the Reports button, and the Reports dialog box appears. There are four report types:

- **Current Tab:** Prints the currently displayed test as a simple text document. Only the screen contents are printed.

- **Typical:** Describes your system in some detail, including the most important indicators of your computer's capabilities. Saved as a .TXT file, this report totals around 25 pages.

- **Technical Support:** Includes Registry information and is fully detailed, weighing in at more than 500 pages.

- **Custom:** Generates custom reports for any System tab you choose (see Figure 20.11). Note that five of the System tabs provide further customization options. Click the Select button to choose your level of detail for that particular tab (see Figure 20.12).

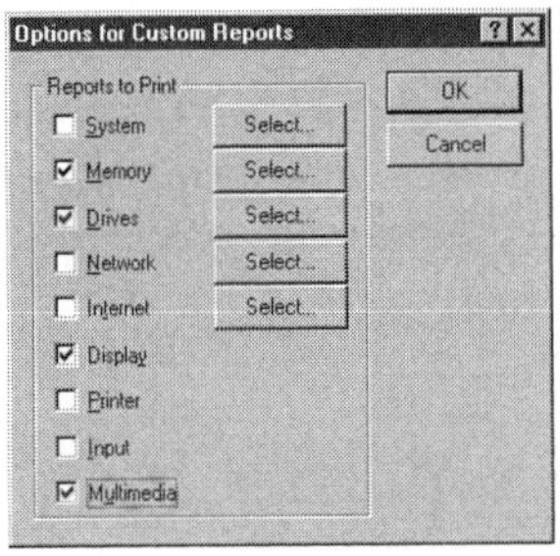

FIGURE 20.11

Custom reports let you specify how many systems need test reporting.

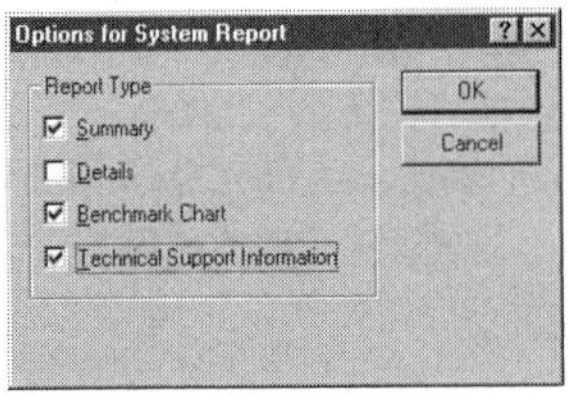

FIGURE 20.12

Determine the desirable level of detail for each system report.

Note that each tab with a Benchmark test allows you to print only the benchmark graph, if you so desire. That's because sometimes the Benchmark test is all you need to determine a component's speed and capabilities. Benchmark graphs will be printed in full color, if supported by your printer. Unless you also select Summary or Detail, very little explanatory information will be printed along with the Benchmark report.

Working with Norton Diagnostics

As mentioned earlier, Norton Diagnostics is DOS-based, and checks the fundamental soundness of your computer's components, such as parallel and serial ports, CPU, and motherboard. It checks raw data flow, hard drive head integrity, and RAM quality. It does not test how your hardware behaves under Windows, nor does it check for software-related compatibility.

Norton Diagnostics is a great tool for running a quality control check on a computer before selling it, or obtaining hard diagnostic data to justify replacing a component as defective.

Running Norton Diagnostics

To begin Norton Diagnostics, restart your computer in MS-DOS mode, and access the folder containing your Norton Utilities files. Type **NDIAGS**, and the Norton Diagnostics opening screen appears. Unless you went out of your way to install a mouse driver for the DOS environment, your mouse will not work. You'll notice that each phase of the test is introduced by messages explaining the test methodology and purpose.

If you simply press Enter when prompted and allow Norton Diagnostics to run all the tests, your system will be busy for 20 to 40 minutes. The opening screen offers three options for running the tests. One, as I just mentioned, is to simply choose Next when prompted, and walk through all basic tests. You can also run any specific test or group of tests from a menu, depending on which resource you want to check out. One final option is to accomplish reporting and printing in one step, by choosing Report from the File menu, and creating a report regimen by selecting which components to test. Using this option, Norton Diagnostics runs a series of tests automatically, since your report options will be chosen beforehand.

Caution: Take care in choosing tests in the comprehensive menu. Some, such as the Comprehensive Memory Test, can take many hours to complete. Most tests can be aborted by pressing the Esc key, but some, such as the Comprehensive Memory Test, may require you to shut off your computer to prematurely end the test.

Note: Your motherboard has a battery which maintains your *CMOS* settings. When it runs out, it takes your system settings with it. Saving a hard copy of your Norton Diagnostics report provides your technician with an easy blueprint to work with. After restoring your battery, she can use the report to set up your system parameters again. These can also be restored in some conditions from a Norton Rescue Disk.

Using Keyboard Controls in the Norton Diagnostics Environment

Use the arrow keys to scroll down and view the entire message. A menu appears at the top of the Norton Diagnostics main screen. This menu lets you choose which tests or group of tests to run. To access this menu without a mouse, simultaneously press the Alt key and the first letter of the menu name you want to open. (Keyboard shortcut letters are also displayed in red onscreen.) Arrow keys move you horizontally across menus, and up and down for menu item selection. Press Enter to select a menu item, or the spacebar to select a check box. For example, use the arrow or Tab keys to highlight the Disable Introduction Messages option, and press the spacebar to select or deselect the option.

Walking Through the Tests

Your System Board and CPU will be tested initially, including clock accuracy, which reflects remaining battery life. After that, ports are checked. Norton Diagnostics examines data flow at various baud rates through each port, and tests the buffered transmissions through a special chip built into your serial port (called a 16550A chip). These tests are quite comprehensive and definitive.

TECHNICAL NOTE

> UART technology is necessary for converting parallel bytes of data flow into serial flow, the type of data flow needed for online transmissions. It is applied to your serial port. UART stands for Universal Asynchronous Receiver Transmitter. This technology needed to be updated to facilitate fast modem transmission speeds. The 16550A chip was invented and deployed on your serial port for this purpose. Once again though, new technology is needed, this time, to facilitate 128Kbps transmission speeds for the modems of tomorrow. Thus, the new 16-650 and 16-750 chips are now found on serial ports of the newest computers.

Using LoopBack Plugs

LoopBack plugs are used during LPT and Serial port testing to increase the accuracy of the tests. They can be ordered from Symantec, although the tests are still of value if you do not use these accessories. In order for your Port tests not to show errors because of the absence of LoopBack plugs, you must specify that you don't want to use them before the tests begin. However, by the time the first screen of the test displays messages about LoopBack plugs, its already too late to gracefully opt out of them. So it's a good idea to check the No LoopBack Plugs option before any tests begin. Then you won't be bothered about them as the tests progress.

To turn off prompts for LoopBack plugs, access the File menu (without a mouse, press Alt+F), then scroll down and choose Options. Use the spacebar to deselect the Use Optional Loopback Plugs check box.

Norton Diagnostics renders a series of tests for each port, active or not. Like most Norton Diagnostics tests, the results are pass/fail. Printing reports will be explained momentarily.

Additional Tests

If you've chosen to walk through the basic series of tests, clicking Next when prompted, you'll also move through IRQ status, RAM, hard drive, and Video diagnostic tests. These are each pretty worthwhile, and won't add more than 20 minutes to your total testing time.

IRQ Status

Testing IRQ status lets you determine what IRQ channel a component is using to send interrupt calls. Interrupt conflicts are a big source of hard-to-trace intermittent errors. When adding new hardware to your computer, you may find that this component is attempting to use the same IRQ that's been previously assigned to another component. Having a way to verify what IRQ channels are available helps you choose which channel to assign your new hardware to.

Most newer hardware is Plug and Play, and thus, able to determine available interrupts during its own installation. However, if a particular component lacks this capability, Norton Diagnostics lets you see what IRQs are available, and which are in use.

Memory Tests

RAM tests are very thorough and detailed, and can verify physical RAM failure, and instances in which RAM is not configured or installed correctly on your computer. Although mixing RAM chip types is a major no-no, not everyone knows not to do this. And not every RAM incompatibility error will present as a fatal, or a non-start condition. You may just see performance denigration and lots of General Protection Faults. You can use Norton Diagnostics to verify faulty RAM chips, errors in chip compatibility, as well as errors in configuration.

Hard Drive Tests

The hard drive tests examine the read/write capabilities of your drive. The drive is made to locate both sequential and randomly accessed data. Norton Diagnostics also tests raw rotational speed (the familiar RPMs, used by hard drive advertisers as a selling point). This test will display somewhat better numbers if an on-board hard drive disk cache is used. This test can be used to verify faulty heads and imperfections in the hard drive's surface area. These indicators warn you of impending hard drive failure, hopefully giving you enough time to back up all your data, before heading south for good. Hard drive tests take longer if your hard drive is particularly large, but are not affected by how full the drive is.

Video Adapter and Monitor Tests

The video test is Norton Diagnostics' most complete, testing your video card's ability to display text and colors in a variety of modes. These tests seem somewhat primitive compared to System Information's Multimedia Benchmark, but they do verify the raw ability of your computer to display clear colors and non-fuzzy text. This test takes longer than any other, and requires you to frequently verify the legibility of text on your screen by pressing a key.

The video mode tests help identify discrepancies between your video card and monitor. In some older configurations, a monitor might be unable to display the same text and color modes that a video card could. These tests help verify compatibility. Also, if you notice symptoms that could represent either monitor or video card failure, these tests help diagnose which component is at fault.

Reports

Quite often, its necessary to print out results of Norton Diagnostics Tests, or create a report to refer to later. You may not need a comprehensive report, perhaps only one or two components were malfunctioning and needed your attention. You can print out a report, or create a file for viewing data by clicking the Print button after completing a test. If you chose to print to a file, a name is suggested that you may either accept or write over, saving under a different name.

If you've already generated a report for one system, and are now creating another report, you don't have to create a new file. Norton Diagnostics will append the existing report with the new information. This allows you to save all your data from one session as one file, simply updating your report as you move from component to component.

You can group together system tests, running them in series without requiring your input for the most part, and generate a single report for this test group. To locate tests that automatically generate reports, select Reports from the File menu and make a selection.

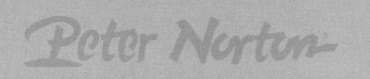

APPENDIXES

Emergency Recovery Techniques

This appendix provides you with quick answers to a selected group of specific problems. These shortcuts give you a direct answer to a direct question as often as possible so that you don't have to wade through Help files or the rest of this book if you've got a problem staring you in the face.

If you have turned to this Appendix because you suspect hardware-related difficulties, turn to the section named "Hard Troubles," near the end of the Appendix.

> **Caution:** If you have purchased Norton SystemWorks because you have already experienced a drive failure or because you suspect a viral infection, do not install Norton SystemWorks yet. Doing so could exacerbate your troubles. Follow the guidelines here (near the end of this appendix) for making repairs through the DOS-based Norton Utilities before you install the SystemWorks software.

SystemWorks Is Installed and Windows Crashes

Use your Norton Rescue set—ideally, your Norton ZIP Rescue Disk set—to reboot your PC and run through the Rescue Recovery Wizard. When the Rescue Recovery Wizard asks whether you want to check for disk problems using Norton Disk Doctor, be sure to allow Norton Disk Doctor to run. It looks for and repairs what may have been the underlying cause of your crash. If you boot with a ZIP Rescue Disk set and suspect Registry damage, allow the Rescue Recovery Wizard to rebuild your Windows Registry. When you reboot normally, immediately run Norton WinDoctor (accessible in your Start menu under Programs | Norton Utilities | Norton WinDoctor) to check for underlying problems.

SystemWorks Is Installed and You Need to Recover a Deleted File

Launch Norton UnErase from the SystemWorks Integrator or from the Start menu, under Programs | Norton Utilities | UnErase Wizard. If the deleted file was recently deleted, select Recently Deleted Files and click Next to continue the Wizard. If the filename appears in the list of deleted files, select it and click Recover.

If the filename does not appear in the list of recently deleted files, click the Back button in the UnErase Wizard and choose to see All Protected Files. The file list sorts alphabetically by default. Select the file's name in the list and click Recover.

If the filename does not appear in the list of all protected files, begin an interactive recovery by backing up in the UnErase Wizard and selecting to see files based on criteria you specify. Step through the Wizard, providing the information of which you are certain, and review the new list of files. If your filename does not appear in the list, right-click the list display and select View UnRecoverable Files.

If the file's name suddenly appears, you will not be able to recover the file through Windows. Quit to DOS, and run the DOS-based version of Norton UnErase from Emergency Disk #2. To do this, boot from Emergency Disk #1, select Norton UnErase, press Enter, and insert Emergency Disk #2 when prompted. You must perform a manual recover to try to get back whatever file fragments have not been obliterated. For details on performing manual recovery, refer to Chapter 15, "Norton Utilities: Getting it Back, Getting it Right: UnErasing and File Compare."

SystemWorks Is Installed and Your Application Crashes

Norton CrashGuard catches about 96 percent of all kinds of crashes. When a crash occurs, the Norton CrashGuard Crash Assistant runs automatically. From within the Crash Assistant, you can save the data you were working on in the crashed application, then restart the application and continue working. Norton CrashGuard protects other running applications so that you can save your work in them, too. CrashGuard can also restart Windows or Internet Explorer if you crash while surfing the Web, and it takes you back to the last URL you were viewing. Most of the Norton CrashGuard Crash Assistant screens are self-explanatory, but refer to Chapter 8, "Norton CrashGuard: When Windows Breaks," for detailed information about the entire integrated component.

SystemWorks Is Installed and Your Drive Failure Seems to Have Occurred Within Windows

Quit any applications that are running, and launch Norton Disk Doctor from the SystemWorks Integrator or from the Start menu, under Programs | Norton Utilities | Norton Disk Doctor. Check the box for Automatically Fix Errors, and let Disk Doctor perform a complete scan of all drives, including surface scans. Norton Disk Doctor repairs any problems it detects and provides you with a report of all errors and repairs.

SystemWorks Is Installed and Windows Is Behaving Strangely

Launch the Norton WinDoctor from the SystemWorks Integrator or the Start menu, under Programs | Norton Utilities | Norton WinDoctor. Begin the WinDoctor Wizard, allowing it to perform all tests. Norton WinDoctor provides you with a summary of problems it detects. Allow WinDoctor to repair all problems using its default repair scheme. WinDoctor advises you when all repairs have been completed successfully.

If repairs fail and Windows continues to behave strangely, it may be necessary to reboot your PC using your Norton ZIP Rescue Disk set. In this case, allow the Rescue Recovery Wizard to analyze your system and, if necessary, rebuild the Windows Registry.

If Norton WinDoctor reports no problems but Windows continues to behave strangely, consider whether you have recently installed new software or hardware. Use the Add/Remove Programs control panel to remove any such software, and see whether Windows behaves properly. If it does, you may have a software incompatibility and should contact the product manufacturer. If you have installed new hardware, contact the hardware manufacturer and obtain technical support. Two hardware devices on your system may be incompatible or improperly configured. If the hardware support technician suspects configuration trouble, advise her or him that you have Norton System Information installed; it may be capable of providing important diagnostic data about your PC.

SystemWorks Is Installed and You Suspect a Virus

If you have installed and configured Norton AntiVirus AutoProtect, it is very unlikely that you have encountered a virus that AutoProtect has missed. Nevertheless, if you suspect you've done exactly that, launch Norton AntiVirus from the Start menu, under

Programs | Norton AntiVirus | Norton AntiVirus, select all drives in the Drives pane by placing a check mark next to each, and click Scan Now. Norton AntiVirus rescans your entire PC and prompts you with respect to any suspected viral activity it encounters.

SystemWorks Is Installed and Windows Won't Start

Boot your PC using your Norton Rescue or Norton ZIP Rescue Disk set. Allow the Rescue Recovery Wizard to test all aspects of your PC and drives. This problem is usually caused by a damaged boot record, and the Rescue Recovery Wizard can easily repair this problem. Also run Norton Disk Doctor to check for file allocation table-related trouble. Repair any problems that NDD identifies.

SystemWorks Is Installed and Windows Seems to Be Performing Worse

This problem is usually caused by severe fragmentation of your application and data files, the Registry, or the Windows Swap File. Run Norton WinDoctor to look for problems and useless data stored in the Registry. Allow WinDoctor to repair problems or remove outdated Registry keys. Then run the Norton Optimization Wizard, and enable it to optimize your Windows Registry and Windows Swap File. (To run the Norton Optimization Wizard, select it from the Start menu under Programs | Norton Utilities | Norton Optimization Wizard.) The Optimization Wizard automatically runs Norton Speed Disk to defragment your entire primary drive. If performance troubles persist after using the Optimization Wizard, run Speed Disk on all other hard drives in your system to eliminate the possibility that their fragmentation is impacting your computer's performance.

SystemWorks Is Installed and You Accidentally Formatted a Hard Drive

Restart your PC using Emergency Disk #1, and select UnFormat from the startup menu. Type the letter of the formatted drive and the switch **/IMAGE** after the word UNFORMAT on the menu's command line, and then press Enter. (For example, UNFORMAT C: /IMAGE.) UnFormat likely can restore your hard drive perfectly using your Image data.

SystemWorks Is Installed and a New Application Behaves Strangely

It may be that the makers of the application missed some software bugs or incompatibilities before the product was released to the public. Run Norton Web Services and use LiveUpdate Pro to search for any available upgrades or patches. If that fails, use the Add/Remove Programs control panel to completely remove the application from your system. Then reinstall the software. Sometimes errors that occur during setup can only be repaired by performing a clean setup.

SystemWorks Is Installed and You Run Out of Hard Disk Space

From the SystemWorks Integrator, select Norton Utilities, then Improve Performance, and, finally, Space Wizard. Allow the Wizard to perform an Express Scan of the full drive. Select discardable files from each screen that the Wizard displays, and allow them to be removed. If this does not provide sufficient drive space, you might want to open the Add/Remove Programs control panel and consider removing applications that you rarely use.

SystemWorks Is Not Installed and You Need to Recover a Deleted File

Boot your PC using Emergency Disk #1, and select UnErase from the startup menu. Press Alt+D to select the drive from which the file was deleted. When Norton UnErase has scanned that drive, press Alt+A to select the folder from which the file was deleted. Norton UnErase shows a list of deleted files in the selected folder. Notice that deleted filenames begin with a question mark. Select the file you want to recover, and press Alt+U to unerase the file. Specify a new first letter for the file's name, and the file is recovered. If the filename does not appear in the list, or if the prognosis for your file is Poor, you must use manual recovery techniques to reconstruct whatever fragments of the original file have not yet been obliterated. These procedures are discussed in Chapter 15.

SystemWorks Is Not Installed and You Accidentally Formatted a Hard Drive

Restart your PC using Emergency Disk #1, and select UnFormat from the startup menu. Select the drive you have accidentally formatted, and be sure to tell UnFormat that you do not have Image data available. UnFormat does the best job it can to reconstruct all the files and folders on your hard drive. When UnFormat finishes, follow the onscreen prompts to quit, and then return to the Emergency Disk startup menu and run Norton Disk Doctor.

You should be aware that after completing this process, your drive will not be bootable, and you will likely not be able to start Windows. You should consider using this process to enable you to recover vital work and data files from an accidentally formatted drive. If you wish to try to boot and start Windows, place Emergency Diskette #2 into a floppy drive, switch to that drive by typing the drive letter, followed by a colon, and pressing Enter, as in **A:**, then type **SYS** following by a space, and the drive letter you want to make bootable. For example, typing **SYS C:** will copy the system files to drive C: (which is usually what you'll want to do when using SYS). Remove the diskette and reboot. Again, the process may only be partially successful—or may fail completely—after using UnFormat, but you will, at the least, be able to retrieve your vital data files, even if you have to reinstall Windows and your software.

SystemWorks Is Not Installed and You Experience Apparent Drive Failure

Boot your PC using Emergency Disk #1, and add the switch **/C** after NDD in the menu's command line. (In other words, **NDD /C**). Press Enter to run Norton Disk Doctor. Enable Norton Disk Doctor to check all areas of all drives, including performing a surface scan. Norton Disk Doctor repairs all problems it encounters and displays a report.w

SystemWorks Is Not Installed and You Cannot Recognize a Hard Disk Even After Booting from Disk

Boot from Emergency Disk #1, and type **/REBUILD** after NDD in the startup menu; then press Enter. (If NDD does not appear on the startup menu's command line, backspace over whatever is there and type **NDD /REBUILD**, then press Enter.) Norton Disk Doctor attempts to rebuild the entire drive. In all likelihood, Norton Disk Doctor will inform you that there are no partitions on your drive. Instruct NDD to rebuild the drive by pressing Enter. Norton Disk Doctor attempts to locate partition information on your drive. When it locates one, it shows you the partition's specifications and asks you to confirm that they are correct. If they are, pressing Enter recovers the partition. If they're wrong, tell NDD to continue searching. Always create an undo file when using the /REBUILD switch with NDD, and store your undo file on a disk. When NDD has completed the rebuild, eject the Emergency Disk and reboot your PC. If your system will still not boot, insert a current standard Windows startup disk and reboot your PC. At the disk prompt, type **SYS C:** and press Enter. This copies basic system files back to your hard drive.

SystemWorks Is Not Installed and You Suspect a Virus

If you think that you have a virus, but you've not yet installed SystemWorks, you should boot from Emergency Disk #1 and select Norton AntiVirus. Follow the onscreen instructions and allow NAV to scan all your hard drives for viruses. If NAV finds a virus, follow its advice to eradicate or quarantine the danger. If no virus is found and you can successfully boot Windows, do so and install Norton SystemWorks. If you cannot start Windows, return to the Emergency Disk menu and select Norton Disk Doctor to check your hard drive for other problems. If NAV has not found a virus, other problems are the seat of your troubles.

Hard Troubles

If you're concerned that you may have hardware-related troubles, there are some simple inspections you can make which can identify and help you eliminate those troubles. Of course, if a chip on your motherboard has failed, just looking inside your computer won't tell you anything. But often times, hardware trouble is much simpler than that, and taking a peek can make the difference. If you're not comfortable opening your computer's system unit, seek the assistance of an experienced colleague or technical support personnel who work for the company from which you purchased your computer.

The first thing to consider when you're going to open your PC is the potential for hardware to be damaged by stray static electricity. Fortunately, the best defense is simply common sense and awareness of the possibilities. The second, and equally vital line of defense is a heightened awareness of exactly the impact you have, both electrically and physically, even if you just reach inside to touch something with no intent of moving it.

Guidelines for Avoiding Static Electricity Damage

It turns out that you are a lot more dangerous to your PC than it is to you; at least in terms of what could go wrong when you open up the system unit. The voltages inside the unit are anywhere from a little less than 3 volts up to 12 volts. These are so low that you won't hurt yourself touching any of them. On the other hand, people normally walk around with static electric charges of several hundred volts, or up to several thousand on a dry, cold day. That is more than enough to totally fry the delicate innards of your computer.

An electric current won't flow unless there is a voltage difference to drive it. Therefore, the actual voltage of your body isn't very important by itself. What matters is how much difference there is between the voltage at your fingertip and the voltage at the places you are about to touch. If you first touch the power supply or an unpainted portion of the metal chassis of your PC system unit, and then touch whatever you want inside, you will by this first step have brought your entire body (including your fingers) to essentially the same voltage as the chips you'll be touching. In this case, no damage will be done.

> **Caution:** It may seem counter-intuitive, but it's vitally important that you keep your PC plugged-in to its grounded power outlet whenever you're looking or working inside it. The ground is central to carrying dangerously high voltages away from both you and your PC. You may read the opposite instruction elsewhere, but don't be swayed by ignorant writers and errant information. Your PC should remain plugged-in.
>
> At the same time, be aware that your PC should be turned completely off before you open the case. In many instances, this just means shutting down Windows, and pressing the power switch. For computers with "soft on" power switches, however (that is, systems that don't ever fully turn off under normal circumstances), it is vital that you locate the power supply on the back of the PC and turn off the main power switch that you will find there.

If you get a shock when you touch the system case, be glad. That shock might have pained you, but it could have killed your PC's inner workings if they had received it instead of you. For not much money you can purchase a static-guard wrist strap and avoid the shocks altogether. The simplest of these are disposable: They're made of paper with a conductive strip attached. You attach one end to your PC's case (it's self-adhesive) and place your wrist through a loop in the other end. And static that builds up across your skin while you work is drained down the wrist strap, so neither you nor your PC get shocked. If you do a lot of work inside PCs, a non-disposable variety is also available.

Looking for Trouble

All of that said, what sorts of hardware trouble can you identify inside your PC? Fortunately, the types of trouble you can easily identify visually are the types of trouble that happen the most.

The most common problem of all involves connections. Not James Burkes' kind; your hard drives' kind. No hardware problem is more common than a cable coming loose inside your PC. So, if you've got a hard drive that has suddenly stopped working altogether—if, for example, you see a message that says `No Boot Drive Available. Insert System Diskette and Press Any Key`—the chances are very good that the only problem you have is something which has worked its way loose inside over time. Of course, if you've recently been working inside your PC and *then* a piece of hardware stops working, you probably just knocked something loose while you were working.

Let me give you an example. Recently, a friend added a new cable modem to his PC. This required him to install a card inside his PC. He inserted the card and found that the cable modem was working perfectly. However, his printer had stopped working. He checked the external connections, checked his software configuration, and spent hours on the telephone with technical support—all to no avail. As it turned out, he had accidentally bumped loose the connector which linked his motherboard to the external parallel port built-in to the back of the system case.

What I ended up doing when he called me for help is exactly what you should do if a piece of hardware suddenly stops working. I looked inside his computer and tried to verify that everything was plugged-in tight. In my friend's case, of course, I checked the printer port connection first, and found the problem right away. If you've opened your PC because your hard disk has stopped working, you'll want to first check to see that the power connector and ribbon cables are tightly plugged-in to your drives. If they appear to be, then gently follow the ribbon cable to its opposite end and make certain that it's tightly seated into the motherboard. If everything seems correctly connected, don't start unplugging and re-plugging cables, thinking you'll make a better contact—it's too easy to forget where connectors go, or what orientation they require. Seek professional assistance from your PC manufacturer or seller if everything is plugged in tight and things are still not working.

If your video display or internal modem or sound card suddenly stop working, it may simply be that the card which provides that functionality to your PC has come loose. In such a case, gently press straight down on the top edge of the card, to re-seat it. You may need to press firmly, but don't be rough. Also, be certain that you don't rock the card from side-to-side. You could snap off the connector, possibly ruining both the card and your motherboard itself.

Finally, if you try to turn your PC on, and nothing happens at all—that is, it seems that your PC isn't getting any power at all—that's probably exactly what's happening. Your power supply has probably "died." Understand, however, that *nothing* inside your power supply is repairable. Power supplies are sealed because the voltages they contain can be deadly. They could easily kill you. So, if you suspect that your power supply has failed, definitely seek professional assistance directly. It is possible to replace a power supply, but it's definitely not a job for inexperienced users.

B

Installation Issues

The process of installing Norton SystemWorks 2.0 does not differ fundamentally from that of installing any other sophisticated piece of Windows 95 or Windows 98 software. Also, much like other software, SystemWorks comes with its own, unique set of installation considerations. We'll explore those considerations and the entire installation process in this Appendix. You'll find information about removing the SystemWorks product from your PC at the end of this appendix.

Installing SystemWorks

If you have AutoPlay enabled on your CD-ROM drive, inserting the Norton SystemWorks 2.0 CD for the first time starts the setup program and presents you with a menu of installation options. In all likelihood, you'll want to choose the first option on this menu and install SystemWorks to your PC. However, there are a few well-produced videos on the CD that will provide you with some good insight into a number of SystemWorks-related issues, particularly computer viruses. If you want to view the videos before installing the product, you can do so; they run directly off of the CD-ROM. Simply click View Product Videos from the initial SystemWorks install screen and then double-click the video of your choice in the window that opens.

Assuming you do eventually choose to install Norton SystemWorks, the first message you'll see from the setup program reflects the most important of those unique considerations I mentioned earlier. This message falls under the general category of *Big Fat Warning You Should Pay Attention To*. It states that installing Norton SystemWorks on a virus-infected or damaged drive can make matters worse. You should repair the damage first and then install.

Like all software, Norton SystemWorks occupies disk space on your PC after it's installed. If you purchased SystemWorks to repair a damaged drive, ironically, installing the product could simply exacerbate the damage. More likely, however, installing the product onto a damaged drive—if the installation worked at all—would simply add Norton SystemWorks to your collection of software that's unusable because it's on a damaged drive. And a virus infection on your drive could infect the Norton AntiVirus component of SystemWorks before you have the chance to use NAV to eradicate the virus! Finally, if you bought SystemWorks to help you UnErase important files that have been lost, you should understand that installing the product could *forever* obliterate those files. (For an understanding of how and why, read Chapter 6, "Norton Utilities: Digging Through the Trash with Norton Protection.")

These considerations have nothing to do with Norton SystemWorks itself; they are simply a reflection of the realities of disk damage, virus damage, and what really happens to files when we delete them. It's just more ironic than it might otherwise be to consider that your disaster-recovery product could be the engine of greater trouble.

> **Caution:** If you have already experienced some form of drive problems, or problems you suspect are related to a viral infection, or if you want to UnErase deleted files, *do not* install Norton SystemWorks. Instead, boot your PC using the disk labeled "Emergency Disk #1," and follow the instructions in Appendix A, "Emergency Recovery Techniques." After you address whatever problems may exist, return here to continue installing Norton SystemWorks.

With your drives in functional shape and no viruses suspected, you can click OK on the Warning dialog box, and continue with the installation. The Norton SystemWorks Setup Wizard steps you swiftly through the process. You are asked to read and agree to the software license agreement, just as with any other product you install. This agreement basically defines what legal relationship exists between you and Symantec, the company that created Norton SystemWorks. It talks about your responsibilities with respect to Copyright law—please don't steal software—and Symantec's responsibilities with respect to warranties, and so on. If you feel you can't agree to the terms, click the No button and SystemWorks Setup will quit; you can't install and use the software without agreeing to the license.

Assuming you find the license to be in order, click Yes, and enter your name and, if you like, your company name into the software. This information will appear in the Norton SystemWorks About box, identifying the name you enter here as the licensee of the software. In the next panel of the Wizard, you can select where you want SystemWorks to be installed on your PC. A default location has been chosen—`C:\Program Files\Norton SystemWorks`—but if you click the Browse button, you can put the software where you like.

Norton SystemWorks setup will next ask you whether you want to install a typical configuration or a complete configuration. If you choose to perform a typical installation, setup installs all the essentials of problem solving, virus protection, and crash protection. To lessen the impact on resources, a typical install will only enable select, vital functionality. This allows you to manually enable additional automated tools at a later time. If you elect a complete installation, all SystemWorks functionality will be installed and enabled, and you'll be given the opportunity—on the next panel—to deselect SystemWorks components which you don't want to install.

Most users should choose to perform a complete installation. You went to the trouble of purchasing Norton SystemWorks; there is very little that is more frustrating than encountering a problem that you can't address efficiently because you chose not to enable some of the suite's components. Of course, if you absolutely cannot spare the roughly 100MB of disk space that a complete installation requires, consider the following alternatives:

- If you never go online, never use floppy disks, and never install software, you could choose to leave Norton AntiVirus uninstalled.

- If, in your entire lifetime, Windows has never crashed on you, you could leave Norton CrashGuard uninstalled.

- If you never have had any trouble connecting to the Internet or an online service, or if you never travel, you could leave the SystemWorks bonus pack uninstalled.

After you select your configuration and decide which components you want to be able to use, the Setup Wizard displays a short confirmation, summarizing your choices. If any of them are incorrect, you can click the Back button until you return to the panel containing the error. Correct the error and then click Next to move forward. Clicking Next at the confirmation panel entitled Start Copying Files begins writing the software to your hard drive. This process can take a good deal of time—perhaps up to a half an hour on an older, slower machine. You can abort the installation at any time, but none of the SystemWorks components will function properly until the installation completes successfully.

After all files have been written to the location you specified in the Setup Wizard, you'll be offered the opportunity to check out the README file. This document commonly contains last-minute changes to the program's documentation, special offers, and any other issues the software designers think you might want to know about before running the product itself. The README file opens—if you choose to see it, of course—in the regular Windows Notepad, from which you can print it if you like. Close the README file after viewing, and the SystemWorks Setup prompts you to reboot your computer. None of the SystemWorks components work until you reboot. Additionally, as a general rule, it's inadvisable to install software while other applications are running. So, go ahead and reboot your PC, activating Norton SystemWorks.

After You Install

After you've installed Norton SystemWorks and have restarted your PC, there are a few steps you'll want to complete. Think of these steps as a vital part of the installation process. They are optional, but you're reading this book because you want my advice, and my advice is: Do it!

When Windows reboots, it finishes recording any changes that the SystemWorks installer made during setup. It may take considerably longer than usual for you to reach the desktop as Norton SystemWorks finishes making its own setup changes and runs Norton Image on your drives (refer to Chapter 10, "Norton Utilities: More than a Mirror, an Image").

You'll also see a small dialog box from Norton AntiVirus indicating that NAV Auto-Protect is fully functional and working. Just click Minimize on this dialog box to continue on to the desktop.

Norton System Doctor will run for the first time and will complete its preliminary scans of your computer, Windows, and your drives. You may receive warning indicators from one or more of the Norton System Doctor sensors, and you should follow the screen prompts to allow Norton SystemWorks to repair any problems it encounters. One sensor warning you will definitely see will inform you that your Norton Rescue information is out of date. Actually, of course, because you just installed SystemWorks, your Rescue information doesn't yet exist. Updating your Rescue disk set is the very first thing you should do after installing Norton SystemWorks. It's an absolutely vital part of your total protection and prevention scheme. To learn more about Norton Rescue, read Chapter 7, "Norton Utilities: Life Preserver on a (Rescue) Disk."

The next step you should take after addressing any problems detected by Norton System Doctor is to begin your free six-month subscription to Norton Web Services and allow LiveUpdate Pro to check for modifications or improvements to Norton SystemWorks itself. LiveUpdate Pro can even update itself, as you'll read about in Chapter 19, "Norton Web Services: Your Current Computer."

Other early steps you might consider include running Norton Disk Doctor, the Norton Optimization Wizard, and Norton WinDoctor—in that order—to double-check for problems on, and to optimize all, your drives and your Windows Swap File. After these steps are taken, you'll know that your entire PC is in working order and that Norton SystemWorks is properly installed and doing its job while enhancing yours.

Removing SystemWorks from Your PC

If you wish to remove Norton SystemWorks from your PC—either in whole or in part—you can do so. Open the Add/Remove Programs Control Panel and select Norton SystemWorks from the list. You'll notice that LiveUpdate and Norton Web Services are also in the list. You can uninstall LiveUpdate any time you want, but to reinstall it, you must reinstall all SystemWorks. Norton Web Services can also be uninstalled at almost any time, but it cannot be removed as long as the Norton Utilities component is installed.

From the SystemWorks uninstall panel, you can select any or all the components that you want to remove. You will be prompted whether you want to remove shared components. If you are deleting the entire SystemWorks suite, it's safe to remove all the shared components in the Symantec Shared subfolder. Whether you remove shared components located in your Windows folder or elsewhere on disk is a determination you have to make on a file-by-file basis. Every PC is different. In general, shared components that appear in the "do you want to delete this component" message box are ones that no other program is using, however, this is not always the case. The Remove Wizard automatically runs once for each of the main components that you elected to remove.

When uninstallation is complete, you may be informed that some components could not be removed. This is usually because they are in use during the uninstallation. After you acknowledge this message and reboot your PC, some of these folders and files will be automatically removed. You can manually remove the remainder, if any, which the Remove Wizard was unable to delete. (Click Details on the uninstallation results screen to see which folders these are.)

To complete a full uninstallation of the Norton SystemWorks suite, you must return to the Add/Remove Control Panel and remove both LiveUpdate and Norton Web Services. Norton SystemWorks can be reinstalled at any time.

The Professional Pack

The Professional Edition of Norton SystemWorks includes a suite of useful utilities that provide some special functionality for power users. The final state of the SystemWorks Professional Pack is subject to change, but what you will read here was the latest available information as we went to press. As of this writing, the Professional Pack consists of a duet of utilities: Norton 2000 and a special version of Norton Ghost.

Installing either of these elements is simple. Just insert the Professional Pack CD into your CD-ROM drive. If your CD-ROM AutoPlay feature is disabled, open the drive using either the Windows Explorer or My Computer and double-click the file called CDSTART.EXE. When the installation program runs, click Install. This opens a customized Windows Help file with buttons that enable you to install either Professional Pack utility as well as any Bonus Pack components you want (you'll read about the latter in the next appendix). Click the button corresponding to the feature you want installed and follow the simple instructions onscreen.

Norton 2000

It's likely no exaggeration that the only issue more hyped than the errantly calculated "turn of the millenium" in 2000 C.E. is the Year 2000 computer "bug," known to almost everyone who hasn't been in a cave for the last five years as Y2K. Unlike the false millenium which will, at worst, generate a few extra hangovers and some disgruntled math pundits, the Y2K problem could indeed have serious and wide-ranging consequences. We'll all know those consequences with certainty in a few months, but there is one thing that we know today: because of the means by which many computers, hardware components and software calculate and maintain dates, the rollover from 31 December, 1999 to 1 January, 2000 could cause thousands of those components and pieces of software to fail.

If your PC or some of its software suddenly fails, the costs could be substantial—or incalculable, depending on how you or your business use computers. Fortunately, Norton 2000 lays the majority of your Y2K concerns to rest, at least as far as your own PC is concerned. Norton 2000 is Symantec's complete Y2K solution, providing testing, analysis, workarounds (when necessary), and cure (when possible) of and for a wide array of Year 2000-related headaches.

Norton 2000 consists of two primary components: the Norton 2000 BIOS Test and Fix and the Norton 2000 Wizard utility. The BIOS Test and Fix is unnecessary for users of Windows 98—the corrections it provides are a built-in part of that operating system. However, for the tens of millions of users still running Windows 95, the BIOS Test and Fix could be a lifesaver, in digital terms. Operating system notwithstanding, all users stand to reap real benefit from the Norton 2000 Wizard utility.

Norton 2000 BIOS Test and Fix

The name "BIOS Test and Fix" is something of a misnomer in that this Norton 2000 component actually can test and fix more. Both a PC's system BIOS and its real-time clock can be tested; these two hardware components work together to provide for many of your PC's date-related needs. If either of these components does not properly handle dates after 31 December, 1999, some or all of your computer's capability to function could be seriously impaired.

Norton 2000 BIOS Test and Fix checks to verify that your hardware does handle dates after the end of 1999 correctly. Moreover, Norton 2000 also guarantees that your PC will operate properly and continuously through the crucial one second over which your PC will switch from 1999 to 2000 C.E. Such a test might seem simple—just set your clock to 31 December around 11:59pm, and watch what happens, right? Wrong. Testing for Y2K compliance in that manner could cause your PC to freeze, and rebooting could cause further date-related problems. Software-expiration triggers could be initiated; any date-containing files you open in this state could be permanently damaged; crucial operating-system support files could themselves be Y2K-incompatible, rendering all of Windows unusable. Not a pretty picture.

Fortunately for users, Norton 2000 BIOS and Fix can complete these tests in a completely noninvasive manner. Neither your operating system nor your applications nor your data files are in danger at any time. Norton 2000 tests the results of rebooting your PC without actually rebooting, and it tests the real-time results of your PC's clock ticking over from 1999 to 2000 without any danger of triggering software expirations or risking the integrity of your operating system.

But problem detection isn't useful without the capability to repair those problems. Norton 2000 can. The BIOS Test and Fix installs DOS-based software that can—on an as-needed basis—permanently correct incompatibilities or provide continuous second-by-second compensation for problems that cannot simply be "cured." Finally, the BIOS Test and Fix alerts you if analysis determines that your BIOS or real-time clock can neither be "cured," nor properly compensated for, in which case you will need to upgrade or replace the incompatible component.

Note: Almost all PCs manufactured in the last few years have BIOSes that can be upgraded by running a special piece of software which can be provided by your BIOS manufacturer. If Norton 2000 BIOS Test and Fix determines that your BIOS requires replacement, you will likely be able to go onto the Internet and quickly locate your BIOS manufacturer and learn how to purchase an upgrade.

Norton 2000 Wizard

The second half of the Norton 2000 suite is the Norton 2000 Wizard. Just as the BIOS Test and Fix checks everything that underlies your software for Y2K compliance, so the Norton 2000 Wizard checks your software and operating system files themselves. This way, you're covered above and below.

The Norton 2000 Wizard has its own knowledge base containing details about the Y2K compliance of most popular software and operating system components and enhancements. Using this, the wizard checks installed software on your PC and produces a detailed report about the degree to which that software is Y2K compliant. In most instances, reports of incompatibility include clickable hyperlinks. These connect you directly to the Y2K-related Web site of the company that produced the problematic software. Each company handles its Y2K issues in a different manner, but most are well-aware of their software's Y2K liabilities. You'll find anything from workarounds to downloadable updates and bug fixes on the different Web sites.

Note: To benefit from this hyperlink capability, your PC must have an active Internet connection. If you use Windows Dial-Up Networking for your Internet connection and it is set to logon automatically, clicking a Norton 2000 Wizard hyperlink connects you to the Internet.

In addition to checking for known application incompatibilities, the Norton 2000 Wizard makes a comprehensive scan of your database- and spreadsheet-related files. As you probably know, these types of files commonly contain date-related information. They may be keeping track of retail inventories, financial transactions, or any manner of other tables or schedules of data which include—or refer indirectly to—calendar dates and times. If these files keep track of dates exclusively in a two-digit format (for example, "99" for 1999), their contents may become corrupted when you either attempt to include date information after 31 December, 1999, or when you open the files at some time after that date.

You can see how this can happen: If the computer sees a date of 10-11-12, should that date refer to 1912 or 2012? Computers have somewhere between little and no ability to understand context, so how these ambiguous dates are actually handled can lead to headaches.

The Norton 2000 Wizard is capable of natively-scanning the most popular database and spreadsheet files. It also has an unformatted file scanner that will check for date-related concerns in files of other types. Macros as well as embedded Visual Basic code are also analyzed. As date issues are detected in your files, the wizard produces a log, tracking those concerns. The log identifies precisely where in each file Norton 2000 has detected date issues and provides an intelligible description of the problem. In many cases, right-clicking a detected problem will provide the option of seeing suggestions by which the problem may be repaired.

The Norton 2000 Wizard reports are fully customizable, allowing you to focus on a particular type of file or a specific date-related concern for which you want to scan. For spreadsheets, the Norton 2000 Wizard will even (optionally, of course) generate a duplicate copy of date-affected documents, color-coding the duplicate to quickly draw your attention to problems in need of correction.

Finally, although you must purchase additional user licenses to do so, the multi-license Norton 2000 Wizard allows you to generate Project Files with which your coworkers—even if they are neophyte users—can safely run and detect Y2K problems on their own workstations. This capability can dramatically reduce the workload of IT professionals who are already overburdened by Y2K issues company-wide.

Norton Ghost

Norton Ghost provides professional power to address a completely different but commonly frustrating problem: how to transfer everything from an existing C: drive to a new C: drive—for example, if you're upgrading to a larger drive or a new PC entirely—without having to reinstall and reconfigure every piece of software you own. Traditionally, such conveniences have been the exclusive pleasure of Macintosh owners. Norton Ghost changes that. With Ghost, a complete copy of any drive, including the Windows Registry and INI configuration files, if relevant, can be quickly made. Restoring a Norton Ghost file to a new drive precisely re-creates the content of the original drive, without all of the restrictions commonly placed on you by other software purporting to provide similar features (like having to partition your new drive into multiple drives, so your new C: drive and your old C: are exactly the same size, thus eliminating some of the reason you upgraded to a new drive in the first place).

Norton Ghost files can also be used as part of your emergency-backup plans. With Norton Ghost, you can restore a drive to its exact condition before some set of problems developed. You can also use Norton Ghost files to restore a complete drive to a new drive if the original suffers from hardware failure.

Finally, although the version of Norton Ghost provided in the Professional Pack has limited features aimed at individual users, a special upgrade path to the full version of Norton Ghost is available which allows IS professionals to create, as it were, a "template PC." This template PC can be configured with the software installation and customizations that are desired for entire workgroups, departments, or whole offices. Using the full version of Norton Ghost, that template PC can be used to create a Ghost file which can be used to create clone after clone (or ghost after ghost) of the original, "standardized," PC. This can dramatically reduce the installation workload on IS personnel. Additionally, because all PCs which are created as ghosts of the original will be configured identically, professional training and support can really be streamlined with the help of Norton Ghost.

Caution: Of course, to use Norton Ghost to automate the configuration of multiple PCs, you must first own the proper number and type of end-user licenses from each of the relevant software manufacturers. It is illegal to use Norton Ghost to generate copies of improperly licensed software.

484

The Bonus Pack

Every edition of Norton SystemWorks includes a Bonus Pack of useful utilities. The final state of the SystemWorks Bonus Pack is subject to change, but what you will read here is the latest-available information. It introduces you to the components that are currently included: Norton 2000 BIOS Test and Fix, Norton Secret Stuff, Symantec WinFax, Symantec Visual Page, and Norton Mobile Essentials.

Installing elements of the Bonus Pack is simple. Just insert the CD into your CD-ROM drive. If your CD-ROM autoplay feature is disabled, simply open the drive using either the Windows Explorer or My Computer and double-click on the file called CDSTART.EXE. When the installation program runs, click Install. This will open a specialized Windows Help file with buttons that will enable you to install any Bonus Pack components you wish. Click the button corresponding to the feature you want installed and follow the simple instructions onscreen.

Norton 2000 BIOS Test and Fix

The Norton 2000 BIOS Test and Fix performs a series of checks to verify that your PC's BIOS (Basic Input-Output System) and its real-time clock are both fully Y2K-compatible. The Test and Fix will watch how your PC handles dates while causing your real-time calendar to roll over from December 31, 1999 to January 1, 2000. On an as-needed basis, the BIOS Fix will correct dates which your BIOS provides to applications. It will also continuously check to see that your real-time clock and calendar properly process dates. By so doing, the Norton 2000 BIOS Test and Fix can render an otherwise Y2K-incompatible system BIOS fully Y2K-compatible.

> Be aware that only users of Windows 95 have need for the BIOS Test and Fix. There is no need for Windows 98 users to install or run the BIOS Test and Fix; the capabilities it provides are included in Windows 98.

Norton Secret Stuff

Norton Secret Stuff is a deceptively simple way to guarantee that no unauthorized individuals can access selected files on your PC or in your email. NSS provides this protection by encrypting the files you choose and allowing you to select a password which is required to decrypt those files. Without the proper password, encrypted files are utterly useless, their actual contents indiscernible and unintelligible to any prying eyes. Norton Secret Stuff provides a level of encryption-based privacy which will more than meet the needs of most users.

Symantec WinFax Basic Edition

WinFax is provided as an enhanced replacement to Windows 95's built-in faxing capability and to provide fax capability for Windows 98 users. (No fax capability is included with Windows 98, and if you upgrade from Windows 95, you may have lost your Windows faxing tools in the upgrade.) From within WinFax you can "print" to your fax-modem from any standard Windows application. WinFax installs, essentially, a print driver that tricks your software into thinking it's printing when, in fact, the WinFax utility has taken over and directed the output to the fax number you select. You can design cover pages to be sent in advance of your actual content, and WinFax can be configured with the telephone number and sender ID data required to make your fax sending comply with federal law.

Symantec Visual Page

Symantec Visual Page is a complete environment for designing not merely Web pages but entire Web sites. Individual pages can be created in an entirely graphical interface, with sophisticated Java and CGI functionality available to designers with no technical knowledge. Individual pages can be "webbed" together into complex structures, all of which can be reviewed visually.

Norton Mobile Essentials

Norton Mobile Essentials is comprised of five major pieces: Before You Go, Location Controller, Connection Doctor (which is also now part of the Norton Utilities themselves), the Norton Connection Troubleshooter, and the Port Monitor. This package of utilities has value for the desktop user as well as the travelling user—Connection Doctor, for example, is a superb tool for troubleshooting *any* online connection. Other pieces, like Before You Go, are obviously targeted at the truly mobile user, but you'll learn about all of them here. As with all of SystemWorks, the various components are at your disposal as you need them; they have been designed to keep out of your way when you don't.

More than anything else, Norton Mobile Essentials, or NME, allows you to establish configurations for different locales which can be immediately selected upon booting. Each time you log on to NME you can select a location which you've defined. All of the subordinate settings which you've configured for that location are globally activated for you. Of course, you don't have to actually move about to make use of this. The location selector can be just as easily used to change configurations for different types of tasks as well as physical places.

Location Controller

The Location Controller is truly the central component of Norton Mobile Essentials. It can replace your standard Windows login. It's through the Location Controller that all of your location-based (or task-based, as we shall see) configurations are maintained and retrieved. When you first reboot after installing NME, you'll find the Location Controller greeting you, as in Figure D.1.

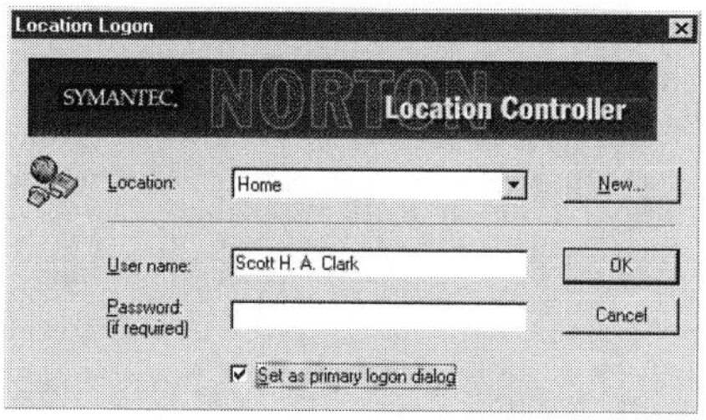

FIGURE D.1
Norton Mobile Essentials Location Logon controls access to your PC and allows you to select the NME location settings you want to use. (You'll read about defining these settings later in this chapter).

If you choose to place a check mark in the box labeled Set as Primary Logon Dialog, the NME logon will replace your standard Windows or network logon. If you choose to leave this box unchecked, you will need to log on to both NME and to your network or workstation.

> **Note:** Of course, if your workstation is not configured for multiple users, then you are not used to logging-on at all; you must log on to use NME features. If you don't wish to use NME features in a given session, you may click Cancel. If you go online during that session using Windows Dial-Up Networking, however, NME will insist that you log on to it.

The first time you log on to NME you have the option of creating an NME password. If you wish to do so, simply type it in the appropriate box below your user name. A password is not mandatory unless your workstation is configured for multiple users and you select NME as your primary logon. In that case, NME will accept your existing user password by default. Notice, also that NME has selected Home as the default location for the machine in Figure D.1. This will not always be the case. When installed, NME will retrieve the various existing locations, if any, from within your modem dialing properties, and those locations will be included for you in the Location drop-down box. The location selected when Windows was last shut-down will be displayed in the NME Location box. You're free to drop the box down by clicking on the arrow at its extreme right and selecting another location. In fact, as you do move from one location to another, this is the primary method you'll use to select configurations when you startup, as you'll see, below. To the right of the Location box is a New button, which launches the New Location Wizard. Let's take a look at how it works.

Adding a New Location

When you click the New button on the Location Controller login (or on the Location Controller screen, accessible from the main NME panel, as you'll read about below) you launch the New Location Wizard. You can see its first panel in Figure D.2. You'll need to enter a new name for each location you create, in the Location Name box. From this first screen, you then determine which settings you want the Wizard to prompt you for as you work your way through it. You can configure a location so that any or all of these tasks will be automatically performed when you login:

- Modem dialing setups, including local area information and, if you like, calling card codes will be set.
- Dial-Up Networking settings, including saved user names and passwords, service provider network configurations, and local telephone numbers will be retrieved.
- A local printer will be set as the default printing device.
- Local Area Network (LAN) connections will be re-established automatically.
- A customized set of applications will launch automatically at startup.
- Time and date settings will be updated to reflect the new location.

To enable any of these features, just place a check mark in its respective box. Click Next, to continue with the Wizard when you've selected the features you want for the new location you're defining. As you read what follows, bear in mind that the Wizard panels which correspond to features you do not enable will not be displayed.

The next panel, shown in Figure D.3, allows you to configure the Country, City (optional), dialing Area Code, and Time Zone for your new location. Selecting a Country in the first drop-down box enables a list of major cities in that country in the City box. Selecting a City automatically enables a list of dialing area codes which are available in that city, as well as selecting the appropriate time zone automatically. Click Next to continue.

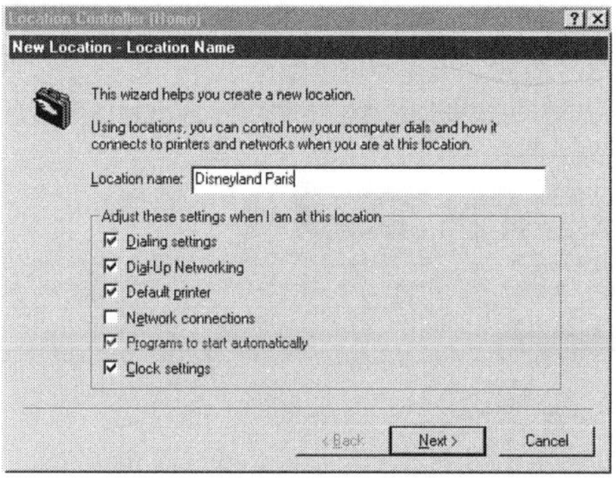

Figure D.2

The NME New Location Wizard creates new logon locations, all with their own customized settings.

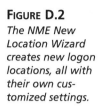

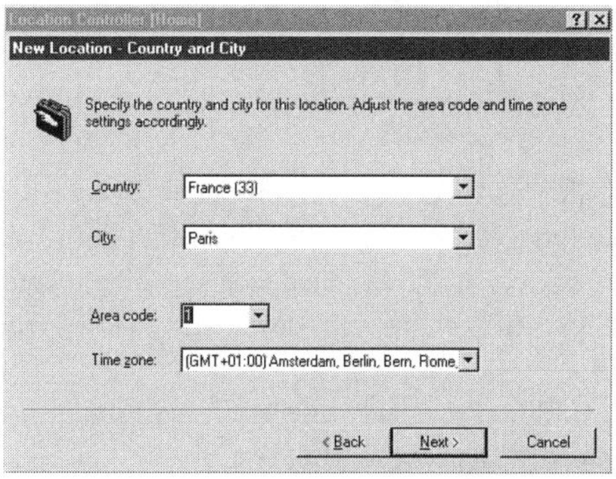

Figure D.3

This panel of the Wizard allows you to Select the Country, City, Area Code, and Time Zone.

Note: If the area code you require for the selected city does not appear in the Area Code drop-down list, you can simply click in the Area Code box and type the code manually. If the city you require does not appear in the City drop-down list, you may leave the city blank, or you can select the closest major city. In either case, you will usually need to manually enter the local area code.

The Dialing configuration panel, shown in Figure D.4, reconfirms the area and country code settings which you chose on the previous panel and allows you to enter codes which may be required for you to properly dial out from the new location. These commonly include codes to obtain an outside or long-distance line from a business or hotel PBX system, as well as deactivating call-waiting if necessary. You may already know that many systems require you to dial such an access code and then wait for a new dial-tone before proceeding. The comma "," is a standard modem code which causes a delay of approximately two seconds. If you require a longer wait, you can enter more than one comma. Thus, "8,,," in the figure indicates that a delay of about six seconds is required to obtain a long-distance dial-tone at this location.

If you choose to disable call-waiting, the drop-down box to its immediate right will enable, allowing you to select one of the most common call-waiting disable codes. If the local code does not appear, simply click in the box and type it yourself.

It's very common, particularly for business travelers, to use corporate calling cards for making long-distance connections to the home office. Placing a check mark in the Dial using calling card check box will open the dialog shown in Figure D.5. From here, you can select your calling card from the drop-down box, enter its number, and click OK to accept your settings.

If your calling card is not present in the drop-down box, click the New button to specify a name for the card you will be using.

You can create a script for your calling card, either for domestic or international uses. For each of the pre-defined calling cards, NME already knows how calls must be made, and will select those settings for you automatically. (You can enter changes if your calling card company has recently modified their dialing steps. Using LiveUpdate on NME will also update any dialing methodologies which are known.) Figure D.6 demonstrates the calling card scripting screen for making an International call via my selected card. Although it looks complex, the beauty of creating the script once and letting the modem do all the work from then on is very appealing.

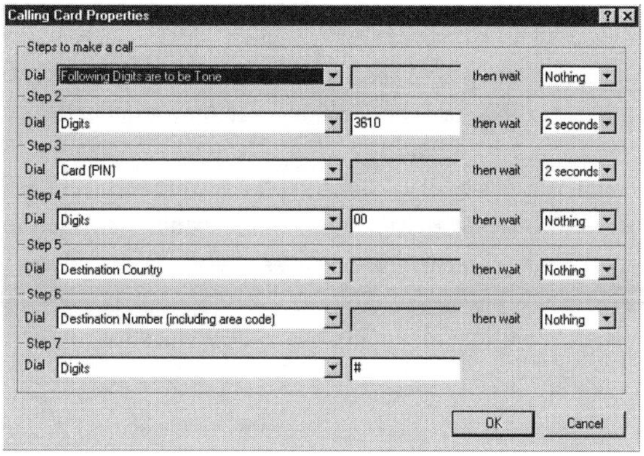

FIGURE D.6

You can create a script for making a calling card call.

Notice that the scripter lets you define up to seven unique steps, allowing you to pause as necessary after each. The steps from which you can select are:

- Entering digits, including commas, as necessary.
- Entering the pre-defined destination number, with or without area code.
- Entering the pre-defined destination area code.
- Entering the pre-defined destination country code.
- Entering your calling card number and PIN.
- Entering digits selectively as tone *or* pulse.
- Entering a "Flash" code.

> **Note:** The data which I refer to as "pre-defined," in the list above is data which NME will automatically extract from the dial-up telephone number you will enter into Windows Dial-Up Networking.

As you select steps from the first column of drop-down menus, data-entry boxes in the second will enable or disable in accordance with the action you've chosen. After each step, you can choose a delay of no time ("Nothing") or from two to forty seconds. You can also instruct the dialer to wait for a "bong," "dial tone," "quiet," "input code," or "done code," depending on your calling card company's system. When the delay specified has been met, the next dialing step will be performed.

Understand that you can create a script for both domestic and international dialing for each calling card you use. The dialing scripts will follow the calling cards. This means that if you dial a number outside the location's country, the calling card's international script will be used. Domestic calls made will use the card's domestic script.

Dial-Up Networking Configuration

The next panel allows you to specify the Windows Dial-Up Networking (DUN) settings you wish to use as this location's default. You may, of course, use more than one DUN configuration at any given location. This is a good example of what I meant earlier when I said that you can use NME to define tasks as well as locations. If you're logging on to your computer with the specific intent of connecting to a given service, then shutting-down, you may find it most convenient to create a separate "location" which uses that service as the DUN default. In this way, when you log on to Windows, you don't have to manually-select anything to quickly make the connection you want. (You'll see more of this later.)

Select any existing DUN configuration from the large drop-down box, as shown in Figure D.7, or click the New button to create a new DUN configuration. Clicking New launches the standard Windows Dial-Up Networking Wizard which will step you through the process of creating the new settings. When you complete the DUN Wizard, you'll be back at the DUN panel, as shown in Figure D.7, with your new location selected.

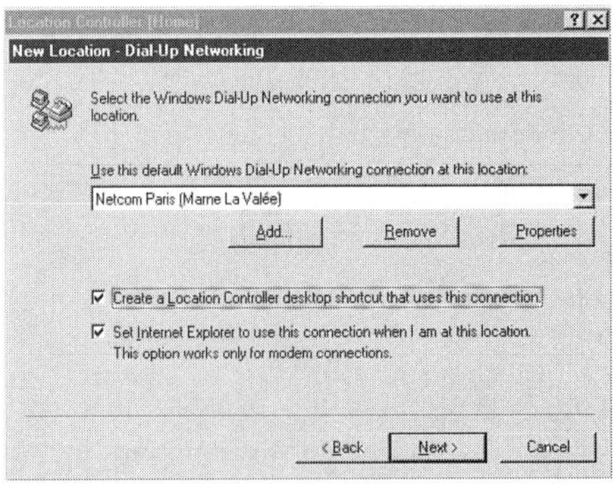

FIGURE D.7

Selecting the default Dial Up Networking (DUN) configuration for this location.

Putting a check mark in the box labeled, Create a Location Controller desktop shortcut that uses this connection, will cause NME to place a shortcut labeled Active Dial-Up Networking on the desktop. Double-clicking the shortcut will dial the related service. No more opening My Computer, then Dial-Up Networking, and then double-clicking on the service you desire!

Placing a check mark in the second box, Set Internet Explorer to Use This Connection will tell Internet Explorer (IE) to automatically connect to the service provider you've selected whenever you launch IE while offline. If you have IE in the taskbar and your user name and password stored within your Dial-Up Networking configuration, this makes getting on the Web from anywhere in the world a "single-click" operation.

Printer Configuration

The next panel of the NME New Location Wizard, shown in Figure D.8, allows you to select a default printer and printer settings for the location. Select an installed printer from the drop-down box or click the New button to run the standard Windows Add Printer Wizard. You can set the default printer settings (resolution, paper size, and so on) for this printer by clicking Properties. Clicking Remove will completely uninstall the selected printer from your PC.

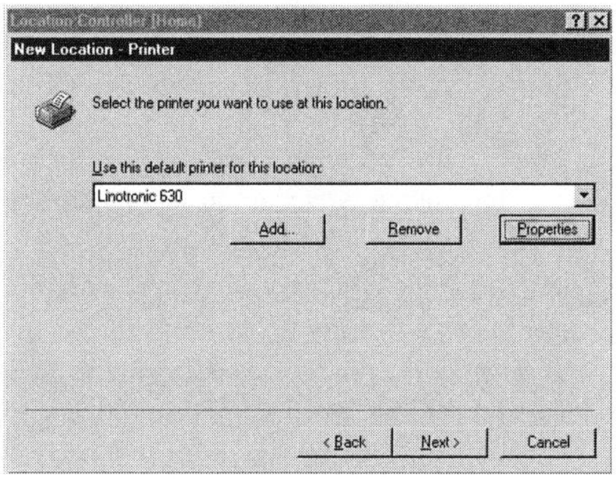

FIGURE D.8

This Wizard panel allows you to configure the default printer and its settings for a location.

Note: If you add a new printer, you may need your Windows CD-ROM or driver diskettes from the printer manufacturer to complete the Wizard successfully.

Configuring Startup Applications

Figure D.9 shows the next Wizard panel, from which you can specify applications you want to automatically run when you startup from this location. Here, too, is an area in which you may find it beneficial to create task-oriented "locations" within NME. You might, for example, commonly want to startup your computer, run Norton Disk Doctor to verify that the airline didn't turn your hard drive into soft mush, launch into and log on to an online service, and begin playing whatever audio CD you have in the drive. The settings you see in the figure below would automatically perform those three tasks. Other times you might want to startup and quickly open a particular Excel spreadsheet. Setting different application settings in a location called "Excel," for example, would let you do just that. In a manner of speaking, then, you can see that NME is providing functionality that is an enhanced version of what is available to you when your computer is configured for multiple users under Windows. With NME, however, your computer can continue to be configured for multiple users, and each user can have multiple working locations or task-based location environments. Configuration and access options which are set under Windows for multiple users—customized desktop, Start menu, access restrictions, and so on—will all be maintained by NME in addition to NME's extended functionality.

Each location can have its own set of startup applications which you define in this panel of the Wizard.

To add a startup application to the list, click Add. It's usually easiest to then click the Browse button and locate the program you want to run. (Be sure that startup applications are on a drive which will be available when Windows starts in this location.) You can use the Parameters box you'll see at the bottom of the application dialog to enter command-line switches or any other codes necessary to launch the program in the manner you require. Moreover, you can enter the path to a specific file in the Parameters box, and that file will automatically be opened when its application launches.

Network Configuration

The next panel, shown in Figure D.10, re-establishes any network connections which you will always want in the new location. One limitation of this panel is that you can only select network connections which are available at the time you run the New Location Wizard. If you try to manually enter the path to a network resource which is not available, NME will advise you that only shared resources may be selected for auto-connection, and your entered path will be deleted.

Assuming the shared resources you require are available, you can add them by clicking New. You'll be able to specify a drive to which you want each resource automatically mapped, and you may enter the user name through which you want to log on to that resource. (You'll be prompted for passwords if they are required.) Once a networking connection is defined, you can modify its settings by clicking Properties, or delete it by clicking Remove.

If you need to log on to a specific Windows NT domain or Novell preferred server, you can place a check mark in the relevant box and enter the domain or server name in the enabled entry box.

This is also a good opportunity for defining task-based "locations" within NME. You may want to connect to different domains or servers, or to different network drives and resources depending on which tasks you intend to perform. NME can make all of these different connections for you through task-based locations. For example, you might have a location defined for "Office-Network Administration" and one for "Office-Department Accounting," each of which would connect you to the relevant network drives, as well as launching applications for those tasks. Bear in mind that you need not define all settings—time, dialing rules, and so forth—for each new location. Unchecking those options in the first panel of the New Location Wizard will skip those panels later in the Wizard.

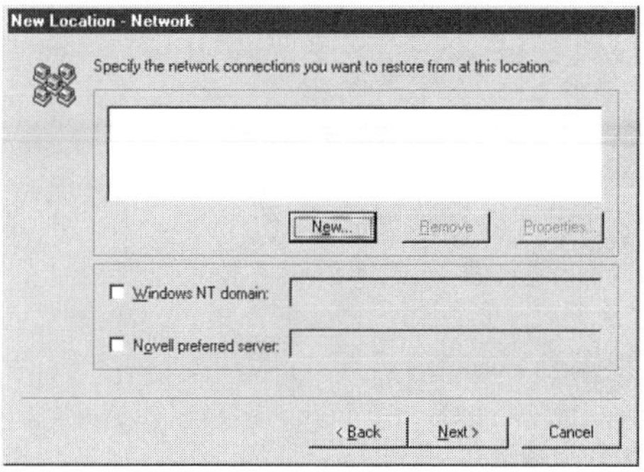

FIGURE D.10
Each location can have its own set of automatic network connections which are defined in this panel of the Wizard.

Time Zone Configuration

The final Wizard panel, shown in Figure D.11, allows you to confirm that you want time zone settings changed when you log on to this location. The time zone you specified—or that NME selected automatically—earlier in the Wizard is displayed, and you can change it if you want to do so. You can also disable time zone updating entirely by removing the check mark from the box.

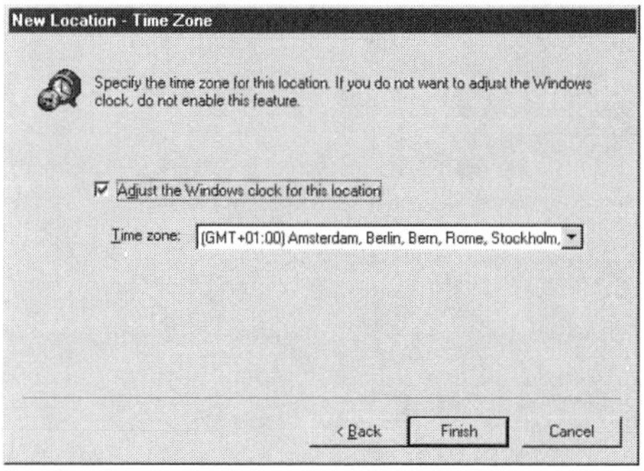

FIGURE D.11
Setting time-zone updating for each location is performed through this Wizard panel.

Other Programs

When Norton Mobile Essentials runs for the first time, it scans your Registry for TAPI-compliant communications software which allows—or requires—synchronization with location-specific settings (such as time). If any such programs exist, their names will appear in the Other Programs tab of the Location Controller, shown in Figure D.12. This tab is not part of the New Location Wizard, but is accessible only when you select

Location Controller from the main NME Integrator, shown in Figure D.13. If no software appears here, then NME has determined you do not have any communications programs which support this feature. (For more information about TAPI-compliance, refer to the documentation for your individual communications software.)

FIGURE D.12

Configuring other software for location-specific operation is performed through this Wizard panel.

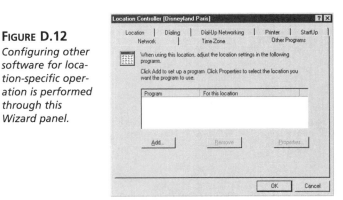

FIGURE D.13

The main Norton Mobile Essentials Integrator gives you access to all primary NME functionality.

Modifying Locations

The Location Controller display shown in Figure D.12 can be accessed at any time via the main Norton Mobile Essentials Integrator (shown in Figure D.13.) As you can see, in Figure D.12, each of the panels of the New Location Wizard is represented as a tab, and the name of the currently-selected location is shown in the display's title bar. Any of the settings which you've made through the Wizard can be modified at any time by selecting the relevant tab from this display. The Wizard itself can be started and new locations added from here as well. You definitely do *not* need to log off Windows and use the New button on the NME logon screen each time you want to add a location.

TECHNICAL NOTE

Norton Mobile Essentials supports dialing exclusively for TAPI-compliant communications software. TAPI non-compliant applications are generally antiquated 16-bit programs, written originally for Windows 3.x or DOS, and are not designed for the multitasking environment of Windows 95 and Windows 98. You may be able to configure NME to support your non-TAPI application through the use of the Interactive Troubleshooter, which you'll read about later in this chapter. If this fails, you will be able to use NME to control all of your location configurations except dialing.

Norton Port Monitor

The Norton Port Monitor, along with Norton Connection Doctor (formerly only part of Norton Mobile Essentials, but now part of the Norton Utilities), can be of great assistance in troubleshooting online difficulties. When opened from the NME Integrator, the Port Monitor will simply and clearly display the status of each COM port on the system, as well as the device or driver which is using the port.

Norton Connection Troubleshooter

Part of Norton Mobile Essentials' online help system, the Connection Troubleshooter can step you through an extensive set of tests and explorations to help you solve connectivity problems. To open the Troubleshooter, click the Troubleshooting button on the NME Integrator, and select whether you're having difficulties with connecting to a service provider or with Norton Mobile Essentials itself, as in Figure D.14. The Troubleshooter will gently walk you through an extensive set of interactive help, asking you questions about the problem you're observing, and making suggestions along the way of diagnostics to run, configurations to modify, and other things to try to get everything righted.

FIGURE D.14

Norton Mobile Essentials' Interactive Troubleshooter will step you through possible solutions to connectivity-related problems.

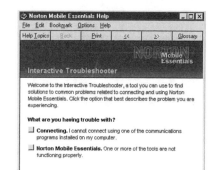

Norton Before You Go

Norton Before You Go, which is part of Norton Mobile Essentials, is itself a small suite of integrated components designed to make sure that your PC and your data—and you—are prepared for work, or play, on the go. Before You Go consists of System Check, SpeedSave, Destination, and Checklist, four tools which can ease traveling burdens from data concerns to packing to finding a rental car! We'll look at each component in turn.

System Check

System Check collects together a variety of installed Norton system-testing utilities and allows you to run them all in preparation for taking your computer on the road. By default, Before You Go will run the Connection Doctor to confirm that all of your connectivity hardware and software is set up properly. Troubleshooting your modem at 3:00 a.m. in a Paris hotel is no way to begin a vacation, believe me!

If you install NME before you install Norton System Works, the System Check will use Microsoft Scan Disk rather than Norton Disk Doctor to perform its drive testing. It's simple to change this, however, so you can use the preferred Norton Disk Doctor utility: From the main Before You Go panel, as shown in Figure D.15, select System Check at the left, and then click Modify at the right.

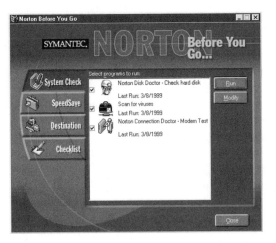

FIGURE D.15
All Before You Go functionality is accessed through this panel.

From the modification panel you can select to Add new applications, Remove applications, or configure the Properties of select applications. Clicking New will display a dialog like you used when configuring startup applications within the Location Controller, at the beginning of this chapter. In this case, we want to configure Norton Disk Doctor as our default disk-integrity checker, so we'll select Check Your Hard Disk in the list of applications, then click Modify. Click the Browse button and navigate to find Norton Disk Doctor. If you accepted Norton SystemWorks' default installation locations, you will find it located at C:\PROGRAM FILES\NORTON SYSTEMWORKS\NORTON UTILITIES\NDD32.EXE. Click OK when you've got NDD32.EXE selected.

> **Note:** If you have extensions for registered file types turned off, the Norton Disk Doctor file will display only as NDD32.

The System Checker will change the description of the program to NDD32. You'll probably want something more memorable, so click in the Description box and type something like, "Check your hard disk." Click OK to accept the new settings.

Incidentally, checking for viruses is a built-in part of the Before You Go System Check. Even if you uninstall Norton AntiVirus, enough components will remain installed to run a basic virus check. "Check for viruses" cannot be deleted, however you can modify it to use Norton AntiVirus's more sophisticated checker if you like. Using the same general procedure as above, click Modify, then browse to locate NAV. If you accepted Norton SystemWorks' default installation locations, you will find it at c:\program files\norton systemworks\norton antivirus\NAVW32.EXE. Click OK and Norton AntiVirus will serve as your NME virus checker.

SpeedSave

The SpeedSave tool is a small disk-based backup program—which is to say that tape drives are not supported—which will allow you to very quickly back up selected files either to floppy or to another drive. The SpeedSave display is shown in Figure D.16, with a backup in process.

FIGURE D.16
A SpeedSave backup is in progress.

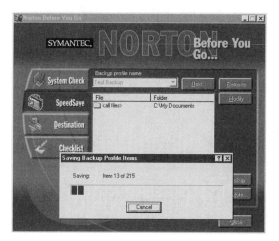

When you click New, a small Wizard will launch, asking you to select what you want to back up—your My Documents folder and its subfolders is the default—and where you want it stored. When you've defined the backup set, you can choose, if you wish, to have a backup performed immediately.

SpeedSave is a great way to either back up local files to the network before you leave the office, or to copy office files to your notebook computer. Any network drive which is locally mapped is accessible for using SpeedSave, so quickly moving your working files or your personal files is a snap.

Once you've defined a backup set, there are a number of different ways you can configure the backup process to behave, as shown in Figure D.17. These options are accessible through the Modify button on SpeedSave's display.

FIGURE D.17
Modifying a SpeedSave backup is simple through this window.

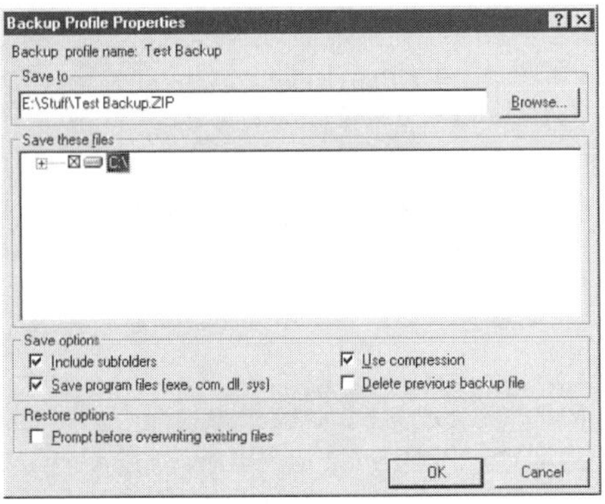

From here you can click the hierarchical plus "+" buttons and select more files for the backup. Placing an "X" next to a folder backs up that folder and all of its contents—including subfolders, only if Include Subfolders is checked, just beneath the drive panel and including executables only if Save Program Files is also checked—and placing a check mark next to a file includes that specific file.

Checking Use Compression will cause all of your selected files to be written to the target drive and folder within a large ZIP file. (Not to be confused with an Iomega ZIP drive.) If you elect to not use compression, a standard Windows folder will be created with your selected files and folders inside.

> **Note:** If you are using Windows 98 Plus!, ZIP files can be opened as normal folders through the use of Microsoft's Compressed Folders tool. This tool alone makes Windows 98 Plus! worth the purchase price.

Finally, Restore Options, at the bottom of this screen will determine whether files are automatically overwritten when you perform a restore, or whether you are prompted to overwrite any existing file. For the most part, you'll want to leave prompting turned *on*. (If you do accidentally restore a file over another and want the original back, you can retrieve the original if you have Norton Protection installed and running. Refer to Chapter 6, "Norton Utilities: Digging Through the Trash with Norton Protection," to learn about Norton Protection.)

To perform a backup at any time, simply run Norton Before You Go, select SpeedSave, and click Backup. To restore previously backed-up files, click Restore and follow the on-screen prompts.

Destination

The Destination guide opens up a world of information about—well, the world. From here, as shown in Figure D.18, you can select a country and, optionally, a city, and the Destination guide will show you information about the electrical and telephonic systems in that part of the world. If you have an active Internet connection, the guide will also search for a Web site featuring your selected city and country, to which you can connect with a single click. A single click will also take you to the Web sites of companies which sell the various conversion hardware required to make your international trip accommodating to your notebook and modem, as shown in Figure D.19. Click Print to print out the guide's data. Click Add to add the selected city and country as a new location in the Location Controller. You can later open the Location Controller and customize the location at will.

FIGURE D.18

The Destination Guide provides access to a wide range of travel-related data.

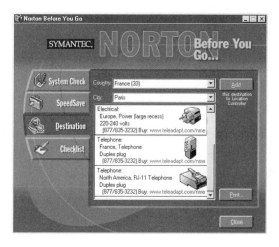

FIGURE D.19
Use Norton Mobile Essentials to secure online ordering of travel accessories.

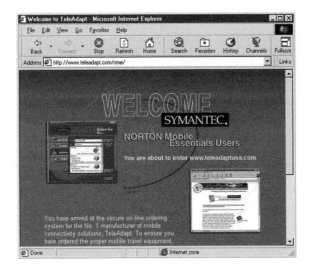

Checklist

At first blush, the Checklist is simply a place to make a list of stuff to do before you travel. But it's actually much more. The Checklist is your access gate to a variety of guides for almost any conceivable travel need. Each guide can be customized, with new data added, and each can be printed. New items can be added, with attached URLs, linking directly to your Web browser. Telephone numbers for businesses as well as their Web pages can be entered, all available from one convenient location. Many existing guides are included, all of which can be customized and augmented by you. Existing guides are:

- Accessories—access to travel-related goods.
- Airlines—major airlines of the world with United States toll-free and International local numbers for most.
- America Online and CompuServe local telephone numbers for the world.
- Auto Rentals.
- Delivery Services worldwide.
- Hotels—telephone numbers and live URLs for major hotel chains worldwide.
- Lost Credit Cards—domestic and international telephone numbers for all major credit cards.
- Traveler's Checklist—where you can, in fact, enter a to-do list.
- Web Sites—providing URLs for major international sources of news, weather, telephone directories, and travel guides.

A Virus Primer

Like an old electrician accustomed to testing a wire by giving it a little "tap" with a bare finger, a lot of people have always been rather casual about viruses. When taking a look at somebody's malfunctioning computer, even power-users just give it the "once over" with an antivirus disk, not expecting to find much. Since the virus scanner was probably 12 months old, its not surprising that they don't. Using the same outdated collection of virus signatures, they scan their own computers, from time to time. Visiting software stores, they glance at the antivirus packages that would promise to clobber every virus within a five-mile radius, and wonder, "Is that really necessary?"

Then they wake up one morning and nothing will turn on.

The Demise of the Five "Nevers"

So, like the electrician with smarting fingers, too many people find out the hard way that lots of their ideas about viruses are outdated. Here are a few of them.

- **You can only get viruses from executable files.** This was a standard mantra for many years. In the golden glory days of "five minutes ago," it used to be true that viruses infected boot sectors, .EXE and .COM, files exclusively. With the advent of macro viruses, that is no longer the case.

- **You cannot get a virus from reading a document.** While it still remains true that you cannot get a virus from opening a piece of standard email or a text file, you can indeed get a virus from opening a Word or Excel file. If that document has a macro virus, your computer can become infected. What's more, Microsoft Outlook has a mechanism for automatically executing macros whenever an email is read. This represents a potential for infection just by opening and reading an email with macros.

- **You don't contract viruses from shrink-wrapped, store-bought software.** Most stores accept returns of computer hardware, and these products often come with driver disks. Many stores simply shrink-wrap the product again, and place it back on the shelf, perhaps after testing. If the customer's computer was infected, it's quite possible for the driver disk to contract the virus as well. That disk is now inside a shrink-wrapped box, ready to be sold to another customer. Additionally, it is not unheard-of for viruses to be present on commercially-prepared software.

- **CD-ROMs do not carry infected programs.** While it's quite true that software manufacturers make every effort to insure that their products are virus-free before shipping, there have been at least two instances of a virus being sent *into the wild* via CD-ROM. The first Word Macro virus, *Concept*, was accidentally distributed on a CD-ROM by Microsoft itself, in the Summer of 1995. The game "Gates of the Underworld. Volume1" contained archived files infected with three potent viruses. These escaped detection because the virus check software they used was not able to check compressed files. Thus the viruses slipped through free and clear.
- **Viruses cannot damage your hardware.** This assurance met with a dramatic demise with the spread of the CIH Virus. It is Windows 95 or 98 exclusive, and activates on the 26th of each month corrupting the BIOS chip, a physical component that must then be replaced. Many computers let you make the BIOS chip unwritable, which, in the event of a CIH virus attack, will save your computer. Nonetheless, the CIH virus recently disabled between 500 and 700 computers worldwide. They needed new motherboards.

Like viruses themselves, the body of knowledge that grows from observing their behavior is always changing.

A Word Against Overreacting

As we'll see in the next section, your computer can experience problems that have nothing to do with a virus. Indeed, one should avoid always thinking "virus" first. There have been many false alarms and panic spread over viruses that did not exist at all. It's important to repeat, for example, that you cannot get a virus by opening a simple text email message and reading it, unless it has macros.

As we explore the types of viruses that are out there, who makes them, and what they can do, realize first and foremost that Norton AntiVirus, an integrated component of Norton SystemWorks, has you covered. Prudent deployment of your antivirus software, especially with regular updating, will keep your computer safe from everything described within this appendix. Norton AntiVirus lets you determine, to some extent, your own level of security against viruses. In these pages, you'll explore virus types and behaviors, not for some morbid interest, but so you can be informed about when extra caution is a good idea.

What Is a Virus?

A virus is a self-replicating program written for the purpose of infecting other computers. Beyond that simple statement, there's much variety on the theme. For example, not all viruses cause obvious damage to your files. Some simply spread, and are discovered only by researchers in laboratory conditions. Since we tend to think of viruses as overtly hostile to our computers, the best way to clarify what a virus is, then, is to compare it to malicious programs that are not viruses.

A *trojan horse* is a file that claims to do one thing, but does another ("Open this game for a good time."). For example, a trojan horse could claim to be a game, but actually contain malicious commands. A trojan horse is not a virus because it does not replicate. The message must be read and acted upon by the victim for the deception to take place. It does not move from one computer to another by stealth, as a virus does. Each victim must respond to the invitation, or a trojan horse goes nowhere.

Note: Norton AntiVirus protects you against all types of malicious files like the ones described here, not just viruses.

A *worm* is a maliciously written program that seeks access into other computers. It uses password-stealing tools to penetrate many systems. Worms often steal or vandalize computer data. They could also work into a bank's computer and transfer funds from one account to another, or erase key documents that would implicate individuals in a crime. A worm is not a virus because, often, worms contain instructions to self-destruct, after the deeds are done. A virus lives to replicate.

Before getting into the nitty-gritty of virus actions, you need to assess your risk level. The following two sections help you determine what level of protection against viruses you ought to deploy in your computing environment. Norton AntiVirus can work with you in implementing your choices. Although some people never adjust Norton's default settings, you can easily customize the program to your own needs and convenience.

Who Is Most Likely to Contract a Virus?

Viruses can attack almost any computer, but there are some behaviors that render you more vulnerable than others. Here they are:

- **Running a computer without regularly updated virus software.**

Tip: Interestingly, running your computer with greatly outdated antivirus software can be more dangerous than none at all, since it lulls you into a sense of false security.

- **High usage of floppy disks**, especially usage of floppies you receive from many sources.

Tip: Even if no one you know would ever intentionally pass you a virus-infected, floppy disk, you cannot be 100% sure from where they got the floppy. Always disinfect floppies and Zip disks, no matter what the source.

- **Many users on one computer.** If these users bring their own floppies (or Zip disks, and other cartridges) to load and unload files, the risk is increased.
- **High Network connectivity.** If many computers share the same files, perhaps uploading and downloading from the same BIN or PUBLIC folder over a network, there's a higher risk of contracting a virus.
- **High dependency on collaborative documents.** If Word and Excel files are traded between coworkers and coauthors, there's an increased risk of seeing viruses.
- **Individuals with a poor understanding of how viruses work.** If you exchange documents or disks, or share computers with someone who lacks knowledge of virus behavior, you yourself are at risk.

Who Is Most Likely to Spread a Virus?

Let's tackle the Typhoid Mary question. Beyond simply contracting a virus, there are those whose behavior or occupation makes them likely vectors for further infection. Of course, in many of these and other cases, there is no intent to do harm. Here are some examples:

- **Traveling salespeople who run demonstrations**, especially those who use a local machine when they drop by to give their demo, or leave behind disks for others to learn more about their product.
- **Tech Support staff** who move from machine to machine in an organization, troubleshooting as they go.
- **Network Technicians** who upgrade or install systems on various machines. Many of the newer viruses are written to be spread across a network. It's considered a challenge amongst virus authors to get a foothold in a piece of software that a Network Tech is likely to use regularly.
- **Disgruntled employees, or ex-employees.**
- And, of course, add to this, **anyone who does not use antivirus precautions** who nonetheless shares floppies, documents, or computers with others.

Once someone learns a great deal about viruses, its common to begin blaming viruses for everything. So, before the graphic details begin, realize first that a computer virus did not cause El Niño, the Gulf War, or the ten common computer problems outlined below.

Ten Computer Symptoms That Resemble (But Usually Are Not) Viruses

When something goes wrong with your computer, a virus attack is not the most likely culprit. Far from it—hardware or driver incompatibility, cross-linked files, and insufficient memory to complete a task are much more common problems.

The following is a short, not at all exhaustive list of computer symptoms that may be viral in their source, but probably are not:

- **You start a program, and partway through, it quits.** Whether the program abruptly exits, or your computer suddenly reboots, this problem could be a video driver error, sound card error, or a response to an attempt to perform a task that you don't have enough RAM to carry out.

- **The audio portion of your program is about to begin, and suddenly, your computer freezes, requiring you to press the reset button.** Probably a sound card error. Check to see if your sound card interrupts are correctly assigned. Check also to see if the program (or Windows) has properly identified your sound card.

- **You are working in a program and suddenly, the colors look really funny.** Probably a video card setting error. If you are running in 256 colors, try increasing to high color or 24-bit mode. If you are running in either of those modes, try reducing to 256 colors. Make sure Windows has properly identified your video card.

- **Trying to run a large program on an underpowered computer.** If software on your machine is demanding resources that you just don't have, the results could mimic a variety of other conditions. Your computer could freeze, multitasking becomes impossible, screens will not refresh, just to name a few.

- **You are working in a program or playing a game, and the figures move very slowly, or become unclear and drop out.** Similar to the above, but more than likely involving an incompatibility with DirectX, a special Windows video mode that provides increased functionality for games and high-definition animation. Many programs attempt to install versions of DirectX on your computer, and some are not savvy enough to make sure you don't already have one. Make sure you are running the newest version of DirectX, and that only one version exists on your computer.

- **You installed a modem, and suddenly your mouse stops working.** Or, suddenly, your computer cannot detect your modem. Either way, your mouse and modem must be configured to select different COM ports. Generally, your mouse stays at the COM port assigned by Windows, while your modem is subject to your own choice in the matter.

- **Over the last few weeks, you've noticed that the text on your screen is fuzzy and harder to read.** Your video card or monitor is showing its age. Replace one or the other. If text always becomes gradually fuzzy after you've had your computer on for a few hours, then its probably the monitor.

- **Your computer gradually takes longer and longer to do things.** Try using Speed Disk, part of Norton SystemWorks, to defragment your hard drive. Also use the Norton Space Wizard to locate all the temporary files on your computer and delete them.

- **Your computer's clock seems to lose time.** Your motherboard has a battery and it *does* run down after a few years.

It's a very common belief that the more severe a problem is, the more likely a virus is the culprit. Hard drive errors, poorly configured drivers and software, and incompatible hardware are responsible for plenty of problems that can drain performance and reduce productivity as fast as any virus can. A hard drive filled close to capacity will display all kinds of errors and performance problems that can look like viruses.

> **Note:** Whenever troubleshooting your computer, remember *Occam's Razor*: Start with the easiest possible solution, test that, and move to the more complex only after the simple solutions fail. Your goal is to get back to work as soon as possible, not justify the existence of every preventative utility on your com-

When It's OK to Jump to Conclusions

These five instances warrant you to "suspect a virus first," before checking other possibilities:

- **Mischievous messages appearing on the screen.** If you boot up your computer, and it pauses to display "The Revolution Is Coming," or something similar, a virus is likely.

- **Your computer's clock displays abrupt and inexplicable changes.** Many viruses use the clock to set up triggers, and some poorly designed viruses manipulate the clock in a way that's fairly easy to detect.

- **An unsolicited musical selection is played through your PC speaker.** One example, the Mozart virus, forces you to listen to 30 minutes of beeps and blips that vaguely resemble something by the Great Composer. Reboot, and *your boot sector will be relocated*, making your files unavailable.

- **Without prior warning, your hard drive is inaccessible upon rebooting.** If this situation was not preceded by sluggish performance, reports of cross-linked files or hard disk error warnings, then you may indeed suspect a virus first.

- **If several other computers besides your own are suddenly acting up.** Many viruses are set to create havoc on a particular day. So take the tip from others who got up earlier than you did and turned on their computer to some bad news. Upon hearing news of widespread trouble, boot up from your Norton Emergency Disk or Norton Zip Rescue set and scan for viruses before booting up normally.

Viruses often launch a full-scale assault against your computer on a particular day. They are programmed to read your computer's clock and calendar, wait for the right day to arrive, and then start destroying files. That's why computer repair technicians often get lots of "virus calls" on certain notorious dates, such as March 6th, and the 26th of any month.

As we'll explore in the following sections, "Types of Viruses," and "How Viruses Behave," viruses use various means to work their way into your system permanently.

There is a common method, however. Most viruses first infect your computer, then set up a trigger event or date, then finally deliver a payload when that date or event is reached.

Types of Viruses

In this section we'll look at the three main virus groups: File, Boot, and Macro. Then you'll learn how each type of virus deploys different means of avoiding detection, and damaging your computer.

File and Boot Viruses

File and Boot viruses have been around since the middle 1980s. File viruses work by infecting a COM or EXE file, while a Boot virus infects the boot sector or the Master Boot Record of your hard drive. (The boot sector of a logical hard drive contains specific information related to the format of that drive; the Master Boot Record contains the physical drive's partition table, which identifies the location of each logical drive.)

File viruses infect their target files by first *loading themselves into memory*, then waiting for a program to be executed. That's why when you run a particular program, it becomes infected.

Boot Sector viruses will write their infected code to the Boot Sector of a logical drive. Similarly, a Master Boot Record virus infects the Master Boot Record and Partition Table of your hard drive. The latter are the first physical sections of your hard drive, and your computer expects to find system information there. Not finding it, you receive an error that your hard drive is not available or unbootable when you try to boot up.

> **Note:** When you suspect a virus, you should reboot from a floppy. Quite often, Boot Sector or Master Boot Record viruses do not deliver their final punch until you reboot. In order for a Boot Sector virus to spread, you must boot up from that infected drive. This is why rebooting your computer should not be some sort of instinctive response to dealing with a virus. When a boot sector virus is suspected, reboot from a Norton Emergency Disk or Norton Zip Rescue set. Then run Norton AntiVirus.

Macro Viruses

Macro viruses deserve their own section, since they are the fastest growing and most threatening class of viruses.

Before exploring the threat of Macro viruses, it's important to review how macros work.

A Macro Is a Set of Instructions

Word and Excel's macro-creation capability empower the user to extend the usefulness of these applications. For example, users can create macros to type a standard final paragraph, perform a spell-check, and print a document. Once created, the macro can implement these three chores with a single mouse-click. Simple macros like these can be created without any programming skills at all.

Macros are a more powerful programming tool than the above example indicates, though. At the heart of Microsoft Office (and thereby, Word and Excel) macros is Visual Basic for Applications (VBA). With this tool, macros can be created to open and close, locate and alter files on your computer, and even delete them.

Templates: A Virus' Free Ride In

When you open a Word or Excel document, you are opening a template, as well. This normal template is a set of macros that provide some of the basic functionality to the program (When you create or open a Word document, the template NORMAL.DOT is opened. In Excel, when you open or create a spreadsheet, PERSONAL.XLS is opened.)

It is very easy to add to these templates by creating macros, and a document infected with a macro virus is simply a document that contains hostile macros. Now when you open a Word document *within Word*, you are empowering that document to carry out the commands of the macros that it came with. That's because any Word document automatically opens with a template, which is simply a set of macros. (Note that you can configure Word and Excel to alert you to the presence of macros in a document as the document opens, allowing you to choose whether or not you want those macros to run.)

How Macro Viruses Work

Once you've opened an infected Word or Excel document in its native application, you've allowed the virus to establish a base of operations to replace your own NORMAL.DOT template with its own hostile macros. Some macro viruses have a relatively benign payload. For example, the WAZZU virus places the word WAZZU somewhere in your document, and randomly relocates three words. But not all are so benign.

In Word and Excel, macros also control the appearance of your menus. Therefore, a hostile macro can rename, remove, or otherwise scramble your menu options. Some drop odd words into your text. Additionally, since VBA is a powerful but easy to use object-oriented programming tool, Word and Excel macro viruses are not limited to playing fast and loose with your documents. They can (and some do) alter other files on your hard drive. It's a piece of cake to design a Word macro that takes down selected files in your Windows folder, or even send a command to erase all files when you open an infected document.

Just like the relatively mild *Stoned* virus became a magic carpet for malicious programmers to build upon, the first Macro Virus, called *Word/Concept*, had a very mild payload, but later became the core of some very ugly creations. These early "benign" viruses could successfully infect documents. This ability became very attractive to more malicious virus creators, who could take apart the code of the less hostile infector, and pack it with a vicious payload.

It's not only ease of creation that attracted virus creators to the macro world. Whether by floppy or Zip disk or via email, computer users exchange far more documents than they do programs. It's not at all uncommon for coworkers to exchange and collaborate on a dozen documents in one day. People rarely exchange programs at such a rate. For this reason, macro viruses have achieved a prevalence far outstripping all but the most dire predictions. They are indeed "everywhere," although many of them are not exceptionally hostile, and many of the hostile ones do not deliver the deadly payload intended.

Java and ActiveX Viruses

Java and ActiveX viruses are a very new field, and thus, we'll cover them later in this appendix, in the section titled "What's Up Their Sleeve Next?"

Virus Classifications

Virus types are often classified according to their characteristics and modes of attack. Some major classifications are described in the following sections.

> **Note:** To read about some of these ugly guys in action, please see the "Examples of Viruses" section later in this chapter.

Multipartite Viruses

Multipartite viruses attack EXE and COM files, as well as the Boot Sector and Master Boot Record of your hard drive, thus combining the effects of both File and Boot infecting viruses.

Polymorphic Viruses

Polymorphic Viruses have a built-in mutation engine. They randomly change parts of their code, altering their "signature." Antivirus software of the scanning nature identifies a virus by comparing its signature to a database of known virus signatures. Polymorphic viruses mutate in order to avoid this identification. (Norton AntiVirus is not burdened by this limitation, as you will see.)

Stealth Viruses

Stealth viruses are masters at disguising their presence and actions. When they infect files, they hide the resulting increase in file size through complex trickery. Stealth viruses sometimes attempt to knock out certain resident-in-memory antivirus software, and disguise their own presence in lower memory regions, while they prepare an attack.

Companion Virus

Once in your system, a Companion virus focuses on a selected executable file that you are likely to use frequently and writes a "companion" program alongside it. When you start the program, you launch the virus' program instead. It does this by switching file names to something similar. You'll end up running, for example, an infected `PSD.COM` instead of the intended `PSD.EXE`.

Slow and Sparse Infector Viruses

Slow Infector and Sparse Infector viruses operate on the idea that you are less likely to be able to trace the source of a virus that gradually eats away at your system. Sparse Infectors only infect occasionally, sometimes only targeting files that fall into a certain specific date or size criteria.

> **Note:** Norton AntiVirus employs a system called Bloodhound Heuristics which monitors your computer for subtle or distinct changes in file characteristics that are indicative of viral activity. Predicting how a virus will behave is a major step towards arresting that behavior. And since it's not possible to know the "signature" of every virus, Norton AntiVirus tracks *activities*, not depending solely on identifying a virus before acting against it.

How Viruses Behave

Now that you've seen that each type of virus has a mechanism that governs its actions, let's look at some examples of their behaviors.

Every virus has events that map out its course of action, as described below.

The Date of Infection

The date of infection is *when* the virus infects your computer. It could live alongside other files on your computer, or infect executable files like COM or EXE files.

Gradual Onset of Symptoms

During the early infection phase, you may notice that programs take longer to load, or show a general sluggishness. You might see files that were not there before, or files that are larger than previously. You may also notice a diminished amount of lower memory. You could, however, see no symptoms at all during this phase.

Trigger Event

A virus establishes a trigger event, determining when it will deliver its payload. Many viruses vary this trigger event, so as to avoid detection and recognition by those who know a bit about viruses. A virus may wait until it has infected a certain number of floppy disks before proceeding. Some wait for a certain date, or keystroke combination, before delivering the final blow.

There are reasons why a virus allows lots of time to elapse before making its presence known in an obvious way.

- A virus has the goal of infecting as many computers as possible. Each new host computer can be counted on to spread the virus to others, via floppies or file sharing of some sort, as long as the virus is not detected.

- If a long time has passed between the date of infection and the trigger event that damages your computer, it makes it very hard to remember what might have caused the virus to begin with. You'll have a harder time tracking down the floppy or file that started the whole mess.

- If a virus remains undetected, it can burrow deep into your system, infecting many files, before administering some sort of body blow to your nice machine.

> **Note:** Some viruses have no trigger event. One particularly devastating virus, known as *Jack the Ripper*, starts working right after infection. It alters your files a few bytes at a time (called data diddling). This slow, inexorable process gradually incapacitates your computer, making it nearly impossible to tell what caused the problem.

Payload

The payload, sometimes called the Warhead, is the end result of the virus' activity on your computer. The payload could be humorous or political messages displayed on your screen, music or noise, or the inability to access your hard drive. One virus makes your printer port inaccessible, while another announces incorrectly that you have to reload Windows.

Viruses' "Peaceful" Coexistence

Let's look at some of the ways that a virus can "coexist" on your computer, all the while planning and preparing an attack:

- It can disguise its presence in files by lobbing off the same number of bytes as it adds to the file when it infects it. The file, therefore, appears the same size. This is sneaky, since unusual growth in file size is an trait looked for by rudimentary antiviral software.

- A virus can mark a file it has infected by adding a tiny code fragment, unnoticeable to simple antiviral software. It can mark a file it has infected by moving the date stamp ahead 100 years. Of course, when you scroll down a list of files and look at the dates, you only see the last two digits. Therefore, an increase of 100 years to a file's time stamp would be unnoticeable to an observer.

- Some viruses know how to disable simple or antiquated antiviral software before proceeding.

Note: It's important for a virus to keep track of the files it initially infects. These files are like a base of operations from which to launch an invasion of your computer. Therefore, "resident" viruses develop means of marking which files are infected, and which it has yet to infect.

Please note that there will probably be no symptoms to indicate that your computer has been invaded by a virus.

How Norton AntiVirus Protects You

Like a general keeping battle plans to himself, it's not possible to intimately discuss proprietary technology for protecting your computer against viruses. What follows is a fundamental look at how antiviral software works. These concepts are important to understand so you can see the necessity of deploying a number of tools against viruses, not just one.

Because viruses are constantly mutating, there is no single technology that holds the answer, or can rid you of viruses forever. That's why a number of tools are discussed here, and that's why Norton AntiVirus includes so many tools, approaching virus defense from so many different angles.

Detection, Identification, Removal, and Repair

Antiviral software has four jobs: virus detection, virus identification, virus removal, and file repair. Because Norton AntiVirus comes in the Norton SystemWorks suite, you'll have the best tool available for each task mentioned above. First, we'll look at detection.

Detecting a Problem

The first indication that you have a virus may simply be that Norton AntiVirus detects something is amiss and prevents you from using your computer until you look at what just happened. If you are sure of yourself, you could decide that the triggering event was not a virus, and continue on your way. Or, you could allow Norton AntiVirus to take further action against the file that caused the problem.

In such a case, NAV has detected, but not identified a virus. Norton AntiVirus scours your computer for virus-like behavior, and finding it, will blow the whistle and make you come and take a closer look. In this way, NAV can protect you from viruses that it has detected, but not yet identified. This is important, because if antiviral software can only protect you from known viruses, you are very vulnerable indeed.

Identifying a Virus

Most often, Norton AntiVirus can register a proof-positive ID on a virus, and tell you its name, rank, and serial number. NAV can proceed to rid your system of the virus. A known virus is vulnerable to good antiviral software, because, beyond just knowing its identity, NAV also understands the virus' behavior, mode of infection, and key qualities that might otherwise make getting rid of it difficult. Positive identification allows Norton AntiVirus to deploy all the necessary tools against a virus, insuring complete eradication.

Virus Removal

Not all viruses say "Fair's fair. You got me," and quietly allow you to slip on the hand-cuffs. Once identified, eradicating a virus requires savvy skill on the part of the antiviral programmer. Creating a program that takes down a particular virus and thoroughly rids you of it in all its manifestations is quite a task, especially for the more complex viruses.

Plenty of viruses know how to encrypt themselves with protective "shells" to escape full destruction, and leave a string of code behind, buying a new lease on life later. Viruses know how to find hidden spaces in existing programs, and leave mutated versions of themselves behind.

File Repair

It's not enough to simply erase a virus, if you have to install all your software again from scratch. In many cases, it's possible to use a file, even if it was once infected by a virus. Norton AntiVirus excels at removing simply the viral code, and repairing missing portions of a file damaged by the infection.

Virus-Fighting Technologies

Speaking in a broad sense, some basic tools that antiviral software deploys to keep your computer safe are discussed below.

Scanners

Virus scanners examine files on your computer and compare them to a set of "signatures" that known viruses possess. Scanners identify known viruses. A virus identified by NAV is pretty much dead in the water. The searchlights are on, the exits are blocked, and all that remains is making sure your file can be repaired, if it can be salvaged.

When you regularly update your Norton AntiVirus files using LiveUpdate, you are adding to and modifying this list of virus signatures that is used to identify viruses. For more information on LiveUpdate, refer to Chapter 19, "Norton Web Services: Your Current Computer."

Integrity Checking

Also called Checksumming, or Change Detection checking, this type of antiviral agent scours your computer for files that appear to have been altered in a way consistent with viral infection. This includes the misreporting of a file size, and files taking up much larger amounts of memory than previously. Files that suddenly appear truncated or "full of garbage code" will trigger this alert as well. The benefit of integrity checking is that it protects you from viruses that are not yet defined. It examines behavior consistent with virus attacks, rather than looking for a virus' identity. The main limitation of Integrity Checking can be false alerts, stopping your system when a program creates a valid change to a file.

Operation Restricting

Also called Behavior Blocking, this type of protection watches activity on your computer. If a file exhibits virus-like behavior, the program will halt the operation, inform you of what just happened, and let you determine how to respond. Examples of this type of behavior are:

- Files that want to "go resident" in memory, usually occupying a tiny segment of lower memory.
- Files that modify their own code in strange, seemingly random ways.
- Suspicious commands, like calls to format a disk (good behavior blocking software knows that operating system files are allowed to make such requests), take over an interrupt, or delete system files.

Note: When a Behavior Blocker encounters suspicious activity, the system will be halted while you determine if the file that triggered the alarm was acting appropriately or not. In Norton AntiVirus, the user has the power to set the sensitivity of Behavior Blocking. If this protective agent triggers the alarm every time a file tries to duplicate itself or writes to a system folder, for example, you'll never get any work done. Worse yet, you'll soon start to ignore the antiviral alerts, or turn them off altogether. However, Behavior Blockers that are not restrictive enough will allow surreptitious virus activity to occur on their watch.

Heuristics-Based Scanning

A much more sophisticated and foolproof application of the above tools, Norton AntiVirus Heuristics examines your data with a grasp similar to Artificial Intelligence models, rather than a simple "search and kill" approach. NAV's Bloodhound Heuristics feature is very adept at differentiating between virus-like behavior and legitimate file changes.

Deploying Antiviral Tools

Antiviral tools will spring into action in two ways. A combination of both of the following approaches is the best:

- **When the user runs the scanner.** Also called "on demand" protection. Some types of virus protection require that you scan your files, using the most current virus signature files available. This takes initiative on the part of the user, either by starting the scanner program then and there, or by setting up a scheduled scan.

- **When a file is accessed.** Manual scanning is not enough. Some sort of virus-checking tool needs to be operating on your computer at all times, ready to step into action anytime a virus tries to access your files. Also called "on-access" protection, it remains resident in memory, and interrupts your activity when truly suspicious activity occurs. When a virus attempts to become resident in memory, you need to know immediately. When your computer is attempting to boot from a disk infected by a virus, your system needs to stop before going any further. That's why some sort of virus protection needs to be in place even at startup, not just when you remember to ask for it.

Handling Viruses When You Are In Charge

In the computer biz, being in charge means people walk up to you and say "You promised me this would work." Far from having an official office, you gradually become aware of the hours you are spending bent over someone else's machine, trying to entice a new level of competency out of both the computer and its user. This is all part of your job, and you are certainly due any accolades that may come your way, but if you find yourself responsible for setting up a virus-free environment, there's a lot more involved than meets the eye.

If you are going to undertake installing antiviral software in an entire environment, be it academic or workplace, you'll need the cooperation, not only of your peers, but the people above you as well. Some users will have to modify their habits, and everyone must faithfully tell you the source of files they install on their workstations. All floppies need to pass muster with you, hopefully before the first virus alert robs you of your lunchbreak. What follows are some tips to help you maintain a virus-free environment, a much taller order than keeping individual computers clean.

- The first rule of medicine is "Do No Harm." Make sure every data source *you* use on the computers in your environment is virus free. Write-protect all the floppies or Zip disks you drag along with you from computer to computer.

- Since virus creators are thinking of more than one computer at a time, you should, too. Therefore, take a reading of the sort of connectivity your environment employs. Do they share lots of documents? Collaborate on the same spreadsheets? Download files from the same server? Whatever flotsam is floating about your environment is your business. It's your job to identify various viral vectors.

Do a "connectivity equation" in your head. First, factor in just the sheer number of computers, people, and shared files of all types. Next, factor in how much interactivity exists between them. Is everybody in the habit of passing around the same set of floppies? Do lots of people "sign off" on an online document before it is considered finished? It's not only the number of "points of connectivity," that are important, but how often those points interact. These are the factors that govern how fast a virus can spread throughout your environment, should one be introduced.

- Educate everybody in your environment about viruses. Let them know how viruses are spread, and the types of behavior they exhibit. For example, people should understand that, just because their computer is functioning well, that doesn't mean it's virus-free. Tell them a little about triggers and payload.

- Everyone should agree not to interfere with background virus scanning, and know how to scan a file before using it, if needed.

- Tell people how to respond, should they encounter a Virus Alert. Make sure they understand what alerts are OK to "click past," and which ones require more attention. Everybody needs to know that they can't just set the Bloodhound Heuristics slider to the least sensitive setting, because the alerts are annoying.

> **Tip:** If working relationships in your environment have deteriorated, for whatever reason, be extra-alert for virus-like activity. This is especially an issue if people were dismissed recently.

- Acquaint people with the behaviors of the most common viruses. For example, they should understand that the sudden appearance of the word WAZZU in their document does not mean they were out too late the night before. Let them know how they should respond, should a virus alert be triggered.

Here's something to remember regarding your own response to virus alerts:

As a rule, everybody in your position underestimates the amount of time a virus alert follow-through takes. Your time is valuable, and it's to everyone's advantage that you get to the heart of the matter quickly. That means you want to find the solution that gets people back to work sooner, rather than later. It's very common for technical people to rely on restoring backups to get things moving quickly, but give Norton AntiVirus the first go. It's amazingly good at disinfecting and restoring files, far better than other software you might have tried previously.

So, let Norton AntiVirus eliminate the virus, and repair the affected files. Run the affected files and make sure they still work, then reboot and do a virus scan again, to make sure the virus is gone. If the once-affected computer passes this test, then you are home free. There's no reason to back up from previously saved files when NAV can get the computer up and running sooner.

> **Note:** Another good reason not to depend on backed up files for virus repair work: Your backup files could be infected, as well. Remember that the initial date of a virus infection can precede the first reported symptoms by several months. Its quite possible that files were conscientiously backed up long before the virus gave any outward indication of its existence.

Examples of Viruses

Here are a few examples of viruses. Listed below are at least one of each main type, as explained above.

- **Jerusalem:** A File Virus, and quite old, having spawned many variants. It installs itself as a Resident Program in lower memory (TSR), and occupies `.EXE` and `.COM` files. On Friday the 13th, it deletes any programs you execute.

- **Hare:** A large multipartite virus, taking up nearly 8KB of space on your hard drive, and 9KB in memory. It strikes on August 22nd and September 22nd. It attempts to overwrite all your files with random data. This is one of the few viruses that truly destroys your files, rather than merely making them unavailable with Boot Sector trickery.

- **Tequila.A:** A multipartite virus. It infects `.EXE` files and the Master Boot Record. It displays a fractal graphic and a message on the screen.

- **Winword/Mentes:** A macro virus that attempts to erase any file on your computer called `C:\LOGIN`.

- **Winword/Talon:** A macro virus that takes over your Tools | Macro menu. When you try to access it, a message is displayed: `This option is not available. Please insert the MS-Office CD and install the help files to continue.`

- **Winword/Nuclear:** A macro virus that creates and infects an AutoOpen macro in Word. When you print your document, there's a 1 in 12 chance the bottom of the document will display: `and finally, I would like to say: STOP ALL FRENCH NUCLEAR TESTING IN THE PACIFIC`. This virus also has a faulty payload that tries to erase important system files. It does, at times, succeed in erasing the `IO.SYS` file.

- **Winword/CAP:** A macro virus is a stealth virus that empties Word's menu items. It alters Tools | Macro so that you cannot quickly open the options and restore the original menu items.

> **Tip:** If you notice any oddly named new macros in your Macros list, a macro virus could have created them.

- **Form:** Overwrites a partition's boot sector, and saves the originals and its own code in the last two sectors of the partition. Since Form assumes that the active partition is a DOS-based FAT16, this virus wreaks more havoc for FAT32 partitions.
- **Barrotes:** Overwrites the partition table on January 5th. This causes your hard disk to appear unreadable. But if you replace the partition sector and eliminate the virus, the problem is solved. You do not have to reformat your hard drive. (Such repairs can be made in seconds with your Norton Rescue set).

That's enough of the little shop of horrors. By looking at the multiplicity and diversity of viruses, you can understand why it's very important to allow Norton AntiVirus to update its files whenever necessary.

Norton AntiVirus deploys a number of tools against viruses. Its not practical to use every tool every day. There are times, however, when you'll need to be 100% certain that no viruses are on your computer.

When Should You Be Certain You Are Virus-Free?

If you use Norton AntiVirus as recommended, making perhaps a few modifications for your own convenience, you'll be as free from viruses as possible. But certain situations demand that you go that extra mile, run the scanner on *all* files, and just make double-sure all goes well. Here are some situations that demand "no-virus" certainty:

- Backing up important files.
- Preparing data to be distributed to others in any medium.
- Creating CD-ROMs.
- Archiving and compressing files for deep storage.

Beyond deploying Norton AntiVirus, which you automatically do upon installing Norton SystemWorks, here are some prudent steps you might want to make part of your routine, if you haven't already. The first set revolve around floppy disks as a contaminant. The next set of tips is more general.

Floppy Disks Are a Big Source

Lots of the older viruses (many of which are still around), level their worst payloads against floppy disks. Up until the advent of macro viruses, floppy disk transmission was still the vector of choice. Therefore, think about implementing the following:

- Make sure all data source floppies are write-protected.
- Scan every floppy before you run it. Even blank floppies you buy in a shrink-wrapped box should be scanned before you do anything else.

- Don't leave floppy disks in the drive when you turn off your computer. When you boot up next, the computer will attempt to boot from the floppy. An amazing number of viruses are spread from booting up this way, even if booting was unsuccessful.

> **Note:** A floppy with a virus may report various types of "unwritable disk" errors. If you get several floppy errors from one batch, even those from a shrink-wrapped box, think long and hard about trusting your data to any floppies from that same source.

Cutting Back on Floppy Usage

Remember that when your computer has a virus, every floppy you've been in contact with for many months back becomes suspect. That's because many viruses linger long on your computer before making their presence known in a dramatic way. Such a time lag makes it hard to know which floppy (if any) was the original vector. Therefore, when a virus is discovered, disinfect all your floppies. If you passed floppies around during the time of possible infection, inform those people.

Undertaking this chore causes one to daydream about a floppy-less world. Indeed, there is a step you can take to minimize your dependence of floppy disks.

Try to move data source floppies to a different medium, if at all possible. For example, if you have some ancient fax program that you are particularly attached to, and it must be installed from a floppy, try moving the installation files to their own folder on a Zip disk. If there are several floppies, then create a separate folder for each floppy disk.

> **Note:** Some programs with multiple disk sources will not let you save installation disks on another medium. That's because the installation script is programmed to search for the "Next Disk" in drive A:, and nowhere else. So, while this solution is attractive, it won't work for everything.

> **Note:** Why is moving data to Zip disks more virus-safe than floppies? Because it's much easier to scan a handful of Zip disks for viruses than an untold number of floppies. You're more likely to do a thorough job and not leave any files unscanned.

Staying Out of Harm's Way

Here are some other sensible virus-aware computing tips that minimize your exposure to viruses:

- If, on a particular day, you hear of other's computers being affected by a virus, boot up that day from your Norton Emergency Disk and scan your computer for viruses. Then boot up normally.

- If someone sends you a Word or Excel document, allow Norton AntiVirus to scan it before opening, or make sure you have AutoProtect running.

- If you are using Word or Excel, enable their own built-in macro virus protection by choosing Tools | Options and selecting the General tab. Placing a check in the box labeled Macro Virus Protection will cause Word or Excel to prompt you for permission to execute *any* macros, including AutoOpen macros.

- Allow Norton AntiVirus to scan any program you download from the Web or an FTP site. Programs in zipped files need to be scanned, as well.

- Use LiveUpdate to download new virus signatures as they become available, to keep your scanning power up-to-date. Be sure to take advantage of scheduled LiveUpdates.

- Pay attention to any Norton AntiVirus alerts you receive via email, or by some other means. To receive regular virus alert notices from SARC, point your browser to: www.symantec.com/avcenter/refa.html.

- Follow through with Quarantined files on your computer. Send them to SARC so they can be scanned. (As discussed in Chapter 7, Norton AntiVirus will move your files to a isolated location on your hard drive, essentially quarantining them, and then prompt you to upload these to the Symantic Antivirus Research Center for evaluation. This is one important line of defense against viruses that you should acquaint yourself with.)

Who Makes Viruses, and Why?

Time was, when you wrote a virus, you had to know a bit of programming. With the advent of macro viruses, you need simply to know how to create and manipulate macros. Acquiring these skills is a far easier task than learning C or C++. Nonetheless, the most notorious viruses require fairly astute programming skills in their creation.

Viruses are created most often by programmers who want to test their ability to circumvent the antiviral security and safeguards. Most virus creators will measure their programming prowess by their ability to infect as many systems as possible. They look for a critical "jump" in infection rate, propelling their creation into widespread notoriety. Most enjoy reading and learning what is being done to stop their own virus from spreading. Like gang members who read the paper to see if their latest shooting has brought them fame, most virus creators want the world to see what they've done. And, like a criminal who is disappointed when his crime is not reported on the news, most virus creators will keep trying until they get it right. They'll burn lots of midnight oil taking apart files and finding the weak spots. This research includes finding the weak spots in antiviral software as well. For example, the Starship virus was written as an elaborate project to elude a popular algorithm used by *Integrity Checkers*.

No viruses are flawless, wickedly masterful creations. Many of them just plain don't work, don't infect well, and, if they do infect, fail to deliver the devastation that was intended. If your computer is infected with a virus, and hangs when a program is supposed to start, that's often because the virus was supposed to do something else at that point, but the programmer lacked the skills to pull it off. But, like an assassin who missed his mark, and is skulking away bitterly in the corner somewhere, he will be back. For example, the first cross-platform virus that could move between Word and Excel, called Strange Days, failed to maintain its ability to cross-infect. The next cross-platform "travelling" macro virus, Shiver, was more clever in its implementation, and could sustain the cross-infection.

Not every virus author wants to take down your computer. Some are content to have a little fun at your expense. This benign intent bodes no better for you, though, because other virus authors will manipulate the code of a successful "nice" virus (for example, the Stoned virus, which simply displayed Your Computer Has Been Stoned on the screen), into something far more vicious. In fact, the New Zealander who originally wrote the Stoned virus unwittingly designed a template used by other ill-intentioned creators to devise a much uglier payload.

What's Up Their Sleeve Next?

The antiviral software of tomorrow will continue to evolve over what you are running with today. Norton AntiVirus is, in fact, particularly forward-looking by virtue of its Heuristics technology and its updatability through LiveUpdate. Nevertheless, if you plan to still be using computers a year from now, it might be nice to know what's in store, and where that extra ounce of caution ought to be deployed. For a moment, think like a virus creator: your goal is to spread your handiwork to as many computers as possible, perhaps bringing the world to its knees, like some sort of comic book villain. What newer innovation can a virus attach itself to, get a foothold in every machine, regardless of its operating system?

Hostile Java Applets

Well, there's Java. Why is it so allegedly wonderful? Because it (supposedly) runs on all platforms. Unfortunately, this flexibility plays right into the hands of virus creators, as well. The creators of Java and the Web browsers that run it are well aware of the security issues involved, and have created a safe environment for Java to run in. As you work online, there are two implementations of Java you are likely to run across: Java applets, and Java applications.

Java applets that you access while Web surfing are not in a good position to take over your computer. They run in a protected memory space, called a Sandbox, far away from system centers. Java applets do not have the authorization to save files to your hard drive, or look for them. They display animations and text, let you run a calculator, or play a game, for example. A Java applet can have a virus, nevertheless. However, your computer won't be infected by it unless you download the file containing the applet, an unlikely occurrence. Security holes can occur, most often in the browsers that allow you to view Java applets. However, browser vendors have been very quick to plug them.

We are told that the future includes Java applications, powerful programs that can run on all platforms. Java applications do have the power to save and modify files on your hard drive. Extremely strict security measures need to be deployed when you run Java applications online. Regardless, Norton AntiVirus does protect you from Java viruses. Just make sure you enable the program to check .CLASS files before you run them (this is the default), and keep Norton AntiVirus updated, and all should be well.

Rogue ActiveX Applets

ActiveX applets are given far more free reign than Java. They enable Visual Basic Script programs, allowing the applet to save and modify files on your computer, as well as monitor CPU activity. ActiveX applets, once enabled, can run scripts from hidden sources, such as other HTML links, without you being apprised of this intent beforehand.

When you access an ActiveX applet, it does nothing at all until its digital signature is verified. Every ActiveX-enabled browser is empowered to examine and verify the authenticity of an applet's digital signature. This makes it hard to create rogue ActiveX applets without a good deal of accountability.

The problem occurs once the digital signature has been verified—perhaps you've run across: "This applet appears to be from the Microsoft Corporation." You are then allowed to click a check box, "Always trust Microsoft," and shoo away any pesky verification issues in the future—the applet has free reign. Whatever script is then invoked by the applet will run on your computer unchallenged.

> **Note:** So, what's out there now? To date, there have been very few Java-born viruses, perhaps only one, known as Strange Brew. Strange Brew tries to infect .CLASS files in your Java folder. The next time any infected Java applet is run from your computer, the virus receives control first. Strange Brew has no payload. It only seeks control of all .CLASS files on your computer. It appears to pave the way for more malicious Java viruses, Strange Brew merely being the code that more dangerous payloads will be allowed to sail in on. The only Rogue ActiveX applets have been created in laboratory situations, to show that the potential danger does exist.

Glossary

Acronym   The bane of a jargon-hater's existence, acronyms are "words" or expressions which are formed by combining letters—usually the first letter of each—from other words. For example, ASCII is an acronym for American Standard Code for Information Interchange, and FAT is an acronym for File Allocation Table.

Allocation Error   Inconsistency between a file's actual size on disk (expressed as the number of clusters used by the file) and the size of the file as represented within the directory entry for the file. A file requiring 10 clusters to store its length, which is reported as using only nine clusters in the file's directory entry, has an allocation error. Norton Disk Doctor can commonly repair this problem.

Applet   A small application designed for the performance, usually, of one or very few related tasks. Examples of applets are the Windows Calculator, Notepad, and small JAVA programs which run within Web pages.

Archive Attribute   A file attribute which is used by backup software to determine whether a file has been created or modified since it was last included in a backup. When a file is first created or later changed, the archive attribute (or "archive bit") is set, indicating that the file needs to be included in the next backup. When the backup completes successfully, the archive bits are "unset" until further changes are made to the files.

AUTOEXEC.BAT   A DOS startup file which was used extensively before the advent of Windows 95 and Windows 98 to load hardware drivers and terminate-and-stay-resident (TSR) software and boot time. Under Windows 95 and Windows 98 the file may still exist to provide compatibility with older programs, or to provide special functionality. See also CONFIG.SYS and Real Mode.

Background   Applications either run in the foreground or in the background. A foreground application receives priority for all of the processor time it requires to complete the tasks you tell it to do. A background task, or tasks, receives very low processor priority, taking advantage of slack time between foreground tasks to operate. For example, Norton Disk Doctor can check the integrity of your hard drives in the background while you work in a word processing program in the foreground. Any time that your word processor needs processing power being used by Norton Disk Doctor, Disk Doctor is paused and that processor time is given to the foreground application. When excess processor time is again available, Norton Disk Doctor will resume working.

Backup   The process of copying files to a device other than the one used for their primary storage (often a tape drive, ZIP drive, Iomega JAZ drive, or CD-Writable), for the purpose of maintaining a copy, should the primary storage device fail or the files be deleted accidentally.

Benchmark   A test performed upon hardware or software to check its performance relative to the performance of other hardware or software. For example, a Pentium II 400 MHz computer's ability to recalculate a spreadsheet might be compared to the ability of an 80486 computer to perform the same task. There are a variety of different tests which assess performance, each of which uses its own scale of measurement. The resulting value of whatever testing that is performed is called the benchmark.

Binary   A numbering scheme, also called "base two," in which combinations of zeros and ones are used to represent values. As with the decimal, or base ten, numbering system, each numerical position, moving from right to left, represents a power of the base. Thus 0001 in binary is the same as 1 in decimal, while 0101 in binary is the same as 5 in decimal, because "101" means one instance of 2^2, plus one instance of 2^0, or four plus one=5.

BIOS   An acronym for Basic Input/Output System, the scheme of code, usually stored in read-only memory chips on a computer's motherboard, which facilitates the moving of data from one hardware device or subsystem to another. A Plug-and-Play BIOS facilitates the dynamic allocation of system resources like memory addresses and interrupt requests to hardware components.

Bit   Originally an acronym for Binary Digit, a bit represents the smallest addressable part of memory. Individual bits are commonly used for maintaining the on- or off-states or yes- and no-states of system features, such as whether a file has been modified since it was last backed-up, or whether a mass storage device, like a hard drive, is writable or read-only. See also File Attribute for more examples.

Block   A block of data is a group of contiguous bytes which are read or written as a body. A "cluster," for example, represents a block of sectors. Within Norton Speed Disk, blocks in the disk map are used to represent the status of contiguous clusters of data during optimization.

Bloodhound Heuristics   A methodology used by Norton AntiVirus to detect not specific viruses, but virus-like behavior. Bloodhound uses an evolving set of common-sense rules to guide its analysis of whether a virus is likely attacking your system. For example, most users would recognize that it would be quite unusual for a word processing application to instruct the operating system to format a hard drive. When such a command is issued, Bloodhound Heuristics intercepts the command, recognizing it as a violation of how the application should normally behave.

Boot Record   On a logical disk, the first sector of disk space used by that partition. The boot record is responsible for maintaining data about the formatting characteristics of the logical drive—bytes per sector, sectors per cluster, and so on. On a bootable hard drive, the boot record also contains the bootstrap loader.

Boot Virus   A virus which infects either a logical drive's boot record or a physical drive's Master Boot Record, usually giving the illusion—or, in a far worse case, showing the reality—that the drive has been erased.

Bootstrap Loader   Located within a bootable logical drive's boot record, the bootstrap loader is a very small piece of code—a tiny program, actually—which tells the computer where to find the operating system files necessary to continue booting the system.

Burning-In   If anything can go wrong with new hardware, it generally will do so right away. Burning-in is the process of continuously running hardware for several days, exercising drive read/write heads and so on, checking for early-life failures.

Byte   A collection of eight bits. Data in modern PCs is always represented in collections of bytes. Roughly one thousand bytes (actually 1,024) is known as a kilobyte. Approximately one million bytes is known as a megabyte. Approximately one billion bytes is known as a gigabyte. (Bytes are always represented as powers of two, into which 1,000, 1,000,000 and 1,000,000,000 do not fit neatly. We therefore round-down to make it easier to talk about these values.)

Cache   A special area of memory used to temporarily maintain values which are likely to be needed by the processor or operating system or application in the near future. A processor cache generally consists of special, super-fast RAM, and holds small amounts of data which the processor is likely to need for calculations in the immediate future. A disk cache is generally a segment of normal RAM which is used to collect values from disk files which are likely to be needed by the OS or an application. In this way, those values are available much more quickly than if they had to be loaded from disk. This is known as read-ahead caching, because the operating system knows how to read data into memory in advance of its actually being needed. Another type of caching, write-behind caching, temporarily holds data that is sent from an application or the OS to a disk, waiting for surplus processor time, during which that data can be written without impacting application performance.

Cache Hit   When data required by the processor, the operating system, or an application is available in a cache. A high rate of cache hits means that the cache is of adequate size and is properly configured to read data ahead of its being requested.

Cache Miss   When data required by the processor, the operating system, or an application is not available in a cache. An excess of cache misses can mean that the cache is insufficiently large to address system requirements. The solution to this is generally to run fewer applications simultaneously or to add physical RAM, or both.

Check Box   A user interface element consisting of a labeled square box into which a check mark can be placed or removed by a click of the mouse. Commonly used to enable or disable multiple options in a dialog box. Contrast with Radio Button. See also Dialog Box.

Circular Logic   See Looping.

CLSID   Within the Windows Registry, a CLaSs ID; a means of distinctly identifying unique objects.

Cluster   A collection of contiguous logical sectors within a logical drive. The cluster is the smallest directly-addressable block of disk space.

Cluster Chain   When a file requires space in excess of one cluster to store its entire length, entries in the File Allocation Table (FAT) will indicate which cluster contains the next segment of that file's data. A fragmented file, for example, might begin in cluster number 5, continue through cluster 8, then skip to 10, then skip to 12, before ending at 14. The FAT sequence represented by 5-6-7-8-10-12-14 represents the cluster chain for that file. See also Defragmenter and Fragmentation.

CMOS   An acronym for Complementary Metal Oxide Semiconductor. Within a PC, the term CMOS is traditionally used to refer to the battery-supported memory in which values about a PC's physical hard disks, other system hardware information, and the computer's real-time clock are stored. If the CMOS battery fails or if CMOS data becomes corrupted, hard drives can become completely inaccessible until the values are restored properly. Norton Rescue can fix this type of problem easily.

COM Port   A serial COMmunications port, commonly used for connecting modems and, largely in the past, mice to a PC.

Compressed Volume File   The singular, massive file which a disk-compression scheme creates and into which all compressed data is stored. The disk compression software causes the compressed volume file to look like a logical drive itself, often hiding the actual logical drive on which the CVF is stored. (At the least, the host drive is usually assigned a new drive letter.) Compression is not available under FAT32.

CONFIG.SYS   A DOS startup file which was used extensively before the advent of Windows 95 and Windows 98 to load memory managing software and real-mode hardware device drivers. Some legacy hardware is still supported through drivers loaded via CONFIG.SYS, but this can dramatically reduce Windows performance. See also AUTOEXEC.BAT and Real Mode.

Context-Menu   A small menu that pops up when you right-click on an object. A context-menu generally provides tools to use on the selected object or information about it, but may also provide global functionality. For example, the context-menu for each sensor in Norton System Doctor also provides access to all of the commands available in System Doctor's main menu.

Contiguous   The state of being physically next to something else. Two books sitting side-by-side are contiguously placed on the shelf. On a disk, cluster number 14 is contiguous with cluster 15, and so on. When a file's entire contents can be stored within contiguous clusters, that file is considered unfragmented. A file which does not fit within contiguous clusters is a fragmented file.

Conventional Memory   The first 640K bytes of memory in a Windows PC. Also known as lower memory. Hardware devices which are controlled by real mode drivers require those drivers be loaded in conventional memory.

Cross-Linking   A potentially disastrous condition in which the File Allocation Table indicates that two or more files are making use of the same cluster. When files are cross-linked it means that at least one file is damaged. Norton Disk Doctor can extract the cross-linked files to new locations on disk, allowing you to open each, determine which file or files are damaged, and extract whatever usable data remains. Keeping your hard drives unfragmented is a good way to prevent cross-linking.

Decimal   A numbering scheme, also called "base ten," in which combinations of zeros and the numbers 1 through 9 are used to represent values. As with the binary, or base two, numbering system, each numerical position, moving from right to left, represents a power of the base. Thus, 1 in decimal is the same as 1 in binary, while 11 in decimal is the same as 1011 in binary, because "11" decimal means one instance of 10^1, plus one instance of 10^0, or ten plus one=11. (1011 binary=$2^0+2^1+2^3$=11 decimal.)

Defragmenter   A utility application like Norton Speed Disk which can relocate and rearrange files on disk so that they exclusively make use of contiguous clusters.

Dialog Box   In general, a small window, subordinate to an application's main window or to the operating system, which displays information—commonly about errors—or asks for your input—commonly to confirm or cancel an action before it is performed.

Directory   See Folder.

Directory Attribute   A file attribute which, when set, identifies the contents of a file as a disk directory (or folder). In Windows, your directory information—filenames, sizes, dates, and so on—is maintained in standard files like all of your other files. The directory attribute defines special handling of these files by the operating system. Norton Speed Disk uses the directory attribute to identify directory files for optimization.

Drop-down box   A user interface element consisting of a list that "drops-down" to display its contents when the list is clicked by a mouse. Drop-down boxes are usually identifiable by the existence of a downward-pointing arrow at their extreme right.

DWORD   A 32-bit numerical value stored within the Windows Registry.

Extension   See File Extension.

FAT   See File Allocation Table.

FAT16   A 16-bit file allocation table, developed originally for DOS 3.3. The FAT16 system had many limitations, not the least of which was an inability to directly address a hard drive of greater than 2GB in size.

FAT32   A newer, 32-bit file allocation table system, developed originally for Windows 95. A FAT32 drive can be extraordinarily large, and makes a much more efficient use of disk space than did FAT16. It does this by making use of smaller clusters, thereby eliminating wasted space from disk. Converting a large hard drive from FAT16 to FAT32 not uncommonly recovers as much as forty percent of the drive's space!

FDISK   A DOS utility program used to create partitions in which logical drives are created.

File Allocation Error   See Allocation Error.

File Allocation Table (FAT)   On a logical drive, the File Allocation Table which keeps track of where files are physically located on disk. The File Allocation Table consists of references to disk clusters, these references together forming cluster chains which trace the location of a given file. Damage to the FAT can result in an inability to retrieve saved files. Norton Disk Doctor can repair a wide range of FAT-related damage, and what NDD cannot repair, Norton Rescue can often reconstruct through the use of Image files.

File Attribute   Individual bits stored within a file's directory entry which are used to identify characteristics of the file to the operating system. See also Archive Attribute, Directory Attribute, Hidden Attribute, Read-Only Attribute, and System Attribute.

File Extension   Developed originally for the CP/M operating system and used later for DOS, file extensions are the three digits—or, sometimes, four digits within Windows 95 and Windows 98—which are used to identify a file's type to the operating system. This information is stored within the Windows Registry and is used primarily in two ways. First, the operating system uses it to know which application to launch when you double-click on a document. Second, individual applications use the file extension to know which method to use to open a file. (The latter is basically an antiquated technique. Most modern applications recognize which methods and filters to apply to a file based on the file's contents. Some applications still use the extension for this purpose, however.)

Filename   The name by which a file is identified in a folder, including an optional file extension. Before Windows 95, filenames were stored using the "8.3" (eight dot three) format, wherein a filename of up to eight characters was followed optionally by a period and a three-letter extension. Windows 95 and Windows 98 both provided the enhanced long filename system, in which a file's name may consist of any length up to 255 characters, including an optional extension.

Folder   Within Windows 95 and Windows 98, a hidden file which consists of filename entries. The operating system recognizes this special file type by looking for the Directory Attribute, and displays these files as directories within the Windows Explorer.

Foreground   Applications either run in the foreground or in the background. A foreground application receives priority for all of the processor time it requires to complete the tasks you tell it to do. A background task, or tasks, receives very low processor priority, taking advantage of slack time between foreground tasks to operate. For example, Norton Disk Doctor can check the integrity of your hard drives in the background while you work in a word processing program in the foreground. Any time that your word processor needs processing power being used by Norton Disk Doctor, Disk Doctor is paused and that processor time is given to the foreground application. When excess processor time is again available, Norton Disk Doctor will resume working. Foreground applications run in the active window.

Fragmentation   A condition that exists when a file cannot be stored on disk in exclusively contiguous clusters. Fragmentation can seriously degrade the performance of your PC as well as hinder successful recovery of accidentally-deleted files. Norton Speed Disk, an integrated Norton SystemWorks component of the Norton Utilities, can eliminate fragmentation.

General Protection Fault (GPF)   An error that occurs when an application makes an instruction or request which the operating system will not allow to be executed. GPFs almost always cause the offending application to be forcibly quit. Norton CrashGuard can intercept and recover from GPFs. (Sometimes also known as IPF, Invalid Page Fault, in Windows 95 and later.)

Heuristics   See Bloodhound Heuristics.

Hexadecimal   A numbering scheme, also called "base sixteen," in which combinations of zeros, the numbers 1 to 9, and the letters A through F are used to represent values. As with the decimal, or base ten, numbering system, each numerical position, moving from right to left, represents a power of the base. Thus 01 in hexadecimal (hex) is the same as 1 in decimal, while A4 in hexadecimal is the same as 164 in decimal, because "A4" means ten (represented by "A") instances of 16^1, plus four instances of 16^0, or one-hundred sixty plus four=164.

Hidden Attribute   One of several file attributes, this one also known as the "hidden bit," which tells the operating system that the file should not be displayed in a normal directory listing. Within Windows 98, hidden files can be displayed with a pastel or "ghosted" icon if you set the View menu's mode to View All Files.

HKEY   Literally a handle to Registry Keys, the HKEYs or "root keys" form the six basic categories into which all other Registry keys fit. The six basic HKEYS— HKEY_CLASSES_ROOT, HKEY_CURRENT_USER, HKEY_CURRENT_CONFIG, HKEY_LOCAL_MACHINE, HKEY_USERS, and HKEY_DYN_DATA—are present on all Windows 95 and Windows 98 systems.

Host Drive   in a system containing compressed volumes, the logical drive on which a compressed volume file is stored.

Image File   A file created by Norton Image, which is used by Norton Rescue, Norton UnErase, and Norton Disk Doctor to recover from damage to a drive's boot record, its file allocation table, or its root directory.

Infection   The process of a virus corrupting either a file or a drive's boot record or a disk's Master Boot Record.

Initialization File   Created originally for Windows 3.x, files, commonly with the INI extension, which tell hardware and software how to configure itself as Windows starts. Much of this information is now stored within the Windows Registry, although INI files still exist for a wide range of purposes. Some INI files, like WIN.INI and SYSTEM.INI are still used by Windows 95 and Windows 98, primarily to provide backwards compatibility with 16-bit applications that are unaware of the Registry.

Interrupt Request (IRQ)   The addressable connections between a device and the main processor are known as interrupts. An interrupt request is a signal from a device to tell the processor to stop whatever it is doing and respond to the instructions the device is issuing.

Keys   Entries in the Windows Registry which are used to identify and categorize the various data values stored subordinate to them. All registry keys are subordinate to the main Registry handle keys, or HKEYs. Each Registry key may have additional keys which are subordinate to it, and each key may also have values which are associated with it.

Legacy   Used with respect to either hardware or software, this is the computer industry's polite way of saying, "antiquated," or "ancient." In general, "Legacy" hardware refers to hardware which is old enough that it is not Plug-and-Play compliant. "Legacy" software generally refers to software written for Windows 3.x or earlier. Contrast with Plug and Play.

Logical Drive   Logical drives are areas of physical disk space which are defined in a disk's partition table. These areas are also commonly known as partitions, although many operating systems and redundant drive (RAID) systems can connect multiple partitions together into one logical drive, represented by one drive letter. Contrast with Physical Disk.

Long Filenames   See Filename.

Looping   See Circular Logic.

Lost Cluster   When the File Allocation Table indicates that a cluster of disk space is in use, but does not associate any specific file with that cluster, the cluster is known as lost. It is not addressable by any normal operating system function. Norton Disk Doctor can identify lost clusters and create new filename entries for them.

Low Memory   See Conventional Memory.

Macro   A series of steps or functions, usually defined within some form of macro language or by watching a user perform tasks and recording those tasks, and generally stored within a document file. If the macro is saved as an "auto-open" macro, then the steps defined within it are executed when the file is opened.

Macro Virus   A type of computer virus which infects macros in document files. These viruses can be executed and cause infection to other files or logical disk damage when the document containing the macro is opened.

Master Boot Record   The first physical sector of a hard disk, in which is stored that disk's partition table and an indication of which partition—known as the active partition—is to be used for booting the system. A small amount of bootstrap code is also located within the MBR.

Maximize   The process of expanding a window from its current size to fill the entire screen.

MIDI   An acronym for Musical Instrument Digital Interface. A standardized method whereby synthesizers and controlling software and hardware communicate with each other to reproduce music. Rather than sending digitized data that is converted into sound, MIDI transmits information *about* the music—note, duration, dynamics, and so on— and the MIDI synthesizer reproduces that music precisely in accordance with those instructions.

Minimize   The process of reducing a window to its smallest size. In the case of an application, this generally eliminates all evidence of the application running except for an entry in the Windows taskbar.

Multipartite Virus   Viruses which can infect both files and boot records.

Offset   With respect to a string a data, any given piece of data may be referred to as being offset from some defined starting point. For example, a byte which occurs 12 bytes from the beginning of a disk sector is referred to as a byte located at offset 12.

Optimize   With respect to the Windows Registry, the removal of unused and redundant keys. With respect to a hard disk, the process of defragmenting files and locating the Windows swap file on a system's fastest drive.

Panel   Within a Wizard, any one page, accessible by clicking either the Back or Next button.

Partition   A logical division within a physical disk. Partitions are most commonly for-matted so that each partition represents one logical drive, and each logical drive has its own drive letter. In some operating systems and in RAID systems, multiple partitions may be linked together to form a single, super-massive logical drive. Partition identifica-tion data is stored within the partition table.

Partition Table   A portion of a physical disk's system information, largely stored with-in the Master Boot Record, containing information about where each partition on the disk starts and stops—in other words, its size—and which partition, if any, is bootable.

Path   A complete description of a given file's logical location on disk, beginning with the letter of the drive on which the file is stored, and ending with the filename itself. As an example, if the system file SHC.DLL is stored within the System folder inside the Windows folder in the root directory of drive C, then its path is
`C:\windows\system\shc.dll`.

Physical Disk   A physical hard disk, contained within its own casing. A physical disk may be partitioned into multiple logical drives, each of which is represented by a different drive letter, or the entire physical disk may be partitioned into one large logical drive, represented by one drive letter. Contrast with Logical Drive.

Plug and Play   A standard method of dynamically assigning system resources such as memory addresses and IRQs, to peripheral devices when the PC is boot. Theoretically, Plug-and-Play compliant devices should be able to share these resources on an as-needed basis, putting an end to the nightmarish configuration conflicts which plagued users before Windows 95. Theoretically. Contrast with Legacy.

Plug and Pray   See Plug and Play.

Polymorphic Virus   A type of virus which changes parts of its own code in an attempt to hide its existence and identity from antiviral software.

Prompt   In DOS, the display which appears to the left of the flashing cursor, indicating to the user where data typed will appear and, often, the currently-selected path. When we speak of the "C Prompt," we're referring to the display of `C:\` to the left of a flashing cursor in a DOS screen.

Protected Mode   A mode of operation in which a processor is able to actively address all areas of memory, including extended memory. Protected mode is the mode in which all of Windows 98 operates, once successfully started. Virtual memory is enabled through protected mode as is multitasking of operations. Protected Mode hardware drivers are loaded by Windows, not by DOS startup files, and provide Windows with more control over the related hardware. Contrast with Real Mode.

Radio Button   A user interface element consisting of a set of at least two labeled circles, into one of which a black selection dot may be placed through use of a mouse-click. Radio buttons are used in circumstances in which the user must select one and only one option from a list of options. Clicking the mouse in any unselected circle will place the selection dot in that circle and remove it from the previously-selected circle. The name "Radio Button" comes from the now-antiquated style of car and home radios in which programmed tuning was made possible by depressing one of several manual keys or buttons. Selecting a radio station in this manner deselected—since only one station may be heard at a time—whatever station was previously on-air.

Read-Only Attribute   A file attribute, also known as the "read-only bit," which tells the operating system that the contents of a given file may not be modified by any application or by the operating system itself.

Read/Write Heads   The tiny electromagnets within a hard drive which are responsible for transferring magnetic impulses to the drive platters and reading those magnetic domains back. It is this process of reading and writing which, respectively, stores and retrieves data from magnetic disks.

Real Mode   A mode of operation in which a processor is restricted to addressing only the first 1MB of memory at any time. Real mode limits the number of processes which can be performed simultaneously to one and provides no support for supplemental (virtual) memory. Real mode emulates the operation of the antiquated 8086 microprocessor. Once successfully started, nothing in Windows 98 operates in real mode unless you have legacy hardware drivers which you must load through your CONFIG.SYS and AUTOEXEC.BAT files. The presence of these drivers requires your processor to switch into real mode every time you use the related device, dramatically reducing system performance. Contrast with Protected Mode.

REG File   A text file used for the exporting and importing of keys and values from the Windows Registry.

Registry   A massive database used by Windows itself and by Windows applications for the maintenance of a plethora of hardware- and software-related configuration data. The Registry is also used to store and access the interface preferences of individual users on a PC configured for multiuser logon.

Rescue Disk Set   A set of floppy disks or an Iomega ZIP drive cartridge which is used to boot a catastrophically-damaged system and effect repairs. A Norton ZIP Rescue set will most commonly consist of a boot floppy and the ZIP cartridge, although may only consist of a bootable ZIP cartridge in systems configured with the ZIP drive as drive A:. Norton ZIP Rescue sets boot the system into Windows itself, giving you access to all of the Windows-based Norton tools. A Basic Rescue Floppy Set boots only into DOS, from which the DOS-based Norton tools are available. Catastrophic damage can be repaired through DOS, then lesser problems repaired when the system can again boot into Windows itself.

Restore   The act of moving files previously backed-up from a backup device like a tape drive or CD-ROM and storing them back on their original primary device, like a hard drive. In the case of a window, the process of expanding a minimized window to its previous size.

Root Directory   The base-level directory in any logical drive's directory or folder tree.

Sector   The smallest physical storage area of a disk. Multiple sectors together form clusters, which are the smallest addressable storage area of a disk. Norton Disk Editor is a "sector editor," which means you can edit on structures as small as a drive's physical sectors.

Seek time   The time it takes for a hard disk's read/write head to move from its current position to the beginning of a file. Seek times are generally expressed as an average of the time required to access files located all over the disk.

SMART Drive   A newer type of EIDE hard drive which contains special hardware designed to allow the drive itself to sense when doom is impending. This information can be reported to the operating system and the user through tools like the Norton System Doctor SMART sensor.

SRA File   A Symantec Registry Archive file can be used to export data from and import data to the Windows Registry through the Norton Registry Editor. See also REG File.

Startup File   A group of any files which are required in order to start a PC. On a Windows system, these are the Windows Registry (which is made up of the contents of the SYSTEM.DAT and USER.DAT files), the WIN.INI and SYSTEM.INI files, and, optionally, the AUTOEXEC.BAT and CONFIG.SYS files for loading antiquated legacy drivers.

Swap File   See Windows Swap File.

System Attribute   A file attribute, also known as the "system bit," which identifies a particular file as being part of the operating system. Files with the System attribute set are not usually displayed in a normal directory listing. In Windows 98, system files can be displayed with pastel or "ghosted" icons by enabling the showing of all files through the Windows Explorer's View menu properties.

Trojan Horse   A program which does not infect other programs but which, when run, causes damage to other files on your system. Trojan horses are not self-replicating, nor do they infect other files, waiting for a trigger to deliver a payload. An example of a Trojan Horse might be a program that let's you play a simple game while it erases your hard disk secretly.

TSR (Terminate and Stay Resident)   Traditionally, a DOS program which loads into memory and remains there while you run other programs. The TSR can usually be invoked at any time by pressing a special key combination, usually known as a hotkey. TSRs commonly provided access to special functions like capturing screen images, or printing files from the DOS prompt.

VFAT   The technical name (an acronym for Virtual File Allocation Table) for Windows 95's and Windows 98's enhanced File Allocation Table system. It provides support for long filenames as well as relocatability for the root directory, making the latter structure more robust in the face of drive damage. The VFAT system as a whole includes the drive's actual File Allocation Tables, its directory structure, as well as several layers of drivers that provide data reading and writing functionality to the operating system.

Virtual Memory   A methodology by which the amount of memory available to a computer is expanded greatly above the amount of physical RAM installed. Virtual memory uses the Windows swap file to provide an area of disk into which data can be temporarily stored while applications are running. The Virtual Memory Manager takes data which an application is not using at any given moment and swaps this data out to disk, making room for immediately-needed data in physical RAM. When the application makes a call to memory to retrieve the swapped data, this call is intercepted by the Virtual Memory Manager. Data is then swapped off of the disk, back into physical RAM, and other data is swapped off to disk as needed. Additionally, Virtual Memory is a major part of Windows' memory-protection environment, whereby—ideally—the inappropriate or disallowed behavior of one application cannot hinder the successful operation of another.

Virus   A program, usually very small, written for the express purpose of causing some behavior, usually damaging, on your PC without your intention. Viruses are self-replicating, and they use this ability to spread from one file to another, attempting to increase the chance that the virus code will remain on your drive. Viruses usually infect files first, then wait for the occurrence of some trigger event—such as a specific date and time—to pass. When this trigger occurs, the virus delivers its "payload," which means that the damage the virus was created to perform is carried out.

Virus Definitions   Files which can be downloaded via LiveUpdate to make Norton AntiVirus aware of the existence of specific viruses. When code matching the "signatures" stored within the virus defitions files is encountered by Norton AntiVirus, NAV knows a virus has been found. NAV can stop the viral code from executing and can isolate and eradicate it from your PC.

Volume Attribute   A file attribute, also known as the "Volume bit," which identifies the entry in a disk's root directory in which is stored that logical drive's volume name, if any.

WAV   A standard Windows format for storing digitized audio. The acronym stands for WAVeform audio.

Windows Swap File   As its name implies, the disk-based file used to provide virtual memory with its on-demand memory swapping functionality. See Virtual Memory.

Wizard   An applet that simplifies some Windows task, commonly configuration-related, by stepping you through the task in small pieces. A wizard presents only selected information at any given moment so as to avoid an overwhelming user interface.

ZIP File   Not an Iomega ZIP cartridge, but a compressed file with the extension, .ZIP. Used to reduce the amount of space required to maintain files on a drive. Under Windows 98 Plus!, all ZIP files function as "compressed folders," which can be opened and manipulated like any other folders. (In the past, a special "Zipping Utility" was required to move files into or out of a ZIP file.) Norton Mobile Essentials SpeedSave defaults to using a ZIP file to backup your selected files.

Index